'A revelation about the core of the marriage'
Raymond Seitz, *Sunday Telegraph*

'A psychological, as well as a political, biography: one which casts new light on the Kennedy years ... Leaming's book is a remarkable help in reading between the lines of one of the most sensational, mysterious and scandalous periods in history' Melanie Reid, *Glasgow Herald*

'The deepest and most rounded account of the Kennedy years from Jackie Kennedy's point of view'
David Robbins, *Irish Independent*

'Leaming offers the clearest picture ever painted of [the Kennedys'] deeply troubled marriage' *Daily Mail*

'A perceptive and well-written book ... Better by far than Seymour Hersh's sensational *The Dark Side of Camelot*'
Sarah Bradford, *Spectator*

'The famously private Mrs Kennedy has met her match and is herein revealed – along with her husband and his administration – respectfully but thoroughly, by an author possessed. Admirably detailed, stunningly successful, and likely to become the definitive biography of the Kennedy marriage, with all the intimacy and international scope implied' *Kirkus Reviews*

'An intimate look at a very private woman. Leaming explores Jackie's complex and often painful inner life with subtlety and compassion. Unabashedly sympathetic toward her protagonist, Leaming provides a fascinating glimpse into the psychodynamics of one of the 20th century's most famous marriages' *Publishers Weekly*

D0543621

'A marvel of clarity, intelligence, sympathy and sound research. Leaming is far too wise to indulge in hero worship, but she is equally too wise to overlook or diminish what is heroic in her subject. For that, and a great deal else, readers must be grateful' *Book Magazine*

'Draws on meticulous research ... Introduces new insights and recollections of the Kennedy years that had been veiled by Jackie's obsession for privacy ... Achingly moving'
Washington Post

'How very very personal Barbara Leaming's *Mrs Kennedy* becomes. It is an intimate portrait of a deeply imperfect perfect marriage, with its dazzling triumphs of historical importance and its private deceits and humiliations behind the closed doors of the private quarters of the White House'
Dominick Dunne

'A fascinating work that isn't just sensational; it makes both Kennedys seem utterly human, flawed and some of it will break your heart' *New York Post*

'Leaming paints a moving portrait of Jackie as she tried valiantly to make her marriage work and find a place for herself and her gifts' *USA Today*

Barbara Leaming is the author of the critically acclaimed *Orson Welles*, written with Welles's cooperation, as well as the *New York Times* bestseller *Katharine Hepburn*. A graduate of Smith College in Russian Studies, she also earned a PhD at New York University and taught for many years at Hunter College in New York City. Her articles have appeared in *Vanity Fair* and the *New York Times Magazine*. She lives in Connecticut.

By Barbara Leaming

Polanski: A Biography
Orson Welles: A Biography
If This Was Happiness: Rita Hayworth
Bette Davis: A Biography
Katharine Hepburn
Marilyn Monroe
Mrs Kennedy: The Missing History of the Kennedy Years

Mrs Kennedy

THE MISSING HISTORY OF
THE KENNEDY YEARS

BARBARA LEAMING

ORION

An Orion paperback

First published in Great Britain in 2001
by Weidenfeld & Nicolson
This paperback edition published in 2002
by Orion Books Ltd,
Orion House, 5 Upper St Martin's Lane,
London WC2H 9EA

Third impression 2004

Copyright © 2001 by Barbara Leaming

The right of Barbara Leaming to be identified as the
author of this work has been asserted by her in accordance
with the Copyright, Designs and Patents Act 1988.

All rights reserved. No part of this publication may be
reproduced, stored in a retrieval system, or transmitted
in any form or by any means, electronic, mechanical,
photocopying, recording, or otherwise, without the prior
permission of the copyright owner.

A CIP catalogue record for this book
is available from the British Library.

ISBN 0 75284 929 8

Typeset by Selwood Systems, Midsomer Norton

Printed and bound in Great Britain by
Clays Ltd, St Ives plc

Contents

List of Illustrations		ix
Author's Note		xi
1	Modus Vivendi	1
2	The Presidency Begins	39
3	Tell Me About Macmillan	60
4	A Family Drama	84
5	The Magic is Lost	105
6	Hall of Mirrors	130
7	In Her Own Right	152
8	Goddess of Power	202
9	Eyes in the Portraits	227
10	A Critical Moment	254
11	Valediction	277
12	Indiscretion	299
13	Private Grief	334
14	A Study in Betrayal	354
15	Alone	383
16	My Dear Friend	410
	Epilogue	416
	Acknowledgments	422
	Notes on Sources	426
	Index	470

Illustrations

All photographs reproduced by courtesy of
the John F. Kennedy Library

The wedding of Jacqueline Bouvier and John F. Kennedy,
    September 12, 1953
Janet Auchincloss
Rose Kennedy
Watching the parade on Inauguration Day, January 20, 1961
Arriving at the Inaugural ball, January 20, 1961
Jackie leaves the White House for her first weekend at Glen
    Ora
Prime Minister and Mrs Caramanlis of Greece arrive at the
    White House during the Bay of Pigs invasion
Jackie with Charles de Gaulle, Paris, June 1961
Jackie with Nikita Khrushchev, Vienna, June 1961
Jackie with Harold Macmillan
The Kennedys with Harold Macmillan, June 1961
Dave Powers and Marlene Dietrich at the White House
The White House swimming pool
Jackie's bedroom at the White House
Kennedy with Mary Meyer
The White House dinner dance of February 9, 1962
Jackie with Bill Walton
Lem Billings and Chuck Spalding
The Kennedys with Harold Macmillan and David and Sissie
    Ormsby-Gore
The Kennedys entertain friends during the America's Cup
    races, 1962
The Kennedy family in Palm Beach, Christmas 1962
The Kennedys with Lee and Stas Radziwill, Christmas 1962

Jackie delivers a speech to the returning Bay of Pigs prisoners, December 29, 1962

Jackie and John Jr have a picnic on the White House lawn, April 1963

Jackie's thirty-fourth birthday party on the *Honey Fitz*, July 1963

Chuck Spalding, Stas Radziwill, and the Kennedys on Jackie's birthday, July 1963

Caroline greets her father at Otis Air Force Base

Caroline, Jack, and Jackie on the *Honey Fitz*, August 1963

Jackie walks behind her husband's coffin, accompanied by Bobby and Teddy Kennedy, November 25, 1963

Jackie and her children leave the White House, December 6, 1963

Author's Note

Had it not been for the fact that Jacqueline Kennedy was married to the President of the United States, it is unlikely that a single book about her would have been written. And yet, in the dozens of books about her, specific details of that presidency have been largely excluded. Even more striking, and of greater consequence, is the fact that the histories of John F. Kennedy's presidency are comparably flawed, missing as they do the story of Jacqueline Kennedy and her crucial role. In an effort to fill the gap, I have tried to tell her story in those years with as much attention to the presidency as to the events of her private life. The role of Jacqueline Kennedy is probably less understood than any other part of the Kennedy presidency; equally, her personal story cannot be grasped without seeing it in the context of the unfolding events of one of the twentieth century's most dramatic presidencies. Her life was changed by historical events in ways she had never anticipated. She, in turn, influenced certain of those events in ways that until now have remained largely unexamined.

The chronicle of any presidency is incomplete without a consideration of the President's private life. That is even more true in the case of John F. Kennedy, because his private life repeatedly put his presidency at risk. Oddly, Kennedy's detractors – those seeking to portray his so-called dark side – have largely excluded Jackie from their versions of events, every bit as much as his apologists have. I would argue that one can come to terms neither with Kennedy's darker aspects nor with his fundamental decency – nor, ultimately, with what was perhaps his most stunning unfinished achievement, his own personal struggle against unimaginable odds for a moral compass – without being intimately familiar with the unusual nature of his life with her.

What follows is Jacqueline Kennedy's story in the White House years told fully for the first time in the larger and inseparable context of the presidency. It is also, quite simply, the story of the Kennedy presidency, with a tremendous missing piece filled in. To view the presidency afresh, rather than start with published memoirs and established histories, I have reconstructed the story from scratch, using the vast documentation produced during the Kennedy administration: letters, memos, transcripts, reports, diaries, and other primary sources. Using Secret Service reports of presidential movements, appointment books, gate logs, and other records, I have tracked the President and First Lady, as well as their intimates and associates, on a day-by-day, often minute-by-minute basis. With the aid of transcripts and minutes of meetings, I listened to what was actually said, by Kennedy himself and by key participants, during the many tumultuous events that made this presidency such an exciting one. I followed the President afterward, whether upstairs to the family quarters or to the Kennedys' weekend retreat in the country, to see him unwind with his wife and close friends. I considered what certain of those friends had to say about the Kennedys, whether in letters or diaries of the period, or in interviews. And I listened carefully to Jackie's own voice, in letters and other documents.

No experience can have been more valuable to me than the opportunity to study Jackie's extraordinarily moving, uncharacteristically frank correspondence with Harold Macmillan, written after her husband's death. As I encountered the passionate, emotionally turbulent, unguarded voice in those letters, and made sense of the allusions, both hers and Macmillan's, to certain defining events in the presidency, I was struck by how little has ever really been known about Jacqueline Kennedy or her intimate life with Jack in the White House years. In telling that story, it is my hope that, as I did, the reader will come to a better and more sympathetic understanding of two flawed but good and remarkable people, both of whom, each in his or her own way, came to exemplify the virtue both valued most: courage.

Barbara Leaming
April 2001

ONE

Modus Vivendi

Shortly before noon on January 18, 1961, two Secret Service cars loaded with baggage waited outside Ambassador Joseph P. Kennedy's Spanish-style mansion on North Ocean Boulevard in Palm Beach, Florida. For the better part of two months, the moldering house and grounds, unofficial transition headquarters of President-elect John F. Kennedy, had swarmed with family, friends, aides, and advisers. On any given day when he was in residence, every spare room had been occupied. Some houseguests had had to double up in maids' rooms, others camped out in odd quarters. For weeks, a formidable press contingent, as well as crowds of the merely curious, had watched visitors pour in and out of the massive, weather-ravaged, iron-grilled gate at the foot of the driveway.

On this particular Wednesday, two days before the Inauguration, the ocean-front house had a lonely, abandoned air. The houseguests, crowds, and commotion had vanished, and the only people in sight were a trio of Secret Service agents. Joe and Rose Kennedy and their brood, which included the forty-three-year-old President-elect, had left for Washington, D.C., where pre-Inaugural festivities had been in full swing for days. This was an event the Kennedy family had been awaiting for much of their lives. Only one family member remained in Florida, and the time was fast approaching when Jacqueline Kennedy, who had put off her departure as long as possible, simply had to leave. The following night, Inauguration eve, she was expected to attend the Inaugural gala staged by Frank Sinatra and Jack's brother-in-law Peter Lawford, the actor, to help pay off the Democratic National Committee's campaign deficit.

Finally, thirty-one-year-old Jacqueline Kennedy appeared at the door. Her brown hair arranged in a bouffant style, she wore outsized dark glasses and kid gloves to complete a traveling costume of a narrow tweed jacket, slim skirt, and low-heeled alligator pumps. To many Americans who had seen dozens of pictures of her during the campaign, a glimpse of the hair, sunglasses, and gloves would have been enough to identify her as 'Jackie.' To people who knew little else about her, that was who she *was*. In fact, like so much in her life, the aim of her signature style was concealment. A chemical straightener disguised the naturally kinky hair she hated. The teased bouffant masked a low hairline. Kid gloves covered large, strong, mannish hands which an early boyfriend had likened to those of a peasant. The cut of her suit jacket artfully concealed the breadth of her shoulders, and her muscular back and arms. The skirt disguised hips she thought much too broad. The shoes were specially cut to make large feet look smaller and more feminine. Sunglasses hid brown eyes set so far apart that her optician had had to special-order a suitably wide bridge. Dark lenses had the additional advantage of guarding emotions that since childhood she had taken tremendous pains to hide.

A Secret Service agent opened the rear door of a large Mercury sedan for Jackie to slip into the back seat. With her Secret Service detail, Jackie tended to be quiet and reserved. Despite her youth, a ramrod straight posture gave her an air of dignity and unapproachability. Once she was in the car, the agent went around to get behind the wheel, while the other men took their places in a follow-up car. There were no friends or family members to see her off or accompany her to Washington. Jackie avoided the intimacy of close friendships, and coolly made a point of keeping people at a distance. By her own design, she was, as she had so often been, alone. In a sign of things to come, as she left at the last possible minute to start a new life in the White House, silent Secret Service agents provided her sole companionship.

These men in their regulation dark suits and white shirts were strangers, and their presence in Jackie's life was a difficult and unsettling accommodation. It was the agents' job to protect her, but, as far as she was concerned, they were a reminder that she had lost the privacy with which she had long sought to protect herself. The prospect of their perpetual presence, she said, appalled her. However considerate and carefully trained the agents were to minimize any sense of intrusion, there remained the fact that for the next four years and more, every time she stepped outside she could expect to see them. It was a situation each new president and his family faced, but for someone like Jackie, fanatically obsessed with her privacy, the idea that she was under constant observation was particularly difficult. As her car rolled down the driveway, she was aware that the agent in the driver's seat, as well as those in the follow-up car, knew some of the most intimate secrets of her deeply troubled marriage, had seen the harsh private reality behind the enchanting family pictures in the press. Jackie's husband of seven years cheated on her compulsively, a fact which was painful and humiliating to her. Now that he was President, she would have to live that nightmare in full view of a group of strangers. Taught to observe and interpret the smallest details, these men would see not just what Jack did, but also whether Jackie was happy or sad, nervous or depressed. They would witness, in short, all the signs of emotion she had spent a lifetime learning to conceal. They would be privy to the body language between her and her husband in places and circumstances where no other outsider was permitted. The fact that her Secret Service detail consisted entirely of men – there were then no female Secret Service agents – was also unsettling. Would they admire Jack's womanizing, as many of his male friends seemed to do? Or would they pity her, though she had worked all her life to avoid pity?

As the Mercury passed through the gate and headed toward Palm Beach International Airport, one of the agents in the follow-up car automatically glanced at his watch and jotted down the time. The moment was a significant one. At exactly six minutes past twelve, Jacqueline Kennedy entered history – the written record of power. Nothing in her life would be the same again. Each time she emerged from her home, whenever she took her children to the park or went for a late-night walk with her husband and the dogs, a member of their Secret Service detail would note down the pertinent information. Jack's movements would be noted even within the White House. Whenever he disappeared from a party with a female guest, frolicked in the pool with girlfriends, or had a visitor in the family quarters when his wife and children were away, that too would be recorded. All phone calls would be cited, the progress of every trip detailed.

Jackie, an avid student of history, understood the uses to which such records could be put by future chroniclers of the Kennedy years. It was one thing to enjoy reading stories of dynastic intrigue, the love affairs of kings and the conflicts of royal wives and mistresses, but quite another to realize that she and Jack would one day be the subject of similar accounts. Jackie also understood that Secret Service agents and the Chief White House Usher, who maintained a book listing every person who went up to the family quarters, were far from the only record-keepers. She herself did not plan to keep a diary, but in Washington a small army of highly sophisticated letter-writers, diarists, and memoirists waited to report on every facet of her husband's presidency. Surely the story of her marriage, sightings of Jack's mistresses, and other scandalous details would be part of that voluminous record.

There were moments already when she felt as if she had become some sort of sideshow, and her every instinct was to revolt against any incursions on her life by the press and public. Days after Jack's nomination the previous summer, Jackie had spoken to Adlai Stevenson, head of the Democratic Party's liberal wing and himself a former presidential candidate, of her distress about her lost privacy. Confronted by a group of tourists as she strolled with Stevenson at the Kennedy family compound in Hyannis Port, Massachusetts, Jackie said, 'I can't bear all these people peering over the fence ... I may abdicate.' 'Steady, kid,' Stevenson replied, 'you ain't seen nothing yet.' At times, the onslaught of curiosity became unbearable, as when newspapers reported where Jackie, then pregnant with John Jr, bought her maternity clothes. She reacted with such hysterical indignation that at least one of Jack's close friends and political supporters, the powerful newspaper columnist Joseph Alsop, stepped in to try to calm her down. Alarmed that she might alienate voters, Alsop risked offending her by pointing out that she had permitted herself to become violently upset about something essentially meaningless. Jackie knew he was correct, but that did not change the way she felt. What Alsop and other friends and advisers of the President failed to understand was that more than mere distress over the fact that people now knew she shopped at Bloomingdale's had prompted her overreaction.

A tormented childhood, in which there had been much to be embarrassed about, had taught Jackie that her emotional survival depended on her ability to keep the world at a distance. By the time she was ready to start school, the marriage of her parents, Jack and Janet Bouvier, had become a battle. Fueled by alcohol, her mother and stockbroker father fought ceaselessly over his infidelities and financial failings. When, as they frequently did, the shouting matches of charge and countercharge took place in front of others, Jackie felt humiliated. Not only did she witness these ugly exchanges, she was a pawn in them. Neither parent hesitated to use Jackie, the older of their two young daughters, to wound the other. When her mother tired of shrieking at her husband, she would pour out her wrath on Jackie. He, in turn, would shower Jackie with praise, his genuine affection compromised by an awareness that his attentions infuriated Janet. Compliments to Jackie were a way to anger his wife, just as Janet's verbal assaults on the child were, as even the household help could see, really an attack on him.

Jackie reacted to the family turmoil with courage and spirit. Constantly criticized by her mother, she fought back. Whether attempting to defend herself or her father, she was in a perpetual state of conflict with Janet and her violent temper. But the trouble at home had an insidious effect. More and more, Jackie retreated from other people. The reason was simple: she wanted to conceal a situation that filled her with shame. Intimacy with outsiders became a threat, feelings something to be hidden. Though Janet would later imply that Jackie was by nature unemotional, in fact she was a turbulent, passionate person, who, since childhood, had applied her own strong will to finding ways to make herself less vulnerable. Her sister, Lee, three and a half years younger, shared her painful home life – a powerful bond – but not her intelligence or sensitivity. Early on, Jackie became a voracious reader and spent inordinate amounts of time alone, retreating into a fantasy world in which her closest companions were the horses and dogs on which she lavished the emotions that were otherwise suppressed. She also learned to channel her passion into an intense response to visual beauty, developing an eye for color and form, an intense appreciation of art and dance. Jackie could be warm and bitingly funny, but other children quickly sensed that she let no one close. She even learned to hide her feelings from her parents. She made a point, partly to annoy Janet, of gushing over her father. Yet the fact that her mother and, increasingly, others saw Jack as a drunken failure and pathetic fool was not lost on such an alert child. Perhaps inevitably, in her eyes it made his love and praise worth less.

Jackie was seven when in 1936 Jack and Janet separated for the first time. The divorce three years later, after several further separations, deepened the child's sense of humiliation, when details of the court case and her father's philandering were reported in the press. To make matters worse, Jackie's picture appeared in print, along with lurid accounts of her home life that included testimony about her own fights with Janet. Jackie had tried desperately hard to conceal all this, and the knowledge that her classmates and teachers had access to some of her most embarrassing secrets sent her further into retreat.

The situation only grew worse with Janet's remarriage in 1942, a month before Jackie turned thirteen, to the wealthy investment banker Hugh D. Auchincloss, known as Hughdie. Seeing that she lived at the Auchincloss estates in McLean, Virginia, and Newport, Rhode Island, most people assumed Jackie was an heiress. In reality, with the exception of room and board provided by her stepfather, she depended on the modest finances of blundering Jack Bouvier. The need to maintain the illusion that she really did belong in her mother's new family gave the teenage girl one more thing to hide. The birth of a half-brother and half-sister to add to Hughdie's own brood from previous marriages triggered a new conflict. Jackie was not a real Auchincloss in terms of wealth, and she had little interest in being thought of as Hughdie's daughter for any other reason. Homely, unintelligent, and utterly lacking in flair or curiosity, Hughdie – the very opposite of dangerous, dissipated Jack Bouvier – held no allure for Jackie. Seeking her identity in her father's French roots, and hoping to differentiate herself from the people around her, she cultivated a passion for all things French, particularly the lives of the French kings and aristocracy. In truth, her father's family background was far from grand. Nonetheless, what began as a form of mourning for an absent parent, as well as an escape from the ordinariness of Hughdie and his narrow, self-satisfied world, became a serious lifelong interest in French history, particularly that of the late seventeenth and eighteenth centuries.

Janet seemed to have attained everything she wanted with her marriage to Hughdie, but her hatred of Jack Bouvier remained undiminished. In his absence, she directed that ill feeling squarely at Jackie. While Lee, fine-featured, petite, and conventionally pretty, looked like their mother, Jackie had inherited their father's exotic looks. She had Jack's broad square face, heavy features, wide-set eyes, large frame, and dark Mediterranean coloring. As though wrestling with a ghost, Janet relentlessly found fault with Jackie's appearance. She pointed with disgust to Jackie's big masculine hands and feet, her broad shoulders and wide hips. Her favorite target was her daughter's kinky hair, which was highlighted by a low hairline also inherited from Jack. No matter what Jackie did with her hair, Janet's criticism of its texture and unruliness persisted. With reference to both her hair and her clothes, Janet accused her of sloppiness and compared her unfavorably to Lee. The conclusion was always the same: Jackie's looks were not feminine. If she failed to find some way of concealing her flaws, no man would ever find her desirable. Indeed, Janet may actually have believed that to be the case. At the same time, it was clear that all Janet could see in Jackie was Jack Bouvier. It was as if, having been sexually rejected by Jack, Janet was sending him a message that she had never really wanted him anyway, that he was as undesirable as the daughter who so strikingly resembled him. Jack didn't get the message, but, unfortunately, Jackie did: her mother found her physically revolting. Step by step, Janet slowly destroyed Jackie's self-image. In time, Jackie came to hate her mother, but more than that she began to hate herself – especially her physical self.

Janet was equally disapproving of her older daughter's mind. Never known for intelligence herself, Janet lived by the credo – shared by many women of her class and period – that men disliked women who had their own intellectual interests and opinions. Frequently she repeated that the worst thing a woman could do was permit a man to see she had serious interests. The skills a man valued in a woman were the ability to make him feel important and fascinating, and the ability to put together an attractive, well-managed house. Disparaging the very things that made Jackie special, Janet criticized her love of books and learning, notably the fascination with French history and culture that, for Janet, served as yet another reminder of Jack Bouvier. Janet taught her daughter that in addition to disguising what she really looked like, Jackie must also conceal how bright she was. Otherwise, there was no chance that she would ever land a husband, certainly not one of the wealthy young men, junior versions of Hughdie, whom her mother viewed as attractive suitors.

Jackie may have resembled Jack Bouvier, but she was also endowed with her mother's strong will, which, ironically, permitted her to stand up to Janet as well as to retain an important skepticism about certain of her values. Still, the incessant attacks left their mark. Much as she fought Janet, Jackie internalized many of her mother's harshest judgments. She was often defiantly sloppy, yet she dressed more and more to disguise her size and strength. She was forever anxiously redoing her hair. She found the boys her mother praised predictable and boring, yet though she didn't particularly want them, she needed to know that they wanted her. In view of what Janet insisted was her utter lack of physical allure, she cultivated seductive mannerisms such as a whispery, baby voice and the habit of looking into a man's eyes so intensely that he felt as if there were no one else in the room. She trained herself to behave in an extremely flirtatious manner and presented herself as a fragile airhead, the antithesis of the strong, clever, curious young woman she really was. Later she would recall that one of the things she had loved best about her junior year in France was that for the first time she felt that she did not have to conceal her intelligence or the fact that she had serious intellectual interests. Nonetheless, when Jackie graduated from college, virtually every aspect of her appearance and manner attested to her mother's victory. Persuaded that no man would be interested if she revealed her true self, she went about in what was in effect a carefully crafted disguise.

By the time Jackie met John Fitzgerald Kennedy at a dinner party in June 1951, just after her college graduation, her belief in her own desirability had been utterly destroyed by her mother. Twelve years her senior, the thirty-four-year-old Congressman from Massachusetts was extremely attractive and amusing, and that first evening at the home of their mutual friends Charles and Martha Bartlett, they seemed to get along, but almost immediately Jackie was off to Europe with Lee on a vacation provided by their stepfather. When she encountered him again, in 1952, an enormous amount had changed in her life. She had won a competition run by *Vogue*, whose prize was the opportunity to work for six months in the magazine's New York and Paris offices. Ever since her junior year abroad, Jackie had longed to return to France and retrieve the sense that it was acceptable to be her bright, intelligent self. But at the last minute, the crippling doubt with which Janet had infected her prevented Jackie from seizing the opportunity. On Janet's advice, she rejected the Prix de Paris and returned to live with her mother and stepfather in Virginia. A family friend, Arthur Krock, head of the Washington bureau of the *New York Times*, found her a job at the *Washington Times-Herald*, the same newspaper where he had previously placed Jack Kennedy's younger sister Kathleen, as well as the beautiful Danish woman said by many to have been the love of Jack's life, Inga Arvad. Both high-spirited young women, who had been close friends, had long since departed the *Times-Herald* but were still talked about there, and Jack Kennedy figured prominently in the newsroom mythology because of his connection to them. Day after day, Jackie was regaled with stories about the adventures of the dashing Congressman and his family. A widely chronicled war hero, he had already written one bestselling book and had announced his intention to run for the Senate in the November 1952 election, with an eye toward the presidency. Meanwhile, Jackie, now twenty-two and eager to escape life with Janet, had rushed into an engagement to a nice if rather predictable young stockbroker, a decision about which she quickly had second thoughts. When she saw Jack Kennedy again, all she had heard at the office invested him with a distinctly romantic aura. He seemed like everything her stockbroker – indeed, all the young men Janet had had in mind – decidedly was not. Soon she called off the engagement.

There was something else that, far more than aura or ambition, gave Jack Kennedy a deep hold on Jackie, one that would last a lifetime. Rich and handsome, he was one of America's most eligible bachelors, pursued by movie stars, heiresses, and a great many other desirable women. When he showed interest in Jackie, it was for her as if a miracle had occurred. Years of scathing criticism of her hair, eyes, hands, feet, shoulders, and sloppy appearance were rendered null and void. Jack's reputation as a playboy, far from being a deterrent, was a great advantage in Jackie's eyes, making it all the more significant that he had been drawn to her. If Jack Kennedy, who could have almost any woman he chose, wanted Jackie, Janet must have been wrong about her desirability – or so it appeared.

Certainly, Janet had been wrong in another respect. Far from being put off by Jackie's intellectual interests, Kennedy was delighted by them. Like Jackie, who had sought an identity in books, Jack, a sickly child often confined to bed, had invented himself out of his reading. Like Jackie, his great obsession was history. While her specialty was French history, his was English, but they shared a particular taste for the eighteenth century. He was thrilled that they seemed to fill in each other's intellectual and cultural gaps in dozens of ways. He was as curious to learn from her about art history and design as she was to share his knowledge of the movies. While he had read every word of Churchill, she was an admirer of de Gaulle. They both loved poetry and competed in memorizing each other's favorite poems. His idea of a present was a book he loved, and he was much given to snatching away the books Jackie was reading if they looked interesting. Jackie, starved for conversation about books and ideas, was captivated when, early on, Jack gave her two of his favorite books as a way of explaining to her who he really was. None of the young men touted by her mother had ever done anything like that. One of these books was John Buchan's *Pilgrim's Way* (*Memory Hold the Door* in the U.K.), from which Jack had derived the credo that public life is 'the worthiest ambition,' politics 'the greatest and the most honorable adventure.' The other was Lord David Cecil's *The Young Melbourne*, set in a world of complex and fascinating political men, the Whig aristocrats of the eighteenth and early nineteenth centuries, who moved constantly and determinedly between episodes of high political seriousness and those of intense pleasure. Their sexual life, Cecil observed, was 'not of a kind to commend them to an austere morality.' Jack, so much older, was clearly the more learned, worldly partner, but Jackie prized the fact that he sought information from her as well. With Jack, no part of her curiosity about the world had to be concealed. Fully accepting the superiority of her knowledge of France and prepared to trust the reliability of her reports, he soon asked her to read and summarize articles on contemporary French politics to assist him in his work. That he not only accepted but actually relished her intelligence was salve to her damaged ego.

Jack and Jackie shared a huge enthusiasm for life, for history and ideas, but also for gossip and fun of every description. She delighted in his extraordinary range of experience, as well as an unpredictability that was completely at odds with everything which Janet valued and Jackie had longed to escape. Unlike the young men she had dated in the past – men who rejected the best in Jackie but also bored her, men who left her with ambivalent feelings about herself – there was nothing dull or predictable about Jack. His interests were diverse, a mixture of the high and the low. He could expound on Churchill, but also do a dead-on imitation of Noël Coward. One minute he might speak of the differences between the British statesmen William Pitt and Charles Fox, and the next of his most recent encounter with the actor Gary Cooper in Hollywood. Janet's life had always struck Jackie as stultifying and vacant. She wanted something more, a life of substance and meaning, a big life that, as she would later say, called on the best in her – and Jack Kennedy seemed to hold out precisely that promise. Fiercely intelligent, full of curiosity and interests, hungry for knowledge and experience, committed despite his love of pleasure to the ideal of public life, he suggested possibilities no other man had. Before long, Jackie was desperately in love.

When he finally proposed in 1953, Jackie did two extremely telling things. She called relatives with the news, but insisted that they keep the engagement a secret until after the publication of the following week's *Saturday Evening Post*, which would feature Jack on the cover as 'Washington's Most Eligible Bachelor' – proof that Janet had been mistaken about her allure. And, in what Jackie later recalled as one of the high points of her engagement, she translated and summarized twelve books on Indo-China to help Jack prepare his first major foreign policy speech as Senator. That sent a further message to Janet: not only did Washington's most eligible bachelor find her sexually desirable, he treasured her intelligence. It also signaled the sort of life Jackie expected to have with Jack. She intended to take an active role in his political career, to work at his side on the great projects that absorbed him.

Jack and Jackie were married in Newport in 1953, and after a honeymoon in Acapulco she returned to Washington with every expectation that she had finally put the years of unhappiness behind her. She plunged into classes in American history at Georgetown University, in order to understand better the issues that faced Jack as a senator. But even before the Kennedys returned from their honeymoon, there had been a sign that something was terribly wrong. Although Jack had wired his parents from Mexico about how happy he was with Jackie, when the newlyweds stopped off in California, Jack suggested that Jackie go on ahead to Washington while he spent a few days alone on the coast. She had married, reflected a long-time female friend of Jack's, with 'eyes filled with dreams.' She did not expect a difficult marriage, assuming that once they were married he would give up his many other women. Her confidence buoyed by his having selected her when he had so many women to choose from, Jackie had blithely dismissed the words of caution offered by one of his closest male friends. In California, she declined to fly home without him, but she was powerless when, back in Washington, he proceeded to behave as if he was still a bachelor. Uninhibited by Jackie's presence, he would slip off with women from Georgetown parties, leaving his young wife stranded and humiliated.

Jackie had entered marriage with deep scars from Janet's assault on her self-image. When Jack began to cheat on her so thoughtlessly, the old wounds reopened. Long told that no man would want her, Jackie blamed herself for Jack's philandering. She did not consider that it might be something in Jack that caused him to behave as he did. As if her mother were still hissing in her ear, she did everything possible to change her appearance and make herself sexually attractive, but nothing seemed to work. She cut off her kinky mop of hair in favor of a short, Audrey Hepburn-style pixie cut. She bought new dresses from Paris in which to recreate herself as the elegant wife of a senator and future president. Yet the infidelity persisted. Any bride would have been devastated, but the situation was much worse in Jackie's case. Jack was supposed to have been her salvation from years of feeling unattractive, but his actions reinforced everything Janet had said. Jackie, who had gone into this marriage in search of sexual validation, found destruction instead. In the first year she suffered a miscarriage, further eroding her sense of herself as a woman. In childhood, the shame of her parents' warfare had caused Jackie to seek emotional isolation; now, the need to conceal the truth about her own marriage drove her to withdraw.

The marriage entered a new phase when, in the summer of 1954, Jack was nearly crippled by a bad back. During their courtship, he had often been on crutches, but in Jackie's eyes that was simply part of the romantic aura that surrounded him. She had barely registered the vague talk that he suffered from Addison's disease, which had to be kept secret lest his political enemies use the information to short-circuit his ambitions. It had merely added to Jack's Byronic air when he spoke of having nearly died in England in 1947 before he found out he had Addison's; or when he mentioned that, as the disease was controlled by the injection of cortisone pellets under the surface of his skin every three months and the daily ingestion of cortisone tablets, his father had set up safe-deposit boxes around the world to ensure that he would never be without cortisone were he to have a crisis when traveling. But when he announced that he was intent on surgery, Jackie was faced with the fact that there was nothing at all romantic about marriage to a man this ill. His condition was so dangerous that his own doctors refused to operate, the wisdom being that sufferers of Addison's disease were too susceptible to infection to risk elective surgery. Jack, who had lived all his life with illness and pain of one sort or another, was so desperate that he found other physicians willing to try.

Jackie had been married for one year when she found herself accompanying her husband to a hospital for an operation she knew he might not survive. As it happened, he developed a post-operative infection and hovered near death. This was followed by months during which he failed to recover, then a second major operation. In the course of some nine months, as Jack lay helpless face down or sat immobile much of the time, with an open wound in his back that refused to heal, Jackie took attentive care of him, and a new kind of peace developed between them. She read to him for hours. They competed in memorizing long passages of their favorite poetry. She taught him to paint, like his hero Churchill. She kept him focused, doing research and talking through ideas for his book, *Profiles in Courage*, which would win a Pulitzer Prize when it was finished. Jackie was his lifeline to a world into which, confined mostly to his father's house in Palm Beach, he could no longer venture. She brought him gossip and made him laugh with acid observations. At a time when for obvious reasons there were no other women in the picture, husband and wife rediscovered and solidified their bond.

The peace did not last. As soon as Jack was able to get about on crutches again, he went off to Europe with his friend Torbert 'Torby' Macdonald and, like a starving man, resumed his compulsive womanizing. By the time Jackie joined him in Cap d'Antibes, it was evident that, whatever she might have hoped, her marital problems had by no means disappeared. Shell-shocked, she returned to America to a life of unending sexual betrayal that she took as confirmation that Janet had been right all along. At the same time, Jack and Jackie were capable in quiet moments of making one another very happy. She became pregnant again and they bought a house in McLean, Virginia, not far from Janet. Lonely and desperate when night after night Jack simply failed to come home, Jackie, who had long disparaged her mother's life as empty and trivial, struggled to lose herself in the minutiae of putting together the perfect house.

The situation reached a crisis when Jackie was seven months pregnant. Still fully intending to play an active role in Jack's political career, she accompanied him to the Democratic convention in Chicago. His speech as he put Adlai Stevenson's name in nomination on August 16, 1956, made him an instant star in his party, and he came surprisingly close to becoming its vice-presidential candidate. Though he lost to Estes Kefauver, his concession speech made another major impact. Everyone seemed to be talking about his great future and, as Jackie watched, his dream of the presidency rushed many steps closer to reality. After the convention, the Kennedys headed east. Jack, unfazed by the fact that his twenty-seven-year-old wife, who had already suffered one miscarriage, was due to give birth in less than two months and had been forbidden by her doctor to accompany him to Europe, took off for the south of France to unwind. Jackie was sent to stay with her mother at Hammersmith Farm in Newport, Rhode Island. Visibly exhausted after the heat and commotion in Chicago and desperately anxious that this baby be delivered safely, Jackie had the additional strain of facing her mother, of all people, with the mortifying news that her husband had deserted her at such a critical time.

In France, Jack made little effort to conceal his activities. At Cap d'Antibes, he sent a male friend to pick up bikini-clad girls on his behalf. On August 21, he took off with friends and a number of girls for a few days of sailing and carousing. Two days after he set sail, Jackie began to hemorrhage and was rushed to the hospital. A Caesarean section was performed, but the baby girl was stillborn. With Jackie's own life in danger, Janet called Hyannis Port, only to be informed that Jack was unreachable. His brother Bobby left immediately for Newport. As it turned out, it was Bobby who told Jackie, when she woke, that her daughter was dead. Jack still had not been located when, two days later, Bobby buried the child in Newport. When the couple's friends called to inquire about Jackie, Janet announced that Jack was off on 'a toot in the south of France.' Jackie, who had never really recovered from the newspaper accounts of her parents' divorce, was crushed when the press reported her baby's death and the fact that Jack, who had just made such a sensation in Chicago, had yet to be reached. Of all the betrayals to which he had subjected her in three years of marriage, this was by far the worst.

Finally, on August 26, Jack checked in with his father. The callousness of his response to the news would be hard to overstate. Sorry as he was, at first he saw no reason to interrupt his holiday. The baby was dead, Bobby had handled the burial arrangements, and there was nothing more that Jack could do. Joe Kennedy brought him sharply back to earth with the brusque order to go home 'at once!' Unrepentant, Jack traveled to Newport, and even then the enormity of his actions appeared to elude him.

For Jackie a turning point had been reached. She could no longer deceive herself that Jack's pursuit of other women would stop. A man who could abandon a pregnant wife, as Jack had just done, and linger with girlfriends after she had lost their child and become gravely ill herself was hardly about to change.

If Jackie were ever to seek a divorce, the time had certainly come. No longer sure that she should or could remain in this marriage, she returned to her mother's house both to recuperate and to decide about Jack.

It was now that the full measure of the damage Janet Auchincloss and Jack Kennedy had done to Jackie became clear. Many women would have walked out on such a husband, no matter how much they loved him. Jackie, in contrast, seemed to see what had just happened as the final, terrible proof of her own inadequacy. Rather than point an accusing finger at her husband, Jackie behaved even now as though she herself were responsible for his infidelity. The entire episode, the loss of a second baby coupled with Jack's careless absence, was the final nail in the coffin of what little self-confidence she possessed. It proved with stunning finality that her mother had been right after all. Jackie was a failure as a woman.

In the end, as if she were convinced that what he had done attested to her own sexual undesirability and that, in view of her shortcomings, any man would probably have done the same, she chose to stay with him. As one of the couple's closest friends would later say, from then on Jackie did not 'demand' fidelity. But that doesn't mean she didn't want a faithful husband. It was just that she appeared finally to decide that she didn't deserve one.

There were also positive reasons for her decision not to seek a divorce. Her marriage did continue to prove her mother wrong in one important way. Jack found her interesting and engaging, as Janet had insisted no man ever would. As they always had, husband and wife still seemed ideally matched in every respect other than the sexual. After three years together, they continued to fascinate and amuse each other. In this area at least, the marriage remained vibrant and Jackie was determined to protect it. If Janet were correct, as she seemed to have been about Jackie's desirability, it was unlikely that any other man would be drawn to her in this way. In 1956, the question of whether Jackie would leave Jack was settled once and for all. The young woman who had entered the marriage with such high hopes had accepted defeat; she made up her mind that she was lucky to have as much as she had, when she could so easily have had nothing at all.

The timing of the crisis, coming as it did so soon after she had witnessed the moment, at the Chicago convention, when Jack's long-held dream of the presidency suddenly seemed capable of fulfillment, surely also played a role in her decision. Close friends of the couple recognized that Jackie, whose imaginative life owed much to her extensive reading of history, had shared her husband's longing for power. To leave him would be to abandon her own dreams of a life of historical significance at the very moment when they finally seemed within grasp.

Jackie's decision not to seek a divorce meant that Jack was free to make a decision of his own. During Thanksgiving at Hyannis Port, he conferred with his father and then informed his family that he wanted to run for president in 1960. For Jackie, the announcement meant that for the next four years Jack would be campaigning and their life together would change dramatically. He would spend those years constantly on the road. He would speak to every group that would have him and charm the local political bosses in the hope that by election time he would have established himself as a national figure. Jackie, aware of the impact his traveling would have on their home life but also still intending to take an active role in his political career, supported the plan vigorously.

Soon after Jack's decision to seek the presidency, Jackie became pregnant for a third time. Fearful of another lost child, she drastically scaled back her plans to travel with him, especially as the pregnancy advanced. The fact that in this period politics came to mean campaigning made it easier for her to reconcile herself to playing a much more limited role. She soon learned that days spent shaking hands in supermarkets or sipping coffee in church basements bored her. Behind the scenes, another factor contributed to her growing reluctance to participate. Jack, encouraged by his inner circle of political operatives known as the Irish Mafia, began to worry that Jackie might prove a liability on the campaign trail. At campaign strategy sessions attended by Jackie, he dissected, item by item, the qualities in her likely to alienate the average American voter. Not without humor, he cited her rarefied interests and pointed to the very clothes, by the Paris couturiers Balenciaga and Givenchy, with which she had sought to reinvent herself for him, suggesting that ordinary people would regard her as a 'snob from Newport.' On more than one occasion, her husband's remarks caused Jackie to run from the room in tears. No wonder she was soon speaking of politics with the tone of anger and disdain usually reserved for her mother. If Jack and his operatives doubted her political skills, she soon doubted them even more. Indeed, on the few trips she took, she seemed increasingly less effective as a campaigner. Had things been otherwise, almost certainly she would have drilled herself to perform, but Jack and his advisers had stripped away another layer of her self-confidence, and she was soon eager to avoid a public role whenever possible.

After months of anxious waiting, terrified that she would lose another baby, on November 27, 1957, Jackie gave birth to a healthy daughter. Friends noticed that from the moment Caroline (named for Jackie's sister, whose full name was Caroline Lee) arrived, Jack seemed to discover long-buried emotional depths, as well as an ability to express them openly. He was besotted with his tiny blonde daughter, and almost from the time she opened her eyes, she was fascinated by him. Jackie's bond with the baby, though outwardly less emotional, was equally strong. Henceforth, the shared intensity of their love for their daughter immeasurably deepened the connection between husband and wife.

Jack's philandering continued unabated. The first summer after Caroline's birth, when Jackie took her up to Cape Cod for the season, leaving Jack at their new Georgetown house during the week, he embarked on an affair so reckless that it threatened to derail his presidential ambitions. The young woman was a receptionist in his Senate office named Pamela Turnure. Her landlady, incensed by the married politician's late-night visits, launched an assault on his candidacy that included letters to the press and important figures including Eleanor Roosevelt, as well as calls to his father and cardinal.

Jack moved Pam temporarily into the home of an old friend
from boarding school days, a divorcee named Mary Meyer.
For the duration of the presidential campaign, the indignant
landlady, Florence Kater, continued to fire off letters about the
Turnure affair, but, though Kennedy's sexual appetites were
not unknown to the Capitol Hill press corps, the era's journalistic
etiquette ruled out most coverage of politicians' sexual lives.
Only when issues such as integrity or competence arose was it
permissible to peek into bedrooms.

Turnure was not the only woman with whom Kennedy was
involved. In these years, whether he was on the road or in
Washington alone, there was always a steady stream of available
women. If no one more interesting was available, he turned to
female staff members, who had grown accustomed to the
candidate's telephone calls at the end of the day. His line was
always the same. Without otherwise identifying himself, he
would say in his unmistakable Boston accent, 'This is your
friend. Would you like to come up later and have a few drinks?'
If the young woman demurred, he would go on to another.
There was always someone ready to say yes.

Jackie complained that in these years she rarely spent two
days in succession with Jack. But out of this situation a *modus
vivendi* evolved that made her troubled marriage somewhat more
tolerable, even if it did not eliminate the anguish of a life with
a compulsively unfaithful husband. In the past, she had been
constantly confronted with Jack's infidelity. During the four
years of the campaign, by contrast, he was home so rarely and
had so much free time on the road that even he found it
possible to restrict his womanizing to periods when he and
Jackie were apart. He continued to cause her tremendous pain,
but without a doubt the philandering hurt less now that Jackie
did not have to witness it. She seemed grateful for whatever
small relief she could find.

Unable to prevent Jack's infidelities, she concentrated on
protecting her dignity. With the many people around her aware
of the sad reality of her marriage, she developed two lines of
defense. With most people, Jackie simply pretended not to know
and left the impression that she was either incredibly naïve or

above such sordid thoughts. In contrast, with certain of Jack's friends, both those who chased women with him and those who abetted matters either as beard or procurer, Jackie sometimes indicated that she knew full well what her husband was up to but did not care. In either case, the pose was easier to maintain with her husband's other women out of view.

Jackie began to train herself to narrow her focus to that part of her marriage that was good and wear blinders to the rest. When Jack was at home with Jackie and Caroline, he was the picture of a devoted husband and father, and increasingly Jackie seemed able to concentrate on these happy times. She was by no means impervious to depression, and in Jack's absence she often descended into perilously dark moods, which she sought to master by riding her horse for hours on end in the vicinity of Hughdie's estate. At other times during days and nights alone, she read rapaciously, stuffing her mind with information with which to divert and intrigue her husband when he came home. She consciously stored up her energy and excitement for the moment of his return, and the better she became at maintaining focus on those hours of his which belonged to her, the more intensity she packed into them and the more vibrant they became. Even as her visible participation in Jack's public life became rarer, she operated more and more as his secret weapon, a source of the images and ideas with which he was forever recreating himself. Often her contributions were directly political, as when she translated portions of de Gaulle's memoirs and read them aloud to him. In his own speeches about America, he was soon reworking the general's marvelous evocation of the image of France.

The perception, soon set in stone, that Jackie hated politics dated back to this period, when she learned to associate campaigning with her husband's infidelity. She had once longed to share fully in Jack's public life, and she paid an immense price for her decision to participate as little as possible. In these years, she abandoned her dream of a life of substance and meaning at her husband's side. She accepted the bargain of a smaller life where the pain caused by his womanizing was more bearable.

Jackie became pregnant again just two months after Jack officially announced his candidacy on January 2, 1960. This meant that she was available to campaign even less, and they lived apart as much as together. Though he was now in the spotlight, Jack engaged in some of his riskiest behavior yet. As a Secret Service agent who later guarded him remarked, he was 'the kind of guy that liked to run through a fire with a full gasoline can.' So he seemed to do during that last year of the campaign. The month Jackie became pregnant, he began an affair with a woman named Judith Campbell, to whom he had been introduced by Frank Sinatra, who soon afterward also put her together with Mafia boss Sam Giancana. The presidential candidate also continued to show up regularly with various young women at the New York nightclub El Morocco, behavior that prompted Joe Kennedy's friend Arthur Krock to warn privately that Jack, whose wife was pregnant after all, had better 'watch his step' or suffer the grave political consequences that would follow a newspaper exposé of his scandalous private life. Joe Kennedy, as cavalier about sexual matters as his son – indeed, his example – fired back that the American people didn't care 'how many times he gets laid.'

On November 8, 1960, Jack was elected President in a close race against Richard Nixon. The following day, Jackie, wearing a bright red coat tightly buttoned over her bulging stomach, stood beside her husband as he made a brief acceptance speech in the Hyannis Armory on Cape Cod. After the election, their life continued much as before. Jack moved restlessly between Washington, Texas, Palm Beach, and New York as he began work on his transition, while Jackie stayed in Washington to await the birth of the baby. Three weeks after the election, shortly after midnight on November 25, Jackie gave birth one month prematurely to their second child. Jack was en route to Florida when he learned that she had been rushed to the hospital. By the time he reached Washington at 4 a.m., his son had been delivered by Caesarean section. John Jr was a sickly baby, who was diagnosed with a lung ailment known as hyaline membrane disease.

One week later, Jackie and the baby were released from the

hospital. They were to leave for Florida the same afternoon, but before they did, Jackie had to fulfill one of the ritual duties of an incoming First Lady, a tour of the White House with her predecessor. While the baby waited with his nurse at the Kennedy residence in Georgetown, Jackie, fresh from major surgery as well as an extremely difficult pregnancy that had taken a tremendous toll on her normally robust health, toured the White House with Mamie Eisenhower. Jackie's doctor's request for a wheelchair had been overlooked, and Jackie, too nervous to protest, climbed stairs and walked long halls as her hostess pointed out the building's every nook and cranny. With the discipline inculcated in her by Janet, Jackie managed to complete the visit without collapsing. Still, the exertion, coupled with the four-hour flight with a sick baby that immediately followed, set back her recovery by weeks.

In Florida, her doctor ordered rest, but there was little chance for it in the chaos of her father-in-law's house. In addition to Jack's work on the transition, Jackie had a tremendous amount to do before Inauguration day. She had to plan their living quarters at the White House, hire staff, deal with requests from the press, and make countless other decisions about the new life that faced her and her family when Jack became President. She was also intensely anxious about John Jr, who failed to gain weight satisfactorily and had trouble sleeping, and uneasy about the need to leave both children in Palm Beach for the time being. Tradition required that the new President wait until the swearing-in ceremony was in progress to move into the White House. Jack and Jackie would have to camp out in temporary quarters at one end of the family quarters during renovations, and a nursery for the children would not be ready for some time. Moreover, she was deeply worried about how, once the children did arrive, she would preserve their privacy so that they could lead some semblance of a normal life.

The hulking Mercury with Jackie in the rear seat pulled up to the terminal at Palm Beach International Airport twenty minutes after it left the Kennedy estate. Here, to greet her, was another reminder of how her life had changed. In addition to press, a small crowd had gathered on Southern Boulevard to watch her departure. Wherever she went, it would be like this. She was merely boarding a plane, yet here were people calling out 'Hey, Jackie!' and assessing her with the same critical glare that Janet had so often directed at her. The public was intensely curious about Jackie, so young and so different from her conservative, grandmotherly predecessors, Mamie Eisenhower and Bess Truman. A great many people had yet to decide whether they liked the stylish new First Lady. As Janet delighted in pointing out, numerous letters to Jackie had criticized her 'messy' hair. But even her detractors evidenced a keen interest, not least perhaps because she had kept such a low profile during the campaign.

As Jackie stepped out of the Mercury to confront the crowd, a faint trace of what an agent later called the 'deer in the headlights' look appeared on her face. Her Secret Service detail helped her through the crowd of excited onlookers to the *Caroline*, the Kennedy family's plane, a twin-engine converted Convair. Jackie climbed the steps and disappeared inside the small cabin, but even now, of course, she was not alone. Her Secret Service detail, the only other passengers, would share the flight to Washington.

As the plane took off that January afternoon, Jackie was at a turning point. Its signs were everywhere: in the crowd at the airport, but also in the gun-toting men in the cabin. Jackie had long been a woman under siege, but in Washington she faced the loss of the two main defensive weapons in her armory. Privacy had protected her in a lifelong struggle against humiliation, first because of the fights in her parents' marriage and later because of the compromises in her own. The constant separations from her husband during the campaign years had permitted her at least the pathetic consolation that she did not have to witness his compulsive womanizing. In the absence of both defenses, Jackie would have to find new ways to protect herself. In the weeks since the election, self-protection had been the common thread in nearly all her major decisions concerning the immediate future.

Aware that by the very nature of things history would afford her no real privacy, she had nonetheless taken steps to limit her public life dramatically. Having long ago abandoned her dreams of power in the interest of holding on to the small part of Jack's life that was unquestionably hers, she presented herself now as a reluctant public figure. She issued a statement that she would not be an active First Lady, and that as much as possible she would pursue a private life devoted to the priorities of her husband and her children. Determined to limit access to that private life, with all its mortifying complications, she ruled out press interviews and photo opportunities. In the interest of further secluding herself, she even attempted to limit her duties as hostess during state visits by directing the Chief of Protocol to encourage foreign leaders to leave their wives at home.

The likelihood that, living full-time with Jack again, she would soon be confronted with his philandering, was much trickier to plan for. Some women in Jackie's situation might have moved to the White House and just waited, hoping against hope that it wouldn't happen, even though, as Jackie did, they knew perfectly well that it would. Jackie was not given to that sort of passivity. She was a fascinating combination of crippling insecurity and iron will. Despite her carefully constructed aura of fey innocence, Jackie was very much a realist, a woman who had lived an emotionally brutal life. Though she worked hard to appear helpless, she was anything but that.

To understand what she was capable of, one had to see her astride one of the massive hunters she favored, galloping headlong across the Virginia hunt country. The mother who had so relentlessly battered Jackie's ego had also painstakingly nurtured her fearless streak. Day after day, since the time when Jackie was little more than a toddler, Janet, herself a champion rider, had put her daughter in the saddle and drilled her for hours, creating an expert horsewoman. The image of the adult Jackie on horseback, strong, wild, and physically fearless, provides the best picture of that part of her character she called on to devise a plan for protecting herself against the constant proximity of her unfaithful husband. That image also suggests why she would have believed herself able to put such a plan into practice.

As Jackie sat in one of the plane's big, upholstered seats en route to Washington, every element of her plan was in place. Her plan would place tremendous emotional demands on her, demands she had never had to live with before. In the past four years, she had simply remained at home while Jack traveled, and pretended that all was well in her marriage. Henceforth, Jackie would be the one to leave and, in effect, make it possible for her husband to pursue other women in her absence. In the past, she had merely been required passively to accept what he was up to. Now, in order to guard against being confronted with things she preferred to avoid, she was going to have to take active steps to make it possible for him to cheat.

Central to her plan was a country retreat close enough to Washington to use on a regular basis. The moment Jack was elected, she had begun to seek the right spot, and while in Florida they had finalized arrangements to rent an estate in the Virginia hunt country just outside Middleburg. In addition to weekends in the country with Jack, she intended to withdraw there with the children several days during the week, in order to give him his freedom at the White House. In the summer, she would spend three months with the children on Cape Cod, at the house they already owned in the Kennedy family compound in Hyannis Port. Jack would remain in Washington during the week, a summer bachelor, and join her on weekends. Her absences had to be part of a routine that was largely predictable, as well as extensive enough to provide an adequate substitute for the freedom he had enjoyed on the campaign trail.

As the *Caroline* descended over a frigid Washington, it remained an open question whether Jackie, for all her carefully considered plans, would be able to manage the new life that faced her. Anyone about to become First Lady would be entitled to feel anxious and pressured. But Jackie's personal resources were already stretched to breaking point. The deeply insecure woman about to arrive in Washington was barely hanging on in a painful marriage that had originally promised to repair the years of damage she had suffered at the hands of her mother. For the past seven years, Jackie had pushed herself beyond the limits of most women – not just to tolerate the humiliation of Jack's infidelity, but also to reinvent herself ceaselessly as the wife she believed he wanted. As if all this were not enough, at the last minute fate had added to her burdens. She had not recovered from the birth of her son before it was time for her to begin her duties as First Lady.

It was nearly 5 p.m. when the *Caroline* landed. Accompanied by Secret Service men, Jackie descended the steps of the plane, her oversized dark glasses in place, as press and another crowd of the curious watched her. A whole new set of responsibilities awaited her at the White House. Jackie, feeling a long way from fresh and confident, had reason to wonder whether she was up to them.

Jackie awoke for the first time in the White House on Friday afternoon, January 20, 1961, alone and terrified. As she lay in the massive, four-poster canopied bed in the Queens' Bedroom at the east end of the second-floor family quarters, her legs were gripped by painful muscle spasms. She was overcome by a strange physical sensation, as if every bit of strength had deserted her. To her horror, she realized she was unable to stand.

Outside her window, Washington, D.C. was buried under more than seven inches of snow. A few hours earlier, under an intense blue sky, Jack Kennedy had stood on a wind-whipped dais and electrified the world with a dramatic Inaugural Address full of stirring poetry and soaring promise. The response had been an outburst of hope that was quite unlike what anyone who had witnessed his narrow victory over Richard Nixon in November might have expected.

After Kennedy was sworn in as America's thirty-fifth president, Jackie had ridden with him in an open car to the White House and stood at his side on an open reviewing stand to watch the marching bands, floats, and ranks of soldiers in the Inaugural Parade. Chilled to the bone in a thin wool coat and delicate ankle-length boots, Jackie had forced herself to remain for almost half an hour, but finally the piercing wind and below-freezing temperature drove her inside the White House. The

President's Air Force aide helped her down from the stand and across the icy path back to the house, where the Chief Usher escorted her upstairs so that she could lie down. Thirty-two thousand participants were scheduled to make their way down Pennsylvania Avenue in a three-hour parade and Jack, visibly exultant on this day of triumph, insisted that he would not leave the reviewing stand until the last soldier had marched past.

Jack was still outside when Jackie awoke from her nap. Frightened at what was wrong with her, she picked up the bedside telephone to summon Dr Janet Travell, her husband's personal physician. Jackie's own doctor had issued strict instructions before she left Florida that she must understand she was still not fully recovered from major surgery and must ration her strength. It was evident that, only hours after the Inaugural festivities had begun, she had already done too much. In her determination to share Jack's happiness, to be beside him at the moment toward which he had been working during all of their life together, she had undertaken more than she was physically up to. Every minute since her arrival from Florida had been filled with packing and last-minute plans for the move to the White House, as well as frantic preparations for several major public appearances. Hair had to be done, dresses needed alteration, and the small house in Georgetown had been so crowded with helpers that she could find no place to escape for even an hour's rest. Finally, on Inauguration eve, she had traveled through a blizzard to attend a gala celebration that had started hours late. By Inauguration day, the punishing cold, coupled with the relentless tension of the preceding hours, had brought her to the point of collapse.

Dr Travell was found outside, watching the parade with the President. When she reached the Queens' Bedroom, she found Jackie visibly ill. Immediately she ruled that Jackie must cancel her plan to accompany the President to that evening's first scheduled engagement, dinner at the home of his old friends George and Jane Wheeler (later Jane Suydam). Instead, Travell ordered supper for Jackie in bed and gave her a Dexedrine to take later in the hope that it might provide her enough energy to get through the Inaugural balls, which were scheduled to begin at 10 p.m. As in so much of her relationship with him, she blamed herself, feeling that she was failing him by not being physically well enough to share in the greatest days of his life. Sick as she was, she would not consider the possibility that she would not be at his side for the formal celebration of his presidency.

Hardly had Dr Travell departed when Jackie's mother burst in to announce that, though Jack was still outside, family and friends had drifted indoors, where there was to be a reception in the State Dining Room after the parade. A lavish buffet had already been set out, with plenty of liquor to warm the shivering bones of people who had been outside for hours. Janet was appalled that her daughter was not downstairs to greet her guests. For years, Jackie had been the target of her mother's lectures about how things ought to be done and the ways in which, more often than not, Jackie fell short of her mother's exacting standards. Janet was capable of extraordinary pettiness and cruelty, her temper compounded by her stupidity. Jackie already felt guilty that she was letting Jack down, and Janet's diatribe only deepened her misery.

Jackie's one comfort, as she lay in bed listening to her mother's demands that she come downstairs immediately and perform her duties as hostess, was that she knew Janet would retreat the moment Jack arrived. He thought Mrs Auchincloss faintly ridiculous and found it difficult to understand how Jackie could take her idiotic ranting so seriously. But then, Jack had not been a child in Janet's household. Whatever faults his own parents had had, he had grown up in a house where both parents, especially the father, lavished praise on their children and carefully nurtured their egos in order to breed a fearless self-confidence that often bordered on arrogance. Janet, stunned that a man like Jack Kennedy would want to marry her ugly duckling older daughter, had from the first been as dazzled by him as Jackie was. She remained at once in awe and 'absolutely terrified' of Jack. To Jackie's delight, Janet never dared try to push her around in his presence.

It was well after six when Jack finally did come in from the parade. As usual, the atmosphere changed the moment he appeared. Jack was always witty and charming, and on Inauguration day he was by all accounts at his most buoyant. Unlike Janet, he was concerned that Jackie had done too much and was quite content that she rest a little longer while he went alone to Jane Wheeler's dinner. With the fierce determination of which she was capable in things that she thought important, Jackie, fueled by Dr Travell's Dexedrine, made sure she was out of bed in time to dress and complete the long process of arranging her hair well before Jack returned to pick her up.

By the time Jack returned from the Wheelers', it was after nine. Vice-President Lyndon Johnson and his wife, Claudia 'Lady Bird' Johnson, were already waiting for the Kennedys on the State Floor. Notified that Jack was downstairs, Jackie, radiant and wide-eyed if uncharacteristically frail, slowly made her entrance. She wore a long, narrow sheath dress of white silk, the bodice embroidered with beads and brilliants and veiled in gauzy chiffon. The President called for a glass of celebratory champagne all around before the foursome left to begin the round of balls. As the White House doors opened, Jackie appeared wrapped in a long white silk evening cape. She held Jack's arm tightly and crossed the Portico with small, tentative steps, as if afraid she might fall. In a hail of exploding flashbulbs, Jack helped her into the presidential limousine.

After an initial stop at the Mayflower Hotel ball, where they paid their respects to former President Harry S. Truman, there was an unscheduled stop at the Statler–Hilton, where Jack briefly went in alone to a private dinner for Frank Sinatra and other entertainers who had appeared at the gala the night before. Finally, they made their way to the Washington Armory, where the main and largest Inaugural ball was already under way.

The Armory was so crowded that someone compared the scene to the New York subway during rush hour, except that the people pushing this way and that were dressed in tailcoats and evening gowns. A path was cleared through the crush for the Kennedys and Johnsons as they made their way to the presidential box, which was hung with red, white, and blue bunting. There, the new President, dashing in white tie and tails, his thick reddish-brown hair boyishly tousled, stood to wave to friends in the swirling sea of revelers below, watched from one side by his proud parents and from the other by his adoring wife.

Though it was Jack who had finally permitted her to escape her mother, Jackie believed she owed the actual marriage proposal, which had been very long in coming, to a trick of Janet's. When, two years after their first meeting, Jack had still not proposed, Janet stepped in. One of Janet's friends had called to say that her daughter was about to go to England for the Coronation of Queen Elizabeth and wouldn't it be lovely if Jackie went along?

Jackie hesitated. She could not bear the thought that her absence might mean a missed chance should Jack decide he wanted to see her. But her mother insisted that the trip would make Jackie much more interesting than if she simply remained in town, by the telephone, available for Jack's calls if and when they came. For many months it had been obvious that Jack was reluctant to discuss marriage. Perhaps if Jackie showed him that she had other things to do and other people to see, he might change his mind. To arouse his jealousy, she must deluge him with letters that conveyed she was having the time of her life without him. It was not a terribly sophisticated strategy, but Janet, an authority on how to snare a rich husband, promised it would work – if anything would.

Prodded by Janet, Jackie composed exuberant letters to Jack about her conquest of London society. She wrote of teas and balls, of dancing with Lord So-and-So when the Duke of Such-and-Such cut in, of her afternoon at the Queen's Garden Party, and other triumphs. She wrote stories and drew whimsical sketches of the Coronation that were published on the front page of the *Washington Times–Herald*. Just as Janet had predicted, Jack made the move which Jackie so desperately wanted. He proposed by telegram, and when her plane touched down in Washington he was waiting at the airport.

Jackie was certain that in this case her mother had been

right, that her newspaper stories and drawings had impressed Jack and that her letters had made him jealous. What she didn't know was that in fact her letters had pushed all the right psychological buttons, evoking as they did an eerily similar stack of letters from England that was among Jack's treasured possessions. Those earlier letters were from his late sister Kathleen, who had moved with the family to London in 1938 at the start of Joseph Kennedy's calamitous tenure as U.S. ambassador to the Court of St James's. To understand Jackie's marriage, how it came about and why it evolved as it did, it is necessary to know something of the passionate private drama of the large, tremendously self-absorbed family she married into, and of the particular role the Kennedys cast her to play.

Joseph P. Kennedy, one of America's seventy-five richest men, had accepted the ambassadorship in the hope that it might be a stepping stone to the presidency. At length, his opposition to the war against Nazi Germany earned him the reputation of an isolationist, appeaser, and worse. He believed that a peaceful world was necessary to economic prosperity and that a war would end in socialism; he was also tremendously reluctant to consider sending his own sons to war. When Britain rejected his appeal to make some accommodation with Hitler, he predicted that the British would be 'badly thrashed' by the Germans and urged his own government to steer clear. The American economy, he believed, would have no trouble surviving a German victory. Reviled in both Britain and his own country as a Hitler sympathizer, an anti-Semite and – the charge that stung the most – a coward, he came home in 1940 with his political future destroyed. His presidential dreams were transferred to the eldest of his nine children, Joe Jr.

The ignominy in which the ambassadorship ended made it the worst episode of Joe Sr's life to date. For his favorite daughter, Kathleen, known as Kick, England had been another matter entirely. Eighteen when she arrived, she quickly conquered the London social scene. She was invited everywhere, pursued by London's most eligible young aristocrats, asked to every select party, dance, and tea. No beauty by conventional

standards, she captivated people with her vitality, clever conversation and an irreverent sense of fun.

Of her four brothers and four sisters, Kick was closest to
scrawny, sensitive Jack, three years her senior and, like her, a
rare bird in the family. Among the Kennedys, Jack and Kick
formed a pair; even in the broad division between older and
younger children, they stood apart from the handsome and
intelligent but boorish Joe Jr, to whom they were close in age
but not in sensibility. Jack and Kick shared friends, were brilliant
at working a party together, and liked to function socially as a
team. After her stint at the *Washington Times–Herald*, Kick
returned to England where, in 1944 at the age of twenty-four,
she married William Cavendish, Marquess of Hartington, heir
to the Duke of Devonshire, one of Britain's richest and most
powerful men.

By the time Jackie came on the scene seven years later, the
family dynamics had altered drastically. Joe Jr, on whom their
father had pinned his political hopes, had been killed in 1944
at the age of twenty-nine, when his plane blew up over the
English Channel on a secret bombing mission. Kick, whose
husband had also died in action, had lost her life in 1948 in a
plane crash in Privas, France, en route to Cannes. Their ghosts
would haunt the Kennedy family. In memory, Joe Jr and Kick
remained always what they had been, young and full of
promise.

On Jack, in particular, the impact of their deaths was
immeasurable. Joe Sr anointed Jack, the second and hitherto
less favored son, to take over the dreams he had invested in
Joe Jr. Jack, who had expected to be a writer or a scholar,
plunged into the political career that was supposed to have
been his brother's; and from the first, Jack's career, like Joe Jr's,
had a whiff of vindication about it. The impact of his sister's
death was less obvious to outsiders. Jack had lost his soul-mate
and partner in the family. Without Kick he seemed oddly
incomplete.

Joe Sr, who had been noticeably closer to Kick than to his
other daughters, desperately missed 'the only one' he felt he
could actually talk to. When Jack brought Jackie Bouvier home

four years after Kick's death, Joe discovered 'a substitute for Kick,' in the words of Betty Spalding, who had been Kick's roommate and later married Jack's friend Charles 'Chuck' Spalding. Jackie, like Kick before her, was someone Joe Kennedy could laugh with, a spunky girl 'unwilling to take any guff' from him or any other member of the Kennedy tribe. 'They had wonderful talks,' recalled Spalding of Jackie and Joe Kennedy. 'He couldn't talk to any of his daughters.' Jackie bantered, she spoke knowledgeably and entertainingly of art and design (subjects the Kennedys knew little about), she did outrageously accurate imitations, and Joe was delighted.

It certainly didn't hurt that Jackie was equally taken with Jack's father. Unlike boring Hughdie, Joe was a riveting conversationalist, a hilarious storyteller, and an expert mimic. He enthralled her with tales of his careers in the liquor business, the stock market, the movies, and politics, and of the many strange and comical characters he had met along the way. Jackie relished Joe's colorful turns of phrase – women invariably were 'tomatoes,' men so stupid they were like 'the donkey that couldn't get out of a phone booth' – and was not afraid to use his own language against him. Not since Kick had any family member teased Joe and flouted his rules.

Jackie recalled Kick in many ways. Like Kick, she was ambitious, adroit in social situations, and, though not conventionally pretty, dazzled nonetheless. There were numerous striking parallels in their life stories. Both had worked at the *Washington Times–Herald*, been recommended to the post by Arthur Krock, hired by Frank Waldrop, and dated journalist John White. Both had spent a crucial year in France, studying the language as well as art and design, and had a passion for all things French. The most important similarity was their transforming effect on Jack. He seemed to connect with Jackie as he once had with his sister.

From the first, both Jack and his father were drawn to Jackie because she could fill the enormous void Kick's death had opened for both men. Still, to some of Jack's friends the very idea that he was dating Jackie was puzzling. They were well aware of Jack's taste in women, his preference for stunning beauties. He had his choice of virtually anyone he desired, and was constantly seen with movie stars and models. With her unfashionably kinky hair and sloppy schoolgirl clothes, Jackie, then in her early twenties and far from the polished, iconic woman she would later become, was very obviously not his type. That he was aware she was no beauty was clear. When a photographer proposed to take her picture, Jack instructed Jackie to turn her face to get a more flattering angle. Jewel Reed, who was married to a former Navy friend of Jack's, remembered being mystified by Jackie. 'I thought, "That's an odd choice for him." I was stunned. I thought she was almost homely.' Betty Spalding had much the same reaction. Jack's ideal woman remained Inga Arvad, the voluptuous, sexually sophisticated Danish blonde with whom he had had an ill-fated affair in 1942. Something other than the physical had drawn him to Jackie, though she never grasped what it was.

Long after they were married in 1953, there would be a good deal of public speculation that Jackie had been chosen as the presidential hopeful's wife because, being refined and polished, she was utterly different from the Kennedys. Much would be made of the notion that for all her usefulness to Jack's future, she had no real place in the Kennedy family. The truth was the very opposite. Jack had been drawn to her precisely because of her multifaceted resemblance to the family 'star,' as Arthur Krock dubbed the lost Kathleen. As such, Jackie, paired with Jack, assumed a central role in the family drama.

If she sometimes seemed alienated in the family, it was because in unwittingly taking over Kick's role with Jack and Joe Sr, she provoked the resentment of Jack's mother and sisters, who saw her as a usurper. Unlike Kick, who was easy and charming with both sexes, Jackie tended to work her magic only on men and found it hard to communicate with most women. It certainly did not help her relations with the Kennedy women that the repertoire with which she entertained Jack and Joe Sr soon contained wicked impersonations of Rose (caricaturing her distinctive giggle, oddly pitched voice, and Irish-American accent) and her daughters.

The precedent of Kick is the piece of the puzzle that is missing from all previous accounts of Jackie's marriage to Jack Kennedy – the simple explanation for what went so painfully wrong. For all of her marvelous rapport with him, Jackie had married a sexually voracious man for whom she functioned, in large part, as a replacement for a vanished sister. Jack and Jackie had a terrific time with one another, shared numerous interests and a sense of humor, and reveled in their ability to function as a team. They completed one another and were like 'two halves of a single whole,' as Jack's prep school roommate and lifelong friend Kirk LeMoyne 'Lem' Billings phrased it. When husband and wife were together, it was evident to friends that he cared about her deeply. But from the first, despite the depth of Jackie's physical attraction to Jack, sex would always be something he sought elsewhere. Though the marriage crushed Jackie's sexual confidence, Jack, in his own curious way, found it eminently satisfying. With Jackie, confirmed by marriage as part of his family, he replicated the charmed life he had enjoyed with his sister. Sadly, she never understood why he had been drawn to her, why he had bothered to marry her, why he could seem so happy when they were together yet betray her so relentlessly. She never grasped that because she was his sister's stand-in, her ceaseless efforts to make herself sexually attractive had to fail. She never realized that the very thing that had brought her together with Jack – Kick's precedent – had doomed the marriage from the start.

On Inauguration night, Jackie talked and laughed with Jack's father in the presidential box at the Washington Armory. Because she reminded him of Kick, in many ways Joe Kennedy favored her over his surviving daughters. Nonetheless, he exacerbated her already difficult situation by encouraging his son to play around and, though he usually delighted in Jackie's forthrightness, he was prepared to hear no complaint. Early on, Jackie had learned an important lesson about life among the Kennedys. Sleeping with women other than one's wife was part of Joe's notion of manly behavior, and he had inculcated that belief in his sons. 'All men behaved that way, they drank and they whored around,' is how Betty Spalding summed up Joe's message to the Kennedy boys. And Jewel Reed remarked: 'I would have thought that any young boy knowing that his father was cheating on his mother would have been really repelled. But they didn't seem to blink an eye. I pondered for a long time. I wondered how in the hell Joe Kennedy sold them this proclivity that he had unless he said, "This is what real men do." '

Alone in the family, Kick had protested at her father's flagrant womanizing, which included having his mistresses to the house. 'The first time I had lunch there I was sitting on Mr Kennedy's left,' remembered Betty Spalding. 'On his right is ... [his] current girlfriend. At the far end of the table is Mrs Kennedy. I thought, "God almighty, this is sick!" ' Things came to a head on the occasion of Kick's twenty-first birthday; Kick refused to invite Joe's mistress to the party and her father exploded in fury. Even when Kick said she would rather call off the celebration than include her father's girlfriend, Joe insisted and spoiled the day. Much as he loved and favored Kick, much as he prized her outspokenness on every other subject, he believed that to capitulate would reflect on his masculine status as 'controller of the family.' So, too, much as Joe adored Jackie, he always insisted on his son's right to stray. Nor was it merely that Jack was his flesh and blood. When Steve Smith, husband of Jack's sister Jean, engaged in extramarital sex, he did so with Joe's blessing.

By midnight, Jackie noticed that the effects of the amphetamine had worn off. When she and Jack left the Armory half an hour later, an aide had to help her through the crowds of well-wishers to the car. Obviously she was in no condition to go on to the other Inaugural balls at the Statler–Hilton, Shoreham, and Sheraton–Park hotels. The limousine dropped Jack and the Johnsons off at their next stop, then took her back to the White House. It was a quarter to one when she passed through the North Gate and was met at the door by Chief White House Usher J. B. West, who escorted her upstairs. Jackie had thought she might have to sleep in her clothes, and she was grateful that Mr West had asked a maid to remain, who helped her unfasten the tiny buttons down the back of her dress.

On Jackie's first night at the White House, she went to bed alone. It was half past three on Saturday morning when her husband's car finally came through the gate.

TWO

The Presidency Begins

On Saturday morning, Jackie started work immediately, despite the fact that two days of Inaugural festivities had severely overtaxed her limited reserves of strength. Before she got out of bed, she called the usher's office to inform Mr West that she would be down that morning to go through all the back rooms of the Mansion to meet the dozens of White House staff members and familiarize herself with their roles. With considerable difficulty, Mr West persuaded her to allow him instead to bring the staff upstairs to meet her in the family quarters, so she would not have to trudge from floor to floor. Jackie finally agreed, but with the stipulation that she must meet each employee individually, not in a large group. As far as she was concerned, there must be nothing perfunctory about any of this. She intended to learn each name, match it to a face, and understand everyone's duties. In Jackie's view, there was no other way properly to run a large house. This house was now her responsibility, no matter how much help she had, and it was by her standards that it would be judged.

Jackie was also on the phone first thing to the director of the National Gallery, keen to arrange a meeting about paintings for the White House. What she had in mind, he learned, was not an appointment a few weeks later, but the next day at the very latest. Along with some silver-framed family photographs and a few other personal talismans which she had unpacked as soon as she arrived, there was already a stack of lined yellow memo pads next to the bed. Jackie was never without them. When she thought of yet another matter she must deal with, she jotted it down on one of the long lists she habitually made.

While she sipped her morning tea and nibbled on toast with honey, her customary breakfast, she began to compose the first of what would become countless handwritten thank-you notes on stationery headed 'The White House.' Gifts had begun to pour in from friends, and Jackie made it a firm rule – one that neither feeling unwell nor the fact that her husband had been inaugurated as President the day before would allow her to violate – that thank-you notes must be written within twenty-four hours of receiving a personal gift. Similarly, if she dined at a friend's home, no matter how late the evening or how many glasses of champagne consumed, she never emerged from bed the next morning without writing a thank-you note first. It was upsetting enough that so many presents were stacked up that not even Jackie could write thank-you notes for all of them immediately, but she would get started on the most important ones.

Not only did she have a long list of tasks; each one had to be performed perfectly. No one pushed Jackie to violate her doctor's orders. No one hinted that the new administration would be in jeopardy if she failed to begin right away. No one suggested that she ought to start work when it was evident that she desperately needed rest. Jackie, trained by her mother, played the role of her own drill sergeant. She was her own harshest and most demanding critic. This morning, there was no need for her mother actually to be there to urge her out of bed. Jackie, though exhausted, did the job herself. By this time, her core of self-doubt had become much more than just a matter of questioning her physical allure; it had spread insidiously to other areas of her life, and she lived in expectation of severe criticism for everything she did. She dealt with this in two ways. Either she flatly and stubbornly refused demands on her time and energy, as she had when she stipulated that she would severely limit her duties as First Lady; or she practiced a relentless and self-punishing brand of perfectionism. At such times, before anyone could utter a word against her, Jackie said it first. Fueled by insecurity, she overworked and over-prepared. No one, not even her mother, could conceivably set the bar higher than Jackie did herself, and she would not rest until she had done all she could to measure up to her own impossible standards. Prior to her arrival at the White House, Jackie had been careful to restrict her official role, but as far as she was concerned, what she did agree to do must be accomplished with panache.

The first major test of her skills was to be a dinner party that Sunday, January 22, only two days after their arrival in the White House. All weekend, in addition to interviewing staff, scrutinizing art and antiques carted over from the National Gallery and the Smithsonian Institute, attending a swearing-in ceremony downstairs in the East Room for members of the Cabinet, and periodically halting everything to greet visitors whom Jack brought up to the family quarters, she tirelessly planned for Sunday night. She went from room to room, upstairs and down, deciding which to use, devising the choreography of entrances and exits, and calculating how things would look from each guest's point of view. She pushed and pulled heavy furniture in an effort to make the spaces more visually appealing. She peered into closets full of china and got down on her hands and knees in dusty storerooms in search of clever props. She conferred constantly with Mr West, whom she had quickly realized would be her most important ally, and whom she soon came to love for all he taught her as well as for his ability to make her laugh in difficult situations. She made voluminous lists on the yellow lined pads that would soon become familiar to the White House staff, and wrote up every minuscule detail with the seriousness of a general readying his troops for a decisive battle. She ignored her doctor's explicit orders to take it easy, breaking off only for the occasional nap, without which not even her monstrously strong will would enable her to press on. Given the fact that she had recently had a baby and been so obviously fatigued by the Inauguration, no one would have thought it odd had she simply postponed the dinner, but Jackie would not consider it. Nor did she consider just letting the evening happen by putting it entirely in the hands of staff.

The elaborate preparations for that first White House dinner party, the evening itself, and its curious aftermath provide a revealing glimpse into the intricate mechanics of the Kennedy

marriage. Outsiders who had heard about Jack's womanizing
were known to speculate that the marriage was a sham. But
the couple's closest friends, such as the Spaldings, regularly had
an opportunity to see something else. When the Spaldings
observed the Kennedys in private — on a weekend, for example,
in their own home at the beach — Jack and Jackie, for all their
difficulties, really did seem tremendously happy together. Betty
Spalding would later say that in the most private situations,
when there could be no question of pretense, it was obvious
there was something 'wonderful between them.' Aware though
Betty Spalding was of Jack's compulsive infidelity, and puzzled
by what seemed like a contradiction in his having chosen Jackie,
she never doubted that the palpable pleasure the Kennedys
took in each other's company was real. That pleasure was
particularly intense when they were hosting an intimate dinner
party for close friends. Jack and Jackie were consummate
performers individually, but it was as a team that they were at
their most dazzling, and they reveled in their joint performance.
That first Sunday night in the White House was to prove no
exception. Jackie, as was her custom, wrote, choreographed,
and stage-designed an evening of pure theater. Jack had only
to make his entrance and hit his marks.

Jack had chosen the evening's guest of honor, Franklin D.
Roosevelt Jr, several weeks previously. Jackie had been in Palm
Beach when she was told that the invitation must go to
Roosevelt, without whose help in the West Virginia primary,
Jack believed, he might never have won the presidency. Coal
miners in that state had disliked the notion of a Catholic
candidate, but Roosevelt's support, carrying as it did his late
father's immense prestige, turned the situation around. Kennedy's attempt to repay the favor by naming Roosevelt Secretary
of the Navy had run into fierce opposition from his Defense
Secretary, Robert McNamara. There had been a time when
Roosevelt was his family's golden boy, but the high hopes for
his political future had never been realized and he earned the
reputation of a dissolute drunk and womanizer who would
'sleep with anything he could get his hands on.' Even Jack had
to accept that, in view of Roosevelt's well-known failings, the

appointment could not go through. The least he could do was make sure that Roosevelt and his wife, Sue, had the position of honor as his first private dinner guests. Sunday would be the first available opportunity, as he had a commitment to appear at a political dinner at the Alfalfa Club on the Saturday.

Both Kennedys were still in Florida when Joseph Alsop had asked them to his Georgetown home on January 21, that same Saturday, to meet his fiancée. The fifty-year-old Alsop, who had a secret life as a homosexual, was about to enter a platonic marriage with a friend's widow, and some people in Washington half-joked that he was motivated by a desire to avoid embarrassment to Jack, whom he expected to see a good deal of socially in the next four years. Alsop, one of the journalists who had excoriated Joe Kennedy when he was ambassador, had first met Jack through Kick. He had known and admired Kick in London and considered her 'a major influence' on Jack. During his early career as a Congressman, Jack had been a guest at a number of Alsop's dinner parties, until his flippant remark that there never seemed to be any pretty girls in attendance irritated Alsop, who cut off further invitations. Jack was reinstated after he took up with Jackie. Despite bad blood with Joe Kennedy, whom he continued to mock, Alsop had been an influential supporter of Jack Kennedy during the presidential campaign and commended him to friends as the first American politician he'd known who had 'the promise of true greatness.' As the President was already booked for the evening of the 21st, Jackie invited Alsop and his fiancée to dinner on Sunday instead. Exquisitely attuned to matters of status and favor, Alsop was certain to appreciate that the invitation was a coup, something to crow about to his vast network of rich and influential friends around the world.

It was what Alsop would say afterward to those people that really mattered to Jackie. Alsop was one of the great Washington gossips, a prolific letter-writer for whom an opportunity to pass on details of the first dinner party at the White House was the equivalent of winning a lottery. Jackie knew that if all did not go well, Alsop, devoted though he was to Jack, would be only too happy to trumpet the news in the morning. Given the fact that there had been no time to bring the White House food and décor up to Jackie's standards, let alone those of the finicky Alsop, there was every reason to believe that the evening might prove a failure. Jackie approached it as a kind of high-wire act, in which a triumph would be all the more valuable and diverting in view of the perils.

As she crossed the hall to greet her guests, she knew she would have to do it alone. Jack had returned half an hour before from a meeting at the house of his brother Bobby, whom he had named Attorney General at his father's urging, and had finished a hot bath moments before Alsop and the Roosevelts drove through the Southwest Gate at a quarter past seven. At this very moment, Jack's valet, George Thomas, was no doubt helping him dress. When Jackie entered the Lincoln Sitting Room, chosen in part for the imprint of history it conferred, it was evident that so far her strategy had worked. Alsop, who wore round horn-rimmed spectacles on a bulldog face, and Roosevelt, jowly and heavy-lidded with a mischievous glint in his eye, were chuckling over the centerpiece: an enormous gold bucket filled with ten pounds of the finest caviar. As Jackie had calculated, the room's intimate proportions made the bucket, an attention-getter in any circumstances, stand out all the more. Another hostess, afraid of appearing vulgar, might have chosen a smaller container, to be refilled periodically so that no one would notice quite how much outrageously expensive caviar had been consumed. In Jackie's design the gold bucket proclaimed: Isn't this fun and exciting! A way to enjoy the extravagance and laugh at the same time, it perfectly captured the week's spirit of ebullience and seemed a promise of things to come. It had another purpose as well. Jackie hoped to stuff her guests with caviar so that by dinnertime they would be too full to care about the execrable White House food. Alsop, the person whose opinion worried her the most, certainly seemed inclined to cooperate. Given to bouts of gluttony, he refused to stop until the bucket was empty and ate so much that, by his own account, he could never again bear the taste of caviar.

One element of Jackie's choreography that didn't quite come off was Jack's signature late entrance. The painter William

Walton, who frequently advised her in matters of taste, had been at the White House that afternoon as she conferred with the director of the National Gallery. Jackie had invited Walton to join them that evening and to bring a female companion – the choice was his – even though the numbers would be off because Alsop's fiancée was ill. In the sort of mishap that mattered to Jackie, Walton had not yet arrived when the door to the adjoining room flew open. With an air of being on the run, Jack bounded in from the Lincoln Bedroom, where he was living temporarily until his and Jackie's rooms were finished. Certainly the absence of two guests detracted from the effect, but the entrance was full of drama nonetheless. Walton and a wealthy widow named Mary Russell, who had worked in the campaign, arrived soon afterward.

While Jack's arrival was the moment guests invariably waited for, it was also what Jackie herself had been looking forward to all weekend. The Kennedys were about to delight their guests with the spectacle of two highly skilled and perfectly attuned actors working together, but to understand the dynamics of those evenings one has to keep in mind that Jack was, as an actress's stage partner sometimes is, Jackie's best and most appreciative audience. Careful as she was to be sure that her guests had a wonderful time, above all she staged those evenings for him.

From the moment Jack appeared, he occupied the position of power in the room. He was noted for his skill as a listener, but as he chatted with others his eyes would often wander to Jackie. He relished her gift for strategy and loved to watch her work a room. Tonight, in Franklin Roosevelt Jr's company, Jackie was wide-eyed, breathy, and flirtatious. She leaned very close to his face, tossed her hair, and teased him. Roosevelt, who counted Jackie among his favorites, adored every minute. With Joe Alsop she was utterly different. He always seemed happiest when Jackie, in the role of a petitioner, humbly sought the benefit of his wisdom. Tonight she asked Alsop to help her select California wines for state dinners, where, despite her preference for all things French, she was expected to serve American products.

That, fortunately, was not the case this evening, as Jackie plied her guests with Dom Pérignon champagne in the hope that they would be tipsy by dinnertime. Champagne glasses in hand, the guests followed on a tour of the family quarters, where she and Jack, nimbly passing the baton back and forth, ridiculed the Eisenhowers' décor: first he explained the his-and-hers television sets constructed in one wall so that Ike and Mamie could watch separate programs as they ate dinner from trays, then Jackie pointed out the nauseating pink-and-green color combination in the former First Lady's bathroom.

Characteristically, Jackie's strongest statement was a purely visual one. She led the group through a small treasure trove of paintings delivered that day from the National Gallery and the Smithsonian. A Renoir, a Cézanne, and a series of George Catlin portraits of American Indians – casually, but also strategically, propped against the walls – offered an idea of the sense of style that Jackie planned to bring to the White House. The guests may not have grasped the calculation that had gone into that moment, but Jack positively reveled in it. Downstairs in the cold, cavernous Family Dining Room, the meal prepared by the Eisenhower-era chef was as bad as Jackie had anticipated. Yet the evening was certified a success when Alsop, full of praise despite the food, merrily pocketed his beautifully calligraphed place card and menu as souvenirs. As usual, Jackie had served her husband well. Seated between Mrs Russell and Mrs Roosevelt, he was the picture of contentment.

The next morning, before light, Jack awoke in the Lincoln Bedroom and picked up the telephone, asking the White House operator to ring Bill Walton at home. He made it clear to the frazzled Walton, roused from sleep, that he was furious about the previous night. It wasn't that he lacked an appreciation for all Jackie had done to make it happen, or had taken anything less than tremendous and very genuine pleasure in their joint performance. Years before, at the family house in Palm Beach and during the war in Washington, he had enjoyed similarly happy evenings when he and Kick, functioning as always very much as a team, had entertained groups of friends. Jack's anger was strictly with Walton, who, he emphasized, was not to make the same mistake again. In future, Walton was not to bring older women to the White House, no matter how wealthy or how hard they had worked in the campaign. If Jackie asked Bill to bring a date to one of her small dinner parties, he was to select one of the women on Jack's list. As this curious pre-dawn call suggested, evenings such as the one Jackie had put together afforded Jack many pleasures, but the sexual thrill was lacking and would have to be provided by somebody else.

The intimate evenings that Jackie arranged with such care were gifts to a husband who more than anything, a close friend once observed, loved to receive presents. As Jack did, she prized the glittering performances for their own sake, but for her they were above all a way to flirt with her husband. However much she blamed herself for his infidelities, perhaps because he gave off such mixed signals, relishing her company one moment and betraying her the next, Jackie never abandoned hope of discovering a solution. As the Kennedys began their first week at the White House, in a way the marriage was precisely where it had been for seven years. Still convinced that a perfect evening or even the right haircut or costume might yet do the trick, Jackie failed to understand the real problem. It had nothing to do with her own lack of physical allure or any other failure on her part. There was no way to fix it. Nothing Jackie did could ever change the fact that she wanted a husband, while Jack sought to replace a vanished sister. As the Alsop/Roosevelt dinner party, so reminiscent of those long-ago evenings with Kick, demonstrated, in that he had succeeded brilliantly.

Jackie, having pushed herself to bring off the evening with flair, had little chance to rest in the days that followed. The very next morning the real work of the presidency began, and Jackie faced countless demands, not a few of them self-imposed. Already the phones had started ringing and the mail was full of requests for the new First Lady's time, whether to attend events, sponsor charities, or pose for pictures with this person or that. She did of course have a team waiting to assist her. After the election, she had hired Letitia Baldrige, a former schoolmate, to run the social office in the East Wing where the First Lady's business would be conducted. Formidably energetic, dedicated, and a fount of clever ideas, Baldrige had been trained by the legendary diplomatic hostess Evangeline Bruce at the U.S. embassy in Paris, where Bruce's husband was then ambassador. Later, Baldrige worked for Clare Booth Luce in Rome where Mrs Luce served as ambassador. With those formidable credentials, Baldrige brought a degree of expertise that proved indispensable in her new role as Jackie's chief of staff.

Jackie also had her own press secretary – which had been, in fact, a source of agitation. First, there had been the matter of why she needed a press secretary at all, for, as Jackie saw it, she wanted less press attention rather than more. If she were to have one, Jackie insisted that the press secretary's principal responsibility would be to find a way to withhold rather than dispense information. But the real reason for her reluctance was the woman whom Jack proposed she hire: Pamela Turnure. Jack had been hounded by Turnure's landlady about his affair with Turnure throughout the campaign, and after numerous attempts she had managed to get into the papers by challenging him at a campaign rally. Questions about the affair continued to dog him after the election, due to this press notice and the landlady's fanatical letter-writing campaign. Though Turnure had no relevant experience or background in press relations, Jack pressed Jackie to hire her. If his wife were willing to hire Turnure, it would put to rest rumors of his affair with his former receptionist.

Before Jackie agreed, she approached Betty Spalding, whose husband was privy to certain of Jack's liaisons. It was not Jackie's habit to confide in the other wives in their circle. She preferred to hide behind acid remarks about people and situations, and conversation tended to stay on the surface. Nor would any of the wives have felt comfortable about bringing up the subject of Jack's other women with Jackie. Any such conversation, Jackie tacitly made clear, was very much off limits. Nonetheless, in this instance, she swallowed her pride and asked Betty Spalding if Jack was indeed having an affair with Turnure. The question was startlingly out of character and Betty, put on the spot, replied truthfully that she didn't know and wouldn't say if she did. The matter, she emphasized, was strictly between

Jack and Jackie. Turnure was appointed not long afterward.

Besides Baldrige and Turnure, one other person was extremely important to Jackie during those first arduous weeks of the presidency. The East Coast society decorator, Mrs Henry 'Sister' Parish II, had come to Jackie's rescue in the past, first at the summer house in Hyannis Port and then in Georgetown where she came in, under somewhat awkward circumstances, to redecorate the house after Jackie's sister Lee had just finished doing it up for her. Brought in to work on both the White House family quarters and Glen Ora, the rented country retreat in Virginia, the former at government expense and the latter at the Kennedys' own, Mrs Parish confronted huge problems, particularly the tremendous pressure of time.

During those first weeks, the need to complete both living spaces as soon as possible was an immense drain on Jackie's limited physical and nervous energies. She was living with the strain of two enormous time constraints. The first and most stressful had to do with Jack. As early as Sunday, Jack had shown signs of restlessness. He complained that the windows in the White House were sealed and expressed the fear that the presidency would make him a prisoner. All day he had gone in and out of the building, as if testing whether he was still free to leave. Nothing was more threatening to Jackie than that her husband might feel trapped with her. With Jack palpably so restless, and with various women who had worked in the campaign now on the presidential payroll and visible about the White House, she was frantic to give him a few days alone each week in Washington before she was confronted with anything she didn't want to see. At the moment, she had no place to go. (Jackie had ruled out the official presidential retreat at Camp David, sight unseen, on the grounds that any place Mamie Eisenhower loved she would surely hate.) The lease on Glen Ora did not begin until February, and before they could move in the redecorating she had ordered had to be finished.

The other major time pressure had to do with the children. Until nurseries had been prepared for them on the second floor and a playroom/schoolroom in the solarium on the third floor, she could not bring Caroline and John up from their grandfather's house in Palm Beach. The longer the work took, the longer Jackie would be without her children. Completing those rooms was very much a priority.

Another great source of stress was Jackie's determination to get everything right in the White House, not just by her own standards, but by those of the many sophisticated visitors who would soon be scrutinizing her every decision. Almost instantly, she grasped how easy it would be to make mistakes. Earlier in the marriage, she had taught herself to put together a stylish small house, but the White House was far beyond anything she, or even her decorator, had ever undertaken. Design elements that had worked perfectly in Georgetown, such as the material for her bedroom curtains, were out of place here. So, Mrs Parish soon discovered, were certain choices she and Jackie made early on. They looked 'perfect for a small house on the Maine coast' but utterly wrong in the official residence of the U.S. President. Even Mrs Parish, a consummate professional with years of experience, admitted that the prospect of the White House terrified her.

Hardly had work on the White House begun when Jackie began to worry that hiring Mrs Parish, famous for her casual and cozy rooms for the very rich, might perhaps have been a mistake. Just as Mrs Parish sensed that too often her proposals were more Maine than grand mansion, Jackie slowly seemed to realize that she needed something more formal and sophisticated than anything she had had before. Jackie was still insecure about her taste, particularly when it would be judged by such stringent standards. With each little thing that didn't work, she became more and more nervous.

The first week, as the family quarters echoed with hammering, was extremely trying. Mrs Parish could not fail to see how anxious her client was, how physically miserable she continued to feel after John's birth, and how lonely for her children. Still, Jackie pressed on as though nothing were wrong. Countless decisions had to be made immediately – colors, materials, wallpaper, trim, and numerous other elements. Every swatch of material, every pot of paint, every piece of furniture had to be looked at, compared, and decided upon. For each room, there were dozens of small decisions to be made. It was physically exhausting work, too, as Jackie moved furniture, climbed up on chairs, peered under tables, went up and down stairs, and lifted pictures.

No matter how overtaxed or pressed for time, Jackie let nothing slide. The very first morning, Mrs Parish arrived with completed plans for the First Lady's bedroom. Jack and Jackie were to have adjoining rooms, and Parish's concept was for hers to be 'severe enough for a man to share.' Jackie instantly rejected the whole idea. She visualized a boudoir crammed with favorite, highly personal objects: books and pictures, a leopardskin throw, an eighteenth-century French bust of a child, a large bed with a draped silk canopy and embroidered silk sheets – a room, in short, designed for seduction. Nor was the bedroom the only change she demanded on the very first day. In view of Sunday's dinner party, Jackie had decided she must have a dining room on the second floor, to offer privacy and provide a more intimate setting for family and private entertaining. And if food was to be served properly upstairs, a small but complete kitchen would have to be installed as well. Since these new rooms could only fit in the space already designated for the nurseries, Mrs Parish would also have to draw up a new set of plans for those rooms, which would now have to be located elsewhere.

By the end of the first morning, an enormous amount of additional work had been added to the list. The changes would be a major expense in both time and money, an especially daunting prospect in light of the minimal $50,000 budget allocated by the government for all renovation work in the second- and third-floor family quarters. This was cause for consternation, as the new kitchen alone would make a substantial dent in the allowance. Jackie, who had a history of battling her notoriously tight-fisted husband over money, realized that if she failed to make the budget cover everything Jack would be furious – another pressure.

Mrs Parish was soon complaining of exhaustion, though she had only the renovations to worry about. Jackie had much else to do besides. In the course of those first few days, she had to preside over three dinners for friends – each prepared with the same meticulous attention lavished on Sunday night's event – as well as two teas, including one for George Balanchine of the New York City Ballet. She also, with scant notice, had to host her first real political event as First Lady, a coffee hour to welcome two American flyers who had been shot down over Soviet air space and imprisoned for seven months before their unexpected release by Soviet Premier Nikita Khrushchev as a good-will gesture to the new American President.

Before her first week at the White House was up, Jack could see that Jackie was overwhelmed and needed help. The following week promised to be even more demanding, with Jackie set to give a party for White House appointees as well as two other small dinners; two nights scheduled for outside parties in the Kennedys' honor; and, capping it off, the children due to arrive at the weekend. As she had no close friends of her own, Jack summoned Lem Billings. It would be Lem's job to reassure Jackie, shore up her confidence, and assist in certain of her responsibilities, not least of which was making certain that the children's rooms were ready.

Lem, one of the oddest components of the Kennedy marriage, promptly notified the New York advertising firm where he was a vice-president that he was needed in Washington and would be out of the office for at least a week. Jackie had long had to share her husband with a great many women, but she also had to co-exist with his numerous, mutually competitive, often sycophantic male friends, chief among them the fiercely loyal but also childish and emotionally demanding Lem Billings. Nonetheless, as she would have been the first to comprehend, in a situation like this, which required an adviser of impeccable taste who knew a good deal about furniture and renovation, Lem could be a tremendous asset.

Three decades previously at Choate, an elite preparatory school in Connecticut, Lem had made Jack the center of his existence. Besotted, he had spared no effort until he became virtually a member of the Kennedy family. Joe Sr liked to remark, with some exasperation, that Lem and his battered suitcase came for Christmas in 1933 and never really left.

Eager to find any foothold in the family, Lem, though secretly homosexual, went so far as to pretend to be Kick's suitor, an attachment neither she nor her friends took seriously. In time, Lem was displaced in his idol's affections by Jack's Harvard roommate, Torby Macdonald. Jack chased girls with Torby, as he could not with Lem. But it was precisely Lem's failure to participate in Jack's philandering that, at length, made him palatable to Jackie in a way that Torby, who routinely procured women for Jack, was not. Early on, when Jack found it hard to adjust to married life, Lem, a constant houseguest, had acted as a buffer. As once he had professed to be in love with Kick, he did everything in his power to attach himself to Jackie as a friend.

Jackie, like Kick, got on well with Lem, though there were moments when she was annoyed by his constant presence in her marriage. They shared a great many interests, and she found his wide-ranging knowledge of art and antiques extremely useful when putting together her houses. At a deeper level, Jackie and the tall, bearish, gravel-voiced Lem were linked by the fact that both longed for more of Jack but had to share him with others. Yet there was an undercurrent of tension in her relationship with Lem. Much as he tried to hide it, he would always be jealous of her status as the one who remained with Jack when he had to go home. Jackie would never cease to be aware that, as was true of all her husband's friends, Lem's loyalty was first and foremost to Jack. Lem might not share or provide girls, but he certainly countenanced them. Even when, as on the present occasion, he came ostensibly to help Jackie, there could be no doubt that he was really there for Jack. He would not have rushed to Washington at a moment's notice for Jackie's sake alone, but he considered it his life's mission to serve his idol.

Lem did his best to lighten Jackie's burden that second week of the Kennedy presidency. Not only did he assist her in every possible way, but also, at a moment when she was concerned about her husband's growing restlessness, his presence did much to keep Jack amused with games, jokes, and songs. Nonetheless, for all of Lem's willingness to play court jester, there could be no escaping the fact that Jack's sense of being imprisoned would soon reach breaking point. That week, Jack began to take late-night walks outside the White House gates, trailed at a distance of about thirty feet by Secret Service agents. On Friday night, he insisted on going out to the movies with his friend Under-Secretary of the Navy Paul 'Red' Fay, who had previously been drafted to escort the actress Angie Dickinson, a girlfriend of the President's, to the Inaugural balls. With a good deal less fuss, Jack could have screened *Spartacus* at the White House, but he wanted to see the new film in a public theater, as anyone might. He longed for a taste of normal life, and he longed for a night out with the boys. Her husband's actions that week heightened Jackie's panic about finishing Glen Ora.

For all of Lem's help and advice, work on the children's rooms continued until the eleventh hour. A snowstorm on the day they were due postponed their arrival, but even then Jackie had to implore the housepainters to work through the night so that the nurseries would be ready on time. While Jack was out with Red Fay, she and Lem filled Caroline's room with favorite dolls and toys, did some work on the third-floor schoolroom, and had a member of staff build a snowman beside the driveway to welcome her.

Saturday afternoon, February 4, Jack and Jackie, accompanied by Lem, left the White House en route to the Marine Air Terminal at Washington National Airport, where the plane carrying Caroline and John Jr from Palm Beach would land. Jackie would have preferred to welcome her children in private, but there was no avoiding the newsmen eager for shots of Caroline and, particularly, the baby. To her mother's dismay, Caroline had become a press favorite during the campaign, but with the exception of official christening pictures John had barely been seen since his birth. Earlier that day, a nursemaid carrying him onto the plane had allowed some first close-ups. But at Marine Air Terminal, when the Kennedys boarded to spend a few minutes alone with the children, Jackie made sure that the baby was hidden in a nest of white blankets before they emerged. Frustrated by their inability to catch a glimpse of John's face as the family group went to the presidential limousine, the newsmen began to joke about what the new baby must look like if Jackie was so determined to hide him.

The children were accompanied by two nurses, as well as their own Secret Service agents – known as the Kiddy Detail – who were to monitor them at all times, except upstairs at the White House or inside Glen Ora and other family houses. Following a tour of the children's rooms, Jack took Caroline by the hand for a visit to the West Wing. In the campaign years, father and daughter had seen too little of each other for Jack's taste, but, he rejoiced, the move to the White House meant they would be together all the time. Later, when Caroline and John had both settled in, Jack and Jackie took a brief walk together on the South Grounds, notably without Lem. Both of them were thrilled that the children had finally arrived, but for Jackie their arrival was also a new source of worry. As in all things, Jackie longed to be perfect as a mother. The realization that she might not have what she deemed an adequate amount of time to devote to Caroline, and the sight of the baby who was still considerably underweight and sleeping poorly, filled her with guilt.

As the second week came to an end, another source of anxiety materialized when Jackie, already concerned that the work in the family quarters thus far lacked the requisite sophistication, discovered that she and Mrs Parish had spent the entire government budget and the family quarters were far from complete. In consultation with Mrs Parish, Jackie – so weary by this point that she remained in bed during some of their meetings – devised a plan to form a committee of wealthy private citizens, known as the Fine Arts Committee, to solicit money and furniture for the White House renovation from their equally wealthy friends. The fundraising plan would permit Jackie not only to complete the family quarters but to extend her touch to the public rooms on the first floor, which she found appallingly shabby. Furthermore, private funds would allow her to decorate in a much more sophisticated style. Excitedly she realized that she would be able to afford the important French antique pieces she had coveted when she lived in Georgetown. Over the years, she had become famous among dealers on the East Coast for taking a fabulously expensive item home on approval, only to have an indignant Jack force her to return it when he learned the price. With this fundraising idea, she would be able to create the house of her fantasies – on a very grand scale.

Once she had the idea for the committee to raise money, she approached Jack. As might have been predicted, he viewed her plan with alarm. Dismayed that, in keeping with what he saw as her spendthrift ways, Jackie had already gone through her entire budget, he was particularly concerned by her sudden interest in the public rooms. As in the campaign years, he worried that Jackie and her Francophile taste might be too rarefied for the American public. It had been one thing to permit her to redecorate the family quarters. Those rooms were off limits to the public, who, as far as he could determine, would not have an opportunity to be offended by anything she did there. By definition, the public rooms downstairs were another matter entirely. He feared an uproar if Jackie's selections of furniture, art, and other elements offended the average voter – the sort of political damage of which he had long suspected she was inadvertently capable. He certainly didn't want a repetition of the brouhaha that had occurred when Harry Truman added a second-floor balcony at the White House. To Jack's mind, the notion of a Fine Arts Committee posed an additional problem. Well acquainted with his wife's tendencies both to spend lavishly and to repaint and refurnish rooms until she got them exactly right, he worried that putting private money in her hands, money she might use unwisely, could create political havoc. Accordingly, Jack announced that he would not even consider the plan until Jackie had made her case to his private lawyer, Clark Clifford, whose political savvy he greatly admired and whose advice he often sought in delicate matters. It was up to her to convince Clifford, when they met over lunch the following Monday. Jack made it clear that if Clifford said no, Jackie would have to accept the White House as it was.

Although Jackie's plan for the White House would change dramatically, at the time she first sought approval for the enlarged renovation project in February 1961, her idea was very simple. She intended to create the most elegant house in America. In essence, she thought of it as a grand private home, a house to reflect her personal taste, decorated and furnished on a scale grander than anything she had ever been able to afford on her own. She understood that she would have to offer a political justification of some sort to obtain Clifford's approval, and at this stage she had worked out a very simple rationale for the project by saying that its purpose was 'to replace unsuitable furniture and furnishings in the White House with appropriate antique furniture in keeping with its history and traditions.' In other words, her argument was that she was going to replace the bad reproductions which filled much of the house with fine antiques because, as she put it, 'These things aren't just furniture. They're history.' She was going to give the house back its history.

Despite her evident physical fatigue after two weeks of flagrant disregard of her doctor's orders, Jackie was brilliant, if calculatedly vague, at the meeting with Clifford. Impressed by her stated goal 'to make the White House beautiful again,' indeed, 'the first house in the land,' the lawyer pointed out the pitfalls. He warned that the White House was 'a sacred cow to the American people' and cited the danger of offending voters. He stressed that every precaution must be taken to avoid controversy. Jackie, insisting that she understood, promised to be careful, and in the end Clifford approved.

From the moment Jackie had grasped the potential of the fundraising plan to enable her to create the house of her fantasies, this had meant one thing: a house decorated under the guidance of Stéphane Boudin, the leading decorator of the day who had done houses for the Duchess of Windsor, Fiat chairman Gianni Agnelli, and other members of international society. Three days after the meeting with Clifford, Jackie brought Boudin, the elfin seventy-two-year-old head of the French house of Jansen, to the White House to make some preliminary suggestions, specifically regarding the State Dining Room and the East Room. Jackie had first been put in touch with the so-called 'decorator's decorator' by her design mentor,

Mrs Charles Wrightsman, when Jack was still a senator, but she had been unable to afford him. Quietly, she had vowed to avail herself of his services as soon as she was in a position to do so. She did not mention this plan to Clifford, of course. Nor had she mentioned it to Sister Parish, whose nose would have been bent badly out of shape by the news that money raised from Mrs Parish's own contacts and clients would be used to import a fabulously expensive French decorator to run the show secretly, while, for appearance's sake, an American continued to be the decorator of record.

Aware that the American public would be offended by the news that she was bringing in a French decorator, Jackie also enlisted the services of Henry du Pont, head of the Winterthur Museum and a renowned authority on American furniture. She told du Pont, as he reported in a letter dated March 18, 1961, to a member of the Fine Arts Committee, that her interest was in making the White House a 'symbol of cultural' leadership, rather than merely treating it as the political symbol it already was. She proposed to furnish the house entirely in the style of a single period, specifically 'the period of the completion of the White House in 1802.' As a 'historic document of cultural life in the United States,' Jackie's White House would show off both the 'skill of the early craftsman' and – what for her was certainly more important, since she would use this to justify the purchase of beautiful eighteenth-century French furniture – also 'the taste of his patron.' Using the example of Presidents Thomas Jefferson and James Monroe, who had bought a great deal of eighteenth-century French furniture for the White House, she would have a historical cover for what was in fact her own personal taste. That Jefferson and Monroe had done it made it politically acceptable for her to do the same – or so she hoped.

Mrs Parish and Henry du Pont would be the public face of the White House restoration project, but behind the scenes Boudin, who to Jackie represented the ultimate in chic and sophistication, would occupy a central role. In the end, she would learn very different, far more important lessons from the master, but for now she was drawn to his celebrated flair for color and his ability to create what Joe Alsop liked to call a 'wonderfully pretty house.' The day Boudin visited, Jack, at her last-minute request, even joined them for lunch, though as yet he had no real idea of what she was up to.

Jackie had rammed through her plan, but in doing so she had put another massive pressure on herself. Sneaking in a French decorator and filling the White House with French antiques was, as she well knew, political dynamite. If it exploded in her face, she would have demonstrated that she was indeed the liability Jack had openly feared. That same week, she had had her first indication of how Jack as President would respond to political fallout whose source was the First Lady or someone in her staff. The Kennedys had hosted their first big reception, for the diplomatic corps, and Letitia Baldrige, unaware of the fact that the Eisenhowers had never served hard liquor at an official party with the press present, made the mistake of serving drinks at open bars in the various reception rooms. There was a fuss in the press as well as among certain politicians, who raised the matter with the President. Jack shouted at Baldrige for an embarrassment that was trivial compared to what Jackie was quietly threatening to unleash.

As the week drew to a close, Jackie, who had also presided over a black-tie dinner in honor of Lyndon Johnson and Speaker of the House Sam Rayburn, was by all accounts at the end of her strength. Having arrived at the White House on the verge of collapse, she had driven herself to do far too much – and after three weeks the end was nowhere in sight. Physically depleted, worried about her children and the potential for embarrassing her husband politically, and overburdened in countless other ways, she faced what was in emotional terms her most difficult undertaking yet. On Friday, she would finally go to Glen Ora with Caroline and John Jr, and give Jack some time to himself at the White House.

THREE

Tell Me About Macmillan

On Friday, February 10, exactly three weeks after the Inauguration, the moment for Jackie to put her plan to deal with Jack's infidelity into operation arrived. Jack would not join her and the children in Virginia until the following afternoon. In the past three weeks, the pressure of waiting for Glen Ora to be ready had proven immense. With each day, there had been further signs that Jack was restless, and the danger had increased that he would begin to cheat while Jackie was still at the White House. Tense as that had been, the moment of actually leaving was surely worse.

The next few hours would require all of Jackie's emotional reserves. Physically exhausted and still not recovered from a major operation, overwhelmed with pressure and responsibility, burdened by demands from all sides on her time, and desperately insecure about everything, she was in no condition to undertake the action she now demanded of herself. She knew full well what her absence would trigger. It was one thing to plan this abstractly in Florida, quite another actually to see it through. Jackie was about to force herself to do something that would bring her great pain, because she could not live with the far worse pain that faced her if she stayed in Washington.

To make matters worse, the afternoon she was to leave she had first to play hostess at an important business luncheon with the *New York Times*'s Arthur Sulzberger and his wife. Jack rarely asked her to do things like this, and he would not have requested it from her this time had it not been extremely important. As she had done repeatedly in the last three weeks, Jackie drove herself to do what Jack needed, and to do it well. When the luncheon was over, Jack escorted the Sulzbergers to the West Wing, while Jackie remained in the family quarters to prepare to spend her first night apart from her husband since he took the oath of office.

At half past three, a large, dark helicopter with a painted white top, piloted by Marines, landed on the South Grounds on a pad about one hundred yards from the White House. Jackie, visibly edgy, came down from the second floor with the children and their nurse and started across the lawn. Before they reached the white cap – as such helicopters were known – Jack emerged from the West Wing. At the sound of the helicopter, he had interrupted a meeting with his science advisers in the Cabinet Room. As this was his family's maiden flight, Jack insisted on taking them aboard and remained for nearly ten minutes.

Not every man would interrupt an important meeting to be sure his wife and children were comfortably settled in for a forty-two-mile trip, but Jack could be surprisingly considerate that way. He wanted personally to acquaint his daughter with the wonders of the great metal bird. But every bit as much as for Caroline, he was there for Jackie. His friends recognized that he was sincerely concerned about the toll these three weeks had taken on her health. His decision to escort her onto the white cap epitomized the tenderness that was one of the things she loved about him. But it also highlighted her dilemma as the wife of a man who sent violently conflicting signals. Even as he made it clear that he loved his wife, she knew he would take advantage of her absence. Was his solicitude an act? Jackie could not know that for Jack, from the outset their relationship had had little to do with sex, everything to do with family. The love Jack expressed that afternoon was for family. To his way of thinking, once the helicopter was gone, anything that followed was strictly sex – 'unrelated and impersonal,' as one friend put it. The sweetness and gentleness with which he saw her off made it frighteningly clear that his capacity for denial was if anything greater than hers.

The flight took half an hour. Jackie had hoped to leave earlier since this would be her first glimpse of Glen Ora, which the Kennedys had rented sight unseen, but by the time the hills of the Virginia hunt country came into view the light was fading fast. There had been unusually heavy snowstorms, and from the air it was possible to see that a lane had been cleared on the two-mile road between Middleburg – founded in 1797 by Katharine Hepburn's great-great-great-grandfather – and Glen Ora. Piles of snow eight to ten feet high loomed on both sides. Bordered by stone walls, the estate had four hundred acres, the main house set out of view from the road down a long, narrow drive. The Secret Service had put up barred gates and wooden gatehouses at the entrance, brought in two trailers for agents' use, and established a communications center in what had once been slave quarters.

As the helicopter descended in the gathering darkness, the battered mansion, surrounded by enormous, gnarled, bare-branched trees, revealed itself. Built in the nineteenth century, with several wings added later, it had three stories, beige stucco walls, and faded white wooden shutters. Tall French doors gave out onto terraces and lawns. The overall effect was of a charming old house in the French countryside. A swimming pool and tennis court were hidden by snow, and there was a guesthouse with a two-story room for parties, as well as a stable from which a local farmer had promised to remove his pigs before the Kennedys arrived.

By the time the white cap touched down on a huge, cleared pasture some five hundred yards from the mansion, it was too dark to explore the grounds. Inside, a high-ceilinged living room, a dining room, a library, and a kitchen occupied the first floor. There were five bedrooms on the second floor, a sixth on the top floor, and many fireplaces. Sister Parish, in addition to her labors in the White House, had done a tremendous amount of work at Glen Ora in the week since the lease began. At Jackie's insistence, most of the rooms had been freshly painted or wallpapered, and there were new wall-to-wall carpets in the living room and children's bedrooms. Jack was already seething at the bills that had begun to arrive. But fighting about money was much easier than fighting about what was really wrong. Defiantly, Jackie continued to spend.

The owner, Gladys Tartiere, had reluctantly agreed to lease the property to the Kennedys after Clark Clifford, who brokered the deal, suggested that it was the least a citizen could do in view of all that burdened a president. Most of her furniture had been carted off to the White House for storage and replaced with pieces from the Kennedys' previous residence in Georgetown. Mrs Parish had had slipcovers made for those few of Mrs Tartiere's sofas and chairs that remained.

Despite the fact that the house was rented, Jackie had instructed Mrs Parish to spend as much as necessary to create a perfect environment. She had a vision of Glen Ora as the place where she and her husband would enjoy strictly private time away from Washington. As such, her view of the house was fraught with contradictions. On the one hand, it would be her retreat while Jack betrayed her. On the other, it was absolutely central to her dream of marital happiness.

What made Glen Ora different from every other part of their life together was that the Virginia hunt country was decidedly Jackie's world. Jack's friends were well aware that, left to his own devices, he would have chosen a waterfront location for his weekend house, possibly Maryland's eastern shore. Jack, who loved to swim and sail, was always happiest near water. The hunt country was landlocked and, to make matters worse, had a single focus. While long discussions of fox-hunting and horse-breeding might be Jackie's idea of heaven, it most certainly was not his.

Nonetheless, Jackie was encouraged by Jack's tender gesture in renting a house in the locale of her choosing. Adding a dollop of romanticism to the steely calculation with which she regarded the place, she had constructed a fantasy of the life they would lead there together. She even imagined that, after he finished playing around and joined her in the country, she and Jack would ride together. In her fantasy, Jackie reverted to the halcyon days of her engagement, when she and Jack rode bareback in the fields around Hammersmith Farm for hours on end. Nostalgia for a more innocent time allowed her to omit the less romantic details. As her mother remembered only too well, after his rides with Jackie the poor fiancé, allergic to horsehair, would come indoors sneezing, watery-eyed, and short of breath. Jackie had made inquiries about horses for Jack while she lay in bed recuperating in Palm Beach. Meanwhile, her mother offered to lend him a gentle horse until something suitable turned up.

For all of Jackie's hopes, that first night at Glen Ora had nothing to do with romantic fantasy and everything to do with the harsh reality of her marriage. As she well knew, in her absence Jack would not have to look far for female companions. On this occasion there was no break in his schedule until 7:45, but as Jackie's absences became well established, the moment her helicopter or car left he would head to the pool or the family quarters with one or more women. It cannot have been easy to live with the knowledge that whatever went on at the White House in her absence she herself had made possible.

There was a light snowfall the next afternoon as a white cap, accompanied by a chase helicopter in case of an emergency, appeared over Glen Ora. Jackie and Caroline, hand in hand, waited in the cleared pasture. As the helicopter descended that first Saturday, its whirling blades created a dense cloud of flying snow. Jackie, in a heavy beige wool sweater and tight brown riding breeches, her hair loose and wind-tossed, watched Caroline rush forward to welcome her father in anticipation of showing him all they had discovered on the property after breakfast. Whatever Jackie had gone through the night before, she was careful to disclose none of it when her husband arrived.

Jack, who had spent the better part of the morning with his advisers on the Soviet Union to discuss strategies for handling the U.S.'s principal adversary, emerged from the white cap with a decrepit black alligator briefcase stuffed with urgent weekend reading matter. Aides followed with plump black briefing books. As would be his custom, Jack had arrived in time for lunch, but first he briefly walked the property with Jackie and Caroline. One destination was the stable, which, despite the farmer's promises, remained full of pigs. To Jackie's annoyance, the delivery of her horses would have to be postponed. After lunch, they spent the day indoors in front of a crackling fire and enjoyed their first real privacy together since the Inauguration. For the moment, it was everything Jackie had dreamed Glen Ora might be. Whether Jack had used his freedom the night before, she cannot yet have known for certain. She seemed determined to spend these hours with him as if the problems that had driven her here did not exist.

Jackie loved to tease Jack that, whether he liked it or not, as the first Catholic President he must attend church every Sunday. She could plead illness, but the President had to show up come hell or high water. Catholic Mass was held at the Middleburg Community Center, five minutes' drive from Glen Ora, and that Sunday locals who hadn't attended in years poured in, along with not a few outsiders. It was ten minutes before twelve that first Sunday, February 12, when the Kennedys drove up in front, where Father Albert Perier and Chief Usher Harold Deering waited to greet Middleburg's new premier Catholic. The service began promptly at noon, and when it was time for Holy Communion everyone naturally waited for the President to go to the altar first. Many eyes, including those of his wife, locked onto him, but he did not rise. Finally, others went forward. Jackie, for her part, cannot possibly have missed the significance of this. A Catholic who has committed a mortal sin cannot take communion before he has attended confession. In his refusal to take communion – so striking that a Secret Service agent remarked on it in his report – Jack, who still observed with full sincerity many parts of his Catholic upbringing, had acknowledged publicly that he was not in a state of grace.

The Kennedys returned to Glen Ora for lunch and spent the afternoon quietly with the children. As Jack was due in Washington the following morning, an important choice confronted Jackie, one she would have to live with for the rest of the presidency. She had to decide whether she really wanted to proceed with her plan. After Jack's conspicuous refusal to take communion, she could not pretend to herself that nothing had happened at the White House in her absence. In a marriage where much was conveyed silently, to let him return on his own would be to establish a pattern of acquiescence, whereas to accompany him would send a very different message. Almost certainly, Jack would continue to cheat, but at least she would have communicated disapproval.

On Monday morning, the presidential limousine, flags flying, waited in front of Glen Ora; Jack had decided to travel by car rather than by helicopter. Up to the last minute Jackie could have chosen one way or the other, but shortly before eleven she sent her husband out by himself. In a gesture as momentous perhaps as her 1956 decision to live with his womanizing, Jackie chose to remain in the country until Tuesday.

Jackie returned to the White House on Tuesday, February 14, in time to prepare for a Valentine's Day dinner party at the Georgetown home of Joe Alsop. Alsop, eager to introduce Jack to Susan Mary Patten, whom he would marry two days later, was determined that the meeting go well. In addition to his passion for the President, Alsop was happily imagining the privileged role he was positioned to play during the Kennedy presidency, so it was crucial that Jack be charmed by his fiancée. That encounter, at a candlelit table set with Alsop's blue Sèvres service and crystal glasses bubbling with Pol Roger champagne, was the evening's central drama. No one can possibly have realized the tremendous impact the evening would have on Jackie.

Among the guests was David Bruce, soon to depart for London as ambassador, so Britain was a natural topic of conversation. Susan Mary knew British society well and had years of practice as a conversationalist. When Kennedy, a connoisseur of gossip, inquired about Harold Macmillan, the Prime Minister he had yet to meet, she had just the story. As a bonus, its source was Lord David Cecil, author of *The Young Melbourne*, Jack's bible.

The anecdote centered on Macmillan's wife, born a Cavendish and an aunt of Jack's late brother-in-law Billy Hartington. Not long after Macmillan had become a Member of Parliament, Lady Dorothy had begun a passionate love affair with another M.P., Robert Boothby. According to Cecil, who was also related to Dorothy, her relatives had decided that, in order to end the embarrassing affair, a wife must be found for Boothby. After they provided a suitable candidate – Dorothy's first cousin – a wedding date was set and the family breathed a collective sigh of relief. But their exultation was premature. Dorothy, determined to keep her lover, joined Boothby and his bride on the honeymoon.

For Cecil, the point of the story was less Dorothy's scandalous behavior than her husband's astonishing reaction. Rather than taking this latest humiliation as his cue to send Dorothy packing oncc and for all, Macmillan continued to love her – a response that, to Cecil, proved what a 'strange man' he really was. Macmillan, who preferred to be alone in his misery, went off to the country for the weekend and was sick out the train window.

Jack, seated only a few feet away from Jackie, exploded in laughter at the punch line, as did others. He appeared utterly charmed by a story whose humor rested on how pathetic it was for a man to continue to love his unfaithful wife. For Jackie, feeling extremely raw after a weekend of secret emotional turmoil, the timing could hardly have been worse. Jack's hilarity hinted at a painful possibility: that he found her own uncon- ditional love equally ridiculous. Had Glen Ora and Jackie's other efforts to sustain the marriage made her pathetic in his eyes?

According to Joe Alsop, Jack would always treasure the story, particularly after Macmillan became someone of whom he was deeply fond. But he was by no means the only one on whom it made an indelible impression. Because of this shattering glimpse into Macmillan's personal life, Jackie would form a strongly emotional bond with a man she had yet to meet, a bond that would eventually encourage her to reach out in her darkest days with a depth of feeling she permitted few to see.

After the dinner party, Jackie began to cancel official engage- ments. On Thursday, she and Jack were due to be guests of the Indian ambassador, Mahomedali Currim Chagla, at a preview of *The World of Apu*, the last part of a trilogy by the renowned film director Satyajit Ray. As the first diplomatic invitation accepted since Jack took office, it was a coup for Ambassador Chagla in the intensely competitive Washington

diplomatic community where such things were closely monitored. As the film was the work of one of India's greatest living
artists, the interest of Mrs Kennedy, a devotee of culture, was
especially gratifying. Hours before the Kennedys were expected,
however, Jackie sent word down to Jack's office that he would
have to go by himself, whatever the diplomatic repercussions.

Ambassador Chagla, notified at the last minute that Mrs
Kennedy had a bad cold, did not conceal his disappointment
when the President turned up at the Dupont Theater accompanied, in Jackie's place, by Senator John Sherman Cooper,
who had been U.S. ambassador to India under Eisenhower,
and his wife Lorraine. The evening was a trial for Kennedy,
who would become famous for walking out of White House
screenings after only ten minutes if the movie bored him. He
could not leave tonight, particularly in view of the affront
committed by his wife, and had to sit through the entire foreign-
language film, which, despite a running time of not quite two
hours, felt by his own account more like three or four. From
the row behind, Senator Cooper watched with amusement as
the President, seated beside Ambassador Chagla, struggled to
hide his restlessness.

When they were released from the theater at half past ten,
Kennedy, laughing with the Coopers about the ordeal, insisted
on showing them the White House. No matter how many
friends he had received in the past three weeks, he retained a
boyish delight in playing tour guide. The Coopers accompanied
him, but demurred when he proposed a visit to the family
quarters. When they expressed their reluctance to disturb Jackie
in her state of ill health, Jack revealed that matters were quite
different from what the Indian ambassador had been led to
believe.

'I don't think she's very sick,' he said with a grin. 'I don't
think she wanted to go.'

When Jack knocked on the door to the Queens' Bedroom,
the Coopers heard Jackie groan, 'Oh, no!' In spite of that, he
opened the door to disclose Jackie as she sat reading in the
four-poster, canopied bed. Though she made her best effort to
disguise her feelings, Jackie, who hated the need to be constantly

'on stage,' was clearly in no mood to share her husband's ebullience. But Jack knew how to handle her at such moments, and teased her about having sent him off alone to the interminable Indian movie. She loved nothing better than to laugh with him, and his account of his struggle to conceal his restlessness soon brought her out of her depression.

The effect was temporary. The next morning, she sent word that she would be unable to appear at a luncheon for Lady Jackson, the economist Barbara Ward, whom Jack had met years before in London through Kick. A follow-up note from Jackie's office said that should anyone ask, the President ought to remember that the Indian ambassador had been told Jackie had a cold and must remain in her room on doctor's orders.

That weekend, Jackie retreated to Glen Ora and took to her bed. The people around her focused on the explanation that her condition was due to complications of childbirth and that a few weeks' rest was all she needed, but in fact, a month into her husband's presidency, she felt unable to bear her new life. The tenuous compromise of the campaign years was a thing of the past, and she found her new plan far more difficult to abide. Added to that, the pressures of her new life were utterly overwhelming, her deep insecurity and feelings of vulnerability making the situation worse.

When, by Sunday, February 26, Jackie showed no sign of returning, Jack flew down from the White House with Dr Travell, concerned that something was seriously wrong. He was aware of the pressure she had been under since the Inauguration, and of how relentlessly she had driven herself. He was also aware that when she arrived at the White House she had not yet recovered from surgery, and that in the intervening weeks she had consistently disregarded the warnings of her doctor. The pressures his infidelity exerted were something that, as always, he preferred to ignore. With the focus squarely on the indisputable fact that Jackie was physically run down from having over-extended herself after John Jr's birth, Jack could avoid consideration of her emotional strain.

Even in the best of times, Jack had grown accustomed to Jackie's sudden dark, introspective depressions. He and Lem comfortably explained away Jackie's 'moods,' as they called them, by deciding that they were just part of her nature, something she had been born with. That was a good deal more convenient for Jack than asking whether it was something in her life with him that caused her repeatedly to grow depressed. If Jackie had always been subject to depression, it couldn't be anything he had done.

On this occasion, Dr Travell, taking her cue from the President, focused on Jackie's physical condition. Since Glen Ora seemed to have effected no improvement, the physician prescribed an immediate stay in Florida, where Jackie could get some sun and rest far from the pressures of Washington. In Palm Beach, she would stay with their friends the Wrightsmans, where her every need would be looked after and she could regain her strength – or so it was hoped. Jack and Dr Travell stayed overnight at Glen Ora, then flew back to Washington on Monday morning. Jackie followed on Tuesday to drop off the children at the White House before heading south the following morning.

With Jackie away, Lem took another leave of absence from his job and installed himself at the White House, where, in a revealing parody of her marriage, he seized the opportunity to act as her stand-in in the family quarters. Jack, who had grown up with five sisters and three brothers, hated to be alone; Lem, like Jackie, excelled in the role of Kennedy sibling. He did it so well that Teddy Kennedy, by his own account, was three years old before he realized that Lem wasn't really his older brother. With Jackie temporarily out of the picture, Lem was decidedly in his element. In many ways, at this time of inexpressible happiness in Jack's life, Lem proved a more congenial sibling than Jackie. By all accounts, Jack, fascinated and delighted by every aspect of this great prize he had just won, had yet to feel the full burden of the presidency. Lem, known for his distinctive booming laugh, fit right in with Jack's ebullience in a way that Jackie, in her depression, did not.

As ersatz First Lady, Lem happily supervised the ongoing renovations on the second and third floor of the Mansion. He arranged small dinner parties, inviting the sort of people not usually on Jackie's list. At Lem's White House dinner parties, one might discover various Kennedys and their spouses, old prep school chums, and, in the interest of making Jack happy, even Lem's *bête noire* Torby Macdonald, whom Lem would always blame for having intruded on his friendship with Jack. Of course, there was another reason why Jack enjoyed the more relaxed atmosphere Lem brought to the White House: Lem turned a blind eye when his friend brought women upstairs.

As Jackie had known he would, the moment she left him alone Jack had resumed what was essentially a continuation of the sex life he had conducted on the campaign trail. 'He couldn't get away from screwing around with other women,' observed Betty Spalding. 'It was a real compulsion with him ... something so deep in that man.' At the White House, some but by no means all of the players were familiar faces. Several young women who had worked in the campaign, and provided sexual diversion for the candidate as well, had moved into jobs in the administration.

In addition, there was an ever-changing supply of fresh faces. Jack had long before taken to referring to many of his women as 'kid,' because he couldn't, often didn't even try to, remember their names. His friend Bill Thompson, his brother-in-law Peter Lawford, and his long-time aide Dave Powers, among others, could be counted on to bring in women for the President's pleasure now that it was difficult for him to circulate widely. Even some of his former girlfriends were willing to pass on an attractive acquaintance whom they thought might amuse him. Everyone seemed eager to make Jack happy, both the people procuring the women and the women themselves. A good many women actively pursued the President, whose proclivities were well known. He had the aura of a movie star, and they were eager to say they had slept with him. Some were social acquaintances of his and Jackie's, some were strangers who sought out an introduction, and some were female members of the Capitol Hill press corps.

From the outset, the Kennedy White House promised to be a veritable seraglio, with women furiously competing for the President's favor. 'There were women that kept score cards,'

said Secret Service agent Larry Newman, 'and they cared not
at all for Jackie's feelings.' Almost everyone who worked at the
White House knew what went on, both with women who
worked there and with outsiders who came in on their own or
were brought in by Powers and others. A hardened attitude
soon developed. 'Some female members of the press were not
circumspect about saying, "I just laid Jack,"' Newman recalled.
'The staff would look like, "'Yeah, you and fifty others and the
Chinese army."'

Jack had his regulars, secretaries who were available at almost
any time. At least one was so naïve that she imagined her
relationship with the President was a serious love affair. Two
of the secretaries built a strong bond of friendship based on
their shared relationship with Kennedy, whom they often visited
together. At work and after hours, they stuck together for moral
support when other female employees ostracized them.

In general, the atmosphere in the White House, taking its
cue from the President, was sexually charged. Kennedy had
made politics glamorous and his administration was filled with
young, attractive people. One woman who worked there would
later remember that everyone seemed to be having an affair or
at least a flirtation, not necessarily with the President. For all
the sexual license, there was one important rule: everyone was
free to turn Kennedy down. Some of the women had learned
this long before they reached the White House, in the days
when Kennedy was still in the Senate or on the campaign trail.
In fact, when a woman did refuse, Kennedy seemed almost to
like her the better for it. 'If you didn't want to play, then he
would try again, because he liked the chase,' recalled Susan
Stankrauff, who worked for Kennedy in the Senate and on the
campaign trail, and later worked for Bobby Kennedy in the
Justice Department. 'Eventually he would figure out it wasn't
worth his valuable time.'

On one occasion during the campaign when he called
with an invitation for drinks, a spirited young woman who
believed fervently in Kennedy but wanted no part in the
sexual shenanigans fired back, 'Friend, I'm too busy typing
up the Senator's speech so he can get elected.' Kennedy,

she remembered, 'laughed like hell and that was the end of it.' He could afford to laugh, for, as everyone in his organization knew, 'if he got turned down, he'd go somewhere else.' There were always others prepared, in many cases eager, to say yes.

Now that he was in the Oval Office, Kennedy continued avidly to pursue employees he had yet to seduce, but in the interest of discretion would usually have Dave Powers make the call. As in the past, women were free to refuse, though, as Larry Newman recalled, 'some of them had trepidations about Powers calling again. But usually that didn't happen if they were in key positions.' A number of women who worked in the White House, admittedly attracted to the President, resisted his advances because, said Newman, 'they just didn't want to put themselves in that position where people could think they were a bimbo.' Though some female employees strongly disapproved of the 'bimbos,' others were more tolerant. 'As long as they didn't take part in any of that and didn't choose to, it wasn't part of their life,' said Newman. 'And to my knowledge, there was no one ever forced to.'

In Jackie's absence, the President, whether at lunchtime or after his last appointment in the evening, could often be found in the pool – a favorite locale for sex because of his bad back – or upstairs in the family quarters with one or more women. That the family quarters were supposed to be his wife's sanctum bothered him not at all. When it was finished, Jackie's bedroom, lovingly adorned with some of her most treasured objects and family pictures, including those of her children, would provide the setting for sex parties. Because of his bad back, Kennedy couldn't use just any mattress. Jackie had one of his special cattle-hair mattresses placed next to her own, and given Jack's fondness for three-way sex her bed, larger than the one in his room, became the obvious choice. No wonder she so quickly came to hate the White House, where the presence of other women regularly defiled her embroidered silk sheets, and where, upon her return, she had to see certain of those women, as well as people who knew what had occurred. These included Secret Service agents, various White House employees, even her friend

Mr West, who controlled the book that noted every visitor to the private quarters. 'It's not that he cheated on her but that everybody knew it,' said Larry Newman, in an effort to explain Jackie's plight, 'and then she's got to appear with him.'

That Jackie found it painful to be at the White House in such circumstances was hardly surprising. And that she was absent when the women sat at her dining table, ran naked through her rooms, or entertained Jack in her bed can have been small consolation. While Lem stood in for her at the White House, Jackie withdrew from nearly everything in her new life, with the exception of her plan to raise money for the White House restoration. At the first meeting of the Fine Arts Committee, Jackie made a presentation without a sign that anything was wrong. It was also in this period, while in Florida, that she enlisted Henry du Pont to play a high-profile role as chairman.

Jackie did not return to the White House until March 8, and then only because her sister, who had missed the Inauguration on account of illness, was due to arrive that evening with her husband, Stanislas Radziwill, a Polish prince who had fled his homeland during the war and reinvented himself as a real estate developer in Britain. The sisters were as competitive with each other as they were close, and Jackie, much as she disliked being First Lady, pulled out all the stops to impress Lee with her new status. There were glittering small dinner parties in the new dining room and a well-timed party in Jackie's honor at the French embassy. The visit's centerpiece was a lavish dinner dance for Lee attended not by political or diplomatic figures, but by seventy-eight friends of the Kennedys. Though her perspective would change in time, at this stage Jackie continued to view the White House as little more than her own, very grand private house. On this maiden occasion, she used the immense state rooms on the ground floor – the State Dining Room, the Blue Room, and the Red Room – for strictly personal ends.

It was soon obvious that however much Jackie wanted to show off at the White House for her sister, she longed to get away. The weeks of retreat had left her rested, but her depression persisted. Soon she took Lee to Glen Ora and then to New York, where they stayed at the Kennedy family apartment in the Carlyle Hotel and spent several days shopping. Jackie said goodbye to Lee in New York and returned to the White House for only a single night before going to Glen Ora for the weekend. On Monday, March 27, she went south again to Florida with the children, this time to spend Easter at the Kennedy house in Palm Beach. Six weeks had passed since Joe Alsop's Valentine's Day dinner party. In that time, the new First Lady had spent only ten nights at the White House, almost all of them during her sister's visit. Now she was off again, and her future seemed highly uncertain.

In January, when she had left Joe Kennedy's Palm Beach house to fly to Washington and a new life she dreaded, she had been determined to protect herself as best she could. She had come with a plan to guard her remaining privacy and cope with the overwhelming problem of her husband's infidelity. At the White House, she had encountered demands and responsibilities that had soon proven too much for her to cope with. Surrounded by women who eagerly awaited her departure so they could swim naked with her husband, and aware that nearly everyone else was watching her keenly and speculating about her life with Jack, Jackie was desperately unhappy. What woman could emerge unscathed from two such months? She was not oblivious to the whispered comments that Jack's womanizing was really all her fault, and that if only Jack had found a better wife things would have been otherwise. She had had to engineer a situation in which he could betray her behind her back, so that he would not have to do so before her eyes. All too quickly, she had come to believe there really was no bright side. Yes, her sister and others were impressed that she was First Lady. Yes, she had given a glamorous dinner dance that everyone in Washington had spoken of with excitement and admiration. But none of that was reason enough to endure what she was enduring. No matter how far from the White House she fled, she had been unable to shake off her depression. As she headed back to the Kennedy house in Florida in what felt very much like defeat, the question was no longer whether she was up to her responsibilities, but whether she was really willing to try anymore.

Jackie had been in retreat for weeks, canceling official engagements, asking Jack or Lady Bird Johnson to substitute for her at public appearances. As she well knew, different behavior would shortly be expected. Jack was due to come to Florida in a few days to celebrate Easter – the first big holiday of the Kennedy presidency – with his family. If, as scheduled, Jackie returned to Washington with him on April 4, she faced her first period of intensive diplomatic obligations.

Beginning with the arrival of Harold and Dorothy Macmillan on April 5, the White House was to be the setting for a series of important visits by world leaders. As the dignitaries were to bring their wives (a daughter in the case of West German Chancellor Konrad Adenauer), protocol demanded that Jackie participate. It also required her to accompany her husband, soon afterward, on state visits to Canada and France, as well as to a hoped-for summit with Khrushchev. Before he made the life-and-death decisions that surely faced him, Jack wanted to size up Khrushchev for himself, while giving the Soviet leader the opportunity to see him clearly rather than relying on second-hand reports.

Repeatedly in six weeks – with the notable exception of Lee's visit – Jackie had canceled appearances that required a few hours at most, usually much less. The duties that confronted her in the coming months would be far more demanding, as well as less handily avoided. When she and Jack traveled abroad, she would be on call hour after hour, for days on end, with little time for retreat. Could she handle it? Would she even try? Could she bring herself to go forward with the plan she had worked out prior to the Inauguration? Sometime during her stay in Palm Beach, Jackie would have to decide.

Late on the afternoon of the 27th, she landed at Palm Beach International Airport. When she was there in January, she had been to all intents and purposes alone. This time, as the *Caroline* taxied to a halt, Joe Kennedy strode across the tarmac to greet her. When the ramp to the plane was in position, Jackie, gripping her daughter's hand, started down first. As she spotted

Joe, her eyes burned brightly. No matter how warm Jackie sometimes seemed in private, her core of reserve was rarely breached. She might flirt with men of power, or gossip with women whose taste she admired; with her sister, there was the incessant whispering that tended to amuse or irritate onlookers. With Joe, Jackie was unmistakably different. As Mr West observed, in Joe's presence Jackie's face was 'animated and happy, as it was when she was playing with her children.'

Two Secret Service agents carried out four-month-old John in a blue bassinet. His English nanny, Maud Shaw, followed. Joe, who had not seen the children since he had had them flown up to Washington at the beginning of February, noted at once that his grandson had gained weight. Miss Shaw had altered John's formula and made a few other changes in his routine, with evident success.

'What have you been doing to him?' Joe asked her delightedly. 'He looks twice the fellow he was. He's doing really well now.'

Jackie, too, fresh from a weekend of riding at Glen Ora, seemed physically improved since Joe had last seen her during her stay at the Wrightsmans'. As twenty pieces of luggage, in addition to a metal box containing Caroline's Welsh terrier, Charley, were unloaded, Jackie and the children, including two of Bobby's sons, piled into Grandpa's car.

A high, crumbling privacy wall protected the Kennedy property from North Ocean Boulevard. The car passed through the large, iron-grilled gate at which, back in January, a Secret Service agent had noted down the precise moment when Jackie, in effect, had entered history. She and Joe got out of the car and headed to the sprawling, dilapidated main house. Its stucco façade had patches of mildewed, peeling paint. Many roof tiles were coated with fungus. The concrete steps leading down to the ocean were in a state of disintegration. Down the hall from the living room, Jackie was shown to the same ground-floor bedroom where she had recuperated after John's birth and made plans for her life in the White House. As she considered afresh how to handle the future, it was fitting that she was back there.

The Kennedy residence, decorated with what one visitor

cattily described as Salvation Army rejects, was the antithesis
of how Jackie wished to live. Unlike others who had married
into the family, she had long existed in conflict with the attitude,
canonized by Joe, that there were more important things in life
than fancy houses and furniture. Yet she always felt happy and
protected here. From the beginning, Jackie had thrilled to the
power that came with having both family leaders – Joe Sr and
Jack – in her corner. Faced with difficult decisions, Jackie would
make them surrounded by the aura of the Kennedys, influenced
by a family drama that had long ago become her own.

Three days later, on Thursday, March 30, Joe returned to
the airport to welcome his son when *Air Force One* arrived. Jack,
as was his custom when he greeted his father, made a fist and
Joe tenderly cupped one hand over his, visibly delighted to see
him. It had been two months since Jack became President, a
day Joe unabashedly regarded as marking his own 'greatest
success.' After the ignominy associated with Joe Kennedy's
ambassadorship to Britain, Jack's election promised the vindication of which the father had dreamed. Anguish over the
wartime charges of cowardice had long superseded a Boston-
Irish boy's rage as the driving force in Joe's life. Winning – at
any cost – had always meant everything to Joe, but never more
so than after his time in London, where he had failed so publicly
and miserably.

It hadn't been easy for him to stay on the sidelines during
the campaign lest the controversy that still swirled around the
father infect the son. Never, perhaps, had Joe's loneliness come
into sharper focus than during the Democratic convention in
Los Angeles, when Jack asked him 'to stay out of sight.'
Accordingly, Joe remained at the house of his friend, the actress
Marion Davies. Jack and Bobby, aware of his distress, dispatched
Susan Stankrauff to answer the phone, have lunch with him,
and generally keep him company. But the phone hardly rang,
Stankrauff recalled, and Joe, 'pouting a little because he'd been
shut out,' finally instructed her to call and summon Jack and
Bobby to dinner. 'They turned him down,' she remembered.
'It was kind of sad.' Joe, for his part, reacted palpably but 'very
quietly.'

His response to Jack's victory was far from subdued. Briefly he came out of hiding, and those who attended the small private reception at the White House on Inauguration day found it hard to forget the sight of a grinning Joe Kennedy as he welcomed guests at the door. 'Oh, he was ecstatic!' Betty Spalding fondly recalled. 'It looked like he owned the house and he'd just built it and he wanted you to come in so he could show it to you.' At the same time, Joe remained sensitive to widespread fears that Jack would be his father's puppet. After the festivities he retreated to Palm Beach, calculating that as long as he was absent from Washington no one could accuse him of undue influence. Still, he conferred regularly with Jack by telephone.

Family lunch that Thursday afternoon was the first occasion on which all had sat down together in the Palm Beach house since Jack became President. Unbeknownst to Jackie, Rose, and the others, Joe had a big surprise planned. For as long as anyone could remember, Joe had sat at the head of the table. When he ordered Jack to take his place, the moment seemed cataclysmic. At first Jack, who revered his father, declined.

Joe grew belligerent. 'Listen,' he thundered, 'you are the President of the country, you sit at the head of the table in this house!'

Jack finally moved with reluctance to the head of the table, a place which he occupied from then on. The scene is important for the light it sheds on the father–son relationship at a time when Jack was wrestling with one of the monumental decisions of his presidency – a decision in which Joe Kennedy, tormented by his past mistakes and hungry for vindication, had an exceptionally strong personal interest. Before Jack returned to Washington, he had to make up his mind whether to go forward with a plan to overthrow Fidel Castro.

The plan had been initiated in March 1960, when President Eisenhower approved a C.I.A.-sponsored covert action to eliminate the Cuban leader. By the time Kennedy took office, the C.I.A. intended to land a strike force of seven to eight hundred Cuban exiles on a Cuban beachhead, six to eight weeks later. Three U.S. Special Forces teams were secretly training the exile brigade in Guatemala. Run, however surreptitiously, by Washington, the invasion plan clearly violated prior U.S. commitments to the United Nations Charter, the Charter of the Organization of American States, and the Rio Treaty, which all explicitly ruled out the use of armed force except in self-defense. As Under-Secretary of State Chester Bowles noted, a U.S.-backed overthrow of the Cuban government would defy treaty obligations that were supposed to be 'binding in law and conscience.' To do so, Bowles judged, would be to blur the vital differences that distinguished the U.S. from the Soviet Union, and thus lose the moral edge.

Characteristically, it was not the moral issue that concerned Kennedy when, eight days into his presidency, C.I.A. Director Allen Dulles asked him to approve the invasion at a meeting in the Cabinet Room attended by Vice-President Johnson, Defense Secretary McNamara, Secretary of State Dean Rusk, and Chairman of the Joint Chiefs of Staff General Lyman Lemnitzer, among others. At a moment when he had an opportunity to state that the U.S. was not in the business of overthrowing foreign governments, Kennedy, whose first question was said always to be the best and most important, asked only whether an invasion could succeed.

Nor did Kennedy engage the question of right conduct when Special Assistant Arthur Schlesinger Jr argued in a February 11 memo that, as the President's 'first dramatic foreign policy initiative,' an invasion 'would dissipate all the extraordinary good will which has been rising toward the new Administration through the world' and 'fix a malevolent image of the new Administration in the minds of millions.' Kennedy, evidently more concerned about his image than about the reasons why an illegal covert operation might tarnish it, directed the C.I.A. only to provide additional cover. Effective cover was also vitally important since the participation of the U.S. in an invasion of Cuba might trigger the Soviets to move on Berlin, a development that could lead to nuclear war. The revised Zapata plan, offered to the President on March 15, was designed not so much to be tactically superior to the previous version – indeed, some argued that it was actually a good deal worse – as to more effectively conceal the role of the United States.

The President's lack of interest in ethics in these discussions went to the very heart of his contradictory nature. He genuinely believed, with John Buchan, in the nobility of politics and public service; this was the idealistic side of Kennedy, which the world had heard in the soaring phrases of his Inaugural Address. As crafted by Theodore Sorensen, that speech inspired a great many Americans to make personal sacrifices for their country and the common good. But Kennedy also had another side, one that manifested itself in both public and private acts. Prepared like his father to do things whether they were right or wrong so long as they served his own needs, Kennedy had a moral Achilles heel. 'The Cuban adventure,' Bowles predicted, would horrify the world all the more in contrast to the high principles on which Kennedy had so recently appealed in his Inaugural Address. To which one might add, with the benefit of hindsight, that the leader who had just initiated an age of idealism in American politics was about to launch the very opposite: an epoch of cynicism.

At length, Kennedy agreed to the revised Zapata plan, but in light of ongoing concerns about the chances for success, as well as for effectively disguising U.S. involvement, he reserved the right to cancel it up to twenty-four hours before the landing. By the time he joined Jackie and the children in Florida, he was inclined to abort the attack. Moral issues aside, it had become increasingly apparent that the operation was tactically unsound, its chances of success estimated by Bowles to be 'not greater than one out of three.' Above all, the prospect of a Soviet retaliation in Berlin weighed heavily on the President.

As he sat down to family lunch that first afternoon in Palm Beach, he had every reason to call off the invasion. In his father's house, however, emotion rather than reason propelled his thinking. Historians have often told the tale of the Bay of Pigs fiasco, but there is always a frustrating hole in the story. As further documents have been declassified and the minutes of important meetings released, it has become apparent that the plan was deeply flawed and that Kennedy had tremendous doubts. Why, then, did he finally agree to an invasion so plainly doomed to fail?

The answer is to be found in Kennedy's devotion to his father and his desire to obliterate his father's legacy of shame. As Joe Kennedy saw it, a quick big win in Cuba would dispel the charge that Kennedys were cowards, while also demonstrating to Khrushchev that Jack was a strong leader. On the other hand, to refuse to go forward with an invasion approved by Eisenhower, the great general and war hero, might revive the charges of cowardice, Jack's own distinguished war record and Joe Jr's death in action notwithstanding. As Bobby Kennedy later pointedly remarked, if Jack 'hadn't gone through with it, everybody would have said it showed that he had no courage.' 'Let us begin anew,' Kennedy had memorably declared in his Inaugural Address, but in view of his powerful bond to his father there can have been few men less able to escape the shadow of the past.

Of all the places where he might have been when he had to make up his mind on the Zapata plan, his father's house was unquestionably the least fortunate. For six days, Jack played golf, watched movies, ate, and just relaxed with his father, and from first to last the main topic of conversation was Cuba. The patriarch may have made the dramatic gesture of relinquishing his place at the table, but his influence continued to be over-whelming. Joe, who had destroyed himself politically by oppos-ing military action against Hitler, pushed hard for a move against Castro. By the time he was ready to return to Washington, Jack, who almost certainly would not have become President but for the spur provided by his father's disgrace, had come around to Joe's way of thinking. He left Florida inclined to proceed with the invasion.

Immersion in the Kennedy family drama also altered Jackie's outlook, as paired with Jack she instantly became central to that drama. Jackie, depressed and self-absorbed, had been at the White House so rarely in the weeks since Valentine's Day as to have been insulated from the rising tensions of the presidency, as well as from Jack's growing sense of his isolation in office at a time when watershed decisions loomed. Nine days in Joe Kennedy's tumultuous presence changed all that. The storm and stress over Cuba seemed to make Jackie look beyond herself for the first time in many weeks. Her husband needed her support. By Tuesday, April 4, when Joe accompanied Jack and Jackie to the airport for the return flight to Washington, she had made up her mind to try again as First Lady.

FOUR

A Family Drama

Late in the afternoon of Tuesday, April 4, 1961, a white cap carrying Jackie, her husband, and their children, along with Peter Lawford, appeared over the South Grounds. After a two-hour flight from West Palm Beach on *Air Force One*, the presidential party had transferred at Andrews Air Force Base for the last brief leg of the trip. As was customary, the white cap came in low and turned with its door to the North Portico before it landed. Marine pilots took immense pride in the precision and expertise with which they ferried the First Family, always coming down in the very center of the landing pad. One passenger compared the experience to being on a giant feather.

A Marine on the ground waited for the blades to stop before rushing up to pull open the door. Jackie, tanned and well rested, headed for the Mansion with Lawford, the children, and a nanny. Jack went directly to the Oval Office, where he would have ten minutes to prepare before heading over to the State Department for a major session on Cuba, at which a number of advisers expected him to decide one way or the other. By rule, the white cap did not depart until the President and First Lady were safely indoors.

The family quarters had been transformed while Jackie was in Palm Beach. The Kennedys' adjoining bedrooms were finally finished, and not without trepidation Jackie went in to inspect them. This was actually the second attempt to complete her enormous, high-ceilinged room on the southwest corner of the second floor. An earlier paint color, which Jackie had chosen herself, had misfired and she had asked that it be redone. This time, she was satisfied. Some of her most cherished personal possessions were arrayed on tables and walls. Jack's cattle-hair mattress sat next to hers, both attached to a single upholstered silk headboard with a draped silk canopy overhead. Small tables on either side had matching white reading lamps, telephones, water carafes, and stacks of books.

Stereo equipment and an extensive collection of popular light recordings were tucked away in the walk-through closet that connected her room with Jack's. The records were a staple of his life. There had been a time when he and Kick always seemed to have a favorite record on, and with Jackie as well he had grown accustomed to hearing Broadway show tunes or something by Noël Coward or Frank Sinatra in the background. A small, portable record player in the West Sitting Room softly serenaded the Kennedys and friends at informal dinners. After guests left, Jack and Jackie almost always played music when they went to bed. As soon as her husband fell asleep, Jackie, in a routine she remembered vividly long afterward, would cross the cold floor with bare feet to turn the music off. Though he usually shared her bed, the second smaller, more simply furnished room provided Jack, who tended to get up first, with a place to review intelligence reports and the morning papers, soak in the tub, play with Caroline, and now and then – despite Jackie's concept of the family quarters as sacrosanct – confer with aides.

The completion of the bedrooms suggested that a fresh chapter had begun. Jackie had gotten off to a shaky start as First Lady, but the new bedrooms promised a second chance. The fact that she and her husband were to share a bedroom again underscored just what it was – her own small portion of happiness with him – that she was so eager to protect.

Jackie had returned to Washington determined to stick to her original plan to undertake as few official duties as possible. But in ways she could not have foreseen, forces had been set in motion in Florida, as Jack conferred with his father, which would forever alter her and her plan. As much as anything she did upstairs, Jack's decisions in the next two weeks would determine the nature of their life together. When he sat down with advisers Tuesday night, it instantly became apparent that his thinking on Cuba had changed in Palm Beach. Suddenly, Special Assistant to the President for National Security Affairs McGeorge Bundy later recalled, Kennedy 'really wanted to do this.' That had not been his attitude when he left. Schlesinger, who before Easter had noted Kennedy's growing skepticism, was among those who detected Joe's influence. But despite expectations that the President would announce one way or another, something kept him from doing so. Emotionally committed to an invasion though he now was, rationally he continued to doubt its chances for success.

At the State Department, Kennedy, desperate for reassurance and still fiercely concerned about the issue of cover, polled his senior advisers on whether an invasion could succeed. When Kennedy asked each man, 'What do you think?' he did not expect long-winded equivocations, only a crisp yes or no. The majority voted yes, with the notable exceptions of Rusk and Senator J. William Fulbright, head of the Senate Foreign Relations Committee, who irritated some with what a detractor characterized as 'a fruitless theoretical argument over whether the invasion was moral.'

It was too late for such thoughtful arguments. At this point, Kennedy was not interested in philosophical questions and Fulbright was rebuffed. Nonetheless, when the session drew to a close Kennedy did ask Schlesinger, who had not been polled, what he thought. The junior adviser made it clear that he opposed the plan and followed up with a memo to warn that Cuba would 'become our Hungary' − a reference to the opprobrium suffered by the Soviet Union after its tanks rolled into Hungary.

It was half past eight before Jack appeared in the private quarters. He and Jackie dined with Peter Lawford, who, in place of Lem, would play court jester in the tense days that followed. Jackie's important duties as First Lady would begin the following day. Nearly two months after Jack's uproarious laughter at Lord David Cecil's story of Harold and Dorothy Macmillan had sent Jackie into retreat, it was the Macmillans who had necessitated her return. Since Macmillan was head of government and not head of state (that position being occupied by the Queen), protocol dictated that Secretary of State Rusk rather than the President appear at the airport that night to welcome them from Jamaica.

At a moment when Jackie was about to try again to live with dignity with a faithless but adored spouse, she met someone who for decades had managed to do precisely that. The anecdote told at Alsop's dinner party was only the start of a long, very sad story. Despite the efforts of her family, Lady Dorothy's infidelity had persisted. For thirty years she continued her turbulent affair with Bob Boothby, who was rumored to have fathered the Macmillans' youngest daughter, Sarah. When Lady Dorothy was with her husband she played the devoted political wife, running his houses, entertaining his guests, traveling with him, and doing all that was needed to further his career. When they were apart – and, more often than not, that was her doing – she spent the time with her lover. Macmillan, deeply moral and religious, regarded marital vows as sacred. Early in the affair, he had a nervous breakdown, and though he recovered, he continued to suffer bouts of depression. Like Jackie, he often took to his bed in despair, finding solace, as she did, in a Jane Austen novel. Finally, declaring that he would never agree to a divorce, Macmillan did his best to accept the situation with equanimity. Knowing that he would never love anyone but Lady Dorothy, he hoped that if he braced himself to do what was difficult perhaps there would be a reward at the end.

Wednesday morning, between an intensive early session in the Cabinet Room and a working lunch in the Family Dining Room, Jack brought Macmillan up to the private quarters. Jackie was introduced to a man whom both she and Jack, in their own ways and for their own reasons, would come to trust as they did few others.

The sixty-seven-year-old Prime Minister had a bushy moustache, baggy eyes, and thinning, unruly gray hair brushed back from a high forehead. His movements were sluggish, his manner stilted. Yet the impression he gave of 'being shot through with Victorian languor' was deceptive, warned Ambassador David

Bruce in briefing papers. As a statesman, Macmillan was in fact 'masterful, dominating, self-confident.' Particularly misleading, thought Bruce, was the Prime Minister's walk, a slow, stiff shuffle that might cause some to think him incapable of swift action. On the contrary, Bruce cautioned, Macmillan was 'shrewd, subtle in maneuver' and could 'featly spring onto his toes like a ballet dancer.' At the same time, an air of unflappability masked the sensitive nature of a man who for more than three decades had struggled in silence with a private grief.

The timing of his entrance into Jackie's life, coming as it did the morning after she and Jack had shared a permanent bedroom at the White House for the first time, could not have been better. Jackie had first heard Macmillan's story just after returning from that terrible first weekend at Glen Ora when she had put her plan into effect, and had heard him ridiculed because of similar accommodations in his own marriage. Seven weeks later, in the midst of her renewed effort to live with Jack's cheating, Macmillan's tremendous personal dignity offered hope that her plan was feasible. What she didn't know was that shortly after the presidential election, Jock Whitney, Eisenhower's ambassador in London, had regaled Macmillan with an account of Kennedy's sexual habits. From the first, both Jackie and her guest were aware of the sadness that linked them.

Because Lady Dorothy was related by marriage to Kick, Jack saw Macmillan as family. And if Jack regarded him that way, Jackie was inclined to do the same. Interestingly, the significance of this tie had not occurred to Macmillan when, the previous November, he had worried about how he was possibly going to get along with this 'cocky young Irishman.' Macmillan, who had enjoyed a friendship with Eisenhower that dated back to the war, suspected he would have little in common with Kennedy, who would see him as 'rather an old horse, ready to be put out to grass.' To make matters worse, the President-elect's father was anathema to Macmillan, who in the 1930s had staunchly opposed appeasement, and he worried that Ambassador Kennedy had inculcated anti-British sentiments in his son. That would be a disaster for Macmillan, who had a huge amount invested politically in the 'special relationship' between Britain and the U.S., and knew that only in partnership with Washington could he attain his goal of East–West détente. Initially, Macmillan reckoned his best chance of connecting with Kennedy was to engage him with interesting ideas. A brilliant letter-writer, he wrote a six-page letter on December 19, 1960, a full month before the Inauguration, to articulate some fundamental principles.

After sounding out various people acquainted with the President-elect, Macmillan decided to use his own connection to Kick to his advantage by sending Lady Dorothy's nephew, Andrew, the eleventh Duke of Devonshire, as his emissary to the Inauguration. Billy and Kick, had they lived, would have been Duke and Duchess, and in Washington Billy's younger brother Andrew and his wife, Deborah, had places of honor at the Inaugural ceremonies. Billy's family had been kind to Kick after his death, and, despite her intention to marry Lord Fitzwilliam, who died with her in the plane crash, had buried her as Billy's widow in the family plot near Chatsworth. For Jack, it wasn't just that the Macmillans were connected to one of his siblings; the connection was to his soul-mate and partner in the Kennedy family. Jack's powerful emotional bond to Kick (equaled only by his tie to his father) led him to treat her relations by marriage as virtually his own.

It pleased Macmillan when, in March, Kennedy reached out to him for advice. Faced with a political crisis in Laos, pressure from his own advisers to intervene militarily, and an impending meeting with Soviet Foreign Minister Andrei Gromyko, Kennedy had, as Macmillan sensed, started to feel the agonizing isolation of office. The impromptu meeting in Key West, Florida, on March 26 had been held at Kennedy's urgent request. He had his advisers lay out to Macmillan their plans for military action in Laos, before the two leaders retreated to confer in private. From the first, as Macmillan told Jackie years afterward, the young man and the old seemed able to talk freely and frankly to each other as though they were lifelong friends. Macmillan liked Kennedy tremendously, and was surprised and delighted that the President seemed to warm to him as well.

Kennedy asked what he thought of the plan, and the Prime Minister declared it a very bad idea. He urged that, rather than intervene militarily, the U.S. ought to push for a ceasefire, to be followed by an international conference with the objective of a neutral Laos. Kennedy, though he did not commit himself one way or another, seemed inclined to agree.

A quick study, Macmillan again used his connection to Kick to his advantage at Key West when he inquired if Kennedy had a preference for British ambassador in Washington. As Macmillan had anticipated, Kennedy asked for another of Kick's in-laws, David Ormsby-Gore. Ormsby-Gore had introduced Kick to his cousin Billy, and his wife, the former Sissie Thomas, had been Kick's best friend in England. As Bobby Kennedy would later say, next to Bobby himself there was no one Jack trusted more than David Ormsby-Gore. In Washington, he would be treated as family every bit as much as ambassador, and his appointment, to take effect in October, would create a situation unprecedented in U.S.–British relations. Thus Kennedy cemented a connection with Macmillan and England, a country his sister had called her 'second home,' where she and Jack had shared halcyon days when he visited. At a moment when, with regard to Cuba, Jack was decidedly under his father's influence, he was also being pulled in a contrary direction.

Up in the White House family quarters, as Macmillan and Kennedy sipped the exceptionally strong cocktails Jackie liked to serve, she relished the fact that the visitor had, by his own account, 'fallen' for her husband at Key West. The two men shared a wry sense of humor, which they often turned on themselves. Both had an intellectual interest in history, and both were fiercely political animals who respected each other's political ruthlessness. Kennedy had decided to take Macmillan's advice and resist the pressure to take military action in Laos. Over time, he would pursue a neutralist solution in the hope that a Communist takeover of the country could be avoided – which, at the time of the Inauguration, Eisenhower had seemed to indicate was the greatest danger in Southeast Asia. Having decided to accept Macmillan's advice, the new

President was anxious about his decision. The budding friendship was strengthened when, in order to assuage Kennedy's concern that Eisenhower would publicly cry 'appeasement' if he rejected calls for military intervention in Laos, Macmillan agreed to urge Eisenhower to refrain from criticism of the decision.

Jackie, spontaneously violating her rule that the country retreat was off limits to anyone from Jack's public life, invited the Macmillans to visit Glen Ora on Saturday before going on to Canada. As it happened, they would be unable to accept her hospitality. The Macmillans had a long-planned lunch date that day with Jackie's neighbor in Virginia, Adele Astaire, Fred Astaire's sister, who had once been married to Dorothy's late brother Lord Charles Cavendish. The lunch ran late, making a visit to Glen Ora impossible. Nonetheless, Jackie's invitation signaled her acceptance of Macmillan as family – a major step.

After the men went down to lunch, Jackie took a walk around Lafayette Square across from the White House, accompanied by Peter Lawford. Then she took a nap in anticipation of her first official responsibility in connection with the visit of a foreign delegation – a tea party in honor of Lady Dorothy, to be attended by the wives of Dean Rusk, David Bruce, and Sir Harold Caccia, the current British ambassador to the U.S. It was the sort of duty Jackie, who vastly preferred the company of men, did least well.

The scandalous stories that swirled around Lady Dorothy Macmillan were legion. By all accounts, it had been she who seduced and relentlessly fueled the affair with Boothby. Not only had she pursued him on his honeymoon with her cousin, but when the marriage ended soon afterward, she made sure he did not marry again, preventing him on at least three occasions from taking a wife. At home with her husband and children, Lady Dorothy was constantly on the phone to Boothby, whose love letters she left about for all to see. Said to be highly sexed, selfish, and cruel, without visible remorse for the pain she had caused, Lady Dorothy made it clear that she and her husband no longer slept together when she announced to her friends, 'I am faithful to Bob.'

The woman who arrived at the White House at half past
five bore no resemblance to her colorful legend. Lady Dorothy
was a benign, grandmotherly figure, stout and frumpy, with a
string of pearls and a nest of white hair. She cared not at all
for clothes or fashion, and her public image was such that one
newspaper nominated her for the title of 'Britain's most super
grannie.' Yet she was known by close friends to be in daily
contact with her lover, and she would rush off to see him
whenever an opportunity presented itself.

The Boothby affair held a special fascination for Jack
Kennedy because, in 1945, Boothby had been engaged to marry
Inga Arvad. Jackie, who had read and in certain cases could
recite from memory Jack's pre-marriage love letters, was fully
acquainted with the volcanic romance between her husband
and Arvad, which had provoked Kick, heretofore first in her
brother's heart, to admit to spasms of jealousy. Arvad's shadowy
past included a stint as a newspaper correspondent in pre-war
Berlin, where Hitler had praised her as the perfect example of
Nordic beauty and invited her to the Olympic Games as his
personal guest. By the time Jack took up with her in 1942, she
was Kick's colleague and pal at the *Washington Times–Herald.*
Then a Naval Intelligence officer, Jack was intoxicated by the
Danish woman's beauty, sensuality, and worldliness. Under
pressure from his father, who attempted to take Arvad to bed
himself, Jack finally and reluctantly had to give her up after it
was disclosed that the F.B.I. was investigating charges – later
disproved – that she was a German agent.

Still carrying a torch for Inga Arvad in 1945, Kennedy was
covering the United Nations Conference in San Francisco for
the Hearst newspapers when word broke in the press of her
engagement to a British M.P. Bob Boothby, also covering the
U.N. Conference, had met Arvad, now a screenwriter at
Metro–Goldwyn–Mayer, three days previously at the Beverly
Hills home of his friends Sir Charles and Lady Mendl. This
time, however, it wasn't Lady Dorothy but the gossip columnist
Louella Parsons who torpedoed Boothby's marriage plans.
When, shortly after the announcement, Parsons ran an item
about Arvad's connection to Hitler, Boothby, horrified by the

likely repercussions to his political career, abruptly broke off with her and rushed back to Lady Dorothy.

That afternoon, as soon as Harold Macmillan left for the British embassy, Jack bounded in to his wife's tea party full of curiosity about a woman who had shared a lover with Inga Arvad. The look on his face when he spotted Lady Dorothy provided Jackie, who adored teasing Jack about anything to do with his past loves, much ammunition.

In the days that followed, talks with Macmillan coincided with secret discussions of the Cuban invasion, and Kennedy could not hide his distractedness from the Prime Minister. Given his fears – articulated in conversation with Macmillan – of being charged with appeasement, his decision not to approve military intervention in Laos would make it harder for him to say no to a move on Cuba.

While Kennedy was in Florida for Easter, Khrushchev had, after weeks of negotiation, agreed to a summit meeting. Khrushchev himself had been anxious to meet the new American President as soon as possible, and on February 22 Kennedy had written to the Soviet leader to say that he had instructed his ambassador in Moscow to pursue the idea of an early meeting. On March 9, U.S. ambassador Llewellyn Thompson met with Khrushchev and relayed a suggestion from Kennedy that they meet in early May. Kennedy, too, was keen to meet his principal adversary face to face as soon as possible, so that he would have some first-hand experience on which to base the great decisions he knew he would soon confront. Better that the two world leaders with access to nuclear weapons should have a sharp, sober view of each other, undistorted by hysteria or preconceptions.

The day before Macmillan's arrival in Washington, with dates finalized for his own upcoming state visit to Paris, Kennedy had cabled Thompson to offer Khrushchev the firm dates of June 3 and 4 for what he termed a 'get acquainted meeting' in Vienna. The primary purpose of Macmillan's visit was to allow Kennedy to confer with America's most important ally in advance of the meetings with the French President, General Charles de Gaulle, and Khrushchev. During the course of the visit, they agreed that, if he could find a suitable pretext, Kennedy should stop in London afterward so that he could sort out with Macmillan his impressions of both men.

In view of all that burdened Jack, Jackie did her best to organize a weekend with his needs in mind. By this time, she had abandoned her fantasy that he would enjoy hunt country life. It had become evident that he did not plan to ride and was bored when she went off without him. Still, weekends were to be a time for privacy and relaxation, and she made it a point to invite houseguests with whom Jack could unwind while she rode with Caroline or neighbors such as Eve and Paul Fout. In good weather, Jack would sit out on the terrace in a rocking chair and chat with friends, his portable record player set up nearby.

Golf was one activity which Jack could enjoy in the vicinity, so on this occasion Jackie invited his journalist friend Ben Bradlee, as well as Chuck Spalding – the latter in case Jack, under intense pressure, wished to talk frankly to someone unconnected to the press. During the campaign, Spalding had abandoned a job in advertising in order to work full-time for his friend. His role, as he saw it, was in part to keep Jack apprised of all he might miss out on as President, from talk of the latest Broadway shows to gossip about the many people they knew in common.

When he and the President were together, the witty, enter-taining Spalding tended to talk the most. Now and then, however, Jack had something he wanted to discuss, and that Monday morning, en route to Washington in the presidential limousine, Chuck listened attentively. Five days before he had to order the air strikes and seven days before the landing, Kennedy described the Zapata plan to his friend of twenty years. Although he had yet to give the official go-ahead, preparations were to begin that day, as the exile troops being trained in Guatemala moved in waves to the staging area in Nicaragua. Kennedy seemed nervous and uncertain to Spalding, who, asked for his opinion, expressed doubts about the plan.

From the moment Kennedy returned to the White House, every item on that week's schedule, including critical talks about

Berlin with the German Chancellor Konrad Adenauer, occurred against the overwhelming backdrop, visible only to Kennedy and his advisers, of the Zapata plan. Enraged by a front-page article in the *New York Times* that reported the coming invasion, Kennedy entered his Wednesday press conference prepared for difficult questions.

'Mr President,' a reporter asked, 'has a decision been reached on how far this country will be willing to go in helping an anti-Castro uprising or invasion of Cuba?'

'First,' said the President, 'I want to say that there will not be, under any conditions, an intervention in Cuba by the United States armed forces. This government will do everything it possibly can, and I think it can meet its responsibilities, to make sure there are no Americans involved in any actions inside Cuba.'

At a meeting later that afternoon, at which details of the invasion were to be finalized, Kennedy reiterated that U.S. involvement must be carefully concealed. Various last-minute changes were reviewed, yet as the session drew to a close, the C.I.A.'s Richard Bissell pointed out that the President had yet to give the clear instruction to proceed. Frustrated by what he saw as his 'ambivalence about making decisions,' Bissell set two deadlines. By Friday at noon, Kennedy had to approve or cancel Saturday's air strikes, which were intended to destroy Castro's Air Force; and by Sunday at noon, he had to approve or cancel the landing of troops the following day, Monday, April 17.

Friday morning, as the first deadline drew near, Jackie was about to go out with Caroline when Jack sent word that he needed her immediately, to accompany him to the Pan-American Union where he was to deliver a speech at the Council of the Organization of American States. Jackie was puzzled, and more than a little irritated, by the unusual request. Jack almost never asked her to attend something like this, certainly not at the last minute. Especially since her return from Florida, he had taken care not to overwhelm her with duties and had been at pains to lessen her burdens rather than add to them, but today he needed her support.

By half past eleven they were back at the White House. As the presidential limousine entered the Southwest Gate, Kennedy ordered the driver to stop. Schlesinger, who had worked on the speech with Kennedy, was also in the car. It was a flawless, sunlit morning and Caroline was at play on the lawn in the distance when Kennedy, his wife, and aide got out. As Caroline dashed toward her parents, Kennedy announced that he wanted to walk down to the pond to inspect the child's ducks. With less than thirty minutes before his moment of truth, he lingered in the warm April air.

At length, the President and First Lady entered the White House together. But then, as if not yet quite ready to pick up the phone, he again went outside with Jackie, this time just the two of them. Jackie could not advise him, as Macmillan had done in regard to Laos, but it was certainly in her power to make him feel less alone in making this terrible decision about Cuba. For six minutes, President and Mrs Kennedy walked together in the bright sunlight on the South Lawn. Finally, he could put off the phone call no longer. Jackie watched him go to the Oval Office. There, as was his habit, he tapped his elaborately carved oak desk as if to summon luck from the wood, and ordered air strikes the following morning.

Experience had taught Jackie that when Jack made up his mind, he tended to prevail. That night, confident that he would have made the right decision, she left him at the White House and flew to Glen Ora armed with numerous books and documents in anticipation of next week's state visit by Greek Prime Minister Constantine Karamanlis. It would be the first diplomatic visit which required Jackie's attendance at both a luncheon and a dinner, which meant she would have to do much more talking than had been required with either the Macmillans or Chancellor Adenauer.

Her homework included Edith Hamilton's *The Greek Way*, which she reread, as well as briefing papers with detailed character sketches of Prime Minister and Mrs Karamanlis. Nothing was left to chance. Did the visitors smoke, drink, or object to those who did? How were their names pronounced, how did they wish to be addressed, and could they be expected to shake hands when introductions were made? What subjects did they like to talk about? What were their interests? Jackie knew that her husband, uneasy about his own lack of languages, hated to communicate through interpreters, so it came as a relief that Karamanlis and his party spoke English.

As on the previous weekend, Jackie had invited guests for Jack. Once he made a decision, he generally didn't look back, and there was no reason to think that this occasion would be different. He would probably be more anxious than ever to forget his pressures. At the same time, the Cuban operation was top secret, and he would surely have a good many calls about it, not to mention the fact that on Sunday he would have to give the 'go' order for the landing. So Jackie had to be extremely careful about whom she invited. Lem could be trusted completely, as could Jack's family. In addition to Lem, who was to join them on Sunday, she invited Jack's youngest sister, Jean, and her husband, Steve Smith, along with Steve Jr, then Caroline's favorite cousin.

Saturday morning at the White House, Kennedy monitored the air strikes and their aftermath. Initial reports suggested that the strikes had achieved their goal of obliterating most of the Cuban Air Force. The cover story invented by the C.I.A. to give the impression that Castro's own people were assailing him also seemed to be working: a bullet-riddled B-26 had landed at Miami International Airport and its pilot, a C.I.A. employee claiming to be a Cuban defector, said he had just stolen the plane and taken part in the bombing. So far, the press and the public seemed to believe it.

By mid-morning, complications began to arise. In response to the dawn attack by eight B-26s on airfields at Havana, San Antonio de los Baños, and Santiago de Cuba, Castro demanded an emergency session of the United Nations. Cuba's Foreign Minister charged the U.S. with aggression against its territorial integrity and political independence, and the Soviet representative warned that Cuba had numerous friends who were prepared to come to its aid, including the Soviet Union. A meeting to discuss U.S. aggression had already been scheduled for the following Monday, but as far as the C.I.A. was

concerned that would not matter, as the invasion would already
have occurred. A session on Saturday, however, took the C.I.A.
by surprise.

To make matters worse, Adlai Stevenson, the U.S. ambassador to the United Nations, had not been properly briefed. It
had been Stevenson's impression that there would be no attack
until after the debate scheduled for Monday, April 17. When
his office contacted the C.I.A. about the air strikes, assurances
were given that they had been carried out by defectors from
the Cuban Air Force and had nothing to do with the U.S.
That afternoon at the U.N., Stevenson cited Kennedy's own
promises at Wednesday's press conference and vehemently
denied U.S. involvement, believing he was telling the truth. It
was only a matter of time before Stevenson discovered he had
been duped, and he was not the sort of person to take that
lightly.

Despite the crisis, there could be no question of Kennedy's
canceling his scheduled departure to join Jackie and her guests
in time for lunch. The U.S. was supposed to have played no
role in the air strikes, and from the outset the cover story had
included the fact that the President would be away from
Washington when the invasion began. At approximately half
past twelve, his white cap left the White House. Kennedy put
on a mask for the world, but at Glen Ora he was unusually
restless and preoccupied. Jackie had planned a trip to the
steeplechase races with the Smiths after lunch, but although
Jack accompanied them he did not last long. After only two
races, Jack, too nervous to make any further pretense of interest,
insisted he must go back to the house to work. Jackie and Jean
Smith stayed on, while Jack and his brother-in-law returned to
Glen Ora.

There, for more than half an hour, Jack furiously whacked
golf balls in the west pasture. He was known for his ability to
turn with ease from business to pleasure, but that talent appeared
to have deserted him. Two things in particular preyed on his
mind. He feared that an invasion of Cuba would trigger a
retaliatory move in Berlin by the Soviets. But he also worried
that if he failed to go through with an invasion approved by

Eisenhower, he, like his father before him, would be branded a coward – and that he simply could not tolerate. That night, just before he and Jackie went to bed, he called Bobby, unique among his advisers in being in a position to understand the demons that drove him, to say he had decided to order the landing.

All the next morning Jackie, aware of the noon deadline, watched carefully, yet Jack made no move to contact Bissell at the C.I.A. He was, however, repeatedly on the phone, and every incoming call seemed to bring more disheartening news. Reporters had picked apart the tissue of lies that made up the supposed Cuban defector's testimony. The plane that landed in Miami had a metal nose; the noses on Castro's planes were plastic. Upon inspection, it was determined that the plane's machine guns had not been fired. As if all that were not bad enough, it now seemed that the initial intelligence reports that the raid had obliterated the Cuban Air Force had been inaccurate. In fact, only five of Castro's planes had been destroyed.

As Sunday morning wore on, Jackie continued to observe. The press routinely clocked Kennedy's attendance at noon Mass in Middleburg, so there was no question of him skipping it lest reporters guess something was wrong. At five minutes to twelve, when he announced he was ready to leave, the phone call to Bissell had not been made. He and Jackie did not get back until half past twelve, thirty minutes after the deadline, and still Jack steered conspicuously clear of the phone. He had lunch with Jackie and the Smiths, then grabbed his golf club and marched outside.

In this highly charged atmosphere, Jackie did something unusual. She rarely played golf with Jack, but now, in view of his ordeal, she reached for a club. The Smiths headed outside after her, and for twenty-four long minutes they all stood in the pasture and hit balls. For many weeks, Jack had been dubious about the invasion's chances, even as he often seemed desperate for a big win against the Soviets. Now, as he pointedly let the deadline pass, it was evident that he remained uncertain. Everything seemed to cry no – everything except a family need for vindication and a desire to show the Soviets he was strong. He had known for some time that tactically the plan was a poor one, and the first missteps can only have reinforced that feeling.

It wasn't reason that motivated Kennedy that day as he worked himself up to approve the landing. Finally, at a quarter to two, a full hour and forty-five minutes past the deadline, Jack threw down his club and headed to the house. Jackie went in after him. He picked up the phone and instructed the operator to get Richard Bissell. When Bissell came on, Jack muttered two words: 'Go ahead.'

After the call, Jack was too wound up to stay at home. Jackie, aware that this was hardly a day to go riding and send Jack off to play golf with the boys, accompanied him to the Fauquier Springs Country Club, where, joined by the Smiths and Lem Billings, they spent two hours on the golf course. Lem, with his songs, jokes, and raucous laugh, was someone with whom Jack always seemed at ease. It was almost impossible for him to be in low spirits if Lem was on the scene. On this occasion, even Lem, for all his exertions, was unable to penetrate Jack's gloom.

All weekend Jack's agitated state of mind had been exacerbated by the fact that a venereal infection was causing him agony each time he urinated. On Friday, Dr Travell had contacted Jack's urologist, who advised that if matters didn't improve by Monday he would start the President on a course of penicillin. At 9 p.m., Jack and Jackie were already upstairs in their bedroom when the phone rang. Jackie saw her husband grow increasingly agitated as he listened to Dean Rusk's appeal to cancel the air strikes, which were scheduled to resume at dawn.

Rusk reported that he had been the recipient of angry words from Adlai Stevenson. The U.N. ambassador felt he had been used and deceived, and warned that further uncoordinated action could only result in political disaster when U.S. lies were exposed. Rusk felt that Stevenson had reason to be furious, and as he tried to offer Kennedy an honest account of what was going on the Secretary of State, to his horror, realized that certain details of the next day's schedule were hazy even to him. The plan had been altered repeatedly, up to the very last minute, and since this was a covert operation there was no final, complete written account. Specifically, up to this point, Rusk had not realized that the landing by sea was to be preceded by more air attacks from Nicaragua. And, Rusk suddenly perceived, it would be evident that those attacks had to have come from outside Cuba.

Jackie, unable to hear Rusk's end of the conversation, heard her husband blurt out, 'I'm not signed on to this!' At that appalling moment, Kennedy had grasped that he too was not entirely clear about all that was to take place. He too had been confused by the Zapata plan's constant revisions. The President had thought, as had the Secretary of State, that on invasion day air strikes would be conducted strictly from the beachhead at the Bay of Pigs.

At this point Rusk argued the need to shift from military to political considerations. He finally persuaded Kennedy to call off the next round of air strikes in the belief that they were not essential. It was agreed that there were to be no air strikes until they could plausibly be conducted from a strip within the beachhead.

When Kennedy got off the phone, his wife watched him sit silently for a moment. Then he shook his head and paced the bedroom in agitation. He was upset, Jackie perceived, not because he had cancelled the air strikes but because the whole operation seemed so out of control. Eventually, both Jack and Jackie managed to fall sleep, but at about half past four that morning, the phone rang. Again it was Dean Rusk. General Charles Cabell, the Deputy Director of the C.I.A., had arrived at Rusk's apartment to appeal for U.S. jets to provide air cover to protect the invading ships as they unloaded.

The troops had begun to land more than three hours previously. Castro was already personally supervising an air and ground response to start at dawn. He was intimately familiar with the terrain, since the C.I.A. had chosen to land at one of his favorite fishing spots.

Rusk put General Cabell on the phone to make a direct request for air cover. Kennedy refused on the grounds that he had undertaken not to use U.S. forces. Though the President didn't know it, it was already too late to keep that promise. An American frogman had been the first to step on shore, to guide the invaders.

After the phone call, Kennedy was too upset to return to bed. Jackie got up with him and they sat together in the pre-dawn darkness, shattered and wondering where all this was headed.

Shortly after nine, Jack, Jackie, and the children climbed into the white cap for the flight back to the White House. For the young couple, it had been a harrowing night, made worse by the fact that they both faced an exceptionally long day. Prime Minister and Mrs Karamanlis were due to arrive at lunchtime for a three-day visit. The Cuban matter would have been hard to handle in any case, but the fact that it was to be played out in front of a foreign leader increased the difficulty a hundredfold. In a few hours, Jackie, never at ease with official duties, was to preside over a large and elaborate luncheon in the visitors' honor. To add to the tension, Rose Kennedy had arrived that morning, eager to attend the administration's first state luncheon, and planned to stay for several days. Jackie, who had had almost no sleep, went straight from the helicopter to the private quarters, where she found the mother-in-law with whom she had never enjoyed the best of relations already ensconced in the Queens' Bedroom.

By the time the President entered his office at half past nine, the stench of failure was in the air. Intelligence reports had seriously underestimated the Cuban Air Force. Three hours previously, one of the invaders' ships, the *Houston*, had been hit. And even as Kennedy was being briefed, word came that one of Castro's Sea Fury planes had hit the *Rio Escondido*, a freighter loaded with vital communications equipment and ten days' worth of ammunition on which the brigade depended. By 10 a.m., it was official that both vessels had been sunk. Without air support, the four remaining ships planned to move out to sea to escape the relentless pounding.

After a session with Dr Travell, who administered penicillin for his venereal infection, the President conferred with Bobby

Kennedy. Bobby, for his part, urged Jack to find some way to win in Cuba now that the U.S. was overtly involved. At one point, Jack, torn between a desire to win and the fact that he had made a public commitment not to intervene, declared angrily that he would 'rather be called an aggressor than a bum.' His remark reflected the dread of a Kennedy again being charged with cowardice, which had been partly responsible for landing him in this mess in the first place. Jack's talk with his brother lasted until shortly before one, when Prime Minister and Mrs Karamanlis were expected in the family quarters.

Upstairs, Jack found Jackie worn and upset. Normally, she would have devoted her attention to making herself glamorous for her debut at a state luncheon. Instead, the young woman who greeted Prime Minister and Mrs Karamanlis appeared dazed and drawn, wearing an ill-fitting black suit that seemed only to highlight her fatigue. Her unwashed hair was lank with hair spray applied in a last-minute effort to make her presentable. Jack, taking over for his wife, gave the visitors a tour of the family quarters that included a stop in the children's room. Despite the crisis, it was essential that he deal with the Greek leader calmly and authoritatively. Karamanlis, after all, had his own priorities and Kennedy, new in office, could ill afford the suggestion that Cuba had affected or was in any way indicative of his ability to treat other important matters.

Seventy-five guests waited in the State Dining Room, where tables were decorated with arrangements of yellow and white flowers. Kennedy, desperate to follow the progress of the invasion, faced a long meal. He was expected to toast his distinguished guests and participate in toasts by the Prime Minister and others. It was past three before he could break away and dash to the West Wing, where the news from Cuba was not good. In addition to the air attacks by Castro at dawn, Cuban tanks had started to appear on the beachhead.

Shortly after ten that night, Kennedy, who had authorized a dawn air strike by six brigade planes against Castro's principal air base at San Antonio de los Baños, went to the family quarters and asked Jackie to walk with him. Instead of limiting themselves to the grounds, the President and First Lady, who had been up since 4:30 the previous morning, strolled out the Northwest Gate. During his first weeks in office, Jack had felt cooped up, and often took late-night walks alone or with friends. But now, in the first real crisis of the presidency, it was Jackie he wanted at his side. Together they prowled the moonlit streets that adjoined the White House.

FIVE

The Magic is Lost

At a 7 a.m. meeting in the Cabinet Room on Tuesday, April 18, Kennedy, his tie askew, listened to a litany of bad news from Allen Dulles. The tweedy, pipe-smoking C.I.A. Director wore floppy bedroom slippers on feet inflamed by gout. Behind him, colored maps of the region were perched on easels. Small magnetic models signified eight U.S. ships, including the aircraft carrier *Essex*, poised in the Caribbean Sea outside Cuban territorial waters. Kennedy had ordered the vessels to stay just over the horizon, out of sight of the beach. News from the Bay of Pigs was sparse, since the communications equipment on which the C.I.A. had expected to depend had been sunk the previous day. It took hours to get any information at all, and by the time a report did come in, more often than not it was out of date. To the President's immense frustration, he and his advisers had to work virtually blind.

Dulles could say definitively that the dawn air raids on San Antonio de los Baños had failed on account of thick haze and low clouds. The exiles were trapped on the beaches, with Castro's men about to surround and crush them. As the day progressed, again and again the C.I.A. would push Kennedy to use the Navy jets on the *Essex*, despite his vow not to involve U.S. forces. Kennedy, adamant, plunged at least one adviser into a fit of agitation when he went up to a map and silently moved a magnetic model away from Cuba to drive home his point.

Jackie remained in seclusion much of the day. That night, she appeared at a few minutes past ten at the top of the staircase to the family quarters, clutching her husband's arm. He wore white tie and tails, she an evening gown. There was a low, continuous beating of drums. The Marine Corps band, resplendent in scarlet dress uniform, played 'Hail to the Chief.' Accompanied by Lyndon and Lady Bird Johnson and House Speaker Sam Rayburn, the Kennedys slowly descended.

A military color guard preceded them into the East Room, careful lest their flags hit the chandeliers. Abigail Adams was said to have hung her laundry there, Union troops to have slept on the floor. That night, the Mansion's largest room held some 840 guests for the annual Congressional Reception.

As there was no receiving line, Jack and Jackie, smiling and waving, circulated among the guests. Now and then they stopped to talk briefly to individual Congressmen and their wives. When the Marine Corps band played the popular show tune, 'Mr Wonderful,' it was the Kennedys' cue to dance.

The President's thoughts are likely to have been far away, for prior to changing into evening clothes he had been given the report from a U.S. reconnaissance mission to determine the situation at Red Beach, one of two landing sites. The brigade had already been defeated, and the survivors were reported to have moved over to Blue Beach. There had been no sign of the troops, only burned tanks and trucks alongside the road, as well as ten to fourteen of Castro's large tanks moving in a convoy with trucks and lorries.

Every now and again, an undercurrent of panic interrupted the revelry. As word spread that the situation in Cuba was moving toward a final disaster, several guests were summoned to an emergency meeting in the Oval Office to follow the reception. At one point Jackie was on the dance floor with Senator George Smathers when Bobby Kennedy interrupted.

'The shit has hit the fan,' Bobby informed the Senator. 'The thing has turned sour in a way you wouldn't believe!'

The tone at the midnight meeting, convened at the request of the C.I.A., was equally hysterical. Several of those present, including Rusk, Johnson, and the President, were in white tie. General Lemnitzer and Admiral Arleigh Burke, Chief of Naval Operations, who had also been at the dance, were in full uniform, laden with medals. Bissell, keen to save the lives of those still on the beach, implored Kennedy to authorize air support. The aircraft on the *Essex*, stripped of markings, were ready to go. Kennedy grew annoyed as he listened to Admiral Burke argue for U.S. air strikes and other backup.

'Burke, I don't want the United States involved in this,' the President insisted.

'Hell, Mr President, but we are involved!' Burke replied.

So the debate raged until a message from the brigade commander, José Perez San Román, arrived from the beach-head. 'Do you people realize how desperate the situation is? Do you back us up or quit? All we want is low jet cover and jet close support. Enemy has this support. I need it badly or cannot survive. Please don't desert us. Am out of tank and bazooka ammo. Tanks will hit me at dawn. I will not be evacuated. Will fight to the end if we have to.'

Kennedy was in a unique position to understand how the brigade commander felt. When he commanded a P.T. boat during the Second World War, his boat had been rammed and sunk by an enemy destroyer. Kennedy remained in the water for about ten hours. Then he landed upon an enemy-occupied island where, without shoes, clothing, or food, he remained for five days before being rescued.

The soldier's plea prompted Kennedy to reconsider. At length, over Rusk's objection, Kennedy reluctantly ordered six unmarked jets from the *Essex* to fly over the Bay of Pigs for an hour at dawn, in order to provide air cover for a B-26 attack from Nicaragua to destroy Castro's tanks. In an important stipulation, the U.S. jets, in the course of defending the B-26s, were neither to seek air combat nor to attack ground targets, and the pilots were to carry as little identification as possible.

The meeting finally broke up shortly before 3 a.m., and no one came away with what they wanted. Certainly, Kennedy's order was a long way short of what the C.I.A. had had in mind. Men scattered, exhausted, depressed, and confused. Some went home, others went to their offices to carry out instructions. Kennedy remained behind to talk with Kenneth O'Donnell, special assistant to the President, and press secretary Pierre Salinger. It seemed to O'Donnell that he had never known the boss to appear 'so distraught.' Kennedy, without putting on his jacket, went outside. Head down, hands in trouser pockets, he walked for nearly an hour.

'He must be the loneliest man in the world tonight,' said O'Donnell, who watched with Salinger from the Oval Office.

It was almost 4 a.m. when the President went upstairs to the family quarters. He had no more than two or three hours' sleep. Wednesday morning, when he inquired how the involvement of the U.S. jets had gone, he was in for a shock. No one had taken into account the one-hour time difference between Cuba and Nicaragua. The B-26s, expecting U.S. air cover, had arrived from Nicaragua an hour early, and Castro had shot down two of the planes.

The order over which Kennedy had agonized had come to nothing, and the entire operation had turned into what one adviser later characterized as a 'comic-opera fiasco.' The President instructed U.S. destroyers in the area to make every effort to rescue members of the brigade from the beach and water, but it soon became apparent that many men had already been captured. In the end, Castro took 1,189 prisoners and there were more than one hundred casualties.

When Prime Minister Karamanlis arrived with his aides for a 10:30 a.m. meeting in the Oval Office, he recognized that he had come at a very awkward moment. Feeling a good deal of sympathy for Kennedy's situation, he volunteered to be passed on to Cabinet members so that the President could focus on the crisis. Kennedy, however, wouldn't hear of it and insisted on conducting the session himself. Following a discussion of topics related to Greece, he invited Karamanlis outside for a private talk without their retinues. As they crossed the threshold into the garden, Kennedy pointed to cleat marks made by Eisenhower's golf shoes. 'No matter what one may think of the political views of General Eisenhower,' Kennedy declared, 'one must confess that as a general he was a most extraordinary man.'

Soon afterward, he launched into a diatribe against Eisenhower, from whom, he noted angrily, he had inherited the plan to invade Cuba – a sore point from the first, as he had felt pressured to do as the war hero intended. When Karamanlis delicately expressed astonishment at the ineptitude of the operation, Kennedy by turns insisted that the whole thing wasn't his fault and vowed personally to accept responsibility because that would be 'in the interest of the American nation.' If Kennedy was testing the waters, Karamanlis's reaction strongly suggested that to accept blame would be best.

At noon, Adlai Stevenson filed a grim report from the United Nations, where the U.S. had received 'virtually no support' in speeches by other ambassadors. White House denials notwithstanding, allies and enemies alike saw that the U.S. was behind the invasion. As a result, Stevenson observed, the Soviets and the Cubans had been able to seize and retain the 'moral initiative,' and the image of the U.S. had been immeasurably damaged throughout the world. 'Whatever happens now,' Stevenson warned, 'we are in for a period of very serious political trouble.'

When Jack appeared in the family quarters at 2:05, his mood stunned Jackie. Her husband was cheerful by nature; she tended to be the dark, despairing partner. Now, she saw a Jack whom she had encountered only once previously. She was reminded of the time of his back operation, early in their marriage, when for months he failed to recover. He had risked everything and ended up worse than before, and sank into a mood so bleak that Joe Kennedy declared that even if his son survived, his spirit might be destroyed. Jack had seemed to lose the will to live, and it had only been through Jackie's efforts, as well as those of family and close friends, that he had finally come back from the brink. It was that frightening Jack of years past who came to her this afternoon.

Full of anger, he raged against the C.I.A., the Joint Chiefs of Staff, Eisenhower, all the people he was eager to blame. Still focused on tactical, not moral, issues, he lashed out at his advisers. He had been assured that the invasion would trigger a popular uprising, but no uprising had materialized. He had been told that at worst the brigade would disperse and 'go guerrilla,' but that had never really been an option. The mountains, some eighty miles from the Bay of Pigs, were separated from the beach by impassable swamps. In fact, the brigade had never been trained to 'go guerrilla,' but had been instructed to fall back to sea if they found it necessary to withdraw. Kennedy felt deceived – or so he kept telling Jackie, and himself. But though, as he insisted, much of the advice had been faulty, it was also the case that he had desperately wanted to believe an invasion could triumph, and was not yet willing to face why his need had been so strong.

On the verge of tears, Jack rested his head in his hands. Then he put his arms around Jackie. Eventually, she persuaded him to rest. He had had only a few hours' sleep the night before, and faced more meetings that afternoon and another late night. He climbed into bed, and Jackie stayed until he fell asleep.

Kennedy was still upstairs when the brigade commander's final message arrived: 'Am destroying all equipment and communications. I have nothing left to fight with. Am taking to the woods. I can't wait for you.' Shortly after that, a report was brought in that Castro held the beach and that the U.S. destroyers Kennedy had sent in to evacuate the remaining members of the brigade were withdrawing at full speed. By the time the President was back at his desk, it was evident that all was lost.

Late in the afternoon, an aide glimpsed the President through a window. Alone in the Oval Office, he was about to meet with a contingent of Cuban exiles, several of whose sons had been killed or captured. Seated in a high-backed rocking chair, Kennedy glanced at the headline of an afternoon newspaper, then let the paper drop to the floor. He would not be permitted to endure his crushing failure in private. That evening he and Jackie were to attend a dinner in their honor at the Greek embassy. Before that, he had to explain the fiasco to Congressional leaders who were even then on their way to the White House.

In the family quarters, a hairdresser dashed back and forth between Jackie and Rose's rooms to prepare the two Mrs Kennedys for the party. Rose, waiting for her son to come upstairs, had a painful telephone conversation with her husband.

Joe had been on the phone constantly with Jack throughout the crisis, less to offer tactical advice than to provide moral support. Now, he confessed to Rose, he felt as though he were dying. A Kennedy in the White House was supposed to mean that sweet vindication was within grasp. Instead, his disastrous counsel in Palm Beach had led Jack, only three months into his term, to feel the ignominy that his father had fought for two decades to live down.

At eight Jack rushed upstairs from a fiery two-hour meeting with Congressional leaders, and a valet helped him change into evening clothes. Jackie nervously dashed from room to room in search of a gift for Prime Minister Karamanlis, who had been so kind that morning. After a day spent watching her husband assailed from all sides, Jackie focused the anxieties which she dared not express on the need to find a less impersonal gift than what had been provided by the State Department. Nothing seemed right. Finally, Jack was ready to go, and as she started toward the elevator she grabbed a porcelain snuffbox from her own collection.

Alone with Jackie that afternoon, Jack had buried his head in his hands and despaired. In the back seat of the presidential limousine, he gave no sign of the emotions that were tearing him apart. Rose, well aware of Jack's state of mind after her talk with Joe, was astonished by his ability coolly to conceal his troubles. Jackie, clutching the tiny snuffbox as if everything depended upon it, demonstrated no such ability. Her own failures she could deal with, but the idea that her husband could fail at anything was a new and deeply upsetting discovery. Jack had always seemed to win – until now.

It had been one thing for the Kennedys to preside over a state luncheon at a moment when all was not lost. It was quite another to arrive at the Greek embassy in defeat. Childlike and endearing, Jackie presented the snuffbox to the Karamanlises. The gesture won the hearts of her hosts, who were acutely aware of the strain she was under. On Monday, she had talked of her love of Greek art and culture, as well as of how exhausted she had been early in the presidency. That night, there could be no missing the toll the past few days had taken, mere weeks before she was due to accompany her husband on his state visits to Canada, Paris, and now possibly Vienna for the summit with Khrushchev. At dinner, the Karamanlises proposed a private holiday in Greece in June, to follow her European tour. In view of what had just happened in Cuba, there was no point in suggesting that the President accompany her, but at least the Karamanlises could make this gesture of friendship to his wife. Jack urged her to accept. After the state visits she would certainly need the rest, and perhaps the prospect of escape to a setting she loved would help get her through the coming weeks.

Jack spent the better part of the evening discussing the history of ancient Greece with Karamanlis, who was awed as much by his mask of serenity as by his erudition. From first to last Kennedy seemed calm and in control, though he was obviously eager to leave as soon as possible. When Jackie and Rose retired with the other ladies after dinner and left the men to their brandy and cigars, it wasn't long before an aide appeared and whispered in Jackie's ear that the President was ready to go. Hardly were they back in the limousine when the mask slipped off. It was nearly 11 p.m. when they reached the White House. Jack didn't bother to escort Jackie and his mother upstairs, but left the car with a quick goodnight and went to his office for a late meeting on Cuba.

Jackie and Rose were still in the back seat together when he disappeared. Since the day Jack had brought Jackie home to meet his family, there had been no love lost between the two women. As Jackie herself would have to do, Rose had constructed a hermetically sealed, safe little life to guard against the hurt of infidelity. Faced with her husband's numerous other women, Rose, recalled Arthur Krock, 'acted as if they didn't exist' – Jackie's strategy exactly. Yet it was Joe, not Rose, to whom Jackie would always be drawn. If she failed to distance herself from Jack's mother, people might see the truth: that she and Rose actually had much in common.

Ordinarily, Jackie would have seized the first opportunity to escape her mother-in-law. Nor was Rose given to showing Jackie any warmth. Yet that night, both women welcomed a chance to talk. It was a measure of Jackie's excruciating isolation that she turned to Rose. She really had no one else in Washington, no one with whom she could be as frank. As the two troubled Mrs Kennedys went up to the family quarters, Jackie poured out all that had happened that afternoon.

Thursday morning, Jack woke up crying. When he was a boy, one of his father's mantras had been, 'Kennedys never cry.' It was such a core family belief that Jackie had taught the same lesson to her own daughter, so she of all people would have known what Jack's tears cost him.

Meanwhile, a jubilant Castro proclaimed 'complete victory over the invading forces.' As to the fate of the men defeated at the Bay of Pigs, there was, reported Wymberley Coerr, Deputy Assistant Secretary of State for Inter-American Affairs, 'no further word.' At a tumultuous 11 a.m. Cabinet meeting, Kennedy seemed 'shattered,' like someone who has suffered 'an acute shock,' aware that much of the world regarded him as an 'amateur.' 'Almost without exception, his public career had been a long series of successes, without any noteworthy setbacks,' wrote Chester Bowles in detailed and penetrating notes on the session. 'Here for the first time he faced a situation where his judgment had been mistaken, in spite of the fact that week after week of conferences had taken place before he gave the green light. It was not a pleasant experience. Reactions around the table were almost savage, as everyone appeared to be jumping on everyone else.'

Kennedy began a monologue on the fiasco. He talked longer than at any previous meeting, between fifteen and twenty-five minutes, but, recalled Assistant Secretary of State for Congressional Affairs Fred Dutton, 'he was really talking more to himself than anyone else.' A kind of war fever erupted in the room. The consensus was that the United States should not be permitted, in Bobby Kennedy's view, to be 'beaten off with her tail between her legs.'

When the President got up from the conference table and walked to his office, Bowles, distressed by all he had just heard, followed. As disclosed in his diary, the Under-Secretary of State worried that the administration lacked 'a genuine sense of

conviction about what is right and what is wrong.' 'The Cuban
fiasco,' he wrote, 'demonstrates how far astray a man as brilliant
and well intentioned as Kennedy can go who lacks a basic
moral reference point.'

Bowles asked Kennedy to forget for a moment their official
titles. He wanted to address the President simply as a friend,
someone who had known him for many years. Yes, said Bowles,
the U.S. had just experienced a massive setback, but history
would be concerned principally with how Kennedy reacted.
Bowles feared that a thirst for revenge, given the climate of
rage he had witnessed, was about to make things even worse.
The emotional pressure to retaliate was intense, but that pressure, Bowles argued, must be resisted. What was needed right
now, he said, was a period of deliberation and sober second
thoughts.

Instead, Kennedy ordered the Defense Department to
'develop a plan for the overthrow of the Castro government by
the application of U.S. military force.' That afternoon, in a
nationally televised speech to the American Society of Newspaper Editors, the President, insisting that U.S. restraint was
'not inexhaustible,' threatened to invade Cuba to safeguard his
nation's security. Told afterward by Assistant Special Counsel
Richard Goodwin that the threats of unilateral intervention had
been unwise, Kennedy said, 'I didn't want us to look like a
paper tiger. We should scare people a little, and I did it to
make us appear still tough and powerful. Anyway, it's done.
You may be right, but it's done.'

The next day, the *New York Times* reported, 'it is clear that
the expedition has involved the United States in a disastrous
loss of prestige and respect. Among high Administration officials
there is recognition that a serious miscalculation was made....
The reviving confidence of United States allies in its qualities
of leadership has been shaken.'

Goodwin thought Kennedy's remarks to the newspaper
editors had at least had the advantage of allowing the President
to exorcise his anger, and indeed, at a scheduled press conference the day after his bellicose speech, Kennedy appeared
philosophical. In a gesture that impressed many observers in

the U.S. and abroad, just as it had when he tested it on the
Greek Prime Minister on Wednesday, he accepted full blame.
Asked by a reporter whether it was true that Rusk and Bowles
had opposed the invasion, Kennedy replied, 'There is an old
saying that victory has a hundred fathers and defeat is an
orphan. I am the responsible officer of this government.'

In private, however, the vitriol continued to pour out. At a
Saturday morning session of the National Security Council, it
seemed to Bowles that 'the atmosphere was almost as emotional
as the Cabinet meeting two days earlier, the difference being
that on this occasion the emphasis was on specific proposals to
harass Castro.' Leading the pack of 'fire eaters' was Bobby
Kennedy, who attacked anyone who suggested that another
move against Castro would merely compound the disaster. The
President, unlike his brother, limited himself by and large to
posing questions, but they were all questions that seemed to
point in one frightening direction. Afterward, Bowles wrote in
his notes: 'I felt again the great lack of moral integrity which I
believe is the central guide in dealing with tense and difficult
questions, particularly when the individuals involved are tired,
frustrated, and personally humiliated.'

The humiliation thus far was as nothing compared to what
faced Kennedy at lunchtime, when he conferred with Eisenhower at Camp David in anticipation of receiving his public
support. Concern that history would compare him unfavorably
to Eisenhower had been a huge factor in Kennedy's decision
to approve the invasion. Now, during a long walk, he had to
endure the general's merciless interrogation.

Kennedy defended himself by pointing out that he had
merely approved a plan recommended by the C.I.A. and the
Joint Chiefs of Staff. Eisenhower refused to leave matters at
that. He demanded to know if there had been any changes
after the Joint Chiefs signed off. When Kennedy mentioned the
cancelled air strike, Eisenhower, with considerable irritation,
asked why he had shifted after the troops were already at sea.
Kennedy's explanation that he feared U.S. cover would be
blown and that that might provoke the Soviets in Berlin elicited
a tirade from Eisenhower, who berated his successor as though

he were a mere boy. The Soviets respected strength, he emphasized, and any sign of weakness would only cause them to press
harder against the U.S. Then Eisenhower proceeded to tear
apart Kennedy's rationale.

'Mr President, how could you expect the world to believe
that we had nothing to do with it?' Eisenhower scolded. 'Where
did these people get the ships to go from Central America to
Cuba? Where did they get the weapons? Where did they get
all the communications and all the other things that they would
need? How could you possibly have kept from the world any
knowledge that the U.S. had been involved? I believe there is
only one thing to do when you get into this kind of thing, it
must be a success.'

Eisenhower did offer tepid support when the two Presidents
met with the press at Camp David. Nonetheless, the private
conversation was a blow to Kennedy, who saw it as the mission
of his presidency to deal effectively with the Soviets. He had
risked everything at the Bay of Pigs in order to appear courageous and strong, yet Eisenhower had just indicated that as a
result of his misstep, the Soviets – indeed, all his enemies –
would view him as weak. For Kennedy, the implication was
clear. The failure to use sufficient force made him vulnerable
to the very charges of cowardice that had ruined his father's
political career and spurred him to move on Cuba in the first
place.

Still reeling, Jack went on to Glen Ora, where Jackie had
taken the children the previous night. He had been scheduled
to spend the weekend on an aircraft carrier observing Naval
maneuvers, but that seemed inappropriate and he had cancelled
at the last minute. Instead, he personally called to invite Chuck
and Betty Spalding, because, he admitted, he just didn't want
to be alone. The Spaldings were waiting with Jackie when the
white cap appeared shortly after four.

Always restless, Jack seemed even more so today. Fifteen
minutes after he arrived, despite his evident fatigue, he went
outside to work on his golf swing with Betty, an expert golfer.
Chuck was recruited to assist. Jackie followed them out to the
pasture. Two weeks previously, she had watched him in this

very field hit ball after ball while he made up his mind. Now, she watched him struggle to come to terms with the outcome of that decision, as well as with his own motives for making it.

He began to chip balls to Chuck, who chipped them back, while Betty made adjustments in Jack's swing. Betty could see at once that his thoughts were not on golf. Usually so buoyant, he was visibly stunned by the debacle – 'the worst thing that had ever happened to him.' 'He wasn't used to making mistakes,' she said by way of explanation for why the defeat had hit him so hard. Chuck, too, would later remember thinking he had never seen Jack like this, despondent and preoccupied with his own error. Whatever he had said publicly on Friday, it wasn't until now that he seemed to accept blame.

'How can I have been so stupid?' Jack groaned over and over. 'How could I have made that mistake?'

Betty was reminded of her own experience at the front during the Second World War when, serving in North Africa with the Red Cross, she had watched an officer deal with a serious mistake. The officer had realized he must let go of it; so must Jack.

'Jack, you didn't make it twice,' Betty said, though she knew her words were inadequate as soon as she uttered them. 'As long as you don't make another one on top of it, you're going to be able to get through this.'

Jackie, watching from the sidelines, looked as if her heart were breaking for her husband. 'She was undone by it,' said Betty Spalding of Jackie's response to Jack's first failure, 'and undone by the fact that he was so upset by it.' Betty also noticed that Jack, in the midst of his ordeal, was beginning to worry about its impact on Jackie. She had endured her share of punishment in the marriage, but at moments such as this it was evident that both partners, Jack every bit as much as she, took pains to be 'sweet and careful of each other.' Said Betty, 'He wasn't experienced in kindness. He wasn't brought up with that and hadn't seen it in his own house. So it was something that really came from him and that I was quite surprised to see.'

No amount of kindness on either side could erase the fact that, by Jack's own doing, his presidency was in grave trouble.

He who had come into office on top of the world had lost
nearly everything in a matter of months.

Three weeks later, as Jackie lay secluded in a bedroom at the
Wrightsman estate in Palm Beach, the Spaldings sat with Jack
by the pool. It was Friday, May 12, and the two couples had
flown down the day before in the hope of giving Jackie a
complete rest before she embarked on extensive foreign travel.
As early as the following Tuesday the Kennedys were due in
Canada, and they were to fly to France at the end of the
month. Alarmingly, the paralyzing depression that had seemed
finally to lift prior to the Cuban adventure had swept over
Jackie again. When the Wrightsmans offered her their winter
residence, Jackie had insisted that, as the Palm Beach season
had ended more than a month previously, the house be opened
only so far as to accommodate a brief stay. The eighteenth-
century parquet floors, some from the Palais-Royal, were bare,
their magnificent carpets rolled up against vividly painted
paneled walls. The museum-quality paintings and porcelains
for which the house was renowned were out of sight, and most
of the furniture was draped with dust covers.

Jackie, her head throbbing, lay in bed with the lights out and
curtains drawn, surrounded by her books on French history
and culture. In the aftermath of the Bay of Pigs fiasco, Jack,
alternating between savage denunciations of both his advisers
and Eisenhower, and despair at his own misjudgments, had
seemed to fall apart before her eyes. Her own fragile self-
possession had shattered.

Only the previous Thursday, in the midst of a state visit by
President Habib Bourguiba of Tunisia, Jack had rushed upstairs
with Arthur Schlesinger Jr's report on the European reaction
to the invasion. Schlesinger, who had been abroad since April
22, reported that 'the first reactions to Cuba were of course
acute shock and disillusion.' In the months since the Inauguration, 'nearly everybody in Western Europe, and especially
perhaps the democratic left, had been making heavy emotional
and political investments in the new American administration.
Everything about this administration – the intelligence and

vision of the President, the dynamism of his leadership, the scope and generosity of his policies, the freshness of his approach to the cold war – had excited tremendous anticipation and elation. The new American President in three months had reestablished confidence in the maturity of American judgment and the clarity of American purposes. Kennedy was considered the last best hope of the West against communism and for peace. Now, in a single stroke, all this seemed wiped away.' 'Kennedy has lost his magic,' one source informed Schlesinger. 'It will take years before we can accept the leadership of the Kennedy administration,' declared another. 'After Cuba,' Schlesinger summed up, 'the American Government seemed as self-righteous, trigger-happy and incompetent as it had ever been in the heyday of John Foster Dulles.'

To add insult to injury, on the very day the Schlesinger report arrived, word came from Moscow that Khrushchev agreed to Kennedy's suggested dates for their meeting in Vienna. The Europeans were aghast that Kennedy had invaded Cuba. Khrushchev, by contrast, sneered that, having gone in, he had not done what it took to win. Khrushchev's response stunned Kennedy, who told Charles de Gaulle that he had assumed any such encounter would be off after the invasion. On the contrary, precisely as Eisenhower had predicted, Khrushchev, sniffing weakness, was eager to swoop in. Of course, if Kennedy now declined the dates, that would be further proof of cowardice. Made restless and upset by these developments, after dinner he went out for a walk with his wife.

But nothing distracted him, and there was concern among White House staff that obsession with his blunder in Cuba had thrown him perilously off balance. McGeorge Bundy complained privately that it was impossible to get Kennedy's attention for essential daily discussions of national security matters. Whenever Bundy appeared – and in recent weeks he had managed to corner the President only three times, for about eight minutes each – Kennedy would rant about that morning's papers and speculate about who in the administration had leaked what. Consumed by a sense of his own disgrace, he simply could not think of anything else.

In the days following his colossal error of judgment, Kennedy, rather than exercising iron self-control and self-discipline, seemed only to grow more heedless. If ever there was a time for caution, this was it. Yet, at a time when he could ill afford anything else to go wrong, Kennedy's private behavior was far from restrained. Two days after the Schlesinger report spelled out what he had lost, he again jeopardized his presidency with an act of remarkable foolishness. He could count on the press not to report most sexual indiscretions, but now he brought into the White House a woman whose extensive association with criminals, had it been discovered, almost certainly would have provoked an avalanche of news coverage.

On Saturday, May 6, Kennedy invited Judith Campbell to the family quarters for the first time. Because of the President of Tunisia's visit, Jackie had not gone to Glen Ora on Friday. Instead, she had accompanied Jack to a dinner in their honor at the Tunisian embassy and went to the country the following day, the children having left separately that morning. Not long after her limousine passed through the Southwest Gate shortly after noon, another White House car was dispatched to the Mayflower Hotel to collect Campbell, who had been staying there since Thursday in a room reserved by Mrs Lincoln. She had traveled by train from Florida, where she had been visiting Sam Giancana and his underworld associate Johnny Rosselli.

The President had lunch with Campbell and Dave Powers in the charming private dining room Jackie had constructed on the second floor. Afterward, he dismissed Powers and took Campbell to his bedroom. First he walked her through Jackie's room, then through the connecting closet where he put on a record – a signal to staff that he did not wish to be disturbed. There was scant opportunity to set a mood, however, for by a quarter to five the presidential limousine was headed to Glen Ora and Judith Campbell was en route to Chicago, where Giancana awaited her.

Kennedy tended to know or care little about the women he slept with, hence the jeopardy in which he routinely placed both himself and his country. By this time it was evident to the agents who guarded him that 'he would have gone to bed with

Mata Hari if that was his night to function.' There is no evidence that Kennedy knew of Campbell's intimacy with gangsters, though the fact that she had been introduced to him by Sinatra should have been cause for concern. Nor, at that point, does Kennedy seem to have been aware that Giancana and Rosselli had previously been recruited by the C.I.A. to assassinate Fidel Castro. He certainly had no inkling that Campbell, who kept meticulous records of her encounters with Kennedy, might have been setting him up on Giancana's behalf. Still, the news that Kennedy was sharing a lover with a Mafia kingpin – let alone one involved in a secret government plot to kill Castro – could have been enough to bring down his presidency, particularly at this extremely delicate time.

It was typical of Kennedy to be at his most weirdly reckless when most in peril. The recklessness continued in Palm Beach. Worried that depression would prevent Jackie from going to Canada though protocol demanded her presence, Kennedy took the huge step of bringing in Max Jacobson, a New York doctor who had a cult-like following and a history of insinuating himself in the lives of rich, powerful, and creative patients, who knew him as Dr Feel Good. Some people saw Jacobson as a savant, even a god; others as 'cunning and relentless,' 'corrupt to the core,' 'a ruiner of lives.' His *modus operandi* was to make his patients so dependent on his injections that they could no longer function independently. When that point was reached, more often than not those lives veered tragically off course. The central element of the Jacobson experience was what the actor Patrick O'Neal described as the doctor's desire to make each injection a rite, in which he fostered the grotesque illusion that he was having sex with the patient via his needle.

Jack had first encountered Jacobson during the presidential campaign, when he was preparing to face Richard Nixon in nationally televised debates. Chuck Spalding, himself a Jacobson enthusiast who kept a collection of hypodermic needles in his dressing room, suggested that Jack pay a visit to the doctor. When Jack agreed, Spalding contacted Jacobson. He stipulated that the candidate's visit be 'private and confidential,' and that the usually crowded and chaotic Upper East Side office, which

was open seven days a week from as early as 5:30 a.m. until
11 p.m., be emptied of all other patients.

Though the blinds were always drawn, a visit to the Jacobson
office was rarely private. In the reception area, patients scanned
the room in search of stars, like tourists at Chasen's restaurant
in Hollywood. Some people remained in the outer office for
hours. Others, usually new patients, were ushered in immediately. The celebrity hunt continued in the rear, where patients
waited for hours, either seated or stretched out on examining
tables from which the interiors of other fluorescent-lit cubicles
were visible. Intrinsic to Jacobson's mystique was his fondness
for injecting patients in full view of one another.

His office, described by one habitué as a 'nut house,' was
notoriously dirty. Wastebaskets spilled over onto floors littered
with broken hypodermic needles and crumpled paper wrappers.
Shelves marked 'METH,' short for methamphetamine, were
crowded with vials of the mood-lifting drug that Jacobson mixed
with steroids, calcium, monkey placenta, and other, undisclosed
ingredients. Jacobson never published his recipes, and some
patients lived in terror that if he died no other physician would
be able to continue his work.

When the presidential candidate arrived, only Jacobson,
his wife, Nina, and a few employees were present. Kennedy
mentioned Chuck Spalding and another patient, the photographer Mark Shaw, then on assignment for *Life* magazine to
cover Kennedy and his family. Kennedy, about to go head to
head with Nixon on national television, complained that he felt
tired and weak. The demands of the campaign had affected
both his concentration and his speech. Jacobson pointed out that
Kennedy's ailments were the most common clinical symptoms
caused by stress. He had just the treatment.

People who experienced that treatment, an injection in the
arm, hand, hip, buttocks, or solar plexus with a one-and-a-half-
inch needle, reported a sense of being lit up from within.
Thoughts raced. Ideas and images came at the speed of light.
A few reported an explosion that traveled from the heels to the
top of the skull. Some could hardly stop moving or talking.
Others dozed off. One patient compared himself to Superman,

another to Michelangelo's Adam touched by the hand of God. Kennedy, for his part, told the doctor that his muscle weakness had vanished and that he felt calm and extremely alert. Jacobson gave him a bottle of 'vitamin' drops to be taken orally before the debate with Nixon.

Max and Nina Jacobson attended the Inauguration, but it wasn't until May 1961 that a call came from the White House. Dr Travell, wary from the first, grilled Jacobson on his methods for treating stress. When Jacobson asked whether this was in reference to the President, Travell said yes. On the morning of Friday, May 12, he received another call instructing him to fly to Palm Beach immediately. Met at his hotel by a government car, Jacobson, who styled himself the 'last doctor in New York to make house calls,' arrived at the Wrightsman estate late in the afternoon, after the Spaldings had left. He was indignant when two security guards, disturbed by his appearance and manner, demanded identification while they called up to the house to make sure he was expected.

Jacobson, who had a powerful chest and biceps and a massive pot belly, cut a hulking, disheveled figure. Large, horn-rimmed glasses with thick lenses magnified roaming, unsettled eyes. He had lost half of a tooth many years previously in a boxing match in Berlin. His resonant voice skidded between a mumble and a shout. A former patient claimed that his thick accent – Jacobson was the son of a kosher butcher in Fordon, a small village on the Polish frontier in western Prussia – made him sound 'like a caricature of Freud.' An actress whose husband had been in thrall to the doctor described Jacobson as 'sinister, like a Vincent Price character.' Though he carried a physician's black leather bag, the pockets of his wrinkled coat and baggy trousers typically bulged with vials, syringes, and tourniquets. His fingernails were stained black by chemicals and he usually stank of medicine and cigarettes.

This was the charlatan who, on Kennedy's order, was led to a porch that adjoined a pretty garden and asked to wait. Jacobson, for his part, had reason to believe he was there to treat the President. Instead, when Kennedy emerged from the garden, he asked Jacobson to see Mrs Kennedy. He had to know whether she would be able to undertake the state visits and other foreign travel that faced them directly.

Jackie gave Jacobson a cool reception. It was evident from the outset that, as the President had said, she was deeply depressed. Reluctant to say what was wrong, she mentioned only a terrible headache. Jacobson, spotting his opening, offered help. He filled a syringe with the contents of one of several varicolored vials and, avoiding his signature theatricality lest Jackie be put off, gave her a shot. Immediately, she seemed to relax. She looked warm and happy, her headache completely gone.

Minutes later, Jacobson and a beaming Jackie went out to find her husband. One look showed Kennedy that Dr Feel Good had worked his magic. Clearly, the shot 'took a lot of strain off of her.' For the moment, the only discernible negative effect was a dry mouth, which caused her to lick her lips intermittently. Chuck Spalding often did the same, and under the circumstances it seemed a small price. Not only would Jackie be able to go to Canada, she even appeared almost excited at the prospect.

Her excitement, like the other benefits of a Jacobson treatment, was transitory. By the time Jackie accompanied her husband on their first trip abroad as President and First Lady on May 16, four days had passed and the doctor's elixir had long worn off. The White House viewed the two-day trip as a dry run for the upcoming European visit. Two matters needed to be carefully monitored. Face to face with a foreign leader on foreign soil, how would Kennedy handle the inevitable questions about the Bay of Pigs fiasco? And how would Jackie manage the exceptionally demanding schedule?

Jackie, enthusiastically received, did well at several events, but at the last minute she canceled what was to have been her most significant contribution, a much-touted interview in French for Canadian television. Twenty minutes before the taping, several French-speaking members of the Kennedy staff were sent in place of the First Lady, who, quite simply, had crumbled under the weight of her schedule and still faced the necessity of hosting a dinner that evening for twenty eminent Canadians.

The cancellation, as her husband perceived, did not bode well for Europe.

He had troubles of his own as well. Soon after he arrived in Ottawa, he seriously injured his unstable back in a tree-planting ceremony. Years of practice at hiding his almost constant pain stood him in good stead. Though he pretended nothing was wrong, the injury, coming so soon before he was to confront de Gaulle and Khrushchev, was a disaster. Back in Washington two days later, Jack hobbled about on crutches – but only in private. Weakened politically by Cuba, Kennedy refused to compound the problem with an image of physical weakness. His injury, coupled with Jackie's cancellation of the television taping, guaranteed that Dr Jacobson would soon be back in their lives.

Jackie remained in the White House a single night before she took the children to Glen Ora, and by the time Jack joined her there on Saturday a new calamity had started to unfold. Newspapers around the world were reporting the latest embarrassment to his administration, and this time the mess was at home. For days the international press had been full of stories about the violence with which a group of black activists was met when it tried to test a Supreme Court ruling that outlawed segregation in terminals, trains, and buses used in interstate transportation. Kennedy, gearing up for Europe, was in no mood for the further complication of the Freedom Riders, whom he regarded as 'an unnecessary burden.' Once again driven by pragmatic rather than moral considerations, his principal concern was the impact on his encounter with Khrushchev of any action he might take in Alabama. Indeed, in Kennedy's view it would be best if he could stay clear of what he repeatedly called 'this Goddamned civil rights mess.'

Kennedy was eager to get the violence off the front pages before he went to France, but he was also gun-shy about sending in the Army to protect the Freedom Riders. During the campaign, he had criticized Eisenhower for permitting the race crisis in Little Rock to reach a point where federal troops had to be sent in. If Kennedy did the same thing now, it would only give ammunition to those inclined to question his leadership. Kennedy had repeatedly called the Governor of Alabama to urge him to accept responsibility for the Freedom Riders' safety, but John Patterson ducked the phone calls. Saturday's headlines trumpeted, 'President Can't Reach Governor.' Two weeks before Kennedy, already enfeebled by Cuba, was to meet Khrushchev, he was further diminished by the spectacle of a U.S. state governor refusing to take his calls. It was an unprecedented insult, one that would be interpreted in Europe as a sign of Kennedy's lack of power and prestige. If he had so little authority in his own country, what would happen with Khrushchev?

Every time the phone rang that weekend at Glen Ora, it brought more bad news. When the Freedom Riders pulled into the Montgomery bus terminal, they were met by an angry mob. As the passengers left the bus, the crowd attacked. Crying 'Get 'em! Get 'em!' they swung baseball bats and lead pipes. John Siegenthaler, the President's personal representative to Governor Patterson, sought to protect one young woman and was knocked unconscious by a pipe. Five weeks after Kennedy, in this very house, had given the go-ahead on Cuba, he reluctantly ordered four hundred U.S. marshals to Maxwell Air Force Base. This at least was better than using uniformed soldiers, which would provide Khrushchev with invaluable propaganda images of U.S. citizens being attacked by their own military.

There was more violence on Sunday as three thousand whites gathered outside the church where Martin Luther King Jr addressed fifteen hundred supporters of the Freedom Riders. A dozen men in business suits, with yellow armbands marked 'U.S. Marshal,' guarded the entrance. Rocks, bricks, and Molotov cocktails flew, and the marshals fired tear gas on rioters. When more marshals proved insufficient, Bobby Kennedy, as Attorney General, asked Jack to send in the military. Finally, Patterson declared a state of martial law and white-helmeted Alabama National Guardsmen were called out. Though the President had avoided sending in troops, it had not been in his power to stop indelible images of racial strife and mob violence being printed in newspapers and magazines around the world for days to come. These images, he knew, would form the backcloth for his sessions with de Gaulle and Khrushchev.

Monday morning, Kennedy returned to the White House alone and sent word to Jacobson that he wanted him there the next morning, when Jackie was due from the country. Instructed to carry an attaché case rather than a physician's bag, Jacobson assumed he was to treat the First Lady. A government car delivered him on Tuesday, shortly after her helicopter landed on the South Grounds at 10 a.m., and after a brief wait a maid led him to Jackie's bedroom. She greeted him with the same icy reserve as in Palm Beach, though she did volunteer that she was nervous about her schedule and responsibilities in Europe. The doctor, careful to seem professional rather than flamboyant, gave Jackie a second injection. Like all of his patients, she had no idea of what was in the shot. When the question was asked, he would laugh and reply, 'You're feeling better, correct? Then that is all you need to know.'

At the close of the session, Kennedy's valet materialized and led Jacobson through the connecting closet. The President, still in agony because of his back, waited in his bedroom. As far as he was concerned, there were two drawbacks to Jacobson's treatment. The shots caused a general lack of control that Jack very much disliked. And, though other patients claimed otherwise, Kennedy insisted to Chuck Spalding that in his own case the drugs impeded sexual performance. Still, he wanted another injection.

Kennedy offered Jacobson a chair beside the fireplace and recounted the tree-planting ceremony in Canada. Since Thursday, he had spent as much time in bed as possible and been treated with Novocain, to no avail. Annoyed by Dr Travell's suggestion that he use crutches openly in France, he vowed not to face de Gaulle as a cripple. He had developed considerable tolerance for pain over the years, but this time it was so severe that he could not imagine being able to concentrate with de Gaulle and Khrushchev. Was there anything Jacobson could do for his back? Jacobson said that he could help, but only if the President obeyed certain conditions. The doctor strictly ruled out alcohol, opiates, and codeine as incompatible with his treatment.

After demonstrating a back exercise, Jacobson gave Kennedy an injection which he promised would not only relieve pain but help with stress as well. Kennedy had spoken only of his injury, but in light of the events in Cuba and Alabama, Jacobson could hardly fail to realize that stress was also a concern. Once before, Jacobson had intervened at a crucial moment in Kennedy's political life. Perhaps what had succeeded with Nixon might work with de Gaulle and Khrushchev as well. Now more than ever, Kennedy sought the air of confidence and euphoria Jacobson could provide.

This was not the first time Jacobson had injected Kennedy, but it was the first methamphetamine treatment administered to him as President. After these shots, old men swore they felt twenty years younger. Despite a heart condition, the aged film director Cecil B. DeMille was said to have thrown off his bathrobe and done a dozen pushups without getting winded. Kennedy merely rose and paced the room, reporting that he felt 'very much better.' Where Dr Travell had failed to bring relief, Jacobson had succeeded instantly and brilliantly, confirming his reputation as a miracle worker. Kennedy wasted no time in inviting the doctor to Paris and Vienna. Determined to make a good showing, he decided to face de Gaulle and Khrushchev under the influence of drugs of unknown composition, even though those drugs robbed him of control.

Kennedy declared that in anticipation of the trip he and Jackie must start treatments at once, and asked Jacobson to stay a few days. Jacobson not only agreed to remain but also refused payment. He returned the next morning to give Jackie a shot before she went to Glen Ora to spend some time with the children and complete last-minute preparations for France. He lingered in Washington to help Kennedy through an address to Congress. Back in New York, he booked a separate flight to Paris in order to avoid press speculation about the presence of a doctor other than Travell on *Air Force One*, let alone a doctor as well known in certain circles as he. By no means discreet, however, he boasted to some of his celebrity patients that he was to accompany the Kennedys to Europe.

On May 30, Jack, who had celebrated his forty-fourth birthday with his father at the Kennedy family compound in Hyannis Port, and addressed some five thousand Democrats at a Party dinner in Boston, boarded *Air Force One* in New York. Jackie joined him, after dropping off Caroline and John at the White House. Once she was on board they were ready to go, but at the last minute Jack decided he did not want to take off without a shot. After much ado, Jacobson was located at a nearby hotel, where he and Nina were waiting to depart on Air France. He rushed to Gate Sixteen, but there was a further delay when a security guard refused to believe the President could be expecting this dirty, alarming individual. Finally, someone on *Air Force One* spotted the commotion and dashed out to get Jacobson. In the presidential stateroom, Jacobson injected Jack and Jackie before the trip that was so dramatically to alter both Kennedys' lives.

SIX

Hall of Mirrors

At half past ten the next morning, May 31, 1961, Jackie squinted in the misty sunlight as she emerged from *Air Force One*. Dressed in a pale blue coat and matching pillbox hat, her dark hair windblown, she paused to take in the scene at Orly Airport outside Paris. A few feet in front of her, Jack was already carefully descending the steps, the only sign of nerves being two hyperactive fingers that twisted a button on his suit jacket. Kennedy had requested the meeting with de Gaulle, but since the Bay of Pigs he had dreaded the day when he would face America's prickliest ally, who had reacted to the fiasco with one devastating word: 'Inept.'

On a red carpet at the foot of the stairs loomed the massive, commanding, seventy-year-old general who unabashedly saw himself as the personification of France. President Charles de Gaulle, aloof and austere, lived by the dictum, formulated twenty-nine years previously, that 'there can be no authority without prestige, nor prestige unless one keeps one's distance.' Convinced that no great statesman ever underestimated the importance of theater and performance, he emulated what he liked to call the 'studied manner' of Caesar and Napoleon. Yvonne de Gaulle, ten years her husband's junior, stood at his side. Small and mousy, she was as self-effacing as he was imposing. As a young wife, Yvonne had washed and pressed her husband's white gloves every night so that he would always look the part of a leader.

Initially, it seemed that Jackie, like her counterpart, was destined to play only a supporting role during the visit. When de Gaulle, notorious for his refusal to speak anything but

French, cheerily addressed Jack in English – 'Did you have a good aerial voyage?' – he seemed to signal that at least for now he planned to make things easy for the young American. Jackie, unlike her husband, spoke fluent French, but after a brief greeting she was led off by Madame de Gaulle to join the ladies, while the men reviewed some troops. At the close of a welcoming ceremony, the two leaders drove off together in an open limousine preceded by fifty roaring motorcycles, while Jackie and Madame de Gaulle followed in a bubbletop Citroën.

In keeping with de Gaulle's conviction that to look powerful is to be powerful, the ten-mile motorcade into Paris was the first of several extravaganzas to which the Kennedys would be treated. De Gaulle had declared a national holiday, and the road teemed with spectators. Kennedy, though in tremendous physical pain, repeatedly stood up to wave, while de Gaulle, disdainful of such gestures, remained seated and offered only occasional grudging acknowledgment of the cheering, flag-waving crowds whom he could barely see without the glasses which vanity disinclined him to use in public. As the motorcade reached the Place des Pyramides, members of the colorful Republican Guard, their glittering gold helmets topped with long red plumes, replaced the motorcycle escort. Enormous black horses tossed their heads, while metal shoes clattered over cobblestone streets. Such national traditions were important to de Gaulle. Confronted by a defeated, diminished post-war France that had 'given up all ambition,' he sought to change the psychological cast of his people, as well as foreign perceptions of his country. He would give France the appearance, the trappings, the façade of power, even if it had not yet retrieved the thing itself. To this end de Gaulle drew on pageantry, art, and architecture as potent reminders of what France had once been – and, with his help, would soon be again.

Met by a one-hundred-and-one-gun salute, the motorcade entered Paris by the Porte d'Orléans, where the crowd swelled hugely. Far more people had turned out than even de Gaulle had anticipated, and to judge by the exuberant cries of 'Vive Jacqueline! Vive Jacqueline!' it was the American First Lady they had come to see. Madame de Gaulle, who religiously cultivated invisibility and took pride in the fact that she went about in public unnoticed, was horrified by the attention directed at her car. Kennedy, who had long feared that Jackie would prove a political liability, appeared by turns stunned and amused. As spectators pressed forward to catch a glimpse of his wife, he jokingly remarked through a translator that he really ought to be jealous.

The reason for the crowd's fascination was no mystery. The previous evening, French television had aired an interview with Jackie taped in Washington. In flawless French, Jackie had said that she was a daughter of France. Not only was she of Gallic ancestry, but she loved France and all things French. She communicated to the French people that their culture was her passion and their taste her ideal. In essence she declared herself one of them, and today as many as a million citizens had come out to welcome her home. All her life Jackie had read and fantasized about France. This rapturous reception was beyond anything she, or anyone else, could have imagined.

There was scarcely time to absorb the full dimensions of her triumph before the cortège reached the French Ministry of Foreign Affairs, the Quai d'Orsay, where she and Jack were to be lodged. Nor could Jackie pause adequately to take in the splendor of the cavernous royal apartments loaded with furniture, tapestries, and paintings from the palaces of French kings. Jack, due at the Elysée Palace in an hour for his first one-on-one session with de Gaulle, closeted himself in the Chambre du Roi, where he was given an injection for back pain and conferred with aides as he soaked in a vast, gold-plated bathtub. Jackie had only half an hour more before she was to join him at a luncheon in their honor. In the Chambre de la Reine, a maid had laid out her clothes for the afternoon and drawn a steaming hot bath in a lavish silver mosaic tub. Alexandre, Paris's most fashionable coiffeur, waited in the wings with two assistants.

While she dressed and had her hair done, Jack went on to the Elysée Palace. Before the Kennedys arrived, Hervé Alphand, France's ambassador to the U.S., had flown in from Washington to confer with de Gaulle. Alphand and his elegant wife, Nicole, had become friends with Jack and Jackie before the election, and saw more of them after the Inauguration than any other foreign ambassador. The ambassador reported that Kennedy, 'upset and lost' following the Bay of Pigs, needed someone to provide a sense of direction. 'He has great admiration for you,' Alphand told de Gaulle. 'He is looking for a guide because he feels a little lost.' De Gaulle, who only a few weeks previously had dismissed Kennedy as 'inept,' took new interest in the young President.

'But no,' France's leader exclaimed, suddenly perceiving an opportunity, 'he is young, courageous, he has no reason to despair' – not with de Gaulle to guide him. Aware that Harold Macmillan, the British Prime Minister, had already been to Washington, no doubt seeking to influence the new President, de Gaulle savored the prospect of taking on the role of Kennedy's mentor himself.

As the two leaders faced each other with only interpreters present, Kennedy's behavior seemed to confirm Alphand's assessment. De Gaulle had told Alphand that since Kennedy had requested the meeting, he would wait to see what Kennedy wanted. Forced to lead the discussion but eager to say little, Kennedy peppered de Gaulle with questions. For nearly half an hour the general held forth on how Kennedy should handle Khrushchev when they met several days later. There was no intimacy to the talks, no evidence of warmth. Kennedy, for his part, felt frustrated by the necessity of communicating through interpreters, which presented an obstacle to his charm, usually a reliable secret weapon. Still, the meeting went the way both Kennedy and de Gaulle, each for his own reasons, wanted. By the time the men left to collect Jackie, Kennedy was pleased because he had not had to betray a lack of experience by saying too much, and de Gaulle was pleased because the younger man really did seem to want his guidance.

It was ten past one when Jackie's car drove through the Grille de Coq. The Republican Guard stood at attention as her husband and de Gaulle came out to greet her. At the sound of trumpets and the sight of the soldiers' splendid uniforms and drawn swords, her eyes lit up with the excitement of a small

child before a present-laden Christmas tree. De Gaulle appeared
no less delighted, though it was Jackie who made him feel that
way. If the husband had impressed de Gaulle as terribly young,
the wife seemed almost a child. Jackie had chosen her costume,
a pale yellow silk suit and matching hat with turned-up brim
worn at the back of her head, for just this effect. The short
A-line skirt and low heels emphasized her girlishness. She
might almost have been a stylish student visiting her doting
grandfather, a role in which, to judge by his eyes and smile,
the usually forbidding de Gaulle was eager to be cast.

Jack had long relished Jackie's sense of social drama. At their
best, her Washington dinner parties were small marvels of *mise
en scène*. Paris would be Jackie's first attempt to deploy her gift
for strategy on a vast public stage. Certainly the cheers that
had greeted her showed that she had handily wooed the French
public. Now, she took aim at their leader. With a sense of
theater to match de Gaulle's, Jackie conceived her meetings
with him not individually but as part of a larger scheme. She
calibrated each appearance to advance the drama step by step,
in terms of what had gone before and was yet to come.

Seated next to de Gaulle at lunch, Jackie underwent a
miraculous transformation. The nymphet metamorphosed into a
highly intelligent woman who engaged the general on recondite
matters of French history and culture. She and de Gaulle
discussed Louis XVI, exchanged views on the duc d'Angoulême,
and reviewed the dynastic intricacies of the later Bourbons.
Enjoying herself tremendously, she leaned very close to de
Gaulle as they talked. Other guests, including Dave Powers and
Kenny O'Donnell, who had previously despaired of Jackie's
political skills, looked on as though at a silent film. Intently as
she seemed to concentrate on the general, however, as always
Jackie's performance was really for her husband, who watched
in wonder.

Jackie had met de Gaulle once before, the previous year, at
the Alphands' in Washington, but this was their first sustained
encounter. It was obvious that the general, who hardly touched
his food, was enchanted. First the *langouste* was taken away, then
the *pâté de foie gras*, then the *noix de veau Orloff*, and during all of

it he barely stopped talking and listening to Jackie. It wasn't, as some thought, her beauty that won him over, nor was it her erudition. Instead, the performer in de Gaulle responded to Jackie's keen dramatic sense, the dazzling variety of a performance built on strong, unexpected contrasts. Had the guest been Eleanor Roosevelt, her conversation would have come as no surprise. But given Jackie's calculatedly juvenile appearance, the effect, as de Gaulle well appreciated, was one of high drama. It seemed safe to assume that Jackie, so knowledgeable about French history, was equally astute with regard to U.S. affairs and wielded considerable influence with her husband. Neither was the case, but by the time lunch ended, the two-handed game of power politics that de Gaulle and Kennedy had been set to play had become very much a threesome.

Kennedy, unaccustomed to Jackie's help on the diplomatic front, sensed her impact when talks resumed that afternoon. De Gaulle added some important insights on how best to approach Khrushchev; he cautioned against military involvement in Southeast Asia, including Vietnam; and he urged Kennedy to forge his own path independent of his predecessor's policies and his advisers' pleadings. Afterward, Kennedy told aides that he and de Gaulle were hitting it off – 'probably because I have such a charming wife.'

Meanwhile, Jackie accompanied Madame de Gaulle on a tour of a pediatric clinic, the sort of obligation she avoided in Washington but appeared thoroughly to enjoy today. Jackie hated for her personal space to be invaded by a crowd, and Secret Service agents soon learned to watch for the telltale widening of her eyes that signaled it was time for them to move in. Her response at the clinic, as well-wishers pushed and shoved to get near, was notably different. Some French television cameramen were so aggressive that they knocked over small children, and at one point Jackie had to be wrenched free from a woman who pleaded for an imprisoned son. The pandemonium left Madame de Gaulle aghast, but Jackie responded with unshakable calm and serenity. Outside, she waved to the cheering crowd as if she had enjoyed doing this sort of thing all her life.

By late afternoon, Jackie had returned to the Chambre de la Reine to prepare for another encounter with de Gaulle. Her evening dress, a skin-tight sheath of pink and white lace, was sleeveless and had a boldly scooped back. It was past eight when she and Jack left the Quai d'Orsay, the latter preoccupied with an unfolding crisis in the Dominican Republic where dictator Rafael Trujillo had been assassinated, purportedly at U.S. instigation. On the front steps, they were greeted by hundreds of exploding flashbulbs and cries of '*Ravissante!*' Following the crowd's gaze, Kennedy paused to stare. His face lit up as he seemed to register what Jackie was up to. She had come to lunch as a sweet little girl, but she would appear at dinner in a different guise: a sophisticated woman of the world, more Hollywood star than Newport debutante.

For a long moment Jack said nothing. Then, 'Well, I'm dazzled.' So was his entourage, including the hitherto highly skeptical Irish Mafia, after the First Lady charmed not just de Gaulle but the fifteen hundred guests who appeared for a post-dinner reception that evening at the Elysée Palace.

Back in the Chambre de la Reine before midnight, Jackie received an injection from Jacobson, who arrived to ensure that the President and the First Lady slept well. It had been an exceptionally long day and the next day's schedule promised to be even more taxing. As Jackie enumerated the wonders of her evening, Jacobson put a finger to his lips and pointed frantically to some molding near the ceiling. This was by no means unusual behavior for the doctor. He was given to bouts of paranoia made worse by his own extensive use of amphetamines, and on this occasion he was sure he had spotted a hidden microphone.

Jacobson moved on to the President, who had been on the telephone trying to make peace between his brother Bobby, the Attorney General, and Chester Bowles, acting Secretary of State. The two were at loggerheads over whether the U.S. ought to take immediate action in response to the Trujillo assassination. After Cuba, the President had ordered a halt to a C.I.A. plan to overthrow General Trujillo, but it now seemed that the order had come too late. There was concern at the White House that the U.S. would be blamed and that the assassination might trigger a Communist takeover. Bobby Kennedy, still bristling at Bowles's position on Cuba, derided him as a 'gutless bastard' for opposing U.S. intervention in the Dominican Republic.

Jacobson returned the next morning, to help prepare Kennedy for the task of explaining the Bay of Pigs fiasco to de Gaulle, which was now complicated by the Trujillo assassination. He also injected Jackie, whose drug-induced exuberance propelled her through a full day of commitments. Scheduled for four hours' rest prior to a dinner at Versailles that promised to be the high point of her trip, Jackie, given energy to burn by Jacobson, insisted on slipping out of the Quai d'Orsay to drive about Paris with a Secret Service agent.

Power, it has been argued, was the single theme in the life of Charles de Gaulle. From young manhood he studied, contemplated, and actively sought power, not simply for himself but for a nation whose destiny he identified with his own. For two days, starting with the motorcade to Paris and continuing through the meals and meetings at the Elysée Palace, de Gaulle had staged a vast pageant of power that made a tremendous impression on both Kennedys. People excited Jack, as a friend once observed, but it was color and form that thrilled his wife. In the sheer extravagance of its effects Thursday night's spectacle, conceived by de Gaulle as the visit's climax, would dwarf everything that had gone before. The dinner in the Hall of Mirrors at Versailles would also be an episode of signal importance in the Kennedys' marriage, as well as one of the great nights of Mrs Kennedy's life.

It was 8:15 when, with flags fluttering, the eleven-car Kennedy motorcade arrived at the palace of the Sun King, which someone once described as 'the greatest expression of absolute monarchy in the world.' Jackie, who had come to lunch the previous day in the guise of a child, then to dinner as a sexy woman of the world, had saved the ultimate seduction for this evening. When she emerged from her car, she was a Frenchwoman. Though Jackie had vowed to wear American clothes as First Lady, tonight she was the embodiment of French fashion. In homage to her hosts, she wore a beaded and embroidered white satin evening gown and matching coat designed by Givenchy, her favorite Paris couturier. Her hair was swept up with leaf-shaped diamond clips to create the glittering suggestion of a small tiara, and her Palm Beach tan, in evidence the previous day, had vanished under pale and beautiful makeup.

Minister of State for Cultural Affairs André Malraux, a well-known romantic adventurer, dashing war hero, and prize-winning novelist whom Jackie had long idolized, escorted the President and First Lady inside. Minutes later, de Gaulle himself, courtly and elegant in white tie, led Jackie up the famous, richly decorated Queen's Staircase to the second floor. As he walked her through the château, Jackie was transported to the terrain of her daydreams. France, emblem of a larger world that both attracted and frightened her, had long been a focal point of her fantasy life. These were the very rooms she had read and dreamed about. These were the scenes pictured and described in the cherished books where she had sought escape from reality. Since childhood, she had been an observer. Tonight, as her reveries of France's illustrious past sprang to life, she was the star of the spectacle.

The Kennedys and the de Gaulles waited in the Queen's Bedroom while one hundred and fifty guests took their seats in the Hall of Mirrors, which extended along the entire west façade of the château. When Jackie entered at last, she saw a candlelit room 240 feet long and 33 feet wide, with a ceiling that soared to a height of forty feet. A vast mirrored wall reflected the geometrical gardens and splashing fountains visible through seventeen high arched windows opposite, as well as a single long slender table in the hall's center, where white tapers flickered in gold candelabra. That the windows also reflected the dizzying images that danced in the mirrors made it hard at times, especially for someone fueled by amphetamines, to separate illusion from reality.

De Gaulle sat between the Kennedys. The diamonds in Jackie's dark hair caught the light as she chatted gaily with her other dinner partner, Malraux, but all the while she closely monitored her husband's conversation. Though the talks had gone better than expected, Jack felt frustrated by the need for an interpreter, and again and again this evening Jackie heard his characteristic dry wit being hopelessly lost in translation. Wanting de Gaulle to see him as she did, to respond to Jack as he had to her, she did something unprecedented: she abruptly banished the official translator and took over herself. From one end of the long table to the other, heads turned and mouths dropped at a stunning breach of protocol reflected in many mirrors. One simply did not dismiss a trained interpreter in the midst of such a discussion, when a single error could affect relations with an important ally.

If Jack was wary, he gave no sign. This was the sort of recklessly brave gesture he associated with Kick, and no one enjoyed the spice of risk and audacity more than he. Besides, like his wife, Jack had had a shot from Jacobson, whose treatments propelled one's confidence to dizzying heights, where no action, however extreme, seemed too dangerous. The scene was reminiscent of Edmond Rostand's *Cyrano de Bergerac*, in which a suitor puts his words into the mouth of an attractive intermediary. From the first, de Gaulle and Kennedy clearly savored speaking through Jackie. Conducted in her whispery voice, the act of translation itself became sexually provocative, an intimate yet public sharing of a woman both men adored.

For two days, Jackie had been warming up de Gaulle. Now she would deliver him directly. Yet in the Hall of Mirrors, not all was quite as it seemed. Jackie aimed to seduce de Gaulle for Jack, but it was equally the case that de Gaulle, with designs of his own, hoped to use her to establish his influence over a weakened U.S. President.

Instantly, Jack and Jackie fell into the team rhythm for which, among close friends, they were renowned. Handed the baton by his wife, Jack shifted to a subject that would permit both men to display themselves at their best. He asked about de Gaulle's contemporaries Winston Churchill and Franklin Roosevelt, on both of whom Kennedy had passionate, well-informed views. Which was the superior wartime leader? Which had de Gaulle liked best personally? Jackie, speaking by turns for de Gaulle and her husband, resembled those fabulous political

women in *The Young Melbourne* prepared to step in and help two
statesmen make overtures to each other.

Many times in the past Jack and Jackie had operated as a
team, but always in private among friends and family, never in
the realm of politics from which early on Jackie had exiled
herself. Tonight, with its heady mix of sex, speed, and illusion,
was the start of something very new. Like Kick, who had
become most herself in England, Jackie began to reinvent herself
in France. She appeared to enjoy the political game as never
before, and the meaning she had once sought in her own life
as an antidote to the emptiness and insularity of her mother's
existence seemed attainable at last. A decade previously, at the
time she won the Prix de Paris, Jackie had failed to seize the
opportunity for a bigger life that France provided. She would
not make that mistake again.

Dinner ended at ten. Two mirrors opened, and the de Gaulles
and the Kennedys vanished. Meanwhile, dinner guests were led
to the Théâtre Louis XV, where they remained seated until the
Presidents and their wives emerged on a small balcony. All rose
to applaud, while the de Gaulles and the Kennedys took their
bows – acknowledgment on both sides that, though the evening's
official entertainment was an eighteenth-century ballet in period
costume, the real virtuoso performance had already taken place
in the Hall of Mirrors.

By the time the two couples said goodbye at midnight, de
Gaulle had reason to believe he had successfully positioned
himself as Kennedy's 'guide.' Malraux led the Kennedys out to
their car. There was a light mist of rain, and hardly had they
driven off when Jack signaled the driver to stop. Overcome
with the emotion of the evening, he and Jackie went for a stroll
amid spraying fountains and huge white classical statues, all
brilliantly illuminated. Something extraordinary had just happened to both Kennedys. At the time of the Inauguration,
Jackie, however proud and delighted for her husband, had been
unable fully and sincerely to share Jack's elation, his sense of
power and dreams fulfilled. Without a doubt she had shared it
tonight, and she began to perceive that she might want to play
an active role in his public life after all. At Versailles, of all

places, she and Jack had finally entered the presidency together.

If Jackie had any doubt about what she had accomplished thus far, the newspapers confirmed that she was the French people's darling. 'Versailles has a Queen,' announced one French newspaper. The previous day, a cartoon had shown the famously strait-laced de Gaulle asleep in a vast canopied bed dreaming of Jackie, whose image floated above. Under the covers, Madame de Gaulle, known to be as prudish and puritanical as her husband, stared daggers at Jackie and exclaimed indignantly, 'Charles!'

All Jackie had to do was express a wish and, evidently, it would be granted. At dinner she had mentioned to Malraux how much she loved the Impressionist paintings at the Musée du Jeu de Paume, and how she wished somehow she could sneak in to see them. Within hours, word arrived that Malraux had ordered the museum closed to the public. For a brief time, it would be open solely for Jackie's private pleasure. The Minister of Cultural Affairs proposed to take her there himself.

If there had been a recklessly brave quality to Jackie's performance the previous night, by the time she left the Jeu de Paume she seemed almost giddy. Jacobson had been to see her and Jack again that morning, and as Jackie emerged from the museum, she who ordinarily shrank from crowds and the press pushed past the police cordons to pose for tourists' cameras. A reporter called out to ask which painting was her favorite. An impish sparkle in her eye suggested she knew full well what she was doing when she named Manet's *Olympia*, the nude that on its first exhibition had provoked a famous scandal.

From there she and Malraux went to Malmaison, the former home of the Empress Joséphine, some ten miles west of Paris. Jackie made the pilgrimage at the urging of Stéphane Boudin, who had worked on the restoration and wanted her to scrutinize certain effects so as better to comprehend some of his ideas for how to redo the White House. It was one thing to study pictures or listen to Boudin describe what he hoped to achieve, quite another – especially given the effects of size and scale central to his theories of power decorating – to see for oneself.

On this last day of their Paris visit, Jack and Jackie lunched

separately, she in the country at the former home of Madame
de Pompadour, he in Paris with four hundred members of the
press at the Palais de Chaillot. Kennedy opened his speech with
the words that would forever define Jackie's conquest of France,
as well as her flamboyant if belated entry into political life. 'I
do not think it altogether inappropriate to introduce myself to
this audience,' the President said dryly. 'I am the man who
accompanied Jacqueline Kennedy to Paris, and I have enjoyed
it.'

Paris transformed Jackie into a figure of international fascination. Everyone, not least Nikita Khrushchev, was intensely
curious about the woman who, according to press reports, had
enchanted the notoriously aloof General de Gaulle. When Jackie
stepped off *Air Force One* at Schwechat Airport in a rainy Vienna,
she emanated a sense of power in her own right.

His wife had been the undisputed star in France, yet Jack
came away gratified that the talks had, in the end, gone well.
At their final meeting, de Gaulle had assured Kennedy that he
had 'a great future,' adding significantly that the French and
American Presidents would no doubt soon be taking 'certain
dramatic actions together.' But Paris had been a visit to an ally
determined to maintain a cordial tone even through dis-
agreement. In Vienna, Kennedy faced the enemy, on whom
State Department briefing papers minced no words: 'The
United States and the Soviet Union as chief protagonists in the
present world-wide struggle find themselves in antagonistic
confrontation in regard to every international political problem
... There is only one major subject on which there would
appear to be a coincidence of interest between the United
States and the Soviet Union, and that is on the assumed
common desire of both to avoid nuclear war.'

Kennedy had also heard certain other things about his
adversary. For one, Khrushchev was said to be highly volatile,
with a hair-trigger temper. The slightest affront, real or
imagined, might set him off. Then, briefing papers warned, his
eyes would narrow to slits, 'like a tomcat about to fight another.'
Kennedy was advised to watch for the telltale swelling of the

vein in Khrushchev's right temple, which occurred when he was about to turn particularly ugly and aggressive. 'If the meeting degenerates into a slug-fest of words,' warned Senate Majority Leader Mike Mansfield, 'with each trying to prove he is stronger and more adamant than the other, then it would have been better had the meeting not taken place.'

De Gaulle, for his part, had told Kennedy not to be misled by Khrushchev's threats, most of which, the general assured, would be bluster. De Gaulle was convinced that for all his posturing, Khrushchev really did not want war. In line with the State Department's assessment that Khrushchev was 'skilled at getting the other man on the defensive,' de Gaulle warned Kennedy not to be drawn into theoretical dispute, in which Khrushchev would surely try to entangle him.

But all this was second-hand. Kennedy, who prided himself on being an excellent judge of character, had yet to face Khrushchev himself. At first, he had expected to face Khrushchev from a position of strength, fresh from a quick and dazzling win in Cuba. When the Bay of Pigs invasion proved to be a disaster, Khrushchev had gleefully confirmed the dates for the summit, and Kennedy was not able to withdraw without seeming to be a coward. By this point, he regarded the Vienna meeting as something which he had been trapped into.

To make matters worse, Llewellyn Thompson, U.S. ambassador in Moscow, had reported Khrushchev's 'obvious pleasure' in Kennedy's blunder. Chester Bowles had it from the Polish ambassador that Khrushchev interpreted the botched invasion 'as a sign of fundamental Kennedy weakness' and saw the new President as 'a soft, not very decisive young man.' Khrushchev had assumed that when the invasion faltered, Kennedy, much as the Soviet leader himself had done in Hungary, 'would send in two, three or four divisions and clean up Cuba' regardless of the cost in human life. As a result of his failure to take that step, Khrushchev expected that Kennedy would be easy to intimidate in Vienna.

When Kennedy flew to Vienna, Max Jacobson traveled on *Air Force One* for the first time. The need to be certain that he had access to a shot before he met Khrushchev had apparently overridden the need for discretion. Clearly, as far as the President was concerned, the possibility that reporters might spot Dr Feel Good posed less of a risk than the possibility that Jacobson might not reach the American embassy residence before Khrushchev arrived at a quarter to one. Despite his desire to assess Khrushchev with a clear eye, Kennedy was prepared to meet his adversary through a haze of drugs if that was what it took to eliminate pain and make energy and confidence soar. Despite the fact that he, and many others, feared that a single miscalculation might lead to nuclear annihilation, he would take drugs which he himself admitted compromised his self-control.

There was another problem. Unlike the Americans who had just completed three days of exhausting talks and ceremonies, the Khrushchev contingent, who had arrived in Vienna the previous day, would be fresh and rested. Kennedy's schedule did not even permit him to go directly to the American embassy. Instead, he had to endure a welcoming ceremony at the airport that lasted until 11 a.m., followed by a forty-five-minute motorcade and detour to pay a courtesy call on the Austrian President.

The schedule was so tight that it was decided Jackie ought to skip the courtesy call and travel separately to the American embassy in order to have time to prepare to go out again before the Soviets came. Given the commotion that seemed to follow Jackie everywhere on this trip, the President's advisers didn't want her departure to coincide with Khrushchev's arrival and distract the attention of the press. Jackie was not scheduled to be introduced to Khrushchev until that evening.

Through rain-splashed windows, Jackie caught her first glimpse of the grim, gray stucco building where she and Jack were to spend two days. Behind the barbed wire, flowering red, white, and lavender rhododendron bushes sagged beneath the relentless downpour. Firs and willows bordered a windy gravel courtyard, at the entrance to which Viennese police tugged at the heavy chain leashes of muzzled Alsatian dogs. Even in the rain a crowd had gathered, and there were cheers and applause as Jackie's limousine passed.

Inside the embassy, there was no time to waste. Jackie had forty-five minutes to bathe and change for a series of appearances that included lunch at a restaurant, followed by visits to a porcelain factory and to Belvedere Palace. Assisted by a maid and by one of Alexandre's assistants, she was nearly ready by the time Jack rushed in at 12:25. Only twenty minutes remained before Khrushchev was due. Like clockwork, no sooner was Jack in his room than Jacobson followed. In five minutes Jackie departed, leaving the courtyard clear when cars flying hammer-and-sickle flags rolled in a quarter of an hour later. There was much press comment on how vital and full of energy Kennedy looked as he bounded down the embassy steps to meet the enemy. The presence of Dr Feel Good was not known.

Khrushchev was short and round, with small, bright, mobile eyes and three conspicuous wens on his face. His bald head was fringed with closely clipped white hair. He too had been extensively briefed on his counterpart's strengths and weaknesses. A psychological profile prepared by the Soviet embassy in Washington during the campaign and given to Khrushchev by Andrei Gromyko offers a fascinating glimpse of the Soviets' first impressions of Kennedy.

According to the report, despite efforts to 'create the impression that he is a strong personality of the caliber of Franklin D. Roosevelt,' in fact 'Kennedy, while not a mediocrity, is unlikely to possess the qualities of an outstanding person. He has, by all accounts, an acute, penetrating mind capable of quickly assimilating and analyzing the evidence of a given phenomenon, but at the same time he lacks a certain breadth of perception, the ability to think a matter over philosophically and make appropriate generalizations. By the make-up of his mind he is more of a good catalyst and consumer of others' thoughts, not a creator of independent and original ideas ... Temperamentally, Kennedy is a rather restrained, dispassionate, and reserved person, although he knows how to be sociable and even "charming."' It was his charm to which the report attributed his success with voters. Particularly striking is the assessment of Kennedy as a 'typical pragmatist' who 'in his political activity ... is not governed by any firm convictions, but by purely

pragmatic considerations, defining his positions ... most importantly, on his own interests.'

Like Kennedy, Khrushchev, despite all he had read and
heard, entered the music room where the first meeting was to
take place ready to make up his own mind about his adversary.
The problem for Kennedy was that Khrushchev seemed to be
able to judge much more quickly. Having taken Kennedy's
measure, he set about systematically to destroy him. The session,
attended by both leaders' advisers, began with an exchange of
pleasantries, after which things immediately went wrong for the
American side. Kennedy tended to be highly controlled in such
encounters, but he had just taken drugs that diminished control.
On this occasion, the result of his hubris was catastrophic. He
abandoned his usual tactic of asking questions and saying as
little as possible until he had his bearings. And he ignored – or
forgot – everything de Gaulle had said about avoiding the
thicket of theoretical dispute from which Khrushchev would
allow no escape.

According to Charles Bohlen, a former U.S. ambassador to
the Soviet Union who attended that calamitous first meeting,
the President let himself be 'drawn into a sort of ideological
discussion with Khrushchev and there, admittedly, Kennedy
was not anywhere near the expert Khrushchev was in the field
of Marxian ideology.' Khrushchev's training as a Bolshevik
agitator made him a master of this sort of argument, and each
time Kennedy tried to regain control of the runaway discussion,
Khrushchev would adroitly turn his words around and paint
him as an opponent of social progress. Kennedy was, as Bohlen
put it delicately, 'out of his depth.' Before the session broke for
lunch, Kennedy had been humiliated in his own eyes and
before his advisers.

After a working lunch, a desperate Kennedy suggested that
he and Khrushchev go out for a walk together and then sit
down alone – that is, with interpreters but no advisers present.
Khrushchev agreed, but the afternoon session turned out to be
even more painful. As Harold Macmillan would later glean,
Kennedy was utterly defeated by his inability to charm Khrushchev. Worse, the ordeal seemed unending. It was shortly

before 7 p.m. when Khrushchev, his footsteps shaking the embassy rafters, finally left.

Jackie, who had abbreviated her afternoon schedule in order to rest before the state dinner, had come in at half past three. Jacobson was waiting in case her husband required another shot. Three and a half hours later, Kennedy finally appeared in their living quarters, pale and exhausted, while Jackie was having her hair set. They were due to leave in an hour. Kennedy told his secretary, Evelyn Lincoln, that he wanted to rest, then did nothing of the kind. He ordered cigars, he paced, he brooded. When Mrs Lincoln asked how the meeting had gone, he replied laconically, 'Not too well.'

His experience at the state dinner in the vast, glittering Schönbrunn Palace, formerly the summer residence of the Hapsburg emperors, was no better. From the moment the Kennedys entered five minutes late, Khrushchev, in high spirits after having run circles around his adversary all day, gleefully seized the upper hand. As photographers shouted requests for a Kennedy–Khrushchev handshake, Khrushchev, affecting the clownish persona he often used to tactical advantage, looked pointedly at Jackie and laughed that he preferred to shake her hand first. Beneath the jollity, his intent was serious. Khrushchev respected power as much as he disdained weakness, and Paris had demonstrated that the First Lady was a force to be reckoned with. Having appraised her husband earlier, he dedicated the evening to an effort to figure out the woman who had bewitched General de Gaulle.

He had assumed from the press accounts that beauty had been responsible for Jackie's success. When he saw her in person, wearing a shimmering silvery-pink sheath evening dress, he decided that the press had it wrong; her looks alone could not account for her triumph in Paris. Khrushchev, far from being disappointed, was intrigued. He attached himself to Jackie, joking, teasing, telling outrageous stories. At one point Jack, fascinated but also alarmed by the strange scene, failed to notice a seated Nina Khrushchev and nearly sat on her lap. Jackie very much held her own in conversation with Khrushchev, and he quickly decided that even her small talk demonstrated intelligence. After her husband's performance, Khrushchev had reason to wonder whether Jackie was more of a partner than he'd been led to believe, perhaps even the power behind the throne. Ready to test the degree of her involvement, he shifted gears and informed her that the President had been wise to cancel an order to send U.S. Marines to Laos. Khrushchev spoke as if he assumed Jackie would be conversant with foreign policy decisions. Jack, who had been listening to every word even as he struggled to be polite to Mrs Khrushchev, was on his feet in a flash to cut this off, his bad back forgotten. Before Jackie could reply, Jack stated that he had never issued such an order. Khrushchev threw Jackie a conspiratorial look that suggested he didn't believe it.

At dinner, Jackie and Khrushchev were the focus of all eyes. As always she had done her homework, though by no means as thoroughly as she had for France. She had read Lesley Blanch's *The Sabres of Paradise*, a highly romanticized portrait of a nineteenth-century Caucasian Muslim leader who conducted a twenty-five-year guerrilla war against the Tsar's army. Jackie, enthralled by the book's atmosphere, asked Khrushchev to tell her more about the Ukraine of that time. But he did nothing of the kind. Where Jackie longed for the vivid and exotic, Khrushchev launched into an arid discourse on how many more teachers there were in the Ukraine under the Soviets than under the tsars. Such recitations had defeated Kennedy earlier, but his wife responded differently.

Soon after he began, Jackie interrupted for all to hear, 'Oh, Mr Chairman, don't bore me with statistics.'

It was not the sort of thing a head of state's wife was expected to say to another leader. And it certainly was not a remark one made to the tempestuous Khrushchev; briefing papers reviewed by the President and First Lady before the summit specifically warned against any public challenge. For a long, tense moment, there was no telling how Khrushchev would react.

To everyone's relief, the vein in his right temple did not pop. Instead, he laughed loudly and appreciatively, and dragged his chair closer to Jackie's. The moment was remarkable. Jackie had just accomplished what Jack had been unable to do all afternoon: she had stopped Khrushchev in his tracks. Khrushchev, far from being annoyed, was delighted by her nerve and unpredictability. Face to face with the piquant personality that had charmed de Gaulle, he was charmed as well. During the musical entertainment after dinner, Khrushchev, assisted by a translator seated just behind them, whispered funny stories in Jackie's ear and took immense pleasure when, every now and then, she covered her lips with a white-gloved hand, threw back her head, and laughed.

Reports of Jackie's newest conquest added luster to the legend that had begun in Paris. Now, she counted two world leaders among her cavaliers. 'First Lady Wins Khrushchev, Too,' declared the next day's *New York Times*. 'Smitten Khrushchev is Jackie's Happy Escort,' announced another paper.

As Kennedy's car approached the Soviet embassy shortly after 10 a.m. the following morning, the crowd called out for Jackie, and was disappointed to discover that the President and Secretary of State had arrived without her.

'Rusk,' the President joked, 'you make a hell of a substitute for Jackie!'

Jack, though distressed by suggestions in the Viennese press that Jackie might have had too much to drink, had reason to hope that once again her efforts would pay off in his talks with a leader hitherto impervious to the Kennedy charm. Any such hope was quickly dashed. No matter how amusing and intelligent Khrushchev had found Jackie the previous evening, this morning he was brutal.

The first day's talks, however difficult, gave no hint of the relentless verbal and psychological pummeling Kennedy now faced. Sitting side by side on a small red damask sofa in the Soviet embassy's second-floor conference room, the leaders began with Laos and the nuclear test ban, then turned to the agenda's most explosive item, Germany. As predicted by de Gaulle, Khrushchev threatened to sign a separate peace treaty with East Germany, and as his voice rose, Kennedy had a glimpse of the violent, vituperative Khrushchev of legend. At their previous encounter, Khrushchev had sized up and humiliated Kennedy; now he set out to intimidate him. Kennedy did himself no favors by facing Khrushchev on speed. Robbed of the control he prized, excitable and hasty, Kennedy over-reacted to Khrushchev, as his advisers later told him. The meeting, he later told David Ormsby-Gore, left him feeling 'savaged,' as if Khrushchev had 'beat the hell' out of him. Worried that Khrushchev would underestimate his deter-mination to honor U.S. commitments in Berlin even if that meant nuclear war, Kennedy requested an additional meeting after lunch. He would have a quarter of an hour to prove he was no coward.

Kennedy spoke first. He made it clear that he hoped to improve U.S.–Soviet relations, but that any interruption of access to Berlin would be intolerable. Khrushchev refused to budge. 'It is not the U.S.S.R. that threatens with war,' he said, 'it is the U.S.' Clenching his fist, he insisted that the decision to sign a treaty with East Germany in December remained 'firm and irrevocable.'

'We are going to negotiate a new agreement with East Germany,' he declared, 'and the access routes to Berlin will be under their control. If there is any effort by the West to interfere, there will be war.'

Kennedy had been warned by de Gaulle about his opponent's tendency to bluff, specifically on this issue. And he had been urged, in the interest of getting the most out of the summit for his country's sake, not to let it degenerate into a 'slug-fest of words.' Yet Kennedy, fueled by Jacobson's cocktail of drugs, traded threat for threat.

'Then there will be war, Mr Chairman,' Kennedy retorted. 'It's going to be a very cold winter.'

Shortly after five on Sunday afternoon, *Air Force One* took off for London, where Kennedy, under the pretext of a private visit to attend the christening of the Radziwills' daughter, had arranged to confer with Macmillan about his talks with de Gaulle and Khrushchev. Jackie departed in a decidedly mixed mood. On the one hand, she had just enjoyed a series of extraordinary personal triumphs unimaginable a few weeks previously. She felt wonderful about herself, excited as never before about her role as First Lady. But Vienna had left the man she loved utterly shattered. Khrushchev had treated him 'like a little boy,' he said. In a perplexing turn of events, Jack had entered the darkest moment of his life to date at the very moment Jackie was suddenly at her brightest.

SEVEN

In Her Own Right

Long afterward, Harold Macmillan would tell Jackie that he would never forget Jack's first visit to London as President. At their first meeting, Macmillan recalled, he had 'fallen' for Jack. In London, Jack made it clear that he trusted Macmillan in a way that would make the relationship uniquely important to both men – and to the world.

On the morning of Monday, June 5, Kennedy arrived at Admiralty House, along with David Bruce and his closest aides. Harold and Dorothy Macmillan had met the Kennedys at the airport the night before, and the leaders had had a chance to talk as they drove together in an open car in a motorcade. En route to the Radziwill house in Buckingham Place, where the Kennedys were to stay, it became evident that Kennedy had had a strong dose of 'reality' in Vienna, though for the moment he did his best to put a good face on things. It wasn't until they met the next morning that Macmillan began to grasp the toll Vienna had taken. Gray with fatigue, Kennedy seemed drained and in acute discomfort on account of his back.

Immediately, Macmillan sensed that the last thing Kennedy wanted was a long, formal meeting, with both leaders' entourages present. That suited Macmillan perfectly. As early as their impromptu meeting at Key West, Macmillan had perceived the benefits of time alone together to talk freely. Then and later, in Washington, no sooner had Kennedy been out of his aides' hearing than he seemed to relax and speak differently. Today, his need for frank, private conversation with a trusted fellow leader who understood his particular burdens seemed greater than ever.

'Mr President,' said Macmillan, 'you have had a tiring day, don't let's have this. Why not come up to my room and we will have a little chat?'

Kennedy was palpably relieved, and the two men went off together. Macmillan had sandwiches and whisky brought in — despite the hour he decided that Kennedy needed a drink — and listened as Kennedy poured out his heart. He blamed himself for his lack of success in Vienna, convinced that Khrushchev had behaved as he did because after the Bay of Pigs he thought Kennedy weak. Kennedy agonized that this perception of weakness might well lead to nuclear war in the next few months and that Khrushchev would only negotiate if persuaded that the U.S., though it had backed down in Cuba, was prepared to fight.

Macmillan, more experienced with Khrushchev, had a different point of view. He wondered whether the Soviet leader's histrionics had been principally 'tactical,' 'an act' designed to 'test the character' of his young adversary. And though Macmillan did not doubt that Khrushchev's performance had been a brutal one, he indicated that he had always rather liked the man personally 'because of his human reactions.' The other Soviets were all 'so dull' by contrast, and Macmillan argued that 'if a person is so alive' as Khrushchev, he cannot be entirely 'dogmatic and theoretical.' Therein, counseled the Prime Minister, lay the hope of human connection, of negotiation. Sensing that the Bay of Pigs disaster had weakened Kennedy as a leader at home, Macmillan worried that he would find it difficult to resist pressure to take military action. He urged the President to find some way to communicate both the will to defend Western interests and a readiness to negotiate. Above all, Kennedy must 'get going some kind of negotiations.'

Whether Kennedy would be able to manage that was another matter. Macmillan, tremendously alarmed by the American's reaction to Khrushchev, later wrote to Queen Elizabeth that Kennedy had been 'completely overwhelmed' and reminded him 'of Lord Halifax or Mr Neville Chamberlain trying to hold a conversation with Herr Hitler.' Given the present cast of characters, Macmillan's reference was loaded with subtext. The impact on the Kennedy family of Joe Sr's impassioned support of the policy of appeasement – a policy Macmillan had opposed to the point of burning an effigy of Chamberlain in 1938 – continued to haunt Jack. Chamberlain, whom his father had backed, was precisely the man to whom Kennedy did not want to be compared. Macmillan worried that the President would devote too many resources to proving that he and his country were strong, and too little to an effort to 'make contact with Khrushchev directly.'

After his own meetings with Kennedy, Charles de Gaulle had told Hervé Alphand that things had gone much as he had hoped. Alphand concurred that de Gaulle had managed to adopt precisely the right tone with no trace of condescension. Confident though de Gaulle may have been in his bid to become the Western Alliance's most influential adviser to the 'lost' Kennedy, in fact he had never really had a chance to outmaneuver Macmillan. Kennedy, by his own account, came to regard Macmillan as someone with whom to share his loneliness. By this point, he was grateful to Macmillan for having come to Key West on such short notice and – in contrast to his father's advice on Cuba – counseled him wisely on Laos. And he was grateful for Macmillan's intervention with Eisenhower the previous April, when Kennedy feared being charged with appeasement in Laos. Kennedy's bond with Macmillan was due to something much more than the often-mentioned 'special relationship' between Britain and the U.S. It was above all personal and familial.

Never perhaps was that clearer than at the small private luncheon following their talk. The two leaders came downstairs, and at a quarter past one Jackie entered, as luminous as Jack had seemed gray. After Paris and Vienna, her picture was ubiquitous in the London press. 'In the pubs the talk is more of "Jackie," the young and lovely First Lady, than of her husband and international politics,' reported the *New York Times*. At today's lunch, however, if one person dominated the occasion, it was Kick. Lady Dorothy Macmillan, who had been Kick's aunt by marriage, had invited other relatives of Jack's late sister, and in their presence he seemed serene for the first time since Vienna.

At two large round tables Jack could see Kick's mother-in-law, the Dowager Duchess of Devonshire, who had insisted that Kick be buried at Chatsworth; Billy Hartington's younger brother Andrew and his wife, Debo, the current Duke and Duchess of Devonshire; as well as Kick's close friends and cousins by marriage David and Sissie Ormsby-Gore. Andrew and Debo Devonshire had attended the Inauguration, and Ormsby-Gore had visited a few weeks later and was due again in Washington in October as Britain's new ambassador. But this was the Dowager Duchess's first opportunity to see Jack since the election, and the first real chance for all to fête someone who, as Kick's brother, remained in a sense one of their own. The Macmillans had not produced them solely for that reason, however. Apart from their associations with Kick, they had been invited to underscore the critically important family connection between the President and the Prime Minister.

After lunch, the leaders conferred again privately until three, when Jack and Jackie went on to the christening of their niece at Westminster Cathedral and the party that followed at the Radziwill residence. That night, the Kennedys attended a dinner in their honor at Buckingham Palace, where the President consulted with David Ormsby-Gore. According to Bobby Kennedy, Jack valued Ormsby-Gore's opinions and recommendations second to none. On this occasion, they discussed what Jack would tell the American people about the Vienna summit in a forthcoming televised address. In a preview of what life in Washington would soon be like, at Kennedy's request Ormsby-Gore actually made some notes on things he might say.

When Jack left for the U.S. on *Air Force One* just before midnight, Jackie remained in London with her sister. In two days they would leave together for a private holiday which had been planned since April, when in the midst of the turmoil over the Bay of Pigs invasion Prime Minister and Mrs Karamanlis had invited Jackie to Greece. A mere eight weeks had passed

since the night of that invitation, yet Jackie was entirely different
from the person she had been then. The Karamanlises' expression of friendship had seemed then to be a way of
helping her through the ordeal of state visits. But far from
being in need of rest, Jackie emerged from Paris and Vienna
exhilarated, with a fresh perspective on what it meant to be
First Lady.

For seven years, her sexual self-esteem had been battered by
Jack's persistent infidelity. In Paris, the admiration of de Gaulle
and Malraux – indeed, of the French people – made her feel
desirable in a way she never had before. There had been further
mob scenes and another public conquest in Vienna. In Greece,
she continued to attract huge international press coverage and
more adoring crowds. In Paris and to a lesser extent Vienna,
her newly acquired power had allowed her to help Jack. Fêted
by the Greek super-rich, offered yachts and villas as well as the
gift of an island closed to tourists for an entire day, Jackie saw
that power could also be pure fun.

One aspect of her life, however, had not altered at all. That
the world seemed to have fallen in love with Jacqueline Kennedy
did not cause her husband to mend his ways. While she was in
Greece, Jack, having addressed the American people on national
television, flew to Palm Beach for the weekend, where the
Wrightsmans again lent him their house. He traveled with an
entourage that included Chuck Spalding and two female staff
members who regularly provided the President with sex. The
girls' status as White House staff permitted them openly to
accompany Kennedy on such a trip, though there were also
four reporters on *Air Force One*. At the ghostly mansion, most
of the priceless eighteenth-century French furniture and art
remained draped in dust covers. The girls added to the air of
incongruity as Sinatra records played on the terrace and the
President, in pajamas, drank daiquiris and spoke to Spalding
about his fears of impending nuclear war.

Kennedy had betrayed Jackie at the first opportunity. Yet
when she landed at Andrews Air Force Base shortly before
midnight on Thursday, June 15, he was waiting in the presidential limousine to greet her. It was a gesture of affection, but

also of respect. As his sister Jean said, Jackie was no longer just his wife, she was a person in her own right.

Full of excitement, Jackie slid into the limousine, threw one white-gloved hand around Jack's neck and kissed him. If she harbored any hope that Europe had finally made her desirable, it was quickly dashed. Made visibly uncomfortable by her kiss, Jack pushed her hand down and barked at the driver, 'Let's go!'

In the end, everything had changed for Jackie in Europe – and nothing.

Jackie soon learned the reason that Jack had remained in the limousine when he came to meet her at Andrews. Forced to use crutches, he wanted to avoid more pictures of the sort that had been taken upon his return from Palm Beach three days before. A previous announcement of the President's back injury had done nothing to prepare the public for television images of him being lifted off *Air Force One* by a crane. The images would have been alarming were they of any president, but public knowledge that as a Senator Kennedy had been out of commission for more than six months in 1954–5 due to back trouble led to fears that the same thing would happen again. White House assurances that his injury was unconnected to the earlier episode did nothing to assuage those fears. At a moment when Kennedy hoped desperately to show strength lest a perception of U.S. weakness cause the Soviets to move on Berlin, images of physical debility were the very last thing he wanted.

The day after Jackie arrived home they went to Glen Ora, where his condition made it impossible to accompany her to the season's big party, the debut of Bunny Mellon's daughter. Bill Walton was drafted to escort Jackie. According to Janet Travell, by this point the President's pain was nearly unbearable.

No amount of pain could prevent him from brooding over Cuba and Vienna. The day after he returned from Palm Beach, he had received General Maxwell Taylor's report on all that had gone wrong in the Bay of Pigs operation. The document, included in a packet of weekend reading, provided food for thought, especially in conjunction with transcripts of the Vienna talks. At Glen Ora, Kennedy alternated obsessively between the two, convinced that his own blunder in Cuba had led to humiliation in Vienna and might in turn lead to crisis in Berlin. Jack had invited Joe Alsop and Phil Graham to Glen Ora, and when they arrived he sat in a rocking chair and read aloud from the Vienna transcripts. Alsop left Glen Ora persuaded that Kennedy really did believe that the failed talks might presage a nuclear war.

Monday morning, Jack and Jackie flew back to the White House. With her husband struggling to find some way to function, Jackie had little choice but to suspend her rules about the separation of public and private spaces, and Jack's afternoon meetings were held in the family quarters, where he remained in bed much of the time. That night, Lyndon Johnson escorted Jackie to the Women's Press Club dinner. By now she and Johnson were great friends, having early on discovered a shared love of horses. Repeatedly during her first months in the White House, the Vice-President had gone out of his way to be sure that whenever Jackie did something he realized must be hard for her, the next day there was a note of warm personal praise from him and his wife. Jackie, for her part, had appreciated this greatly.

Jack remained upstairs as much as possible until Wednesday, when Prime Minister Ikeda of Japan arrived in Washington. Following a luncheon in Ikeda's honor, he and Kennedy conferred as scheduled on the presidential yacht, which Jack had rechristened the *Honey Fitz* after his maternal grandfather. The day trip did Jack no good, for that night he developed a sore throat, chills, and fever. When at midnight he seemed considerably worse, Jackie took his temperature. It was 101 degrees.

By the time Janet Travell came in, it had gone to 103 and later spiked to 105. Aware that this was 'not a simple viral infection,' Travell worked on Kennedy all night. She took blood cultures and began large doses of penicillin. In light of his two prior Addisonian crises and the fact that stress was known to provoke such crises, she increased the amount of corticosteroids he took regularly. She also prescribed an intravenous infusion and cold alcohol sponge baths. By 6 a.m. his temperature was back to 101.

There could be no concealing the fact that the President was ill, but when Travell released details to the press she omitted the worst news about his temperature. Instead, she said – 'truthfully,' she later emphasized – that it had been 101 both when she arrived and in the morning. Nor did she allude to fears of an Addisonian crisis, as Kennedy always made every effort to hide his Addison's disease.

On Thursday morning the crisis seemed past, yet the President remained very ill. He canceled all appointments, and that night Jackie, ready to tackle her duties as First Lady as never before, went alone to a dinner in the Kennedys' honor at the Japanese embassy, with the Johnsons in tow. By Friday, Jack was able to hold some meetings in the family quarters, and the following day he went to Glen Ora with Jackie and Lem. Kennedy attended Sunday Mass in Middleburg in an effort to dispel international alarm over his condition, the fever episode having occurred so soon after the disturbing images of him being removed from *Air Force One* by a crane.

Kennedy's physical weakness had begun to seem emblematic of his weakness as a leader, so he was right to try to put out pictures that showed him on the road to recovery – and strength. In view of recent developments, even staunch friends had begun to doubt his capacity to lead. That very same day, Sunday, June 25, Harold Macmillan confided to his diary that he could 'feel in my bones that President Kennedy is going to fail to produce any real leadership. The American Press and public are beginning to feel the same. In a few weeks they may turn to us. We must be ready. Otherwise we may drift to disaster over Berlin – a terrible diplomatic defeat or (out of sheer incompetence) a nuclear war.'

Once again Jackie stepped in to help her husband when he needed her, but this time with a bold new sense of self and certainty of direction acquired in Europe. President Ayub Khan of Pakistan was due to arrive on July 11. In the past, Kennedy himself had assumed responsibility for state dinners, but on this occasion Jackie took over for her ailing husband. The event she designed, a *tour de force* of political image-making, would mark her U.S. debut as the President's partner in international diplomacy, as well as a fascinating turning point in the Kennedy marriage.

Ayub Khan was of the utmost importance to Kennedy, since both Pakistan and India were critical to U.S. hopes of preventing a Communist takeover of Asia. Originally scheduled for the fall, the visit had been brought forward after Lyndon Johnson's urgent report following a visit to Karachi in May. Johnson argued that President Ayub, who had taken power in a bloodless military coup three years previously, had an important perspective on Soviet efforts to exert influence in Pakistan and its region that Kennedy ought to hear first-hand sooner rather than later.

The Bay of Pigs fiasco had complicated efforts to persuade Pakistan and other underdeveloped nations in Asia and Latin America that the U.S., far from being opposed to social change or revolution per se, had in fact been born in revolution and continued to believe in revolutionary ideals. It was no accident that Kennedy, in his forty-fourth birthday speech in Boston, stressed that he was going to Vienna 'as the leader of the greatest revolutionary country on earth.' 'Our knees do not tremble at the word revolution,' he insisted. 'We believe in it. We believe in the progress of mankind.' In Vienna, however, Khrushchev had adroitly turned the President's words around so that he seemed to send a very different message. As Kennedy pored over the transcript of their first meeting, he could not help but be struck by the fact that he came across as a fierce adversary of social change.

In her plans for the state dinner, Jackie set out to convey to Pakistan – indeed, to all the underdeveloped nations for whose hearts and minds Washington was vying with Moscow – the message Jack had failed to put across in Vienna. Ordinarily such dinners took place in the State Dining Room, but on this occasion Jackie chose a highly unusual setting. Some months earlier, the director of Mount Vernon had sent word that the First Lady might wish to use George Washington's Virginia home for a private party. In a memo, he indicated that it was hers for the asking in the spring or summer and assured that it was 'fabulous in the early evening with the setting sun and the beauty of the river.' Now, as Jackie considered what to do about Ayub Khan, she thought of Mount Vernon. Its director had proposed a small private party, and her task was to orchestrate a large state dinner, but from the outset she realized that the location was precisely what she needed. Despite numerous logistical difficulties, Jackie would hear of no other venue.

Then and later, most people seemed to assume that Mount Vernon appealed to Jackie because of its sheer beauty. In fact, the reason for her choice was vastly more revealing. Paris had awakened a new political instinct in her, which was first expressed in her concept for the Ayub Khan dinner. At a stroke, she found a way to remind Pakistan and, through press pictures, the watching world that the U.S. had been born in revolution. She used Mount Vernon to create an image that powerfully and dramatically advertised the U.S. as, in Jack's words, 'the greatest revolutionary country on earth.' To drive home the point, she commissioned a pageant in period costume by the Army's Colonial Color Guard and Fife and Drum Corps, in which men known since Washington's day as the President's Own fired muskets in a Revolutionary War-era military drill.

Kennedy came from a family that recognized the importance of the image. Long before Jack had evinced his own mastery of print and television, his father, upon becoming U.S. ambassador to the Court of St James's, had used press photographs of his own large brood to portray the Kennedys as attractive and appealing. With the Ayub Khan dinner, Jackie added a novel element of sophistication, and in this as in so many other things Jack was her most discerning audience. No one better appreciated what Jackie was up to, or the skill needed to bring it off. The more ideas she had, the more immersed in her plans Jack became. Soon he was making suggestions of his own – e.g., that guests be transported to Mount Vernon by boat instead of car – and, as in France, the collaboration seemed to spark a new intensity of feeling between husband and wife.

Kennedy, said Angier Biddle Duke, Chief of Protocol, liked to see attention paid to his wife, and there was plenty of it from an enchanted Ayub Khan, as he danced attendance on Jackie at one table while the President, at his happiest and most relaxed for weeks, chatted with Ayub's daughter at another. As at Versailles, when she interposed herself between her husband and de Gaulle, at Mount Vernon Jackie again spoke for Jack – this time, not with words but with the visual images that were her forte.

As the evening drew to a close, limousines pulled up to take guests down the long drive to the Potomac for the return boat trip. Jack and Jackie were about to enter the presidential limousine when he put his arm around her shoulder, and together they turned to look back at Mount Vernon. He saw that the dinner had been a real coup, and he was tremendously grateful. For his wife, it represented a good deal more. While Paris had shown the world a new Jackie, Mount Vernon had richly realized the promise she had long sensed. Only the year before, she had confided to Joe Alsop that Jack's political power had no meaning for her because she had done nothing to earn it. After the dinner at Mount Vernon, that would no longer be the case. Casting aside that preoccupation with the trivial that Janet had bequeathed to her daughters, Jackie was ready to do things that mattered and allow her actions to have scope and consequence. She had finally discovered a role in the Kennedy presidency, a way to earn power in her own right. And she did not intend for it to be a one-time experience.

She remained in Washington until the end of Ayub Khan's visit, and late Friday, July 14, flew with Jack and the children to Hyannis Port. There, in the course of the summer, she would work out her plans for the fall. Drawing on the visual skills that had permitted her to make the Ayub Khan dinner so much more than the merely glamorous event many people mistook it for, she would continue to use imagery on behalf of her politically beleaguered husband. Jack agonized that he looked weak to the world, so Jackie would make him seem otherwise. Like de Gaulle, she set out to change perceptions. Mindful of de Gaulle's lessons in the psychology of power, she would create settings and events, use décor and high culture, to give the Kennedy presidency, enfeebled by failures in Cuba and Vienna as well as Soviet threats on Berlin, the veneer of an authority it did not yet truly possess. Her efforts would buy time as Jack worked to build real power as President.

There was an enormous amount to do, and little time to do it. If Jackie were to work effectively in the fall, she who had previously taken scant interest in foreign policy and never expected to play more than a passive role would have to know all the main characters and what was at stake case by case. So she read memos, studied position papers, devoured books – all in the interest of helping Jack, who, in Washington during the week, joined his family on weekends. Many people would later attribute the impact she made to her beauty and charm, and though she certainly possessed both qualities, more often than not the basis for her triumphs was in fact meticulous preparation and exceptionally hard work.

Meanwhile, in Jack's absence, Jackie was determined to devote as much time as possible to Caroline and John Jr. She was particularly concerned about her daughter and believed that the past spring, during which she had often been away or unwell, upset, and distracted, had taken a toll on the three-year-old. The summer provided an opportunity to make up for all that, especially since the children were her principal companions during the week. Aside from Caroline and John Jr, Jackie, who had no intimate friends and whose adoring and very much adored father-in-law was away in Cap d'Antibes with Rose, tended to spend weekdays in solitude. Most mornings she would drive Caroline to the Allen Farm in nearby Osterville so the child could ride her pony. Sometimes, on the way back, they would stop at local antique shops. Before lunch, Jackie liked to water-ski on Nantucket Bay. Occasionally Caroline would ride in the speedboat manned by a Secret Service agent, but more often Jackie went out alone. Strong and vigorous again after many months of ill health, she would pull herself up on her skis and, holding onto the towline with muscled arms, leap back and forth over the speedboat's wake.

Often, at lunchtime, Jackie would take Caroline and some Kennedy cousins on a short picnic cruise on Joe's boat, the *Marlin*. After a nap back at the house, she would read and work on the folders that came up by courier from the White House. Everything stopped punctually at a quarter to three, when the ice cream van arrived, bell ringing, and was waved past the wooden sentry booths by Secret Service men. Children would materialize from all directions, and almost always Jackie would appear through the hedge to buy a Popsicle for Caroline.

The tourists completely defeated Jackie that summer. She felt as if she were living in a fishbowl, with people peering in at her with enormous eyes. For her daughter's sake, however, she tried to live as normal a life as possible. On one occasion she took Caroline to a church fair, and there were visits to the aquarium and an amusement park. In the evenings, mother and daughter might walk down to the news shop. On more than one occasion, Jackie, upset by tourists, hopped into a car with a Secret Service agent, leaving Caroline to pedal home on her tricycle protected by a member of the Kiddy Detail.

Later, Jackie would recall these months as a keenly sensual time. She took pleasure in the sun, the water, the simple summer foods, the sense of indolence that would overcome her at times – but most of all the excitement of waiting for Jack. At times it was as if she and the children spent the week in a fever of anticipation. Friday evenings, after being informed by a Secret Service agent that *Air Force One* had arrived at Otis Air Force Base, Jackie and Caroline, sometimes with John Jr in his carriage, would race to the main house. A helicopter pad had been installed on the lawn, and by the time the white cap came into view, all the Kennedy cousins on the grounds, as well as neighbors and tourists on the periphery, would be gathered as close as possible.

For Jackie, it was the start of the best part of the week. But her delight was as nothing compared to that of Caroline. The child's aim was to get her father out of the white cap and over to their own house as quickly as possible so that he could change into a sweater, khaki trousers, and sneakers and take her off to buy her weekly allotment of candy in town. His back was so fragile that to walk any distance was usually impossible, so Joe had provided a golf cart. Unlike Glen Ora, where Jack felt closed in and bored much of the time, Hyannis Port was very much his element and he seemed instantly to unwind. He had no problem with the tourists. In fact, he rather liked the attention, and on such nights even Jackie, serene in his company, appeared not to mind it either.

Saturday mornings, Jack would go out early with Caroline. They would head off on the golf cart to visit Bobby, play with cousins on the lawn, or go down to the beach for a swim. By lunchtime they were back to collect Jackie and their guests, usually Lem Billings or Chuck and Betty Spalding, for fish chowder – Jack's favorite – and a cruise on the *Marlin*. The baby, too young for prolonged exposure to the sun and salt air, stayed behind with the nanny, Miss Shaw. On board, Jackie would watch happily as Jack told stories to his daughter, who snuggled on his lap. Sometimes they would transfer to a speedboat, so that Jackie could water-ski while the President drove. Or they would land at a nearby island to picnic and swim off the beach. They would stay out until late afternoon, coming home for the Saturday matinée in Grandpa's basement screening room. In the evenings, Jack would play backgammon with Lem or his brother Teddy. There would be trays of frozen daiquiris, as well as lobster and corn, and often a late film screening. Sundays, after church, Jack and Jackie liked to sit on the patio to read the papers before going out again on the *Marlin*. It was in many ways a splendid life, made even better by Jack's sincere gratitude for all Jackie had done and planned on his behalf. Jack, easily bored, tended to be excited by anything new, and at the moment there could be no doubt that Jackie had his fond attention.

She still did not have his sexual interest, however. No matter how the relationship had changed or how idyllic those weekends were, Jack's promiscuity persisted. Monday mornings, when Jackie accompanied him on the golf cart to the helicopter pad, she sent him back, in effect, to his numerous other sexual partners. That summer, there were White House visits by Judith Campbell, night-time cruises on the Potomac with various women, as well as sex parties in both the pool and the family quarters. Jackie seemed to live for the weekends and ignore the rest, though she did at times betray resentment in acid remarks to the Spaldings and others about Dave Powers. 'She knew that he was usually the one that called the girls or brought the girls in,' said Larry Newman in explanation of Jackie's unsparing attitude to Powers, to whom she tended to be noticeably unfriendly.

Meanwhile, the crisis over Berlin escalated. If the Bay of Pigs had taught Kennedy anything, it was that in the end the burden of decision was his alone. Spurred by his advisers to prove that he would protect Berlin with force, he alternated between public saber-rattling and private bouts of anxiety about its consequences. 'What could we do in the next 6 months that would improve the population's chance of surviving if a war should break out?' Kennedy wrote in a memo to McGeorge Bundy. 'What should we ask the citizens to do at this time and what should be required of them in case of attack?' To Eleanor Roosevelt, he wrote, 'The prospect of a nuclear exchange is so terrible that I conceive it would be preferable to be among the dead than among the quick.'

De Gaulle's warning about Southeast Asia notwithstanding, advisers pushed Kennedy to swoop in for what they promised would be a quick, easy victory over the Communists in Vietnam. These calls had begun in the aftermath of the Bay of Pigs invasion when Walter Rostow, Deputy Special Assistant to the President for National Security Affairs, wrote in a memo, 'There is one area where success against Communist techniques is conceivable and ... that area is Viet-Nam ... a clean-cut success in Viet-Nam would do much to hold the line in Asia while permitting us – and the world – to learn how to deal with indirect aggression.' Such a success, Rostow suggested, might ease 'the acute domestic tensions over Cuba.' Now, after the disastrous Vienna summit, Robert Komer of the National Security Council staff picked up the chant. Komer sent Kennedy a memo recommending action in Vietnam as a means of shoring up America's image against a crisis in Berlin: 'I believe it very important that this government have a major anti-Communist victory to its credit in the six months before the Berlin crisis is likely to get really hot.' The President, who, said his friend Charles Bartlett, had 'a horror of involvement on the continent of Asia, a deep horror,' resisted these entreaties.

Kennedy finally made up his mind about Berlin on July 20, choosing to follow Macmillan's advice to signal both a determination to defend Western interests and a willingness to negotiate. After a meeting with the National Security Council, Kennedy wrote to Macmillan: 'Our central problem at this juncture is to protect our mutual vital interests without war if possible and to put ourselves in the best position if war should be forced upon us.' While he rejected calls to declare a state of national emergency, Kennedy did plan 'a significant buildup of military strength.' He would ask Congress for a supplementary defense budget of more than three billion dollars, increase draft calls from the present 8,000 to 25,000 per month, and ask Americans to build nuclear fallout shelters. These measures, he hoped, would 'convey to the Soviets, while they are still in the process of making decisions, convincing evidence of our firmness of ultimate purpose.'

The next day, Kennedy flew to Hyannis Port, where, having reached a decision, he felt considerably better. Even his physical health seemed to improve, and the weekend that followed was the best of the summer. He and Jackie sailed and swam together. There were picnics with his sisters and brothers, and a happiness they wished would never end.

The lessening of tension was temporary. On July 25, Kennedy addressed the nation, and Moscow's response was swift, sharp, and not at all as expected. Reacting to Kennedy's warnings rather than his bid for talks, Khrushchev sent word by John McCloy, Kennedy's Adviser for Disarmament, that he considered the President 'in effect had declared preliminary war' by presenting an ultimatum on Berlin which if rejected could mean war. Macmillan, terrified that saber-rattling on both sides might lead to nuclear destruction, and convinced that Khrushchev sought an opening to permit him to keep face in front of his more militant opponents at home, urged Kennedy to continue to press for negotiations.

On Sunday, August 13, Jack and Jackie were about to sail to Paul and Bunny Mellon's for lunch when word arrived that Khrushchev had moved in Berlin. In an effort to cut off the flow of people from East to West, East German troops and police threw up a barrier of barbed wire and rubble that was the start of what would come to be known as the Berlin Wall. At first, no one was sure what was happening. Did the Soviets intend to cut off Allied access to Berlin? Was this to be the start of a war? To test the situation, Kennedy ordered 1,500 troops in armored trucks into Berlin along the autobahn. For forty-eight hours Washington held its breath until they arrived safely.

Kennedy, careful to follow up with an effort at conciliation, directed Secretary of State Dean Rusk to 'take a stronger lead' on Berlin talks. Still, matters did not progress as the President would have liked. Despite Khrushchev's personal assurances in Vienna, the Soviet Union announced its intention to resume nuclear testing. Five days later, Kennedy, insisting that he had no choice, ordered the resumption of U.S. underground testing. But, following Macmillan's advice, he continued to press for face-to-face negotiations between the U.S. and the Soviets. He who had been taught a lesson in disgrace at the Bay of Pigs understood that his adversary must not be humiliated. Even if the matter of access to Berlin was non-negotiable, the U.S. must show a willingness to compromise. Thus, amid the hurly-burly of threats and counterthreats, on September 3, Rusk instructed Ambassador Thompson to propose talks to Soviet Foreign Minister Gromyko.

As the summer drew to a close, Kennedy's estimate of his presidency was tinged with disappointment and despair. He disclosed his mood in a private conversation with the *New York Times*'s Elie Abel, who had been approached by a publisher to do a book about the major decisions of Kennedy's first term. Abel had an appointment to discuss access, and as Kennedy was running late and about to leave for the weekend Abel was asked to wait in the President's bedroom. In the meantime, a good many people rushed in and out to get papers signed or to ask a question before Kennedy departed. Dave Powers served Bloody Marys, the sound of a helicopter's rotating blades wafted through an open window, and a snapshot of Caroline wedged into the frame of a mirror fluttered in the breeze. Finally, the President turned to Abel, who described his project.

Kennedy's response was revealing. 'Why,' he asked bitterly, 'would anyone write a book about an administration that has nothing to show for itself but a string of disasters?'

That summer, Jackie reconsidered her plans for the White House specifically in terms of Jack's needs. Her concept had changed radically since the lunch in February with Clark Clifford, when all she had in mind was finding a way to make her fantasy house a reality. As the time approached for her return to Washington in the fall of 1961, she was already indignantly denying that she had ever thought of the White House as a 'house' and insisting that from the first her intent had been to create formal rooms of state. In fact, there had been a decisive shift in Jackie's thinking. She found her inspiration in a paper by two historians, L. H. Butterfield and Julian P. Boyd, which had been submitted on April 24, 1961, as a critique of her short-lived plan to decorate the White House in the style of a single period. The paper had made the point that the White House was three things – the 'headquarters of the Executive Department of the United States Government,' the 'home of the elected leader of the nation and of his family,' and finally, 'a museum.' When Jackie formulated her original plan, her focus was squarely on the White House as her 'home.' She had no interest in its political function, and as for its purpose as a museum open to tourists, that served best to bolster her argument, which she no doubt sincerely believed, that a tasteful house would make American visitors proud.

After her visit to France, Jackie became concerned less with the White House as her home than the White House as the headquarters of the Executive Department. As such, according to the paper by Butterfield and Boyd, it was important not just as a 'functioning center' – i.e. an office – but as 'a symbol of national power and purpose.' This conception became the new focus of Jackie's renovation project. The woman who had presented her original plan to Henry du Pont in cultural terms, dismissing the political as outside her sphere of interest, now set out to make the White House the symbol of a power her husband's troubled presidency had yet to achieve on its own.

Jackie had once been drawn to Boudin's ability to create a

'wonderfully pretty' house. Now she became far more interested in his theories of decorating as a statement of power. The heroic proportions Boudin favored would provide the Kennedy administration with a much-needed image of strength; his highly finished style would lend a glaze of discipline and control. While Jackie's original focus had been on the private rooms upstairs, with the ground-floor public rooms forming an after-hours extension for essentially private entertaining, henceforth she concentrated on the state rooms: a political stage on which to enact the drama of the Kennedy presidency. Certainly Jackie would continue to give private parties, and certainly the house would provide a lovely setting for such occasions, but that was secondary to the serious business of creating a setting which would project Jack's power as a leader. The White House, which Jackie had once believed ought to be comfortable, cozy, and inviting, would be deliberately formal, finished, and above all intimidating. Rather than putting people at ease, those rooms would impress upon them the grandeur and power of the presidency – and of Jack.

Over the next nine months Jackie would be resident illusionist, conjurer of an image so dazzling and distracting as to shift public attention from her husband's disastrous record. Before Cuba, he had offered the world an image of youth and hope. Jackie would recast him as a mature, self-possessed leader who was already achieving great things. The image she crafted in those months no more corresponded to reality than would the image of Camelot after his death.

Nor, given Jackie's accomplishments, was there much truth to the image of herself she also worked hard to create – an image that has never been challenged – as a non-political First Lady. Certainly she had been that when she arrived in the White House the previous January, but since Paris she had metamorphosed into one of the most public and political First Ladies yet. When she returned to Washington after the summer, her role would be absolutely central. The post-Bay of Pigs image, for whose creation she was largely responsible, was the cover Jack needed for his own slow, painful steps to real leadership.

To make that image work, Jackie paid a price. She had to act as if all she did was social rather than political. Despite her own personal transformation, she had to profess still to be a woman who disliked and played no role in politics. If she acknowledged or took credit for an illusion of power where in fact there was none, her efforts to help her husband would fail.

The season's first diplomatic visitors would be the President of Peru, Dr Don Mañuel Prado, and his wife. Jackie had been engaged for weeks in meticulous plans for their reception. Characteristically, she reached for a visual image to put across her message simply and eloquently. For Ayub Khan, she had staged the dinner at George Washington's house in order to remind the world of America's revolutionary past. Now, she sent word from Hyannis Port that she wanted the 1869 G. P. A. Healy portrait of Abraham Lincoln, among the most celebrated paintings in the White House collection, moved to the State Dining Room. Hanging over the marble mantelpiece, it would offer a reminder of America's own Civil War, fought to liberate an oppressed segment of the population. With no other painting to compete for attention in the great white and gold room, Lincoln's portrait conveyed precisely the notion of sympathy with the oppressed and support for social progress that Jack wished to send to Latin America.

After the Bay of Pigs invasion, the image of the Kennedy administration as rapacious gangsters out to restore the exploitative past of the Batista years had become prevalent in Latin America. Jackie hoped to eradicate the image of her husband as a weak and incompetent bungler, as well as the perception of him as a buccaneer who disregarded international law and sought to undermine social justice for the benefit of the rich and powerful. Her goal was to create an image of a mature, confident, and confidence-inspiring leader with highly sophisticated tastes – a statesman rather than a pirate. To that end, she enlisted two singers from the Metropolitan Opera, Roberta Peters and Jerome Hines, whose presence at the White House would identify Kennedy-era America as a nation of culture, delicacy, and refinement. On this and subsequent occasions,

Jackie's promotion of high culture would, among other purposes, lend an air of substance and dignity to an administration that the world then perceived in very different terms.

Jack hated to wear tails, but Jackie was insistent. Just as the White House must look like the residence of a man of power, she and Jack, more than seeming just young and attractive, must appear truly out of the ordinary. Aware of Señora de Prado's reputation for elegance, Jackie ordered a striking new evening ensemble from New York. Meanwhile, memos flew back and forth by courier between Hyannis Port and Washington, Letitia Baldrige worked feverishly in the East Wing, and by the time the Kennedys boarded *Air Force One* at Otis Air Force Base in Massachusetts on the morning of Monday, September 18, for the flight to Washington, every element seemed to be in place. The children had been left at Cape Cod with Miss Shaw, because Jackie was not due to take up permanent residence in Washington for another few weeks.

In countless ways an utterly different person from the depressed, confused young woman who had left for Paris at the end of May, Jackie had a purpose and a sense that she knew what to do in her campaign to repair the damage to Jack's image. Her arrival in Washington that September of 1961 would mark a new beginning, as, for the first time, she considered that 'the best' in her was being called upon. Unexpectedly, she had the life of meaning and significance she had dreamed of, and, nervous as she was in anticipation of her many duties, she fully intended to enjoy it. The fact that her opportunity had come as a result of Jack's crisis cast a shadow over that pleasure, but she did her best to concentrate on the fact that she had found a way out of the triviality and superficiality that were the sum total of her mother's and her sister's lives – and to focus on the work ahead rather than on the fact that she would be again put in the position of having to facilitate her husband's infidelity. She faced enormous challenges in the months to come, but as *Air Force One* headed south, she was tremendously excited about finally emerging as the person she had always hoped to be. She savored the prospect that her intelligence, her discipline, and her skills were about to be put into play.

It was nearly half past ten when the white cap carrying the Kennedys touched down on the South Lawn at the White House, and the President was greeted with news of a crisis. Dag Hammarskjöld, Secretary-General of the United Nations, had died in a plane crash in the Congo. Knowing that this could be the opening the Soviets had been awaiting to change the structure of the United Nations, Kennedy immediately went into meetings. If Jackie had needed a reminder, after three months away, of how tension-filled life at the White House was, she had it. When she went up to the family quarters to check on the renovations made in the course of the summer, she was immediately confronted with a crisis in her own domain. It was as nothing compared to the news Jack had to deal with, but Jackie was astute enough to recognize the sort of thing that might well undermine all her careful work.

Jackie had a note from Letitia Baldrige, not about the state dinner the following evening, but about a small, seemingly inconsequential luncheon scheduled for Thursday, September 21. Peter Lawford was in Washington at work on Otto Preminger's film *Advise and Consent*, based on the Allen Drury novel about Capitol Hill politics. By this time, his connection to the Kennedys rather than his acting ability had become the basis of Lawford's precarious Hollywood career, and sadly he knew it. Jack was genuinely fond of Lawford, and also loved to mingle with movie people, like his father, who had never lost his taste for Hollywood. In the past few weeks, Lawford had been Jack's regular companion in the evenings, and he had proven as useful at providing women in Washington as he always was in Hollywood. Many of the summer bachelor dinners in the family quarters presided over by the brothers-in-law had included one or more women whom Lawford had picked up that day for the President's amusement. The fact that Lawford was less careful than he might have been about whom he brought in seemed not to worry the President, even though on one occasion the woman turned out to be the secretary of one of Kennedy's chief Congressional opponents. Typically, far from holding the oversight against his brother-in-law, Jack was eager to show his appreciation for all the women who had worked out very well indeed, and agreed easily to give a luncheon for Preminger and the other actors in the film.

Persuading Jackie had been more difficult, but she too was fond of Lawford, and the fact that one of the guests would be the actress Gene Tierney, a one-time girlfriend of Jack's, provided an incentive. Jackie could be cold as ice to any woman who posed a new threat, but she was always eager to meet her husband's former girlfriends, particularly when she was confident that Jack's passion was long dead. She would talk intently to these women, as though in search of the secret of their former allure so that she might appropriate it for herself. She also loved to read their passionate letters to Jack, who preserved such documents with the care and determination of an archivist. That Tierney had also been married to Oleg Cassini, Jackie's official designer, made the prospect of a meeting even more intriguing.

By 1961, Tierney was a poignant figure. When Jack was involved with her just after the war, she was the great beauty best recalled from the film *Laura*. Following her romance with Jack and her divorce from Cassini, there had been a sad romance with Aly Khan, two psychological breakdowns, and more than two years in mental hospitals. At forty, though her perfect beauty was gone, she remained attractive, and a year previously had married a Houston oilman. *Advise and Consent*, in which she had a small role, was to be her comeback. Jack had seen her once after the breakdowns, and she had been tremendously grateful for his solicitude. His agreement to the luncheon was in part motivated by the opportunity it presented to be kind to Gene by having her and her husband to the White House. The rest of the company – Henry Fonda, Charles Laughton, Walter Pidgeon, Don Murray, Lew Ayres, and Preminger himself – would no doubt prove amusing. Jackie's only real objection was that she had so much else scheduled that week, including a dinner that same night at the Peruvian embassy. In the end, she agreed for Lawford's sake.

The memo from Baldrige gave Jackie reason to regret her decision. Baldrige reported that when she had called Lawford at his hotel to make arrangements, Frank Sinatra had been present and there had been no way to avoid including him.

Jackie loathed Sinatra, with whom she had just endured a weekend at Hyannis Port. Sinatra's presence at the Cape had been so disconcerting that, uncharacteristically, Jackie had failed to conceal her jealousy at Jack's interest in one of the women Sinatra had brought with him. Jackie's palpable upset had been so unusual that everyone noticed, representing a huge defeat for a woman who prided herself on her ability to disguise her emotions, particularly with regard to her husband's other women.

Jackie had long made it clear that Sinatra was not welcome at the White House. He had worked hard on the campaign and felt that a public gesture of appreciation was his due, but to his dismay none had been forthcoming. Aside from Jackie's personal dislike of someone she regarded as a crude, boorish thug who brought out the worst in her husband, there was a more serious aspect to her objections. During the campaign, she had tried with some but by no means complete success to make Jack understand that his association with Sinatra and the Rat Pack was utterly wrong for his image. In her view, that was even more true after the Bay of Pigs disaster. The last thing Jack needed was to associate with a man linked in the public mind with the Mafia – certainly not in this of all weeks, as Jackie launched a full-scale rehabilitation effort.

In her careful plans, she was doing everything possible to put Jack across as a statesman. Even though it was his image that Jackie was struggling to repair, Kennedy hated being told what to do, and insisted that the invitation stand. She saw all her efforts going up in smoke, as, tied to Sinatra, Jack would present himself as a swinger at best and a gangster at worst, precisely the sort of man who would have gone into Cuba to help the mob retrieve its gambling interests – as Latin Americans in particular believed the motive of the invasion to have been. Hoping to avoid press coverage of Sinatra's visit, Jackie sent orders that the luncheon was to be strictly 'off the record.' Jack, for his part, could not conceal his delight at the thought of an afternoon with Sinatra, whose means of gaining entrance despite Jackie's ban amused him. Sinatra's presence posed a further problem, whose solution was insignificant at the time. In need of an extra woman who would be both amusing to Sinatra and socially acceptable, Jackie took Jack's suggestion and invited Mary Meyer, the divorced sister-in-law of his friend Ben Bradlee.

When Max Jacobson arrived that afternoon, he found the White House in full crisis mode. Jack, dealing with Hammarskjöld's death, and Jackie, up in arms about Sinatra, seemed very much in need of his treatments, and he agreed to remain in Washington overnight. Jacobson had become nearly indispensable. Methamphetamine injections, not illegal at the time but extremely dangerous nonetheless, enabled Jackie to sustain the high level of performance she demanded of herself, against the backdrop of a marriage that continued to be a source of constant pain. She planned to help her husband throughout the fall, week after week, with visitor after distinguished visitor. Whenever she did, Jacobson would fly down to assist. So long as he was present, the White House would be bearable. Then she would go off on schedule and leave Jack free – all with a little help from Dr Feel Good.

At a quarter to twelve the following morning, both Kennedys set out to attend the welcoming ceremonies for the Peruvian President and his wife at Andrews Air Force Base. While Jack held meetings during the afternoon, Jackie completed final arrangements for the state dinner. Just before the guests arrived, Jacobson injected both Kennedys to be sure they were at their most charming and assured. At 8 p.m., the President, in white tie and tails, started down the red-carpeted formal stairs from the second floor, Jackie at his side wearing a mustard yellow silk skirt and black sleeveless top. As usual, the Marine Corps band greeted his appearance by playing 'Hail to the Chief.' As the Kennedys reached the bottom of the stairs and posed with President and Señora de Prado for photographs, they turned to look at each other in an exchange of delighted smiles while cameras flashed. This was the image Jackie wanted the world to see. This was how the President of the United States must be perceived – not just glamorous and handsome, but also assured and in command. The young woman whom Jack had once feared would be a political liability had turned out to be the very opposite, stage-managing everything perfectly, from the Lincoln portrait and the opera singers after dinner even to their own behavior with each other.

The success of the state dinner seemed to heighten Jackie's anger about Sinatra, whose presence was antithetical to everything she had just so magnificently accomplished. Still, she had no choice but to endure his visit. Defeated two weeks previously when she lost her composure during Sinatra's stay at the Cape, she did not want to repeat her mistake. Ordinarily, the *Advise and Consent* luncheon would have been the sort of private event at which Jack and Jackie seized the opportunity to shine together. On this occasion, Jackie had no interest in performing. Instead, she planned to keep her eye on Sinatra – who had been loud and obnoxious in Hyannis Port – and on the clock. The Kennedys were due at the Peruvian embassy at eight, and the President was scheduled to deliver a critically important address at the United Nations the following week. Jackie hoped the luncheon would end before anyone in the press room got wind of it.

Things got off to a poor start when the Kennedys entered a quarter of an hour late and Sinatra called out, 'Hey, Chickie baby!' A far cry from the dignified strains of 'Hail to the Chief,' with which the President had been greeted two days previously, 'Chickie baby' was Sinatra's nickname for Jack. From then on, Jackie had her work cut out for her. Ordinarily, her attention would have been riveted on Gene Tierney; ordinarily, in an effort to amuse her husband, Jackie would have bantered with Charles Laughton or Henry Fonda. But she did none of that. From first to last, she focused on Sinatra as a potential source of trouble.

Unfortunately, far more lasting trouble was erupting elsewhere in the room. If Jackie, usually a dynamic hostess, seemed somewhat withdrawn and preoccupied, Mary Meyer, the extra woman invited at the last minute, more than made up for it. Jack had known the forty-year-old Mary since both were teenagers at boarding school, and he could see that she was giving the performance of a lifetime. After a bit of sweet and solicitous small talk with Gene Tierney, he spent much of the meal quietly taking in Mary's act from a distance, as she focused on the sixty-three-year-old actor Walter Pidgeon with a laser-like intensity. A pretty, petite blonde with blue-green eyes and emphatic dark eyebrows, Mary was behaving as if the meaning of her life depended on Pidgeon's response to her. In a curious way, it did.

Some twenty years earlier, young Mary Pinchot, newly out of Vassar and living with her mother on Park Avenue in New York while trying to make a name for herself as a journalist, had briefly dated Pidgeon, then at the peak of his success. The exceedingly popular *Mrs Miniver*, in which he co-starred with Greer Garson, had just been released, and he had appeared in the previous year's winner of the Academy Award for Best Picture, *How Green Was My Valley*. At the time, Pidgeon was twice as old as Mary, but his age mattered much less than his fame. Fame had been the motive for Mary's desire to write, as it would be for her efforts to establish herself as an artist in later years. She craved fame the way other people thirst for love, and the fact that her dates with Pidgeon landed her in the Broadway gossip columns had been a powerful aphrodisiac. In the end, the relationship had been nothing more than a fling, but, because of the press coverage, it held huge personal significance for Mary. She learned that hitching her wagon to a prominent man might prove a quicker route to fame than anything she accomplished on her own.

Three years later, in 1945, Mary thought she had found such a man when she married Cord Meyer, a decorated war veteran who had attended St Paul's, Yale, and other élite schools. Arrogant and aristocratic, he had grandiose ambitions, and was certain that he was in the running to head the post-war world government that people connected to the One-World movement were then predicting. At the very least, he knew he would rise to the top of American politics. Mary, persuaded – as were many of the couple's friends – that Meyer's dreams were sure to come true, was happy to put aside her own personal ambitions to serve what she told herself was his far greater talent. The young woman who had been thrilled to see her name in the gossip columns when she dated Walter Pidgeon believed with all her heart that she and Cord Meyer would soon make headlines together.

Things did not work out as Mary had hoped, and in the course of a miserable marriage that spanned more than a decade she watched as her husband's literary and political promise amounted to little. Meyer was adept at masking a sense of failure with an air of superiority. When his dreams of becoming a great leader did not materialize, he joined the C.I.A. Believing, like others drawn to the agency in its early days, that he was not subject to the rules that governed ordinary human beings, he plunged deep into the world of covert operations. By the time the marriage ended in 1958, he had become a deeply embittered, abusive drunk. Mary, once so full of dreams for herself and her future, had ended up a pathetic, oppressed housewife with a philandering husband.

Other women in Mary's position might not have been so eager to face an old lover after twenty years. When Pidgeon first knew her, Mary had been young and fresh, but she had picked the wrong man and, finally, didn't even have a marriage to show for it. Nonetheless, Mary was tough. Had she not been, she would never have survived thirteen years with Cord Meyer. In spite of all the heartache and disappointment of her life, she felt that she had to convince Pidgeon, who attended the luncheon with his wife, that she really was on top of the world. One abiding fear fueled Mary's every word and action that day. Under no circumstances must Pidgeon be permitted to leave with an impression that her life had been a failure. In the three years since her divorce, she had reinvented herself with a fierce, almost frightening desperation. The luncheon was to be an important test of her new persona.

Having spent the better part of her adult years surrounded by Meyer and his C.I.A. associates, Mary derived inspiration from them. Dazzled by their talk of infiltration operations, assassinations, drug experiments, and brainwashing techniques, she recast herself in their image: a wild outlaw of a woman in the guise of an aristocrat. Having imbibed from her husband the credo that ordinary rules of conduct did not apply to superior, privileged people such as themselves, she worked hard to leave an impression of utter unpredictability, of being capable of anything. She was conspiratorial and self-mystifying. She exuded an air of danger and furtiveness that caused people to wonder whether she was high on drugs. She was contemptuous of convention, particularly in matters of sex and drugs, and conducted herself with seeming impunity. Some found the new Mary exciting, others thought her off-putting and even frightening. The delicate, fine-boned blonde had cultivated a tough edge, her soft refined voice calculatedly at odds with the shocking things she loved to say.

Jack Kennedy had no clue to the motive for Mary's performance, but he was mesmerized nonetheless. He had seen her do a version of this before, but never with such a degree of urgency. During her marriage, Jack's focus had been squarely on Cord Meyer, whom he disliked. In the years since the divorce, Jack had been on the campaign trail much of the time and had not had much chance to observe her metamorphosis. To seize his sexual interest, as she unquestionably did that afternoon, she had to have made him see her in a whole new way. Certainly it was not Mary's pose as a bohemian artist, another of her masks, which seduced Jack. Suddenly, Jack saw Mary as dangerous because, like the C.I.A. men she imitated, she could not be controlled. She didn't run from danger, but actively sought it out – and that excited him immensely, though he tended to prefer much younger women. Mary, intent on dazzling Walter Pidgeon, had unwittingly ignited Jack's desire, and he would go after her as soon as he had a free moment.

Jackie, too, appears entirely to have missed the awakening of her husband's interest in Mary Meyer. She was busy monitoring Sinatra, and before the luncheon was over had found new cause for indignation. Someone mentioned that the President had given Preminger permission to shoot some scenes at the White House. Jackie said nothing, but after lunch she insisted that Jack inform Lawford that he had changed his mind. Meanwhile, Preminger, on whom Mary's blazing performance had also made a strong impression, had offered her a walk-on part.

Following that night's dinner at the Peruvian embassy, the Kennedys were due to leave town for two weeks. As Jack had

had no real vacation all summer aside from weekends at Cape Cod, the original plan had been for them to spend two weeks in Newport. As a result of Hammarskjöld's death, Jack decided to go to New York the following Monday in order to block Soviet efforts to install a so-called 'troika' at the United Nations that, he believed, would profoundly undermine the organization. Newport would have to be postponed, and in the interim the Kennedys went back to Hyannis Port. Sunday night, Jack flew to New York with Peter Lawford. In a sign that the White House well understood her political potency, Jackie, newly interested in international diplomacy and eager to participate, followed on Monday morning. She watched Jack deliver what Eleanor Roosevelt later called a 'courageous and excellent speech' that persuaded delegates to reject the Soviet proposal. The Kennedys passed the night in the family apartment at the Carlyle before they left for Newport, where they were to spend their longest continuous time together since those first, trying weeks at the White House before Glen Ora was ready. In contrast to that episode, their time together in Newport was, for Jackie, sheer joy.

Anxious as Jackie had been to escape the insularity of Newport society, she had always responded intensely to the beauty of her stepfather's estate overlooking Narragansett Bay. Miss Shaw brought Caroline and John up from Cape Cod, and Jackie's mother and stepfather temporarily moved out of the massive, gray-shingled main house to permit the First Family to vacation in privacy. There were horses for Jackie and Caroline, water and beaches for Jack, and plenty of guest bedrooms for his friends. Nearly every morning, he and his daughter went off to a neighbor's estate for a swim in the heated pool. At lunchtime, family and friends would cruise on the *Honey Fitz*, where Jack, perched on a battered leather swivel chair, would watch Jackie, in a bathing suit and cap and the upper section of a wetsuit, water-ski off Bailey's Beach or in Potter's Cove. At such moments, they seemed the picture of happiness. Yet it changes the way one looks at that picture to know that silently Jack was planning a tryst with Mary Meyer.

Monday morning, October 2, Jack seemed hardly able to

tear himself away from his family. Instead of beginning his journey back to Washington by helicopter, he sailed the *Honey Fitz* with his wife and daughter and some guests to Quonset Point, where *Air Force One* waited at the Naval Air Station. It was nearly four in the afternoon when Jackie returned to Hammersmith Farm. Originally, she had been scheduled to go to Washington with Jack that afternoon, since on Wednesday there would be a state dinner in honor of the President of the Sudan at the White House. Instead, Jack arranged with his father for her to use the *Caroline*, so that she could fly back to Washington at the last possible minute. To Jackie, he insisted that there was no reason to tear herself away from Newport at a moment when it was so beautiful just because he had to return to work.

As soon as Jack reached Washington on Monday, the real reason for his solicitude became clear. This was his first opportunity to follow up on the *Advise and Consent* luncheon, and he used it. The urgency with which he acted suggested the intensity of the impression Mary Meyer had made. A call was placed to invite her to the White House for Tuesday evening, October 3, at half past seven. Had Jackie returned with her husband as planned, that invitation could not have been issued.

At the luncheon ten days earlier, Mary had been so intent on Walter Pidgeon that she was oblivious to the fact that Jack was watching her. In the course of more than twenty years, she had encountered Jack in dozens of social situations and he had consistently reacted as if she were a comfortable old friend, someone he obviously liked but did not regard as a potential lover. When he placed Pamela Turnure temporarily in her house during the contretemps with her landlady, he made it clear that he regarded Mary as a woman of his own generation, fit only to provide a haven for his young girlfriends. In short, that October evening, Mary had no reason to expect anything more than the pleasure of being included in another White House dinner party.

When Mary entered the Yellow Oval Room where drinks were to be served, Jackie's presence was everywhere. Kennedy had been playing a record of Italian songs, undoubtedly his wife's. Books by André Malraux, a history of the Spanish Riding School that Jackie had been given in Vienna, a study of Meissen china, and some volumes from her Greek holiday were stacked on tables. On the walls were paintings by Eugène Boudin and Berthe Morisot. Only Jackie herself was missing, and as the minutes passed it became evident that she must be still in Newport. Mary took a moment to comprehend the reason for the invitation. Well aware of Jack's proclivities, she was taken aback nonetheless at this sudden spark of sexual interest after twenty-five years. When it became evident that she was the only guest, she abruptly made her excuses and left.

Mary did not reject Jack so much as cut things off before an actual proposition occurred. She might have been reckless and wild, but she was not stupid. She knew how much Jack delighted in the chase. Given her desire for something a good deal more substantial than what Jack usually had in mind, she realized that the smartest response was not to let him get what he wanted too quickly. Indeed, from the moment of Mary's abrupt departure from the White House, the chase was on. Fascinated ten days previously, the President was even more interested in her now.

Jackie flew in from Newport the next day, pleased to have had the extra day at Hammersmith Farm and ready to resume her program of political image-making. Reporters and photographers pressed in on all sides as, dressed in a fitted white wool suit, her bouffant hair covered with a blue silk scarf, Jackie stepped off the plane, in good spirits after a long holiday with her husband. She can have had no idea that, a few hours previously, he had taken the first step toward an affair with Mary Meyer, drawn to a newly-perceived recklessness and taste for danger in her that matched his own. This affair would not be with an office worker whom Jackie could ignore and hold at an emotional distance, but with a member of her own social set, someone she saw often in private circumstances. More and more, he would go after women in their milieu, intensifying Jackie's isolation and leading some of those women to titter among themselves that half the female population of Georgetown had either had sex with Jack or been asked to.

The visit of the Peruvian President was only the start of Jackie's crowded official schedule that fall. In the course of the season, besides her ongoing work on the White House restoration, she was scheduled to host approximately one major event per week. That day she was returning for a state dinner for the President of the Sudan, and in the weeks that followed there would be receptions for the leaders of Finland, India, and the Commonwealth of Puerto Rico, as well as the annual White House Judicial Reception and a dinner in honor of Harry Truman. Besides all this, she was to appear at high-profile cultural events, including concerts, plays, and museum and gallery exhibits. For each of these events Jackie devoted many hours to extensive preparation. In addition to official briefing papers, she immersed herself in each country's history, literature, and art. Though she made it look effortless, she greeted Jack's visitors with a full awareness of their interests, politics, likes, and dislikes, and could carry on a knowledgeable discussion about their countries and cultures. She was determined that if a slip were to be made and a visitor offended, it would not be by her. The days and weeks when many people assumed she was idly vacationing included a highly disciplined regimen of intensive study. Repeatedly, heads of state left Washington as intrigued by Jackie's intelligence and diplomatic skills as de Gaulle and Khrushchev had been. In view of those triumphs, it was decided that she would make further state visits, to Venezuela and Colombia with Jack, as well as to India and Pakistan on her own.

Besides her official work on Jack's behalf that fall, Jackie began an intensive schedule of private entertaining. Even though she had assumed a much more active public role than originally planned, she still believed it was her duty to divert her husband from the pressures of official life. She saw evenings as Jack's 'time for happiness,' and she took her obligation very seriously. Almost nightly when in residence at the White House, she would invite Jack's close personal friends and other guests to intimate dinners and, on occasion, larger parties, all designed with his pleasure in mind. Jack would arrive in the private quarters on the second floor of the Mansion from his West

Wing office at about 7:30 most weekday evenings to discover that Jackie had a treat ready and waiting. Most of the time, she conceived these evenings as a kind of surprise – not in the sense that Jack was unaware of the dinner, but rather that the workings of the evening were generally her own carefully crafted confection which he had only to sit back and enjoy. No one loved being made a fuss of more than Jack did, and on such evenings Jackie lavished attention on him.

Rarely in the next two years would Jack and Jackie spend the evening alone. Virtually every night during the presidency, Jackie orchestrated some sort of light entertainment for her husband. Jack might have to leave their guests at nine o'clock and disappear into his bedroom to read a position paper or study briefing papers for a meeting the next morning, but in between his arrival in the private quarters at 7:30 and that moment, Jackie would have offered him something fun. This required a tremendous amount of hard work, especially considering that these little jewels of entertainment occurred almost daily.

Jackie took special care with the guest lists for these dinners, unless Jack had specified whom he wished to see. Sometimes, she assembled a casual evening of close friends with whom he could relax, gossip, and laugh. On other occasions, she went to great lengths to assemble an ever-changing cast of characters whom he would find amusing and interesting. Knowing that he could easily feel trapped within the confines of the presidency, she searched far and wide for people who would give him a sense that he was still in touch with the varied tastes and interests that his office made it so much harder for him to pursue. In these years, Jackie was constantly on the phone to social connections in Washington, New York, and Palm Beach, as well as to her sister in London, picking their brains to find out who was in Washington at any given moment, and who might welcome a chance to fly in from Paris or Rome for an evening with the President. On her yellow pads she scribbled the names of possible guests. Who was a particularly good storyteller, she demanded to know, and who had the best gossip? On Jack's behalf, she sought out the most brilliant and beautiful people in the world, a mix of characters to add flavor to his evenings and keep his mind off his burdens for a few precious hours.

In this, Jackie assumed the role that Kick had once played to such immense effect in Jack's life. Just as Kick had once been Jack's most important supplier of a seemingly endless stream of intriguing new friends, both in America and later in England, now it was Jackie who imported writers, playboys, princes, and beautiful women to sparkle at her dinner table. But unlike Kick, whose introductions often resulted in deep and lasting friendships, Jackie for the most part provided only people who would be passing diversions in Jack's life. In part this was because by the time Jack became President he had established a long-standing set of close friends and confidants, not a few of whom had come to him through Kick.

Jackie went back and forth to Newport until October 26, when she brought the children back to the White House. The day marked a sea change in Washington as David Ormsby-Gore, the new British ambassador to the U.S., finally presented his credentials to the President. His arrival profoundly shifted the city's political and social dynamics. It was as if Jack had suddenly acquired another brother, but this one older, wiser, and more seasoned, with a deeply grounded moral sense. Hervé Alphand's privileged relationship with the Kennedys was as nothing compared to the access Ormsby-Gore enjoyed, and the French ambassador's nose was soon very much out of joint. The Kennedys' friendship with the Ormsby-Gores was to be different in quality from their relations with most other couples in their social set as well. Usually it was the husband who was Jack's friend, but in David and Sissie's case the friendship would truly be that of a foursome. The Ormsby-Gores, who had been close to Kick and made no bones about their disapproval of Joe Kennedy's treatment of Rose, would be equally warm and sympathetic to Jackie.

They arrived at an interesting time in Jackie's life, when the details of her trip to India and Pakistan were being finalized. Early in the presidency, she had played the most minimal role in Jack's political calculations. Such was Jack's reassessment of her abilities, however, that when Ambassador John Kenneth Galbraith proposed in September that she make an official visit to India, he loved the idea. Only four months after Jack had had to bring in a doctor to ensure that Jackie was able to travel abroad with him, he believed her fully competent to go out on her own, and not just to any foreign country but to a strategically important, explosive region whose leader was notoriously prickly. Berlin was the sole complication, so it was agreed that she would go after the situation cooled down.

When Khrushchev, citing Kennedy's willingness to negotiate, lifted the December deadline for a separate treaty with East Germany, tensions eased dramatically. Jackie's trip was soon scheduled; she would leave on November 20, a week after the season's last state dinner. In the interest of not offending Ayub Khan, Nehru's rival in the subcontinent, it was decided she would go to Pakistan as well. Upon her return, she was to accompany Jack to Latin America – a taxing schedule immeasurably complicated by the fact that Nehru was due in Washington for a diplomatic visit, by all estimates the most important of the season, just before Jackie's departure. The burden was on her to begin a friendship with Nehru on U.S. soil, if the trip to India were to be a success.

The advance word on Nehru's attitude to her husband was not encouraging. According to briefing papers, Nehru was coming to the U.S. to size up the new young President. In light of the Bay of Pigs and other missteps, Nehru, sensing that Kennedy was under immense pressure 'from the Pentagon and within the Department of State,' wondered just how much in charge of foreign policy the President really was. His skepticism intensified after a meeting with Khrushchev, who painted a portrait of an inadequate leader who exercised surprisingly little control in his own country.

Galbraith informed the President that, for their first meeting, Nehru did not want a formal state visit, but preferred instead something more informal, with less fanfare, preferably in a home setting rather than at the White House. Kennedy suggested inviting him to Hyannis Port, but Jackie insisted on Hammersmith Farm in Newport. Instinctively she understood that at this stage in the reconstruction of Jack's image, he needed a more imposing setting than one of the Kennedy beach houses in which to meet a skeptical Nehru. While she would certainly have been much happier greeting the Indian leader at the White House, at least Newport itself, and the massive main house and sweeping lawns of her mother and stepfather's estate, would open the visit with an appropriate impression of prestige and power.

On his arrival at Hammersmith Farm, as might have been expected, the elderly Nehru instantly responded to Jackie. Before his arrival, she had gone into the garden with Caroline and had the little girl pick a rose to present to the Prime Minister. The effect was charming, and the frail old man, dressed in white cap, white leggings, and homespun beige tunic, seemed ready to be enchanted. Jackie had prepared herself carefully, as she always did for a state visit, and nervous though she was she had the right materials at hand to win over the legendary statesman. Her suggestion that Nehru should stop first at Hammersmith Farm was a clever idea, but she was not in control of the other details of the visit. In a miscalculation that set the tone for all that followed, hardly had Nehru arrived and been introduced to Jackie than he was whisked off to a working lunch with Kennedy, Galbraith, and a retinue of advisers. Instead of taking full advantage of the informality of the locale, which Nehru himself had requested, and letting Jackie soften him up before talks began, the Americans rushed him into an atmosphere of business before the ice had been broken.

The lunch did not go well for Kennedy. To make matters worse, the afternoon badly shook Jackie's confidence and left Nehru's daughter, Indira Gandhi, full of indignation. The cantankerous, outspoken Mrs Gandhi, the third generation of the Nehru family to serve as President of the ruling Indian National Congress Party, made no secret of her resentment at being sent off with the President's wife, child, and friend (Lem Billings) when vital matters were being discussed elsewhere. The two women did not hit it off, to say the least, and by the time the meal was over Jackie had begun to have second thoughts about her own trip to India two weeks later. Before they all flew to Washington that afternoon on *Air Force One*, Jackie communicated her doubts to Galbraith and the Indian ambassador to the U.S. Mrs Gandhi, for her part, was waiting to spill out her discontent at the first possible opportunity.

When they arrived at Andrews Air Force Base, Nehru gave a vivid hint of what might have been by taking matters into his own hands after the welcoming ceremonies. Abandoning the President to his daughter, he attached himself firmly to Jackie. At the White House, he and Jackie emerged from the helicopter and, whispering in each other's ears, walked arm in arm across the South Lawn as if they were the most intimate of friends. But once more scheduling posed a problem, and by the time Jackie had another chance to work her magic on Jack's behalf, it was too late. She would not be able to spend any substantial time with the Prime Minister until after he had met with the President for talks.

The next day's meeting was a disaster: Nehru was taciturn, Kennedy uncharacteristically loquacious, and the result, as Nehru later reported to Macmillan, was that he found his host boring. The real problem with the visit was undoubtedly that the President was distracted by the situation in Vietnam. Nehru had come to Washington determined to see for himself if Kennedy was under the sway of militaristic advisers, and he arrived at a moment when the President was indeed facing unrelenting pressure from the Pentagon and the State Department to do something he very much wanted to avoid: commit U.S. troops to fight in South Vietnam. Kennedy, torn between a post-Bay of Pigs reluctance to take any military action and the old fear of being perceived as cowardly and weak, had resisted such advice for six months, but in October he had grudgingly agreed to allow General Maxwell Taylor and Walter Rostow to undertake a personal inspection tour of South Vietnam. As chance would have it, the 'Report on General Taylor's Mission to South Vietnam,' as the document was called, landed on Kennedy's desk three days before Nehru arrived in Newport, and the need to absorb and respond to its jolting but by no means unexpected recommendation that the

U.S. send combat troops did much to put Kennedy off his game.

Helping to undermine the President's focus were the phone calls that came in throughout Nehru's visit from Judith Campbell, who was trying to arrange to see him in Los Angeles the following week on his first visit to the West Coast as President. There would come a day when Harold Macmillan would excoriate Kennedy for depleting his powers by 'spending half his time thinking about adultery, the other half about second-hand ideas passed on by his advisers' – an apt description of much that went wrong during Nehru's ill-starred, week-long visit.

Nehru's cool reaction came as a blow to Kennedy, who was always at a loss when his charm failed. If Nehru was charmed by anyone it was Jackie, with whom he finally had an opportunity to talk at length at dinner that evening. But no matter how brilliantly she performed, when she returned to the family quarters at midnight she announced that she wanted to put off her trip. Acutely aware of the importance of the mission, she knew that she needed more time to prepare, as well as more experience. If she postponed the trip until after the Latin American tour in December, at least she would have one more foreign visit under her belt. Jack, who at dinner had experienced the difficult and disagreeable Mrs Gandhi for himself, called Galbraith at 2 a.m. to say that Jackie's trip was off until January.

Things had been moving very quickly for Jackie – at times, perhaps, too much so. The night after Nehru left, a major White House event celebrated her new life. Eight months previously, she had emerged briefly from a deep depression to give a private dinner dance for her sister at the White House. On Saturday evening, November 11, she gave a second private dinner dance for Lee. On this occasion, after years of being humiliated by Jack's cheating, Jackie would show her sister how beautiful, desirable, and powerful she had become. The eighty-nine carefully chosen guests who poured into the Blue Room were personal friends and acquaintances of the Kennedys, and included internationally prominent social figures such as Gianni and Marella Agnelli, whom Jackie wanted to think well of her.

On this glittering night of all nights, when the Piper-Heidsieck 1953 champagne flowed until four in the morning, the First Lady was courted, praised, flattered, and admired. But even as she was confidently working the crowd, flirting, giggling, whispering to this one or that, her husband was propositioning one of her guests.

Unlike his first attempt in October, on this occasion Jack actually had an opportunity to put the question to Mary Meyer – and she had an opportunity to refuse. Far from being offended, Mary was delighted to have been asked, and made that abundantly clear by immediately telling various friends who were present. In effect, Mary had set the course of her relations with Jack Kennedy. From the outset, she seems to have been most interested in the flattering thought that the President desired her, and in her ability to trumpet the news and assure herself the attention she craved.

Mary was surely aware that for a forty-year-old woman to refuse the President's advances would instantly remove the danger of seeming too eager. As Jack well knew, Mary was no prude and had said yes often enough to other men. Rather than bringing the dalliance to an end, Mary's refusal heated things up considerably. For Jack, the chase did not mean, as it does for some men, flowers, love letters, and the like. His approach was a good deal more basic. The only flattery he offered was his own willingness to try again and again. As he was extremely busy that fall, his next attempt might have to wait a bit, but in such matters his memory was phenomenal. Meanwhile, there was no urgency, as there were always plenty of other women ready to say yes.

As it happened, one result of Mary's eagerness to tell others what had just happened was to make Jackie seem ridiculous to some of the very people she hoped to impress. Well into the evening, as heavy drinking began to take its toll on a good many guests, Bobby Kennedy saw Gore Vidal, who had been crouching beside Jackie, steady himself by putting his arm on her shoulder. Perceiving a sign of disrespect, Bobby stepped in to move Vidal's arm, and an ugly fight ensued. The Attorney General's efforts were misdirected; if he was concerned about

Jackie's dignity, he would have done better to keep an eye on his brother.

It was nearly dawn before Jack and Jackie went to bed. At 8:25 a.m. on Sunday, a white cap was called to take the Kennedys, the Spaldings, and several other guests to Camp David at 10:35. In fact, the group would not take off until shortly before noon. Before they left, a disturbing scene unfolded in the family quarters.

'That was when everybody was hitting up,' recalled Betty Spalding, who was present when Max Jacobson arrived. By now his presence at the White House was routine, hypodermic needles and mood-lifting drugs an integral part of both the President and First Lady's lives. That morning, there was no pretense that Jacobson was there on account of Jack's bad back. 'It was cranking everybody up after an enormous night,' Spalding explained, 'shooting us with this stuff and sending us all up to Camp David.' Dr Feel Good had been called in to help the Kennedys and their friends enjoy their outing in the Cacotin Mountains after a night of hard drinking.

As several couples casually sat around the bedroom, Jacobson moved from person to person and injected them in full view of one another. Behind closed doors and beyond the stately image Jackie had worked so hard to create, this was what the presidency had come to after ten months. Given the climate at the White House, all but one individual in the room seemed to regard such behavior as normal.

Betty Spalding, the sole dissenter, watched transfixed: 'It was the damnedest performance I ever saw. I thought, "These people are crazy to be doing this!"' She knew about Jacobson from her husband but had never actually met the doctor, and from the first his appearance and manner did not inspire confidence. As Jacobson tried to insert a fresh needle in the syringe, he jabbed his own finger with the point. When the needle fell on the floor, he did a mad little dance around it in an effort to distract attention from his blunder, though no one but Betty seemed to notice or care. Presently, she watched him inject the First Lady, whose highly controlled personality seemed to make her an unlikely candidate for drugs. And in view of

Jack's medical history, Betty considered him lucky that the mixture of Jacobson's shots and other doctors' medication didn't kill him.

Betty watched Chuck get a shot, but when her turn came she did her best to put Jacobson off, saying that she had 'a lot of allergies' and didn't know how she would respond. Perhaps because she was so badly hung over, Jacobson managed to persuade her – for the first and last time – at least to accept 'a very light dose.' Thus, the President and First Lady and several of their friends went to Camp David high on speed.

At the time, the President was between crucial meetings on the Taylor Report. The first session, at which McGeorge Bundy had had reason to doubt that Kennedy completely understood all he approved, had taken place on Saturday, before the dinner dance. The second was scheduled for the following Wednesday, November 15. Kennedy, for his part, was unequivocal. He did not want to send troops to Vietnam. He thought that unlike Korea, where there had been a clear case of aggression opposed by the U.S. and others at the U.N., the Vietnam conflict was a good deal more ambiguous. When his advisers had pushed for a move on Cuba, he hadn't been sure whether they were right or wrong. By contrast, this time he was convinced they were mistaken and that if he followed their urgings, the U.S. would be heading toward disaster. Despite tremendous pressure, Kennedy knew he had to find the strength to continue to resist, as well as to articulate an alternative policy on Vietnam.

In this light, the Sunday morning drug-taking scene at the White House was anything but a private event of concern to no one except the participants. If ever Kennedy needed to focus calmly, intensively, and with a clear head, to scrutinize every word and comma in the Taylor Report, to grasp and assess all the modifications made in the past few days and marshal his own arguments in anticipation of the next meeting, it was during those next few days. He had the intellectual capacity, and he knew he must act before it was too late.

The episode provides a fascinating example of the tremendous effect of Kennedy's reckless and arrogant personal behavior on public affairs. His role models remained those eighteenth-century English aristocrats who, as David Cecil wrote in *The Young Melbourne*, did not 'let their pleasures interfere with ... more serious activities.' 'After eighteen hours of uninterrupted gambling,' wrote Cecil of one of Kennedy's favorite figures, 'Charles Fox would arrive at the House of Commons to electrify his fellow members by a brilliant discourse on American taxation.' While such passages formed a basis for Kennedy's self-image, he was unable to live up to them. Fox brought it off – perhaps – but in this and other critical instances, Kennedy could not. Arriving at Camp David high on drugs after an all-night party, he was in no condition to make judgments that, as we now know, led to the tragedy of the Vietnam War.

Jackie had never visited Camp David, and Jack had had only a glimpse during his painful encounter with Eisenhower after the botched operation at the Bay of Pigs. The better part of Sunday was spent exploring the possibilities of the presidential retreat, followed by a film screening in the private theater. Monday morning, as they waited to go back to Washington, Kennedy and Betty Spalding sat together surrounded by some baggage. He had unburdened himself to her after Cuba, and now again he made no effort to hide his agitation as he studied the Taylor Report, on the fly as it were. Intensely aware of the extent to which Cuba had weakened him even within his own government, Jack, in despair, suddenly threw the report at Betty and said he had no idea 'what the hell' he was going to do about Vietnam.

In contrast, the mood that night at the White House was one of Olympian authority and assurance, when Jackie staged the last of the season's state dinners, a musical evening in honor of Governor and Mrs Luís Muñoz-Marín of Puerto Rico. In a cultural coup, the Kennedys hosted a concert by Pablo Casals. The celebrated eighty-four-year-old cellist had refused to perform in the U.S. since 1928, in protest at Washington's recognition of the dictatorship of Francisco Franco in Spain. That an artist of such legendary principle had agreed to end his boycott out of admiration for what he saw as Kennedy's ideals made for the sort of grand political symbol any leader would have relished, as well as a spectacular conclusion to Jackie's fall program of pageantry.

With the India trip postponed, Jackie looked forward to three weeks of relative calm until she and Jack were to leave for Latin America. The praise for the Casals dinner had barely died down when she took the children to Glen Ora on Thursday, the first time she had been there since the spring. On this occasion, Jack would not join her later that weekend. On Thursday he embarked on a four-day political trip west, the first extended domestic travel of his presidency.

In Seattle, he delivered a speech at the University of Washington, then went on to address a political dinner for Senator Warren Magnusen. Shortly after 10:30 p.m., he closed the door of his suite, which adjoined that of Dave Powers, at the Olympic Hotel. The second floor, reserved in its entirety for the presidential party, presumably shut down for the night. In addition to local police and firemen, at least seven Secret Service agents were on the floor, two posted in front of the President's door at one end of the hall. There had been no indication that late-night visitors were expected, so the Secret Service instructed the policemen on guard at the elevator that no one was to be admitted.

Not long after the floor was sealed, agents Larry Newman and Roy Kellerman heard a commotion near the elevator, as if an unexpected visitor were protesting noisily at being stopped. As the agents ran to the scene, a tipsy man and two attractive, well-dressed women turned the corner, accompanied by police.

'I'm bringing these two girls in to see the President!' the stranger boomed.

By this time, the policemen had recognized the women as expensive call girls, and the tipsy man as a local Democrat of some prominence. They were only too happy to pass the mess on to the Secret Service, who refused to let the trio pass. A standoff ensued, with Newman and Kellerman moving to inspect the prostitutes' purses.

'Who do you work for?' the tipsy man demanded of Newman.

'I work for God,' the agent replied.

The prostitutes, completely cool, silently watched the furious

back and forth – in Newman's words – 'like a tennis match.'
The tipsy man, however, was anything but cool, and before
long his indignant protests brought Dave Powers out from his
suite.

'Hi,' said Powers, quickly taking charge. The matter was now
out of the agents' hands. 'Thank you. I'll give you a call, pal,'
said Powers, who had deftly choreographed the whole scene so
that the tipsy man would be prevented from personally presenting the call girls to the President.

As the door closed on his face, the tipsy man called after the
prostitutes, 'You remember, if you talk about any of this night,
you'll wind up in Stillicoom!' Stillicoom was a state mental
hospital.

Finally, Powers and the women disappeared, but not before
policemen and firemen on the floor, not to mention the hotel
staff, knew what was going on. The President of the United
States, the man with the beautiful young wife with whom half
the world had fallen in love, was to spend his first night on the
road with a pair of expensive hookers.

Meanwhile, Jackie spent a quiet weekend at Glen Ora, where
she rode and watched the hunter trials. On Monday afternoon,
she sent the children to the White House with their nurse and
drove back on her own in order to shop at leisure in a
Georgetown antique shop. That morning, Jack returned from
Los Angeles, where he had enjoyed a rendezvous with Judith
Campbell and partied with Frank Sinatra, Peter Lawford, and
Angie Dickinson.

Wednesday afternoon, Jack and Jackie flew up to Hyannis
Port with the children. Though Jack now sat at the head of the
table at Kennedy gatherings, Joe remained the head of the
family. Thanksgiving was celebrated under his roof, before he
and Rose decamped for Palm Beach. At Cape Cod, the
Kennedys ice-skated in the family rink and Jackie went off at
intervals to practice golf with the local pro. She had been taking
lessons all fall in anticipation of accompanying Jack in the
spring when, it was hoped, his back would finally permit him
to play. As in so much she did, both large and small, it was
evident that she still sought to change herself, as if hoping to

hit on the one crucial element missing from her marriage. The only alteration Jack made after the Seattle trip was to have Dave Powers, rather than a local intermediary, bring in the prostitutes.

Back in Washington after the holiday, Jackie resumed her long weekends at Glen Ora with the children. Jack had not been there since the spring when he came down for a single Sunday night on December 3. The following weekend, he also spent only one night in the country, having remained in town not for the usual shenanigans but to dine at Joe Alsop's with Kick's sister-in-law, the Duchess of Devonshire. It was a measure of Jack's affection for the Devonshires that he did something quite uncharacteristic, in asking the National Gallery to permit him to bring the Duchess for a private visit after dinner. Afterward, he took her back to Alsop's house, where he lingered happily until the wee hours.

In Washington, in the days before she and Jack left for Latin America, Jackie made a point of spending as much time as possible with Caroline and John. As on other occasions, in an attempt to approximate a normal life she insisted on taking them to public parks such as Montrose Park and the playground on Q Street in Georgetown. In what was known in the argot of the Secret Service as a 'spontaneous movement,' she, the children, and their protectors would arrive without advance notice or advance men, catching people in the park off guard and getting the Kennedys in and out before word of their presence spread. The agents' primary fear for the children was a kidnap attempt. In the event that cameras materialized, Jackie's principal concern was that no pictures be taken of the children. In addition to protecting them from the burden of a premature celebrity, she worried that the more recognizable Caroline and John became, the harder it would be for them to go out for walks with their nanny.

Jackie had much else on her mind as the moment of departure drew near. She had done a great deal on behalf of Jack's presidency in recent months, but in the days that followed considerably more would be required. From the first there had been abundant opposition both inside and outside government

to Kennedy's Latin American trip, especially his plan to visit
Venezuela, where, three years previously, Richard Nixon had
been greeted by a stone-throwing mob. In light of that incident,
recalled Sue Vogelsinger, a White House press assistant who
accompanied the Kennedys to Venezuela, 'there was more than
a little concern on the part of the Secret Service that something
could indeed happen.'

The prospect of a stone-throwing mob was negligible compared to the potential horrors in Caracas, where a fully-fledged
assassination attempt on the President or members of his party
was reported by U.S. intelligence to be in the works. Two days
before Jack and Jackie left, the C.I.A. notified Bobby Kennedy
that a planeload of Cuban agents was en route to Venezuela
'to carry out sabotage during President Kennedy's visit and, if
possible ... make an attempt on the President's life.' The
following day, Venezuela sent assurances that, while the enemy
did indeed plan 'serious disturbances,' as well as a 'personal
threat' to the President, local security should be enough to
forestall any danger. That same day, a telegram from the U.S.
embassy in Caracas noted ominously that, in view of the security
focus on Kennedy, assassins might be tempted to target someone else in his party. That could well mean Jackie, particularly when she was with Venezuela's First Lady while their
husbands conferred separately. Almost certainly, however, the
gravest danger would come during the Kennedys' motorcade
through downtown Caracas, a hotbed of anti-government sentiment.

Despite pressure from many quarters, Kennedy refused to
cancel the trip, though up to the last minute his security advisers
reserved the right to cancel the motorcade. He saw the visit as
part of an ongoing effort to persuade the world's underdeveloped
nations of the United States' commitment to democratic revolution. As such, Kennedy chose to go to two countries, Venezuela and Colombia, whose leaders were champions of
progressive reform, and hoped that his presence would send a
message throughout Latin America, where Castro had been at
pains to portray the U.S. as an evil exploiter. During his visit,
the President planned to draw attention to the accomplishments

of the Alliance for Progress, a program of social reforms which he had initiated.

Jackie's participation would be a great advantage, both because of her star status and because she knew enough Spanish to address crowds on the President's behalf. Her maiden attempt at political image-making after Europe, the Ayub Khan dinner at Mount Vernon, had conveyed a related message of social change, so the Latin American trip formed a fitting conclusion to her first season as an active First Lady. In view of the danger both to her husband and herself, tremendous courage was required to go through with it.

The atmosphere was exceptionally tense as the Kennedys left the White House on Friday morning, December 15, en route to Puerto Rico, their first stop. When the President discovered that an aide had provided an incorrect weather report, causing Jackie to pack the wrong clothes, he exploded to a degree well out of proportion to the offense. It was shortly past four when Governor and Mrs Muñoz-Marín, who had been the Kennedys' guests three weeks previously at the Casals concert, greeted them at the airport in Puerto Rico. The crowds' enthusiasm meant the trip had started well, but that first night, with its ceremonial dinner in the Kennedys' honor, was also a time of waiting.

When *Air Force One* took off for Caracas early the next morning, it had not yet been decided whether to risk the motorcade. The plan called for the Kennedys to land at Maiquetía Airport, where a fleet of cars would take the party through the city to La Carlota Airport on the other side of town. There they were to board a Marine helicopter for the next brief leg of the trip, to an Alliance for Progress-backed housing project located in a rural area more hospitable to President Rómulo Betancourt. To avoid the threat of violence in the city, all they had to do was take the helicopter directly from Maiquetía. At virtually the last minute, however, Kennedy's security people chose to proceed with the motorcade. Kennedy, fully aware of the peril, concurred. The Venezuelan government 'had a gun every ten feet all the way into town, which is about a thirty-mile trip,' remembered Sue Vogelsinger. 'So it was scary.'

In Caracas, the drive through the crowded, treacherously

narrow downtown streets was an ordeal, as some twenty thousand troops, brandishing rifles, pistols, and machine guns, struggled to hold back the pushing, screaming crowds. Police motorcycles roared on either side of the presidential limousine, on whose running boards stood Secret Service men. One agent, Larry Newman, later compared the frantic, fast-paced motorcade to running a gauntlet. 'Jackie! Jackie!' the Venezuelans shrieked when they spotted her. Ostensibly they were welcoming, but there was also a gut-wrenching sense that at any moment they would force the car to stop, or that an assassin would suddenly spring forth whom Betancourt's military, for all its conspicuous weaponry, would be powerless to stop in time. Jackie betrayed no fear, yet nothing in her experience had prepared her for the electric tension of the seemingly interminable ride. As they approached the end of the last city street, she, like everyone else in the presidential party who had been counting the seconds, breathed a sigh of relief.

At 7:30 a.m. on December 18, 1961, when *Air Force One* returned to the U.S., Joe Kennedy was waiting on the tarmac at Palm Beach International Airport. His opportunities to bask in the glory of the Kennedy presidency were frustratingly few. Unlike Rose, who came to the White House often, Joe tended to steer clear lest it be said that Jack was his puppet. In Hyannis Port, he was always beside himself with delight when Jack's helicopter landed on or took off from the family lawn, and he never missed an opportunity to greet *Air Force One* when Jack arrived in Palm Beach. Despite the physical distance that Joe calculatedly maintained, father and son did talk on the phone constantly, and Joe kept close tabs on Jackie as well. When she took her first steps as an active First Lady, he called her office regularly to discuss her press coverage.

Joe knew what it was to lose the two people he loved most, Joe Jr and Kick, and he was ecstatic at the safe return of Jack and Jackie from a trip which had threatened to be extremely dangerous. Jack had long ago taken over his older brother's part in their father's plans, and Jackie had become like a daughter to the old man. In a celebratory mood and mindful of issues of succession, Joe decided that the time had come for Jack's son, who had just celebrated his first birthday, to make his entrance onto the family stage. Miss Shaw had already brought both children to the Spanish-style house on North County Road, just down the beach from Joe's, that Jack had borrowed from Colonel C. Michael Paul for the duration of the presidency. Jackie, off duty until after the Christmas holidays, planned to stay in Palm Beach while Jack went briefly to Washington before meeting Macmillan in Bermuda to discuss nuclear testing, Berlin, and other matters.

Joe saw Jack off on *Air Force One* the following morning with the kind of symbolic gesture he relished. While Jackie and Caroline remained behind, Joe swooped tiny John up into his arms. His unprecedented inclusion of John Jr in the ritual at Palm Beach International Airport was an event of deep personal significance to Joe, comparable in its way to the moment when he relinquished to Jack his place at the family table. The tableau of three generations of Kennedy men announced the continuation of the dynasty, and expressed in a single, highly charged dramatic image the old man's dreams for the future.

EIGHT

Goddess of Power

༄

On the morning of Tuesday, December 19, 1961, Jackie and Caroline drove to the Kennedy mansion to take a swim while Joe, who had seen Jack off at the airport earlier, went to his regular golf game. Soon after they arrived, Joe returned early and unexpectedly from the Palm Beach Country Club.

At the airport, Joe had seemed flushed to Evelyn Lincoln, who also thought his steps 'a little unsure.' Then, at the country club, he felt faint as he leaned over to pick up his ball after the sixth hole. He told his niece Ann Gargan to tee off while he rested on a bench. When he got up, she could see that his balance was shaky, so she sent for a golf cart to transport him to her car. While they waited, he appeared disoriented, his speech jumbled. Suddenly he panicked about young John. Where was he? Had he forgotten the boy and left him somewhere? Had something happened to his grandson while in his care? Joe had no memory of driving him home after the airport.

Back at the house, Joe insisted that he felt better when he saw Jackie and Caroline. Jackie, whom he favored in many ways over his surviving daughters, always put a smile on his face. He promised to join her in the pool as soon as he had changed. Ann, however, persuaded him to take a nap. Upstairs, Joe slept for only about five minutes. When he woke, he could neither move his right side nor speak. An ambulance was called to take him to St Mary's Hospital, which was located some fifteen minutes away from the Kennedy mansion, and there it was determined that he had had a stroke. He might not pull through, doctors warned Rose, and if he did survive he was unlikely ever to recover fully.

Jack, in Washington, said he would fly down as soon as *Air Force One* was ready. Secret Service agents, ordered to report immediately, left cars parked haphazardly outside the White House in order to board a special bus to the airport. Jack dashed from a National Security meeting to the flight, on which his brother Bobby and sister Jean were to accompany him. Another sister, Eunice, flew down separately. Pat Lawford came from Los Angeles and Teddy Kennedy from Boston. En route, the President disciplined himself to work on 1962 legislative planning with an aide, as it was the only way to control his emotions. Shortly before 8 p.m., *Air Force One* landed in West Palm Beach.

Jackie was waiting in the lobby at St Mary's, where a nun said Joe had been given the last rites of the Catholic Church. When Jack and Jackie reached his third-floor suite in a wing donated by the Kennedy family, doctors asked them not to go in. After considerable difficulty, the staff had finally managed to get Joe to sleep and they preferred that he not be disturbed. At length, Jack, Jackie, and Bobby did manage to see him for a quarter of an hour. Joe recognized them but was unable to speak.

Jack had lived his forty-four years with a father to whom he could reach out whenever he needed affirmation. Now, whether Joe lived or died, he had lost that advantage at a moment when each day seemed to bring fresh pressures. It was not that Jack any longer counted on Joe's day-to-day advice, but he remained utterly dependent on his encouragement and support. Jack could rely on Bobby for many things, but the younger brother was unseasoned, as well as hot-tempered and immature. His loyalty was indispensable and his advice would prove increasingly important, but the succor Joe routinely provided was beyond Bobby's capacity.

In a very different way, from the time of Jackie's earliest days in the family, Joe had been a central figure in her life. Now, she and Jack clung to each other in grief. Joe made it through the night, but by Wednesday morning he was said to be near death. Jack and Jackie slipped out of the hospital and, careful that no reporters followed, went to St Edward's Church.

Ordinarily the President and First Lady's church appearances were carefully orchestrated photo opportunities, but today's visit and others to come were anything but hollow displays of piety. Jack and Jackie wished to be alone as they lit candles and knelt side by side to pray.

Three times on Wednesday they returned to the hospital, and by the end of the day it was evident that Jack was emotionally and physically drained. But he was still President, and this evening nine advisers were expected for a working dinner and briefing session in anticipation of the conference with Macmillan in Bermuda scheduled for the next day. At seven, when Dean Rusk, McGeorge Bundy, Charles Bohlen, David Bruce, and others came in, Jackie joined them for dinner. A working meal was usually her cue to disappear, but on this occasion she could relieve Jack of some of the pressure for an hour or so. Her unusual step gave him time to recover, postponing the start of briefings on vital issues until she withdrew.

It wasn't until Harold and Dorothy Macmillan landed in Bermuda that they received news of Joe Kennedy's condition. From the Governor's house, where the talks were to take place, Macmillan sent word that he would understand if the President postponed the meeting. He offered to travel to Palm Beach right away or to Washington at a later date, whichever Kennedy preferred. Late that night, it was decided that, as Joe's condition appeared to have stabilized though there remained no hope of full recovery, the President would indeed go to Bermuda. Jackie remained at Joe's bedside in her husband's place.

As it happened, Jack's anxieties about his father, far from impeding talks, seemed to permit him to form an even stronger bond with the Prime Minister. Despite the many factors that made Macmillan the polar opposite of Joe Kennedy, he was uniquely suited to fill the emotional chasm in Jack's life. Twice in moments of crisis Kennedy had reached out to the older, more experienced leader, with whom he had an extremely meaningful family connection. With Joe suddenly out of the picture, it was not at all surprising that he would look to Macmillan as a new father figure.

Macmillan, for his part, had a great deal to offer. Much as he liked and admired Kennedy, whom he praised in a letter to the Queen as 'a very effective, even ruthless, operator in the political field,' he worried that the President did seem 'more interested in short-term than in large and distant problems.' In his diary, Macmillan went a good deal further: 'There is a marked contrast between President Kennedy "in action" on a specific problem (e.g. Congo, West Irian, Ghana) and his attitude to larger issues (the nuclear war, the struggle between East and West, Capitalism and Communism, etc.). In the first, he is an extraordinarily quick and effective operator – a born "politician" (not in a pejorative sense). On the wider issues, he seems rather lost.'

In Bermuda, Macmillan took it as his mission to shift Kennedy's perspective to precisely those 'large and distant problems' with which the Prime Minister believed a great leader must be concerned. Joe Kennedy had taught his son to win at any cost. Macmillan, of a very different cast of mind, pressed him to rethink his 'concept of the role of being a head of government' and to gaze 'two or three years into the future and, if possible, even longer.' A veteran of two world wars, Macmillan believed that war, nuclear or conventional, no longer provided an option for sane people. To reduce armaments was the only rational approach.

Whether Macmillan would have been quite so effective under other circumstances is impossible to say; his words, coming as they did at a time when Joe Kennedy's influence was suddenly removed, made a huge philosophical impact. Adding to the intensity of the experience for both men were the 'country house conditions' in which the conference was held. Kennedy and Macmillan lived under the same roof, ate all meals but breakfast together, took long walks, and had lots of time to talk. It seemed to Ormsby-Gore that Kennedy's instincts were similar to Macmillan's, but that the Prime Minister had thought out his positions in ways the younger man had yet to do. 'I think that not many people had talked to President Kennedy in quite those sweeping terms before,' Ormsby-Gore remembered. 'And I think that this did add a dimension to his thinking.' As far as

Macmillan was concerned, no topic was more important than that of nuclear testing. Even Berlin, discussed passionately and at length, struck the Prime Minister as 'small beer compared to the destruction of humanity.'

One immediate problem facing Kennedy was whether to follow the Soviets in resuming atmospheric nuclear testing. Only recently, Atomic Energy Commission Chairman Glenn Seaborg had informed Kennedy that the commission 'as a whole' believed that 'in view of the limitations of underground testing and in light of the comprehensive nature of recent Soviet tests, national security considerations require that the United States embark upon a program of atmospheric testing at the earliest appropriate time.' Kennedy went to Bermuda in part to request permission to use Christmas Island, a British territory in the central Pacific, for atmospheric testing. Macmillan, determined to avert the resumption of testing, warned Kennedy not to be drawn further into the arms race.

At Bermuda and in letters afterward, Macmillan urged Kennedy to try 'to break the cycle' and 'put a stop to all this folly.' He advised him to do 'everything possible to control events and not merely follow them.' Reflecting that 'it is not the things one did in one's life that one regrets but rather the opportunities missed,' he pushed Kennedy to militate for a summit with Khrushchev and some form of test ban treaty – if not a comprehensive ban, then at least one on atmospheric testing. He argued that it was their duty 'to try and bend history' to ensure that mankind did not obliterate itself, that it was their personal obligation to end the arms race. An under-lying theme in all he said was his and Kennedy's responsibility as world leaders to act, and to base their actions not just on what was politically and personally expedient but on what was right.

Kennedy left Bermuda on December 22, 1961, convinced of the need to find some way to break the deadlock between East and West. Nonetheless, distrustful of the Soviets, he rejected the notion of a summit. Macmillan, conceding that the Soviets were given to 'trickery and bad faith,' insisted that it was at least worth a try, but Kennedy remained doubtful. Pressed on the matter of Christmas Island, Macmillan claimed that he had to confer with his Cabinet. That, it turned out, was merely a way to buy time, during which Macmillan worked on Kennedy in marvelous, often moving letters that opened with the salutation 'My Dear Friend.' The Prime Minister's aim was to come up with a plan whereby he and Kennedy would reach out to Khrushchev together, and achieve a breakthrough in time to avoid the resumption of U.S. testing. Meanwhile, the Bermuda Conference and the letters from Macmillan that followed began the important process of recasting Kennedy's thinking. The effects may not always have been apparent, but a seed had been planted.

Instead of Joe, Jackie was on the tarmac at Palm Beach International Airport on Friday night when *Air Force One* touched down. After a stop at the hospital, Jack went home to try to get some sleep, only to awaken in the morning to the news that Joe had contracted pneumonia and was barely clinging to life. Jack and Jackie went off to pray together, and did so again the following morning when Joe had so much trouble breathing that doctors had to perform a tracheotomy. By now it was Christmas Eve, and though Jack and Jackie finally went home to hang Christmas stockings for the children, they soon returned to Joe's hospital suite and lingered till almost midnight. For eight days, he hovered between life and death, and not until December 27 did doctors suggest the immediate crisis might be past. That day the *Honey Fitz* sailed for the first time since Jack had come to Florida. The next morning, Jack and Jackie brought Caroline to see her grandfather. Afterward, Jack slipped off to St Edward's to pray alone.

His father had survived, yet the sight of him helpless, drooling, frustrated, and angry was unsettling. Joe Kennedy, formerly so proud and powerful, had lost all his magnificent dignity. Once a riveting conversationalist, he could do little more than make shrill, incoherent noises. Jack, in a moment of desperation, wondered aloud to Jackie if it had been the right thing to fight and pray to keep his father alive, imprisoned in a contorted, useless body. He told her that if he were ever in a similar state, she must do nothing to preserve his life.

Rather than return to Washington after the New Year, Jack decided to conduct the presidency from Florida for the time being. While he was in meetings, Jackie sat at Joe's bedside. When Jack's departure could be put off no longer, she agreed to stay behind until Joe was discharged from hospital. Finally, on Monday, January 8, 1962, Joe was driven through the iron-grilled gate on North Ocean Boulevard. Two days later, Jackie, satisfied that at least Joe was back in his own bed, flew to Washington with the children in time to attend her husband's second State of the Union address, and resume her official duties.

Following the almost unbearable tension of the trip to Venezuela, Jack and Jackie had shared a wrenching emotional experience in Florida. Day after day, they had gone back and forth to the hospital, conferred with doctors, agonized constantly. They had knelt and prayed and wept together. Jackie had done her best to take as much of the burden off Jack's shoulders as possible. She had fussed over his father and lightened Joe's spirits in a way no other member of the family seemed able to do. Unquestionably, the three tumultuous weeks since Joe's stroke had drawn Jack and Jackie closer together than ever, yet even now she remained in his eyes more a soulmate than a spouse. In the days that followed, his choice of sexual partner pierced to the very heart of the carefully constructed private life in which his wife expected to feel safe.

On the morning of Sunday, January 21, having attended a gala dinner in Washington the previous night to celebrate the anniversary of the Inauguration, Jack and Jackie, accompanied by her sister, joined Caroline and John at Glen Ora. Monday morning, Jackie, Lee, and the children stayed in the country, while Jack returned to the White House. That evening a presidential car collected Mary Meyer in Georgetown. Evelyn Lincoln signed her in at the White House at half past seven. Jack had wanted to get Mary into bed since after the *Advise and Consent* luncheon in September, some four months earlier. On this night, by her own account, he finally succeeded.

From the moment Kennedy had watched Mary show off for Walter Pidgeon, danger had been her principal attraction.

There was no controlling her and no predicting her actions. The experience of having seen his father go from a vibrant, powerful man to a helpless invalid from whom all pleasure had been snatched in an instant had caused Jack to be even more strongly drawn to the sort of danger Mary represented. Betty Spalding and other friends would later say that he had always been preoccupied with notions of dying young and taking one's pleasures while one can. His father's plight only intensified such feelings. More than ever, risks made him feel alive. More than ever, he seemed intent on living while he could – at full intensity. Now he had invested those feelings in Mary, whose calculated decision not to have sex with him right away made him prize success with her all the more.

As for Mary, it was perhaps inevitable that she would eventually succumb. For much of her life she had sought fame, and almost always in the same way, via an attachment to a man. There was a frightening precedent in the story of her older half-sister, the failed actress Rosamund Pinchot, who only managed to attract the headlines she had long chased when she committed suicide because of mistreatment by her lover, the Broadway producer Jed Harris. Like the sister she idolized, Mary craved attention and saw sex as a way to get it. (Ironically, Mary too would find fame only in death, when, after her unsolved murder in 1964, the story of her affair with Kennedy began to emerge.) The shadow of Rosamund's suicide hinted at the desperation behind Mary's pose of reckless indifference, a desperation that made her more dangerous than even Kennedy probably imagined.

Later, many people would ask whether Mary was bothered by what she was doing to Jackie, a woman she not only saw socially, but whose marriage to a compulsive philanderer in some ways mirrored her own. Not only had Mary lived with the humiliation of Cord Meyer's betrayals, she too had lost a child to death. Mary was well aware of Jackie's anguish when the Kennedys' baby was born dead in 1956, as the Meyers were then their neighbors in Virginia. But even to ask such a question about Mary is to misunderstand the character she had invented for herself in the aftermath of divorce. As far as Mary was concerned, rules that might have stopped another woman in her position from embarking on an affair with Jack Kennedy simply did not apply to her. Sleeping with another woman's husband and even sharing that man with another of her friends fazed Mary not at all. She thought of herself, and wished to be thought of, as beyond such mundane considerations.

If Mary couldn't have cared less how Jackie felt, she cared greatly how her ex-husband would react. Cord Meyer regarded Kennedy as his social and intellectual inferior, and could not comprehend how Jack had managed to become President while he, for all his youthful promise, had never gotten further than the upper reaches of the C.I.A. In short, Meyer was wildly jealous of Kennedy, and Mary could be confident that news of her latest affair would prove a bitter blow. Toward the end of her marriage, Mary had had an affair with an Italian she met on vacation. She had told everyone that she planned to leave Cord for her lover, and then had to live with unspeakable embarrassment when the Italian dropped her. Her affair with Jack Kennedy, a man who occupied a position Cord Meyer believed ought to have been his, had the potential to redress that handsomely.

Jackie came in from Glen Ora on Wednesday in anticipation of flying down to Palm Beach with Jack the next day for a long weekend with his father. He had been eager to visit at the first opportunity, as he had not seen Joe since he was discharged from the hospital. Before Jackie left Washington, she sent out invitations to a dinner dance on Friday, February 9, 1962, conceived to lift Jack's spirits. She was right to think he would need cheering up after the visit, since the scene that greeted them in Palm Beach was no pretty picture. Jackie was convinced that Joe had suffered several small strokes previously and in the hope of a sudden death had discarded his medication. He had not gotten his wish. Confined to a wheelchair, a tangle of oxygen equipment nearby, he was clearly finding it difficult to adjust to the nightmare that was now his life. He seemed particularly ashamed of a deformed right hand, which someone had attempted to conceal with a scarf. It did little for Joe's self-esteem that some well-meaning visitors pretended to overlook

On September 12, 1953, Jacqueline Bouvier married John Kennedy, her "eyes filled with dreams."

The spectres haunting Jackie's marriage: Janet Auchincloss and Rose Kennedy.
Jackie saw marriage to Jack as an escape from her own mother; later, she began
to fear that her life might become like that of her mother-in-law.

inauguration day, January 20,
1961. Watching the parade
from the first row of the
viewing stand are Jack's
parents, Rose and Joseph
Kennedy, Jackie, Jack, and
Lyndon and Lady Bird
Johnson.

Jack and Jackie arrive at
the Inaugural ball at the
Washington Armory. Not yet
fully recovered from the birth
of her son John, Jackie was full
of unease about the life that
faced her as First Lady.

Three weeks into the preside[...] a depressed Jackie, accompa[...] by Caroline, leaves by helico[...] to spend her first night at Gl[...] Ora, the Kennedys' country retreat.

When Prime Minister and Mrs. Karamanlis of Greece arrived at the White House [...] April 1961 for lunch with th[...] Kennedys, the calamitous B[...] of Pigs invasion was in prog[...]

With French President Charles de Gaulle at Versailles in June 1961. During her time in Paris, Jackie found the sense of purpose she had sought since childhood and returned home with the dynamics of her marriage radically changed.

With Soviet Premier Nikita Khrushchev in Vienna in June 1961. Convinced that it was not Jackie's beauty that had captivated de Gaulle, Khrushchev set out to discover what her role in the presidency might be.

The Prime Minister and the First Lady. A day would come when Macmillan would address Jackie, as once he had addressed her husband, as "my dear friend."

The Kennedys with British Prime Minister Harold Macmillan and his wife, Lady Dorothy, immediately after Kennedy's disastrous meeting with Khrushchev. Jackie's fascination with the Macmillans' turbulent marriage had been sparked even before she met them.

Long-time aide Dave Powers was often the one who delivered President Kennedy's women of the evening – some of them regulars, others brought in for a single occasion. Marlene Dietrich came to the White House for what was by her own account a brief interlude with the President, a man considerably her junior.

The White House swimming pool was a favorite sexual trysting place. The President's father made him a gift of the murals designed to create the fantasy that he was swimming in the harbour at St. Croix, the effect heightened by romantic lighting and a wall of mirrors.

No room at the White House was more lovingly constructed than the bedroom Jackie shared with Jack. In her absences, this room too sometimes served as a trysting place for Jack and his other women.

Jack with Mary Meyer. Jackie would come to regard the liaison as the most threatening of her husband's many affairs.

A private dinner dance at the White House for the Kennedys' friends on February 9, 1962. That night, a guest inadvertently caught the President upstairs with Mary Meyer.

Jackie with Bill Walton. One of the most painful aspects of Jackie's marriage was that their friends were aware of Jack's infidelity. Though Walton was Jackie's friend as well as Jack's, he frequently served as beard for Jack's women at private evenings at the White House.

Lem Billings (left) was Jack's boarding school roommate and oldest friend. He served as a kind of third wheel in the Kennedys' marriage. Though he did not participate in Jack's womanizing, Lem was often present when Jack entertained other women in Jackie's absence. Chuck Spalding (right), one of Jack's closest friends in the White House years, became increasingly involved in the President's philandering.

Jack and Jackie with Harold Macmillan and Sissie and David Ormsby-Gore, British ambassador to Washington. Like Macmillan, both Ormsby-Gores became close friends of the Kennedys, and stayed loyal to Jackie.

During the 1962 America's Cup Races, the Kennedys entertain friends on a naval destroyer named for the President's late brother Joe. At this very moment, the Cuban Missile Crisis was about to explode, and a desperate Jackie was reaching breaking point over Jack's relationship with Mary Meyer.

Palm Beach, Florida, December 25, 1962. The Kennedys celebrate their last Christmas together. Seated in the background is the President's father, incapacitated by a stroke. Jackie had just become pregnant with her second son, Patrick.

Christmas 1962 was a happy one, as Jack basked in the victory of the Cuban Missile Crisis. The Kennedys are on their way to a cruise on the *Honey Fitz*, one of several presidential yachts. In the rear are Jackie's sister and brother-in-law, Lee and Stas Radziwill.

Jackie delivers a speech in Spanish to the returning Bay of Pigs prisoners on December 29, 1962. The occasion marked the symbolic end of her work to restore Jack's prestige after the debacle of the Cuban invasion a year and a half earlier.

Jackie and John Jr. have a picnic on the South Lawn of the White House in April 1963. Jack was again on his own politically, as Jackie's attention was focused on another difficult pregnancy.

(left to right) Chuck Spalding, Steve Smith, Jack, Stas Radziwill, David Ormsby-Gore, Jean Smith, and Jackie on the *Honey Fitz* off Hyannis Port, celebrating Jackie's thirty-fourth birthday and the signing of the test ban treaty in Moscow that week. This was, perhaps, the last truly happy weekend of the presidency.

Chuck Spalding, Stas Radziwill, Jack, and a beaming Jackie at Hyannis Port on her birthday – ten days before the birth of Patrick.

Caroline greets her father at Otis Air Force Base in Massachusetts. On August 7, 1963, Jackie gave birth prematurely to Patrick Bouvier Kennedy, who lived less than forty-eight hours. In the days and weeks that followed, Jack flew back and forth between Washington and Cape Cod as if he could not bear to be parted from Jackie, Caroline, and John.

Caroline, Jack, and Jackie on the *Honey Fitz*. The weekend of August 24–25, 1963, was gray and cold, as a grief-stricken mother and father clutched their surviving children and each other. An international crisis was brewing in Vietnam, and the President's distraction that weekend would have formidable consequences.

Jackie insisted that despite security fears she would walk behind Jack's coffin in the funeral procession in Washington on November 25, 1963. Jack's brothers Bobby and Teddy accompany her.

On December 6, 1963, Jackie leaves the White House with Caroline and John to start a new life without Jack.

the paralysis. Jackie, instead, made a point of reaching for his twisted hand and covering the frozen side of his face with kisses. Her visits, Joe's chauffeur observed, left him 'high as a kite' and her warmth, noted his nurse, did much to help him 'not be ashamed of his condition.'

Back in Washington, the guest list for the dinner dance had swelled to more than one hundred names. These events had become a coveted invitation, and by now everyone in Washington society was angling for one. Finally, Jackie decided that only seventy-five people would actually be given dinner. They included regulars like Lem Billings and the Spaldings, who were also to spend the night at the White House; the Ormsby-Gores and the Alphands, the only foreign ambassadors with entrée as close personal friends; old friends of Jack's such as Flo Smith and Fifi Fell; and other members of the inner circle. At 10 p.m. a second wave of forty guests was to join them for dancing, and on that list was Mary Meyer.

Though the evening had been designed to please Jack, Jackie too enjoyed the respite from the ceaseless tension of the past two months. Eager to be happy, at least for a night, the First Lady was quickly out on the dance floor to do the twist, which was then the rage. Her partners included Averell Harriman and Robert McNamara. Jack ducked in and out of the crowded ground-floor state rooms. Creating a sense of high drama, as he loved to do, he would whisper briefly to someone then vanish for a time, only to reappear and talk in hushed tones to someone else. Before long, all eyes were on the President, and word spread, precisely as he intended it to, that something big was in the works. Finally, he took Ben Bradlee aside – was *Newsweek*'s cover still open? Kennedy insisted he could not yet say what the scoop was, then leaned over to whisper details to his sister Jean.

At any moment, he expected word of a top-secret swap of prisoners at the Glienicker Bridge, which linked East and West Berlin, in which Colonel Rudolf Abel, an East German spy held by the U.S., would be exchanged for U-2 pilot Gary Powers, who had been shot down over the Soviet Union. Each time Kennedy disappeared, it was to seek an update on the

progress of the spy exchange. His pleasure in teasing Bradlee
only to give him the exclusive at last, to the frustration of other
journalists present, was open and unabashed. As it happened,
he was playing two high-stakes games that night, and even
those guests eventually let in on the first would remain in the
dark about the second. For Jack, that was part of the thrill.

Earlier, Betty Spalding, walking with a cane due to a skiing
injury, had gone up to the third floor to rest a stiff, painful hip.
With a noisy party under way two floors below, there was no
one else on the third floor, which housed various guest rooms
as well as Caroline's schoolroom. At length, Betty was making
her way back down to the dance when she was surprised to see
two others arrive upstairs.

'Up comes Jack and Mary Meyer,' Spalding remembered,
'headed for that place where Jackie had a nursery school on
the third floor for the kids. I figured they were going in there
for a little sexual action.' When the couple spotted Betty, they
were completely unfazed, and just kept walking. Two weeks
previously, Jack had slept with Mary when his wife was at Glen
Ora. Now he took matters a significant step further. While
Jackie was downstairs, he slipped off with his lover to the room
where Caroline and her friends attended school. Jackie, for all
her Sisyphean efforts, was back where she had been early in
the marriage when her husband, uninhibited by her presence,
would disappear from parties with women.

Betty's appearance as Jack and Mary headed into the children's schoolroom that night gave Mary an opportunity to
prove her total lack of concern for any standards of behavior.
Many women would have been embarrassed to run into another
woman in such a situation, but not Mary. Now that the chase
was over she had reached the point of maximum danger, when
all her imagination would be needed to keep Jack's interest.
She knew she was not his only lover, but she gave every
indication of making sure she stayed in the front rank. No one
seemed to care if she was a painter, but people would care that
she was the President's mistress, and holding on to that status
became the most important thing to her. Her willingness to
show contempt for Jackie by slipping off with her husband had

been a kind of love call to Jack, a signal that, like him, she was a superior person who did as she pleased. Jack, with his taste for tough, hard-edged party girls, had found precisely what he was looking for in Mary. Judith Campbell had looked and sounded exactly like the moll she was, but Mary, with her fine features and soft blonde hair, looked every inch a lady – until one saw her fail to blink an eyelash at the sight of Betty Spalding.

The brazen encounter with Betty, followed by a quick act of sex in the children's room, was a way to sustain Jack's interest by demonstrating how far she would go. Another mother – for Mary had two children of her own – might have protested at Jack's peculiarly tasteless choice of setting for the tryst. Certainly, there were numerous other third-floor rooms to which he could have led her, had it occurred to him that it might be preferable not to have sex amid children's toys and books. When Mary failed to object, she showed that she was no ordinary mother and that, like Jack, she took her pleasures where and when she wished. Like Cord Meyer and his friends, on whom she had modeled her outlaw persona, she enjoyed shocking people, and the fact that Betty Spalding had spotted them would only have heated things up for Mary. Though Betty's disgusted reaction did not bother Mary, she would not forget it. Mary would lie in wait for the moment when she could signal her contempt for Betty after that silent moment in the hall.

Five days after Jack and Mary disappeared upstairs to the schoolroom together, Jackie gave a small Valentine's Day dinner party at the White House attended by Fifi Fell, the *Manchester Guardian*'s Max Freedman, and the Bradlees. A year after Jackie had reacted so strongly to the story of Harold Macmillan's 'strange' acceptance of a beloved spouse's infidelity, her painful personal circumstances were more like his than ever. Her public role, however, was utterly different from what it had been. After dinner, the Kennedys and their guests watched *A Television Tour of the White House with Mrs John F. Kennedy,* her first major solo performance as First Lady. Taped one month previously, after she returned from caring for Jack's father, the show was aired on all three networks. A year before, Jackie had barely been able to function without her husband. Tonight, though Jack had a cameo role, from first to last the stage was hers as she escorted an estimated twelve million viewers through the newly restored White House to point out all that had been done and was yet to come.

Jackie presented the restored White House as both a source of national pride and, importantly, the emblem of the Kennedy presidency. In a shrewd act of historical appropriation, she used the inspirational symbolism of that great building on behalf of the administration, forever linking them in the minds of many. There had been a time when Jack, perceiving the makings of a political disaster, had feared her taste would be too rarefied for most Americans, but the program proved him wrong. In the days that followed, more than two million dollars in contributions poured in from ordinary citizens captivated by Jackie's vision for the White House. If Jackie still wondered whether she was up to her solo trip abroad, which loomed in March, the reaction to her work on the White House must have shored up her confidence.

She would need every bit of confidence she could muster, given the recent drastic deterioration of U.S. relations with India. Five weeks after Nehru's visit to the U.S., he had ordered an invasion of Goa, a Portuguese colony on India's west coast. At midnight on December 17, 1961, as the Kennedys were winding up their Latin American trip, thirty thousand Indian soldiers had seized Goa, as well as the nearby Portuguese territories of Damao and Diu. Secretary of State Dean Rusk immediately called the Indian ambassador to protest, and at the United Nations Adlai Stevenson demanded a withdrawal. But the most important expression of disapproval came from the President himself. 'The effect of the Goan episode on the relations of our two countries ... has not been good,' Kennedy wrote to Nehru. Citing 'its impact on American opinion,' he hinted that the invasion, coming as it had as a 'shock' to many Americans, could result in a cessation of aid to India. Kennedy insisted he did not wish to see that happen. The criticism infuriated Nehru, and in the three weeks prior to Jackie's visit a wave of anti-U.S. sentiment swept India. When Jackie first agreed to go to India and Pakistan, she had not bargained for anything like this.

Nehru remained fond of the First Lady, of whom he kept a framed photograph, arm in arm with him on the White House lawn, in the entrance hall of his home. He insisted that in New Delhi Jackie stay under his roof, in a suite previously occupied by Edwina Mountbatten, wife of the former Governor General of India, who was reputed to have been Nehru's mistress. Still, there was no telling what sort of anti-U.S. demonstrations or other unpleasantness President Kennedy's wife might encounter in India. The prospect was especially troublesome because of the large international press contingent which followed her everywhere. Their presence ensured that news of even the tiniest demonstration or diplomatic false step on either side would instantly be flashed around the world.

It would be very easy for Jackie to make a misstep, scheduled as she was to go on to Pakistan, India's adversary, for a visit with Nehru's arch-rival, Ayub Khan. The need to avoid making either leader jealous of her attentions to the other required an exceptionally delicate balancing act. All in all, it attested to Jack's confidence in Jackie's diplomatic skills, as well as to her own courage and determination to serve him well, that in the end neither he nor she chose to cancel the trip.

After one final postponement due to a bad cold, Jackie, accompanied by her sister, arrived in New Delhi, via New York and Rome, on Monday, March 12, 1962. She spent the night in a guesthouse provided by the U.S. embassy, before moving to the Prime Minister's residence. For forty-eight intensely demanding hours, she shared five meals, long walks in the garden, and bantering conversation with Nehru, for whom she played the little girl, a role carefully chosen from her repertoire on the basis of their previous encounter. In a moment that typified her strategy, Jackie, who had just displayed matchless courage in Venezuela, went so far as to jump into Nehru's arms at the sight of a snake that danced for its charmer in the garden outside her suite. In the past, she had delivered bravura performances for world leaders, but then she had to be on stage only for bursts of time and always with Jack nearby. In New

Delhi, by contrast, she was required not only to perform full out for days at a stretch, but also to make it appear effortless, as though she were having the time of her life.

From the day after Jackie arrived, the international press was flooded with accounts of glorious banquets and ceremonies, images that encouraged readers to think of the visit as mere play. In fact, because of her mission's highly sensitive political nature, her days, particularly those spent under Nehru's roof, involved a tremendous amount of work. Nehru, well aware that Jackie had been sent to soften him up, relished the skill behind her performance, her ability to effect political ends even as she cast herself as determinedly apolitical.

On March 15, Jackie began five days of travel, and enthusiastic crowds greeted her everywhere. She was cheered, garlanded with flowers, pelted with rice, and sprinkled with rosewater. One ancient woman, withered and toothless, anointed her Goddess of Power. Jack received reports on her progress, and it was evident that Jackie by her very presence did much to take the bitterness out of U.S. relations with India. She, in turn, lamented that Jack could not be with her, especially when she visited the Taj Mahal, built in the seventeenth century by a heartbroken Moghul emperor in memory of the woman he loved. When she returned to New Delhi there was a final gala evening, a dinner at the U.S. embassy to thank her host. In the morning, Nehru accompanied her to the airport and sang her praises to reporters. Henceforth, visitors to his upstairs sitting room observed Jackie's picture displayed alongside those of Mahatma Gandhi, Edwina Mountbatten, Motilal Nehru (his father), and the poet Rabindranath Tagore, the individuals closest to Nehru's heart.

Jackie had no time to savor her success. The very fact that her visit had been so successful required her to make sure that her time in Pakistan went equally well. In Washington, she had been advised to take into account Ayub Khan's acute sensitivity to possible U.S. favoritism toward India. At the same time, she must not offend Nehru with any hint that she enjoyed her visit to Pakistan more. So from the time Ayub met her at the airport in Lahore, the First Lady had to be careful not only of how she actually behaved, but also of how her actions and statements might play in the international press.

Again she crafted a flawless performance. The fragile, flirtatious little girl she affected to be for Nehru simply would not do with Ayub, who demanded something edgier and more romantic. At Mount Vernon, she and Ayub had discovered a shared passion for horses. His Jackie was a bold, fearless equestrian, and in Lahore she instantly fell into character. In the motorcade from the airport, Jackie, rather than sitting demurely, stood side by side with Ayub in the rear of the open car as Jack himself might have done, and the unprecedented air of daring and excitement set the tone for all that followed. At the Governor's Palace, Ayub offered her a flashy, high-spirited bay gelding named Sardar from his stables, and soon the Prince and the First Lady were galloping side by side in a dashing display of horsemanship. Ayub seemed to find her physical courage as enchanting as his rival had found her fragility. At the big party in Lahore that night, he paid tribute with a pearl necklace set with diamonds, rubies, and emeralds. That was only the first gift. Moments later, a fantastically costumed groom led out Sardar and presented him to Jackie.

In Washington, Jack was delighted by the fact that Jackie had been able to play two such colossal egos as Nehru and Ayub against each other in a manner that permitted both men to emerge happy. Glowing reports from John Kenneth Galbraith and Walter McConaughy, the U.S. ambassadors in India and Pakistan respectively, delighted the President.

As usual, gratitude for her efforts did nothing to cramp his style. On the very day Jackie had lamented his absence at the Taj Mahal, he had had a rendezvous with Mary Meyer in the White House. And even as Jackie was excitedly wiring home about Sardar, Jack was preoccupied with Judith Campbell. Over lunch with the President on March 22, F.B.I. Director J. Edgar Hoover had disclosed that Campbell, not the first woman whose involvement with Kennedy he had had occasion to monitor, had significant ties to the Mafia. Kennedy's bitter dealings with Hoover dated back to the war, when the F.B.I. had found out about his affair with the suspected Nazi spy Inga

Arvad. In later years, Hoover's files had overflowed with reports of Kennedy's 'extracurricular activities,' often with prostitutes.

What made the Campbell affair stand out was her simultaneous involvement with Sam Giancana, a target of the F.B.I.'s Top Hoodlum Program since 1958. Could it have been merely coincidental that one individual, Frank Sinatra, had introduced Judith to both Kennedy and Giancana? Sinatra was known to wish to ingratiate himself with the Mafia, as well as to boast of personal influence with the Kennedys, so it would have come as no surprise had he acted at Giancana's instigation. But what would Giancana's motive have been? Did he hope to blackmail the President? Did he seek immunity from federal prosecution?

In Jackie's absence, Kennedy had planned to spend the weekend of March 24–25 at Sinatra's compound in Palm Springs, California, but the Attorney General, incensed by the possibility that Sinatra had set his brother up, urged Jack to cancel his visit. Jack obliged by arranging to go instead to Bing Crosby's estate in Palm Desert. As for Campbell, the President, confronted with evidence from White House logs of seventy instances of phone contact, called her for the last time after his lunch with Hoover and broke things off.

Still fuming over Hoover, Kennedy left town as planned the next day. Jackie had wired to advise him to see Indira Gandhi in Washington that weekend, but Jack replied that he had to be in California, though he didn't say why. He spoke at the University of California at Berkeley, was briefed on the missile program at Vandenburg Air Force Base, then flew to Palm Springs with Dave Powers that night. He kept his promise and pointedly avoided both Sinatra and Campbell, yet it quickly became apparent that he was not going to abandon the behavior that threatened his presidency. It is possible that he had no idea what he was getting into when he started an affair with Judith Campbell. But there can be no doubt that he knew exactly what he was doing when he arranged for Peter Lawford to bring Marilyn Monroe to the Crosby estate. He had first encountered Monroe on his trip to California in November, and seen her again at a party in New York in December. Judith

Campbell was unknown to the public at large. Marilyn was one of the most celebrated women in the world. And it was no secret, certainly not to someone who devoured *Variety* and anything else to do with the movie business, as Jack did — and certainly not to the brother-in-law and carousing partner of Marilyn's friend Peter Lawford — that she was very sick.

One year previously, Marilyn's confinement in a New York psychiatric hospital following the end of her turbulent marriage to Arthur Miller had made international headlines. After her release, she had reverted to drink and drugs, and she had been on a downward slide ever since. In reaction to Miller's remarriage, on February 17, Marilyn had consumed an enormous quantity of pills and alcohol. Two and a half weeks before Lawford delivered her to Kennedy, she had appeared at the Golden Globe Awards drunk, drugged, and disheveled. This was the woman, recently diagnosed as a 'borderline paranoid addict,' with whom Kennedy spent a night in Palm Desert, though the Director of the F.B.I. had just put him on notice to watch his step or jeopardize the presidency.

While in Palm Desert, the President was entertained in a very different way by Jackie's further telegrams on the matter of Sardar. She sounded as if nothing on earth mattered more to her than that horse. Her pleas for special treatment, including permission to forgo the customary quarantine, amused rather than irritated Jack. He had relished the headstrong Kick when she demanded her way no matter what, and similarly delighted in Jackie at her most spirited and stubborn. Jack and Jackie loved to tease each other, and he responded with a long, comical telegram of his own to assure her that the government had dropped all its other work on domestic and international affairs in order to devote full-time attention to Sardar.

This affectionate raillery aside, Jack remained serious about Jackie's accomplishments in India and Pakistan. He, more than most, knew that her difficult and important diplomatic mission had been anything but the jetsetter's holiday depicted in some press reports. Instead of merely coming to Andrews Air Force Base with the children when Jackie flew in from London on the night of Thursday, March 29, he surprised her with an official reception committee, complete with receiving line, worthy of a returning diplomat. Fiercely protective despite all he himself did to hurt her, Kennedy had found a way to convey just how highly he valued her work of the past three weeks.

Faced with a crowded spring schedule which would conclude with a trip to Mexico, Jackie lingered at Glen Ora with the children for a week before the annual Congressional Reception on the evening of April 10. The previous year's party had coincided with the unfolding Bay of Pigs invasion, and Jack had yet to recover from his blunder. Now, lest that humiliation be forgotten, a Cuban military tribunal, ignoring pleas for clemency from the Organization of American States and several Latin American leaders, had sentenced the prisoners held since the attack to thirty years of hard labor and set a ransom of $60 million. When Dr Miró Cardona, chairman of the Cuban Revolutionary Council, asked for an opportunity to discuss the matter, Kennedy invited the exile leader to an off-the-record meeting in the family quarters before the Congressional Reception. Jackie returned to find her husband faced with the sad task of breaking the news that the U.S. could not permit itself to be forced to negotiate with Castro or pay a ransom. She took Caroline out to ride her pony while Jack had his difficult talk upstairs.

They were still on the South Lawn when Jack, having finished his discussion with Cardona, went to the Oval Office to see Roger Blough, chairman of the U.S. Steel Corporation, who had requested an urgent appointment. The President, concerned that a rise in steel prices would trigger inflation, had been working with industry leaders to make sure that did not happen. He had put his prestige on the line and persuaded the unions to limit their wage demands in order to permit management to hold down prices. On April 6 and 7, the last of those contracts had been signed, and Kennedy had thought that his dealings with Big Steel, as the industry giants were known, were at an end.

When Blough announced that U.S. Steel had raised its price by six dollars per ton, or 3.5 percent, Kennedy was furious, convinced that U.S. Steel had used him to persuade the workers to cut back their demands then played him for a patsy. 'He fucked me,' the President said afterward to Arthur Goldberg, who had personally handled the delicate negotiations with the unions. 'They've fucked us and we've got to try to fuck them.' His aides also took the price rise as a personal insult. Theodore Sorensen, for one, later called it 'an affront to the office of the Presidency and to the man who held it.'

Fresh from his meeting with Cardona, Kennedy had been hit with an unpleasant reminder of the extent to which the Bay of Pigs fiasco had hobbled his presidency. U.S. Steel would never have dared to double-cross a strong leader. The administration, in Bobby Kennedy's view, could not afford to lose this one. If they could force the steel companies to back down, it would be a first significant step toward the real power and authority that had eluded this presidency for the past year. But how were they to do it? That was the question that absorbed the President as, convinced the event must be jinxed and vowing never to preside over another, he changed into black tie for the Congressional Reception.

On the anniversary of the Bay of Pigs, Kennedy, recalled Clark Clifford, did not wish 'to lose a public struggle that would reveal him to be weak.' Thus the admittedly 'tough' plan of attack he and Bobby soon devised. In March, the President had been outraged when J. Edgar Hoover once again intruded on his personal life. Now, a little less than three weeks later, he emulated the F.B.I. Director in his dealings with the steel barons. The idea was to dig up dirt, to look into the records of top executives in order to learn who had been with them on business trips. Unfaithful to Jackie as Kennedy habitually was, he set out to discover evidence of his adversaries' infidelity to their wives. He explained the strategy to Under-Secretary of the Navy Red Fay: 'Do you know what you're doing when you start bucking the power of the President of the United States? ... Do you want the government to go back to hotel bills that time you were in Schenectady to find who was with you? Too many hotel bills and night club expenses would be hard to get by the weekly wives' bridge group out at the Country Club.'

Kennedy went on television to criticize the price hikes, and in the days that followed there was huge public pressure on U.S. Steel, as well as Bethlehem Steel, which had joined them, to back down. There was the specter of antitrust proceedings and a probe of market practices, but Kennedy's most powerful weapon was the threat to expose embarrassing aspects of certain executives' private lives. Not long after F.B.I. agents, on Bobby's orders, swept in to seize business and personal records, the steel companies capitulated. They reversed the price increase and the administration experienced its first big – though ruthlessly accomplished – win.

The week after the steel crisis, the Kennedys flew to Palm Beach to spend Easter with Joe, who was scheduled to begin an intensive rehabilitation program in New York the following month. Jackie remained with him when her husband returned to the White House on April 27 for a round of talks with Macmillan. As Lady Dorothy was not on this trip, it was agreed that there was no need for Jackie until the last day.

For Macmillan, the four months since the Bermuda Conference had been disappointing ones. He had appealed to Kennedy for a new peace initiative, and on February 7, 1962, the leaders had written jointly to Khrushchev. Echoing the language that Macmillan had used with Kennedy, together they invited Khrushchev to join them in accepting 'a common measure of personal obligation to seek every avenue to restrain and reverse the mounting arms race.' Macmillan hoped Khrushchev would respond in time to prevent the U.S. from resuming its own nuclear tests. When Khrushchev did reply, his answer, proposing that the three heads of state go to Geneva to open negotiations, was not what Macmillan had hoped. Fearing that unless their respective foreign ministers had made some concrete progress first, a summit could turn out to be nothing but an empty show, Britain and the U.S. declined. Khrushchev angrily replied that they weren't really interested in progress on disarmament so much as in diverting blame for the resumption of U.S. tests. The charges prompted Kennedy to answer in a February 24 letter to Khrushchev, written without consultation with Macmillan. On March 2, Kennedy publicly announced that the U.S. would resume testing in late April.

Macmillan was furious that Kennedy had failed to consult him before responding to Khrushchev. At first, he contemplated confronting Kennedy to tell him he must do what was right and not give in to political considerations. 'Eisenhower did not bother so much about the politicians,' Macmillan railed in private. 'He did what he thought was right ... But Kennedy came up through Congress and he is much more conscious of political pressures. Of course, it is true that he cannot get a treaty through unless the Senate agrees.' In the end, there was no confrontation. Instead, even after tests had been announced, Macmillan persuaded Kennedy to make one final joint appeal to Khrushchev, in a letter dated April 9. The effort failed, and two days before Macmillan was due in Washington, the U.S. resumed tests at Christmas Island.

Since the Bermuda Conference, there had been some temporary discord between the allies – notably Macmillan's distress at the February 24 letter, as well as his sense that Kennedy was driven by strictly political considerations – and the Prime Minister was left with a sense of personal failure when U.S. tests resumed. Yet the fact remained that Macmillan had exerted immense influence over Kennedy, who had repeatedly agreed to reach out jointly to Khrushchev. Clearly, the meeting had had a huge impact, and not everyone in Washington was happy about it. Such had been the Prime Minister's influence in the past four months that, prior to his visit on April 27–29, various members of the State Department did their best to persuade Kennedy to pull back.

Briefing papers drafted by Joseph Sweeney, Officer in Charge of United Kingdom–Ireland Affairs, and cleared with Secretary of State Dean Rusk, Under-Secretary George Ball, Acting Assistant Secretary of State William Tyler, and others, took a patronizing tone toward Macmillan, who was portrayed as a dotty, much diminished leader whose opinions were not to be taken very seriously: 'Our purpose in the Washington talks with the President and the British Prime Minister is clear. We want to be friendly toward the Prime Minister who is under emotional strain on disarmament and hard pressed politically. We want to listen to his views with sympathetic understanding ... We want him to leave Washington without having induced us to modify our views, but with a satisfied feeling that he has had a very worthwhile and pleasant exchange. The British need these discussions and we do not ... They may attempt to attach greater importance to these talks than we do.' That was the State Department speaking. Much to its chagrin, the President attached tremendous importance to the talks and took what Macmillan had to say very seriously indeed.

Kennedy and Macmillan first met privately, which, as they had discovered at Key West thirteen months previously, allowed them to talk freely and frankly. In this case, the arrangement allowed them to decide where they wanted the meetings to go before they joined their advisers. Kennedy's opening remarks in the Cabinet Room, followed by those of Macmillan, made it abundantly clear that they had already discussed and pretty much worked out the large issues. Essentially, they were reporting on their joint decisions to their aides, including Rusk, Ball, Tyler, Sweeney, and others on the U.S. side who opposed Macmillan's influence. Kennedy and Macmillan agreed on the dangers of a premature summit meeting, though the Prime Minister emphasized that 'we should not lose contact with this strange character,' as he called Khrushchev. Both leaders hoped that Khrushchev might yet relent on the crucial matter of inspections – long a sticking point – without which any meaningful treaty was impossible. 'The whole thing changes at a word from Khrushchev,' Macmillan declared. 'The thing is to get to him.' So far, unfortunately, they had not.

Jackie returned in time to have Macmillan to lunch in the family quarters on Sunday, the last day of the visit. At a moment when her husband was under pressure to distance himself from the British, she made a point of emphasizing the personal nature of the connection by inviting, besides the Prime Minister himself, only David and Sissie Ormsby-Gore. That afternoon, with warmth and affection on both sides, Kennedy and Macmillan discussed many topics, from the politicians that each had to deal with domestically to the books they happened to be reading. Jack had just finished Barbara Tuchman's *The Guns of August*, an examination of the misjudgments that had led to the First World War, and a good part of the conversation was devoted to it. As he fondly watched the President and the Prime Minister talk as they would 'in their own houses with their best friends,' Ormsby-Gore, in the unique position of being close to both leaders, was struck that Jackie's intimate lunch seemed to have 'really set the seal on their friendship.' It was her gift always to know just what to do with the people who meant most to Jack.

On Tuesday, May 8, Jackie was expected in Groton, Connecticut, to christen a submarine. She took the opportunity to travel to New York a day early, in order to surprise Jack's father on the occasion of his first attempt to walk on his own. In a display of the monstrous will that had driven him all his life, Joe had battled relentlessly to speak and move in however limited a fashion, though he often felt angry and dispirited by the excruciatingly slow pace of progress. To make matters worse, he was often an uncooperative patient. Such was the case when, before Jackie came in, the doctor urged Joe to walk, and Joe's face reddened as he screamed, 'No, no, no.' Defiantly he seized the hook-handled, hospital-issue cane and hurled it at the wall. At length, Joe grudgingly accepted the cane, but as he began to rise he heard a familiar breathy voice.

Astonished, Joe fell back into his wheelchair as Jackie ran to kiss him. 'I heard you were going to walk today,' Jackie said, 'and I just had to come.' She knelt and Joe, fighting tears, held her with his functional left arm. But the tears were not to be suppressed, and Jackie, declaring how very proud of him she was, patted his and her own eyes with a handkerchief. 'Aren't we foolish?' she laughed, before signaling to one of her two Secret Service men. The agent produced a long, thin mailing tube, and Jackie challenged Joe to guess what it contained. Out slipped an elegant, shiny black walking stick with a formidable silver head. Jackie had guessed that the impressive walking stick, a reminder of better days, would make Joe feel good about himself.

Clutching her gift, Joe attempted to stand. His therapist, taken by surprise, moved to catch him, but the First Lady signaled to leave him alone. She hooked her arm in Joe's, kissed the distorted side of his face and announced it was time for a walk. As they made their way up and down the corridor, Jackie, full of praise, promised he could do it. When the doctor feared his patient might have attempted too much, Joe refused to stop. With Jackie there, he propelled himself beyond the point anyone had thought possible.

When he returned to his wheelchair, Jackie knelt and reminisced about the many times he had pushed them all to win. She kissed his hands and declared that he had had his own victory today. On the verge of tears, she hugged him and announced, 'You are a magnificent man.' As she left, Jackie, still struggling with her emotions, nodded to staff members rather than speaking. From the very beginning, Joe, in his own exceedingly peculiar way, had been the one who looked out for her. Now, she gracefully slid into the role of his protector.

NINE

Eyes in the Portraits

A Secret Service supervisor came down the hall at the White House in search of agent Larry Newman, then assigned to protect the President. It was Newman's skill as a tennis player that was required, and it wasn't the President he was to work for, but the First Lady.

'I can't do this,' Newman grumbled.

'Yes you can.'

Before long Clint Hill, an agent who regularly guarded Mrs Kennedy, appeared with a tennis racket and a can of balls, and Newman, still dressed in his blue suit and wingtip shoes, went to collect her.

'I just want to rally,' said Jackie as they walked to the tennis court. She neither commented on the obvious fact that the young man was inappropriately dressed nor made any attempt at small talk. Agents weren't supposed to initiate conversations with a President or First Lady, but Jackie more than most created 'an aura around her' that ruled out any such contact. Something about the way she moved and looked made her seem 'rigidly in control of the space around her.' Clearly, one violated that space at one's peril. And the Secret Service man noticed something else at close range. Though seemingly self-absorbed, Jackie missed little. 'She was introspective,' he observed, 'but her antennae were out there.'

The tennis court was on the South Grounds, where Newman loosened his tie and stripped off his jacket. Then he removed his .38 and, lest it frighten her, hid the revolver under his jacket on the bench. They walked out onto the court and soon Newman, slipping and sliding in his wingtips, and sweating

profusely due to the humidity, was rallying with the First Lady.
The image is comical on the one hand, but it also highlights
Jackie's terrible isolation in Washington. In the following
months, she would spend many hours playing tennis with a
young man to whom she was barely required to speak. Newman
was one of the agents who, in Seattle a few months before, had
watched unhappily as Dave Powers ushered two prostitutes into
the President's suite. That and subsequent experiences with
Kennedy helped form his attitude to the First Lady, to whose
detail he was soon transferred. 'We had a lot of feeling for
Jackie because we knew she was kind of walking uphill on this
whole thing,' Newman recalled. 'I just never felt good about
denigrating a woman that way.' When he began to escort Jackie
to Glen Ora, Newman, who knew what went on in the White
House pool or family quarters as soon as she left, lived in fear
that she would suddenly ask to turn back en route. The Secret
Service man was forever picturing himself on the radio alerting
the other agents that Mrs Kennedy was on her way back.

Newman did not believe that Jackie, as she sometimes liked
to pretend, was unaware of what her husband was up to. 'Jackie
had her sources in the White House,' Newman explained. 'It's
like a hotel or a business, everybody knows what's going on.'
Still, impressed by her dignity, he and the other agents took
it upon themselves to shield her as much as possible from
embarrassment and hurt. 'She was a person you wanted to
protect,' Newman reflected. 'We didn't feel sorry for her, but
we liked her because she to us at that time was what a First
Lady should be.'

It was no secret at the White House that of all the social
events staged by Jackie, the one in which she had the greatest
personal stake was the dinner in honor of André Malraux on
Friday, May 11, 1962. That Malraux had responded so strongly
to Jackie in Paris meant the world to her. In the months since
he had accepted an invitation to the U.S., she had worked and
planned tirelessly to be certain that the visit confirmed his
estimate of her intellect and taste. At a dinner party given by
the Wrightsmans in January, she had confessed to Hervé
Alphand that she feared Malraux would be bored in Wash-

ington. Alphand suggested that she put together an evening of the very finest American artists whom her guest might hope to meet. When Jackie worried whether it might be best to invite only those who spoke French, Alphand urged her to do nothing of the kind. All she needed to do was fill the White House with luminaries, and Malraux would be thrilled.

That day, Malraux accompanied Jackie to the National Gallery of Art in Washington, and, as they had at the Musée du Jeu de Paume, the Minister of Cultural Affairs and the First Lady animatedly discussed art history. Later, at the White House, she introduced him to some of America's most distinguished artists – a list on which she had worked for months. There were the novelists Robert Penn Warren and Saul Bellow, the poet Archibald MacLeish, and the critic Edmund Wilson. Franz Kline, Andrew Wyeth, and Mark Rothko represented painting, Leonard Bernstein music, and George Balanchine dance. From the theater came Tennessee Williams, Elia Kazan, and Arthur Miller (accompanied by his new wife). At the First Lady's table, Malraux sat on one side of Jackie, Marilyn Monroe's craggy-faced former husband on the other. Jackie presided over the evening looking radiantly happy in a shocking pink strapless silk dress that bared her beautiful shoulders.

After dinner, the violinist Isaac Stern, accompanied by Eugene Istomin on the piano and Leonard Rose on the cello, performed in the East Room. At previous White House concerts, Jack had been known to burst into applause at the wrong moment. On two occasions, during a pause between movements, Jack rushed on stage to thank the musician, who whispered frantically that more was to come. Lest Jack embarrass himself in front of Malraux, a code was devised whereby an aide opened a door to signal that the performance had indeed ended.

The Malraux dinner reiterated that the White House vigorously supported the arts, but it was also the case that Jackie brilliantly used the arts to lend prestige to her husband's presidency. Malraux himself understood just how profoundly she had been transformed by her visit to Paris, and how much an evening such as this owed to that experience. Late that night, he signaled approval by whispering in her ear an offer to allow the *Mona Lisa*, the jewel of the Louvre's collection and a particular favorite of Jackie's, to be exhibited at the National Gallery of Art in January. As Jackie well knew, the *Mona Lisa* never traveled. To send it to Washington would be a spectacular gesture of affection and respect for the First Lady.

Jackie was in an exceptionally good mood when she decided to ride in the Loudon County horse show the following weekend. Sardar had finally arrived, and she was eager to show him off. No sooner did she announce those plans, however, than Jack suggested that her participation would somehow embarrass the administration. Press pictures of her in elegantly tailored riding clothes, surrounded by all the obvious signs of wealth at such an event, might alienate many voters. Repeatedly, Jackie had proven her effectiveness on his behalf, and he had had every indication that the American people, far from being put off, were proud of her elegance and glamor, yet for some reason he reverted to his old view of her as a political liability. He went so far as to consult National Security Adviser McGeorge Bundy about whether her appearance might be a public relations disaster.

Bundy laughed off the President's anxiety, which was indeed ridiculous, especially when he was on the point of participating in a public event that really would endanger the administration, as well as embarrass his wife deeply. On the same day as Jackie's event in Loudon County, Saturday, May 19, there was to be a Democratic Party fundraiser at Madison Square Garden to pay off Kennedy's campaign debt. It took the form of a party – ten days in advance of Kennedy's forty-fifth birthday – and, in addition to various other entertainers, Peter Lawford had asked Marilyn Monroe to attend.

Jack, delighted at the prospect of being publicly serenaded by the sex goddess, overlooked the inevitability of scandal on account of Marilyn's much-publicized troubles with her film studio. Twentieth Century–Fox, notified of her intention to appear at the Kennedy gala, informed her lawyer that she would be in breach of contract if she took time away from director George Cukor's *Something's Got to Give*, a production already badly behind schedule. It was a foregone conclusion that the President's name would be dragged into any court action, so this was something Kennedy should have steered clear of from the first.

Marilyn's problems at Fox pointed to an even worse error in judgment in recruiting her for the gala. The absences that had stalled Cukor's production were due in large part to her extremely fragile state of mind. Marilyn, who had attempted suicide many times in the past, had been found in a drug coma as recently as April 11. She would finally succeed in taking her own life less than three months after the event at Madison Square Garden. Though no one could have anticipated exactly when and if Marilyn would manage to kill herself, it was evident even to casual observers that she was a walking time-bomb.

It was one thing for Kennedy to bring such a woman to a private house in Palm Desert, but quite another to put her on stage in front of television cameras with no way to control what she would say or do. Nonetheless, shortly before noon on Thursday, May 17, Peter Lawford, representing the President of the United States, collected Marilyn from the Fox lot and personally escorted her to New York. During rehearsals, Kennedy was informed by a nervous production person that Marilyn's interpretation of 'Happy Birthday' was likely to be over-the-top. He laughed, saying that she should sing it any way she liked. He would soon have reason to regret those words.

On the day of the gala, Jackie rode in the Loudon County horse show with none of the adverse public reaction her husband had feared. Later, much would be made of her absence from Madison Square Garden, as though somehow it had been a comment on Marilyn, an expression of disapproval. In fact, Jackie almost never accompanied her husband to party political events, and there is no indication that anyone ever considered that she might be present at Madison Square Garden.

In the course of the evening, Lawford, as master of cere-monies, made a running joke of Marilyn's legendary lateness. Finally, she slithered into the blinding spotlight, wearing a white fur and a dress so tight she could barely cross the stage. Geisha-like, she approached the microphone at the front, and as she threw off her fur appeared almost naked in a gauzy flesh-toned dress embroidered with rhinestones. She flicked the mike with one fingernail, then, shielding heavy-lidded eyes with both hands, searched the audience of fifteen thousand for Jack.

Her performance was funny to many, but in ways most viewers could not have suspected Marilyn was enacting a painful personal drama. Devastated by Arthur Miller's recent remarriage, she was sending a message to the celebrated playwright and political hero: If you don't want me anymore, Kennedy (whom she knew Miller admired) does. To be sure that Miller watched, Marilyn, always the strategist, had drafted her aged former father-in-law, Isadore Miller, to escort her to the gala.

The moment Marilyn started to sing, it became apparent she was high. She closed her eyes, she licked her lips, she ran her hands up her thighs and over her stomach, aborting the gesture at her breasts. All the while, her trademark breathy singing voice made 'Happy Birthday' seem lewd. This was the second part of her message to Miller. Marilyn had struggled to reinvent herself as a serious actress, she had longed to be a good, decent wife and mother, and yet here she was right back where she had been when he first met her, a sexual joke, a powerful man's erotic toy. Marilyn's performance was the desperate scream of a dying woman. Its other intended audience was Ralph Greenson, her psychiatrist, who, on vacation in Europe, seemed to have abandoned her. To the psychiatrist, as to the ex-husband, Marilyn declared by her actions: See how bad I can be now that you have left me.

After 'Happy Birthday,' Marilyn sang Kennedy's praises to the tune of 'Thanks for the Memory':

> *Thanks, Mr President,*
> *For all the things you've done,*
> *The battles that you've won,*
> *The way you deal with U.S. Steel,*
> *And our problems by the ton.*
> *We thank you so much.*

After the Bay of Pigs and other missteps, Jackie had bought time for him to bring off his first big win – over U.S. Steel. His very public prize was Marilyn.

Kennedy and Lawford must have known that Marilyn would create a sensation, and no doubt the riskiness of the enterprise excited the President. But they had failed to calculate just how far Marilyn would go, or the impact she would have. Broadway columnist Dorothy Kilgallen, commenting on the telecast, described her act as 'making love to the President in direct view of forty million Americans.' Had someone less celebrated performed as Marilyn did, it probably would have been quickly forgotten. But the possibility of sparks between the sex goddess and the President instantly captured the popular imagination. On stage afterward, when Kennedy joked that he could now 'retire from politics after having had "Happy Birthday" sung to me in such a sweet, wholesome way,' there was more than a touch of ruefulness in the humor.

In the past, Kennedy and his father had shrugged off suggestions that his adulteries might be exposed. For all the whispers, all the rumors true and false, nothing substantial had yet materialized in the press. The gala finally put a recognizable public face on all that people had heard, guessed, or imagined about Kennedy's womanizing. Many months of gossip and speculation coalesced in the vivid image of Marilyn Monroe, who, mythical creature that she was, came to stand in the popular imagination for all the President's women. She and Kennedy had met for the first time six months previously and in the interim spent only a few hours together, including their night in Palm Desert, yet such was the suggestive power of her Madison Square Garden performance that rumors soon abounded, and persist to this day, of a relationship of many years' standing.

The huge interest in Marilyn's performance made it seem possible that whispers of a priapic presidency were about to find their way into print. Kennedy's decision to put her on that stage dared journalists to look into his sex life, and now the first order of business was to stop any stories. It appears to have bothered him not at all to lie about whether he had slept with Marilyn. Among the people he turned to for help was William Haddad, Inspector General of the Peace Corps. Formerly a *New York Post* reporter, Haddad had extensive press contacts. 'See the editors,' Kennedy instructed him. 'Tell them you are speaking for me and that it's just not true.'

Following the Saturday night gala, Kennedy spent the better part of Sunday in New York. He gave speeches, attended a reception at the mayor's residence, and squeezed in two visits to his father at the rehabilitation center. It was half past seven when *Air Force One* returned to Washington. Instead of going directly to the White House, he boarded a helicopter for Glen Ora. He returned alone Monday morning, with Jackie due that evening in anticipation of the season's last state dinner the next day. At the White House, there were repeated calls from Marilyn, eager for the President to invite her to Washington. Needy, desperate, and unstable, Marilyn, who was known to keep calling at all hours of the day and night until she got what she wanted, was nothing if not persistent.

'He wanted to stop it,' recalled Senator George Smathers, 'because it got to be to a point where it was somewhat embarrassing.' Finally, Kennedy sent Bill Thompson, one of his procurers, to Los Angeles to try to control her. From then on he made a point of refusing Marilyn's calls, and at length she got the message. 'She stopped bothering him,' said Senator Smathers, 'because he quit talking to her.'

Jackie, in keeping with her policy, 'If you ignore it, you're above it,' arrived on schedule and appeared at her husband's side all week as though Marilyn's performance had never occurred. Yet to some observers, thoughts of Marilyn were unavoidable when Jackie presided over the state dinner for President and Mrs Félix Houphouët-Boigny of the Ivory Coast wearing a white, floor-length strapless gown adorned with silver sparkles and crystal beading that curiously evoked the movie star's glittering costume at the gala. Wednesday, Jackie went to a lunch for Senate wives, and Thursday night again she appeared in public with Jack at President Houphouët-Boigny's dinner in their honor at the Mayflower Hotel. Then she returned to Glen Ora where, on Tuesday, May 29, she gave a family birthday party for Jack.

At a moment when half the world seemed to be speculating about Kennedy's relationship with Marilyn Monroe, it was his dealings with the increasingly erratic Max Jacobson that were fast becoming a topic of great concern in the family. Certainly, Jacobson's displays of paranoia were cause for alarm. Convinced he was being spied on, he insisted that the paintings in the White House were 'bugged.' Once, as he walked from the West Wing to the elevator that led to the family quarters, he raved, in the presence of several agents, that the Secret Service had 'eyes in the portraits' and that men 'in the wall' monitored his every word. On another occasion, Jacobson marched up to a White House policeman, indicated a portrait and demanded, 'Is that one bugged too?'

Jacobson's utter lack of discretion had also become a serious problem. He never tired of boasting of his connection to the Kennedys, and in one instance he actually convinced Kennedy, then in New York, to drive past his office at an appointed hour so that certain patients could see that the President was indeed one of them. Given to feelings of persecution exacerbated by his own considerable drug use, Jacobson flew into a temper and offered to resign when, after the birthday party, Bobby demanded a sample of the drugs Jacobson was regularly pumping into the President and First Lady. As Jacobson refused to say what was in the shots, Bobby planned to have the sample tested in an F.B.I. laboratory. The President assured Jacobson that he would be kept on no matter what the tests disclosed.

By this time, Jackie, too, was devoted to Dr Feel Good, and never perhaps was the reason clearer than on the evening of Friday, June 1, 1962, at the last private dinner dance of the White House social season. The First Lady had organized the black-tie evening as a gesture of thanks to John Kenneth Galbraith for his kindness in India. Fifty-one guests, less than half the number who attended February's dinner dance, occupied six round tables. Jack, clearly enjoying himself immensely, shared Table Six with Flo Smith (a former flame who never failed to make him roar with laughter), Bill Walton, television news

executive Blair Clark, and other friends. But it was Table Four
that offered a bracing picture of the dismal fate Jackie had
spent years trying to avoid. For all the humiliation she had
suffered at Jack's hands, she had done everything in her power
at least to be spared the lot of Rose Kennedy, who had been
forced to sit with Joe's mistresses at her own table. Tonight, the
presence at the First Lady's table of Mary Meyer, who at the
last dinner dance had slipped off with Jack to his daughter's
schoolroom, proved that Jackie had definitively lost that struggle.

As soon as the social season was over, Jackie fled Washington.
She had put her personal stamp on the White House and it
had provided the setting for some of her greatest triumphs, yet
its association with Jack's cheating caused her to loathe the
place. On Wednesday, June 6, accompanied by Secret Service
agents Clint Hill and Larry Newman, she spent three days in
New York, where she attended the theater, dined at Le Club
with Truman Capote, and saw Dr Jacobson.

One could always tell when Jackie had just had an injection
by the way she intermittently licked her lips. Her drug use had
escalated to the point where she wanted shots all the time, even
when alone on a private trip that involved no official duties.
She did not, however, visit Jacobson's office near the Carlyle.
'He would go sit in the lobby of the hotel until he got a call
and then he would go up,' Newman recalled. Jacobson's role
in the First Lady's life distressed her Secret Service agents, who
worried that in the event of a Congressional inquiry they would
be asked why they had permitted such a person upstairs even
though he was Mrs Kennedy's guest.

'We knew he was going up to see her and giving her shots,'
Newman remembered. 'But that wasn't our call.' The agents
did, however, make a point of subtly harassing Jacobson. They
stared stonily and addressed him disrespectfully. 'Once in a
while we checked his valise just to give him a hard time,' said
Newman. 'Of course, there was just a bunch of bottles in there.
It looked like he made Kool Aid in different shades. We just
looked in it like we were looking for a gun. We didn't really
talk to him. It's in the air, like between animals. He knew we
didn't like him.' But the First Lady liked – or at least needed –

Jacobson very much, and in the end that was all that mattered.

Jackie spent the better part of the month at Glen Ora. On Wednesday, June 27, she returned to the White House for two nights before the state visit to Mexico, her last major official duty before the summer. In conjunction with U.S. plans to undermine Castro – a covert operation authorized the previous November under the code name Operation Mongoose – the President and First Lady's three days in Mexico were expressly designed to shake the Cuban leader's confidence by creating an impression, through extensive pro-Kennedy demonstrations organized by the U.S. State Department, that Mexico, far from being a Cuban ally, was in fact 'solidly with the United States and the West.' Addressing the Mexican people in Spanish, Jackie continued her effort, begun at Mount Vernon, to counter the impression of the U.S. as opposed to revolution and social progress *per se*. The effect of her nationally televised talk, a State Department observer reported back to Washington, was 'astounding.'

Her trip, the finale of nine months' work on her husband's behalf, had real personal significance as well. In those months, not only had Jackie immeasurably helped Jack, she had also carved out the big, interesting life she had coveted early in her marriage, before Jack's constant adulteries forced her to step back. At last, all her talents were being called on in the service of something important. But even as her political partnership with Jack neared a state of perfection, the escalating chaos of their private life robbed her of what should have been a wonderfully happy moment. Jackie had long coped with her circumstances by spending many hours alone and out of sight. Starting with Paris, she had accepted a far more public life, and by the time she returned from Mexico she was desperate to retreat.

That she was especially tense and on edge became clear early on the evening of Friday, July 6, when she and the children, after a week at Camp David, traveled to Andrews Air Force Base, where they were to meet the President in anticipation of flying up to Cape Cod together on *Air Force One*. A thick curtain separated the white cap's passenger compartment from the

cockpit, where Larry Newman sat with the Marine pilot. Before
the flight, Jackie had stipulated that, in order to avoid the press
at Andrews, she wanted the chopper to touch down at *Air Force
One*'s tail. That way she could get Caroline and John on board
without being photographed.

Her orders made perfect sense to Newman, who, based on
extensive personal observation, had concluded she was 'the
mother of all mothers with those children.' He understood and
respected her wish to shield them from publicity, and instructed
the pilot to obey her wishes. At the same time, the Secret
Service man's priority was to ensure her and the children's
physical safety, so he listened carefully when, moments before
landing, the pilot pointed out a problem.

'Sir, we've got some wind here off the ground. I'm going to
have to put her down in front.'

'What's the safest bet?' asked Newman.

'In front.'

'Do it,' said Newman.

Soon, the chopper was safely on the ground – in front of *Air
Force One*. Newman opened the curtain and entered the passenger compartment to explain the change. What he saw and
heard took him by surprise. The First Lady, usually so polite
and reserved, had turned into a harridan. Stamping with rage,
she cursed and swore. 'She chewed me out,' recalled Newman,
'up one side and down the other. I mean it was bloody blue!'

'It's not the pilot's fault,' the agent declared. 'I did it. The
other landing was insecure.'

Jackie, unappeased, continued to swear. She didn't care about
safety. She didn't want to hear about the wind. All she cared
about was that her orders had been disobeyed, and she and the
children would have to cross the tarmac in sight of the press.

Her outburst was part of a pattern of unease with her Secret
Service agents all that July. At the Cape, Jackie used every
opportunity to push her protectors back. She demanded that
their follow-up car stay at a greater distance from her own. She
objected to a follow-up boat when she water-skied. 'Drowning,'
she said tartly, 'is my responsibility.' She insisted that the agent
on the pier stand further back, where she couldn't see him. She

refused to be shadowed closely in town. She laid down the law, and her list went on and on. A good many of her complaints concerned the children, but at heart the problem seems to have been that Jackie herself could no longer bear to be watched by these men who knew exactly what her husband did in her absence. Worse, by this time they also knew something else. With the men in her detail, it was impossible to pretend, as she did with certain of her husband's male friends, to be beyond hurt with Jack. The agents could see the truth for themselves. They saw her rush out to join him on the beach. They saw the way she ran to catch up with him in the water. They saw her walk beside him at night. Trained to observe closely and well, they had visual evidence of how strongly she felt, though time and again Jack recoiled from physical intimacy. In private moments, something about the Kennedys' body language reminded one agent of siblings. 'You would think they were a brother and sister if you saw them walking along,' remembered Larry Newman. 'They communicated in their own language. They were just happy walking along and talking. They weren't up nose-to-nose or anything like that. I think that would have made Kennedy wet his pants.'

Unwilling to spend another summer in the family compound, where she insisted she felt too exposed to the public, Jackie had urged Jack to accept the singer Morton Downey's offer of the use of a secluded property at Squaw Island, some three minutes' drive away. There, she would pass the month of July. In August, with funds accumulated from the summer sublet of Glen Ora and the rental of her house in Hyannis Port to Jack's sisters Eunice and Pat, she planned to take Caroline to the Italian resort of Ravello, where Lee and her husband had rented a villa.

Meanwhile, Jack would be spending four nights on his own at the White House each week, before joining Jackie for weekends. On the first such night, Monday, July 9, the appearance of both procurers, Bill Thompson and Dave Powers, on the presidential yacht established a tone. Powers, especially, was a source of resentment among the Secret Service agents, who worried that one of the women he delivered might have it in mind to compromise or physically harm the President. The visitors, whisked in without so much as having to disclose their names to those who protected Kennedy, might be carrying listening devices, cameras, or poison-filled syringes. The Judith Campbell episode had proven that outside forces might take advantage of the President's sexual compulsions to plant one of their own in the White House. At the very least, with so many strangers in and out of the President's bed, matters threatened to spin dangerously out of control.

Once, an agent and a White House policeman stationed downstairs at half past two in the afternoon, not far from some cabinets loaded with riot guns, looked on aghast as an unknown girl wearing only a terrycloth bathrobe emerged from the elevator to the family quarters.

'Where's the President?' she asked matter-of-factly.

Before the Secret Service man had a chance to think he replied, 'He's in the Oval Office.'

'Thank you,' said the girl, heading toward the West Wing as if it were the most natural thing in the world to wander freely about the White House in a bathrobe.

'No, no, no,' the agent shouted in consternation, as he and the policeman rushed to stop her. 'You can't go over there!'

Determined to restore at least the semblance of order, the men turned her around, put her in the elevator, and sent her back upstairs.

A strange sense of foreboding permeated Washington during these months. 'He loves pleasure and women too much,' Hervé Alphand, the French ambassador, wrote in his diary that summer of 1962. 'His desires are difficult to satisfy without making one fear a scandal and its use by his political adversaries. That may happen because he doesn't take sufficient precautions in this puritan country.'

Others, like former Secretary of State Dean Acheson, worried about an impending international crisis. Kennedy, Acheson told his old boss Harry Truman, had come to remind him of an Indian snake-charmer. 'He toots away on his pipe and our problems sway back and forth around him in a trance-like manner, never approaching, but never withdrawing; all are in a state of suspended life, including the pipe player, who lives only in his dream. Some day one of these snakes will wake up; and no one will be able even to run.'

As the summer began, Kennedy, by no means immune to a sense of foreboding, focused on Berlin. In a July 5 letter to the President, Khrushchev, who had begun again to make noises about a peace treaty with East Germany, proposed the withdrawal of American, British, and French troops from West Berlin. There was now every sign that a new crisis might be astir in Berlin, which Kennedy had viewed for some time as a likely trigger for nuclear holocaust. Only later would he learn that the real peril that July of 1962 was actually a good deal closer to home. Khrushchev, setting the stage for a showdown, was making final arrangements to ship nuclear missiles to Cuba.

At half past five on Monday, July 16, Kennedy met in the Oval Office with Dean Rusk, Foy Kohler and Charles Bohlen (the new U.S. ambassadors in Moscow and Paris respectively), and others to finalize his written reply to Khrushchev. Kennedy's purpose in writing was firmly to reject the Soviet proposal that Allied troops be withdrawn from West Berlin. Under the influence of Barbara Tuchman's *The Guns of August*, he remained mindful of the misjudgments that can precipitate war, and that understanding saturated his message to Khrushchev. 'In reading the history of past wars and how they began,' Kennedy wrote, 'we cannot help but be impressed how frequently the failure of communication, misunderstanding and mutual irritation have played an important role in the events leading up to fateful decisions of war.'

In the present case, the potential for disaster was much greater because the miscalculations of either nation could 'threaten the very existence of the race itself.' Kennedy displayed a grasp of all that was at stake, as well as the need for clear thinking and carefully considered decisions on both sides. Given the potential consequences, it was supremely important that neither leader act hastily or emotionally. In the interest of precision, having expressed his views in writing, he also planned to communicate them verbally when he handed his letter to Anatoly Dobrynin, the Soviet ambassador, on Tuesday.

Kennedy's meeting with Rusk and the others was the last on his schedule for Monday. He left the Oval Office at twenty past seven and headed upstairs for the night. Ten minutes later, Mary Meyer signed in. Secret Service agents tended to be frustrated when Dave Powers made it impossible for them to check the purses of the various women he delivered to Kennedy. There was no such impediment to looking into Mary's purse, but her status as a member of the Kennedy circle made such a probe seem unnecessary. A familiar guest, she was unlikely to bring in anything that might pose a threat. Had she been checked on this occasion, however, it would have been discovered that she was carrying six marijuana cigarettes. Marijuana, as it happened, was very much Mary's second choice of hallucinogen this evening, her avowed desire being to turn the President on to L.S.D.

By this point in her affair with Kennedy, Mary found herself in the position many of his sexual partners did. She had known him long enough to be aware that his interest tended to be fleeting. In Lem Billings's words, Jack 'liked a new face and he liked to change around.' Mary could harbor no illusion that she was the only (other) woman in his life, or that she was without formidable competition: movie stars, great beauties, young girls, expensive hookers, and many others all vying for their turn with the most powerful man on earth. Still, at forty-one, Mary had been pitched into the great drama of her life and, having been deeply embarrassed when the man for whom she had planned to leave her husband ditched her, she did not wish to repeat the experience with Jack. Knowing that it would be difficult to keep his attention, wanting to add spice to the time he spent in her company, Mary seized on hallucinogens as the way to his heart. She described some of her own acid trips and Jack, who loved such mad talk, said he'd like to try it. In the aftermath of the White House dinner dance when she and the President slipped off together, Mary traveled to Cambridge, Massachusetts, to ask Timothy Leary, the Harvard psychology professor who was high priest of the burgeoning psychedelic movement, to teach her to conduct an L.S.D. session.

She appeared at Leary's faculty office unannounced and explained that she had related her own L.S.D. experiences to 'a very important man' in Washington. Her noted friend wanted to try acid, Mary reported, but as 'a public figure' could hardly come to Leary himself. She went on to suggest that her interest was no mere casual search for sensation but had a serious political aim. She had heard Allen Ginsberg say that if Khrushchev and Kennedy took acid together, they would end world conflict. Feeding drugs to world leaders, with or without their knowledge, in order to make them gentle and peace-loving was a prevalent counterculture fantasy, more an attitude than anything meant seriously. Mary, however, had taken Ginsberg's fanciful remarks literally, for she, unlike the Beat poet, actually had access to the President. Careful to leave no doubt that she was talking about someone at the very highest level of government, she deluged Leary with questions: Did he agree it would be 'good for the world' if a powerful person turned on with his wife or girlfriend? Didn't he think 'the world would be a better place if men in power had L.S.D. experiences?'

After years of listening to Cord Meyer and his C.I.A. colleagues, men who planned assassinations and the overthrow of governments because they, not some higher authority, thought it ought to be done, Mary seems never to have considered that drugging the President and altering the course of history according to a whim of her own might be wrong. Such men were not governed by the law – and neither, as Mary now saw herself, was she. Her delusions of superiority, like her ex-husband's, were fueled by a dark, secret fear of inferiority. Life had not worked out for either of them as they had believed it should. Had they looked beyond their own festering bitterness and resentment, they would have been confronted with the appalling possibility that they were not so superior in the first place. For Mary, as for Cord, it was essential at all costs to hold the mask firmly in place, to keep telling oneself that the world had no right to tell superior people what to do. For all her talk of ideology, her real reason for wishing to drug the President was a far more personal one. At a moment when Mary had very nearly abandoned her lifelong pursuit of the spotlight, Jack

Kennedy had seen her with new eyes and revived her hopes. He had become her main chance, and, like her late sister Rosamund, she was prepared to take extreme measures rather than have those hopes dashed once again.

At length, she and Leary went to the professor's house, where they ate hallucinogenic mushrooms and talked of her awareness, as a long-time C.I.A. wife, of government experiments with drugs used for brainwashing, espionage, and warfare. Unlike the bad guys at the C.I.A., Mary emphasized, she planned 'to use drugs for peace.' Leary had an 'uneasy' feeling about Mary, and sent her home with an armload of reading matter on psychedelic research along with the admonition that she wasn't ready yet to run an acid session.

In lieu of L.S.D., Mary acquired marijuana from her friend Jim Truitt, who worked as assistant to Phil Graham, publisher of the *Washington Post*. With Truitt she did not hesitate to identify Kennedy as both her lover and the man whom she sought to introduce to hallucinogens. She not only confided details of her affair to Truitt, who repeated them to Graham and others, but also later regaled him with an account of getting stoned with the President.

It goes to the heart of Kennedy's nature that only hours after he emphasized to Khrushchev the need for clear thinking and carefully considered decisions, he went upstairs and smoked three of the joints Mary had smuggled in. In the weeks to come, as the Cuban Missile Crisis brought the world to the brink of nuclear war, Mary enjoyed regular intimate access to the President despite the fact that she had boasted of her intent to feed L.S.D. to men in power.

From her own, purely personal point of view, turning Kennedy onto pot seemed to do the trick. Mary's recklessness had enchanted him, so much so that when she called the White House at 6:43 the following morning, he wanted to see her again that night. He arranged to meet her at a dinner party at Joe Alsop's, where Bill Walton, who often did this sort of favor for Jack, would serve as beard.

If evidence were needed that Kennedy could ill afford to have his judgment clouded by drugs, it came that morning when he entered the Oval Office to news of a plane-buzzing episode in the Berlin corridor. The incident was a further sign that real trouble might be brewing in Berlin, and he registered a protest to Anatoly Dobrynin when the ambassador appeared at 6 p.m. to collect the letter to Khrushchev. Then, after a swim, the President went to Joe Alsop's house, where the twenty dinner guests included Bobby Kennedy, Charles Bohlen, and McGeorge Bundy.

Presumed to be Bill Walton's date for the evening, Mary made less effort to conceal her presence in Jack's life from then on. He, for his part, did astonishingly little to hide it either. Although, as friends noted, Mary certainly 'wasn't the only one who was sleeping with him,' her relationship with the President stood apart. In addition to an intense sexual connection, she also enjoyed his friendship – a combination sadly beyond his wife's powers. That summer Jack entertained Mary Meyer openly and unabashedly at the White House. A pattern was established whereby Mary would turn up in the Oval Office and at gatherings of the President's friends, where her presence in Jackie's absence was accepted as a fact of life. The pointed casualness with which Mary flitted in and out of Jack's weekday life in this period made it impossible that Jackie would not have found out what was going on.

Squaw Island, however, was Jackie's turf. There, private life as she conceived it went on as if Mary did not exist. On Saturday, July 28, a flotilla set out from the Kennedy pier in Hyannis Port in celebration of Jackie's thirty-third birthday. Jackie, the center of attention in a shocking pink bathing suit, had thirty-three guests for lobster lunch. Among them were Joe and Rose, the Spaldings and their twin daughters, as well as various Kennedys and their children. There was swimming and water-skiing, and by the time they headed back, amid thirty-knot winds and three-foot-high waves, Jack had finally agreed to something he had previously resisted. Gladys Tartiere had indicated that she would not renew the lease on Glen Ora when it ended early the following year. Jackie wanted to buy some land nearby at Rattlesnake Mountain, but Jack, who disliked the hunt country, had hesitated. In honor of Jackie's birthday, he gave in, promising to make an appointment that week to set the purchase in motion.

Monday morning, Kennedy returned to the White House, where he arranged to see Mary Meyer that night. As if he and Bill Thompson had not recently finished trying to deal with Marilyn Monroe, Kennedy had Mary and Bill, mistress and procurer, enter together at half past seven, just as he was concluding an off-the-record meeting with Clark Mollenhoff, an investigative reporter who would come closest in the President's lifetime to taking the lid off the scandals.

Jackie had one last weekend with her husband before leaving for Italy. While she prepared for the trip, Caroline, whose first time abroad this would be, spent the better part of Saturday morning, August 4, with Jack. First, they watched the golfers tee off at the Hyannis Country Club. Then they drove to the compound to visit Joe and tour the property on a motor scooter. By the time they boarded the *Marlin*, Jackie and Joe were waiting. The foursome, anchored near Egg Island, picnicked on a sandbar. When Joe got tired, they dropped him off at the Kennedy pier for a servant to drive him home. Jack and Jackie took the *Marlin* back out and anchored off the breakwater, where parents and child swam happily together for nearly an hour.

Sunday would be their last day together, and to mark the occasion Jack and Jackie included eighteen-month-old John in the family party. The baby, who was still too young to be taken sailing most of the time, was due to leave the next day with Miss Shaw to stay with his grandmother in Newport while Jackie was away. Shortly after noon, in a rare outing that included just the four of them, they took one of the presidential yachts, the *Patrick J*, and did not return until nearly 5 p.m.

While the Kennedys were out on Nantucket Sound, Peter Lawford had called from Los Angeles with the news that Marilyn Monroe had taken her own life with a drug overdose, and the idyll was shattered. Lawford, the last person to talk to Marilyn on the phone, suddenly found himself part of a lurid story guaranteed to grab headlines. On Saturday, August 4, Marilyn had accepted Lawford's invitation to join him and several friends for dinner. When he called later to ask where she was, Marilyn, in thick, halting speech that meant she was drunk or drugged, perhaps both, said she could not attend. But it was her parting comment – 'Say goodbye to Pat, say goodbye to Jack, and say goodbye to yourself because you're a nice guy' – that led Lawford to alert her attorney to check on her. Had it not been inevitable that Marilyn's connection to Kennedy would be endlessly rehashed in the press because of her performance at Madison Square Garden, the hapless involvement of the President's brother-in-law in her death would have made it so.

Jack and Jackie had dinner together at home, after which he paid a call on his father. Later, she accompanied him on a walk to Teddy Kennedy's house nearby; it was nearly half past ten when they returned. Jack flew to Washington the next morning. Jackie and Caroline, due to spend the night in New York, stopped off first to say goodbye to Joe. But he was asleep, so Jackie, who still liked to take a potshot at Jack's surviving sisters, wrote a typically playful note – 'Please put a picture of Jack & me & Caroline & John right by your favorite chair where Eunice will see it – & nail it down so she can't take it away & put Timmy there instead' – before they left.

By early evening, Jackie and her daughter were settled in at the Carlyle. As far as she was aware, Jack was planning to stay in that night. At 7:50 p.m., when she had every reason to assume he would be upstairs even if he had stopped for a swim first, she called the White House. The President, she was informed, was out. In fact, Mary had arrived for the evening twenty minutes previously. It was nearly half past eleven before Jack summoned a car to take her home.

There was mounting concern among Kennedy's advisers that the Republican Party would make promiscuity an issue in 1964. Instead of attempting to curb the President, however, they focused on Jackie. They worried that her decision to spend a few weeks in Italy on her own for no purpose other than private pleasure might suggest that the Kennedys' marriage was less than ideal. Lest anyone interpret the holiday as a sign of trouble, the White House made a point of informing the press that her trip coincided with a period during which the President, who would be speaking in various parts of the country, would be unable to join her at Cape Cod on weekends. That was true, up to a point. Kennedy would indeed be away, in Maine the first weekend and California the next, but he was scheduled to do relatively little work in either place. Nonetheless, the White House went out of its way to create an impression that, with her husband off working, Jackie hoped to assuage her loneliness in Ravello. Though she planned to remain for a third week if all went well, for now the public was told only that she would be away for two weeks.

When Jackie and Caroline arrived on Wednesday, Ravello was packed with press from around the world. From first to last, Jackie took immense care to do nothing to embarrass her husband. In line with Washington's insistence that her visit to the glamorous resort be kept 'low key,' Jackie had brought only a maid, as well as her Secret Service detail which included Clint Hill and Larry Newman. As no secretary or press aide accompanied her, the American embassy in Rome sent a young woman named Mary Taylor. Jackie's new assistant was instantly struck by her meticulous attention to propriety, with regard to both her own behavior and that of anyone associated with her, either as friend or employee. 'She was very concerned about who she was and how she acted and how the people around her acted,' Taylor recalled. 'She wanted everyone to comport themselves in a good manner.' Jackie left no doubt that as First Lady it was essential she make 'a good impression' on Italy and on the world, and initially it seemed as if the visit would play exactly as she hoped. Reporters confined themselves in large part to accounts of Jackie's arrival, as well as colorful descriptions of Ravello and its history.

Secret Service agents had arrived well in advance to consult with Stas Radziwill on security. Built on the side of a cliff high above Amalfi and the sea, the Villa Episcopio, formerly the residence of King Vittorio Emanuele III and currently owned by the Duca di Sangro, posed little problem, as it was accessible only through gates. Provisions did have to be made for the beach house across the bay, where Jackie and the others swam, as well as for chase boats when she sailed or water-skied. Fiat beach cars transported the Radziwills and their houseguests up and down to the water, where they were loaded onto motorboats to the beach. Besides Lee and Stas, those in residence when Jackie was present included Gianni Agnelli and his wife, Marella, who had both been guests at the White House; *Paris–Match* photographer Benno Graziani and his wife, Nicole; and *New York Times* foreign affairs columnist C. L. Sulzberger.

Jackie's first important test came two days into her stay. Lee became ill and a physician was summoned from the U.S. naval station in Naples. Jackie, determined not to offend their host nation, requested that a local doctor also be called lest it be said that her party had a low opinion of the Italian medical profession. As wife of the President of the United States, Jackie insisted, her duty was 'to cement relations' with Italy rather than undermine them.

Lee's indisposition did not hamper her guests' enjoyment, and on Sunday night a party of five, led by Stas Radziwill and guarded by Secret Service men, descended the mountain in the dark. They proceeded on foot, using steep old stone steps through a grape arbor, lest the sight of the Fiat beach cars alert the press. Their destination, one of several outdoor nightclubs, had many small, colored lights strung up near the wharf. There Radziwill commandeered a slatted, candlelit table and some folding chairs. No sooner had the waiter brought wine bottles and glasses, however, when to Jackie's consternation the estab-lishment was overrun with press. On all sides, photographers shouted in different languages, vying for pictures. Jackie's Secret Service detail had learned to watch for the telltale widening of her eyes when she felt her space being threatened. Such was the case tonight, as it became apparent that Jackie was about to insist they all return to the villa. The agents didn't want to see her evening ruined, so Clint Hill moved in to handle things. Of all the agents, Hill, the lead, clearly had 'the best rapport' with her.

'Let them have one picture,' Hill proposed. 'Let me see if that'll work.'

With Jackie's approval, Hill persuaded the invaders to leave her in peace in exchange for a single opportunity to photograph her and her party. As soon as the wine bottles were removed, in the interest of propriety, the herd of photographers, who were permitted no closer than ten feet from the table, moved in. Agnelli smiled into the cameras and Radziwill languidly dangled a cigarette between two fingers, as Jackie, in white Capri pants, a silk shirt, and sandals, posed with evident nervousness.

There followed an exceedingly odd scene, as the photographers removed themselves from the nightclub area and formed a semicircle on the cobblestone pavement, sitting in silence, legs crossed, directly facing Jackie's table. As the water lapped at the wharf, one by one the men placed their box cameras and flashes on the cobblestones five feet in front of them, a signal to Jackie that they planned only to watch. Positioned thus, they resembled nothing so much as 'a bunch of football players listening for the play,' Larry Newman remembered, and, as Jackie and her friends were prepared to ignore them, they sat there all evening.

Monday morning, the party went sailing on Agnelli's sleek two-masted racing yacht. Clint Hill traveled on board, other agents on chase boats. Eager to be included in everything, Caroline, on whom Jackie lavished attention throughout the trip, made a face when she realized that on this one occasion she was to be left behind with her Radziwill cousins and a maid. Again that evening, the children remained at Villa Episcopio when Jackie, the Radziwills, the Agnellis, and others sailed twenty-two miles to Capri – a two-hour trip – for midnight supper at the home of fashion designer Irene Galitzine. After dinner, Jackie and her party took a walk to the town square. Pursued as always by press, they sailed at 2 a.m, with guitar music and dancing on deck.

Tuesday morning, as Jackie slept late, reporters saw her daughter at play on the beach alone. Later there was more sailing and more press photographs of her and Gianni Agnelli that, through clever framing and cropping, made it appear as if she and the legendary playboy were by themselves. In fact, as Jackie's Secret Service detail could plainly see, Marella

Agnelli, the Radziwills, and others were very much present. Despite some highly misleading images that would soon appear in print, it was never anything less than 'a proper trip,' avowed Larry Newman. 'It was just beautiful people enjoying themselves.' Besides, the Secret Service agent pointed out, 'I never saw anything of untoward desire or activity on her part toward another man.' Nor, Newman observed, was it Jackie's style to get even with Jack by carrying on, as some would later suggest she had done, with Agnelli in Italy. 'She was above all that,' Newman insisted. 'She didn't burn that kind of a fire.'

Meanwhile, Jack was off to Maine, where, after devoting a sum total of eighteen minutes to official duties, he left for Johns Island with Chuck Spalding, Torby Macdonald, and other pals for three days of fun and games. When the President returned to Washington, the sex scandal Alphand and others had feared finally seemed about to occur – though, contrary to anyone's expectations, with poor Jackie as its focal point.

On Tuesday and Wednesday, American newspaper readers were treated to hints in words and pictures that the First Lady was up to no good with Gianni Agnelli. First, the pictures of Jackie, Agnelli, Radziwill, and two others in the outdoor night-club plunged Kennedy into a fit of anxiety, and he called Jackie at 3 a.m. on Wednesday. Those images were as nothing compared to the shots of Jackie and Agnelli that materialized the next day, alongside stories that made it sound as if, with the exception of a guitarist to serenade them, she and the playboy had been alone on the yacht from Capri. Descriptions of Caroline making a face when her mother went off on Agnelli's yacht and of the child alone on the beach the next morning contributed to the sense that something was amiss. 'Less Agnelli, more Caroline,' Kennedy famously telegrammed his wife, in addition to placing another 3 a.m. call. Not that he believed for one moment that she was really fooling around with Agnelli. Above all, he was concerned with the potential political consequences. Nor, significantly, can the press really have believed any of it. They knew perfectly well that Agnelli's wife and others had also been present. Nonetheless, the stories and images, in their own peculiar way, finally broached the unspeakable by hinting that all was not well in the Kennedy marriage. As yet unable or unwilling to spotlight the President's liaisons, certain members of the press, bursting to say what they knew or suspected, sought a kind of relief by casting aspersions on his wife.

In reaction to Jack's calls and telegram, Jackie made every effort to do as asked. Henceforth, she tried to keep her evenings with the Radziwills and their guests out of view. Meanwhile, on Friday, Jack began a round of speechmaking that included stops in Pierre, South Dakota, Pueblo, Colorado, and Fresno, California, before he landed at the Beverly Hills Hotel on Saturday afternoon. Twenty-five minutes after checking in, he and Dave Powers headed to Peter Lawford's house in Santa Monica, where they spent the better part of two days on the beach with women provided by Lawford. By this time, Jackie had decided that she did indeed wish to remain in Italy for a third week. Unfortunately, her announcement revived the speculation that had just begun to die down. Indignant, one hundred women who called themselves the Concerned Citizens of America threatened to picket the White House when Jackie returned. 'Would you not better have served the nation and the President by remaining here at home by his side?' they demanded in an open letter. 'We have honored you greatly with the position of First Lady of our land. We ask only that you not violate the dignity of that title.'

Matters came to a head the following weekend. On Sunday, August 26, the President, on a visit to his father in Hyannis Port, awoke to newspaper stories of Jackie's visit to a nightclub, where, dressed in tight red pants and top, she danced the twist with the Duca di Sangro until 3 a.m. Again, Kennedy had no reason to doubt that the evening had been an innocent one. Nonetheless, always the politician, he moved swiftly and skillfully to restore an image of family happiness. He called his mother-in-law to invite himself to Newport that very day, and before he left made sure to alert the press. Accordingly, photographers were present when the white cap landed in a pasture at Hammersmith Farm, where young John, whom Jackie rarely permitted to be photographed, was waiting to greet his dad.

Jackie's wishes notwithstanding, a first extended look at the younger child was just about the only thing Jack could think of that was guaranteed to nudge her trip out of the news.

That afternoon, as Kennedy and his son, hand in hand, headed up to the main house, the press was notified that he planned to give John a swimming lesson at Bailey's Beach Club. Half an hour later, John looked on as Kennedy got into the pool at Newport's most exclusive club and signaled the boy to jump. For a moment John stood poised at the edge, then with a great scream of delight leapt in. Cameras clicked furiously as he hit the water and his father's adoring arms closed around him. Had John balked or made a scene, the carefully staged photo opportunity might have misfired. But he had given a performance that could not be faked. In a split second, he had given the world a picture of perfect trust. Part of what made the image so compelling was that, calculated though it was, the strong feelings depicted on both sides were authentic. Pictures of the episode appeared in many newspapers the next day, whereupon the White House announced that Jackie and Caroline were due home on Friday, in time for the family to spend the Labor Day weekend together.

Jackie was to return to all the same problems that had driven her into hiding at the beginning of July. Nonetheless, before she flew home, she had Mary Taylor send a telegram to Jack saying, 'I can hardly wait to see you.'

TEN

A Critical Moment

When Jackie arrived in Newport on the evening of August 31, anticipating a quiet reunion with her husband, she discovered that Jack was in the midst of a crisis. A few hours earlier, while still in Washington, he had been handed evidence that the Soviets were secretly building defensive, surface-to-air missile sites in Cuba. By the end of a holiday weekend outwardly devoted to trips to Bailey's Beach, cruises on the *Honey Fitz*, and related pleasures, he would have to decide how to respond, if at all, to this shattering information. Should he make Khrushchev aware that he knew what was going on? Should he draw a line in the sand and warn his adversary not to install offensive missiles capable of striking U.S. targets?

Beyond the obvious political implications, the President's dilemma had huge personal significance for his wife. Jackie's efforts on behalf of Jack's beleaguered presidency had been leading to the critical moment when he would have an opportunity to prove himself indisputably a strong leader. His earlier blunders had encouraged Jackie to take an active role in his political life. Now, again, a crisis in Cuba was about to transform both her public and private circumstances.

The trouble had started while she was in Italy. On the evening of August 22, C.I.A. Director John McCone, who had replaced Allen Dulles in the wake of the Bay of Pigs fiasco, briefed the President on new intelligence from Cuba. Since late July, an unusually large number of Soviet ships had delivered military cargoes to Cuba, with more vessels currently en route from the Black Sea. Soviet bloc personnel from these ships were now engaged in 'some form of military construction' at several locations. Exactly what it all meant, no one in the administration could yet be sure. Most believed that the buildup was purely defensive. McCone, however, held the minority position that the Soviets planned to introduce medium-range ballistic missiles. Yes, he agreed, defensive missiles were indeed being installed, but less to fend off an attack than to prevent U-2 surveillance from detecting the arrival of offensive missiles aimed at the U.S. Nothing would be known for certain until the next U-2 flight. On August 29, a U.S. spy plane flew over Cuban construction sites and took pictures.

The results, presented to Kennedy a few hours before he left for Rhode Island, documented at least eight different surface-to-air missile sites, some of which looked as if they might be operational within two weeks. Even with that information, it remained unclear whether McCone or the others were right. That weekend in Newport, Kennedy was faced with the task of making the first major decision of the unfolding crisis – whether to put Khrushchev on notice – with frustratingly incomplete knowledge. To make matters worse, on the very day Jackie returned, Republican Senator Kenneth Keating, basing his remarks on leaked information about the military buildup in Cuba, had criticized the President for lacking the guts to stand up to Castro. These and similar charges by other Republicans touched a nerve, not merely because of the debacle at the Bay of Pigs but because of Joe's wartime reputation as an appeaser and a coward. As at the time of the Bay of Pigs, the Kennedy family drama would be very much a factor in the crisis Bobby soon dubbed 'Cuba 2.' This time, besides hoping to obliterate his father's legacy of shame, Jack was no less concerned about his own.

By the time Jackie saw him off on the morning of Tuesday, September 4, Jack had made up his mind on at least one thing. That day, the White House released a statement on Cuba to the press, but its intended audience was really Khrushchev himself. Noting the influx of weapons from the Soviet Union, as well as the presence of anti-aircraft missiles, torpedo boats with ship-to-ship guided missiles, and some 3,500 Soviet technicians either already in Cuba or en route, the President made it clear that the U.S. did not yet possess evidence of Soviet combat forces or offensive weapons such as ground-to-ground missiles. But, he cautioned, 'Were it to be otherwise, the gravest issues would arise.' In short, Kennedy served warning that he would not tolerate the presence of offensive missiles in Cuba.

Soon afterward, Anatoly Dobrynin sent word that he wished to see the Attorney General. That evening at the Justice Department, in addition to handing Bobby Kennedy a private letter from Khrushchev that signaled interest in an atmospheric test ban treaty, Dobrynin conveyed strong assurances that Khrushchev had no plan to send ground-to-ground missiles or other offensive weapons to Cuba. Mindful of the political importance to Kennedy of the upcoming mid-term Congressional elections, Khrushchev promised to do nothing to disrupt U.S.–Soviet relations prior to the election. According to Dobrynin, Khrushchev very much liked Kennedy personally and vowed to make every effort not to embarrass him. Khrushchev was lying about the missiles, of course; the first Soviet shipment of medium-range ballistic missiles was due in Cuba that weekend. Still, the strong, direct nature of Khrushchev's message, delivered privately in conjunction with a personal letter, led Kennedy to give it credence, though he went to bed that night, and many nights thereafter, unsure.

Kennedy spent the evening in the Oval Office in anticipation of conferring with Bobby after Dobrynin left. The following evening, however, he was free. Mary Meyer signed in shortly before 7:30. Jack was in his office when she arrived, but left for the pool ten minutes later. Unlike Judith Campbell who, afraid that her carefully set hair would not survive the water, had reacted with horror when he suggested they start their sessions in the pool, Mary loved to swim naked, having often done so as a girl to shock onlookers. A late summer hiatus in his affair with Mary, when they had both been away separately, provided a natural opportunity to break it off, but Jack did not. Jackie would not be back in Washington until October 9.

The next day, September 6, Dobrynin summoned Ted Sorensen to the Soviet embassy to convey more assurances from Moscow. On Khrushchev's behalf, he reiterated that prior to the Congressional elections nothing would be done to complicate the international situation. All they had undertaken in Cuba thus far, Khrushchev insisted, was 'defensive in nature and did not represent any threat to the security of the United States.' McCone, for his part, did not trust the Soviets. On Friday, the C.I.A. Director interrupted his honeymoon in France to urge the President to schedule more reconnaissance flights to gather information on what, despite the sweet talk from Khrushchev, he continued to believe was a buildup of offensive missiles. Though virtually all of the C.I.A.'s own analysts disagreed with McCone, Kennedy shared his suspicions. Before going to Newport for the weekend, he sent a message of his own to Khrushchev by asking Congress for 'stand-by authority to order 150,000 military reservists to active duty.'

The following week, the Soviet news agency Tass cited Kennedy's request to Congress as evidence that he planned 'an act of aggression.' The Soviets warned that a military move against Cuba or Soviet vessels headed there would trigger war. At the same time, they disclaimed any intention of transferring offensive missiles to Cuba, reminding the U.S. that it was already well within their power to launch a nuclear attack on the U.S. from their own soil. In a September 13 press conference, Kennedy dismissed rumors of an imminent U.S. invasion as Castro's frantic effort to prop up a troubled régime, and insisted that the U.S. would strike only if Cuba became an offensive military base for the Soviet Union. At the present time, he said, the stream of Soviet arms and military personnel into Cuba notwithstanding, conditions had yet to reach a point that would justify U.S. intervention. Still, the President made it clear that he would not hesitate should threatening conditions develop. He had no idea that the first shipment of offensive missiles had already arrived in Cuba, or that even as he left Washington on Friday evening, September 14, for a ten-day vacation at Hammersmith Farm, the Soviet freighter *Poltava* was en route with a second shipment of medium-range ballistic missiles.

Kennedy had scheduled his fall vacation to coincide with the finals of the America's Cup races, the premier international yachting competition. The U.S. had held the Cup since 1851, when the yacht *America* had won at Cowes, England. Thereafter, the races had been held in the ocean off Newport. At the last race, in 1956, the U.S. had won against the English challenger. This year's competition would be the first of Jack's presidency, and he and Jackie hosted an extended house party at Hammersmith Farm. Australia was the challenger, and its yacht, the *Gretel*, would compete in three events against the U.S. vessel, the *Weatherley*. On the night before the final races began, the Kennedys attended a black-tie dinner for three hundred hosted by Ambassador Harold Beale of Australia.

The setting was the Breakers, an ersatz Renaissance palace built in the nineteenth century by Cornelius Vanderbilt. Seated side by side at the main table beneath an ornate ceiling painting of 'Aurora at Dawn,' the Kennedys, whose ninth wedding anniversary had passed two days previously, seemed at times to inhabit a world of their own. Dressed in a blue strapless chiffon gown gathered at the bosom with an antique diamond pin, Jackie, consummately seductive, leaned over to touch her husband's arm and whisper in his ear. She turned her chair so that her face was inches from his and maneuvered her shoulders to close off the rest of the room. Again and again, Jack's eyes lit up as he erupted in laughter at something she said. Such moments offered a unique window on the marriage. After nine years, Jack and Jackie were still very much a team, as amused and engaged by each other as ever. At the same time, she was still struggling to win his desire as she had long ago earned his love.

Jackie had undergone many metamorphoses. She had started as a freckled schoolgirl with short, kinky hair and heavy eyebrows, who often dressed with shirttails out or in a Vassar student's sweaters and kilts. In the marriage's troubled early months, she tried to make herself over à la Audrey Hepburn, with a pixie haircut. By the time she reached the White House, Jackie had been masquerading as an elegant mock little girl, a look she used to effect in Paris in 1961. Tonight, with her shoulders bared and her hair pinned up, it was evident that she had lost considerable weight since the Inauguration. The style of her evening clothes had shifted markedly as well. Stiff fabrics had been abandoned in favor of soft chiffons, demure necklines replaced by strapless dresses that emphasized her shoulders and back. She had also changed her makeup in an effort to highlight the sensuality of her wide mouth.

Frustratingly, her efforts came to naught, for, as the scene at the Breakers attested, Jack remained the passive object of her seductive charm. After nine years, things were as they had always been. Much as he loved Jackie as family, he continued to have sexual relations with an ever-changing cast of characters – and by this time he had been carrying on with Mary Meyer for nearly eight months. Worst of all, from Jackie's point of view, he seemed utterly blind to the hurt he was causing her.

The next day, Jackie was similarly demonstrative on the open sea, when, along with the Ormsby-Gores, Assistant Secretary of the Treasury James Reed and his wife, Jewel, and some twenty-five other friends, the Kennedys watched the first race from the deck of the U.S. destroyer *Joseph P. Kennedy Jr*, named after Jack's brother. Dressed in a fitted navy suit with gold buttons, a silk scarf tied over her hair against a furious wind, she perched on the arm of Jack's chair. Her arm draped around his shoulders possessively, she cuddled against him as one friend or another came over to talk. When her husband moved to the ship's rail for a better view, Jackie curled up on the ground at his feet like a cat and leaned against him as he monitored the progress of the American and Australian sloops, while the flag whipped in the wind above the deck. At that moment she seemed so desperately in love, and so desperate in that love.

On Wednesday, September 19, with one race remaining, the President went to Washington overnight to meet with the President of Rwanda and hear the C.I.A.'s latest estimate of the Cuban situation. McCone was still in France, but the consensus of C.I.A. analysts was that the military buildup was purely defensive. A Soviet decision to introduce offensive missiles in Cuba, they insisted, 'would indicate a far greater willingness to increase the level of risk in U.S.–Soviet relations than the U.S.S.R. has displayed thus far.' Before Kennedy returned to Newport on Thursday, he heard from McCone, who continued to sound alarm bells. In the meantime, bad weather and concerns about a possible incident had meant that U-2 flights were either useless or not conducted at all, so there was no more hard evidence either way than there had been at the end of August.

Kennedy flew back to Newport via Harrisburg, Pennsylvania, where he spoke at a Democratic fundraising dinner for the Congressional campaign. The rest of his stay at Hammersmith Farm was devoted to cruising on the *Honey Fitz* and swimming at Bailey's Beach, and on Sunday he and Jackie flew to Hyannis Port to visit his father. On Saturday, they watched from the deck of the *Joseph P. Kennedy Jr* as the Americans won the third and final race and retained the Cup. Jackie returned to Washington with her husband on the evening of Monday, September 24, to spend her first night in the White House since July. She would remain for only two nights, long enough to take Ayub Khan, on a private visit to the U.S., to see Sardar and spend the day riding with him at Glen Ora. That evening she accompanied Jack, Rose, and a host of other Kennedys to a benefit for the Kennedy Foundation, the family charity, followed by a late supper party hosted by the Ormsby-Gores at the British embassy. Wednesday morning, she returned to Hammersmith Farm and the children, with Jack due to follow on Friday for one last weekend. After that, his weekends during October and early November, as well as a good many weekdays, were to be devoted to campaign trips in anticipation of the mid-term Congressional elections.

Saturday afternoon, Jackie had word that a new crisis, this one on the home front, would keep Jack in Washington all weekend. The previous day, he had had a visit from Bobby Kennedy and Assistant Attorney General Burke Marshall, who announced that a confrontation seemed likely over an attempt by a black veteran of nine years in the Air Force named James Meredith to register at the University of Mississippi. Segregationist Governor Ross Barnett vowed to block Meredith or go to jail in the attempt. Bobby, determined to handle the matter on his own, had been in the thick of negotiations. But the talks failed, and a court ruling directed Barnett to admit Meredith by October 2 or be held in contempt.

Barnett continued to refuse, and it seemed that only federal intervention would get Meredith into the university. Any federal force, the Attorney General recognized, was likely to encounter state troops bolstered by a 'civilian army' of segregationists who had rallied to the Governor's call. Other considerations aside, in terms of the Cuban crisis the timing could hardly have been worse. As at the time of his summit meeting with Khrushchev, the President's authority was to be clouded by the profound embarrassment of a violent confrontation between the U.S. government and its own people. In the midst of efforts to deal effectively with Khrushchev on Cuba, the world would be treated to the ghastly spectacle of federal and state forces at war in Mississippi.

By the time Jackie heard from her husband, he had decided that if Barnett failed to back down he would go on television that night to explain why he had to order troops to Mississippi. Max Jacobson was flown in to give him a shot before he went on camera. Three times during the day, the President talked on the phone with Barnett. Negotiations proceeded in fits and starts, and by 7 p.m. it looked as if an accord had been reached. Barnett made it clear that he wanted no one to know he had accepted a deal, whereby he and his people would gather at the Oxford campus while Meredith quietly enrolled in Jackson. Barnett, it was agreed, would tell his followers that he'd been tricked and that it was simply too late to do anything about it.

Kennedy canceled his television spot and repaired to the family quarters. Before the President went to bed, Bobby called to say that Barnett had cancelled the deal. If Barnett failed to make himself a hero by blocking the integration of the University of Mississippi, he was determined to become a martyr by forcing his adversaries to use federal troops. Though this was exactly what the administration was eager to avoid, Kennedy signed a proclamation shortly after midnight ordering all those who had obstructed justice in Mississippi to 'cease and desist.' Next, he signed papers officially putting the Mississippi National Guard on federal service. He retired for the night in the belief that a showdown was inevitable.

Sunday morning, Bobby was back on the phone, playing

'hardball,' as he had done at the time of the steel crisis. He notified Barnett that his brother planned to go on television to explain his actions to the nation, and went on to say that the President would disclose the secret deal Barnett had agreed to. Almost certainly, as the Governor could not fail to see, that would ruin his reputation with his segregationist followers. Chastened, he was ready to negotiate again. He and the Attorney General agreed that Meredith should be registered at Oxford, and that Barnett would do what he could to 'preserve the peace.'

The Justice Department ordered federal marshals, already assembled at Memphis, to move to Oxford with tear gas and other riot equipment. Before the President went on television, he wanted to be sure that Meredith was safely on campus and that Justice Department officials had the situation under control, so several times he changed the time he planned to speak. Meanwhile, in Oxford, Assistant Attorney General Nicholas Katzenbach directed marshals to surround the Lyceum Building, where, as Sunday had been ruled out for religious reasons, Meredith was to be registered the following day. A crowd of jeering students threw rocks and bottles. After Katzenbach personally escorted Meredith to a dormitory room at Baxter Hall, the mob yelled, 'Go to Cuba, nigger lovers, go to Cuba!'

Back in Washington, it had been decided Kennedy would go on television at ten. He had two speeches prepared. One had been written in the event that there were battles in progress in Oxford, the other if there were peace. As technicians set up lights and cameras in the Oval Office, Kennedy, along with Marshall and the Attorney General, monitored the situation from the Cabinet Room. Katzenbach filed periodic reports from a pay phone in the Lyceum Building. The crowd on campus seemed to grow more threatening as the evening progressed.

As the appointed hour for the broadcast drew near, Kennedy was pleased that Meredith was now on campus and no tear gas had been used. Burke Marshall and Bobby Kennedy remained in the Cabinet Room when the President left to deliver his conciliatory speech. Two minutes before he went live on air, Katzenbach notified the Attorney General that the situation had changed drastically. A fully-fledged riot had erupted. 'I'll do something to try to stop the President,' Bobby replied. By the time he reached the Oval Office, it was too late.

'Good evening, my fellow citizens,' said the President, sitting at his desk. 'The orders of the court in the case of Meredith versus Fair are beginning to be carried out ... This has been accomplished thus far without the use of the National Guard or other troops.' When he returned to the Cabinet Room, he discovered that, contrary to the picture he had just painted, the campus had become a battlefield. 'I haven't had such an interesting time since the Bay of Pigs,' he remarked as, once again, circumstances spun out of control. Bobby, half in earnest, half in jest, anticipated the press release that would accompany his own dismissal: 'The Attorney General announced today, he's joining Allen Dulles at Princeton' – a reference to the disgraced former C.I.A. chief who lost his job after the botched invasion. Obviously, both brothers feared that another disaster was in the making.

The first gunshot was fired at approximately 11 p.m. Snipers soon wounded three marshals, and many more casualties followed. At various times during the evening, an unoccupied car, a bulldozer, and a fire truck came crashing into the Lyceum Building. The President insisted that marshals were not to open fire unless Meredith's life was threatened. Amid a swirl of contradictory reports, word reached the White House shortly before midnight that the mob had stormed Meredith's dormitory, and it seemed that the riot was about to include a lynching. Still, after much discussion, it was decided that there was no way to remove Meredith. Then came word of the first death, a reporter for the London *Daily Sketch* found shot in the back.

Around midnight, rifle and shotgun fire echoed in the background as Katzenbach asked for the Army's assistance. The Attorney General said that it would take an hour for troops to arrive from Memphis, but the night wore on and casualties mounted with no sign of the Army. The President, enraged, telephoned Army Secretary Cyrus Vance. 'Where are the troops?' he demanded. 'They arrived at the airport twenty-five minutes ago,' Vance replied. 'The hell they are,' Kennedy exploded. 'I've just talked with people at the airport and they're not there.' Several times in the hours that followed, Kennedy was assured that the soldiers had arrived when in fact they had not.

Besides his worry about how the Army would fare, the President agonized about how all this was going to play with voters. As the Attorney General recognized at the time, particularly because he was so close to the President, there could be no public finger-pointing at the military. Exasperating as the Army's performance undeniably was, planning and execution of the entire confrontation had been the Attorney General's responsibility.

Heard to whimper in the course of the ordeal, Bobby was devastated that he had let his brother down. By the time the troops showed up it was after 4 a.m. More than half of the three hundred marshals had been injured, twenty-eight had sustained gunshot wounds, and two people – the British journalist and a local repairman – were dead. The Army seized the places where snipers had hidden, and order was restored.

Just after 5 a.m., the telephone woke Jackie at Hammersmith Farm. Tortured by what he saw as his own failure to send in troops earlier and convinced that at least one life might have been saved had the Army arrived punctually, Jack told her that he expected to be pilloried by press and public in the morning. Joe Alsop once pointed out that Kennedy, otherwise scornful of criticism, was highly sensitive if he believed it to be accurate. In this case, there was no question that he thought he had another debacle on his hands. Before trying to get a few hours' sleep, Kennedy wanted to talk to his wife. Jackie listened as he offered, in the words of an aide, 'a dismal account of the night's happenings.'

The President was back at his desk shortly after 9:30. By then, Meredith had registered at the University of Mississippi. Despite the deaths, the previous night was being depicted as a success, as the press reported the story as a tremendous effort to provide one American with justice. Rather than noting that the President had obviously been unaware of the riot in progress as he delivered his televised address, or focusing on the inadequate planning, news accounts tended to depict the violence as the segregationists' regrettable reply to Kennedy's words of conciliation.

In the pre-dawn hours, when his outlook had been bleak, the President had unburdened himself to his wife. That night, when he finished work at half past seven and returned to the family quarters with a sense of relief and disaster averted, he spent the evening with Mary Meyer.

Three months had passed since an edgy Jackie had left for the summer amid an outburst of profanity over the prospect of being photographed at Andrews Air Force Base. The ceaseless scrutiny of her complicated life had become intolerable, and seemed no less so on Tuesday, October 9, as she emerged from a plane at Andrews en route to the White House. This time, when photographers closed in on her and the children, Jackie dispatched a Secret Service man to confiscate the film. At a moment when she was about to step back into the spotlight, it was a symbolic gesture at best, but one that indicated her mood as the season began.

Jack, waiting for her in the family quarters, had just made a momentous decision. For the past week, McCone had been arguing for further U-2 flights over Cuba to gather hard information on Soviet activity, despite the danger that newly operative surface-to-air missiles were now in a position to shoot down U.S. reconnaissance planes. McCone had gone head to head with National Security Adviser McGeorge Bundy, the former arguing that the presence of offensive missiles in Cuba was now 'a probability rather than a possibility,' the latter that the Soviets would never go so far. Kennedy, concerned about the lack of hard information on the one hand and the possibility of an international incident on the other, finally made up his mind based on intelligence reports of a mysteriously restricted area in a remote part of Cuba suddenly filled with Soviet military personnel, added to the reported delivery of missiles which if fired from that area could hit many major American cities. Not long before Jackie returned, the President, siding with McCone, approved a U-2 flight.

For a good half hour, Kennedy lingered with his family, catching up on all their news as if he were nothing more than an ordinary, adoring parent. The next day, he continued to take time off from his work to spend with the children. John had left the White House in July still very much a baby but had returned, a month shy of his second birthday, an ebullient, photogenic little boy. A few minutes before 11 a.m., the President emerged hand in hand with his son. Feet carefully laced into 'big boy' shoes, John, beaming from ear to ear, fought to keep pace as they crossed the South Lawn to the 'lopaca' – his word for the helicopter. A love affair between parent and child was in full bloom, and, family friends said, it was hard to tell who was the more besotted.

The flight to Andrews Air Force Base was a brief one, and there, with the impeccable manners instilled by his mother, John stood at the President's side as he welcomed President Sékou Touré of Guinea. Later, Caroline appeared in the Oval Office, and the President clapped his hands with delight as she and John performed some dances. The happy scene, memorialized by a photographer, attested to Kennedy's boundless and unabashed pleasure in his family's return.

As always with Kennedy, things were a good deal more complicated than they seemed. Besides making a point of integrating the children into his crowded schedule, Jack found a way to see Mary Meyer at the White House that evening, although Jackie was back and he would not return from a campaign event in Baltimore until late.

Two weeks previously, when she was in Washington to see Ayub Khan and attend the Ormsby-Gores' party, Jackie had inspected preliminary plans for the redevelopment of Lafayette Square, the charming nineteenth-century square directly in front of the White House. Months earlier, she had intervened to halt a scheme, developed under Eisenhower, to replace the townhouses with modern office blocks. She had enlisted Bill Walton to come up with a way to reconcile the genuine need for governmental office space and her own desire to preserve the historic and aesthetic qualities of the old square. It had been no easy task, but at length the architect John Warnecke had drawn up plans that would retain the lovely townhouses, siting the new buildings behind them. Jackie, delighted by all she saw, had instructed Walton to organize a celebratory dinner party to take place the night after she returned from Newport.

As it happened, Jackie's dinner party provided Jack, whose schedule prohibited him from attending, with an opportunity to see Mary, by arranging for her to be Bill Walton's date. The fact that he would not be present at the meal himself took matters to a new level. Not only did he produce his mistress at the family table, as his father had been known to do, but he asked his wife to wine and dine her in his absence. Worse, Jackie would be doing so in front of at least two people, Walton and James Truitt, who, as a beard in the one case and drug supplier in the other, had had a hand in the affair.

Jackie was in the family quarters with her husband when seven guests congregated in the Yellow Oval Room at eight. Besides Meyer, Walton, and Truitt, Warnecke and Federal Aviation Agency Administrator Najeeb Halaby were present. Jack joined them for drinks but soon headed downstairs and across the South Lawn to the white cap which would take him to Baltimore, where he was to give a campaign speech at the Fifth Armory. The grotesque evening that followed in the newly redone President's Dining Room was one few wives could have forced themselves to endure with dignity. Jackie, with the steeliness that served her well in such circumstances, managed to be pointedly gracious to Mary, as if this were not the woman who had been sleeping with her husband all summer. Shortly after ten, the unmistakable roar of helicopters signaled that Jack was back in time to see his mistress before the evening ended.

Jack was neither stupid nor unfeeling, yet he seemed oblivious to his own cruelty on this and similar occasions. If his decision to put his mistress at that table indicated that this was to be a harsh season for Jackie, it sent a very different message to Mary. She no longer had reason to wonder whether her liaison would continue after Jackie returned. Jack had demonstrated the lengths to which he would go to see her, even if it meant humiliating his wife. Mary, euphoric, was soon off to see Timothy Leary. Over bottles of Dom Pérignon at Boston's Ritz-Carlton Hotel, she boasted of how well her secret affair was going and discussed the next step in her scheme to 'brainwash' powerful men in Washington with L.S.D.

The day after the dinner party, Jackie remained at the White House with the children while Jack flew to New York to start four days of campaigning. He was still in suspense over Cuba, as a tropical storm had made it necessary to postpone the reconnaissance flight. In the meantime, McCone had shown Kennedy photographs that purported to document crates on board a ship that had arrived in Cuba early in October, which were said to carry unassembled Soviet medium-range bombers. The President's response had been swift and sharp; he told McCone that he wanted the information withheld until after the elections. The Republicans were already hitting hard with charges that he was soft on Cuba. If information about the crates found its way into the press, Kennedy warned, that would inject 'a new and violent Cuban issue' into the campaign and his own 'independence of action' would be impaired. McCone said it would be impossible to do as Kennedy asked, since the pictures had already been disseminated to the intelligence community and several other commands, and were to be reported in the next morning's C.I.A. bulletin. He did agree to word the report to indicate 'a probability rather than an actuality,' as the photographs disclosed only crates, not the bombers themselves. Additional talk about secrecy issues gave Kennedy time to mull over all he had just seen and heard, and McCone took notice when the President suddenly remarked, 'We'll have to do something drastic about Cuba.' Nothing could be decided until there was hard evidence, and that would have to wait until the weather improved.

While Kennedy was on the road, Republicans continued to charge, based on unconfirmed refugee reports, that the Soviets were establishing offensive missile bases in Cuba. Republican Senator Homer Capeheart of Indiana, for one, called for an immediate invasion. Moscow, however, persisted in its staunch denials, the latest at a lunch between Ambassador Dobrynin and Chester Bowles, now Ambassador at Large. In Indiana on Saturday, in words not unlike his father's at the outset of the Second World War, Kennedy publicly took issue with Senator Capeheart: 'These self-appointed generals and admirals who want to send somebody else's son to war ought to be kept at home by the voters.' The echo suggests that Joe's political downfall was on Jack's mind as he waited to see whether Khrushchev had been telling the truth. As chance would have it, Joe was due at the White House on Monday for a first visit since his stroke, a tacit admission that there was really no reason for him to steer clear anymore. Paralyzed and unable to speak, a pitiful shadow of his former self yet a tumultuous presence nonetheless, he was unlikely any longer to be labeled the President's puppeteer. Yet, in a less immediate sense, that was exactly what he remained. His visit would have packed a powerful emotional charge at any time, but coming as it did in the midst of a second unfolding crisis in Cuba, it highlighted the extent to which painful issues attached to the father continued to drive the son.

By the time Jack returned to the White House at 2 a.m. Monday morning, the reconnaissance mission had flown after a five-day delay, and 928 photographs were under analysis at the National Photographic Intelligence Center. Two additional U-2 flights were to follow later in the day. The results from the first mission were still not ready at 11:30 when Jack, again accompanied by young John, prepared to greet Prime Minister Ahmed Ben Bella of Algeria, who was arriving in Washington for a day of meetings. That afternoon, Jackie, in the deep pink Chanel suit with navy lapels she had first worn for her proud arrival in London from India and Pakistan, collected both children after their naps and set out by car to meet Joe at the airport. Jack was waiting when they returned, and he and Jackie escorted the old man in his wheelchair to the Lincoln Bedroom, where she had installed a hospital bed and made other arrangements for his comfort. She had also asked several female members of the presidential staff whom Joe had known since Jack's days in Congress to pop in. He had an early dinner with

his son and daughter-in-law, as Jack, who had had little sleep
the previous night, needed to retire early.

At a quarter to nine the next morning, Tuesday, October 16,
the President, in dressing gown and pajamas, read the papers
in bed propped up against pillows. Jackie, in the adjoining
room, was preparing to spend much of the day with Joe, as she
and Jack were to attend a dinner party at Joe Alsop's that
evening while Joe ate with the children. There was a knock at
the President's door. As he looked up to see McGeorge Bundy
crossing the off-white carpet, he indicated the newspaper and
grumbled about its headline, 'Eisenhower Calls President Weak
on Foreign Policy.' He was on the point of complaining about
what he saw as Republican election-year mischief when Bundy
cut him off.

'Mr President,' said Bundy, 'there is now hard photographic
evidence, which you will see later, that the Russians have
offensive missiles in Cuba.'

'He can't do that to me!' Kennedy exploded.

Bundy had had a call from the C.I.A. the previous night,
informing him that analysis of the reconnaissance photos indicated three medium-range ballistic sites near Cristobal, in Pinar
del Rio province. The U.S. now had evidence of eight large
medium-range ballistic missile transporters and four erector
launchers in tentative firing positions. In short, McCone had
been proved correct. Bundy, for his part, had decided to wait
until morning to tell the President. Later he would explain that
he felt that since Kennedy had just returned from a strenuous
trip, a good night's sleep would be the best preparation for all
that faced him in the days ahead.

As his outburst indicated, Kennedy took the news about the
missiles personally. From the start, his dialogue with Khrushchev
on this matter had been cast in distinctly personal terms, with
Khrushchev sending word that he liked the President and did
not wish to hurt him before the election, and Bobby conveying
that Soviet missteps in Cuba would upset his brother. The
President tended to see world affairs as a struggle between great
men. Inevitably, he interpreted Khrushchev's betrayal as a
personal insult, a comment less on American weakness than on

his own. The blow was made all the worse by his father's looming presence down the hall. On the basis of 'Cuba 1,' Khrushchev seemed to think that Kennedy, a coward like his father, would never dare go in and destroy the missiles.

In view of Joe's condition, Jack wanted him to have no inkling of what was going on. Nor did he want the Soviets to guess that he knew about the missiles, for that would severely limit his options. He did, however, tell Jackie, whom he instructed to proceed with her day as if nothing had happened. She was also to keep to her Wednesday and Thursday schedule, which included a press preview of the plans for Lafayette Square and an overnight trip to attend a New York University reception in honor of her work on behalf of culture and the arts.

In the Oval Office, the President notified his press secretary only that there would be a good deal of traffic at the White House that week. If journalists inquired, Salinger was to deny that anything special was going on. Kennedy was more forthcoming with Charles Bohlen, who arrived to pay his official farewell call before he left to take up his new post as ambassador to France. Bohlen came with the expectation of a talk about de Gaulle, but it was the Soviet Union and Khrushchev that Kennedy was eager to discuss. Bohlen, one of America's premier experts on Soviet matters, had been the translator in Roosevelt's talks with Stalin at Yalta and later served as ambassador in Moscow. That night he was to be the guest of honor at Alsop's dinner party, and Kennedy, though expecting to see him there, welcomed an opportunity to confer in private.

'Chip, come here and look at these,' said Kennedy of the reconnaissance photographs arrayed on his desk. The pictures, difficult for a layman to decipher, were a source of immense frustration to Kennedy, who thought they looked less like a missile site than a football field. Both men agreed that the U.S. would have to eliminate the bases. The only question was how. Bohlen urged Kennedy to pursue a diplomatic course first.

Kennedy continued to weigh his options when he met with advisers in the Cabinet Room. The C.I.A. deciphered the reconnaissance images for an audience that included Bobby Kennedy, Dean Rusk, Robert McNamara, Lyndon Johnson, and McGeorge Bundy, among others. Most seemed stunned that the Soviets had gone so far as to install offensive missiles in Cuba. For the President, a major lesson of the Bay of Pigs operation had been that no major action must be taken without every aspect being discussed 'in full detail.' Having been badly burned when he deferred to the expertise of others, Kennedy probed the C.I.A. men with questions.

One theme of Kennedy's questions was the enigma of Khrushchev the man. Why had he lied? Why had he decided to install the missiles? What was the advantage? What did he want and what bargaining chips would such knowledge give the U.S.? Rusk came closest to offering an answer when he suggested that Khrushchev, angry about U.S. Jupiter missiles stationed in Turkey, meant to show the Americans how it felt to have enemy missiles so near. He also suggested that Khrushchev might want to provoke Kennedy to act in Cuba, thereby giving the Soviets justification to move in Berlin. Rusk, though he was determined to eliminate the Soviet missiles, urged extreme caution. 'I think we'll be facing a situation that could well lead to a general war,' he emphasized. 'Now with that we have an obligation to do what has to be done, but to do it in a way that gives everybody a chance to pull away before it gets too hard.' Given the extent to which Khrushchev had deceived him, Kennedy placed little hope in diplomacy. Assured that there were no nuclear warheads yet, he weighed three options: a strike against the missile bases, a wider air strike on military targets, and air strikes followed by an invasion. At the very least, he vowed, 'We're going to take out these missiles.'

Later in the day, Assistant Secretary of State for Inter-American Affairs Edwin M. Martin seized Kennedy's interest with a suggestion that the direct threat posed by the missiles might not be the principal issue. Far more important, Martin proposed, was the 'psychological factor that we have sat back and let them do it to us.' The repercussions would be especially significant, Kennedy agreed, in light of the fact that one month previously he had vowed in public that the U.S. would strike if Cuba became an offensive base for the Soviet Union. His own statements about where the U.S. would draw the line, the

President concluded, compelled him to attack. But why, he continued to wonder, did Khrushchev appear to risk war over Cuba, especially when he already had it in his power to launch intercontinental missiles against the U.S. from Soviet soil? Concluding that he didn't know enough about the Soviets and wanted to hear what specialists had to say, Kennedy went upstairs to dress for dinner. Fortunately, two such specialists were to be among Alsop's guests that evening.

France had a reputation as one of the touchiest high-profile diplomatic posts, and Alsop, who possessed a taste for such gestures, had planned the evening to show de Gaulle that Bohlen was important enough for the Kennedys to appear at his farewell party. To be sure de Gaulle got the message, Alsop had put Hervé and Nicole Alphand on the guest list. It was therefore impossible for Kennedy to cancel lest he alert the French ambassador that he was in the throes of a crisis.

Usually, the Kennedys arrived at Alsop's house in high spirits, but this evening was markedly different, though neither the host nor his guests, with the exception of Bohlen, knew why. Given Jack's absorption in the current crisis, the requirements of Jackie's role were also a departure. Ushered onto a terrace where drinks were served, Kennedy barely greeted Alsop, Phil Graham, and the other guests before making a beeline for Bohlen, whom he led to the far end of the garden where they could not be overheard. Meanwhile, it fell on Jackie to distract the group. While Kennedy wondered aloud to Bohlen whether he should approach Khrushchev directly, how much time remained before the Soviet weapons were operational, and what the international repercussions would be in the event of a U.S. strike, Jackie did her best to make utterly fascinating small talk. Later in the evening, Kennedy moved on to Isaiah Berlin, a renowned authority on Russian intellectual history. After he had picked the Oxford professor's brain on Khrushchev, the Russian cast of mind, and related subjects, he dismissed him with the remark, 'You must go and sit next to Jackie. She wants to bring you out.' As always, Jack could rely on her to pick up the baton and intuit exactly what he needed – in this case, to take Berlin off his hands.

Thursday night, Jackie returned from New York University to discover that Joe Kennedy had been waiting for an hour to dine with his son. Three times word had been sent to the Oval Office that dinner was ready. Finally, ten minutes previously, Jack had returned to the family quarters in a temper following a meeting with Andrei Gromyko, and had still not appeared in the dining room. For over two hours, the Soviet Minister of Foreign Affairs had told 'more barefaced lies' than Kennedy could recall ever having 'heard in so short a time.' Again and again, he had insisted that the armaments sent to Cuba were 'only defensive.' The President had had to resist an urge to open the center drawer in his desk and produce the reconnaissance photographs, knowing that if he did so he would sacrifice the element of surprise should the U.S. attack.

That morning, he had reviewed the results of new U-2 flights and the information had been seriously disturbing. More missiles had been discovered, they had a longer range than expected, and to make matters worse they were 'pistol pointed' at the U.S. That was not all. The crates spotted earlier had been unpacked and, precisely as feared, contained Soviet jet bombers capable of dropping nuclear bombs on the U.S. Indeed, as of that morning the C.I.A. insisted that it must now be assumed there were nuclear warheads in Cuba. Kennedy's advisers were thunderstruck, as all their plans had been based on an assumption that the missiles were not operational. Suddenly everything had to be rethought. In this atmosphere of chaos and confusion, Llewellyn Thompson, now Ambassador at Large, proposed something new: a blockade against the shipment of offensive military equipment to Cuba, coupled with a demand that equipment already in place be dismantled. Others continued to press for an air attack, the option still favored by the President.

By the time he joined Jackie and his father, the blockade option had begun to attract him as more likely to avert a nuclear war by giving Khrushchev a chance to pull back. He wanted to discuss it further, but whatever he and Jackie chose to talk about in the President's Dining Room, there could be no reference to any of this in front of Joe. They had a hurried dinner, and afterward Jack rushed off to make a call.

At 9:45 p.m., members of the Executive Committee devoted to the missile crisis arrived. Kennedy had instructed them to use the family gate in order to bypass the press. Lest a parade of cars attract attention, Bobby had transported ten men in his vehicle, four in the front and six in back. They emerged like clowns from a circus car and were soon proceeding down the second-floor Center Hall to the Yellow Oval Room opposite the children's rooms.

Their presence signaled a disruption of the boundaries Jackie had established early on between those spaces dedicated to the presidency and those to family life. It was commonplace for heads of state and other dignitaries to be received in the Yellow Oval Room for drinks and to meet the President's family, but such visits to the First Lady's sanctum tended to be highly orchestrated and afforded guests a sense of privilege. This impromptu gathering was an entirely different phenomenon. The family quarters resembled a spacious apartment, and it would have been impossible for Jackie to ignore the turbulent session that raged past midnight in a room whose inner doors, opposite the fireplace, led directly to her husband's bedroom.

Jack did not go to bed until early Friday morning, as he had gone downstairs to dictate a memo after Bobby and the others left. Scheduled to make campaign appearances in Cleveland and Chicago the next day and determined not to cancel lest his absence raise questions, he had directed his advisers to present both positions – blockade versus military strike – when he returned after the weekend.

A few hours later, Kennedy met with the Joint Chiefs of Staff, who reacted with horror when he indicated his preference for a blockade. 'It will lead right into war,' protested General Curtis LeMay, who preferred an immediate military strike. Given Kennedy's sensitivities, LeMay hit where it hurt when he declared, 'This is almost as bad as the appeasement at Munich.' Kennedy suppressed his anger until after the meeting. Then, recalled Deputy Secretary of Defense Roswell Gilpatric, he was 'choleric,' 'beside himself.' Fuming over the pointed reference to his father's blunder when he applauded the Munich

Pact, Kennedy went upstairs to say goodbye to Joe, who was scheduled to go home that afternoon. The encounter was a poignant one, at least for the son. From the first, his political career had been driven by a desperate need for vindication, but even as President he had yet to achieve that either for Joe or for himself.

Kennedy headed out to the South Lawn and had just climbed into the white cap which would take him to Andrews Air Force Base, where *Air Force One* waited for the flight to Cleveland, when he spotted Jackie. After what he had just gone through with LeMay, then Joe, she who knew his feelings better than most saw one last chance to comfort him. As she raced across the grass, her hair blew in the gust from the whirling blades. Jack came back down the steps and Jackie flew into his arms, whereupon, recalled Dr Janet Travell, who witnessed the scene from her office, 'they stood motionless in an embrace for many seconds.'

ELEVEN

Valediction

Early on the morning of Saturday, October 20, 1962, the phone rang at Glen Ora, where Jackie had taken Caroline and John for the weekend after seeing Joe off at the airport. It was Jack calling from Chicago to tell Jackie that his advisers' presentation was ready. After he conferred with them, he would have to decide between a blockade and a military strike. He intended to cut short his trip and tell the press a bad cold had forced his return. Meanwhile, he instructed her to go to the White House immediately. 'He wanted Jackie and the children to be there when he was making these awful decisions,' recalled David Ormsby-Gore. He sought her emotional support, certainly, but he also wanted her there because no one could predict Khrushchev's response. In the event of a nuclear attack, Jack planned for his wife and children to accompany him, along with certain essential members of government, to an underground shelter in a Virginia mountain.

Late that afternoon, Jackie returned to a White House consumed by war fever. Small white envelopes with pink identification cards had been distributed to employees who were to be admitted to the nuclear shelter. Among them were women who had slept with the President at one time or another. Some recipients were honored to go with the Kennedys. Others hated the idea of leaving their own families behind. Meanwhile, after a two-and-a-half-hour session with advisers in the Yellow Oval Room, Kennedy tentatively settled on a blockade coupled with an ultimatum that all missiles be withdrawn. If Khrushchev refused, there would be an air strike. The President, emphasizing that 'our world position will be much better if we attack only the missiles,' ordered the military to be ready in three days. A speech to announce the blockade, if and when Kennedy gave the go-ahead, was in the works, but he reserved the right to change his mind.

As at the time of the Bay of Pigs, Kennedy reached out to his wife as a final decision drew near. Saturday night, though it was no longer possible to shut out the crisis entirely, he retreated to the cocoon of beauty and serenity she had created in the family quarters. When Dave Powers visited, he discovered the President reading softly to Caroline, who lay nestled in his arms.

Sunday morning, preparations for a blockade were in progress, but when the President and First Lady went to Mass, he had not completely ruled out a surprise air attack. He continued to weigh arguments that only an immediate air strike would knock out all the missiles. The second a blockade was announced, Kennedy knew, the opportunity for surprise would be lost and the missiles could be camouflaged. After church, Jack and Jackie returned to the family quarters, where he listened to presentations by General Maxwell Taylor and General Walter Sweeney Jr. The latter would be in direct charge of an air strike if one were ordered. Certain though Sweeney was of success, he was careful to point out that even under optimum conditions it was unlikely that all missiles would be obliterated. Taylor chimed in, 'The best we can offer you is to destroy 90 percent of the known missiles.' Up to this point, the possibility of wiping out every missile had been the sole factor that prevented the President from ruling out a surprise attack. Told that some would probably survive, he finally and definitively made up his mind in favor of a blockade. He would issue his ultimatum Monday evening.

While the session with the generals was in progress, Ormsby-Gore appeared in the family quarters. Kennedy had directed his old friend to 'come unseen' shortly before lunch. The British ambassador waited until Taylor and Sweeney emerged from the Yellow Oval Room at half past twelve. Then he went in and met with the President alone. In the intense hour that followed, for the first time Kennedy spoke of the missile crisis to someone outside the U.S. government. He showed Ormsby-Gore the reconnaissance photographs and reviewed his options. Which, Kennedy asked, did Ormsby-Gore favor – blockade or air attack? Ormsby-Gore chose the former, on the grounds that the latter would damage the U.S. politically since few people around the world would consider the provocation of the missiles 'enough to merit an American attack.' Only then did Kennedy disclose he had just reached the same conclusion. He would send word to Macmillan – the first foreign leader to be contacted – later that day, and to de Gaulle and other allies the next day before he went on television.

Kennedy believed a blockade the more responsible choice. Still, he recognized that Khrushchev might respond with what Rusk chillingly called 'an immediate, sudden, irrational' nuclear strike. Alternatively, the Soviets might retaliate by seizing Berlin, in which case Kennedy's plan was, in his words, 'to fire our nuclear weapons at them.' Jackie appeared at 1:30 and they all went in to lunch, where she asked Ormsby-Gore to return to the White House with Sissie for dinner on the eve of what promised to be the most difficult and dangerous days of Jack's presidency.

While Jack spent the better part of the day in meetings, Jackie was left to rearrange their social schedule as discreetly as possible. A large dinner dance in honor of the Maharaja of Jaipur and his wife, who had entertained Jackie in India, loomed on Tuesday night. Guests were flying in from various European cities, and the Jaipurs themselves were to stay in the White House family quarters. A small dinner party was scheduled for the night before – the night of Jack's speech, as it turned out – to be attended by Lee Radziwill and the Grazianis, who would be in Washington for the Jaipur party. Without going into details, Jackie instructed Mr West to prepare to cancel the dinner dance and move the Jaipurs to Blair House, the government guesthouse. As for the dinner party, she decided to go ahead, hoping that her sister and the Grazianis might divert Jack after his speech, while they and the world waited for Khrushchev's response. Her major problem was to make sure that no one suspected a crisis was brewing. To her relief Mr West, nothing if not discreet, knew better than to ask questions. In contrast, there was no need to hold anything back that evening with the Ormsby-Gores. Both were acutely conscious of Jack's burdens, and it was a tremendous comfort to have them present as he prepared to embark on what would prove to be the final chapter of a family drama in which David and Sissie had been key players since the days of Joe's ambassadorship.

On the morning of Monday, October 22, the President attended a round of meetings. After a last session on contingency plans for U.S. action in Berlin at half past twelve, he went upstairs to see Jackie. He had wanted her nearby as he agonized about the missiles, and now that he had made up his mind, he wanted to be sure that she and the children were safe when he went on the air at seven. Most staff members in possession of pink cards knew there was more than a 50 percent chance that, in the event of a nuclear attack, they would not be able to reach the Virginia shelter in time. So Jack asked Jackie to leave before his speech and wait in a location close to the shelter. If there were a nuclear strike, she and the children would have time to seek refuge even if he did not.

Jackie wouldn't hear of it, insisting that she would remain at the White House no matter what. If Khrushchev did fire missiles, she would come to the Oval Office and 'share whatever happened' to Jack. Husband and wife spent the next two and a half hours together. They would have no more time alone until after his speech. Jackie had just expressed a willingness to die at her husband's side, yet before he went downstairs he made a point of arranging for Mary Meyer to dine with them that night by adding Bill Walton and 'one more woman' to the guest list Jackie had composed when she returned from Newport.

When the President returned to the West Wing, he went into a series of meetings that concluded with a highly-charged encounter with Congressional leaders from both parties dismayed by the idea of a blockade. Senator Richard Russell, an influential Georgia Democrat, demanded a military strike. The longer Kennedy waited, Russell warned, the more likely Khrushchev was to convince himself that the U.S. was afraid to fight. 'We're either a first-class power or we're not,' Russell said. 'You have warned these people time and again, in the most eloquent speeches I have read since Woodrow Wilson, that's what would happen if there was an offensive capability created in Cuba. They can't say they're not on notice.'

Even Senator William Fulbright, who had opposed an invasion at the time of the Bay of Pigs, declared that in light of the presence of offensive missiles he now favored 'an invasion, and an all-out one, and as quickly as possible.' Kennedy, visibly fatigued, oddly unfocused, and unresponsive to the blistering criticism, delivered a punch-drunk performance that did not bode well for his television address. 'If they want this job, fuck 'em,' the President cursed as he left. 'They can have it. It's no great joy to me.' Scheduled to go before the cameras half an hour later, he headed upstairs to change clothes.

While Kennedy was arguing with the Congressmen, Secretary of State Rusk presented Ambassador Dobrynin with the President's personal letter to Khrushchev, as well as the text of the speech he was soon to give. When Rusk disclosed that the U.S. knew about the missiles, Dobrynin appeared to age about ten years. Simultaneously, in Moscow, copies of the letter and the speech were delivered to the Soviet Foreign Ministry. By the time the President went on the air, his ultimatum was already in enemy hands.

Kennedy read the better part of his speech rapidly and unemotionally, projecting the authority that had been absent from his session with the Congressmen. Publicly accusing the Soviet Union of having lied about the missiles, Kennedy announced 'a strict quarantine on all offensive military equipment under shipment to Cuba' and promised further action if surveillance showed that offensive military preparations continued. 'The 1930s taught us a clear lesson,' he went on. 'Aggressive conduct, if allowed to go unchecked and unchallenged, ultimately leads to war.' The U.S. would ask that an emergency meeting of the United Nations Security Council consider a resolution for 'the prompt dismantling and withdrawal of all offensive weapons in Cuba, under the supervision of United Nations observers, before the quarantine can be lifted.' Kennedy warned that his government would 'regard any nuclear missile launched from Cuba against any nation in the Western hemisphere as an attack by the Soviet Union on the United States, requiring a full retaliatory response upon the Soviet Union.' He called upon Khrushchev 'to halt and elim- inate this clandestine, reckless, and provocative threat to world peace and to stable relations between our two nations.'

'My fellow citizens,' Kennedy declared, 'let no one doubt that this is a difficult and dangerous effort on which we have set out. No one can foresee precisely what course it will take or what costs or casualties will be incurred. Many months of sacrifice and self-discipline lie ahead – months in which both our patience and our will will be tested, months in which many threats and denunciations will keep us aware of our dangers. But the greatest danger of all would be to do nothing.'

After the eighteen-minute address, Kennedy went to his office and called Macmillan on a special secure line. It was half past midnight in London. At the time of 'Cuba 1,' Kennedy had been constantly on the phone to his father, less for tactical advice than for moral support. During 'Cuba 2,' Macmillan took Joe's place, frequently staying up until 4 a.m. in anticipation of Kennedy's call. Afterward, chroniclers of the Cuban Missile Crisis would ask just how much practical advice the President sought and received, but the question entirely misses the point. The purpose of those conversations, as Macmillan would later tell Jackie, was to allow her husband to talk to someone who, because he too was a head of government, sympathized and understood. If it was tactical advice Kennedy wanted, Ormsby- Gore was there to offer it on the Prime Minister's behalf. Repeatedly, Kennedy called London in quest of something intangible. At a moment of overwhelming pressure, contact with Macmillan assuaged his sense of isolation.

It was also true that by the time of the missile crisis, Kennedy had internalized Macmillan's belief that it was a great leader's personal obligation to avoid the insanity of war *if possible*. While Macmillan had little impact on the specifics of Kennedy's minute-by-minute tactical decisions, the Prime Minister's philosophical influence was a guiding force in his resistance to demands for immediate military action.

'You must have had a very hard time,' Macmillan ended their first telephone conversation. 'I feel very sorry for you and all your troubles. I've been through them. I only want to tell you how much we feel for you.'

Buoyed up by the man he had learned to call 'dear friend,' Kennedy retired to the family quarters, where Jackie and six guests waited. Lee was there, as well as the designer Oleg Cassini, and Benno Graziani and his wife. So were Mary Meyer and Bill Walton, who had watched Jack's speech together at Walton's house and come to the White House afterward. In view of the crisis, any resentment Jackie felt toward Mary would have to be suppressed.

Given Mary's crackpot plan to achieve world peace by slipping L.S.D. to men in power, Jack's having made it possible for her to be present at this critical moment boggles the mind. And there was more: When the President's mistress and their beard arrived at the White House, a military aide had taken them aside to convey his instructions. If in the course of the evening word came of an impending nuclear assault, Meyer and Walton were to be rushed to the underground shelter in Virginia, along with Jackie and the children.

By the time the dinner party ended after midnight, there had been no retaliatory action, in Berlin or elsewhere. Still, many people went to bed uncertain whether they would wake up the next morning. At a meeting of the President's advisers on Tuesday, October 23, Rusk articulated everyone's fears when he dryly remarked, 'I think it very significant that we were here this morning.' Whether they would still be there the following day was another matter.

Late in the day, the Organization of American States voted unanimously to support the U.S. action, yet as the hour approached for Kennedy to sign a proclamation ordering the blockade, it was evident that he was uneasy. Under Jackie's influence, he was known to be fastidious about his appearance. On this occasion he was uncharacteristically disheveled and, as one observer noted, seemed older than his age for the first time in his life. He had reason to be anxious. Shortly before he entered the Oval Office, he had received word that Khrushchev had instructed Soviet ships to run the blockade. Alone with Bobby after the signing, the President wondered aloud whether he had done the right thing. The blockade was to begin at 10 a.m. the next day, October 24, and if the information proved accurate a clash was inevitable.

'It looks really mean, doesn't it?' Jack asked. 'But, on the other hand, there wasn't any other choice. If he's going to get this mean on this one, in our part of the world, no choice. I don't think there was a choice.'

'Well, there isn't any choice,' Bobby confirmed. 'I mean, you would have been, you would have been impeached.'

'Well, I think I would have been impeached,' Jack echoed.

In the midst of this grim conversation, Kennedy suddenly remembered he was due upstairs. Jackie had canceled the dinner dance for the Jaipurs, but had decided to go ahead with an informal dinner for fourteen. As on the previous night, her intention was to take Jack's mind off his troubles, but she had reason to wonder whether even this more modest event was a good idea. In the course of the evening, she realized that Jack and David Ormsby-Gore had wandered off together, abandoning the rest of the group. She eventually found them in the Yellow Oval Room, crouching over photographs of the missile sites spread out on the white carpet, methodically studying each image in order to decide which to release to the press.

At 10:30 p.m., a visibly shaken Bobby Kennedy appeared. He had just come from a meeting with Dobrynin, who continued to insist that as far as he knew there were no missiles in Cuba. Asked whether Soviet ships planned to proceed despite the blockade, Dobrynin had replied ominously that such had been their instructions one month previously and he assumed they had 'the same instructions at the present time.' Jack agreed to Ormsby-Gore's suggestion to move the line of quarantine closer to Cuba, in order to delay a confrontation and give Khrushchev more time to reconsider. Despite objections by the Navy, the President ordered that ships be intercepted not 800 but 500 miles from Cuba. Even so, a clash seemed likely sometime the following morning when the first vessel, menacingly accompanied by a submarine, would reach the quarantine zone. The moment could trigger the world's first nuclear confrontation.

Wednesday morning, the atmosphere in the family quarters was extremely tense. Great numbers of lives, indeed the existence of all mankind, might depend on Kennedy's decisions in the next few hours. Meanwhile, Jackie discovered that young John had developed a fever in the night that had reached 104. Jack expected the first ship to cross the quarantine line at about half past ten, and before that happened he again asked Jackie to move closer to the underground shelter. Again she refused. While her husband conferred with advisers in the Cabinet Room, she bundled John into a White House car and took him to the doctor.

The day that followed was marked by violent swings of emotion. When she saw Jack next, at lunch, the news seemed encouraging. At the last minute, all six Soviet ships had abruptly either 'stopped or turned back.' The enemy appeared to have retreated from the faceoff. By the time Jack came upstairs for dinner, however, he had reinterpreted the ship movements. The ships, he suspected, carried either missiles or secret material that Khrushchev did not want to fall into enemy hands. In the interim, other ships – these, Kennedy guessed, carrying nothing of military importance – had been spotted moving toward Cuba, and might yet provoke an incident. It now looked as if the first challenge to a Soviet tanker would take place at approximately two in the morning.

After the Kennedys dined with their friends Charles and Martha Bartlett, a letter arrived from Khrushchev: 'The Soviet Government considers that the violation of the freedom to use international waters and international air space is an act of aggression which pushes mankind toward the abyss of a world nuclear-missile war. Therefore, the Soviet Government cannot instruct the captains of Soviet vessels bound for Cuba to observe the orders of American naval forces blockading the island. Our instructions to Soviet mariners are to observe strictly the universally accepted norms of navigation in international waters and not to retreat one step from them.'

In short, Khrushchev was confirming that he had ordered his ships to run the blockade – the worst possible news.

With 2 a.m. fast approaching, Kennedy, still in the Oval Office, ordered the challenge to the Soviet tanker to be postponed for a few hours while he sent a message to United Nations Secretary-General U Thant, who had suggested that Kennedy suspend the blockade and Khrushchev agree not to send in any ships while both sides talked for a week or two. At the time, Kennedy had responded with skepticism, on the grounds that such an arrangement would give the Soviets time to finish building the missile sites. Now, Kennedy asked U Thant to request Khrushchev to 'hold up' his ships for just forty-eight hours, so that both sides could come to terms on the conditions for any negotiations – conditions that, as far as he was concerned, would have to include a halt to work on the missile sites. He left no doubt in his message to U Thant that if Khrushchev refused to talk, the challenge to the first ship would proceed. He followed up with a personal letter to Khrushchev urging him to 'take the necessary action' to cool the situation down. The letter was delivered to the Soviet embassy in Washington at a quarter to two, whereupon Kennedy finally joined Jackie upstairs.

Thursday morning at six, the U.S. intercepted a Soviet vessel to demand its name, point of origin, destination, and type of cargo. Told that this was the *Bucharest*, that it was from the Black Sea bound for Havana, and that its cargo was oil, the U.S. sailors waved it on then followed it toward Cuba. Kennedy decided to let the ship go lest an incident distract Khrushchev before he replied to U Thant. As Kennedy told Macmillan that evening, if Khrushchev failed to respond by Friday afternoon, the U.S. would search the next Soviet ship that crossed the line.

On Friday, word came that Khrushchev had agreed. He would keep his ships out of the quarantine zone for forty-eight hours. As Kennedy knew, this wasn't much of a concession, as no Soviet vessel was due to reach the blockade during that time, but at least it seemed to signal a willingness to negotiate. Whether or not the preliminary talks proved fruitful, Kennedy hoped to use this lull in the tension to rest with his family. That afternoon, Jackie and the children left for Glen Ora. The President was to follow the next day. The break, he calculated, would serve him well if the conflict dragged on for weeks. When he talked to Macmillan that evening, he reported rumors of Khrushchev's interest in a settlement that would have him remove the missiles in exchange for a U.S. pledge not to invade Cuba. The President emphasized that at this point it was still all 'rather unofficial and unreliable.' Even as he was on the phone, however, a letter arrived that made the offer very official indeed. Khrushchev expressed a willingness to withdraw the armaments if Kennedy recalled his fleet and vowed not to attack Cuba or encourage others – presumably Cuban refugees – to do so. Those were acceptable terms, and Kennedy went to bed hopeful that the crisis was at an end.

Saturday morning, he discovered it was not so. Newspapers reported that 'Premier Khrushchev told President Kennedy yesterday he would withdraw offensive weapons from Cuba if the United States withdrew rockets from Turkey.' Kennedy guessed at once that Khrushchev had released a second, different letter to the press. Indeed, it had been broadcast over Moscow radio and a copy delivered to the U.S. embassy there. 'He's put this out in a way to cause maximum tension and embarrassment,' the President told aides. 'It's not as if this was a private proposal, which would give us an opportunity to negotiate with the Turks. He has put it out in a way that the Turks are bound to say that they don't agree with this.' Kennedy recalled that, more than a year ago, he had talked about withdrawing the Jupiter missiles because they were 'obsolete and of little military value.' More recently, when he seized on them as a possible bargaining chip in the Cuban crisis, Thomas Finletter, the U.S. ambassador to N.A.T.O., had warned that the Turks 'set great store' by them as a symbol of U.S. determination to protect Turkey. National Security Adviser McGeorge Bundy argued that to withdraw the Jupiter missiles now, after Khrushchev's latest move, would give the appearance of selling out an ally.

Secretary of State Rusk thought a missile trade would smack of blackmail. Kennedy perceived a different problem: Khrushchev had put the U.S. in the absurd position of appearing to attack Cuba 'for the purpose of keeping useless missiles in Turkey' – a position highly unlikely to win international support for an air strike.

That afternoon, Kennedy was informed that a low-altitude daylight surveillance mission approved a few hours previously had encountered Cuban ground fire and that one of the U-2 planes had failed to return. Then came a report that the aircraft had been shot down, its pilot killed. General Taylor called for an attack on the missile site that had targeted the plane, and Defense Secretary McNamara judged an invasion of Cuba 'almost inevitable.' With the nuclear powers set to collide, Kennedy made a last effort. He responded to Khrushchev's letter of the previous night as if the more recent public letter did not exist. Kennedy embraced the proposal, which he made a point of crediting to Khrushchev, that the U.S. undertake not to invade Cuba in exchange for a Soviet promise to dismantle the missile bases and remove all offensive weapons. That much Kennedy was prepared to put in writing. Meanwhile, he sent an oral message to Dobrynin via Bobby Kennedy, who also delivered the letter; the President was ready to remove the Jupiter missiles and would quietly do so once Moscow and Washington came to terms on Cuba. The offer, he stressed, must be kept secret. If word leaked out, the U.S. would consider it null and void. The President wanted to avoid the appearance of a *quid pro quo* but was not about to let obsolete missiles stand in the way of peace.

Once Bobby had made the offer, they could do nothing but wait. At an evening session of the Executive Committee, Kennedy seemed relatively calm. Asked by someone unaware of this latest development whether the U.S. planned to take out the missile site that had shot down the plane, Kennedy insisted, 'We don't know if it did yet.' Clearly he did not wish to stir things up, preferring to wait at least until Monday to hear from Khrushchev.

The answer came a good deal sooner. Early on the morning

of Sunday, October 28, Moscow radio announced that Khrushchev and Kennedy had reached an agreement. In a letter to
the President, Khrushchev promised to discontinue work on
the weapons construction sites as well as to dismantle, crate,
and return offensive arms to the Soviet Union. It was a stunning
victory for Kennedy. Macmillan spoke for many when he told
the President, 'It was indeed a trial of wills and yours has
prevailed.' Only a few close advisers knew of Kennedy's secret
offer to remove the Jupiter missiles. Had the trade been made
public, almost certainly it would have diminished his image of
having stared Khrushchev down.

The outcome of the crisis registered in the West as a major
defeat for Moscow. In contrast to the Bay of Pigs, this time
Kennedy had done everything right. In forcing Khrushchev to
retreat, he had put to rest the old charges of Kennedy weakness
and cowardice and attained the vindication his father had long
yearned for. Encouraged by Macmillan not to crow but to use
victory to positive ends, Kennedy wasted no time in asking
Khrushchev to join him in giving 'priority to questions relating
to the proliferation of nuclear weapons, on earth and in outer
space, and to the great effort for a nuclear test ban.'

Numerous vital details of the deal remained to be taken care
of, but that afternoon a white cap rose over the White House,
taking the President to Glen Ora. At the time of 'Cuba 1,'
Jackie more than anyone had observed him at his nadir. She
had watched him make every wrong decision. She had seen his
tears and done all she could to help as he waited for a second
chance. During 'Cuba 2,' she had made it clear that she
preferred to die at his side than go on alone. Now that Jack
had succeeded so brilliantly, his first instinct was to share his
happiness with her. It was very much a gesture that he did not
send for Jackie and the children, as he otherwise might have
done. He could stay at Glen Ora only for four hours and would
hardly have time to unwind, but he made a point of going to
her. As the white cap landed, Jackie waited in the field, the
huge white-shuttered stucco house behind her. The moment
represented everything she had been working toward since
Paris.

When Jackie returned to the White House the next day, she planned a pair of victory celebrations for the following week. One was a dinner party for twelve, the other a large dinner dance ostensibly to welcome back General James Gavin, former U.S. ambassador in Paris but really, as it evolved, a gathering of friends to toast Jack's success. The dinner party began as an effort to reassemble a few of the people who had been at Joe Alsop's farewell dinner for Charles Bohlen. In a sense, that evening had marked the start of 'Cuba 2,' and it seemed fitting to celebrate with some of those who had been present. The first names on Jackie's list were the Alsops and the Isaiah Berlins (though Mrs Berlin had not been present at the Bohlen dinner). When Jackie contacted Alsop, she learned that C. L. Sulzberger, whom she had met in Ravello, and his wife would be staying with him that night, so they had to be invited as well.

The addition led Jackie to think she might include some others who had not been there on the 16th. She asked Arthur Schlesinger Jr and his wife, friends of both the Alsops and the Berlins, and Schlesinger suggested that she invite the playwright S. N. Behrman, whose wit Jack was likely to appreciate. Since Behrman was to come alone, Jackie, in need of an extra woman, asked her sister, Lee Radziwill, to come as well.

By the time Jackie left for Glen Ora on Friday, her office had sent out invitations. When she returned, she discovered her sister would not be able to attend after all, meaning that the list was now one woman short. Jack proposed a substitute, and on Wednesday a last-minute invitation went out to Mary Meyer for the following evening. In the thick of the missile crisis Jackie had suppressed her resentment, but the idea of sharing a small, sentimental victory celebration with Jack's mistress was just too much. By Thursday, she had found a way to express her displeasure, as usual by digging in her heels about some other matter.

Arrangements were being made for President and Mrs Kennedy to fly to Hyde Park, New York, for the funeral of Eleanor Roosevelt on Saturday, November 10, 1962. Not only was Mrs Roosevelt a revered figure in her own right, but her son was Jack's close friend, as well as the man who had done so much to bring about his decisive victory in the West Virginia primary. Nonetheless, in the hours before Mary Meyer appeared in the family quarters, Jackie angrily refused to travel to Hyde Park. For the moment, it seemed that this was to be one of those times when she simply would not be budged.

When people started to arrive at half past seven, Jack and Jackie were still at odds. Caroline, wandering the second-floor hall in her nightgown, was the only Kennedy in sight when guests emerged from the elevator. Jack was running late. He had just wound up an interview with columnist Walter Lippmann and rushed upstairs to dress without pausing for an evening swim. A butler ushered the guests into the Yellow Oval Room, where the President, in 'a glow of absolute happiness' over Cuba, joined them a few seconds later, as caviar and crabmeat were being passed around. There was still no sign of Jackie. When she did finally make her appearance, her mood was in marked contrast to her husband's. Ordinarily an expert hostess, on this occasion Jackie seemed 'a little ill at ease' to Sulzberger, who wondered whether she might be pregnant. Tonight the dazzling teamwork that usually made the Kennedys' dinner parties so much fun was pointedly absent. Jack, eager to talk politics and foreign policy with the men, proceeded as if he and Jackie had been handed the scripts of entirely different plays.

After dinner and much victory talk, the gentlemen emerged from their brandy and cigars to join the ladies – including Jackie and Mary Meyer, the latter notably 'pretty' tonight – in the sitting room. By then, Jackie was able to contain herself no longer. She put on Jimmy Dean's popular record, 'P.T. 109,' about Jack's Second World War exploits. Over and over, she sang along to the silly song about the young Navy officer's heroism. No one but Jack seemed to understand quite what she was up to, and before long he excused himself and went to bed. A night that had begun in celebration ended with Jackie deflating all the talk of Jack's greatness.

Two days later, when Mary Meyer returned for the dinner dance, at least two of the guests, Betty Spalding and Sissie Ormsby-Gore, had decided they were fed up with the way Jack insisted on embarrassing his wife. Significantly, both of Jack's critics were women, both had been close to Kick – with whose anger at Joe's philandering they sympathized – and both sincerely adored Jack, with whom they had enjoyed a long friendship independent of his association with their husbands. Indeed, Betty and Sissie were much closer to Jack than to Jackie, and it was precisely because they prized his friendship, as he did theirs, that their censure carried so much weight.

In Betty's case, years of discomfort with Jack's promiscuity came to a head that night. For one thing, the Meyer affair had gone on too long and too publicly. But Mary was far from the only problem. The office girls, the prostitutes, the procurers, the drugs – it had become too much. 'I didn't approve of the way he behaved,' she remembered. 'It was sick.' Two decades after Betty, invited to lunch by Kick, had first been appalled by the sight of Joseph Kennedy's mistress at the family table, she had to accept that Jack, in his way, was every bit as objectionable as his father. Sissie Ormsby-Gore too was 'disgusted' by what Jack was doing to Jackie.

'They had turned that place into a brothel, hadn't they?' said Betty Spalding of what Kennedy, Dave Powers, and the others had accomplished at the White House. Not everyone thrived in that environment as well as Jack. Fresh from his triumph over Khrushchev, Jack seemed on top of the world, but the same could hardly be said of those on whom nearly two years of profligacy had taken its toll. Several of the female employees who had been sleeping with the President, including one who had reluctantly aborted his baby, had finally decided to leave. The marriages of several of his friends had been ruined after the husbands aped his womanizing and their wives refused to follow Jackie's example and look the other way. A number of the President's associates were bedazzled by the image of him, in Fred Dutton's words, 'like God, fucking anybody he wants to anytime he feels like it.' Kennedy made them feel like 'a bunch of virgins, married virgins.'

'Jack had appeal for women,' recalled Jewel Reed, contemplating the collapse of her own marriage, 'but he had far more appeal for men. Men who were older, wiser, more senior than he were very, very much drawn into his thinking. He was the alpha, without any question at all.' Under his influence, friends would 'strip away their own personal values, compromise their integrity and become, certainly intellectually, all but hostages to him,' she observed. 'It was as if he emasculated them. They emerged deprived of original loyalties ... I think the wives of these men would understand perfectly what I am saying.' The men, forced to choose between Kennedy and their families, were drawn ineluctably to the former. In such cases Kennedy's appeal 'had a homosexual effect,' Reed insisted, though the men involved 'weren't homosexual.' Since the America's Cup races in Newport, Jewel had left Washington at her husband's request. Jim Reed had declined a solo invitation to the dinner dance that night.

The Spaldings, though they came to the dinner dance as a couple, had been having problems of their own, in which Jack's toxic influence played a role – another reason for Betty's change of heart. Chuck had embarked on an affair with Nina Jacobson, the doctor's wife, and Betty, in contrast to Jackie, refused to ignore her husband's infidelity. It wasn't long before word spread that the Spaldings' marriage, which had produced six children, was in trouble.

In a symptom of the debauched atmosphere at the White House, one of the other female guests approached Betty.

'Do you mind if I sleep with Chuck?' the woman asked, her question a travesty of politeness.

'I don't give a goddamn what you do!' Betty shot back.

Untouched by the turmoil, Jack, surrounded by Bill Thompson, Torby Macdonald, Bill Walton, and other chums, was enjoying himself. Still, there would be no dancing till dawn, and this dinner dance broke up earlier than the previous three. The Kennedys had a funeral to attend the next day, as Jackie had agreed to accompany Jack to Hyde Park after all. Meanwhile, when the Spaldings returned to Connecticut, Betty told her husband that she found the scene at the White House 'terrifying' and did not wish to go back. Nor, for the moment, did she plan to see her old friend Jack. 'I didn't want to be around him anymore,' she recalled. 'I didn't care if he was

President. I didn't like the way he treated Jackie.' And she didn't like the effect that the malign atmosphere of Kennedy-era Washington had on her own life.

Despite Jackie's evident pride in Jack's handling of the Cuban Missile Crisis, the weeks that followed were tense, unhappy ones. Friends and employees noted a good deal of dissension over money, often an indication that other matters were upsetting her. She demanded a more generous budget, Jack replied that her expenses were already out of control, and she went on defiantly to spend even more. Her ambitious plans for the house at Rattlesnake Mountain in Atoka, Virginia, became a source of strife. Jack had no real interest in the construction project beyond the consideration that, with the lease of Glen Ora at an end, they needed a convenient weekend retreat. Jackie, by contrast, never tired of referring to Atoka as the first house she and Jack would build together, and as such she had a great deal invested in it emotionally – far more, at any rate, than he seemed to comprehend. While Jackie fantasized about the splendid life they would have there, Jack derided the hunt country setting as 'pretty deadly' and complained to Charles Bartlett on a visit to the property, 'Can you imagine me ending up in a place like this?'

Other prospects, by contrast, excited him greatly. There was to be one last, very special victory celebration, but that had to wait until after a press conference on November 20, 1962, at which he announced that the outstanding issues of the missile crisis were over. Before leaving to spend Thanksgiving with Jackie and the children at Hyannis Port, he contacted Macmillan to suggest that they meet in Nassau on December 19–20, to make plans for the post-missile crisis world. On Friday, December 7, the President went off to deliver speeches in Nebraska and New Mexico. Then, instead of joining his family at Glen Ora for the weekend, he went on to Palm Springs, California, to enjoy his first time on the loose since 'Cuba 2.'

It was 12:10 p.m. when *Air Force One* touched down at Palm Springs Municipal Airport. The mayor, city manager, and members of the city council were on hand, but the welcoming ceremony didn't take long. Seven minutes later, Kennedy and

Powers were in a car headed for the Bing Crosby estate in Palm Desert, where Peter Lawford, as was his custom, had assembled a collection of women. By a quarter to one, the car had driven up the dirt road past some state police posted below. With the exception of a Sunday morning trip to church, Kennedy would not emerge until Monday.

Saturday evening, when two Secret Service agents stationed in front of the house checked the pool area, the source of a good deal of noise, a disconcerting sight greeted them. The President and his friends were naked, as were the women around the pool, a number of European stewardesses among them. On one side Kennedy sipped a drink and chatted with some women, while across the water Dave Powers was having sexual intercourse in full view. As if that were not enough, Powers later shouted, 'Hey, pal,' as he mooned the President before dashing into the house, collecting some of Crosby's suits, and leaping into the pool with them. Kennedy laughed so hard he nearly fell out of his chair.

The laughter died down and the celebration turned ugly when a drunken Peter Lawford went too far with one of the women. Clearly she didn't want to do what Lawford had in mind, and his refusal to back off frightened her severely. Confronted with this nasty scene, the Secret Service men, usually disinclined to intervene in what was after all Kennedy's 'show,' decided on their own to remove her. 'We got her out and nobody said anything,' remembered Larry Newman, 'and we didn't give a shit if they did ... It was just the right thing to do.'

After Jack returned on Monday, December 10, Jackie spent the better part of the week in Washington, where she and the President attended Isaiah Berlin's lecture on the nineteenth-century Russian intelligentsia, hosted the annual White House staff Christmas party, and went to the ballet and theater together. Friday, she took the children to Florida to prepare for Christmas, while Jack went to Nassau. A year had passed since the Bermuda Conference, when Macmillan had stepped into the emotional chasm Kennedy faced at the time of his father's stroke. In the interim, the Prime Minister had been a source of invaluable counsel and support, providing Kennedy with the philosophical ballast that, it could be argued, permitted him to triumph in 'Cuba 2.' It would be no exaggeration to say that only Jackie and Bobby had done more to help Jack regain his footing in the traumatic aftermath of the Bay of Pigs.

In the weeks since 'Cuba 2,' Kennedy had repaid the favor by appearing to betray Macmillan politically, canceling a program dating back to Eisenhower's presidency that would have allowed Britain to purchase Skybolt 1000-mile-range air-to-ground missiles, then under development by the U.S. When Defense Secretary McNamara proposed terminating the Skybolt program for technical and economic reasons that had nothing to do with the British sale, it failed to occur to Kennedy, euphoric after 'Cuba 2' and absorbed in his own immediate needs, that the move would be devastating to Macmillan. Two points had been central to the Prime Minister's foreign policy agenda. One was his country's special relationship with the U.S., the other an independent nuclear deterrent that made Britain a player, along with the U.S.S.R. and the U.S., in negotiations for a test ban treaty. The decision to abandon Skybolt called both into question – a massive public humiliation and a potentially fatal political blow.

By the time Kennedy reached Nassau, having had a long talk en route with David Ormsby-Gore, he accepted that he had fences to mend. Macmillan, determined to sustain the friendship but also to remain firm, held out for a credible substitute for Skybolt in Polaris submarine-to-surface missiles. In Nassau, the leaders' relationship was tested, and in the end Kennedy, over the objections of his advisers, agreed to give Macmillan what he needed, though considerable political damage had already been done.

Then, suddenly, the unexpected occurred. The previous April in Washington, Macmillan had declared, 'The whole thing changes at a word from Khrushchev.' Out of the blue, that word arrived, in a letter to Kennedy from Khrushchev which indicated that he might be willing to accept the inspections that had been a sticking point in the negotiations thus far. Macmillan saw the opening that might finally lead to a test ban treaty.

The combination of the letter's fortuitous timing and the President's feelings of guilt over Skybolt gave Macmillan the ammunition he needed to enlist Kennedy as his partner in launching a major new drive toward détente and a shift in the direction of East–West relations. A meeting which had begun with dark foreboding ended with both leaders excited about the possibility for real progress.

Jackie found Jack in a very good mood when she and the children met him and David Ormsby-Gore at Palm Beach International Airport on Friday afternoon, December 21. They all drove to the Paul house to drop off Ormsby-Gore, whose wife was also to spend Christmas with them, then went directly to see Joe. So much in the lives of both father and son had been resolved in recent weeks, and that night there was more excellent news when Castro finally signed an agreement to release the Bay of Pigs prisoners in exchange for $53 million in medicine and food. The prisoners began to leave Cuba on the 23rd, and the last group arrived in Miami on Christmas Day. Two days afterward, the brigade leaders visited the Paul house. In a gesture that suggested how deeply personal all this was for him, the President had insisted that he wanted to confer with them in his home, where Jackie and the children could meet them.

Jack had an emotional one-hour meeting with the exiles around a long dining table. Then he introduced them to Jackie, who, for reasons of her own, was similarly emotional as she greeted them in Spanish and called in the children to say hello. No less than for her husband, 'Cuba 1' had been a watershed for Jackie. Jack's needs in the aftermath of the Bay of Pigs had compelled her to rethink entirely how she planned to live as First Lady, and accomplish things she had previously not even imagined. Though she had done it for him, she had discovered that she loved her new role for the size it gave her life. 'Cuba 2' represented another turning point – for Jack, and for Jackie.

Jack's handling of the crisis had proven he was strong. Consequently, the illusion of authority, power, and prestige that Jackie had worked so hard to create was no longer as necessary.

It was time for the conjurer to seek a new role, though she had
no idea what that might be.

Two days later, on December 29, 1962, when Jackie addressed
a rally of some fifty thousand Cuban exiles at the Orange Bowl
to welcome the prisoners to Miami, her remarks, delivered
softly but passionately in Spanish, were in effect a valediction.
About to withdraw from the public role 'Cuba 1' had thrust
upon her, she would not appear at her husband's side before
another such crowd until November 1963, in Texas.

TWELVE

Indiscretion

On January 8, 1963, Jackie posed for photographers at the National Gallery in Washington. Her shoulders were bare, her dress a dramatic column of soft mauve chiffon embroidered with pearls and crystals. Her diamond earrings glittered. She had flown up from Palm Beach that afternoon to accept custody of the *Mona Lisa* from André Malraux.

Jackie had returned from Florida with a secret. Amid the tumult of conflicting emotions that followed 'Cuba 2,' she had become pregnant. Her pregnancies had always been difficult, and this time she worried desperately from the outset that she would suffer another miscarriage. In any event, the news, known only to Jackie, her husband (who shared her delight), the Ormsby-Gores, and a few others, had immediately allowed her to put off any decisions about what was next. Now that she was pregnant, she and Jack would turn back the clock to those first months after the Inauguration when he had operated largely on his own.

By this time, work on the White House was largely complete, with the exception of a few last details. Stéphane Boudin had flown in from Paris to attend the *Mona Lisa* festivities and oversee the completion of the last of the state rooms, the Blue Room, which was to open to the public on January 21. In none of the state rooms was the shift in Jackie's original plans for the White House, or the transformation in her sense of herself and her capacities, more apparent. 'The Blue Room was Boudin's masterpiece,' she would later say. 'It is a formal reception room, and so you have to have a sense of state, ceremony, arrival, and grandeur.' Nothing could have been more emphatically at odds with her own original concept of comfort and prettiness.

The tentative, uncertain young woman whose voice can be heard in Jackie's first letters about the renovation project just two years earlier would never have had the nerve to go through with this most extreme of all the state rooms. She had begun the project as very much a private woman preoccupied with issues of taste. By the time the Blue Room was completed, she had become a fully-fledged political image-maker. Although she continued to worry about Jack's approval, she was utterly certain of what she was doing. Under the influence of de Gaulle and with the practical mentoring of Boudin, Jackie had set out to create a stage on which to present the image of her husband's presidency as one of grandeur and power, certainty and stability. For all of Jack's fears that her White House project would backfire politically, in fact it had served him brilliantly and been tremendously popular with the American public. Jackie had created an image of her husband as a powerful and mature statesman, which helped him buy the time he needed actually to become that statesman and leader. Now that he had emerged from the missile crisis with his international prestige enormously enhanced, it seemed an ideal moment to step back and leave the finished stage to him.

As Jackie later told Joe Alsop, her work on behalf of the presidency had called upon the best in her. It had provided the meaning and sense of significance she had quietly sought all her life. Yet, as she prepared to withdraw, she was known to insist glibly that she had had it with being First Lady all the time and was eager to take the veil. Such remarks, like the pose that she didn't really care about Jack's cheating, were defensive. It was safer to pretend still to be the person she was before Paris than risk vulnerability by admitting what her work had meant to her.

For some time, it had seemed inevitable that one of Kennedy's many affairs would provoke a crisis. Now, soon after Jackie had informed her staff, without explanation, that she planned dramatically to cut back her schedule for 1963, the Damoclean sword of scandal and embarrassment which Jack had placed over both their heads threatened to come crashing down.

On January 12, 1963, *Washington Post* publisher Phil Graham, who had an extensive history of mental illness and alcoholism and was in the throes of a major breakdown, walked out on his wife and, accompanied by a girlfriend, traveled to Phoenix, Arizona, where an Associated Press convention was in progress. The head of the organization was about to address a roomful of newspaper publishers when a drunk and disoriented Graham headed to the lectern. In the midst of a tirade of gibberish and obscenity came the real showstopper: mention of Graham's close friend, President John F. Kennedy, and his liaison with Mary Meyer. Graham knew all about the affair from conversations with his assistant, Mary's friend Jim Truitt.

At first, as Graham rambled on, no one in the audience moved, transfixed by the spectacle of a powerful man cracking up in public. Finally, when Graham began to take off his clothes, the wife of an A.P. official had the presence of mind to coax him from the lectern. In one respect, it was too late. Someone in a position to know had spoken publicly of the affair between the President and Mary Meyer in the presence of reporters.

Immediately, the President received two calls, one from someone who had witnessed the incident and sought to warn him, the other from Graham himself, who had been taken back to his hotel. On the basis of his talk with Graham especially, Kennedy perceived a disaster in the making. All his instincts told him one thing: Graham, a very sick individual, had to be brought under control at once. He had another urgent phone conversation, this time with Jim Truitt, and sent a government jet carrying Graham's doctors to remove him from Phoenix without delay. The decision to use a government plane was a mark of how seriously Kennedy took the threat Graham posed. The doctors' mission proved to be no simple task. Graham had to be forcibly tranquilized and, when he landed in Washington, he insisted that he was a prisoner and tried to escape. They managed to get him first to George Washington University Hospital and then to Chestnut Lodge, a private psychiatric hospital outside the city. Afterward, Graham's wife, Katharine, wrote to the President, 'He would and will die at the thought that he might have hurt you in any way. I hope he didn't – too much ...'

In the days that followed, miraculously, no reference to the incident appeared in print. In conversation with Timothy Leary, Mary Meyer attributed the silence to conspiracies, though in fact the newspaper people who had witnessed Graham's sad performance were merely protecting one of their own. The decision to keep the episode out of the papers, however, did not prevent it from quickly becoming the talk of Georgetown.

Despite the close call, as well as the fact that much of élite Washington was avidly discussing Graham's outburst, Kennedy did not break off, or even cool, his affair with Mary. He prized her company too much to end the relationship, though almost certainly that would have been his course of action had Graham named one of his other sexual partners. He had not hesitated to get rid of Judith Campbell, for instance, when his relationship with her became problematic. On January 29, a week after the Graham incident, Mary came to the White House family quarters for the usual session while Jackie was at Glen Ora. Jackie's ability to put up with Jack's liaisons was based in part on the conviction that they were strictly about sex and 'didn't mean anything to him.' Evidently, this affair was different.

This was a very bad period for Jackie, characterized by the tears, depressions, and days in bed that had blighted her early months as First Lady two years previously. Preoccupied with details of the new house in Atoka, she became nearly hysterical when Gladys Tartiere, in keeping with the Glen Ora lease, reminded her that the house had to be returned in exactly its state when the Kennedys took possession. At considerable expense, Jackie would have to tear out the carpets, wallpaper, and other elements of decoration that she had added.

By the end of January, Jackie's low spirits had begun to worry Jack. At his suggestion, on February 3 she went to New York for a week to shop. In the past, a bit of time away from Washington had often done the trick. On this occasion, soon after she arrived her Secret Service detail notified the White House that she was exhausted and planned to return. Jack urged her to stay on, pointing out that since he had taken office, they had not had a real weekend in New York together. He would join her on Saturday and they could go to the theater, see friends, and, for two days at least, forget that they were President and First Lady. Cheered by the prospect, Jackie agreed.

It soon became apparent that Jack had another reason to go to New York. When he arrived at the Carlyle at 5:20 on Saturday afternoon, the assistant manager escorted him upstairs to Suite 34-B. He stayed barely long enough to greet Jackie before ducking out and taking the elevator to 29-A, where Phil Graham, having talked his way out of Chestnut Lodge, was installed. Graham's brief stay at the psychiatric hospital could have done little to improve his condition, so it was essential that Kennedy make every effort to prevent his friend from making any more damaging statements in public. Next time, Graham might not be so fortunate in his audience. The President talked to Graham for a good twenty minutes, a conversation that made Kennedy so nervous that when he departed he inadvertently left behind some classified documents.

While Jackie dressed for the evening, Jack walked over to the nearby home of his sister Jean. He wanted to see Caroline, who had been brought to New York by her mother so that she could spend a few days with Jean's son, Steve Jr. After a visit, he returned to collect Jackie for dinner at their favorite New York restaurant, Le Pavilion, with Chuck Spalding and Lee and Stas Radziwill, before going on to see *Beyond the Fringe*. The hit show from Britain had a number of jokes about Kennedy and Macmillan, and no one laughed harder than Jack. After the theater, the group went on to Flo and Earl Smith's Fifth Avenue residence, where Jack's long-ago girlfriend, now the wife of a considerably older and very wealthy man, introduced him to a number of young New York beauties who might be of interest as sexual partners. Flo Smith, who on occasion still slept with Jack herself, often introduced him to women, though in the present instance, as Jackie was with him, the pretext was to find extra women for the White House dinner dance on March 8.

In the morning, Hyde became Jekyll again. Letting Jackie

sleep late, Kennedy went to his sister's house to take Caroline and Steve Jr for a walk in Central Park, returning in time to escort Jackie and Lee to a late Mass. Afterward, Jackie was in a terrific mood, buoyed by this rare reminder of normal life. The trio abandoned their limousine and walked to the fashionable restaurant Voisin, where Stas Radziwill and Chuck Spalding joined them. Lunch, full of laughter and good cheer, was dominated by talk of the fifty-mile hikes Bobby and others had undertaken in response to the President's call for an increased level of physical fitness.

Jack bet the two men one thousand dollars each, to be donated to charity, that neither could walk fifty miles. The bet was accepted; a setting, Palm Beach, and a date, February 23, were agreed upon. Somebody suggested they bring Max Jacobson to energize the woefully out-of-shape Radziwill, who was by then far too involved with Jacobson for his own good. So caught up was everyone in the spirit of the afternoon that even Spalding concurred, though his affair with Nina Jacobson meant that he and Dr Feel Good were no longer on speaking terms.

Late that afternoon, the Kennedys flew back to Washington. Jackie was exhausted and, though the Bradlees had been invited to dinner, slept though the evening and the entire next day. The trip to New York seemed to have done her no lasting good, for in the days that followed she was again tearful and emotional. As the time approached to accompany Jack to Palm Beach, where in the hope of boosting her health and spirits she planned to stay on an additional week by herself, the source of Jackie's malaise came into sharp focus.

On February 20, the day before the Kennedys left, invitations went out to a dinner dance on March 8. Mary Meyer's name appeared on the list, clearly put there by Jack; after the Graham incident, Jackie would certainly not have included her. Neither Graham's outburst, nor the whispers Mary's presence would doubtless provoke, nor the inevitable embarrassment to his wife, deterred him. It was bad enough to invite Mary to White House social events when her affair with the President was supposedly a secret. To do so after it became public knowledge was humiliating in the extreme.

Three lines down on that same list was a painful reminder of the life decisions that had brought Jackie to this pass. For the first time on any White House guest list, Betty Spalding's name appeared alone. Since Betty's calamitous last trip to Washington, her marriage had come apart. Not for her the compromises that Jackie had made to keep her marriage alive. Unusually, Betty was not exiled, as other wives were when their marriages ended. In most cases, the men were Jack's friends but the women were not; dumped by their husbands, for the Kennedys they ceased to exist. Betty, in contrast, was a long-time family friend in her own right, through Kick, and she would continue to receive invitations to the White House while the Kennedys saw Chuck Spalding separately.

As it happened, Spalding was on *Air Force One*, along with the Radziwills and the Ormsby-Gores, when the Kennedys left for Florida the following day. Fueled by Dr Jacobson's shots, Spalding and Radziwill won the bet by completing the fifty-mile hike. Jack flew back to Washington at the end of the weekend, and Jackie followed a week later. Upon her return, she discovered that any hope she may have had that Mary Meyer would refuse to appear at the dinner dance was futile. Jack's mistress, brazen as ever, had accepted the invitation as if Phil Graham had never blurted out her name. In another reminder that not every woman was prepared to accept Jack's behavior, Betty Spalding, true to her vow to stay away from him, had sent regrets. If Jackie had not yet and probably never would reach the point Betty had with Chuck, she had arrived at some sort of personal breaking point. 'If you ignore it, you're above it,' had been her policy, but now, three months pregnant, she could no longer turn a blind eye to her husband's relationship with Mary Meyer. On Wednesday, March 6, two days after she returned from Palm Beach, Jackie struck Mary Meyer's name from the list of those asked to dinner. Offering the excuse that the guests of honor, World Bank head Eugene Black and his wife, had invited too many of their own friends, she relegated Mary to those invited only for dancing at 10 p.m. To cancel the invitation altogether would have caused far too much gossip, but at least this way Jackie would be spared the ordeal of having Mary at her table.

That evening, at dinner with Ben Bradlee and his wife – Mary's sister and brother-in-law – Jackie inadvertently communicated some of her tremendous upset. Bradlee's comments about how hard he'd found it to portray Bobby Kennedy in a *Newsweek* article led Jackie to speak of how in 1956, in Jack's absence, Bobby's friendship had been a real comfort when her baby daughter was delivered stillborn. As she told the story, she seemed to catch herself, as if realizing that this raised the highly sensitive question of why her husband would have been away at such a moment. Obviously, Jackie didn't want to disclose that Jack, cavorting in Europe, had refused to return when he learned that the baby was dead, so she brushed it off with the remark, 'We couldn't get hold of Jack at the time.' The Bradlees, unaware of her current pregnancy, were in no position to perceive the full subtext, but Jack certainly was. That she had told the story at all highlighted her fear of losing another baby, and in her own way she had forced the painful issue of Mary Meyer at last. Before Friday's dinner dance, Jack, having finally grasped that the affair was just too much for his pregnant wife to handle, promised to end it.

The night of March 8 was cold and wintry, the White House grounds blanketed with snow, as fifty guests took their places at five large round tables for dinner. Jackie's defenses were already up, though it would be more than an hour and a half before Mary arrived from a dinner party at Bill Walton's, one of four such dinners attended by those asked only for dancing. As if in anticipation of the whispers that were to greet Mary's first public appearance at the White House since Graham's outburst in Phoenix, Jackie worked hard to maintain her dignity in front of her companions at dinner. Adlai Stevenson, to judge by his subsequent report of their conversation to Marietta Tree, had the mistaken impression that Jackie had been remarkably candid. In fact, when Jackie wasn't trying to give people the idea that she was oblivious to Jack's adulteries, she liked to indicate, usually to men, that she knew and didn't care. Despite Stevenson's belief that he had elicited an unprecedented confession, Jackie was actually saying nothing new and not being particularly honest when she claimed to be unconcerned about how many women Jack slept with as long as he realized it was wrong. To anyone familiar with her pattern, as Stevenson was not, it would have been evident that her comments in this regard were the very opposite of confidences, that the truth of her feelings was the very opposite of what she said. One assertion that Stevenson heard that night, however, Jackie seems never to have made before. She claimed that her troubles with Jack were over for the present.

When Mary, escorted by her and Jack's old friend Blair Clark, arrived at ten, she seemed to have gone out of her way to draw stares. Given the chilly weather, she cut a peculiar figure in a summery, pastel chiffon dress. Those watching for sparks between the President and his mistress had to wait two hours before he made his move. At one minute past midnight, as recorded by the Secret Service detail that monitored Kennedy's every step on the public floors of the White House, he disappeared to the pool area. Mary joined him, but their meeting was nothing like those they had enjoyed there in the past. Jack abruptly ended the affair, using the Graham episode as an excuse. Five minutes later, the Secret Service men watched Kennedy walk back to the dance floor. Mary left the building and, coatless, wandered about in the snow until the bottom of her dress was soaked. Ninety minutes later, wet and bedraggled, she drifted back to the party, where her worried escort had been searching for her.

Kennedy had already turned his attention elsewhere. His promise was limited to a relationship that, because it involved more than just sex, had become intolerable to his pregnant wife. Jackie was not so naïve as to think that Jack would transform suddenly into a faithful spouse, so when she told Stevenson their troubles were over, almost certainly she was referring strictly to Mary. As in the past, much as she loathed the situation, she knew she would find a way to live with Jack's other women, though she had probably not expected that he would give her an opportunity to start that same night.

At half past one, about five minutes before Mary returned

from her walk, the Secret Service again clocked the President into the pool area. On this occasion, he was accompanied by one of the numerous beautiful women at the party. They were together for eighteen minutes: the sort of quick act of sex, typical of Kennedy, that George Smathers once likened to a rooster getting on top of a hen so briefly that afterward the poor little hen, feathers ruffled, is left to wonder 'what the hell' just happened to her. Nor, as certain guests noticed, was Kennedy finished for the night. At twenty to three, the rooster disappeared to the pool area with yet another hen for all of twelve minutes.

Mary was among the last to go home, lingering with Blair Clark as if unable to accept the finality of what Jack had said. When Mary was a teenager and Jed Harris dropped her sister Rosamund, Rosamund had gone into the garage, turned on the engine of her car, and committed suicide, thereby achieving the headlines that had previously eluded her. Anyone who knew that Mary's sister had taken her own life, or that on another occasion her father had attempted to kill himself, might well have worried as she prepared to leave the White House that night. For all of her arrogance, for all of her contempt and cruelty toward others, Mary was a woman who walked on the edge. She had given every indication that she was willing to do whatever it took to hold Jack's interest, and now that he had ended their affair there was no telling what her response might be. At the time, she seemed intent on calling attention to the fact that she was in the throes of some secret drama, lingering outside, returning from her walk with a wet dress, all of it guaranteed to broadcast that something was going on. For Mary, seeking the spotlight had always been what the game was about.

She was noticeably tipsy by the time her escort finally called for their car and Jackie, in a gesture of triumph, came out to the North Portico with Jack to see her off. In forcing the end of her husband's most disturbing affair, Jackie had done all she could, short of walking out, to make her own life tolerable. Any further alteration would have to be the product of changes in Jack. That she expected none became clear the next day. She took Caroline and John to Camp David, initiating what would be her weekly routine for three months until it was time to go to Cape Cod for the summer. In essence, she resumed the design for living with which she had come to the White House two years previously, arranging to give Jack at least one or two free nights a week in the White House. He, for his part, refrained from confronting her with his other women once again.

To Jackie's surprise and delight, despite her initial unhappiness at having to use the official presidential retreat until their new house was ready, Camp David turned out to be the setting for much happiness. Principal among its attractions was privacy. Once inside, the Kennedys could live entirely out of sight of curiosity-seekers. The children were free to play outdoors without people staring or taking pictures, and Jack and Jackie didn't even have to leave the grounds, which had a private chapel, to attend Mass. In expectation of a new baby, the foursome seemed to radiate special joy. Both children were of an age to do new things. Jack and Jackie took particular pleasure in Caroline's ability to participate in excursions to historical sites, and were equally touched that John was old enough to learn his father's routines. Like clockwork, by lunchtime on Saturday, the boy would start to scan the sky for the 'lopaca.' Once the Marine helicopter was in its hangar, he loved nothing better than to sit with his father in the pilot's seat and pretend to fly.

When the Kennedys did venture from the property, it was often to travel by helicopter to the battlefields of Gettysburg and Antietam, where they indulged the passion for Civil War history that absorbed them that spring of 1963. The Secret Service would have cars waiting when the white cap carrying the Kennedys, the Ormsby-Gores, and other houseguests touched down. The President would get behind the wheel of one car, his wife and daughter at his side. As they toured the site, they would vie to determine whether he or she knew more historical facts. In anticipation of his arrival Saturday afternoon, Jackie would have spent many hours with whichever Civil War book she had discovered that week, only to have Jack snatch it away as soon as he came in. To watch them like this – sharing intellectual pleasures, competing fiercely, delighting in their children – was to be reminded that for all Jackie's anguish, her private life with her husband could also be intensely happy.

The Kennedys' shared intellectual passion for the Civil War was in part an effort to find a substitute for the dynamic political partnership that had immeasurably enriched their life together. Jackie was to preside over a few state dinners that spring, but in contrast to the previous year's crowded schedule her days were free. She devoted a good deal of time to the completion of the house in Atoka, Virginia, but the discovery of how much she and Jack liked Camp David removed any sense of urgency. She even confided to Mr West that they would have been perfectly happy at the presidential retreat after all, and had had no need to undertake the expense of a new house.

Jackie had just wound up her collaboration with Stéphane Boudin on the last of the state rooms at the White House. As a personal favor, Boudin recommended paint and colors for Atoka, and the discussion naturally reverted to the domestic sphere, the creation of a 'pretty' house, which had been Jackie's desire before her metamorphosis into a political creature. The contrast to her previous collaboration with Boudin was marked, and encapsulated all she had just lost in stepping back. There had been a time when she was content to constantly redecorate her house in Georgetown, but could she really go back to being that person again?

On March 18, Jack went to Costa Rica to meet with Central American leaders, his first solo trip abroad as President. Jackie had ruled out foreign travel for the duration of her pregnancy. The Kennedys' joint trips to Europe and Latin America had been among the defining experiences of Jackie's life, yet on the very day Jack left, her own activity was what it might have been had she never joined her husband on the political stage: she went to New York to buy furniture for Atoka. On other occasions, it was evident that she still longed for the active, influential life. As Jack conferred informally with David Ormsby-Gore about British–American efforts to secure a test ban, over dinner or when the two couples were at leisure together in the

White House or at Camp David, Jackie would listen attentively, even take notes. No detail seemed to escape her.

Unfortunately, the hope generated by Khrushchev's letter of December 19, 1962 had long since, in Ormsby-Gore's words, been 'run into the sand.' By March 1963, Macmillan was painfully aware on the one hand that Khrushchev seemed to have faltered, and on the other that Kennedy's advisers (whom the Prime Minister privately dubbed 'the rats') were urging the President to drop the push for a test ban treaty, which, they insisted, would amount to nothing and damage him politically. Worse, at times he seemed inclined to heed their advice.

Nothing was of greater urgency to Macmillan than to jump-start negotiations. On March 16 he completed a long, eloquent letter, undoubtedly the most important of his correspondence with Kennedy, to urge that together they make a bold new approach to Khrushchev. 'What, then, are we to do?' Macmillan asked with reference to the deadlock since December. 'Of course, there are very strong arguments for doing nothing. Strong logical arguments, strong political arguments. But this is not the spirit in which you, who carry the largest responsibility, before God and man, have faced your duty, nor that in which I have tried to do the same. I have a feeling that the test ban is the most important step that we can take towards unraveling this frightful tangle of fear and suspicion in East–West relations – important in itself and all the more important for what may flow from it.'

In short, Macmillan was urging Kennedy to make a choice, to give precedence to moral considerations over practical ones. As the Soviets had long recognized, Kennedy tended to be governed by the latter. The right thing might not be the easiest or the most expedient in political terms, but Macmillan challenged Kennedy to disregard the counsel of his own advisers, as well as much that he had been taught by a father unburdened by ideals. He pressed the younger man to reach beyond the mere self-interest that had motivated both Joe Kennedy's isolationism in the 1930s and his war fever at the time of the Bay of Pigs. There could be no denying that if Kennedy accepted Macmillan's urging, he would be taking two big political risks. One was that Khrushchev would never sign a test ban, the other was that even if Kennedy and Macmillan secured a treaty, the U.S. Senate would not ratify it. The latter in particular would be a massive setback as Kennedy prepared to run for re-election. Macmillan's letter was delivered by David Ormsby-Gore on March 21, the day after Kennedy returned from Costa Rica.

One week later, fully aware that his decision could cost him a second term, Kennedy made the difficult choice Macmillan had challenged him to make. He overrode his advisers' objections and wrote to Macmillan suggesting that they write jointly to Khrushchev to propose sending special emissaries to Moscow. With those momentous words, Kennedy finally stood ready, as he had announced in his Inaugural Address, to begin anew.

At the very moment Macmillan was helping Kennedy to find himself morally, the Prime Minister's government was rocked by a scandal of precisely the sort that Hervé Alphand and others had been expecting in Washington. The three months since their meeting in Nassau had been unkind to Macmillan. Despite the brilliant negotiations that had won Polaris missiles for Britain and sustained the concept of an independent nuclear deterrent, the confusion over Skybolt had damaged him politically – damage that Kennedy, for his part, deeply regretted. Then, on January 14, de Gaulle vetoed Britain's entry into the European Economic Community, another great blow. But the scandal that threatened to bring down his government was, of all things, sexual in nature. In March, Macmillan's preoccupation with the test ban treaty meant that he paid too little attention to that scandal – with disastrous results. He was in the throes of composing the final draft of his March 16 letter to Kennedy when he groaned in his diary that he had had to spend much of a day trying to deal with the 'silly scrape' in which his Secretary of State for War found himself. John Profumo was rumored to have shared the favors of the model Christine Keeler with Captain Yevgeny Ivanov, Assistant Naval Attaché at the Soviet embassy in London. As Macmillan well understood, the sexual angle was the least of the trouble. Ivanov was said to have used Keeler to pry atomic secrets from

Profumo. Macmillan had known about those charges since February and, while Profumo privately denied it all, the rumors refused to die.

Things came to a head on March 21 – the day Ormsby-Gore delivered Macmillan's letter to Kennedy – when a Labour M.P. rose in the House of Commons to demand that Profumo publicly address the accusations. Macmillan tended to be a shrewd judge of men and their motives, but in this case he too readily accepted Profumo's claim that there had been no impropriety. Macmillan resented being distracted from the test ban by a matter so sordid, and it is likely that his private difficulties with Lady Dorothy left him reluctant to discuss sex. The next day, in the House of Commons, Macmillan sat beside Profumo on the Front Bench, a signal that he, for one, believed him.

In fact, Profumo was lying about his relationship with Keeler, inconceivable though it was to Macmillan that a Minister could lie to Parliament. The affair had begun two years previously at Cliveden, home of Lord Astor, during a house party in honor of Ayub Khan (then en route to Jackie's historic state dinner at Mount Vernon), which included a nude romp in the swimming pool. Profumo was, however, being truthful when he denied having divulged any nuclear secrets. Macmillan, determined to get back to the important business of the test ban, assumed that Profumo's testimony would put the matter to rest, but instead the fact that Profumo, visibly supported by the Prime Minister, had lied to Parliament created a new and more serious problem.

'It is hard to overstate the atmosphere of political squalor in London today,' Arthur Schlesinger Jr reported in a confidential memo to Kennedy on March 25, following a three-day visit. The cumulative effect of the Profumo case and other sex scandals, Schlesinger wrote, 'has been to reinforce the impression that the Government is frivolous and decadent, and that everything is unraveling at the seams.' In London, Joe Alsop wrote home, 'no one except the Irish servants at the Turf Club talked about anything at all except sex.' It simultaneously excited and frightened Alsop, whose own secret life had brought him very close to ruin several times in the past, that under the influence of the Profumo affair, suddenly everyone's sex life seemed vulnerable to scrutiny. At a London dinner party, he reported, 'we started on sex with the first course and never left the subject for more than about five minutes.' As the evening progressed, Alsop heard things about the sex lives of prominent individuals 'that even made my limp, thinning and normally non-erectile hair stand straight up on end.'

The U.S. embassy in London provided Kennedy with constant updates on the scandal that threatened to destroy Macmillan. In conversation with Chuck Spalding, he made it clear that in theory such a thing could happen to him too, but he insisted that in reality he had nothing to worry about because he always took 'precautions.' If anyone knew that Jack scorned even the most basic precautions, it was Spalding. Still, in a kind of *folie à deux*, Spalding willed himself to agree that, despite the warning bells of Phil Graham and Profumo, Kennedy had nothing to fear.

Kennedy devoured each new memo on the Profumo scandal, yet his own flagrant and reckless sexual behavior persisted as if there were no lesson in the tale of the government official, the model, and her Communist contact. He might have asked himself what he knew about the women he saw on trips or those Dave Powers, Bill Thompson, and others delivered to the White House; he might have taken a belated lesson from the Judith Campbell episode. A history of life-threatening illnesses, as well as the premature deaths of a brother and sister, had long haunted Kennedy with thoughts of an early death and seemed to drive him to enjoy life at full intensity while he could. At the same time, there was often something fatalistic, even suicidal, about his efforts, as if, fearful that his existence was to be a short one, he was weirdly determined to make it so.

Kennedy did not share Macmillan's conviction, expressed in his diary with regard to Profumo, about the different standard of behavior to which men in public life must aspire. The Prime Minister's profound influence on Kennedy's public actions had as yet had no impact on his private morals. That the two remained utterly unconnected in his thinking was evident on March 28, the day he answered Macmillan's letter about the test ban and agreed to come down on the side of right conduct. Jackie was due to spend the night away from the White House. Literally one minute after her car passed through the Southwest Gate, Jack, as if thumbing his nose at the warning provided by events in Britain, began a two-and-a-half-hour pool party.

In his letter to Macmillan, Kennedy enclosed a first draft of the proposed joint appeal to Khrushchev, and soon revisions were flying back and forth. When the Kennedys went to Palm Beach for Easter, Macmillan expressed the wish in his diary that they agree on a final draft while the President remained far from Washington and 'the rats' who continued to oppose London's influence. A second, very different decision faced the Kennedys that weekend. In deference to Jackie's wishes, there had been no public announcement of the pregnancy. As late as April 10, when she flew to Florida with Joe a day ahead of her husband, Jackie had continued to deny to most friends that she was pregnant. By this time even she recognized that the moment was fast approaching when a statement had to be made, but, mindful of the frenzy that would ensue, she was in no hurry.

The vacation had a rocky start when Joe, disoriented by the prospect of flying on a government jet rather than the *Caroline*, became violently upset, screaming and stamping his foot, shortly before takeoff. The rest of the trip was little better. By the time they reached Florida, Jackie, who had done her best to remain serene, was a nervous wreck. The whole point of the government plane had been to provide a taste of what Joe had missed. Now that her plan had backfired, Jackie, in the hope of sparing his dignity, pretended he had taken the government plane as a favor to her. In the limousine afterward, she tearfully offered thanks. 'It was a difficult trip for you, and I know you'd have been more comfortable on the *Caroline*; but it was grand of you to go through with what you did just to be with me.' She rested her head on his shoulder and added, 'If I'd only known, Grandpa, I wouldn't have put you through it for the world.' Joe hugged her with his good left arm and caressed her cheek.

Jack arrived on *Air Force One* the following afternoon for an extended weekend, with houseguests Red and Anita Fay. Accompanied by Fay and several Secret Service agents, Jack visited St Edward's Church early that evening. Before taking communion on Easter Sunday, it was essential that he confess – and given the previous day's skinny-dipping session, there was plenty to tell. On one prior occasion, as soon as Kennedy began to speak the priest had piped up from behind the confessional screen, 'Good evening, Mr President.' Now, in an effort at anonymity likely to fail, Kennedy took care to sandwich his confession between that of two agents.

The weekend was precisely the sort of holiday Jackie needed as she steeled herself to approve a statement about her pregnancy. She cruised on the *Honey Fitz*, waded with the children in the ocean behind the Paul house, and strolled along the beach to visit the Wrightsmans. But she stayed home when Jack and young John raided a local toy store for the planes that had become the boy's obsession. On another occasion Jack disappeared to Lilly Pulitzer's shop to buy a selection of the sleeveless cotton shift dresses which were then the craze in Palm Beach, as a surprise for her and Caroline. On Easter day, they attended a special private Mass at the Kennedy estate on North Ocean Boulevard and reconvened that evening under the patriarch's roof for a big, joyous family dinner.

In that setting, two Easters previously, Jack, urged on by his father, had decided to approve the invasion of Cuba. This year, the day after Easter, in a measure of how he had developed as a statesman, he and Macmillan finally agreed on the wording of their letter to Khrushchev. 'We all have a duty to consider what are the needs of security,' they wrote, 'but we also have a duty to humanity.' Admitting that previous talks had reached an impasse, they proposed 'to break out of this' by sending 'very senior representatives who would be empowered to speak for us and talk in Moscow directly with you.' By the time Kennedy flew back to Washington on *Air Force One* on Wednesday, April 17, the message had been delivered in Moscow.

By then, Jackie had also reached a decision of her own. Now four months pregnant, she had pushed aside fears of an early miscarriage but continued to hate the thought of publicity. Scheduled to stay in Palm Beach for a further week with Caroline and John, she sent Jack to Washington with her consent to make an announcement. Not long after he arrived, he presided over an hour-and-a-half pool party on the eve of the public statement that he and Jackie were expecting a baby.

The announcement sent the public into raptures. The huge interest in John Jr's birth was as nothing compared to this. Jackie's tenure as First Lady had made her a star in her own right, her every activity a source of national fascination and pride. The country – indeed, the whole world – seemed to have fallen in love with her children as well. Caroline and John had become America's little angels, and Jackie's pregnancy would be a national event, the excitement and anticipation shared by all. Jackie flew north in time to host the annual Congressional Reception, a ritual both she and her husband had come to associate with gloom, coinciding as it had with the Bay of Pigs in 1961 and the steel crisis in 1962. The previous year, Jack had said half in earnest, half in jest, that he planned never to attend another. This time, the mood was dramatically different. In the aftermath of 'Cuba 2,' there was a feeling that Kennedy, having recovered his footing at last, might be about to alter the course of East–West relations and lay claim to his rightful place in history. Jackie, in her first public appearance since the pregnancy was announced, became the focal point of all that hope and happiness.

Jackie could rest assured that Jack had given up Mary Meyer, for in the interval since the March 8 dinner dance he had passed his mistress on to Chuck Spalding. His gesture accomplished three things: he eliminated a problem, rewarded a pal, and reassured Jackie, who soon learned of the Spalding–Meyer affair, that he had kept his promise. Mary accepted the end of her affair with the President with surprising equanimity, at least on the surface, discovering in Spalding a means of suppressing her sense of rejection and failure beneath a characteristic gesture of contempt. Betty Spalding had been visibly disgusted at seeing Mary enter the White House schoolroom with Jack the previous year. An affair with her husband was the perfect revenge, an opportunity to show Betty the same contempt she had shown Jackie.

For Jack's forty-sixth birthday on May 29, Jackie planned a surprise party, a night-time cruise down the Potomac on another of the presidential yachts, the *Sequoia*. She invited Jack's brothers and sisters, as well as friends including Chuck Spalding, Lem Billings, Jim Reed, George Smathers, and Bill Walton. By now, Jack had made sure that Mary Meyer was well established in Jackie's mind as Spalding's, so at the last minute when Spalding asked if he could bring Mary on the *Sequoia*, Jackie agreed. She even had an assistant call Mary directly to issue an invitation. It would be the first time Mary had been asked to join the Kennedys for the evening since Jack broke off the affair. At the party, as far as Jackie could see, he appeared perfectly content to leave Mary to Spalding. When at one point he did slip off, it was with the wife of another guest.

Jackie left the next day to spend the Memorial Day weekend at Camp David. She returned on June 3 for her last official appearance before the baby was due, a state dinner in honor of the President of India, Dr Sarvepalli Radhakrishnan. Two days later, Jack, on a five-day trip west, stopped off in El Paso, Texas, to confer with Governor John Connally, Senator Ralph Yarborough, and Vice-President Lyndon Johnson. In an effort to smooth over the political infighting that had destroyed party unity among Texas Democrats, Kennedy promised to return in November.

The President went on to California, where on Friday, June 7, he attended a fundraiser at the Beverly Hilton Hotel in Los Angeles. Afterward, he retired to his suite to wait for Jesse Unruh, Speaker of the State Assembly and one of the most powerful men in California politics. Kennedy knew Macmillan had been fighting for his political life in recent days. Profumo had resigned, having confessed that he had indeed had an affair with Christine Keeler. Because Macmillan had conspicuously supported the War Minister in the House of Commons, there were widespread doubts about his judgment and competence. In London there was talk of 'a loosening of grasp in the Prime Minister in recent months.' There were hints that certain Tory politicians were on the verge of labeling Macmillan 'an electoral liability,' and that the Profumo affair might lead the Conservative Party's rank and file to call for his resignation. There were rumors of further sex scandals involving high government officials and whispers that Macmillan's problems at home had left him unable to face anything to do with sex. Kennedy's knowledge of what scandal had done to his counterpart did not stop him from welcoming Jesse Unruh's delivery of several girls for the evening. And Unruh, unlike the Democrat in Seattle whom Dave Powers had halted at the door, had the political clout to present the girls personally to the President.

The next and last stop was Honolulu, where Kennedy was to speak to the U.S. Conference of Mayors and lay a wreath at the Pearl Harbor Memorial. En route, he was in a foul mood, distressed that a press photograph of a Secret Service agent pushing a presidential aide into the pool at the Beverly Hilton would be bad for his image. Considering what he had been up to at the hotel, his concern seems silly, even more so in view of his plans for the evening. About ten minutes after the President retired to a guesthouse at Makalapa Naval Base, an aide delivered two girls for his pleasure.

Kennedy had reached a dramatic turning point in his development as a leader when he responded affirmatively to Macmillan's March 16 plea to restart the drive for a test ban treaty. By June, he was ready to make his chosen course of action public. He flew Ted Sorensen to Hawaii to work with him on the final draft of the speech in which he would announce the proposal which he and Macmillan had jointly made to Khrushchev. While he was still in Honolulu, a message arrived from Khrushchev accepting the proposal. Thus, the speech turned from the revelation of an offer into a statement that special emissaries would soon go to Moscow for high-level discussions with the aim of reaching an early agreement on a comprehensive nuclear test ban.

Kennedy's commencement address at American University in Washington on June 10, 1963, was much more than just an announcement of this dramatic development. The speech, considered by some to be the finest of his presidency, set forth the credo that world peace was 'the most important topic on earth' and its pursuit his most urgent task as a leader. The man

who spoke those words was very different from the fledgling
President who, two and a half years previously, had delivered
an Inaugural Address that inspired millions, then swiftly con-
tradicted its spirit with his actions in Cuba. At the time of the
Bay of Pigs invasion, Chester Bowles had lamented that
Kennedy lacked 'a basic moral reference point.' The commencement address – the peace speech, as it would come to be
known – suggested that that was no longer the case. Kennedy
had touched on certain of these themes before, but the crucial
difference this time was his commitment to act despite the
political consequences to himself. It seemed quite possible that
the Senate would refuse to ratify a treaty, potentially a devastating blow to his hopes for a second term. Kennedy was
willing to take that chance. Far from the politician he had been
at the start of his presidency, determined to win at any cost,
here was a statesman ready to risk his own re-election in pursuit
of ideals.

'I speak of peace because of the new face of war,' he declared.
'Total war makes no sense in an age when great powers can
maintain large and relatively invulnerable forces and refuse to
surrender without resort to those forces. It makes no sense in
an age when a single nuclear weapon contains almost ten times
the explosive force delivered by all of the Allied air forces in
the Second World War. It makes no sense in an age when the
deadly poisons produced by a nuclear exchange would be
carried by wind and water and soil and seed to the far corners
of the globe and to generations yet unborn.'

There were powerful echoes of Macmillan throughout the
address, and anyone who has read the 'dear friend' letters,
especially the impassioned appeal of March 16, cannot fail to
see the Prime Minister's influence in bringing Kennedy to this
point. If the Cuban Missile Crisis freed Kennedy of the shadow
of the past and restored his credibility as a leader, the peace
speech gave evidence of a stunning moral and political transformation. Significantly, Chester Bowles, who had fallen from
power as a result of disagreements with the President and the
Attorney General, would hail the address as a critical turning
point in Kennedy's presidency. There had been a time, accord-

ing to Bowles, when the administration lacked 'a genuine sense of conviction about what is right and wrong.' On the basis of the peace speech, Bowles considered that Kennedy, about to develop 'real greatness as a President,' had found himself morally at last.

The profound developments in Kennedy's political morality, it soon became apparent, were in conflict with the pragmatic code that drove his private life. The most visible sign of the evolving struggle between public and private codes of behavior was the action Kennedy took immediately after he delivered the American University speech. Directly after his return to the White House that morning, Kennedy phoned Joe Alsop. Since his old friend Hugh Fraser, Macmillan's Secretary of State for Air and a great friend of Kick's, was dining at Alsop's that night, would Alsop mind if he invited himself along as well? Alsop was delighted to agree, as it was a source of tremendous pride that his remained one of the few private houses in Washington to which Kennedy still came two years into the presidency. Then Kennedy dropped his bombshell. As Jackie was at Camp David, would Alsop mind asking Mary Meyer? Twelve days had passed since the birthday party aboard the *Sequoia* when Mary, escorted by Chuck Spalding, had recrossed Jack's radar screen. His call to Alsop, on the very day that Bowles was saying Kennedy seemed to have found himself morally, was a first step toward resuming an affair that had profoundly hurt and threatened his wife, to whom he had promised that he would not see Mary again.

If the first request had pleased Alsop, the second delighted him utterly, since there would be much gossip value in the news that Mary was to be Jack's dinner partner. Not a day passed before Alsop, as was his habit, was trumpeting the news halfway around the world. Strangest of all, Kennedy must have known he would do that. If he wanted to see Mary Meyer so badly, why didn't he ask her to the White House privately and avoid talk that sooner or later was bound to reach Jackie's ears? The wish to meet Mary at Alsop's house suggests that he may have been uneasy about the encounter and hoped it would be enough just to talk and laugh across a dinner table in the presence of others. That he was nervous is also strongly suggested by what he did next. Not long afterward, he called Alsop back to say he'd be unable to come after all, as he was experiencing 'a bit of a bother' with his back due to a 'taxing weekend trip to Hawaii.' By that time, Alsop had already asked Mary, who accepted without hesitation.

Jack's cancellation left Alsop with the task of finding a dinner partner for her. He invited David Bruce, U.S. ambassador to Britain, who was in Washington without his wife to talk to Kennedy about his visit to Britain at the end of June, as well as the political implications of the Profumo affair. The topics were linked because, despite the fact that Kennedy and Macmillan wanted to meet one last time before the start of test ban negotiations, a number of administration figures were urging the President to steer clear lest he be tainted by Macmillan's problems. In any event, no sooner had Bruce accepted Alsop's invitation than Kennedy changed his mind yet again. In a call that suggests he was fighting an inner battle over whether to see Mary, he said he would come at eight, but only for a drink.

Finally, Kennedy 'stayed so long,' Alsop wrote to Evangeline Bruce, 'that he might almost as well have stayed to dinner anyway.' It is this totally unprecedented hesitation to fulfill his own desires without concern for right or wrong which is so striking about Kennedy's back-and-forth with Alsop over Mary Meyer. This was simply not the sort of thing which had ever seemed to concern him before, and it was all too obviously connected to the moral commitment he had made that day in his speech at American University.

In addition to Mary Meyer, David Bruce, and the Frasers, Alsop's guests included David and Sissie Ormsby-Gore. Sissie, who made no bones about her disgust with Jack's infidelity, cannot have been pleased to attend an event that reunited the President with his mistress. Jack, for his part, paid a good deal of attention to the beautiful Lady Antonia Fraser, in whose presence, Alsop reported, he resembled 'a small boy wondering whether to plunge a spoon into a fresh dish of peach ice cream.'

But it was Mary Meyer who really had the President's attention that night, and before he left he invited her to the

White House on Wednesday evening, when Jackie would still be at Camp David. For three months, Jack had kept his promise to a wife physically and emotionally incapable of handling this particular affair. Given her condition and her fears of losing her baby, as well as the fact that she asked so little of him, the decision to break his word was to court disaster.

The next morning, Kennedy awakened to a chorus of public praise for his speech. There was one discordant note, a telegram to Bobby Kennedy from Martin Luther King Jr that called on the administration to find a 'just and moral' solution to 'the nation's most grievous problem' – civil rights. King had spoken out along similar lines in the *New York Times*, urging the President to address race as a moral issue, in terms 'we seldom if ever hear' from the White House. King argued that the administration's major new civil rights legislation would fail to pass if Kennedy did nothing more than introduce it before going off to Europe.

As chance would have it, King had chosen his moment well. Macmillan had done the groundwork in guiding Kennedy to give precedence to moral over practical concerns. After the previous day's breakthrough in international matters, Kennedy realized he was ready to do the same on the domestic front. He had disappointed King before, but he suddenly decided to go on television that night to speak about racial problems. Immediately, the men around him voiced opposition. The civil rights bill already presented enough of a political danger, they argued. The President should not make matters worse with a personal commitment. Besides, the timing was hasty. No speech had been drafted or vetted, and, given the topic's extreme political sensitivity, especially in the South, to go on the air so spontaneously seemed foolhardy. As with the test ban treaty, Kennedy overrode his advisers. For the second consecutive day that week, he chose publicly to risk his own re-election in the pursuit of ideals.

Kennedy's address to the nation began at eight. Speaking in large part extemporaneously, he announced plans to send sweeping civil rights legislation to Congress the following week, but emphasized that law alone cannot make men see right. 'We are confronted primarily by a moral issue,' he declared. 'It is as old as the Scriptures and is as clear as the American Constitution. The heart of the question is whether all Americans are to be afforded equal rights and equal opportunities, whether we are going to treat our fellow Americans as we want to be treated.' It was the first time Kennedy had spoken of civil rights as a moral, rather than merely a legal, issue.

The evening following his civil rights speech, despite his promise to a pregnant wife, Mary Meyer was due to arrive at the White House at eight. On Wednesday, June 12, 1963, between accepting congratulations on the previous night's speech that included a rapturous telegram from King, the President did a bit of last-minute scrambling when he learned that Jackie had decided to return that evening. Had she heard about the dinner at Alsop's house? In any case, before she and the children appeared, Kennedy asked Bill Walton to come to dinner as well.

It was half past seven when the car carrying Jackie and the children passed through the Southwest Gate. Jack was still in his office, and since he stopped off for a swim before heading upstairs at a few minutes past eight, Jackie had to welcome Mary when she and Walton arrived in the family quarters.

It is difficult to conceive what this horrific evening must have been like for Jackie, six months pregnant, fearful for the baby she was carrying and consumed with memories of the terrible days in 1956 when her first child was stillborn and Jack had thoughtlessly sought his own pleasure in Europe. The shock was far more than just Mary Meyer's presence, which was a clear signal that he had either resumed the affair or planned to. When Jack had learned that Jackie was on her way back to the White House that evening, he could easily have called Mary to cancel. Instead, he had allowed her to come as scheduled and had contacted Walton to serve as a perfunctory beard who fooled no one, certainly not Jackie. Why had he not simply canceled the invitation? Why had he chosen to force Jackie to face a situation which she could hardly fail to understand?

Jack could be callous, indifferent, irresponsible, and above all much given to denial, but Jackie had never had reason to believe that he wished to hurt her or took the slightest pleasure in doing so. This evening, the inescapable conclusion presented itself that Jack wanted her to know he had broken his promise about Mary Meyer, a promise Jackie had pressed him to make about no other woman in his life. What pleasure could Jack possibly have expected from such an evening? Certainly it wasn't sex. As there would be only the four of them at dinner, he was not about to slip off with Mary to his daughter's schoolroom. Nor could he have anticipated an amusing evening of pot-smoking, which, in more conducive circumstances, Mary had provided in the past.

During her years of suffering at Jack's hands, Jackie had always had one thing to cling to, one thing she seemed always in her heart to know: that Jack never set out to hurt her. He had never taken pleasure, as Joe Sr was known to do, in his wife's pain and humiliation. Jackie had never doubted, certainly not in recent years, that Jack loved her. But her belief in that love was dependent on the certainty that he really believed, as he often insisted to friends, that his womanizing had nothing to do with his feelings for her. Jack's denial of the impact his infidelity had on Jackie was in a way as sustaining to her as it was to him. All that seemed to be changed as the appalling possibility presented itself that Jack had designed this evening to hurt her, to put wife and mistress at the same table and watch Jackie's face when she realized that Mary was back.

In a long list of terrible nights, this surely stood out as the worst. There could be no question that Jack, despite his usual willful blindness to Jackie's feelings, might be unaware of what his affair with Mary had come to represent to Jackie. It was the single instance in which Jackie had drawn the line, the one time she had forced on her husband the understanding that his unfaithfulness did indeed cause her great pain.

As Jackie prepared to leave the White House two days after the dinner with Mary Meyer, her whole world was in crisis. Already preoccupied with fears for her baby, she now had reason to question whether the love which had long been her only certainty was in doubt. By all accounts, there had once been a time when Joe Kennedy loved Rose, before he began to take pleasure in being openly cruel to her. Had such a change just occurred in Jackie's marriage? After Wednesday evening's dinner, how could she believe any longer that Jack did not intend to hurt her? And if he did, how could she continue to believe in his love?

At 2 p.m. on Friday, June 14, Jackie's car drove through the Southwest Gate, heading for Camp David. Six hours later, Mary Meyer signed in at the White House and the President resumed their affair.

Before Kennedy left for Camp David the next day, the White House received an urgent report from Ambassador Bruce on the situation in London, which Mrs Lincoln included in the President's weekend reading book. Bruce's long telegram so upset Kennedy that at length he removed it from the binder and gave it to Jackie to read. 'Whatever estimate I had formed of the political situation in Britain when I left here six days ago has been altered by what has occurred in my absence,' Bruce wrote. He had returned to find Macmillan 'under heavy attack. On Monday next he must make the most difficult speech, followed by interrogation, of his long career in the House of Commons.' Some thought he had colluded with Profumo in telling 'a palpable lie,' others – the majority – that he had been naïve or stupid in believing the War Minister's denial of his affair with Christine Keeler. In either case, one woman had 'precipitated a political crisis,' as well as 'the possible downfall of a Prime Minister.'

'In his vigil this weekend,' Bruce reflected, 'I do not doubt that the Prime Minister, a resourceful man, will draw up a brilliant brief for delivery to the Commons. But even if he gains a personal success, his former prestige will, because of the inexorable impact of events, be beyond complete restoration. Democracies are as cruel as other systems of Government in attributing blame to their political leaders. A sacrifice is increasingly demanded here, and the appointed lamb for the altar is the Prime Minister, who must already have appreciated the sad truth that no ingratitude surpasses that of a democracy.'

At Camp David, Jack watched Caroline ride her pony and visited the hangar with John Jr, where father and son, as was their custom, climbed into the chopper, donned helmets, and pretended to fly. But, as Jackie would later recall, her husband was 'deeply depressed' by Macmillan's predicament, a topic he returned to again and again in conversation. Apart from his strong feelings for the Prime Minister, whom he regarded as a 'hero' and mentor, the topic was a loaded one: both Kennedys knew that Jack regularly engaged in behavior that, at any moment, could result in a similar fate. Frustrated by his own inability to help Macmillan, Kennedy seized on the need to bring something at once more personal and more extravagant than the standard State Department gift when he visited Birch Grove, the Macmillans' country house in Sussex, two weeks later. He enlisted Jackie, who came up with the idea of a vermeil dressing set for Lady Dorothy and a desk set for the Prime Minister.

By the time Jack arrived at Camp David on Saturday, Jackie had outwardly mastered her emotions, and, as she had so often done before, concentrated on the tremendous pressures Jack faced. Perhaps it was simply easier that way. At the same time, thinking about the Macmillans would surely have kept alive the very questions raised by Mary's reappearance. To what extent had Lady Dorothy's relations with Bob Boothby been motivated merely by selfishness, or had there been a point where deliberate cruelty entered the picture? Thoughts of Macmillan's unfaithful wife, though presumably confined to the matter of selecting a gift for her, were not likely to distract Jackie from her own troubles.

Jackie remained alone with her thoughts at Camp David on Monday, while the President returned to the White House to the news that Macmillan had delivered a spectacular performance in the House of Commons. Calling the Prime Minister's speech and the debate that followed 'one of the most dramatic parliamentary occasions in recent history,' Bruce reported that Macmillan had won a vote of confidence but lost control of the Conservative Party nonetheless. The 'general expectation' was that he would 'have to go sooner or later,' but no move to oust him was likely prior to Kennedy's visit. If in any sense Bruce, fresh from the evening at Alsop's house with

Kennedy and Mary Meyer, had intended his reports as a warning, the point was not taken. That night, hours after Macmillan had barely averted his downfall, Kennedy held a two-hour pool party.

In light of the Profumo affair, an objective observer might have gasped at the suicidal idiocy of Kennedy's ongoing pool parties. The President had a different view, congratulating himself on emotion-free and, in his view, danger-free couplings. In fact, one of his regular girls that spring posed a grave threat to the presidency. By May, Ellen Rometsch, a dark-haired twenty-seven-year-old German model, had become a great favorite of the President, who, according to Bobby Baker, said she gave 'the best oral sex' he ever had. Bill Thompson had discovered her at Baker's Quorum Club in Washington. Members of the key club, located in the Carroll Arms Hotel, entered through a door with a large gilded 'Q' or − for those who preferred not to be observed − through an unmarked door near the hotel newsstand. Within, scantily clad hostesses were available for 'dates' with politicians and lobbyists. Baker, who also held a powerful position in the U.S. Senate as Secretary to the Senate Majority, provided girls to promote his own shady and far-ranging business activities, as well as to influence government decisions. During her tenure as a Baker girl, Rometsch, who bore a faint resemblance to Elizabeth Taylor, numbered various prominent Capitol Hill figures among her lovers. After Thompson first delivered her to the White House, she visited on ten occasions. Beyond the fact that Rometsch came from Bobby Baker, Kennedy knew nothing about her background or her other lovers. Nor, despite what had happened with Profumo, did he wish to.

When Jackie arrived back the next day, she had Bruce's long telegram with her. Jack had left it behind at Camp David. As he was due to depart for Europe the following Saturday night, this would be their last week together at the White House that spring. By the time he returned, she would be at Cape Cod. As the week drew to a close, Jackie did not go on ahead to Camp David as usual. Instead, Jack accompanied her and the children at lunchtime on Saturday, so that they could enjoy a few hours there together before he returned to Washington for his flight to Germany.

Back at the White House a few days later, she completed last-minute preparations for the summer and issued instructions to set up a nursery for the new baby in the tiny room known as the high-chair room, where Miss Shaw fed Caroline and John. She ordered rugs and directed that John's old crib be taken out of storage and repainted. On Wednesday, as soon as they left for a week at Hammersmith Farm, Mr West was to begin work so that everything would be ready in the fall. Jackie's habitual defenses against emotions she could not handle kicked in. At a moment when her life threatened to implode, Jackie immersed herself in routine, detail, and organization. Nothing must be neglected, no minuscule detail overlooked. As the old certainties about her relationship with Jack threatened to desert her, she seemed determined to do what she had always done: make herself feel in control of what she could.

In Berlin, the President delivered his '*Ich bin ein Berliner*' speech, and the tumultuous reception presaged that, as the previous European visit had been Jackie's triumph, this trip was to be his. From there he made a sentimental stop in Ireland, where he was greeted with immense feeling and returned it in kind. Expected at Birch Grove early on the afternoon of Saturday, June 29, he sent word at the last minute that he would be a bit late, having decided to stop first to visit Kick's grave at Chatsworth. The Duke and Duchess of Devonshire were waiting when the President's helicopter landed, and the trio drove to the family estate that would have been Billy and Kick's. Until her death, Kick had been Jack's other half, and in the years since she had subtly shaped his life through a wide range of friends and family connections. At St Peter's Church, he walked up a gravel path to the Cavendish plot at the top of the graveyard and stood at the grave, where Billy's mother had placed the graceful inscription: 'JOY SHE GAVE / JOY SHE HAS FOUND.' After a quarter of an hour, he and Kick's brother- and sister-in-law returned to the car. It was time to see Macmillan, Kick's uncle by marriage, the alternate father that in death she had bestowed on Jack.

The Prime Minister personally collected Kennedy at Gatwick Airport, grateful for an opportunity to shift back to what was truly important: a celebration of the talks in Moscow to begin on July 15, as well as a good deal of last-minute tactical planning. He valued loyalty tremendously and was touched by Kennedy's readiness to lend prestige to an embattled friend, despite politically motivated advice to stay away. Kennedy had not forgotten that Macmillan once did the same for him. When Kennedy arrived from Vienna defeated and diminished by his encounter with Khrushchev, Macmillan had done all he could to help. How different was the John F. Kennedy who came to England in June 1963, as a result of both 'Cuba 2' and the bold actions that, inspired by Macmillan, he had taken afterward.

At Birch Grove, where the President's gifts were received with the tenderness with which they had been selected, Macmillan had a distressing glimpse of Kennedy's physical condition. He had grown exceedingly fond of the President, and was shaken to see a young man so horribly crippled with pain yet so determined to go forward. In the Prime Minister's study, it quickly became apparent that Kennedy could not sit in a regular chair, and an aide was hurriedly dispatched to find a rocker. After they talked for a while, Kennedy went upstairs to prepare for dinner. He was to spend the night in a room that, fittingly, had once belonged to Macmillan's American mother.

Before Kennedy reappeared, he received unsettling news from Washington, suggesting that soon London might not be the only world capital embroiled in scandal. Bobby Kennedy called to report an article in that day's *New York Journal–American*, which opened alarmingly, 'One of the biggest names in American politics – a man who holds "a very high elective office" – has been injected into Britain's vice-security scandal.' A model associated with Christine Keeler through Stephen Ward, the man who had introduced Keeler to Profumo, claimed to have been a bedmate of a top U.S. politician. Bobby hadn't actually seen the article but gathered that the 'big' name had been withheld – for now. In view of the sums Keeler had recently been paid to tell her story in the *News of the World*, that could change at any moment. Further testimony from other women was sure to follow. Particular names were unlikely to mean anything to the President. In many cases, he hadn't even bothered to learn them in the first place. But he knew enough to make sure Bobby cut this off quickly.

The President did not reveal his troubles to his host, but as he and Macmillan talked that evening, the Attorney General went to work. He called Courtney Evans, his liaison at the F.B.I., to say that his brother had 'expressed concern' about the allegations. Evans, in turn, called his man in New York who read him the *Journal–American* piece, the result of a twenty-minute transatlantic taped interview conducted by James D. Horan and Dom Frasca with Maria Novotny. Novotny, then under contract for her story to the *News of the World*, claimed to have information about a top U.S. official's involvement with a Chinese-American woman who had worked for Harry Alan Towers in New York and Stephen Ward in London. 'Like our Mr Profumo,' Novotny declared, 'your man also has access to government secrets.' Thus, in addition to sex, there was the specter of a security breach. Towers, who had been arrested on white slavery charges, had skipped bail and fled 'behind the Iron Curtain.' Novotny declined to name the Chinese-American. The next day, eager to learn the official's name before it appeared in print, Bobby Kennedy brought Horan and Frasca to Washington.

That afternoon, Sunday, June 30, Kennedy left for Italy, the last leg of his trip. If he was worried about scandal, he gave no sign. He and Macmillan had talked of great things, of changing history and the exhilaration of waiting to see if their gamble paid off in Moscow. They agreed to meet again before Christmas or in the New Year at the latest. In the meantime, they would be in touch by phone, telegram, and letter. Neither man knew it, but this would be the last time they saw each other. Later, Macmillan would describe his final impression as Kennedy went off to his helicopter: 'Hatless, with his brisk step, and combining that indescribable look of a boy on a holiday with the dignity of a President and Commander-in-Chief, he walked across the garden to the machine.'

While Kennedy was in Italy, where he had a tryst at the

Villa Serbelloni on Lake Como with the wife of one of his and
Jackie's jet-set friends, Bobby interrogated the reporters who
had broken the *Journal–American* story. Who was the top official
in the article? Frasca replied it was the President of the United
States – the last thing Bobby wanted to hear. The reporters
went on to say that Kennedy's contact with the Chinese-
American woman had occurred 'prior to his election to this
office.' There was 'no evidence of a protracted relationship,'
the incident being limited to 'a personal indiscretion.' Then
they played the tape of their interview with Novotny. When it
was finished, Bobby indignantly demanded to know if they had
printed the allegations 'without any further check being made
to get to the truth of the matter.' Frasca insisted he had
additional sources that must remain confidential. After the
meeting, Bobby ordered an investigation 'to determine the exact
periods of time' the Chinese-American woman may have been
in the United States.

Following talks with Italian leaders, as well as with the newly
elected Pope Paul VI, Kennedy returned to the White House
at 2 a.m. on Wednesday, July 3. The family quarters were
empty. Jackie and the children, still in Newport, were to leave
later that day for Cape Cod. He had a few hours' rest,
then taped a statement about his European trip for use in a
forthcoming television special. Later, he met with aides to
review some points about the test ban treaty talks.

The Attorney General had less lofty issues to handle on his
brother's first day back. The *Journal–American* article was bad
enough, but now there was far more damning evidence about
another of the President's sordid relationships. This was no
one-shot affair that may or may not have occurred before he
took office. Ellen Rometsch had regularly attended pool parties
that spring, and she had made the mistake of talking about
them to an F.B.I. informer. On the day of the President's return,
J. Edgar Hoover summoned Bobby to his office and laid out
some of what he knew. The case eerily echoed the Profumo
affair, for even as Rometsch had been carrying on with the
President, she was alleged to have shared her favors with,
among others, a Soviet attaché in Washington. That detail

provided the angle the mainstream press needed to cover the story. To make matters worse, Rometsch came from East Germany, and there were rumors, never substantiated, but devastating to the President nonetheless, that she was a spy for the Communist German Democratic Republic. This was everything Kennedy's Secret Service agents had long feared might happen as a result of the many anonymous women being ushered in and out by the President's procurers. If the story broke, especially in the climate created by the Profumo affair, Kennedy would be ruined.

At 7:05, the President, who had much to reflect on, went out alone for a short walk on the South Grounds. It was a hot July evening and he intended to join Jackie at Cape Cod the next day. Soon, he headed indoors to the pool, where Mary Meyer arrived fifteen minutes later. In view of what Hoover had just revealed, Ellen Rometsch must never be admitted again. But as far as Jack was concerned, that had nothing to do with Mary Meyer. For three months, he had tried to stay away from her. Now that their affair was on again, he had wasted no time in arranging to spend his first night home with her. He and Mary remained in the pool until ten past nine, when they went up to the family quarters for dinner.

THIRTEEN

Private Grief

By the time Jackie arrived at Cape Cod that July, after a week with her mother in Newport, her life had begun to seem perilously close to Rose's. For years she had insisted on the distinction between her own marriage and that of her mother-in-law. Now, with Rose nearby in the Kennedy family compound, it was sometimes hard to see the difference. This was an especially difficult moment in Jackie's life, as her pregnancy had caused her to retreat from the diplomatic partnership she had forged with her husband. Had she made a terrible mistake in giving up, with so little thought, so much of the power she had won in her own right? Jack had just made an immensely successful solo trip to Europe and had seemed to relish having the spotlight to himself after the ambivalent experience of their trip together two years before. Jackie must have wondered – for she had long known that Jack did not like to share the spotlight – if he was glad to have her out of the picture. Was she about to become like Rose, the object of laughter from both her family and outsiders as she continually relived her own glory days at the American embassy in London?

With the exception of Rose's obsessiveness about churchgoing and religion, there was a distressing similarity between Jackie's life and that of her mother-in-law during the long summer weeks at the Cape when Jack was in Washington: the insistence on routine, the exercise taken daily at the same time, the long hours spent reading, the need for time alone. Rose would travel on her own to Europe, where, in contrast to the life she led with her family, she wasn't treated as a joke. These trips had their uncomfortable parallel in Jackie's own escapes to Europe

and New York. In the presence of her husband and children,
Rose might seem a ridiculous figure, but away from her family
she could be reasonable and intelligent, eager for experience
and knowledge. In her private cabin by the beach, she spent
long hours devouring serious books – much like Jackie. Jackie
of all people knew that this was not the Rose people talked about,
the absurd creature who lived with her husband's mistresses
constantly in and out of her house. Rose's example suggested
the possibility that one day Jack's feelings for Jackie would
become what Joe's were for Rose. If it were true that Jack had
reached the point with Mary Meyer where his intention was to
hurt and ridicule his wife, then any meaningful difference
between the two Mrs Kennedys had ceased to exist.

With Mary Meyer, Jack had come closer than ever to
behaving like his father. Jackie was smart enough to have
quickly picked up that one of Mary's principal defenses was her
display of contempt for others. Had Mary's contempt for Jackie
infected Jack? Had her haughty laughter at Jackie, at her
pretensions and her difficulty in connecting with people, made
Jack see her as being like Rose?

As Rose pursued the carefully plotted routine of her days,
just a mile or so away Jackie went through routines of her own.
Like her mother-in-law, Jackie craved solitude. That summer
of 1963, rather than stay in the Kennedy compound, she and
Jack had rented an isolated house called Brambletyde on Squaw
Island. Jackie was the one who had first been drawn to the big,
gray-shingled house set at the end of a long dirt road on the
tip of a peninsula, with only the beach and water beyond.
When she brought Jack out to see Brambletyde, he quickly fell
in love with the romantic location, where one heard the
perpetual lash of waves against rocks and the whip and snap of
the American flag outside the master bedroom window. They
thought perhaps they would buy the house, but, unable to come
to terms with the owner, they negotiated a rental instead.

It was to this isolated location that Jackie, almost seven
months pregnant, came to await the birth of her baby. She
arrived tense and troubled. No matter how much care she had
taken to repress such thoughts, no matter how much effort she

made to underscore her own distance from Rose with her snide imitations of her mother-in-law's voice and mannerisms, no matter how often she led the laughter at Rose's expense, there seemed every possibility that one day she would find herself living the same cruel life with Jack that Rose lived with Joe. Was that what Jack's return to Mary Meyer meant?

The first signs from Jack when he joined her on the Fourth of July were calming. Despite the fact that he had spent his first night back from Europe with Mary at the White House, when he arrived at Hyannis Port the following day he gave every indication that his feelings for Jackie were what they had always been: love and concern. Watching him that evening, it would have been difficult to believe that he could ever have considered hurting a wife to whom he was so obviously attached by the deepest bonds. No sooner had the President's chopper touched down at the Kennedy compound at 5:10 p.m. than Jack, pointedly forgoing the customary hello to his father, hurried out to Brambletyde. His rush to be alone with her and the children away from the mob of relatives was the sort of gesture sure to assuage Jackie's fears. An hour later, her anxieties for the moment set aside, Jackie and Jack drove back to the compound to join the family, who were celebrating both the holiday and the birth that day of Bobby and Ethel's eighth child, Christopher.

By the next morning, Jackie seemed a new person. She slipped immediately into the comforting rhythms of summers past, when all that mattered were the hours when she and Jack were together and she could ignore whatever he did in her absence. She slept late, then spent the morning alone while Jack and their houseguest Lem Billings took John Jr into town. The President himself drove the convertible to a toy store, where they purchased kites to take advantage of the winds that swept the peninsula. At lunchtime, Jackie and Caroline joined the group for a picnic lunch on the *Honey Fitz*. In the afternoon, Jackie watched as Jack and Lem showed the children how to fly kites. Afterward they swam off the *Marlin*, and on Sunday afternoon Jack announced that his back felt the best it had in two years and that he wanted to play a few holes of golf. There was celebration all around, as previously his back had kept him away from a game he loved. Immediately they drove to the Hyannis Golf Club, and Jackie walked around the course with him for five holes. Their happiness together made it hard for her to imagine that they could ever really become like Joe and Rose.

As soon as Jack returned to Washington on Monday morning, the worrying and waiting resumed. In summers past, Jackie had spent her days in anticipation of the weekend when, in effect, life began. This year, pregnancy intensified and complicated the sense of expectation. She seemed to feel safe only on weekends when Jack was with her.

Jack had made certain that Jackie was not actually alone as she waited for the baby that summer. From the start of the pregnancy, she had been so anxious that Jack had arranged for her obstetrician, Dr John Walsh, to spend the first part of the summer at Hyannis Port. Dr Travell was to take over when Walsh left. Though Jackie planned to give birth at Walter Reed Hospital in Washington in September, a hospital suite waited at nearby Otis Air Force Base in case something went wrong. In addition to her doctor, she had her Secret Service detail, particularly Clint Hill, for support, and she took the added measure of bringing her personal secretary, Mary Gallagher, to the Cape for the first time.

Like Rose, Jackie's great tranquilizers had always been routine and physical activity. The comfort of doing the same thing at the same time, day in and day out, seemed to calm and order the lives of both Mrs Kennedys. Where Rose had her golf in the summer, Jackie had always had her water-skiing, though this summer she was supposed to avoid strenuous physical activity. To the alarm of the Secret Service men, she did continue to swim in the choppy waters near the house. On one occasion, agents dashed to the rescue when a canoe with Jackie and the children caught in some mud and she stood up to try to dislodge it herself.

More often than not, Jackie could be found in her room or on an adjoining sun porch. She painted and read. She dictated to Mary Gallagher. She fired off letters, memos, and Christmas lists. She answered queries that came in on courier flights from Washington. She ordered a dress for the baby's christening in October and sent thoughts to Mr West about the new nursery under construction in the family quarters. She worked on the scrapbook of the White House restoration project which she planned to give Jack on their tenth wedding anniversary in September. In short, she retreated into whatever details she could find to fill her days and her thoughts, so as to avoid having to think about all the things she feared.

When Jack returned the second weekend, he brought David and Sissie Ormsby-Gore. Naturally, conversation focused on the test ban negotiations scheduled to begin in Moscow on Monday. The talk was a reminder of how much the past two years, since that fateful trip to Paris together, had added to her relationship with Jack. The bond had deepened and intensified in ways that would have made the very thought that his interest in Mary could be designed to hurt her seem silly and baseless.

Kennedy and Ormsby-Gore spent hours that weekend, as Jackie and Sissie listened, trying to anticipate what would happen in Moscow. Already there had been a snag. Khrushchev had delivered a speech in Berlin in which he appeared to renege on his earlier offer to allow inspections. Macmillan had wasted no time in writing to Kennedy, arguing that while they ought to see 'whether an accommodation can be reached to get the full ban,' they must 'not let slip the very big prize of the modified ban.' That is, if the two sides couldn't agree to a ban on all tests – both underground and atmospheric – the 'second prize' of a ban on atmospheric tests alone would be well worth having, not just for itself but for the sake of the other important changes in East–West relations to which it might lead, such as nonproliferation agreements to keep nuclear weapons out of the hands of the Germans and others. That in turn was likely to make the Soviets – who, given their experiences in the Second World War, deeply feared the prospect of a nuclear-armed Germany – more accommodating in the matter of Berlin.

Khrushchev's last-minute change of heart with regard to

inspections was the sort of thing Kennedy's advisers had warned about when they opposed Macmillan's plea for a renewed initiative back in March. Kennedy had risked a great deal politically in siding with the Prime Minister, and he was under intense pressure now. Earlier that week, he had instructed U.S. Special Envoy Averell Harriman, about to leave for Moscow, to try for a partial ban in the event that a full ban was not achievable.

If the President needed a reminder of why he was doing this, he had it that weekend in the screening room at Brambletyde. As the Kennedys and the Ormsby-Gores watched film of his recent speech in Berlin, he remarked on how disturbed he had been by the thought that if he had asked his audience 'to cross into East Germany and pull down that wall,' almost certainly, 'sheep-like,' they would have gone. Kennedy found that terrifying. Given his feeling that another Hitler could easily emerge, clearly nonproliferation agreements and other safeguards were essential.

From the moment talks began on July 15, it was evident that a full test ban was out of the question. Negotiations for even a partial ban would be hard fought. By the time Jack returned for a third weekend at the Cape, with Lem Billings and Jim Reed in tow, he was full of anxiety about the fitful progress in Moscow. Friday evening at six, Jackie accompanied him to St Francis Xavier Church for the christening of Bobby and Ethel's son. Jackie, who hated to be gawked at, especially when pregnant, survived the ordeal well, including the family gathering afterward at the compound. But the next morning, Jack rushed downstairs upset and alarmed, telling Jim Reed to get hold of Dr Walsh immediately.

When Walsh couldn't be reached, Jack's agitation grew. It was nearly an hour before Reed found him. Walsh, it seemed, had gone out for a walk without saying where. When he finally arrived, Kennedy breathed fire and fury. In the future, someone must always know where the doctor was. After examining Jackie, Walsh reported that her complaint was nothing serious. She was merely exhausted. Nonetheless, the episode, harrowing for all, had stripped away even Jack's usual surface calm. That

morning, all the underlying tension about the pregnancy, Jack's
as well as Jackie's, had furiously burst forth.

Worried as he was about Jackie, Jack flew back to Washington
on the night of Sunday, July 21. As President, he had to be in
Washington as the delicate negotiations in Moscow reached
their final, critical moments. She was fine, she assured him, as
he left her in Dr Walsh's care.

The husband who exploded with rage at Jackie's doctor
continued not just to see Mary Meyer, but also to risk the sort
of scandal that would be devastating to his wife in her current
delicate state. The solicitude was sincere, for whatever Jackie
may have feared Jack remained locked in denial that his
involvement with Mary Meyer or any other woman had anything to do with his wife. That this was so would become clear
in just a matter of weeks. But if his concern for her was real,
so were his coarseness and recklessness. That summer, in
addition to Mary, there were two film actresses whom Dave
Powers delivered to the family quarters. Before long, remembered Larry Newman, who was on duty that night, one actress
'came down mad, crying. Her hair was wet. I don't know what
the hell went on.' Nor, by this time, were the President's
procurers above approaching women in tour groups at the
White House. 'Say, you're a beautiful woman,' an aide said to
one. 'Would you like to meet the President? If you do, I could
arrange that.' Taken aback, the visitor, who knew no one else
in the group, threw herself on the mercy of another tourist, a
Navy ensign, whom she asked to escort her off the White House
grounds.

Late on Wednesday, July 24, Kennedy met with his advisers
to consider last-minute complications in the talks; there was a
real danger that at this late date they might not reach an
agreement. Macmillan directed Ormsby-Gore to postpone the
start of his vacation and remain at the President's side until
negotiations were completed. Finally, at 5:15 p.m. in London
on Thursday, Macmillan could bear it no longer and picked
up the phone to make the case himself. When Kennedy took
the call, Macmillan explained that he had asked Ormsby-Gore
to go to the White House. 'Don't worry,' Kennedy broke in.

'David is right here. It's been worked out and I've told them to go ahead.' Even as they spoke, the treaty was being initialed.

Upon hearing the news of the signing, Macmillan hurried off to find Lady Dorothy. The woman who had hurt him so profoundly was the person with whom he wanted to share this great and historic victory. After he told her the news, he burst into tears. Later, he telegrammed Kennedy, 'I found myself unable to express my real feelings on the phone tonight ... I do understand the high degree of courage and faith which you have shown.'

Jackie turned thirty-four that weekend. The Ormsby-Gores, in high spirits, flew up with Jack from Washington, and on Sunday, July 28 – Jackie's birthday – Averell Harriman, carrying an enormous tin of caviar sent by Khrushchev, arrived from Moscow to report to the President. Though Jack continued to worry about the confirmation fight in the Senate, the tension of the previous weekend was gone. No one was happier for Jack than Jackie, no one more aware of the meaning of his struggle, under Macmillan's guidance, to pursue this particular course. His great achievement served as a reminder of all that was good and decent in him. It offered hope that the transformation in his public life might one day find its echo in his marriage.

The good feeling over the treaty fed into the birthday festivities. Jackie, immensely proud of her husband, asked Sissie, once Kick's friend and now hers as well, to be her baby's godmother.

August began on a note of jubilation. Everyone, Jackie included, had been swept up in the wait for the test ban treaty and then the celebrations. She seemed more at peace than she had for many weeks. Before Jack had left the weekend after the treaty was agreed, he had promised the children that he would bring a surprise next time. By Friday, August 2, they were so excited that Jackie took them out to Otis Air Force Base to meet *Air Force One*. When John caught sight of his father coming down the steps, he broke away from Jackie and Caroline. His tiny red sneakers streaked across the tarmac, and he hurled himself into his father's arms – an image later printed in newspapers around the world. The Kennedys flew to Hyannis Port by helicopter, but not until they were at Brambletyde did Jack produce the surprise, several puppies to divert the children while they waited for the baby. By this time, all the talk of a new brother or sister had made Caroline, especially, very impatient.

The next day, the family enjoyed a lunchtime cruise on the *Honey Fitz*. Around four, Jackie went home for a nap while Jack went off with Red Fay to play golf. Not long after he returned, the weekend took a sudden, dark turn with the news that Phil Graham had committed suicide that afternoon. For Jackie, all the pain and embarrassment associated with Graham's outburst in Phoenix was revived in an instant. Her feelings for a friend notwithstanding, Graham would always be for her the man who had publicly revealed Jack's affair with Mary Meyer. Diagnosed as a manic depressive, he had been committed to Chestnut Lodge again on June 20, the week after Kennedy resumed his affair with Mary Meyer. For six weeks he had lobbied intensively to be released for a weekend, and finally that morning, August 3, he had been granted a pass. He and his wife drove to their farm in Virginia and, after lunch, went upstairs for a nap. Graham soon got up, went to a ground-floor bathroom, and shot himself with one of the guns no one had thought to remove. At the sound of gunfire, Katharine Graham rushed downstairs to find her husband dead.

The news was too much for Jackie, seven and a half months pregnant and desperately worried about her baby. Graham's suicide seemed to dredge up all of her fears about Mary Meyer, all the dark possibilities that had been in play since that terrible dinner with Mary and Bill Walton at the White House. Her composure of the past two weeks evaporated. On Sunday morning, she remained at Brambletyde when Jack attended Mass. At noon, she did not go out on the *Honey Fitz* with everyone else. Struggling for mastery over her turbulent feelings, she composed an eight-page condolence letter to Katharine Graham that, for Jackie, had the effect of temporarily making the episode seem to be about something other than Mary

Meyer. She distanced her own pain by willing herself to focus on another's.

Kennedy must have made the connection between the news of the suicide and Jackie's sudden change of mood. The previous March, aware that she was at breaking point, he had promised to give Mary up. In June, he had seen her face at that ghastly dinner when she realized that the mistress was back. He also knew that physically and emotionally his wife was extremely fragile. Just two weeks previously, he had demonstrated how seriously he took her fears about the baby when he exploded at Dr Walsh. Yet when he returned to the White House after the weekend, he arranged to see Mary Meyer that same night. She arrived at 7:40 and spent the evening with him.

The next day, Tuesday, Kennedy left the White House at a quarter to three to attend Phil Graham's funeral at the National Cathedral. The other mourners were already seated when he walked up a side aisle to take his seat. The dramatic last-minute entrance was hardly necessary to focus all eyes on him, since few in attendance would have been unaware of Graham's revelation six months previously. In a sense, the episode in Phoenix had been the start of a sad trajectory that had ended here. Once again, hours after Mary Meyer had left the President's bed, half of Washington seemed to be talking about them.

The following morning, August 7, Jackie, who had not gone to Washington for the funeral, was in Osterville watching Caroline ride her pony when she felt a stabbing pain. Her Secret Service agents immediately called Dr Walsh to meet them at Brambletyde, where he examined her and decided to take her to Otis Air Force Base Hospital at once. A helicopter was ordered at the Kennedy compound. As Dr Walsh helped Jackie into a car for the short drive, Dr Travell, who was also in attendance, asked if Jackie wanted her to call the President.

Jackie's response was sharp and immediate: 'No!'

It was as if she couldn't bear to take the chance of being rebuffed as she had been in 1956, when she was rushed to the hospital under similar circumstances and Jack was off in Europe.

Back then, he had been on a yacht with some girls. This time, too, as he had broken his word about Mary Meyer, Jackie had reason to fear that his interest lay elsewhere.

By the time they got to the landing pad in front of Joe Kennedy's house, Jackie was pleading over the chopper's roar, 'Dr Walsh, you've got to get me to the hospital on time! I don't want anything to happen to this baby.' Walsh patted her hand as she got out of the car, but she was beyond soothing.

As they approached the helicopter, Jackie cried out, 'This baby mustn't be born dead!'

'Mr President, don't worry, Jackie will be all right,' Dr Travell said on the phone from Squaw Island. She had just told him that Jackie had left for the hospital forty-five minutes earlier, and that at this minute Dr Walsh was preparing to perform a Caesarean section.

'How about the baby?' the President asked, anxiety apparent in his voice.

'Fifty-fifty.'

'I'm coming up as fast as I can.'

Air Force One and other planes were unavailable, so aides found a Lockheed Jetstar to fly the President to Otis Air Force Base immediately. Everything he said in these rushed, desperate minutes made it clear that, like Jackie, his fears were focused on the possibility that the baby might die, and he knew he had to be with Jackie if and when that happened. In 1956, she had endured the death of a baby without him. Neither of them seemed able to bear the possibility that the experience might be repeated.

As Kennedy hurried aboard a helicopter at 12:15 p.m. for the first leg of the trip, he seemed to one aide to have set a test for himself: to reach Jackie's side before the baby was born. It was 12:30 when the eight-passenger Jetstar took off from Andrews Air Force Base headed north. In Massachusetts, the Caesarean delivery was already in progress.

The small plane was full. Kennedy had hastily summoned a few aides, including his secretary, Mrs Lincoln, and Jackie's press secretary, Pamela Turnure, and new social secretary,

Nancy Tuckerman. All would later remember how striking the silence had been during the flight. Normally, the President would read or dictate, if only to distract himself. On this occasion, Turnure noticed, 'he just kept sitting and staring out of the window, and obviously his thoughts were completely with her.'

Turnure would recall being struck by how similar this scene was to the anxious plane trip from Florida to Washington in November 1960, the night that Kennedy, then President-elect, had received word that Jackie was giving birth to John Jr. In fact, that night in 1960 had been very different, however upset he was not to have been with Jackie for the delivery. He had had little to feel guilty about, having left her just a few hours previously to return to work at his transition headquarters. If, then, there had been echoes of 1956, it was simply a matter of innocent bad timing. This time, the parallels to his horrifying behavior in 1956 were unmistakable.

It is to 1956, not 1960, that these terrible hours must be compared. That 1956 was uppermost in Jack's mind is evident from his focus on the fear that the baby would die. Unlike at the time of John's birth, this time, as in 1956, Jack had been thoughtlessly carousing with another woman while his frightened wife worried about their unborn child. Less than forty-eight hours previously, Mary Meyer had visited him at the White House.

In 1956, he had seemed oblivious to the thoughtlessness and cruelty of his behavior. He was a man who had been taught to take his pleasures as and when he wished, without guilt of any kind. In August 1963, Jack Kennedy was no longer the same man. Most importantly, of course, he had had the experience of loving two children of his own; it was also true that in the years of his presidency he had come to feel a need for direction which his own father had not given him. While his father's lessons – for good and bad – had helped him in his long battle to win the presidency, once he was in office it quickly became apparent that those lessons were woefully inadequate preparation for becoming the statesman he wanted to be, for winning the place in history he desired. Feeling this lack, he had come under the influence of a new and very different sort of mentor, and by the time of that long plane ride up the Atlantic Coast his standards of behavior were changing. His father had drilled into him that he must be a man, with all the selfishness that entailed; Harold Macmillan had for two years pressed him to become a moral man.

As his own actions hinted on the day of the American University speech in June, Kennedy's newfound political morality was coming into conflict, however unconscious, with the private behavior in which he had been coached by his father. The man who sat staring out the window in silence had continued to betray the wife who adored him, in direct contravention of a promise he had made to her, but his urgent need to reach her side now suggested that he was feeling an emotion with which he had heretofore had little acquaintance: guilt.

The plane was still airborne when, at 12:52 p.m. on August 7, 1963, Dr Walsh delivered a four-pound, ten-and-a-half-ounce boy. The Jetstar touched down at Otis a few minutes before 1:30. Jack arrived at the hospital to be greeted with the news that he had already failed his wife: the baby had been born in his absence.

Jackie's secretary Mary Gallagher, who had no idea what Dr Travell had told him, was confused when she encountered him in the hospital corridor. After a quick 'How's the baby?' he headed off in search of Jackie, as if everything depended on his reaching her as soon as possible.

A few minutes later, he followed as she was wheeled from the delivery room to her room. There was a small sitting room next door, and he waited there with his sister Jean until she woke. She was said to be fine, but the premature baby had hyaline membrane disease, the same lung ailment that had afflicted John. As Jackie slept, Jack mobilized the powers of the presidency to secure the best medical treatment. A renowned specialist flew in to consult with Dr Walsh and the decision was made to move the infant to Children's Hospital in Boston. Prior to the transfer, the Base chaplain baptized the little boy Patrick Bouvier Kennedy. Jack and Jackie had agreed in advance that if they had a son, he would be named for the President's great-grandfather.

By the time Jack went in to his wife, he had decided that the best thing he could do was try to protect her. Preferring to take the whole burden on himself, he did not disclose the seriousness of Patrick's condition, telling her that the baby had to be transferred but downplaying the gravity of the situation. Jackie had no reason to doubt him, as John, though sickly at birth, had grown into a robust two-year-old who radiated health.

When Jack wheeled the incubator into Jackie's room, he gave no hint that this might be her only chance to see and hold Patrick. He put the baby in her arms, tiny and fragile, with a shock of dark hair like his mother's and wrists so thin that the identification tag seemed ready to slide off. A few minutes later, their son was in an ambulance to Boston. Jack waited with Jackie until Luella Hennessey, who traditionally cared for Kennedy wives after they gave birth, arrived from Hyannis Port where she had been with Ethel. After a quick visit to Squaw Island to check on Caroline and John, he returned to spend another half hour with Jackie before flying to Boston.

At Children's Hospital, Kennedy was told that Patrick had handled the trip well and nothing more could be done until the next day. He went to see his son in the incubator before retiring to the Ritz-Carlton Hotel, and in the morning spent another twenty minutes with Patrick before returning to Jackie, who had been reading congratulatory telegrams and clipping news articles about the baby. Masking his anxiety, Jack spoke only of what had in fact been an encouraging report from doctors. At noon, he was off again to Squaw Island, but hardly had the helicopter landed when word came that suddenly Patrick was much worse. In the hope of keeping his lungs open, doctors planned to try a pressure chamber used in open-heart surgery. Jack chose not to tell Jackie but did call her mother, who arranged to meet him in Boston.

Thirty minutes later, Janet Auchincloss met Jack at Logan Airport. Together, two people who, each in his or her own way, had done much to hurt Jackie in the past proceeded to Children's Hospital. On this occasion, Jack seemed to fear for his wife every bit as much as for his son. 'Nothing must happen to Patrick,' he told Janet, 'because I just can't bear to think of the effect it would have on Jackie.' In the hospital elevator, a doctor informed Jack just how bad the situation was. Afterward, he conferred with medical staff for nearly two hours.

Finally, at 4 p.m., Jack was driven to the Ritz-Carlton. Too restless to remain there, he soon returned to the hospital, where for an hour he watched alone as Patrick struggled to breathe. Periodically, Jack steeled himself to call Jackie and pretend all was well. Desperate to do something when, for all the power of his position, there was nothing he could do, he finally decided to spend the night at the hospital. At 2 a.m. on Friday, August 9, a Secret Service agent awakened Dave Powers with the news that Patrick's condition had deteriorated. Powers told the President, who went to his son at once.

For the next two hours, Jack, dressed in a white surgical cap and gown, held the baby's tiny fingers. He was still touching them when Patrick died shortly after 4 a.m. The infant's heart had given out under the strain of his struggle to breathe. When it was over, Jack looked down at the son he had come to love and said softly, 'He put up quite a fight.' Then he paused and added, 'He was a beautiful baby.' Afterward, Jack went to his room and asked to be left alone. When Powers closed the door he could hear the President sob.

Early that morning, Jack made arrangements for Patrick's burial. He asked Richard Cardinal Cushing, a devoted family friend who had married Jack and Jackie ten years earlier, to conduct the service. He also ordered a casket. Then he braced himself to face Jackie. It was nearly 9 a.m. when Jack, accompanied by Bobby who had come up from Washington the previous day, ran a gauntlet of photographers outside Children's Hospital. Inside the car, he broke down – and one cameraman caught it on film. Before they left, the President sent an aide to ask that the image not be published, telling him, 'I'm asking it as a favor to me.'

At Otis Air Force Base, Dr Walsh had told Jackie the bad news as soon as she woke up. Jack had so successfully concealed Patrick's condition from her that she was utterly unprepared.

She was still weeping when Luella Hennessey and Mary Gallagher came in to tell her the President was on his way. Immediately, Jackie fought for control, enlisting the two women to wash her face, comb her hair, and prop her up in bed with some pillows. Five times Jackie had been pregnant, and three of those children had been lost.

When the door opened shortly before 9:30, Jackie had no idea what to expect. Both in person and on the phone, Jack had hidden his own anxiety. She had not seen his suffering or tenderness with the baby, nor had she been told of them. So how was she to interpret his apparent lack of emotion? Was he indifferent, as he had been seven years before when their daughter was stillborn? Or had he been trying to protect her? At this point, she really had no way of knowing. Thus she refused to let Jack see her tears, and thus the urgency with which she composed herself in anticipation of his arrival. In a decade of marriage, she had often self-protectively concealed her emotions behind a carefully constructed mask. Now, in the event that Jack really was indifferent, Jackie donned that mask again.

When Jack entered, she was taken by surprise. As she later described the scene, he fell to his knees beside her bed and burst into loud, wrenching sobs. He wept for the son they had just lost, but also for the baby girl to whose death he had failed to react for seven years. He wept for the decision to go to Europe over a pregnant wife's objections, and for the refusal to come home. And he wept for his own callousness this time. Jack had felt grief before, notably for Kick and to a lesser extent Joe Jr, but with Patrick's death he overcame the inability to feel guilt that had allowed him – otherwise so kind and caring a man – repeatedly to betray his wife. In those hours with his dying son, he had discovered an emotion that would immeasurably complicate his life with Jackie from then on.

Jackie's mother and other family members assembled at Otis. Lee, who had been on an Aegean cruise with her lover, the Greek shipping tycoon Aristotle Onassis, sent word that she would be there soon. It was almost twelve when Jack left for Squaw Island. Later, he told Jackie that John was too young to

understand Patrick's death, but Caroline, who had been excited
about the idea of a new baby brother, reacted with tear-filled
eyes, although she did not cry. After a quick visit to Jackie,
Jack, seemingly unable to stop moving, went to see his father
and then went to dinner with the children. It was nearly half
past nine when he announced that he was going back to see
his wife for a third time that day.

That night, cordoned off together on a dark military base,
Jack seemed to reach out to Jackie in a way he never had
before. While it was obvious to Luella Hennessey, who knew
them both well, that husband and wife consoled each other as
no one else could, she also felt that it was Jack who needed
comforting the most. As he stayed into the night ostensibly for
Jackie's sake, it was her strength he drew on. Finally, after she
fell asleep, he returned to Squaw Island.

The next day, Jackie was too weak to go to Boston for the
funeral. Jack went with his brothers and sisters, as well as
Jackie's family. The funeral Mass was held in a chapel in the
Cardinal's residence that accommodated no more than sixteen
people. Besides Cardinal Cushing, the only non-family member
was Francis Cardinal Spellman, who came from New York.
Before the Catholic funeral Mass for children known as the
Mass of the Angels, Jack approached the white casket, taking
out a St Christopher's medal he'd carried since Jackie gave it
to him a decade before. St Christopher is the patron saint of
travelers. As Patrick had embarked on a journey on which his
parents could offer no protection, they had agreed to place the
medal in the casket.

As Cardinal Cushing said the Mass, Jack wept openly. The
service closed with a prayer written especially for Patrick by
the Cardinal. Afterward, the Kennedys, Janet, Lee, and the
others filed out, leaving Jack alone with Cardinal Cushing. The
Cardinal watched him go up to the casket, where he was
overcome with grief. 'He put his arm around the casket of little
Patrick,' Cardinal Cushing recalled, 'and I can tell you in all
honesty he tried to take it with him. And he wept.'

'My dear Jack, let's go, let's go,' said the prelate, who began
to cry himself. 'Nothing more can be done.'

After the casket was lowered into the earth at nearby Holyhood Cemetery, Jack touched the ground and muttered that it was terribly lonely there.

Afterward, he flew to Jackie, who had been under sedation. They comforted each other until it was time for her to rest again. He, for his part, seemed unable to rest. The moment she fell asleep, he was off to see Caroline and John, and for the remainder of the weekend he shuttled incessantly between Brambletyde and Otis. On Sunday he brought the children, first Caroline and then John, to see their mother. Late Sunday night, John and his father left the hospital to be greeted by a mob of photographers outside. From the moment of Patrick's birth, the world press had staked out the hospital entrance. Unlike his sister, who had adopted Jackie's distaste for the press, John adored being photographed and tonight was no exception. 'Daddy, I think they took my picture!' he exclaimed. The President, wearing dark glasses, smiled, his first light moment in days.

The press contingent, dubbed 'vultures' by Nancy Tuckerman, who had replaced Letitia Baldrige as Jackie's social secretary, was still waiting on the morning of Wednesday, August 14, when Jackie was due to be released after a week in the hospital. White House staff, prepared to sneak her out the back door if she preferred, asked if she felt up to walking past the press.

'Yes, I can do it,' Jackie replied firmly. She believed that going out the front door, however painful and unpleasant, was 'the right way to do it.'

By the time the President arrived, Jackie was dressed. A sleeveless pink shift she had often worn when pregnant hung loosely on her fragile body, ordinarily strong and athletic. Her face, pale and strained, was without makeup, hair tucked hastily behind her ears. When she was ready to leave, instead of putting on dark glasses as was her custom, she chose to confront the cameras without them, as though to let people have a look and be done with it.

Unexpected as the first sight of her was when she emerged into the blazing sun shortly before eleven, it was something else that caught people's attention. Some reporters noted it, so did certain friends when they looked at press pictures afterward. Jack was holding Jackie by the hand. One old friend was instantly struck that in all the years she had known them, she had never seen him do that before; indeed, he was known to walk a few feet ahead of his wife. Jack, slowly accompanying Jackie to the car, never once let go of her hand.

When they returned to Squaw Island, Jackie spent the afternoon resting on the sun porch next to her room, coming downstairs briefly to watch Caroline and John play with the puppies. There had been one canine addition while she was in the hospital, an Irish wolfhound puppy which the President had brought from Ireland. It was a chaotic but happy scene as the children laughed and tumbled over the grass with the dogs. Jackie was too exhausted to remain for long, and soon she retreated upstairs.

Presently she sent word asking that the flag outside her window be lowered. Ordinarily she loved to hear it whip in the wind, but today the sound was unbearable. In the days that followed, despite the brave face she had put on in public, it would be a sign of all she was going through privately that no flag flew over Brambletyde. To certain observers, it was Jack who 'seemed even more broken' by Patrick's death. But then, he had to deal with guilt as well as grief. Jackie had mourned for their stillborn daughter in 1956, seven years before, while Jack had only just begun.

On Thursday, August 15, the day after Jack brought Jackie home, he went to Washington to meet with Henry Cabot Lodge, who was about to leave for Vietnam to replace Frederick Nolting as U.S. ambassador. Lee would stay with Jackie overnight, and Jack returned in time to drive Jackie and the children to nearby Barnstable Airport the next day to see Lee off on her flight back to Greece. After Lee's plane left, the President's convertible, trailed by Secret Service, pulled into a drive-in ice cream stand where, like any ordinary father, Jack ordered four cones. Later, when the children had gone to bed, he read aloud from Harold Macmillan's condolence letter, perhaps the most moving of the entire 'dear friend' correspondence. Both

Kennedys were aware that the Prime Minister had himself known great personal pain, and it was that suffering which underlay the message's wisdom. His words about their son's death, Jackie later told him, bound them both more powerfully than ever to the man who had become a kind of second father to Jack. From the first, Macmillan had been drawn to the best in Kennedy, the core of kindness and sensitivity that often seemed dramatically at odds with other, less savory aspects of his character. Macmillan had seen Kennedy in deep despair after his disastrous meetings with Khrushchev in Vienna, but he knew that what he and Jackie had just endured was far worse.

'The burdens of public affairs are more or less tolerable, because they are in a sense impersonal,' Macmillan wrote from experience. 'But private grief is poignant and cruel.'

FOURTEEN

A Study in Betrayal

After the Bay of Pigs fiasco, Jack had summoned the Spaldings to Glen Ora to share his anguish. With an even heavier heart, he asked them to Brambletyde on Jackie's first weekend back from the hospital. With them, no pretenses were needed. Nine months previously, Betty had decided she didn't want to be around Jack anymore, but in the present circumstances, she and Chuck came to Squaw Island together to comfort old friends.

From the minute they arrived, it was evident that Jack was a changed man. 'He was so overwhelmed by it,' said Betty Spalding of his reaction to the baby's death. 'I didn't think that something like that would ever hit him.' That Saturday, for the first time in memory when the President was at Cape Cod, the *Honey Fitz* lay at anchor all day. While Jack talked to Chuck, Jackie spoke with unusual candor to Betty.

Jackie was reeling, not just from the loss of a son but also from the effect it had had on Jack. Desperately trying to sort out her own feelings, she spoke of his arrival in her hospital room after the baby died, how he had knelt by her bed and wept. When Jackie said that she had 'never seen anything like that in him,' Betty, acquainted with Jack's response to the stillbirth in 1956, was in a unique position to understand. This time, Jackie had been 'stunned when he burst into tears. She couldn't believe it ... She was very touched by it and thought, "Maybe now I'm getting through to him."' After the earlier episode when he had acted 'like such a jerk,' Jackie had chosen tacitly to accept his cheating, a monumental decision. But now, she confided, she had begun to wonder whether he might yet change and they might have a different kind of marriage at last.

In the aftermath of tragedy, Jackie had begun to hope again. And it struck her visitor that she had reason to hope. In the past, Betty had witnessed both Jack's innate kindness and his appalling insensitivity. He was at heart, she judged, 'a kind, observant, thoughtful man,' who had been grotesquely 'distorted' by his father's example and teaching. 'He was deeply emotional,' she said of Jack, 'but everything was kind of screwed up because of the Old Man's ethics and behavior.' From Joe, Jack had learned that one's own needs came first and one ought never to feel even a trace of guilt. From Patrick, by contrast, he had just had a very different lesson. In recent months, he had translated moral convictions about peace and civil rights into public acts. But whether his private morals would alter as well remained to be seen.

When the Spaldings left on Sunday, Jack remained at home with Jackie and the children. By evening, she felt strong enough to go out for a boat ride with Teddy and Joan. After half an hour, they were back. Jack had to return to the White House in the morning for his first full work week since Patrick's birth, and although Jackie would be in good hands with Luella Hennessey, he was reluctant to leave.

On Monday, August 19, Kennedy returned to face two crises. Bobby had already stepped in to handle the first. While the President and First Lady had been preoccupied with their son, the F.B.I. had been investigating charges that Ellen Rometsch was a Soviet bloc spy. Bobby, eager to short-circuit Hoover's inquiry, had moved to have her 'rush deported' before F.B.I. agents quizzed her about her sexual services to the President. She was scheduled for deportation from the United States two days later. That, the Attorney General hoped, would put an end to any threat she posed to the administration.

The second crisis was something the President was going to have to handle himself. The rapidly disintegrating situation in Vietnam was about to explode. In the last weeks of August, Kennedy's blinding grief and his duty as a leader were poised to collide.

From the first, Kennedy had had a bad feeling about Vietnam. Aside from his belief that South Vietnam must fight its own war, Kennedy's focus on U.S.–Soviet relations meant that he was far more concerned with Cuba and Berlin, where Moscow had a clearly defined interest. In South Vietnam, the interested parties – or so Washington assessed – were Hanoi and Peking. Prior to 1963, Kennedy 'had not paid a great deal of attention' to Vietnam 'except sporadically,' recalled National Security Council member Michael Forrestal. Each time he approved increased military aid to the Diem regime – the most important occasion being in December 1961, when he exceeded the number of U.S. military personnel permitted by the 1954 Geneva Accord – he had done so reluctantly, despite the entreaties of advisers such as Walter Rostow to increase the U.S. presence. Following a meeting on January 3, 1962, between Kennedy and the Joint Chiefs of Staff, Deputy Secretary of Defense Roswell Gilpatric wrote, 'In the discussion concerning South Vietnam the President re-emphasized the importance of the U.S. not becoming further involved militarily in that area. The President also emphasized the importance of playing down the number of U.S. military personnel involved in Vietnam and that the U.S. military role there was for advice, training and support of Vietnamese Armed Forces and not combat.' At a session on April 6, 1962, with Averell Harriman, then Assistant Secretary of State for Far Eastern Affairs, Kennedy made it clear that he wished 'to seize upon any favorable moment to reduce our involvement, recognizing that the moment might yet be some time away.'

Kennedy's advisers persisted in the belief that the U.S. must assume responsibility for defeating the Viet Cong guerrillas, and that, given the right commitment of forces and equipment, the battle was eminently winnable. Members of the President's staff, the State Department, and the Defense Department all pushed hard for 'increasing the effort.' By 1963, when the number of U.S. military personnel in Vietnam exceeded 16,000, political advisers and military officials promised that the U.S. strategy was, in Forrestal's words, 'showing signs of being successful.'

As in 1961, Chester Bowles, now the President's Special Representative and Adviser on African, Asian, and Latin American Affairs, marched to a different drummer. Bowles warned that U.S. support for 'an unpopular Vietnamese régime with inadequate roots among the people' could be a disaster in the making. Like Rostow, he evoked the Bay of Pigs invasion, but to a very different end: 'I hesitate to play the role of Cassandra again in regard to Vietnam and Southeast Asia,' Bowles told the President on March 7, 1963. 'However, I remain deeply concerned about the outlook there ... I see nothing in the present course of events to dispel my conviction, expressed to you and the Secretary on several occasions, that this situation may ultimately prove as troublesome as Cuba in its effects on the Administration's position at home and abroad.'

That spring, Diem's repression of Buddhists had 'forced' Kennedy, in Forrestal's words, 'to pay more attention' to Vietnam. On May 8, the birthday of Gautama Buddha, police hurled grenades at a crowd of Buddhists. Nine people were killed. On June 11, the day after Kennedy's American University address, photojournalist Malcolm Browne's unforgettable image of a Buddhist monk's self-immolation in protest at government repression – a government the U.S. was working to uphold – crystallized Kennedy's doubts. He shuddered when Madame Nhu, Diem's scurrilous sister-in-law and confidante, seemed to speak for the régime in her ridicule of the Buddhists for having 'barbecued' a monk. Madame Nhu, who served as the epicene, unmarried Diem's unofficial 'wife,' went so far as to claim that Browne had bribed the Buddhists to drug and burn an old man. She clapped her hands and gleefully offered matches and gasoline to other monks, indeed to any American journalists, who wished to set themselves on fire.

For Kennedy, such episodes drove home the point that the U.S. role in Vietnam was misguided on every possible level. At a time when he was basking in the glory of the test ban treaty, Vietnam threatened to burden the administration with an involvement as damaging as the Bay of Pigs. Now that he was asking the American people to rethink Cold War attitudes, intervention in Vietnam looked like a contradiction, a reversion to past policies.

On Tuesday, August 20, at the Congressional leaders' breakfast, Senate Majority Leader Mike Mansfield handed the President a long, thoughtful memo written in view of two further self-immolations by Buddhist monks, as well as a disturbing *New York Times* article, 'Vietnamese Reds Gain in Key Area,' which indicated that, contrary to the optimistic picture painted by Kennedy's advisers, things were going very badly. David Halberstam reported substantial deterioration in the Delta – an area containing most of Vietnam's population and resources – despite twenty months of U.S. buildup of the Vietnamese forces. Mansfield argued that 'the changing of Ambassadors' was a perfect moment to reconsider U.S. policy in Vietnam. 'The die is not yet finally cast but we are very close to the point when it will have to be,' he wrote. 'Therefore, we may well ask ourselves, once more, not the tactical question, but the fundamental question: Is South Vietnam as important to us as the premise on which we are now apparently operating indicates?' For Mansfield, the answer was no. 'Vietnam,' he told the President, 'is not central to our defense interest or any other American interest but is, rather, peripheral to those interests.' And, he went on, 'the way out of the bind is certainly not by the route of ever-deeper involvement.'

Kennedy read the memo before he went to bed. Wednesday morning, August 21, he was given an intelligence report that seemed to confirm the wisdom of reversing course in Vietnam. Contrary to assurances that Buddhists would be left in peace, police and army personnel had raided Buddhist pagodas. Some Buddhists had been killed or wounded, a great many arrested, religious statues and holy relics desecrated. At 10 a.m., Kennedy attended a stormy meeting on Vietnam. By this point his advisers fell into two camps, both dedicated to the proposition that it was America's duty to win the war, but at odds over Diem's viability. Harriman led a contingent that had previously decided that Diem and his influential brother, Ngo Dinh Nhu, had to be replaced if U.S. efforts were to succeed. For the Harriman group, the assault on the pagodas was the last straw.

The other camp believed that, whatever the limitations of Diem and the Nhus, this was hardly a time to consider a change in régime.

After the meeting, Kennedy, detached and preoccupied after only two days back in Washington, arranged to fly to Cape Cod – and Jackie – just for the night. He had never before done that sort of thing in the middle of the week, and most certainly not in the midst of a crisis such as the one brewing in Vietnam.

At a moment when Kennedy's guard was down, the Harriman group seized the opportunity to make a dramatic change in policy on Vietnam. 'Cuba 1' had taught Kennedy that despite anything the experts said or promised, no important decision must be made without discussing every aspect 'in full detail.' His handling of 'Cuba 2' proved how well he had learned that lesson. It is no defense to say so, but he would never have permitted the Harriman group to move in his absence had he been on top of his game. But he was still in deep mourning for his lost son, and in the days that followed Harriman used that vulnerability to full advantage.

That weekend, the big, gray-shingled house on Nantucket Sound was, said houseguest Bill Walton, 'full of sadness.' Kennedy, after spending Wednesday night with Jackie, had gone back to Washington Thursday morning, but returned Friday night. Despite the fact that Walton had often acted as beard for Jack with Mary Meyer and other women, he was very much Jackie's friend as well, someone with whom both Kennedys were comfortable. The somber mood was not helped by tempestuous weather, which kept everyone locked indoors. Jackie confided to Walton that Jack, who had so wanted another son, felt 'the loss of the baby in the house' as much as she. Indeed, that Saturday, while Jackie rested, Jack took Walton to his study and pored over condolence letters from world leaders. He read certain messages over and over, and wondered aloud how to respond. Exactly two weeks after he had buried Patrick, the President, still plunged in grief, seemed unable to focus on anything else. Endlessly he returned to the subject, as if nothing else mattered. In the past, Walton had not been alone in the awareness that Jack seemed terribly uncomfortable when Jackie expressed physical affection. Now, by contrast, Walton watched in wonder as 'she hung onto him and he held her in his arms.'

While Jack was at the Cape, also absent from Washington were such principal decision-makers as National Security Adviser McGeorge Bundy, Secretary of State Dean Rusk, Defense Secretary Robert McNamara, and C.I.A. Director John McCone. On Saturday morning, August 24, only the anti-Diem faction, consisting of Harriman, his protégé Forrestal, and Assistant Secretary for Far Eastern Affairs Roger Hilsman, was present to receive word from Saigon. In the aftermath of Wednesday's assault on the pagodas by Ngo Dinh Nhu, several Vietnamese generals wanted to know where the U.S. would stand if they decided to remove Nhu and his outspoken wife from the government.

Harriman and the others immediately perceived a chance to unseat Diem. Forrestal wasted no time in notifying the President that Nhu had been unmasked as 'the mastermind behind the whole operation against the Buddhists.' He referred to sentiment in Washington that Nhu could no longer be left in power and noted that 'Averell and Roger now agree that we must move before the situation freezes.' Quite what he meant by the latter he did not specify until Roger Hilsman completed a draft of a telegram to Ambassador Lodge that suggested giving Diem the opportunity to eject Nhu and his coterie. 'But if he remains obdurate,' the telegram went on, 'then we are prepared to accept the obvious implication that we can no longer support Diem. You may also tell appropriate military commanders we will give them direct support in any interim period of breakdown central government mechanism.'

In short, the Harriman–Forrestal–Hilsman document, if approved by the President, gave the green light to a military coup. Late that afternoon, Forrestal sent a copy to Brambletyde and urged Kennedy to respond immediately because, he insisted, the situation in Saigon 'may not remain fluid for long.' 'Harriman, Hilsman and I favor taking this action now,' said Forrestal, who was eager to move before the Pentagon or other supporters of Diem found out what they were up to, and proposed to send the telegram to Saigon that night.

Approached by Harriman and Hilsman on a golf course, Under-Secretary of State George Ball indicated that he would need Kennedy's clearance to send it. Ball called the President at Brambletyde, where he had been obsessively rereading condolence letters and holding on to Jackie like a drowning man. In a state of distraction that seems to have prevented him from grasping the full implications of the request, Kennedy said that if senior advisers such as Rusk and Gilpatric signed on, they could go ahead. Those words would reverberate in both his administration and his marriage, as well as profoundly influence the course of history. Following his talk with the President, Ball contacted Rusk, Forrestal talked to Gilpatric, and Harriman got in touch with Richard Helms at the C.I.A. In each case, the individual contacted was left with the distinct but false impression that Kennedy had already given his approval. Rusk, Gilpatric, and Helms reluctantly concurred, as they thought, with the President. The telegram authorizing the overthrow of Diem went out shortly after 9:30 that same night.

On Sunday, August 25, the sky over Brambletyde was still dark, but the rain had stopped. Jack went out on the beach with Walton. He undid the kidney-shaped back brace he wore over his trunks and soaked in the water, preferring to bathe rather than swim. Meanwhile, in Washington, a telegram arrived from Lodge. Not only did he heartily agree with yesterday's green light of the proposed coup, he asked permission to go a step further. As the chances that Diem would turn against his brother were 'virtually nil,' Lodge proposed that they take their demands directly to the renegade generals, without so much as a word to Diem. 'Would tell them we prepared to have Diem without Nhus,' telegrammed Lodge, 'but it is in effect up to them whether to keep him.' The Harriman faction was careful to approve Lodge's request before Forrestal forwarded the text of the ambassador's message to Brambletyde late in the day. Thus, a private tragedy, the death of young Patrick, had had monstrous public consequences, for it is unlikely that in any other circumstance the President would have so entirely missed what was going on.

In effect, Kennedy had authorized a coup in South Vietnam with scant knowledge of the generals he had agreed to back. Over the next two weeks, some in the administration, including his brother, argued vociferously that the telegram should never have been sent. General Maxwell Taylor, the President's senior military adviser, who hadn't seen a text until after it went out, called the actions of the Harriman group an 'egregious end run.' Unfortunately, by the time Kennedy realized he had made a huge mistake, it was already too late. When the White House suggested it was having 'second thoughts,' Lodge retorted alarmingly, 'We are launched on a course from which there is no turning back.' Kennedy, in a struggle for control, replied, 'there is one point on my own constitutional responsibilities as President and Commander in Chief which I wish to state to you in this entirely private message, which is not being circulated here beyond the Secretary of State. Until the very moment of the go signal for the operation by the Generals, I must reserve a contingent right to change course and reverse previous instructions.' Lodge shot back that he understood the President had the right to reverse course, but added: 'To be successful, this operation must be essentially a Vietnamese affair with a momentum of its own. Should this happen, you may not be able to control it, i.e. the "go signal" may be given by the Generals.' In other words, the coup, if and when the generals chose to proceed, was already out of U.S. hands. At length, Kennedy breathed a sigh of relief when word reached the State Department that 'this particular coup' – whatever that might mean – was off.

The same weekend that Kennedy had allowed the infamous telegram to be sent, Lee Radziwill had invited Jackie to complete her recuperation on Aristotle Onassis's yacht, the *Christina*. The President was opposed for two reasons, both to do with image. For one, Onassis had had legal skirmishes with the U.S. Maritime Commission and the Justice Department. For another, there had already been speculation in the press about Onassis's affair with Lee, and a scandal involving Lee would certainly cast a shadow over her sister. But soon Jack turned his thoughts to what would be best for Jackie, and decided that if she wanted to go perhaps it would be all right. The White House had announced that she would not undertake any further official duties until the first of the year, so a trip abroad might be ideal. He and Jackie agreed that she would travel to Greece in early October, though there was to be no public statement for the time being.

The minute word spread within the administration, a number of voices were raised in protest. Besides the matter of Onassis's legal problems, his extensive business dealings with the U.S. government through Victory Carriers, a New York-based shipping firm in which he held a major stake, raised conflict-of-interest issues. Jackie's trip promised to turn into an ethical and political nightmare.

'You have an election year coming up,' Kenny O'Donnell reminded the President, 'and it may not look right to have this sort of trip.'

'We will cross that bridge when we come to it, and that's final,' Kennedy replied. 'I want her to go on the trip. It will be good for her, and she has been looking forward to it.'

Kennedy was similarly unreceptive to a recommendation by Henry Labouisse, the U.S. ambassador in Greece, that Jackie avoid appearing on Onassis's yacht. While not wrong in itself, Labouisse declared, it was bound to leave 'a poor impression.' The President was prepared to make only a single concession to public opinion. He asked that both Stas Radziwill and newly appointed Under-Secretary of Commerce Franklin D. Roosevelt Jr be present on the cruise, the former to quell rumors of an affair between Lee and Onassis, the latter to represent the U.S. government.

For Jackie, besides a chance to regain her health, the trip would provide an opportunity to consider what was next for her. In the aftermath of the Cuban Missile Crisis, she had put off any such decisions when she learned she was pregnant. Had Patrick survived, those decisions would have been postponed for five or six months more. Still, the scrapbook she had worked on that summer as an anniversary present for Jack suggests that she had already given a good deal of thought to her work and what it meant to her. Since childhood, Jackie had been known for the beauty and thoughtfulness of the scrapbooks she produced for special occasions. Interestingly, in this case she did not choose to commemorate the ten-year anniversary with images of children or family life. Instead, at a moment of withdrawal from serious political involvement, it was her work on the White House that she chose to memorialize. Far more than mere pictures of a house, these images were a meditation on the possibilities that, for all its shortcomings, life with Jack Kennedy had afforded her, a portrait of the person their partnership had allowed her to become.

On Thursday, September 12, 1963, she and Jack celebrated their anniversary with family and friends at Hammersmith Farm. He came up from Washington, though it was the middle of the week. The year before, it hadn't seemed to matter that they spent the evening apart, but in the aftermath of tragedy, it was very important that they be together on the anniversary day itself. Jack's emotions were still very tender, but in other people's presence he used his famous wit to keep them concealed. After dinner, he made a great joke of his own penny-pinching. He read aloud from a list of possible gifts prepared by one of Jackie's favorite antique dealers, with mock admonitions to 'steer her away from that one' if the item was particularly expensive.

Very different were Jack's tone and demeanor when, in private, he gave Jackie a gift chosen with great care and feeling. On that terrible morning at Otis as he knelt beside her bed and told her about the little boy he had come to love, she had begged that Patrick not be forgotten, and asked him then to give her something that would be their private reminder, not of Patrick's loss, but of his life. That night, Jack produced a slender gold ring with small green chips of emerald to represent the fighting Irishman he'd seen as Patrick waged his courageous fight to live. Jack slipped the ring onto his wife's little finger, next to her wedding band. Jackie, in turn, gave her husband a St Christopher's medal to replace the one he had put in Patrick's coffin.

Jackie spent another ten days in Newport, then flew to Washington with Jack and the children on Monday, September

23. Although he was scheduled to leave the very next day for a week's trip west to highlight the administration's policies on conservation, she needed the time to settle Caroline and John back into the White House and complete her own preparations before she went to Greece on October 1. Jack went directly to a meeting with Defense Secretary McNamara and others while Jackie took the children to the family quarters, where the tiny room that was to have been Patrick's nursery confronted her. In the hope of sparing her feelings, Mr West had obliterated every trace of the redecoration. Above all, he reasoned, she must not come back to an empty crib. Not a word about the matter was spoken, but when Jackie looked in, the high-chair room had been restored as exactly it had been when she left in June.

The following day, Jack faced two significant tests. He had taken a political risk in pushing for a test ban treaty that the Senate might well refuse to ratify. Now that the vote was taken, fourteen more votes were cast in favor than the two-thirds majority required for ratification. It was a tremendous political victory for the administration.

The second front was personal. When Kennedy boarded *Air Force One*, Mary Meyer was among the passengers. For once her presence was entirely innocent. She and her sister were part of a group scheduled to accompany the President on the first leg of his conservation trip, to the Pinchot Institute of Conservation Studies in Milford, Pennsylvania, which Mary's cousin, Gifford Pinchot Jr, had donated to the nation. The President gave a speech, then drove with the sisters to the home of their aged mother nearby. Six minutes after he stepped out of the car to pose for a photograph, he was en route to Minnesota. The first encounter between Jack and his mistress since Patrick's death offered a reminder of all that had happened between them in the past, and all that must not happen again.

He did not plan to give up other women entirely. It remained a fundamental factor in the Kennedy marriage that Jack could not seem to find sexual satisfaction with his wife. Whatever Jackie may have hoped in recent weeks, no amount of guilt on his part would ever change that. Early Saturday afternoon, when the President wrapped up a ten-state tour, he and Dave Powers made the customary weekend stop at the Bing Crosby estate, where Peter Lawford and company joined them.

On Monday, Kennedy, accompanied by Lawford, returned to a White House that had been inundated with angry letters in response to the announcement of Jackie's trip. Though some were from the usual cranks, others expressed the apparently sincere distress of people who had mourned young Patrick Kennedy and felt betrayed, even mocked, by the First Lady's vacation on the yacht of a notorious playboy. There was considerable agitation about her expensive tastes and fondness for luxury. A chorus of fault-finders asked why, if she was well enough to go to Greece, she hadn't returned to her duties as First Lady. Why couldn't she be a good wife and stay at home to care for her busy husband? If she needed a vacation so badly, why didn't she take one in the U.S.? There was more. Had Jackie heard about Onassis's scandalous affair with Maria Callas? Did she realize that accepting the hospitality of such a person diminished her as First Lady and her husband as President? As at the time of her trip to Ravello, it was Jackie at whom criticism was directed.

After months at the beach, where she'd spent most of her time with her hair pulled back in an elastic band, Jackie spent Tuesday morning with Kenneth, her New York hairdresser. Haile Selassie, Emperor of Ethiopia, was arriving that day, and lest he be offended by the timing of her departure on the very day he arrived, it had been explained that Mrs Kennedy, still in mourning, was going to Greece to recuperate with her sister. Unfortunately, the press had been playing her trip rather differently, so her presence at the welcoming ceremony for Selassie was obligatory. When Jack came upstairs to collect her at half past eleven, he exploded, angrily instructing her maid to see if Kenneth was still in the building. Jackie's haircut made her look far too jet-set. The hairdresser, discovered in Mary Gallagher's office on the third floor, was brought back. 'What are you trying to do,' Kennedy asked, 'ruin my career?' Jackie's hair was promptly combed out and rearranged into a much more conservative pageboy style. When she put on a new hat,

Jack erupted again. The maid was sent for a replacement.

Minutes before the train pulled in, Jack and Jackie emerged from the presidential limousine. Jackie, clutching a bunch of red roses, had managed to compose herself after the altercation, and when Selassie stepped off the train it became apparent that months away from diplomatic duties had not caused Jackie to lose her touch. She quickly charmed the Emperor, whom she invited to tea that afternoon when he came to confer with the President. Before the motorcade left for Blair House, Selassie told her he was 'very deeply touched' that she had come despite the fact that she was still grieving. Shortly after the state dinner began, Jackie slipped out by a back elevator and left for the airport.

In her absence, Jack spent a great deal of time with both Caroline and John. He played with them in the morning, let John visit his office by day, and took both children swimming in the White House pool by night. On Thursday, John accompanied his father to Andrews Air Force Base, where *Air Force One* awaited in anticipation of a brief trip to Arkansas. Miss Shaw had come along to take John back to the White House after the President left, but first Kennedy insisted that the boy have a few minutes in the cabin before takeoff. The nanny watched John take his usual seat, strap himself in and − when he heard his father say he couldn't come to Arkansas − begin to wail. Eventually he had to be carried off the plane, still howling. The next day, newspaper photographs set off an angry outcry, many readers mistakenly assuming that John's tears were for his absent mother.

After that, it was open season on Jackie. No sooner had she boarded the *Christina* on Friday, October 4, than newspaper reports of all-night revelry prompted complaints that such behavior was inappropriate for a woman in mourning. In addition to Onassis, there were a dozen people on the yacht, including Lee and Stas Radziwill, Franklin Roosevelt Jr and his wife, Onassis's sister Artemis, and Irene Galitzine. Wherever the *Christina* stopped, photographers were waiting for Jackie − alerted, it was rumored, by Onassis, who thought personal publicity good for business.

To make matters worse, the disapproval of Jackie's holiday was not limited to the press and the public. The President's critics in Congress were soon making political capital of the situation. Representative Oliver Bolton of Ohio railed that it was 'improper' for the First Lady to accept Onassis's 'lavish hospitality.' He pointed out that four of Onassis's tankers had been built with U.S. aid, that the U.S.-insured mortgage on one vessel was already overdue, and that a $1.5 million payment on another was expected presently. 'Would it not be the subject of bitter criticism,' asked the Republican Congressman, 'if an American ship owner with ships in mortgage default to the Maritime Administration were to turn over to the disposal of a presidential party a luxury ship at a personal cost of many tens of thousands of dollars?' And he added: 'Why doesn't the lady see more of her own country instead of gallivanting all over Europe?'

Kennedy monitored the uproar, but during the two and a half weeks Jackie was gone, other matters preoccupied him. The day after she left, he took what he hoped would be a significant step toward clarifying the situation in Vietnam. Upon reflection, he was deeply dismayed that he had authorized a military coup. As he well knew, his state of distraction at the time was no excuse. Now, having sent McNamara and General Maxwell Taylor to Vietnam to make recommendations based on first-hand observation, on October 2 the President decided emphatically to cut off support for a coup for the foreseeable future. In doing so, he thought he had rectified his own mistake. The next day, the C.I.A. received word that the Vietnamese generals had resumed their coup plans. To all intents and purposes, it was out of Kennedy's hands. All he could do was wait to see whether the generals' actions would presage a disaster for the U.S., as the Bay of Pigs operation had done.

Nor was Vietnam the only matter to have gone awry. The Ellen Rometsch affair threatened to surface again in connection with a Senate probe of Bobby Baker. A lawsuit by a disgruntled vending machine contractor had set off an avalanche of newspaper stories, and Mike Mansfield had called Baker into Senator

Everett Dirksen's office to answer questions about influence-peddling. Rather than appear, Baker resigned as Secretary to the Senate Majority. That did not stop Republicans on the Rules Committee from demanding a full investigation. Delaware Senator John Williams, for one, called for Baker to answer hard questions about the exchange of money and sex for votes and contracts, dealings that often took place at the Quorum Club. The President had reason to fear that such an inquiry would lead inevitably to the Baker girls, one of whom was Ellen Rometsch. The clearest sign that the Kennedys anticipated trouble was the fact that the Attorney General, having previously resisted an F.B.I. request to put a wiretap on Martin Luther King Jr, finally gave the go-ahead. The President might soon need Hoover in his corner.

It was no accident when, on the very day Baker's resignation caused such a stir on Capitol Hill, the President sent for Stanley Tretick. For eighteen months, the *Look* photographer had been trying to persuade the White House to let him do a story on the President and John Jr. When Kennedy suddenly agreed, Tretick naturally assumed it was because the First Lady was absent, and in part that was true. Almost certainly, Jackie would never have approved the shoot, which resulted in the famous images of John as he crawled in and out of a secret door in the desk where his father was at work. With the Ellen Rometsch story threatening to explode, the President would benefit from a national magazine photo spread that depicted him as a devoted father and family man. Kennedy suffered an additional jolt when Harold Macmillan unexpectedly announced his resignation. On October 7, after months of wondering whether it might be time to step down, the Prime Minister had decided instead to stand for re-election. That same night, he fell ill. In the absence of his personal physician, a team of doctors discovered an inflammation of the prostate gland. Though it would not be known until after he had been operated on whether the tumor was malignant, Macmillan immediately assumed the worst. Caught up in his own dark imaginings, Macmillan, on whom the strain of the Profumo affair had taken a deep personal toll, decided he was finished and might die. The operation, on

October 10, discovered that in fact his tumor was benign, but by then the race to replace him was already in progress and the resignation announcement could not be rescinded. At a time when events in Vietnam threatened to derail recent progress with the Soviets, and when a Profumo-like sex and security scandal imperiled his presidency, the loss of Macmillan's steadying influence was a serious blow to Kennedy.

Meanwhile, Jackie had sailed as far as Istanbul, with stops at Lesbos, Crete, Ithaca, Skorpios, and Smyrna. Afterward, she and her sister went to Morocco to visit King Hassan II. Finally, on October 17, though it was well past the children's bedtime, Jack was waiting with both Caroline and John when Jackie's plane landed at National Airport. He let go of their hands and both children ran as fast as they could toward the plane. Caroline dashed up the steps to hug and kiss her mother, while John was in such a hurry that his little legs gave out and he had to half-crawl the rest of the way. When the President reached the cabin door, Jackie stepped back just enough so that press gathered below saw only her white-gloved hand reach round his neck and pull him to her.

Jackie came home upset about the uproar her trip had provoked, but to her astonishment Jack ignored it. Other problems absorbed him. He could talk to her about Macmillan, but some subjects – notably Ellen Rometsch - were obviously taboo. Macmillan, already more than a little rueful, was to submit his official resignation to the Queen the following day. Jackie understood fully what Macmillan had meant to her husband, and the tremendous sense of loss, not just practical but also emotional, that he had to cope with now.

She also knew that he was still suffering over Patrick, whose grave he planned to visit that weekend. Before he left, he asked Jackie a favor. She didn't have to answer right away. While she was in Greece, Texas Governor John Connally had come to Washington to discuss the visit Jack had agreed to make the previous June. To Jack's considerable irritation, not only had the trip been expanded, but the Governor insisted that he bring the First Lady. Jackie had not accompanied her husband on a single domestic political trip since he became President, but he left no doubt in her mind that he hoped this time she would agree to go.

Jack faced a difficult re-election campaign in 1964, particularly in the South. The morally driven choices he had made in his push for a test ban treaty and civil rights legislation had angered conservatives, which meant that Texas was sure to be hostile territory. When Connally pressed him to bring Jackie, he saw that the trip could serve as a dry run for her involvement in the campaign. For the first time, both Kennedys considered the tantalizing possibility that she might be his partner in domestic politics as she had previously been on the international front. At Camp David that weekend, Jackie realized that this might be the opening she had been looking for. By the time she returned to the White House after the weekend, she had decided to agree to go to Texas.

On Thursday, October 24, U.N. Ambassador Adlai Stevenson had an ugly experience in Dallas, where he had gone to deliver a speech. Right-wing protestors incensed by the test ban treaty, among other matters, had distributed handbills with the President's picture and the legend: 'WANTED FOR TREASON, This man wanted for treasonous activities against the United States.' The protestors heckled, shoved, and spat at Stevenson, and pelted him with eggs. One hit him in the head with a placard. 'Are these human beings or are these animals?' Stevenson demanded when police finally rescued him from the mob.

The incident was the talk of a dinner party that night given by Jackie in honor of Irene Galitzine. Franklin Roosevelt Jr, one of the guests, held forth on Stevenson's ordeal, and when Jackie mentioned her plan to accompany Jack to Dallas, he warned her to think twice. Dallas, known as 'the most anti-Democrat city in Texas,' was in a frightening mood, and this was not the first such scene to have occurred there. During the 1960 presidential campaign, a group of right-wing women known as the Mink Coat Mob had hit and spat at Lady Bird Johnson. In conversation, it became evident that Jackie, disturbed by the assault on Stevenson, was already wavering. Jack, she said, very much wanted her to go, but in the end she would follow her doctor's orders. She had just had a baby and might not be ready for such a physically demanding trip. At the same time, when Jackie talked to another guest, Hervé Alphand, about Charles de Gaulle's impending visit to the U.S. after the first of the year, it became equally evident that she longed to be an active First Lady again. The Texas trip would be an important first step in that direction, but she worried seriously whether it might be more gruelling than she could stand.

Jack barely waited until dinner was finished before he disappeared and left Jackie with their guests. While she did her best to keep the peace between Roosevelt and Alphand – the former, who had had too much to drink, launched into a tirade against de Gaulle – Jack turned his attention to Vietnam. Earlier that day, he had had word from Saigon that a coup was imminent. It felt unpleasantly like those early months of the presidency, when it seemed as if underlings were running the show. In the morning, he would have McGeorge Bundy notify Ambassador Lodge that the President demanded forty-eight hours' notice of any coup attempt.

At the time of the Bay of Pigs invasion, Chester Bowles had recognized that Kennedy, for all the fine words of his Inaugural Address, had no real concern that backing the overthrow of Castro would mean defying obligations that were supposed to be 'binding in law and conscience,' as well as losing the moral edge over the Soviets. This time, Kennedy did understand that U.S. support for the coup was wrong and might immeasurably damage the new course in East–West relations which he and Macmillan had worked so hard to establish. Questions of right conduct now mattered to Kennedy, but it remained to be seen whether, having given the go-ahead to the generals two months previously, he would be able to regain control.

After lunch on Friday, October 25, Jackie took the children to the new house in Virginia, which had been rented to tenants for the summer. Though she could have gone there the previous week, she had gone to Camp David instead, preferring to spend her first weekend at Atoka – the first house she and Jack built together – with her husband. Jack, accompanied by Lem Billings, was to join them late Saturday afternoon after speaking at Amherst College. Despite all the delays in moving in, as well as Jack's blatant lack of enthusiasm, Jackie regarded Atoka as their house in a way none of the others had ever really been and had high hopes invested in it. She wanted every element to be perfect, and in anticipation of Jack's arrival she devoted hours to hanging her collection of Moghul miniatures on one dining room wall. Jackie, who had started the collection after Nehru gave her a miniature that depicted a burglar overtaken by princesses as he breaks into a palace, joked that the pictures lent the house the air of a harem.

When Jack stormed in on Saturday, he was in no mood for harems, or anything to do with the new house. The Ellen Rometsch story had broken in the press. Headlined 'U.S. Expels Girl Linked to Officials,' Clark Mollenhoff's exclusive article in the *Des Moines Register* promised to set off an American equivalent of the sex and security scandal that had destroyed Britain's Secretary of State for War and fatally weakened Macmillan. Before leaving Washington, Kennedy had been on the phone about the Rometsch matter to Bobby as well as Bill Thompson, who had brought her to the White House in the first place.

The President's feverish conversations with his brother continued at Atoka. Bobby detailed Mollenhoff's assertions that Rometsch, described as a 'part-time model and party-girl,' had been 'associating with Congressional leaders and some prominent New Frontiersmen.' Kennedy and his team didn't know it, but in his private diary Mollenhoff had already specifically linked her to the President. Though Mollenhoff did not actually name Kennedy in the newspaper article, he left no doubt that he was pointing to the top. He reported that 'the high rank' of Rometsch's male companions had incited the Senate Rules Committee, concerned about espionage, to schedule a hearing for the following Tuesday. Why, Senator Williams (Bobby Baker's scourge) planned to ask, had Rometsch been deported the previous August? If the Senators were able to answer that, Kennedy's liaison with a 'party-girl' and suspected Soviet bloc spy would be disclosed, his presidency in serious jeopardy. In light of Mollenhoff's contention that Rometsch felt let down by her powerful Washington friends, Bobby sent an associate, LaVern Duffy, to Germany to placate her. The investigation had to be cut off before the Rules Committee convened on Tuesday. All weekend, the phone rang at Atoka as Bobby reported on his efforts to avert disaster.

For reasons Jackie could not fathom, Jack's tour of the new house, punctuated by the incessantly ringing phone, went poorly. She was soon in a mood as grim as her husband's. Atoka was a disaster. Jack complained about the lack of closet space, the need to abandon his own room whenever they had a houseguest, the sexually suggestive Moghul miniatures. He seemed to hate everything about the place, and Jackie believed it was his disappointment in the house she had designed that made the weekend such a miserable one.

In the course of several phone conversations, Jack and Bobby settled on a strategy that, however underhanded, had proven successful in the past. When the President went to war against Big Steel, his most powerful weapon had been the threat to expose private lives. Now, he used that tactic with Senate leaders. The Attorney General, urged on by his brother, marshaled F.B.I. files on the sexual indiscretions of Senators and Congressmen. If anyone knew the sort of salacious material – not all of it accurate by any means – contained in J. Edgar Hoover's archives, it was Jack and Bobby. Though Bobby admitted that some of the material was based on 'lies' by various Capitol Hill call girls, he and the President had no compunction about using it indiscriminately.

Monday morning, in meetings with Courtney Evans and Hoover respectively, Bobby communicated his and the President's dismay over Tuesday's hearing. Professing concern for 'the reputation of the United States,' though he and Hoover both knew he was really trying to save his brother, Bobby made the case that the F.B.I. Director ought to apprise Senate leaders of the damaging personal information about legislators that would be made public should the Rules Committee poke its nose into the Rometsch matter. Bobby made it seem as if the sexual secrets would come out as a matter of course, when in fact his tacit threat was to release them himself. At first, Hoover

demurred. Then, realizing how useful it would be to have the
President and the Attorney General in his debt, and not a little
grateful for the approval to put a wiretap on Martin Luther
King Jr, he did in fact talk to Mike Mansfield and Everett
Dirksen. Over lunch at Mansfield's home, Hoover stunned the
Senate leaders with a litany of scandalous revelations, some
true, others false, about politicians on both sides of the aisle.

Accordingly, the Rules Committee, contrary to its original
plan, confined itself solely to further scrutiny of Bobby Baker's
shady finances. By then, however, the national press had picked
up the *Des Moines Register* story. On Tuesday, October 29, the
very day the White House scared the Senators into silence, the
New York Times published its own article on Rometsch. It was
only a matter of time before someone told the tale of the
President and the party-girl.

That day, Kennedy had distressing news from Saigon. Despite
the President's efforts to withdraw his approval, Ambassador
Lodge reported that a coup attempt appeared imminent. Nor
were the Vietnamese generals willing to give Kennedy the forty-
eight hours' notice he demanded. They agreed to notify the
embassy no more than four hours in advance, which, Lodge
told the President, 'rules out my checking with you between
time I learn of coup and time it starts. It means U.S. will not
be able significantly to influence course of events.' Nor, Lodge
emphasized, was it in the White House's power to stop the
coup 'short of informing Diem and Nhu with all the opprobrium
such an action would entail.' Even so, Kennedy refused to
believe he had permanently lost control until, at half past three
on the morning of Friday, November 1, the phone rang and he
learned that a coup was in progress. As it turned out, General
Paul Harkins, head of the Military Assistance Command in
Saigon, sardonically observed, the plotters had notified the U.S.
only four minutes before they struck.

In the family quarters, Jackie watched as, for two and a half
excruciating hours, her husband waited for news. She had
observed a similar scene at Glen Ora at the time of the Bay of
Pigs adventure. Though in the intervening period of more than
two years Jack appeared to have recovered dramatically and

definitively from that pre-dawn ordeal when he felt his presidency slipping away, the same thing seemed to be happening again that morning. And again, there was a sense in which he himself was to blame. He had given his agreement to a coup, no matter how many times he had tried to rescind it.

Finally, at 6 a.m., McGeorge Bundy arrived in the family quarters. According to a telegram from the C.I.A. station in Saigon, the generals had demanded Diem's resignation and threatened to bomb the palace if he refused. A further telegram described a desperate call from Diem in which he learned of the U.S. attitude to the coup. Lodge, whose heart was with the generals, had replied noncommittally, 'I do not feel well enough informed to tell you. I have heard the shooting, but am not acquainted with all the facts. Also it is 4:30 a.m. in Washington and the U.S. government cannot possibly have a view.'

Kennedy most certainly did have a view. He was appalled, not least by Lodge's cordial invitation to the generals to gather at the U.S. embassy after the coup where the ambassador planned to receive them himself. At a 10 a.m. meeting in the Cabinet Room, Kennedy told Dean Rusk to notify Lodge that it would be unseemly for the generals to call on the embassy 'in a large group' as though 'reporting to headquarters.'

After lunch and a nap, the President sent Jackie and the children to Atoka with a promise to join them on Saturday. As the fighting in Saigon raged on, General Harkins reported that it was impossible to say which side had the advantage. Kennedy stipulated that should the coup succeed, he expected the rebels to guarantee the safety of Diem and his family, keep reprisals to a minimum, and treat those arrested in a humane fashion. That evening, he was informed that Diem and Nhu, asking for safe passage out of the country, had surrendered and been taken into custody. Kennedy went to bed worried that the international community would blame the U.S. for the coup.

When he awakened on the morning of Saturday, November 2, the situation was far worse. Word had come that Diem and Nhu had committed suicide by taking poison en route to the generals' headquarters. As at the time of the Cuban Missile

Crisis, Bundy had decided not to inform the President until morning. At 9:30 Kennedy entered the Cabinet Room, where all his top advisers on Vietnam were gathered. He had just taken his seat when Forrestal handed him Lodge's latest telegram. As the President read it in silence, he 'literally blanched,' McNamara recalled. Far from having taken their own lives, Diem and Nhu had been murdered. Kennedy 'leapt to his feet,' remembered General Maxwell Taylor, 'and rushed from the room with a look of shock and dismay on his face which I had never seen before.'

He gave instructions to cancel his scheduled trip to Chicago that afternoon for the Army–Air Force football game and to schedule another meeting for 4:30 p.m. to discuss Vietnam. Then, distraught, he went upstairs to the family quarters. In August, Kennedy had held himself responsible for his son's death; now he accepted responsibility for Diem. He had not intended that Jackie should go into labor prematurely or that Diem should be killed, yet he felt that in some way his actions had led to both. Since that terrible night just before Patrick was born, Kennedy had avoided being alone with Mary Meyer. Now, his resolve shattered. He was alone upstairs when he picked up the phone and summoned her to the White House. His previous invitations had been motivated by desire; this one, it is not too much to suppose, was born of self-loathing. To reach out to Mary Meyer now was a confession of guilt, a signal of unutterable self-disgust, a statement to himself as much as anyone else that this was the kind of man he really was.

It was shortly after 1 p.m. when Mary signed in and took the elevator to the second floor, as she had done many times in the past. For more than three hours Jack remained with her. He did not come downstairs until eighteen minutes after the second Vietnam meeting was to have begun.

The conjunction of the assassination of Diem and the resumption of Kennedy's affair with Mary Meyer brings into sharp focus the excruciating moral crisis in which the President found himself in November 1963, twenty days before his assassination. For all that his father had indisputably given Jack – boundless and unqualified love not the least of it – he had failed to equip

him with anything resembling a moral compass. It was only
with Joe Sr's removal from the scene in December 1961 that
Jack's intensive moral education began, under the tutelage of
Harold Macmillan. Even in adulthood Jack had depended on
the emotional succor Joe Sr provided, which made him highly
susceptible to the fierce campaign for his soul that Macmillan
waged passionately and tirelessly over a remarkable two-year
period.

It was a campaign that, as Macmillan himself understood,
would have had little hope of success had Jack Kennedy lacked
a fundamental core of decency, what David Ormsby-Gore
called with characteristic understatement, 'the right instincts.'
As Betty Spalding was reminded at the time of Patrick's death,
Jack had been endowed by nature, as had his sister Kathleen,
with a sensitivity and kindness that his father's influence and
training had grotesquely distorted. Had these instincts been
lacking, Macmillan might not have succeeded so brilliantly in
helping the President develop the beginnings of a moral sense.
Macmillan's task was made easier by the fact that he was
pushing Kennedy in the direction of his own best instincts,
while his father had steered him away from a decency that
came naturally. By the time of the American University speech
in June 1963, Kennedy had begun, under Macmillan's influence,
to take the first tentative steps toward becoming a moral leader.
Macmillan's influence in this regard would begin to be felt in
Kennedy's personal life as well. Almost certainly, the crisis over
his private behavior that Patrick's death triggered owed much
to the corresponding upheaval in Kennedy's political thinking.

With the death of Diem and the call to Mary Meyer, Kennedy
had reached a crossroads. Certainly, Mary's reappearance at
the White House indicated that it was going to be difficult,
perhaps impossible, for Jack to turn his life around, as he had
hoped to do after Patrick's death. Joe Sr had taught his sons to
act strictly in terms of their own needs and desires. Now that
Jack had learned the meaning of guilt and recognized how
much he had harmed Jackie, how could he live with himself
when, as on the present occasion, he continued to indulge
himself by doing things that caused her great pain? He wished

to think of himself as a decent man who loved his wife, yet how could a decent man persist in hurting her so? Twenty days before his death, the dilemma was at its harshest.

On a political level, as well, there was no telling whether Jack, who had spent the better part of his career as a pragmatist disguised as an idealist, would seize the opportunity to become a great leader governed by principles of right conduct. He had taken his first steps in that direction, but to confirm them he would have to utterly reinvent his *modus operandi*. Whether he would have succeeded, or whether he would have returned permanently to the easier ways to which he had long been accustomed, no one will ever know. All that is certain is that Kennedy's fumbling and indecisive leadership over Vietnam in September and October 1963, coupled with his gesture of resignation to his own weakness when he summoned Mary Meyer, indicated that tremendous obstacles to the expression of his moral sense lay ahead. Certainly he had the chance for greatness – and the material. That Macmillan chose to believe in him is perhaps the most potent argument that in the end he would have found the strength to become all he was capable of. But less than three weeks from death, Jack Kennedy, both politically and personally, was very much in the throes of a moral crisis, one that would never be resolved.

It was dark that Saturday by the time Jack flew to Atoka. Such were his spirits that he and Jackie might as well as have been in the pasture at Glen Ora in the devastating aftermath of the Bay of Pigs invasion, except that this situation was considerably worse. Then, he had been furious with himself for having miscalculated. This time, he felt shame for the wrong he had done. As Forrestal would recall, the deaths of Diem and Nhu 'shook him personally, bothered him as a moral and religious matter.' Shortly after he arrived, word came from the C.I.A. that snapshots were being offered for sale to the international press that showed 'Diem and Nhu covered with blood, apparently bullet riddled, lying dead on floor of armored vehicle with hands tied behind them.'

Kennedy had been talking to Ormsby-Gore about following up the test ban treaty with a trip to Moscow, a logical next step, but the assassination of Diem and Nhu altered everything. Vietnam, to which he had paid scant attention, suddenly threatened to undermine all he still hoped to accomplish with regard to détente. Seeing Jack in such distress, Jackie made a firm and final commitment to accompany him to Texas. For days she had vacillated, but his anguish over the Diem assassination made up her mind. He was in trouble; he needed her; as always, she would do what she could to help.

Jackie and the children returned to Washington on Tuesday, and two days later the White House announced her plan to visit Texas. As this was to be her first domestic political trip with the President, inevitably there were questions. Did Jackie's decision mean she planned to campaign actively in 1964? 'Say I'm going with my husband on this trip,' Jackie instructed her press secretary, 'and that it will be the first of many that I hope to make with him, and if they ask about campaigning, say yes that I plan to campaign with him and that I will do anything to help my husband be elected President again.'

Details of the Texas visit, which had been extended to two days, were yet to be worked out when the Kennedys spent a third, considerably more serene weekend at Atoka. Though Kennedy's conversations with Ben Bradlee, their houseguest for the weekend, showed that he was still worried about the Bobby Baker inquiry, without a doubt he was in a much better mood. He and Jackie spent a good deal of time outdoors with the children, the only impediment to her enjoyment being roads too muddy to accommodate horse trailers belonging to her friends. The White House photographer had come down to Virginia, and Jackie rode Sardar while he filmed. Jack, surveying the scene, sat on the terrace and enjoyed the late fall sunlight. Young John, dressed in an army helmet, a toy machine gun slung over his shoulder, marched happily back and forth. Jackie tried, without success, to teach him to salute properly for the camera. Despite her efforts, he persisted in saluting with his left hand, much to everyone's amusement. A weekend of quiet pleasure, it would be their last together as a family.

On Monday, Jackie spent an extra day in the country in anticipation of a trip that promised to change her life every bit as much as Paris had. Jack took the children back to Washington, since Caroline had school, and as a special treat he took John, who loved military pomp as well as any chance to spend time alone with his father, to the Veterans Day ceremony at Arlington National Cemetery. Jackie returned in time for a performance of the Black Watch Tattoo on the South Lawn late Wednesday afternoon. Up on the Truman balcony, Caroline perched on the right arm of her father's chair, her arm around his shoulders. Jackie sat to his left, with John on her lap. David Ormsby-Gore sat just behind, as they all watched the military drills and listened to the drums and mournful bagpipes of the Royal Highland Regiment. The next day, the President was to begin a five-day solo trip. After addresses to the conventions of the A.F.L.–C.I.O. and the Catholic Youth Organization in New York, he would go on to Florida, where visits to Cape Canaveral and U.S. Strike Command Headquarters were scheduled before his return late Monday night. In the meantime, Jackie and the children would spend the weekend at Atoka.

Thursday morning, before the President left to open a new highway in Maryland en route to New York, he held a press conference that touched on two volatile issues. In the course of responding to a question about the following week's meeting in Honolulu to assess U.S. policy in post-coup South Vietnam, Kennedy stated his position simply: 'I don't want the United States to have to put troops there.' He seemed less sure of himself when he fielded a question about Bobby Baker. Acknowledging that Baker was under investigation, Kennedy said, 'I think we will know a good deal more about Mr Baker before we get through. Other people will be investigated as time goes on.' And so they would have been – notably the President, had he lived.

The day after he made those remarks, Kennedy left New York accompanied by two of the girls who had regularly attended White House pool parties. His back had been bothering him again, so he asked Dr Jacobson to fly down to Florida separately to treat him that weekend. Jacobson, as always, was delighted to oblige. Also present was Torby MacDonald, who had been linked by investigative reporter Drew Pearson to the

Baker inquiry. Jack, Torby, and the girls flew on *Air Force One* to Florida. At a moment when it was obvious that the Baker inquiry might soon shift to Kennedy himself, he still saw no need to exercise caution. He spent part of the weekend, the last of his life, as he often had, tempting the fates. Nor was his self-annihilating behavior limited to high-risk sex. That weekend, though warned of grave peril in Texas, he forbade his Secret Service detail to ride on the running boards of the presidential limousine.

On Sunday, November 17, Kennedy sat by the pool at his father's house in Palm Beach with a report which had been delivered to the White House on Friday and sent down for his perusal. The previous March, he had asked Professor Richard Neustadt, an outside consultant, to investigate the crisis provoked by the cancellation of the Skybolt missile program. It had not been Kennedy's intention to damage Macmillan politically, and he wished to understand how such a thing could have happened. Neustadt's analysis of the crisis was more than just a dissection of why government had malfunctioned. The sequence of events he examined amounted to a study in betrayal, a portrait of a President too absorbed in his own needs to consider those of his friend and mentor. The same could be said for much that Jack had done to Jackie through the years. Perhaps that was why, after she returned from Atoka on the afternoon of Wednesday, November 20, Jack gave her a copy of the Skybolt Report when he came upstairs for lunch.

'If you want to know what my life is like,' Jack told his wife, 'read this.'

He went back to his office at 4 p.m. Jackie put the Skybolt Report aside to take with her to Texas in the morning.

FIFTEEN

Alone

That evening, Jackie went to the annual Judicial Reception, though it had previously been agreed that she would not attend. The night before, at Atoka, she had decided that it might provide a good warm-up for Texas. At 6:30 p.m. on November 20, 1963, Jackie came downstairs to greet seven hundred people in the East Ballroom in her first such appearance since her son's death. Despite some last-minute jitters, she was as poised and effective as ever. Jack, preoccupied with Vietnam and a meeting with Henry Cabot Lodge to follow the Texas trip, stayed only twenty minutes. Not long afterward, Jackie left with Bobby, who escorted her back to the family quarters. In keeping with her rule that evenings were Jack's 'time for happiness,' more often than not there were dinner guests. This evening, the last they spent together in the White House, she and her husband dined alone.

Despite Jack's conviction that her presence in Texas would be an advantage, Jackie remained apprehensive. If her partnership with Jack worked, she would once again have an important role and serious work to challenge and excite her. But several factors militated against success, not least a lack of experience in domestic politics. Jackie's record as a campaigner was nonexistent, compared to her spectacular accomplishments on the international scene. To make matters worse, the torrent of personal criticism provoked by her recent trip to Greece suggested that a possibly substantial and certainly vocal segment of the American populace regarded her negatively. The only way to find out was to test the waters, which meant that both Jack and Jackie –

each for his or her own reasons – had a tremendous amount staked on this trip.

It was a measure of Jackie's gift for strategy that, rather than flinch from the nasty letters, she made a point of learning from them. Jackie had always been a planner by nature, for whom every performance had to be meticulously worked out in advance. Whether it was an intimate dinner party with a few close friends or a vast state dinner, everything was scripted, nothing left to chance. She didn't just happen to say the right thing, though by the time she did all trace of the many hours spent poring over briefing papers, memos, and other background material had been eradicated. Her effects might have seemed effortless, but improvisation was anathema to her. Having created 'Jackie' characters to suit de Gaulle, Khrushchev, Nehru, Ayub Khan, and others, she crafted her new role with the people of Texas in mind.

Reviled for her expensive tastes, she would wear only relatively simple costumes that had been seen and photographed before. Told she showed too much independence, she would be sure always to play second fiddle to Jack. Perceived as threatening, she would do her best to look and act as much as possible like an ordinary American wife, although still the pretty and appealing Jackie the audience had come out to see. Criticized for her fondness for luxury, she would make a point of traveling without the personal maid, hairdresser, and press secretary who customarily hovered in attendance. Pamela Turnure would be on the trip, but Jackie saw to it that her press secretary was temporarily reassigned to the President's team. Reporters would have to do without Turnure's usual periodic bulletins on the First Lady's clothes. Jackie calculated that the panache that had worked so brilliantly in Paris was unlikely to play well here. For this audience, from first to last she must be a supporting player not a co-star. Or, as Pamela Turnure summed up, 'I think she wanted to be the woman to accompany John Kennedy to Texas.'

This was to be Jackie's first visit to Texas. They were to make five stops in two days – Houston, San Antonio, Fort Worth, Dallas, and Austin – then spend Friday night and Saturday at

Lyndon and Lady Bird Johnson's ranch in the hill country
outside Austin. All of Jackie's anxieties seemed to focus on a
short speech she was to give in Spanish to a Latino political
action group in Houston, though she had successfully delivered
many such speeches in Latin America and, more recently, at
the Orange Bowl in Miami. After dinner, Jack called Donald
Barnes, a State Department translator who had traveled with
them in Latin America, and asked him to be ready to accompany
them on *Air Force One* in the morning. Though it served the
President for his wife to do well, the thoughtful gesture of
having Barnes there for her, both as a reminder of Latin
America and as reassurance that she'd be equally good in
Texas, exemplified the kindness that in spite of everything she
saw as his core self.

Earlier, he had handed her the Skybolt Report. In the guise
of a dry government study, it was in the end an explanation of
how the President had thoughtlessly harmed someone he cared
about deeply. Besides Jackie, he also wanted Macmillan to read
it. At his request, McGeorge Bundy had called David Ormsby-
Gore for an opinion as to whether this was a good idea, and
Ormsby-Gore had agreed that it was. Jack planned to send the
Prime Minister a copy as a Christmas present. But why give it
to Jackie? By her own account, she was struck by the gesture,
as it was not Jack's habit to ask her to read such documents.
On the other hand, in the beginning he had been known to
give her books, notably *Pilgrim's Way* and *The Young Melbourne*,
as a way of giving her an insight into his true self. In the final
days of his life, was he doing the same? At a moment when the
President's involvement with Ellen Rometsch threatened to
break in the press and embarrass Jackie in unthinkable ways,
was he trying to say that he had never meant to hurt her?
Jackie kept the Skybolt Report with her to read 'in snatches'
on the trip.

As the Kennedys went to bed in the family quarters one last
time, much in their private lives remained unresolved. Despite
Jack's crisis of guilt after the death of their son and Jackie's
hope that he and the marriage might change, he had already
reverted to his former ways. He had been back to the Bing

Crosby estate, revived his affair with Mary Meyer, and spent his final weekend in Florida with two girls who had been regulars at White House pool parties. It looked as if he and Jackie were about to resume a political partnership, but how his unfaithfulness would affect their work together remained to be seen. In the past, she had been miserable about his other women, particularly Mary, and it seemed likely that she would be again when she returned to the White House full-time. And no matter how well things went on their first foray into domestic politics, could Jackie or the marriage have withstood the sex and security scandal that almost certainly faced the President after he returned from Texas?

Though 'Cuba 2' and the test ban treaty had been personal triumphs for Kennedy, the course of his presidency was highly uncertain. The assassination of Diem had thrown everything into chaos. Could Kennedy possibly resolve the tremendous conflict between U.S. support for the coup and his newfound convictions about right and wrong? After his feckless handling of Vietnam, notably his utter inability to control the men who worked for him, the leadership qualities he had supposedly proven in 'Cuba 2' were open to question again.

Friends would look back on this moment and remember things very differently. With great sorrow and much wishful thinking, they would focus on the remarkable and genuine transformations of the past year. They would tell the tale as if the Kennedy presidency had found its triumphant resolution in the Cuban Missile Crisis, and as if Jack and Jackie's marital problems were resolved in the healing aftermath of Patrick's death. They would do their best to forget that an entire year followed 'Cuba 2,' a year which witnessed the debacle in Vietnam, and that in the three and a half months after Patrick's death Jack continued his adulteries, especially with Mary Meyer. For better or worse, on the eve of the trip to Texas the truth about the Kennedys' lives was far more complicated.

Air Force One left Andrews at 11:05 a.m. on Thursday, November 21. Jackie spent much of the nearly four-hour flight working on her Spanish speech with Donald Barnes in the gold-carpeted conference area. Shortly before they landed, she left to change into a simple, short-sleeved, white wool dress. In that carefully considered costume, Jackie looked every inch the conservative wife of an affluent American businessman, rather than the jet-setter who had aroused so much ire. Even more than her clothes, it was how she acted when she emerged from the plane that sealed her success. As she came through the door to face the Johnsons, the Connallys, and many others assembled on the tarmac, she paused as though unsure quite how to react to a vast welcoming party. For a moment, it was as if de Gaulle, Nehru, Ayub Khan, and all the others had never met her at an airport. She waited a beat before a 'big, hesitant smile' appeared on her face. The emphatic hesitation, as if she wasn't sure the crowd was here for her, was utterly disarming. As Lady Bird Johnson perceived, it drew people's interest. It signaled humility. It conveyed that Jackie understood that her triumphs around the world didn't count here. It declared that today she was ready to let the people of Texas decide.

The crowd cheered and screamed her name as she followed Jack down the steps from *Air Force One* and received a bouquet of yellow roses at a brief welcoming ceremony. Afterward, the Kennedys were escorted to an open car for a forty-minute motorcade to the School of Aerospace Medicine at Brooks Air Force Base, where Jack was to speak. Jackie noted that the back seat was slightly raised so that the crowds could see the President. Lest the wind ruin her hair, she asked to ride on the low jump seat in front of her husband and let Governor Connally share the rear. To everyone's relief, the crowds along the motorcade route were not only substantial but also exceedingly friendly.

Jackie performed her scene at the Air Force base exactly as scripted, which meant she had no lines or action. She needed only to stay in the background and look the part of an adoring helpmeet. Afterward, they flew to Houston. Upstairs at the Rice Hotel, Kennedy asked Dave Powers how he thought the Houston crowd today compared to the one he had drawn on a solo visit in 1962. 'Mr President,' said Powers, 'your crowd here today was about the same as last year's, but a hundred thousand more people came out to cheer for Jackie.' Kennedy beamed. They had hardly begun, but already Jackie was a sensation. Her fears that the recent backlash against her would be a problem had proven unfounded.

That night, they dined in their suite. Presently, the Johnsons came down from the floor above. Lady Bird had been working for days to make the Kennedys' visit to the ranch something both would enjoy. It was easy to guess that Jackie would want to ride, since their shared passion for horses had formed a bond between the First Lady and the Vice-President from the outset. But what would Jack care to do? When Lady Bird asked, he surprised everyone by saying he wished to ride with Jackie. After John was born, Jackie had dreamed that she and Jack would spend weekends at Glen Ora riding together, and had even taken steps to find him the perfect horse. Her fantasy had been dashed when Jack had not warmed to life in the hunt country, and she was left to ride mostly by herself or with Caroline. Few things could have more clearly signaled his delight in her having accompanied him to Texas than the decision to ride with her. That day, Jackie had entered his world, the world of domestic politics, and he in turn proposed to join in hers. As soon as the Johnsons left, Jack confirmed his intentions by directing the White House to send his riding trousers via courier to Bergstrom Air Force Base in Austin. They were to be placed in a sealed package addressed to George Thomas, the President's valet, which would be picked up on Friday after the Dallas visit was over.

On that note, Jackie, having changed into a simple black velvet suit with pearls, headed downstairs to deliver the speech she saw as her test. On the mezzanine floor, the Kennedys entered the ballroom together, where some seven hundred members of the League of United Latin-American Citizens had assembled. Jack spoke first, a short speech about the Alliance for Progress. 'In order that my words will be even clearer to you,' he concluded, 'I am going to ask my wife to say a few words to you also.' Jackie picked up the baton and continued in Spanish.

The audience was delighted. Afterward, Jack alone sensed that Jackie was oblivious to her triumph. When he tried to reassure her by quoting some positive remarks he'd heard,

Jackie nervously dismissed them by saying people could hardly tell him anything else. Later, on *Air Force One*, he sought out Donald Barnes. Moments later, he headed back to inform Jackie that Barnes confirmed she had been terrific and that everyone had been 'very impressed.'

It was shortly past midnight when the Kennedys arrived at the Texas Hotel in Fort Worth. Despite the hour and the fact that it was hot and rainy, a huge crowd awaited. In their suite, Jack's special mattress, which traveled with him everywhere, had already been put in place. But it covered only half the king-size box spring, and due to a misunderstanding a complementary mattress had not been provided for the First Lady. Too exhausted to protest, Jackie, though reluctant to be apart from her husband, decided to sleep in the smaller bedroom. Jack was in a good mood, despite a pain in his stomach. Jackie had performed beautifully, and he wanted to be sure she knew it.

'You were great today,' he reassured her.

Later, Jackie would remember their embrace. They were so tired as they leaned against each other that she suddenly thought they were like a pair of bookends. Finally, Jack got into bed, and Jackie headed to the other room. He told her not to rush in the morning. He was scheduled to speak in an open parking lot across the street before their first appearance together. She didn't have to come downstairs until after the speech, when she was scheduled to join him at the Fort Worth Chamber of Commerce breakfast in the Grand Ballroom.

Before Jackie turned out the light in her room, she did something that strongly suggests she had come to believe his praise. She unpacked her pink wool Chanel suit with navy lapels and a matching pillbox hat, and carefully laid them out for the morning. She had dutifully packed a number of conservative costumes, but had also included one that was ever so slightly different – just in case. Who can say whether she would have unpacked it if the day had not gone so well, or if Jack had not been so determined to let her know she'd been wonderful? In any event, Jackie had her confidence back.

If she still had any doubts in the morning, Friday's papers

dispelled them. 'She has been nothing less than sensational on her first domestic trip outside Washington as a political, campaigning wife,' wrote one commentator. 'She has become an instant political pro and may turn out to be the President's secret weapon in the 1964 campaign.' 'It was apparent from the time his plane landed that the big thing going for him was his wife,' declared another. 'The crowd ... applauded the President, but it was obvious they had eyes only for her.'

Jack's experience Friday morning seemed to confirm what the newspapers were saying. When he addressed the crowd in the parking lot, he was greeted by cries of 'Where's Jackie?' His own dramatic instincts kicked in and, far from being annoyed, he seemed to enjoy stoking the anticipation. 'Mrs Kennedy is organizing herself,' Jack improvised, setting up her entrance. 'It takes her a little longer. But of course she looks better than we do when she does it.' After his speech, he headed for the hotel kitchen, from which he was to enter the ballroom. There was no sign of Jackie, and he sent word upstairs. The ballroom, recalled Liz Carpenter, Lady Bird Johnson's press secretary, 'was packed in great expectancy with all television cameras trained on the door where it was supposed the President and Mrs Kennedy would enter.'

When, after a delay, the door swung open and the President made his entrance, Jackie was nowhere to be seen. As he marched to the head table and sat down, the room erupted in whispers and, said Carpenter, 'much expectation about Mrs Kennedy ... everyone was eager to see her.' One Connally aide, who had sold numerous tickets to the event, wondered aloud whether the First Lady would show up at all. After everyone at the head table had been introduced, Raymond Buck, head of the Fort Worth Chamber of Commerce, announced, 'And now, an event I know you've all been waiting for!' He turned and indicated the kitchen door – Jackie's cue.

Hers was a star's entrance delayed until the last moment for maximum effect. Some 2,500 people were on their feet, cheering and applauding. Many stood on chairs for a better look. Newsmen shouted to female colleagues in search of an adjective for her suit's precise shade of pink. Jackie, smiling shyly and with eyes locked on her husband, slowly crossed the ballroom. Eager as she was to please the crowd, as always her performance was for no one other than Jack. To the end, he remained her best and most appreciative audience, the only audience that mattered.

At the head table, she took her seat without anyone seeing her lightly touch his hand. Jack, falling into the team rhythm, remained deadpan. People wondered: Was the President annoyed with his wife for having kept him waiting? Poker-faced, he let the curiosity boil until, after a short gift-giving ceremony, he rose to address the room. Jack waited a beat, then began, 'Two years ago, I introduced myself in Paris by saying that I was the man who accompanied Mrs Kennedy to Paris. I am getting the same sensation as I travel about Texas.' With that tribute, Jackie knew, as did the entire room, that the Kennedys had a new act. In the beginning, they had delighted private dinner guests with their teamwork. In Paris and other foreign capitals, they had performed brilliantly together on the world stage. After this morning, the Kennedys would be taking their show to the American people.

When they were back upstairs, Jack asked if Jackie would accompany him to California in two weeks. Without hesitation, she agreed. Then Kenny O'Donnell came in with the *Dallas Morning News* and their high spirits were abruptly shattered. A full-page advertisement with a funereal black border, headlined 'Welcome Mr Kennedy to Dallas,' contained a diatribe against the President's policies. Shortly before they were to leave for Dallas, the sight revived the fears of violence that had nearly kept Jackie from Texas.

She regained her composure on *Air Force One* and by the time they reached Dallas's Love Field – a thirteen-minute flight – she was ready to pick up where she and Jack had left off at breakfast. By then, as one reporter would say, Jackie had become 'almost the focus of the trip.' In a 'departure from protocol,' it was she, not the President, who emerged first from the plane's rear door. She was momentarily perplexed when someone handed her a bouquet of red roses, instead of the yellow ones she had been given in San Antonio, Houston, and

Fort Worth, but there was no time to puzzle over a small detail. To the astonishment of the *New York Times*'s Tom Wicker, she headed over to the crowd gathered behind a chain-link fence, and for nearly ten minutes joined her husband in shaking people's hands. 'I don't know that I ever saw Mrs Kennedy do this any other time,' Wicker reflected. Clint Hill, at Jackie's side, monitored the outstretched hands for weapons. At one point, despite her efforts to stick close to her husband, she and Jack became separated. Accompanied by Hill and another agent, Paul Landis, Jackie started toward the limousine, then asked where her husband was. Told he was still shaking hands, Jackie returned to the fence, intent on doing what was needed. As she passed *Newsweek*'s Charles Roberts, he asked how she liked campaigning.

'It's wonderful,' Jackie replied. That, too, was a departure.

Finally, Jack broke away from the crowd and they headed over to the dark blue Lincoln convertible where John and Nellie Connally had already taken the right and left jump seats. Jackie was to share the back seat with the President. This morning, concerned about her hair again, she had been hoping that rain would necessitate a plastic bubbletop. But the sky was clear and bright and at 11:55, they headed into Dallas in an open car.

Jack sat to her right, the bouquet of red roses on the seat between them. Since Jack had ruled out Secret Service men on the running boards of his car, Jackie's agents rode with his on the follow-up car, Clint Hill on the Cadillac convertible's left front running board and Paul Landis on the right rear. Vice-President and Mrs Johnson, accompanied by Senator Ralph Yarborough, followed in a Lincoln convertible. The motorcade's destination was the Trade Mart, where the President was to address a luncheon, and the trip was scheduled to take forty minutes. On the way into town, when Kennedy spotted a sign that said, 'Please, Mr President, stop and shake our hands,' he told the driver to pause. By the time the President got out of his car, Landis had jumped off the follow-up car and assumed a position beside him to monitor the crowd. 'It worked,' exclaimed the woman with the sign. 'Our sign worked!'

But the crowds en route were as nothing compared to the

crush downtown. For Jackie, all this suddenly felt very familiar. Afterward, she would remember that it had reminded her of the frenzy of trips she and Jack had taken abroad. The city struck her as 'hot, wild' – like Mexico and Venezuela. She longed to put on dark glasses against the burning sun, but Jack told her not to; he wanted people to see her. As they drove slowly through the downtown center, cheers and applause mingled with the gunning and occasional backfire of Dallas police motorcycles flanking the limousine. On Main Street, recalled Paul Landis, 'the crowd lined both sides of the street, and in several places was right out onto the street leaving barely enough room to get through.' On four occasions, the motorcycles on Jackie's side had to drop back behind the follow-up car. Hill rushed forward and jumped onto the left rear bumper of the President's car, just behind Jackie. Other agents ran alongside in an effort to control the surging crowd.

Relief seemed to be in sight when the motorcade turned right, onto Houston Street. Jackie heard Nellie Connally say they would soon be there. The Governor's wife, pleased that all had gone well despite much trepidation, remarked, 'Mr President, you certainly cannot say that Dallas doesn't love you.' Making a left on Elm Street, the limousine, proceeding at eleven miles per hour on a slight downward incline, neared an underpass. The crowd had thinned noticeably, and Jackie, waving to people on her left, was pleased by the thought that 'it would be so cool in that tunnel.'

About then she heard what she took to be the backfire of one of the police motorcycles.

Jack heard it too, for he abruptly stopped waving and looked to his right, then at her. Jackie, still looking out her side of the car, seemed fine, so he turned back and started to wave again. A fraction of a second later, Jackie, unaware that her husband had just checked on her, briefly turned to the right, toward the school book depository, before she resumed waving.

The agents riding the follow-up car had heard the noise as well, but Landis alone thought he recognized the report of a high-powered rifle.

'What was it? A firecracker?' asked John Ready, who occupied the right forward position on the running board.

'I don't know,' Landis replied. 'I don't see any smoke.'

Another loud noise followed.

'Oh, no, no, no,' moaned Connally.

The Governor's sobs caused Jackie to turn. Jack seemed to grab his own throat with both hands. Though she didn't know it at the time, a bullet had entered from the rear at the base of Jack's neck just to the right of his spine, exited below the Adam's apple and hit Governor's Connally's right shoulder.

'My God, they are going to kill us all,' Connally said.

Nellie took the Governor in her arms and dragged him down in an effort to get them both out of harm's way.

'Jack!' Jackie shouted.

Frantic to save him, Jackie tugged at his left arm, first with her right, then with both white-gloved hands. His arm wouldn't budge. In fact, he had not been reaching for his throat at all. The bullet had caused a spinal trauma that made both arms snap up, elbows out, hands below chin, in a sudden, involuntary movement. Despite her efforts, his arms remained frozen. From the vantage point of the follow-up car, Jackie appeared to have wrapped her right arm around his shoulders.

As in a nightmare, she could not pull her husband down before the next shot five seconds later.

Her face was very close to his when the bullet hit.

'I love you, Jack!' she cried.

Blood and human matter flew in all directions. As his brain split asunder, his arms unfroze. A fragment of his head flew out the back of the open limousine. Blood rained on the Connallys. The Governor glanced down at his trousers and saw a thumbnail-sized chunk of Kennedy's brain.

Clint Hill, running, had been struggling to get up onto the rear of the limousine when the third shot was fired. As Hill jumped onto the left rear step, Jackie screamed, 'They've shot his head off!'

Hill saw her turn and climb onto the trunk 'as if she were reaching ... for something that had been blown out.' Dave Powers, watching from the follow-up car as Jackie crawled on hands and knees, feared she would fall off and be crushed.

Finally, she turned to Hill, who, by his own account, 'grabbed her and put her back in the back seat, crawled up on top of the back seat and lay there' in an effort to shield her and the President with his own body.

Below, Jackie held her husband face-up on her lap. The car's pale blue interior was spattered with blood. A skull fragment with a patch of hair lay near the red roses. The right portion of Kennedy's head and part of the brain were missing. Jackie held the top of his head in a conscious effort 'to keep the brains in.'

For six minutes, sirens blasting, they sped to the hospital.

'Jack, Jack,' she sobbed, 'what have they done to you?'

'He's dead, he's dead,' she could hear someone yell.

Jackie continued to talk to him. She asked whether he could hear, she repeated that she loved him. Yet she sensed he was dead. By the time the limousine screeched to a stop behind Parkland Memorial Hospital, she had accepted it as a fact. Hill jumped off the car to disclose a hatless Jackie curled over the President, her hair matted with gore. She cradled his head in her arms. There were Secret Service men everywhere. Some were crying, others begged her to get out.

In order to reach the President, the agents first had to remove the wounded Governor and his wife. Then agent Emory Roberts asked Jackie to let them take her husband. She would not budge. Meanwhile, Roberts had seen Kennedy's head and knew what he must do. He turned to Roy Kellerman.

'You stay with the President,' Roberts told the other agent. 'I'm taking some of my men for Johnson.'

As the shooting had occurred when both Kennedy and Johnson were in town, there were immediate fears of a conspiracy to murder the Vice-President as well. Soon, agents were hustling the Johnsons past the presidential limousine and into the hospital. 'I cast one last look over my shoulder,' Lady Bird remembered, 'and saw in the President's car a bundle of pink, just like a drift of blossoms, lying on the back seat. It was Mrs Kennedy lying over the President's body.'

Meanwhile, Paul Landis reached over and attempted to help Jackie up.

'No, I want to stay with him!' Jackie insisted.

Clint Hill was more effective. He opened the left rear door, took her by the arm and coaxed her to let go.

'Cover up his head,' someone said.

Before Hill draped his jacket over Kennedy's face and upper chest, Dave Powers looked in and cried, 'Oh, no! Mr President! Mr President!'

'How badly was he hit, Clint?' a reporter asked.

'He's dead,' Hill said curtly.

Hill and others lifted him out the right rear door, and as they did several red roses clung to the President's body. A young nurse tried to lift his head onto the emergency cart, but Jackie pushed her away and did it herself. As agents wheeled her husband in, Jackie ran alongside, but despite her efforts Hill's jacket slipped off Kennedy's face. By the time they reached the trauma unit, the white sheet beneath was soaked with blood.

Kennedy, still alive but in extreme shock, lay on his back. He was unresponsive and made no voluntary movements. Dr Charles Carrico, a surgical resident, detected a few faint sounds that he took for heartbeats. There were sporadic attempts to breathe but no palpable pulse. 'From a medical standpoint,' the physician recalled, 'I suppose he was still alive in that he did still have a heartbeat.' That being the case, Carrico tried to restore breathing with a tube down the throat.

Jackie requested a priest. Believing that Jack was dead, she allowed herself to be coaxed out of the room. As she drifted into the narrow hallway and the door closed, a policeman rushed up with a folding chair.

'I'm not going to leave him,' she said.

When Dave Powers saw her covered with blood and brain tissue, he burst into tears. The door opened again and a nurse asked if anyone knew the President's blood type. Kellerman read off the information from a card in his wallet. Moments later, another nurse reported that Kennedy was still breathing.

Jackie stood and asked, 'Do you mean he may live?'

No one replied.

Ignoring the grim faces, Jackie clutched at hope. She told herself Jack might yet survive and promised, whatever his condition, to remain with him always. 'I'll take care of him every day of his life,' she thought. 'I'll make him happy.' Suddenly she was frantic to get back inside the room. She remembered one of his back operations when, despite her promise not to leave his side, 'bossy' doctors had forced them apart 'for hours and hours.'

Determined not to let that happen again, Jackie re-entered the trauma unit. By this time there was so much blood on the floor that nurses had surrounded the cart with sheets so the medical staff would not slip. Jack, ashen, lay stripped to the waist, a sheet over his lower body, which still wore a back brace, an Ace bandage, and undershorts. The tube in his mouth had been connected to a machine. Bits of brain tissue stuck to the drapes of the cart. Someone asked Jackie to leave, but Admiral George Burkley, the President's personal physician who had been in the motorcade, intervened.

'It's her prerogative,' Burkley insisted.

Despite the blood on the floor, Jackie dropped to her knees and prayed. Her white kid gloves, buttoned at the wrist, had red stains. Pistol cocked, Clint Hill hovered nearby. Jackie was kneeling when a surgeon, Dr Malcolm Perry, entered and took charge of the resuscitative measures.

Perry and an associate decided to perform a tracheotomy. It took between three and five minutes to cut an opening in the President's neck directly above the quarter-sized bullet wound, and insert a tube in the windpipe. Intermittently, Perry looked up to retrieve an instrument from the tray and caught a glimpse of Jackie. When she wasn't praying, she wandered about, staring vacantly, hands clasped in front of her. At one point, she approached Dr Marion Jenkins, an anesthesiologist. Nudging him with her elbow, she handed him a piece of her husband's brain.

Pandemonium erupted when the doctors could not detect a heartbeat. 'Apparently,' recalled Dr Charles Baxter, who had assisted in the procedure, 'this had ceased during the tracheotomy.' Dr William Clark, a neurologist, and Perry took turns administering closed-chest cardiac massage. It presented an appalling spectacle. 'With each compression of the chest,'

Jenkins recalled, 'there was a great rush of blood from the skull wound.' Soon, 'a great deal of blood was running off of the table' on Kennedy's right side.

While Perry continued the chest massage, Clark scrutinized the head injury. He judged that the magnitude of the wound and loss of brain tissue were such that nothing more could be done. 'Literally,' recalled Baxter, 'the right side of his head had been blown off.' By this point, the physicians agreed, the patient was dead. Yet for a few minutes more, resuscitative activity continued.

Baxter assured Jackie that they would not declare him dead until he had had the last rites. Father Oscar Huber, one of two priests waiting in the corridor, told the doctors to go first, however. As the head wound, not the neck injury, was the cause of death, the task fell to the neurologist. Clark declared the President legally dead at 1 p.m. on November 22, 1963.

The atmosphere changed abruptly. Now it was the physicians who felt like intruders. Most left quickly, though a few – Baxter, Clark, Jenkins – still had tasks. Before the priests entered, the widow approached the body, over which a sheet had been drawn. Jack's foot, white and bloodless, protruded, and she leaned over and kissed one toe. After kissing his stomach, she pulled the sheet down to study his face. Jack's eyes were still open, and his mouth, she thought, looked 'so beautiful.'

Finally, she kissed his lips and wept.

Father Huber joined Jackie on the right side of the cart. As he said the last rites, she reached under the sheet to hold Jack's hand. Softly, she joined the priest in prayer. Afterward, she went into the corridor to wait while nurses prepared the body for the trip to Washington. As extensive bleeding persisted, they wrapped four sheets around the head, and when blood continued to ooze through, took the further precaution of securing a plastic mattress cover to put in the casket.

Jackie, determined to see her husband one last time before the casket was closed, sat just outside the door. Meanwhile, the Johnsons had been taken to a tiny room with billowy white sheets for partitions. 'The Vice-President was worried about Mrs Kennedy,' recalled agent Rufus Youngblood, and asked to see her. For his own safety, the Secret Service refused to let him leave the room, so at length he sent Lady Bird.

Led to the emergency area by some back stairs, she found Jackie in the corridor. 'You always think of her – or someone like her – as being insulated, protected; she was quite alone,' Lady Bird remembered. 'I don't think I ever saw anyone so much alone in my life.'

Lady Bird threw her arms around Jackie and muttered, 'God help us all.'

Shortly thereafter, Kenny O'Donnell went to Johnson.

'He's gone,' O'Donnell said.

As there was much concern that the Vice-President might also be targeted, O'Donnell urged him to fly to Washington immediately.

'How about Mrs Kennedy?' Johnson asked.

O'Donnell explained that she refused to leave without the body.

'I am not leaving until Mrs Kennedy and the body are on board,' Johnson declared.

Finally he agreed to wait on *Air Force One*, with shades drawn to frustrate any potential gunmen.

After the Johnsons left, Jackie entered the trauma room to say goodbye to Jack. His clothes and possessions had been put into two paper shopping bags. Naked, his head swathed in sheets, he seemed oddly 'little' to her now. Determined to give him something, as he had given Patrick a St Christopher's medal, Jackie decided to put her wedding ring on his finger. But when she tried to remove her left glove, she found that blood had stiffened the leather, and she had to ask a policeman to pull it off.

Out in the hall again, Jackie was beset by doubts brought on by the sight of her bare ring finger.

'Do you think I did the right thing?' she asked O'Donnell.

He tried to reassure her, but in the frenzy of the moment Jackie wondered whether that ring, which she had worn for ten years, was the closest thing she had to a memory of her husband.

Shortly after 2 p.m., William Greer, the agent who had been driving the limousine when Kennedy was shot, emerged from

the trauma room with the two paper shopping bags. Behind
him, on a rubber-tired gurney, was a dark red bronze casket.
Jackie attached herself to its right side. 'She was walking with
her left hand on the casket and a completely glazed look on
her face, obviously in shock,' remembered Charles Roberts, the
Newsweek reporter. 'It was deathly still in that corridor as this
casket was wheeled out. I had a feeling that if somebody had
literally fired a pistol in front of her face that she would just
have blinked.' As agents slid the casket into the back of a white
hearse and drew the curtains, Admiral Burkley tried to talk
Jackie into riding in front with him. She preferred to stay with
the casket, and in the end Burkley and Clint Hill joined her in
the rear for the ten-minute drive to Love Field.

The ramp to the rear entrance of *Air Force One* proved too
narrow, and agents had tremendous difficulty lifting the casket
into the plane. Finally, it was strapped down in the left rear
portion of the aircraft, where crew members had ripped out
four seats and a partition.

Jackie, who had followed the agents up the ramp, spent a
few moments with the Johnsons, then took one of two seats
across the aisle from the casket. Johnson, who was assigned the
presidential bedroom when he came on board, had insisted that
it rightfully belonged to Jackie. She was reluctant to leave the
casket, but Lady Bird convinced her, and soon she had her first
privacy since the shooting. She remained alone in the private
quarters for ten minutes.

Meanwhile, preparations were under way for Johnson's
swearing-in. Shortly after Jackie retired to the bedroom, federal
judge Sarah T. Hughes came on board to administer the oath.
The ceremony was to occur in the conference area prior to
takeoff. As many people as possible crowded in, while others
watched and listened through the door to the main cabin. Only
Jackie was missing, although she had said she wished to attend.
Johnson, who very much wanted her there, sent Kennedy's
Congressional liaison, Larry O'Brien, to see if she felt up to it.
When he entered the private quarters, she was still in the
bathroom preparing.

'I will be ready in a moment,' she said.

The bathroom mirror had offered a first glimpse of what she looked like. Though a nurse at the hospital had given her a towel to clean her face, she had been far too preoccupied to care how she looked. Now, in preparation for the swearing-in ceremony, she wiped Jack's blood off with a Kleenex and combed the gore out of her hair. As soon as she finished, she felt she had made a mistake.

'Why did I wash the blood off?' she thought. 'I should have left it there, let them see what they've done.'

Jackie, who had so often had to hide her feelings, wanted the world to see her pain, to grasp the full horror of what had happened to Jack. She still wore the blood-spattered pink suit. Both stockings were saturated with blood from kneeling in prayer on the hospital floor. Mindful of the inevitable photographs, she decided not to change for the swearing-in.

Moments later, Jackie entered the conference area, where, en route to San Antonio, she had worked on the little speech in Spanish that had caused her such anxiety. Now, Liz Carpenter noted, she was 'ashen and quivering – almost as though she were in a trance.' 'She was in what appeared to me to be almost total shock,' recalled Charles Roberts. By this time, the small, crowded space had grown warm and stuffy. Jackie stood on Johnson's left, Lady Bird on his right, as he put his hand on the Bible and said in an uncharacteristically soft voice, 'I do solemnly swear that I will faithfully execute the office of the President of the United States, and will to the best of my ability, preserve, protect, and defend the Constitution of the United States. So help me God.' Then he turned and kissed his wife's forehead.

Following a moment of silence, the new First Lady squeezed Jackie's hand and said, 'The whole nation mourns your husband.' Afterward, she walked her back to the private quarters and sat with her as *Air Force One* took off. Jackie refused Lady Bird's offer to send someone in to help her change.

'I want them to see what they have done to Jack.'

Lady Bird returned to her husband, and Jackie resumed her vigil at the casket.

'It's going to be so long and so lonely,' Jackie said to no one in particular, in a voice that could barely be heard.

Soon, Dave Powers, Kenny O'Donnell, and Larry O'Brien arrived to keep her company. Admiral Burkley came back to broach the matter of an autopsy.

'Well, it doesn't have to be done,' Jackie shot back.

'Yes,' said the admiral, 'it is mandatory that we have an autopsy. I can do it at the Army hospital at Walter Reed, or at the Navy hospital at Bethesda, or any civilian hospital that you would designate.'

After some consideration, Jackie ruled that, as Jack had been a Navy man, his body ought to be taken to Bethesda Medical Center.

When *Air Force One* landed at Andrews Air Force Base at 6 p.m., security was tight, the nation on full military alert. Dallas police had a suspect in custody – Lee Harvey Oswald – but there were rumors of a larger plot. Government officials 'just didn't know quite where they were for a long period of time nor were they certain more assassinations hadn't been planned,' recalled Washington journalist Nancy Dickerson. Johnson feared, in his own words, 'an international conspiracy.' Not only had both the President and Vice-President been in Dallas, but Secretary of State Dean Rusk and five other Cabinet members had been en route to Tokyo for a joint Cabinet meeting with the Japanese. The timing aroused suspicions that the assassination had been planned to coincide with a power vacuum in Washington, and there was anxiety on *Air Force One* that the Soviets might act before the new President reached the White House.

Rusk, who with the others had immediately headed home, worried about a plot by the Cubans or the Soviets. Was there some connection to the recent assassination of Diem and his brother in Vietnam? Or to the U.S.-inspired assassination plot against Castro? Acting Secretary George Ball wondered whether Dallas might be 'the beginning of a Soviet move' or 'the first step in a coup attempt.' The former seemed very much a possibility when government files showed that Oswald had spent thirty-two months in the Soviet Union until his return to the United States in June 1962. In view of these concerns, the public had been banned from Andrews, and access to the landing area limited to government officials and press. Secret Service agents prepared to guard Johnson with rifles out.

Inside the plane, as the passengers waited for Jackie and the casket to go out through the rear, Bobby Kennedy, who had entered in front, could be heard.

'Where's Jackie?' he demanded, pushing his way through the crowd. 'I want to be with Jackie.'

Bobby looked neither left nor right, Liz Carpenter remembered, and his face was 'streaked with tears.'

At the rear door, on which all lights and cameras were focused, there was a delay as a yellow forklift prepared to remove the casket. Finally, Jackie emerged into the glare, the image more eloquent for being silent. The same pink suit that just that morning had brought cheering Texans to their feet while a delighted Jack looked on provoked involuntary gasps of horror as onlookers saw his blood on her skirt. At length, escorted by Bobby, she followed the casket into the rear of a battered gray Navy ambulance for the forty-five-minute drive to Bethesda.

It was nearly seven in the evening when the motorcade reached the hospital. Jackie was taken to the presidential suite on the seventeenth floor, while agents accompanied the casket to the morgue.

'She was very much in command of herself,' recalled Nancy Tuckerman. 'Obviously she was in a certain amount of shock, but she could operate and she could make sense, and she realized that she had to make certain decisions.' The first problem was what to do about her children. Jackie's mother, who had come to the hospital, had already taken Caroline and John to her own home in Georgetown. Janet reported that they had had dinner and were preparing for bed, but Jackie insisted that they spend the night at the White House. Both children were returned within the hour.

Next, she took up the arrangements for Monday's funeral. 'They were not expecting to hear it from her,' Pamela Turnure remembered, but soon instructions were sent to Bill Walton and Chief Usher J. B. West 'to find out how Lincoln's funeral

had been done.' Both men had been instrumental in helping
Jackie put together the White House early in the presidency.
Now they would help her prepare it for the final pageant of
the Kennedy years.

Jackie's most important decision, with monumental implications for the days ahead, had to do with the funeral procession.

'I am going to walk behind the casket,' she insisted.

Would Lyndon Johnson do the same? Would foreign dignitaries? Such a risk seemed foolhardy, even irresponsible, to
many people. The Secret Service and the F.B.I. were quick to
advise, 'Under no circumstances should the American President
take that risk.' The State Department had already discouraged
foreign delegations, and in the hours that followed, Dean Rusk
and George Ball would agonize over the possibility that an
assassin might strike down one or more heads of state on U.S.
soil.

At Bethesda, the autopsy was complete by 11 p.m. The
undertakers took over. A new casket was delivered; the original
had been damaged when it was loaded onto *Air Force One*.
Kennedy's valet arrived with the clothes in which he was to be
buried. Meanwhile, Jackie, impervious to a sedative provided by
Dr Walsh, missed her wedding ring. Admiral Burkley retrieved it
for her.

It was after 4 a.m. Saturday morning when Jackie finally
returned to the White House, which, according to her orders,
had been draped in black bunting. As the casket was carried
in, some of the office girls who had been with Jack since his
Senate days gathered on the balcony to watch. The casket
rested on a catafalque in the East Room, where an altar boy
in a white cassock lit four candles. After a Roman Catholic
priest said a prayer, Jackie knelt, threw her arms over the flag-
draped bronze casket, and rested her head there. Then, as staff
members sobbed, Bobby took her arm and guided her to the
family quarters.

By Saturday morning only a few world leaders – Britain's
new Prime Minister, Alec Douglas-Home, Chancellor Ludwig
Erhard of West Germany, and President Eamon de Valera of
Ireland – had announced plans to attend the funeral. Everything

changed after Hervé Alphand contacted the State Department
to ask if Charles de Gaulle would be welcome. The French
people had responded passionately to the assassination, and de
Gaulle, who had tremendous affection for Jackie, wished to
stand beside her.

The State Department called back in half an hour to say
that the U.S. was touched by de Gaulle's gesture and
awaited his visit with gratitude. In fact, de Gaulle, who had
been the target of at least nine assassination attempts, was
absolutely the last person they wanted in Washington at that
moment. In one notable instance, fanatics had nearly blown
up his limousine; in another, machine-gun fire had narrowly
missed the General and his wife en route to their country
house. There were fears that were he to march in the funeral,
his great height would make him a conspicuous target. But it
was also the case that as one of the last two surviving members
of the Big Four of the Second World War – Roosevelt and
Stalin were dead – de Gaulle's decision would no doubt inspire
other leaders. And so it did. Hardly had Paris announced, at
12:30 p.m. Washington time, when many other world capitals
did the same.

In the midst of what was rapidly shaping up to be a security
nightmare, a message from Ambassador Foy Kohler in Moscow
caused the greatest concern. At a moment when there was
widespread suspicion that the Kremlin might be behind the
assassination – following which the Soviet Union had immediately gone onto a state of national alert – a tearful Nikita
Khrushchev had arrived at the American embassy to sign the
condolence book.

Afterward, in a private talk with Kohler, he expressed 'deep
personal regret and shock' at the death of Kennedy, for whom
he had 'great admiration and respect.' Khrushchev mentioned
that he and his wife had written to Mrs Kennedy. Devastated
that she had been 'sullied' by her husband's blood, he planned
to send his number two man, Anastas Mikoyan, First Deputy
of the Soviet Council of Ministers. Mindful of U.S. suspicions,
Khrushchev spoke pointedly of 'Lenin's condemnation of "nihil-
ist" activities' directed against the Tsar's person. In short,

Khrushchev wanted it understood that he had had nothing to do with the shooting.

That didn't mean everyone in Washington believed him – Rusk for one continued to fear that the assassination had Communist origins – or that Moscow's emissary would be safe from revenge-seekers. Kohler, in the interest of preventing matters from heating up, urged the State Department that, 'if facts permit,' U.S. authorities should portray Oswald as a 'madman' with a 'long record of acts reflecting mental unbalance' rather than dwelling on his Marxist connections. In a meeting with Ambassador Anatoly Dobrynin, Llewellyn Thompson warned that it would be unwise for Mikoyan to speak on American television. He also pointed out that 'the public had been highly aroused by the assassination of President Kennedy, that in any country there were crackpots, and it was always possible there could be unpleasant incidents.' So Mikoyan's visit, Thompson urged, ought to be brief.

Jackie, insulated from these machinations, persisted in her controversial plan to 'walk behind Jack' on Monday. She chose St Matthew's Roman Catholic Cathedral for the service expressly because it was eight blocks from the White House. Rain or shine, she planned to walk to St Matthew's through a heavily populated area of the city, whether other mourners joined her or not. As St Matthew's had limited seating – by contrast with the Shrine of the Immaculate Conception in northeastern Washington, which accommodated 2,500 but could not be reached on foot – the guest list had to be trimmed mercilessly.

Meanwhile, seventy-five family members and friends joined Jackie and the children for a private Mass in the East Room, believed to be the first Roman Catholic Mass celebrated in the White House. Afterward, she retired to the family quarters, leaving government officials past and present, including former President Eisenhower, to file past the casket throughout the day.

Harold Macmillan was too ill to travel to Washington. He sent the Duke of Devonshire, who had stood in for him at the Inauguration three years previously. Macmillan, in a first public appearance since his illness, would go to the House of Commons on Monday to deliver a eulogy.

On Sunday, as Jackie was about to accompany the casket to the Capitol for a day-long public viewing, and as de Gaulle, Mikoyan, and others prepared to descend on a jittery Washington, violence erupted in an unexpected quarter. Millions of Americans were watching television in anticipation of the cortège and saw Lee Harvey Oswald killed by a mysterious gunman while in police custody in Dallas. Even to those who doubted that the Kennedy assassination was part of a larger conspiracy, the vertiginous jolt of Oswald's murder suggested further madness in store.

The Johnsons, who had attended St Mark's Episcopal Church on Capitol Hill heavily protected by Secret Service agents and rifle-toting police, were waiting in the Green Room at the White House for the Kennedy family when they learned that Oswald had been killed. There was scarcely time to absorb the news before Jackie appeared with Caroline and John. She was dressed in black, the children in matching light blue wool coats with velvet collars and red Oxford shoes.

Less than an hour after Oswald's murder, Jackie, who would not be told of it until later, appeared at the North Portico, holding Caroline with her left hand and John with her right. For five extraordinary minutes, as the casket was put into position by pallbearers, Jackie, in bright sunlight, cut a stoical figure.

Like her decision not to remove the bloodstained suit and stockings on her return from Dallas, the children's presence was a statement. Given her past behavior, one might have expected her not to include them in the public ceremonies. But on this occasion, she who had fought ceaselessly to protect her children's privacy wanted the world to see their loss. To a nation reeling from the murders of Kennedy and Oswald, Jackie, in her bearing, offered a much-needed image of composure and quiet courage in the face of violence, of dignity and stability against chaos.

Oswald's death heightened official anxiety about her eight-block walk the next day. Perhaps if de Gaulle could be persuaded not to march with Jackie, other world leaders would again follow his example. Rusk personally met the General at Dulles Airport on Sunday evening, hoping to convince him not to put himself in danger. De Gaulle, trailed by aides, bodyguards, and a French police inspector, swept off the plane in a voluminous overcoat.

'It is a tragedy,' he said in English, but shifted to French when Rusk thanked him for coming. 'I am only executing the will of the French people,' he replied. 'The emotion is intense throughout France.'

Told of Oswald's murder, de Gaulle grew visibly upset and speculated about a police conspiracy. In light of that, Rusk asked, would de Gaulle consider being driven to the funeral tomorrow?

'No,' the General answered emphatically, 'I shall walk with Mrs Kennedy.'

The pressure not to march intensified early Monday morning after the French consul in Lausanne, Switzerland, received an anonymous telephone call to warn about an attempt on de Gaulle's life in front of St Matthew's. There was also much concern about the ailing Mikoyan, who had received anonymous death threats that morning. At Rusk's behest, Llewellyn Thompson made a last-minute appeal, emphasizing that Mikoyan's age and health provided excellent reasons for him not to walk the half-mile route along 17th Street and Connecticut Avenue. Mikoyan, after consulting Khrushchev, insisted that he would walk with Mrs Kennedy.

Nor did the F.B.I. or Secret Service ease up in their efforts to dissuade the new President. Johnson made it clear that the perilous walk was something he wanted to do. When it became apparent that Johnson, de Gaulle, Mikoyan, and all the rest planned to march, George Ball and Deputy Secretary of State for Political Affairs U. Alexis Johnson manned a communications center in the State Department building, ready to deal with assassination attempts. At a Cabinet meeting, Rusk and others openly expressed their fears.

Church bells tolled as foreign dignitaries, including eight heads of state, ten prime ministers and much of world royalty, assembled in front of the White House at 11:25 a.m. Ten minutes later, Jackie, dressed in black, descended the steps of the North Portico. Silent and still, she stood behind the black caisson, escorted by Bobby Kennedy on her right and Teddy Kennedy on her left.

Moments before the procession, she turned briefly and, through her veil, saw Lyndon and Lady Bird Johnson, followed by a limousine carrying Caroline and John. Beyond them stretched a parade of leaders and historical figures from ninety-two nations, such as rarely gathered in one place. Given the danger, Jackie's walk to the cathedral had come to represent much more than a widow's grief. In the leaders' decision to march, they emulated her refusal to permit terror to rule.

Finally, as bagpipes played, Jackie started to walk. She held Bobby's hand but soon let go and continued alone.

SIXTEEN

My Dear Friend

'You have shown the most wonderful courage to the <u>outer</u> world. The hard thing is really to feel it, <u>inside</u>.' Three months after the assassination, Harold Macmillan wrote those words to a desolate Jacqueline Kennedy.

As long as Jackie remained at the White House, she had continued to exercise astonishing emotional discipline. On December 6, she moved with the children to a borrowed house in Georgetown, where the horror finally came crashing over her. It was as if, having managed one last time to do exactly what Jack needed, she had exhausted her own strength and spirit.

She had an enormous amount to cope with: grief, the horror of having witnessed Jack's murder, the trauma of nearly being killed herself. All that would have been enough to test anyone's limits. But for Jackie, there was something else. With Jack dead, she faced all of the unresolved questions, the agonizing doubts and uncertainties that had haunted her marriage. While her husband lived, she had held out hope, even in her darkest moments, that he might change. Any such hope died with him, leaving her to find a way to live with the brutal truth and puzzling contradictions of their life together.

A woman of deep and tumultuous emotions, Jackie had long inhabited a marriage and a milieu which required her to hide those feelings. For the first time, she was bereft of defenses. The emotional distance she had long cultivated had deserted her. At the age of thirty-four, she was confronted with a chaos of uncontrollable emotions, and she was unable to restrain her wild sobs even in the children's presence. When she left the house it was usually to visit a church to pray, or to drive in the darkness to Arlington National Cemetery to stare at Jack's grave. She agreed to go to Florida for Christmas in the hope of providing a semblance of normality for the children, but she returned three weeks later still boiling with rage and bitterness.

On January 31, 1964, ten weeks to the day since the assassination, she reached breaking point. In the morning, she and the children were to leave their temporary quarters for a house she had bought just across the street. With the move, life without Jack would become permanent. Late that night, Jackie was overcome with the need to tell someone how much she had loved Jack and how happy they had been together. Perhaps she just wanted to remind herself one last time, so that his loss would not seem quite so final. She would have to find someone who could believe in the reality of that happiness and the love she had felt in spite of everything. Given the nature of her marriage, she knew there was almost no one she could trust to understand.

Early in Jack's presidency, even before Jackie had met Harold Macmillan, the story of his love for the unfaithful Lady Dorothy had inspired in her a powerful feeling of connection. He had been in her mind at the very end, in Texas, as she read the Skybolt Report, which Jack had given her hours before he died. If there was anyone who might understand, it was he.

On the surface, Macmillan seemed a strange choice of confidant for a woman so rarely given to speaking from the heart. He was more than three decades her senior, and, as she herself remarked, she did not really know him very well. He had been Jack's intimate, not hers. Moreover, as she knew, he was extremely reticent about personal matters and exercised formidable control over his own much-troubled emotions.

Still, she risked it. In private life, Macmillan had known something very like her own harsh experience of love. Yet she recognized, based on his dealings with Jack, that he remained capable of deep feeling and extraordinary generosity. As her first letter would make clear, she had been struck by his response to the Skybolt crisis. In the end, Jack's careless betrayal had in no way diminished the Prime Minister's feelings for him.

It was close to midnight when she sat down to write. She began by talking of Macmillan's extraordinary partnership with Jack. She wanted him to know how Jack had felt about him and their collaboration. They had worked for the finest things in the finest years – a time she movingly called 'the days of you and Jack.' She wanted Macmillan to know how much her husband had loved him.

That only reminded her of how much had been lost. Embarrassed, she promised that she let no one else see her bitterness. But why, she wondered, was Jack gone when de Gaulle, on whom there had been so many assassination attempts that he traveled with his own supply of blood, lived on? Why was the eighty-eight-year-old Adenauer still here, when her husband was not? Jackie raged that so much of what Jack had hoped to do, so much of what he and Macmillan had planned, remained unfinished. What sort of justice was this, when the good men suffered? In her anguish, she allowed herself to be caught up in the 'what ifs': What if Jack had been content to live an ordinary life with her, rather than caring so much about his place in history? Would he still be with her now? Did history matter anyway?

Crying out in pain, she told Macmillan how much she had loved Jack, how happy their life together had been. She was lost without him. She wrote as if consumed by emotions that she hid from the world but could no longer endure alone.

Macmillan was deeply saddened and alarmed by Jackie's letter, even as he was pleased that she had turned to him. He read and reread her words, and pondered them deeply before replying two weeks later. He understood that her decision to contact him conferred a certain responsibility. On the basis of their few encounters, he knew Jackie well enough to grasp how alone in the world someone of her character and sensitivity must be to have revealed herself so.

Seated at his table at Birch Grove that February, Macmillan composed a letter of ineffable delicacy and sensitivity. Opening with the salutation, 'My Dear Friend,' he instantly made it clear that Jackie had been right to turn to him. He reminded her that this was the way he had initiated his correspondence and friendship with Jack, and by using those same words now he was telling her that the affection they had shared was hers for the asking.

He had clearly been disturbed by the self-deprecating way in which she insisted in her letter that she had been an observer, not a participant, in Jack's work. The truth, he knew, was far more complicated. As Jackie had reminded him of his own great partnership with Jack and all they had tried to accomplish together, Macmillan reminded her that she too had been Jack's partner in working for the best things. No matter how brief that partnership, she must always remember that their years together had been splendid ones.

It was Macmillan's sense of how isolated Jackie seemed, with all her questions, confusion, and bitterness, which made him worry most. Gently, he offered to serve as a sort of safety valve or lightning rod, someone to whom she could speak frankly. He had suffered much in private and knew what it was like to live without the possibility of release. When he reminded her that Jack had trusted him, implicit was a promise that Jackie could do the same. Lest she worry that she was imposing on him, Macmillan stressed that it would ease his pain as well by making him feel he could still do something for Jack. If, however, she chose not to write again, he promised to understand.

For months, Macmillan heard nothing more from Jackie. At first he had no idea that many times over the winter she returned to his letter, reading it again and again, committing to memory his suggestion that he might be able to help Jack by being the recipient of her letters. She had come to think of his letter as her rock, the most important letter of her life. All that winter, she would sit alone and pour out her despair and rage in letters to Macmillan. Each time she finished, she would destroy what she had written before sending it. Finally, she asked David Ormsby-Gore to tell Macmillan why there had been no response. She told herself that these unsent letters would get her through the winter, and that when spring came she would feel better and be ready to explain herself.

On June 1, 1964, Jackie finally put a letter in the mail to Birch Grove. She told Macmillan that without the outlet of all

she had written to him that winter, she would surely have
destroyed herself by keeping everything inside. By then, the
worst hysteria had abated, and she decided that Washington
was too full of memories of life with Jack. Accordingly, in the
fall she moved to New York, where, for the children's sake, she
began to force herself to put all thought of her husband out of
her mind. It was a conscious decision embarked on with
enormous discipline, and by spring 1965 she believed she had
indeed managed to forget him. Jackie had turned down previous
invitations to Kennedy tributes but, confident that her emotions
were finally under control, she agreed to attend the dedication
of Britain's memorial to Jack at Runnymede, the meadow where
King John signed the Magna Carta in 1215. The Kennedy
Memorial Trust, under David Ormsby-Gore's direction, had
built a memorial on a portion of land to be ceded in perpetuity
by Queen Elizabeth to the United States. Jackie asked Ormsby-
Gore to invite Macmillan to speak.

When Lyndon Johnson offered a presidential jet to transport
Jackie, her children and brothers- and sisters-in-law to England,
she asked him not to send *Air Force One* lest it provoke unwanted
memories. Pointedly, she requested the 707 whose interior least
resembled the plane in which she had brought Jack's body back
to Washington. On Friday, May 14, Queen Elizabeth, Prince
Philip, and the Kennedy party crossed the meadow to some
stone steps that led up a forested hill. At the crest, all observed
a moment of silence as Jackie and the children inspected the
large stone with plaque affixed. It was the first time she had
seen Macmillan since Jack's death, and his tender words at the
ceremony were almost too much to bear.

Two days later, Jackie, the children, and the other Kennedys
went to Birch Grove for Sunday lunch, and the photographs
of Jack there, the gifts she had helped him pick out for his visit,
and the rocking chair he had used because his back hurt so,
pierced Jackie's heart. All the agonizing emotions she thought
were forgotten surged up again. The terrible sense of how much
of Jack's work remained unfinished overwhelmed her, along
with a feeling that there was nothing she could do about it. At
the same time, watching Caroline and John, she was struck by

the burden they bore on their seven- and four-year-old shoulders of always representing their father well. At a moment of great pain, Jackie was swept away with pride in both children, and the experience changed everything for her.

Jackie returned from England with her memories and emotions alive again, but full of peace and a new sense of purpose. In the aftermath of her trip, she wrote to Macmillan. She understood now that there was one more thing she could do for Jack, she told him, one thing it was in her power to complete on his behalf. She could make his children the people he would have wanted them to be. And, Jackie told her dear friend, if she could do that and the children grew up to be all right, that would be her vengeance on the world.

Epilogue

While her children did indeed provide Jackie with the sense of purpose she needed in order to go on with her life, she continued to struggle to come to terms with the loss of Jack. There remained the question of what was to become of her, what she was to do with the rest of her life. She was after all a very young widow, only thirty-four at the time of the assassination.

The woman who had entered the White House insisting that she hated politics had become a highly skilled diplomat in the course of the Kennedy presidency. For all of her public insistence on minimizing the seriousness of her work, she had had an extraordinary apprenticeship as Jack's partner, and there was every reason to think that she might wish to continue on her own. It came as no surprise when Lyndon Johnson proposed to offer Jackie an embassy. The most obvious choice was Paris, but he was willing to let her have her pick of virtually any major country in Europe or Latin America. Johnson had always been personally fond of Jackie, had observed and encouraged her as First Lady, and had a history, unlike Kennedy, of offering professional encouragement to the women around him.

In early 1965, on the advice of her brother-in-law Stas Radziwill, Jackie was seriously inclined to consider Johnson's offer. In addition to a sense that somehow she was continuing Jack's work, an ambassadorship also offered hope that she had a meaningful future of her own. When she was pregnant with Patrick and at work on the new house at Atoka, she had realized that a life dedicated to trivial things was no longer for her. By November 1964, Bobby Kennedy had left Johnson's government and been elected by the state of New York to the United States

Senate. Jackie had been instrumental in launching him, devoting much of her restless energy to helping him assume his brother's mantle. Therein lay the complication for her own personal hopes. Bobby and Lyndon Johnson regarded each other as political enemies; both saw Jackie, the most potent symbol of the Kennedy presidency, as a major prize for any politician seeking to claim Kennedy's legacy.

She quickly became a pawn in their struggle, but early in 1965 she seemed uncharacteristically oblivious to the needs of people she would consider more important than herself, daring for a short time to think primarily of herself and her future. She went so far as to raise the issue of the ambassadorship to Joe Alsop when he visited her in New York. As soon as he returned to Washington, Alsop, who had transferred his romantic investment in Jack Kennedy to Bobby, wrote to express his horror at the thought that she was seriously considering Johnson's offer. Jackie, still emotionally fragile and uncertain, reacted as if she had accidentally touched a hot coal. As if ashamed to have even considered an ambassadorship, she wrote a contrite letter to assure Alsop he was right. Then, as if to prove she had dropped the idea and knew her proper place, she abruptly launched into a long discussion of a carpet in which Joe had expressed an interest. This passage in the letter is, with hindsight, tremendously sad, signaling as it does the abandonment, under pressure, of Jackie's hopes for an independent political role.

In the aftermath of her decision to refuse the ambassadorship, Jackie seemed to dismiss all thought that she could herself do anything actively to advance Jack's historical legacy. She retreated to the care of her children, and to the trivial things that she had hoped to put behind her: a life of shopping and decorating, luxurious travel, and whiling away her days.

She would later say that in these years she had consciously taken steps to make herself interested in things again. For a time she had tried to recreate Jack in Bobby, feeding him a rich diet of book after book as if to give him a crash course in the intellectual understanding he lacked in comparison to Jack. But as much as she cared for her brother-in-law, he could never be what Jack had been, her second self. Finally, in an attempt to fill the emptiness, she embarked on several brief love affairs, culminating in a relationship with David Ormsby-Gore, whose wife, Sissie, had died in May 1967. In November 1967, Jackie and David (then Lord Harlech), united in their sense of mutual grief and loss, traveled to Cambodia together with an entourage. The expressed aim of their visit was to see Angkor Wat and the ruined town of Banteai Chhmar; Averell Harriman described the trip as being, in addition, a U.S. effort to 'renew contacts with the Cambodians.' As always in such circumstances, Jackie performed impeccably, but the trip put an end to any hope that, after four long years of grieving, she would ever discover a replacement for Jack. If David Ormsby-Gore could not take Jack's place, no one ever would.

Early in 1968, Harold Macmillan came to New York – swooping into her life, Jackie exulted, like some great bird that did more to free her than anything she herself had tried or planned. His appearance, she later said, shook and changed all her thoughts, and suddenly she knew what had to be retrieved. Macmillan was just emerging from his own period of grief, the deaths of his beloved grandson and brother having been followed, in May 1966, by the loss of Lady Dorothy, whom he had loved, as Jackie had loved Jack, despite the pain of years of flagrant infidelity. Jackie and Macmillan talked about world issues in her apartment on Fifth Avenue, she went to hear him lecture at Columbia University, and gradually she was filled with an exhilaration that she had not experienced since her years in the White House. The man whom she, like her late husband, had learned to call 'dear friend' brought her back to life after four tormented years, and together they realized that they had much important work still to do. As she would later declare, his visit made her breathe an air she had forgotten. Talking to Macmillan, Jackie refound a sense of larger purpose. She had come to terms with the fact that Jack could never be replaced, but Macmillan made her see that she might find again that sense of meaning which her life had had in the years of the presidency. Greatly distressed by the extent to which the Vietnam War was undoing the things the President and the Prime Minister had worked to achieve, Jackie, like Macmillan, was hungry to engage again with the great world. They would take Bobby as their instrument.

In recent months, Bobby had been under increasing pressure to challenge Lyndon Johnson for the presidency in a bid to end the war. To the annoyance of many, he had as yet done nothing to that end. Macmillan talked to Bobby in Jackie's presence. A month after Macmillan's visit, she wrote to urge Bobby to seek the presidency. Two weeks later, on March 16, 1968, Bobby announced he would run. In England, Macmillan thrilled to the sight of a newspaper photograph of Jackie and the children at the window of her apartment, watching Bobby march down Fifth Avenue following his declaration. Macmillan rejoiced that she had rediscover ed her sense of engagement, but also that, as in the days when Jack lived, there was reason to hope again.

Less than three months later, on June 5, 1968, Jackie was awakened in the early morning hours to be told that Bobby had been shot as he celebrated his victory in the California primary. She flew to Los Angeles on a borrowed private jet to find Chuck Spalding waiting for her. Bobby was still clinging to life, but all hope was gone. Later, she would remember the sound of a television, with the voice of Macmillan reciting a eulogy for both Jack and Bobby. His words were so tender and beautiful that some stations played them over and over, an endless loop of grief.

Jackie's reaction to Bobby's death was one of inexpressible fear. All thought of purpose and engagement disappeared, as the terror she had known in Dallas swept back over her, accompanied by a desperate sense that she must do something to protect her children. In a letter to Joe Alsop on September 8, 1968, she said that she hoped never to love or care about anyone again. One month later, on October 20, she married Aristotle Onassis on the Greek island of Skorpios. It was a marriage conceived in terror, for, as her letter to Alsop made clear, she had no concern with love now. Onassis, with his unlimited resources, private island, and security force, could protect her and her children from the violence that threatened to destroy the entire Kennedy family.

The response of the American public was cruel. Headlines

and stories reviled Jackie for having tarnished the memory of her martyred husband. The implication, only thinly veiled, was that she had sold herself. How could she possibly have married this toad of a man? What reason could there be other than greed? The anger was frightening in its intensity. The heartache America had felt when Jackie stood at the door of *Air Force One*, her pink suit spattered with her husband's blood, was abruptly forgotten. So was the pride and admiration that surged when she marched with such courage down Pennsylvania Avenue. Guarding Jack's memory had been the thing that mattered most to her, and she had risked her life for it at his funeral. She would have died rather than defile it – and yet, as she sought to protect her children, that was exactly what America accused her of.

As always, Macmillan was there for her. At a moment when her countrymen turned on her, Macmillan, less than a year after they had shared the intoxication of renewed hope, offered Jackie reassurance that she had not betrayed Jack. On November 11, 1968, he wrote with wishes for her happiness, as well as the hope that she would continue to regard him as a friend. As always he spoke with indirection and consummate tact, expressing his admiration and respect for her by placing himself in the role of supplicant for her friendship. That the great moral figure in Jack's life understood her decision gave her comfort.

Jackie called Macmillan her lifebuoy – the person who intervened repeatedly to save her from drowning. He had supported her in the months after Jack's assassination, when she did not know if she had the strength to go on. For a brief moment in 1968, he had brought her back to life and hope. Four years later, he re-emerged at a time when John Jr, nearing his twelfth birthday, needed to know his father better. The Kennedy Macmillan had known was neither the apologists' saint nor the detractors' devil, and by Jackie's own account there was nothing in all those long years that moved her so much as the sight of the seventy-eight-year-old former Prime Minister reminiscing about Jack on American television, while young John, old enough to listen and understand, watched. In letters and conversations, Macmillan had never ceased to struggle with Jack, to press him to become the man and the leader he was capable of becoming had death not intervened. Macmillan could afford to be highly critical at times, for he saw and prized the very best in Kennedy. Nothing meant more to Jackie than for John to hear about his father from someone who, like she, had suffered at his hands yet understood, as the Skybolt Report made clear, that he had never intended to hurt them. As both she and Macmillan well knew, John's father had not been a perfect man, but he had had a core of goodness and decency. With Macmillan's help and her own, he had tried to be better. Now, the knowledge that her son could see and hear Macmillan talk of Jack brought a kind of peace.

In December 1972, Macmillan, his hand too shaky to write, dictated a letter thanking Jackie for her deeply moving message about watching the television program with John. He assured her that he had thought about her continuously all those years, and about all the 'anxieties, disasters and triumphs in which I have played a small but deeply sympathetic part.' To the end exquisitely reticent about personal matters, Macmillan emphasized that it was hard to convey how much Jackie's friendship and understanding had always meant to him, but given all that had passed between them he felt certain that she would be able to 'read within the lines of these stilted words.'

Their friendship continued for another fourteen years, until Macmillan's death at the age of ninety-two in 1986. Jacqueline Kennedy Onassis died of cancer in 1994, at the age of sixty-four. The time she once spoke of to Macmillan as 'the days of you and Jack' remained the best of her life.

Acknowledgments

My first and most important debt is to Helen Langley of the Bodleian Library at Oxford University. Early in my research, I contacted her because I knew that Jacqueline Kennedy had written some letters to Harold Macmillan, though at the time I had no idea that they would be of any particular importance. Helen Langley, in her reply, let me know that the letters were crucial and not to be overlooked, and went out of her way to facilitate my access to the letters, which were then still closed to researchers. I will never forget her face when we finally met in Oxford after I had seen the letters, and she asked whether I felt that the trip had been worthwhile. The letters were pivotal, and deeply influenced my understanding of both the personal and the political dynamics of the Kennedy presidency.

I am also greatly indebted to the archivists and staff at the John F. Kennedy Library in Boston, Massachusetts. The Kennedy Library, with its towering glass wall overlooking the water, is simply one of the most exciting places I have ever visited. It contains a vast and complicated collection that has been organized with immense care and intelligence. The archivists and staff were unfailingly generous with their patience and guidance. On more than one occasion, while I read and made countless photocopies, they agreed to remain open in driving snowstorms long after they had every reason to go home. As an undergraduate and graduate student, my field of specialization was Russian studies, so my work at the Kennedy Library was a particular delight. Mystery after mystery posed in long-ago seminars on Soviet politics and history was solved as I read documents marked 'Top Secret' and 'Eyes Only The

President.' Of the thousands of documents I found at the Kennedy Library, the ones that made the strongest impact on my understanding of Jacqueline Kennedy's story were the detailed memoranda of the conversations between Kennedy and Khrushchev in Vienna in 1961. Photographs and newsreels alone give the impression simply of a beautiful young woman and her dashing husband taking Europe by storm. The reality was strikingly different, and it was only as I watched Kennedy lose control of his meetings with Khrushchev and felt his mounting sense of alarm that I began to understand something of the tremendous pressure Jackie operated under in those years, and to grasp the full dimensions of her achievements. For that and so much more I thank the Kennedy Library, where I would like to single out Megan Desnoyers, June Payne, Maura Porter, Allan Goodrich, and James Hill for their many kindnesses.

Thanks too to the archivists and staff at the Lyndon Baines Johnson Library in Austin, Texas, where Linda Seelke guided me through the collection and made numerous invaluable suggestions. The collection has a richness and texture that is very much a reflection of Lyndon Johnson himself. It is as different from the Kennedy Library as Johnson was from Kennedy, and for this reason I am convinced that it is essential to work in both archives if one is to assemble anything like a complete picture of the Kennedy years. For this book, some of the most poignant material was to be found in Austin, where I read the Secret Service's internal report on the assassination, which included the extraordinary testimony of Jackie's agent, Clint Hill. The experience of listening to Hill vividly describe what he saw below him in the back seat of the presidential limousine as he lay outstretched atop the open car forever altered the way I thought of Jacqueline Kennedy. At the Johnson Library, in addition to Linda Seelke, I would like to offer special thanks to Bob Tissing, Alan Fisher, and Charlaine Burgess.

I am also grateful to the archivists and staff at the Library of Congress in Washington, D.C., where I have worked many times in the past. Although I examined a number of different collections for this book, I learned most from the Joseph Alsop

Papers. Alsop's letters and records offer a detailed glimpse into the vanished world of Georgetown in the early 1960s. A prolific letter-writer, Alsop made real to me a milieu in which it was by no means unusual for equal passion to be devoted to debates over military intervention in Vietnam and the proper placement of a monogram on a glass. At the Library of Congress, I am especially indebted to Jeffrey Flannery for his interest in my project.

In addition to these three institutions, where I conducted my most important research, I am grateful to the staffs of various other archives and libraries. These include the Franklin D. Roosevelt Library; the Massachusetts Historical Society; the Vassar College Library; the Beinecke Rare Book and Manuscript Library, Yale University; the John Gray Library at the Kent School; the Louis B. Mayer Library at the American Film Institute; Columbia University Library; the Smith College Library; and the Princeton University Library.

I would also like to thank the people I interviewed who were so generous with their time and insights. The names of those whose remarks are quoted or paraphrased in the text are cited in the notes.

This is my third book with Ion Trewin, my editor and publisher at Weidenfeld & Nicolson in London. I can no longer imagine my writing life without him at its center. Ion is an unfailing source of strength and sharp critical judgment. This book in particular has benefited enormously from his insights, suggestions, and criticism. Ion has a great editor's ability to inspire, to create the drive that makes a complex project possible. No one I know has more enthusiasm for a project he cares about – or more generosity of spirit when it comes to doing what is necessary to make it happen. He also makes the process great fun.

Allegra Huston, who first came into my life when she was a very young editor at Weidenfeld, has now edited five of my books. She knows the inside of my head better than I do, and she has the ability to find thoughts in there that I didn't know I had. She has countless gifts as an editor, but none greater than her capacity to give herself to the material completely.

Every line of a book seems to imprint itself on her brain to be retrieved at will. The result is that she has an unrivaled sense of structure. Allegra is relentless and brave. Added to this are her brilliance and imagination – and a gift for friendship that is the greatest talent of all.

This is my first book with Fred Hills at The Free Press, but I have done two other books at Simon & Schuster and it has felt like coming back to a very familiar place once again. Fred was enthusiastic about the project from the first and remained so all the way through. I am grateful to him for his many suggestions during the writing and after the first draft. I thank him for making it possible for me to undertake a project that has meant a great deal to me.

Lois Wallace has been my agent from the beginning and without her I would not have a career as a writer. She gave me some excellent advice when I was first considering this project, read the manuscript with great care, and made many suggestions. After so many years, a thank-you seems woefully inadequate.

I do not know how to begin to thank my husband David. Without him there would be no book. There is no one on earth more generous – and no one I could imagine it possible to love more.

Finally, to Mallet and Pierre: Your patience has not always been infinite, but you have done your best, I know. Tomorrow, Steep Rock!

Barbara Leaming
May 2001

Notes on Sources

The basic sources for reconstructing the activities of the President, the
First Lady and the people around them include the following: the
President's Appointment Books for January–June 1961, July–December
1961, January–June 1962, July–December 1962, January–June 1963, July–
November 1963; United States Secret Service records for the President,
the First Lady, and their children; Diary Record Books of the White
House Police for 1961, 1962, and 1963; United States Secret Service records
of Presidential Movements; United States Secret Service Appointment
Records, White House police post/gate logs, and United States Secret
Service Appointment Records, White House police attachments to
post/gate logs; White House telephone memoranda and toll tickets; trip
logs and flight records; Summary of Trips of President John Fitzgerald
Kennedy; and the Presidential Appointments Names Index. These records,
combined with the materials cited in the notes that follow, as well as
thousands of other pieces of evidence, including letters, memos, diaries,
photographs, movie and newsreel footage, and the testimony of witnesses,
allow one to follow the Kennedys day by day, hour by hour, often minute
by minute.

Abbreviations:
JFK = John Fitzgerald Kennedy
JBK = Jacqueline Bouvier Kennedy (also used after her marriage to
   Aristotle Onassis)
JFKL = John Fitzgerald Kennedy Library
LBJL = Lyndon Baines Johnson Library
FDRL = Franklin Delano Roosevelt Library
LC = Library of Congress
BLO = Bodleian Library, Oxford
MHS = Massachusetts Historical Society
BP = Blair Papers, University of Wyoming
UK = University of Kentucky

WCT = Warren Commission Testimony
SSIRT = Secret Service Internal Report Testimony

Publication details for books are given only on first citation.

Chapter 1: Modus Vivendi

1 departure: Secret Service Memorandum, From: President Elect Detail, Subject: The departure of Mrs John F. Kennedy from Palm Beach International Airport, West Palm Beach, Florida, on January 18, 1961, Date: January 19, 1961.

2 tended to be quiet and reserved: Larry Newman, author interview.

3 passed through the gate: Secret Service Memorandum, From: President Elect Detail, Subject: The departure of Mrs John F. Kennedy from Palm Beach International Airport, West Palm Beach, Florida, on January 18, 1961, Date: January 19, 1961.

5 Alsop's intervention: Joseph Alsop to JBK, August 4, 1960, LC; JBK to Joseph Alsop, n.d., LC.

5ff JBK's family background: John Davis, *The Bouviers*, Farrar, Straus & Giroux, New York, 1969; John Davis, *Jacqueline Bouvier: An Intimate Memoir*, John Wiley & Sons, New York, 1996; Kathleen Bouvier, *Black Jack Bouvier*, Pinnacle Books, New York, 1999; Mary Van Rensselaer Thayer, *Jacqueline Bouvier Kennedy*, Doubleday, New York, 1961; Carl Sferrazza Anthony, *As We Remember Her: Jacqueline Kennedy Onassis in the Words of her Friends and Family*, HarperCollins, New York, 1997; Gore Vidal, *Palimpsest*, Random House, New York, 1995.

5ff JBK's relationship with her mother: Betty Spalding, author interview.

7ff JBK's self-image and lack of self-confidence: JBK to Joseph Alsop, August 31, 1964, LC; Joseph Alsop to JBK, September 9, 1964, LC.

9 JBK meets JFK: Janet Auchincloss, interview, JFKL; Senator Albert Gore, Sr., interview, JFKL; Charles Bartlett, interview, JFKL.

9ff JBK's early relationship with JFK: Jane Suydam, author interview; Roland Evans, interview, JFKL; Dinah Bridge, interview, JFKL; Betty Spalding, author interview; William Douglas-Home, interview, JFKL; David Ormsby-Gore, interview, JFKL; Jean Mannix, interview, JFKL; Jewel Reed, author interview; Janet Auchincloss, interview, JFKL; Lem Billings, interview, JFKL; Charles Bartlett, interview, JFKL.

9 Inga Arvad: Inga Arvad, unpublished memoir, MHS; Inga Arvad correspondence with JFK, JFKL.

10 called off the engagement: Lem Billings, interview, JFKL; Charles Bartlett, interview, JFKL.

10 JFK's women: Lem Billings, interview, JFKL.

10–11 JFK's love of books: JBK to Joseph Alsop, January 14, 1967, LC.

10ff JFK's character: Charles Spalding, interview, JFKL; Dinah Bridge, interview, JFKL; Joseph Alsop, interview, JFKL; Arthur Krock, interview, JFKL; Lem Billings, interview, JFKL; Charles Bartlett, interview, JFKL.

11 'the worthiest ambition': John Buchan, *Memory Hold-the-Door*, Hodder & Stoughton, London, 1940. (US title: *Pilgrim's Way*).

11 'not of a kind': David Cecil, *The Young Melbourne*, Bobbs Merrill, New York, 1966.

11 JBK's knowledge of France: Hervé Alphand, interview, JFKL.

12 the best in her: JBK to Joseph Alsop, August 31, 1964, LC.

12 wired his parents: JFK to Rose Kennedy, September 15, 1953, in Amanda Smith, ed., *Hostage to Fortune: The Letters of Joseph P. Kennedy*, Viking, New York, 2001.

13 suggested that Jackie go on ahead: Jewel Reed, author interview.

13 'eyes filled with dreams': Jane Suydam, author interview.

13 did not expect a difficult marriage: Jane Suydam, author interview.

13 problems in early marriage: Dinah Bridge, interview, JFKL; Betty Spalding, author interview; Mary Pitcairn, interview, BP; Jewel Reed, author interview; Jane Suydam, author interview; Lem Billings, interview, JFKL.

13 change her appearance: William Walton, interview, BP.

14 Addison's disease: Vernon S. Dick, M.D., to William P. Herbst Jr, M.D., March 20, 1953; Dr William P. Herbst Jr, medical file on John F. Kennedy 1953–63; 'Management of Adrenocortical Insufficiency During Surgery,' *A.M.A. Archives of Surgery*, Volume 71, 1955; India Edwards, interview, LBJL; Janet Travell, interview, JFKL; Arthur Krock, interview, JFKL; Kay Stammers Menzies, interview, BP; Charles Spalding, interview, JFKL.

14 the operation: Roland Evans, interview, JFKL; Richard Cardinal Cushing, interview, JFKL; Janet Travell, interview, JFKL; Lem Billings, interview, JFKL; Charles Spalding, interview, JFKL; Charles Bartlett, interview, JFKL.

14 attentive care: Betty Spalding, author interview; Janet Auchincloss, interview, JFKL.

15 JFK's recuperation: Andrew Dazzi and John Harris, interview, JFKL; Janet Travell, interview, JFKL; Arthur Krock, interview, JFKL; Charles Bartlett, interview, JFKL.

15 1956 convention: William Douglas-Home, interview, JFKL;

Arthur Krock, interview, JFKL; Torbert Macdonald, interview, JFKL; Charles Spalding, interview, JFKL; Senator George Smathers, interview, JFKL.

15 exhausted: Charles Bartlett, interview, JFKL.

16 JFK in France: Senator George Smathers, interview, Senate Historical Office.

16 sent a male friend: Mary Ann Nordman, author interview.

16 'a toot': Betty Spalding, author interview.

16 'at once!': Betty Spalding, author interview.

17 did not 'demand' fidelity: Betty Spalding, author interview.

18 longing for power: Betty Spalding, author interview.

18 constantly on the road: JBK, interview, LBJL.

18–19 JBK and politics: Charles Spalding, interview, JFKL.

19 run from the room: Betty Spalding, author interview.

19 anxious waiting: Roy Heffernan, M.D., interview, JFKL.

19 birth of Caroline: Janet Auchincloss, interview, JFKL; Luella Hennessey, interview, JFKL; Maud Shaw, interview, JFKL.

19–20 Turnure affair: Florence Kater to Eleanor Roosevelt, April 30, 1959, and June 18, 1960, FDRL.

20 'This is your friend': confidential source, author interview.

20 Jackie complained: JBK to Joseph Alsop, n.d., LC.

20 pretended not to know: Jewel Reed, author interview.

21 knew full well: William Walton, interview, BP.

21 de Gaulle memoirs: Hervé Alphand, interview, JFKL.

22 'the kind of guy': Larry Newman, author interview.

22 Krock's warning: Arthur Krock, interview, BP.

23 arrives at Palm Beach International Airport: Secret Service Memorandum, From: President Elect Detail, Subject: The departure of Mrs John F. Kennedy from Palm Beach International Airport, West Palm Beach, Florida, on January 18, 1961, Date: January 19, 1961.

24 'deer in the headlights': Larry Newman, author interview.

25 to encourage foreign leaders: Angier Biddle Duke, interview, JFKL.

27 not recovered: JBK to Joseph Alsop, January 1, 1961, LC.

27 arrival in Washington: Secret Service Memorandum, From: President Elect Detail, Subject: The departure of Mrs John F. Kennedy from Palm Beach International Airport, West Palm Beach, Florida, on January 18, 1961, Date: January 19, 1961.

27 unable to stand: Mary Van Rensselaer Thayer, *Jacqueline Kennedy: The White House Years*, Little, Brown & Co., Boston, 1971.

27–8 JBK leaves reviewing stand: Janet Auchincloss, interview, JFKL; Charles Spalding, interview, JFKL.

28 Wheeler dinner: Jane Suydam, author interview; Arthur Krock, interview, JFKL.

28 Dexedrine: Mary Van Rensselaer Thayer, *Jacqueline Kennedy: The White House Years*.

29 target of her mother's lectures: Betty Spalding, author interview.

29 'absolutely terrified': Betty Spalding, author interview.

30 JFK on Inauguration day: Charles Spalding, interview, JFKL.

31 JBK's trip to England: Janet Auchincloss, interview, JFKL; Lem Billings, interview, JFKL.

31 waiting at the airport: Janet Auchincloss, interview, JFKL.

32 Joseph Kennedy as ambassador: Isaiah Berlin, interview, JFKL; Hugh Fraser, interview, JFKL; Arthur Krock, interview, JFKL.

32 the Kennedys in England: Dinah Bridge, interview, JFKL; Torbert Macdonald, interview, JFKL.

32–3 background on Kick: Hugh Fraser, interview, JFKL; Dinah Bridge, interview, JFKL; Betty Spalding, author interview; William Douglas-Home, interview, JFKL; Jewel Reed, author interview; Torbert Macdonald, interview, JFKL; Kathleen Kennedy correspondence with JFK, JFKL; Lynne McTaggart, *Kathleen Kennedy: Her Life and Times*, Doubleday, New York, 1983.

33 JFK and Kick: William Douglas-Home, interview, JFKL; Betty Spalding, author interview; Joseph Alsop, interview, JFKL.

33 death of Joe Jr: Arthur Krock, interview, JFKL.

33 'the only one': Betty Spalding, author interview.

34 'a substitute for Kick': Betty Spalding, author interview.

34 'They had wonderful': Betty Spalding, author interview.

34 'tomatoes' and 'the donkey': Betty Spalding, author interview.

34 JBK in the Kennedy family: Dinah Bridge, interview, JFKL; Betty Spalding, author interview; Mary Pitcairn, interview, BP; Jewel Reed, author interview; David Ormsby-Gore, interview, JFKL.

35 more flattering angle: Jewel Reed, author interview.

35 'I thought': Betty Spalding, author interview.

35 'star': Arthur Krock, interview, JFKL.

35 JBK and Rose Kennedy: Betty Spalding, author interview; Jewel Reed, author interview.

36 'two halves': Lem Billings, interview, JFKL.

36 'All men behaved' Betty Spalding, author interview.

37 'I would have thought': Jewel Reed, author interview.

37 'The first time': Betty Spalding, author interview.

38 Jack stays out late: Joseph Alsop to Flo Smith, January 26, 1961, LC; Joseph Alsop to Robert Kintner, January 29, 1961, LC; Joseph Alsop, interview, JFKL.

Chapter 2: The Presidency Begins

39 Mr West persuaded her: J. B. West, *Upstairs at the White House*, Coward, McCann & Geoghegan, New York, 1973.

40 made it a firm rule: Mary Barelli Gallagher, *My Life with Jacqueline Kennedy*, David McKay Co., New York, 1969.

41 soon came to love: JBK to Joseph Alsop, July 28, 1983, LC.

42 'wonderful between them': Betty Spalding, author interview.

42 JFK's debt to Franklin Roosevelt Jr: Roland Evans, interview, JFKL.

42 'sleep with anything': Betty Spalding, author interview.

43 excoriated Joe Kennedy: Joseph Alsop to Mrs Goodhue, December 10, 1963, LC; Joseph Alsop, interview #2, JFKL.

43 'a major influence': Joseph Alsop to Lady Elizabeth Cavendish, December 22, 1960, LC.

43 arrangements with Alsop: Jacqueline Kennedy to Joseph Alsop, January 1, 1961, LC.

44ff dinner party: Joseph Alsop, interview, JFKL; Joseph Alsop to Mrs James Flood, January 31, 1961, LC; Joseph Alsop to Ann Patten, January 23, 1961, LC; Joseph Alsop to Billy Patten, January 23, 1961, LC; White House file for January 22, 1961, dinner; Joseph Alsop, *I've Seen the Best of It*, W. W. Norton, New York, 1992.

45 California wines: Joseph Alsop to Mrs James Flood, January 31, 1961, LC.

47–8 background on Letitia Baldrige: Letitia Baldrige, interview, JFKL.

48–9 hiring of Pamela Turnure: Betty Spalding, author interview.

49 limited energies: Letitia Baldrige to Jessica Daves, February 4, 1961.

49 signs of restlessness: Charles Bartlett, interview, JFKL; Ralph Horton Jr, interview, JFKL.

50ff redecoration of family quarters: Joseph Karitas, interview, JFKL; Larry Arata, interview, JFKL.

50 'perfect for a small house': Apple Parish Bartlett and Susan Bartlett Crater, *Sister: The Life of Legendary American Decorator Mrs. Henry Parish II*, St Martin's Press, New York, 2000.

51 'severe enough': J. B. West, *Upstairs at the White House*.

51 complaining of exhaustion: Apple Parish Bartlett and Susan Bartlett Crater, *Sister: The Life of Legendary American Decorator Mrs. Henry Parish II*.

52 good-will gesture: Llewellyn Thompson to Dean Rusk, January 21, 1961; Dean Rusk to Llewellyn Thompson, January 23, 1961.

52 appointees: White House file for January 29, 1961, reception.

52 background on Lem Billings: *The Billings Collection*, privately printed.

53 neither she nor her friends took seriously: Betty Spalding, author interview.

54 implore the housepainters: Joseph Karitas, interview, JFKL.

55 devised a plan: Mrs Charles W. Engelhard Jr to Henry du Pont, n.d, LC.

55–7 background on White House restoration: JBK correspondence with David Finley, LC; Minutes of the Fine Arts Committee, LC; White House press releases; Mark Hampton, *Legendary Decorators of the Twentieth Century*, Doubleday, New York, 1992; Clark Clifford, *Counsel to the President*, Random House, New York, 1991; James Abbott and Elaine Rice, *Designing Camelot: The Kennedy White House Restoration*, Van Nostrand Reinhold, New York, 1998; John Walker, *Self-Portrait with Donors: Confessions of an Art Collector*, Little Brown & Co., Boston, 1974.

56 viewed her plan with alarm: Joseph Karitas, interview, JFKL.

57 'to replace unsuitable': Clark Clifford to JFK, March 11, 1961.

57 'beautiful again': Clark Clifford, *Counsel to the President*.

57 Boudin visit: Letitia Baldrige to JFK, February 9, 1961.

58 'symbol of cultural': Henry du Pont to David Finley, March 18, 1961, LC.

58 style of a single period: L. H. Butterfield and Julian P. Boyd, 'The White House as Symbol,' April 14, 1961, LC.

58 'the period of the completion of the White House in 1802': Henry du Pont to David Finley, March 18, 1961, LC.

58 'historic document ... patron': Henry du Pont to David Finley, March 18, 1961, LC.

59 Jack shouted: Letitia Baldrige, interview, JFKL.

59 dinner in honor of Johnson and Rayburn: White House file for February 9, 1961, dinner.

Chapter 3: Tell Me About Macmillan

60 Sulzberger luncheon: White House file for February 10, 1961, luncheon.

61 'unrelated and impersonal': Betty Spalding, author interview.

61–3 background on Glen Ora: Glen Ora file, Clifton Papers, JFKL.

63 Clark Clifford suggested: Clark Clifford, *Counsel to the President*.

63 his rides with Jackie: Janet Auchincloss, interview, JFKL.

64 to discuss strategies: memorandum drafted by McGeorge Bundy, 'The Thinking of the Soviet Leadership,' Cabinet Room, February 11, 1961. Background on situation with Soviets: Llewellyn Thompson to Dean Rusk, January 24, 1961; 'Current Intelligence Weekly Review,' January 26, 1961; Llewellyn Thompson to Dean

Rusk, February 1, 1961. Background on Kennedy–Khrushchev relationship: correspondence between the two leaders, including the then secret 'Pen Pal' letters. Khrushchev's first letter to Kennedy is dated November 9, 1960 and the last October 10, 1963. Also invaluable was the voluminous cable traffic between the U.S. embassy in Moscow and the State Department.

64 principal adversary: Isaiah Berlin, interview, JFKL.

65 did not take communion: Secret Service report cited in President's Appointments Book, Sunday, February 12, 1961.

66 Alsop's dinner party: Joseph Alsop, interview, JFKL; JBK to Joseph Alsop, February 15, 1961, LC; Joseph Alsop to Colin Falconer, March 10, 1961, LC.

66–7 David Cecil's anecdote: Joseph Alsop, interview, JFKL.

67 'strange man': Joseph Alsop, interview, JFKL.

67 always treasure the story: Joseph Alsop, interview, JFKL.

67–8 Ambassador Chagla event and aftermath: Letitia Baldrige to JFK, February 16, 1961; Letitia Baldrige to Evelyn Lincoln, February 16, 1961; Letitia Baldrige to JFK, February 17, 1961; John Sherman Cooper, interview, UK; JBK, interview, UK.

69 'on stage': Larry Newman, author interview.

69 Barbara Ward luncheon: Letitia Baldrige to JFK, February 4, 1961; Letitia Baldrige to JBK, February 9, 1961; Letitia Baldrige to JFK, February 16, 1961; Letitia Baldrige to JFK, February 17, 1961; Barbara Ward, interview, JFKL.

69 retreated to Glen Ora: Wilma Holness, interview, JFKL.

69–70 JBK's depressions: Lem Billings, interview, JFKL; Betty Spalding, author interview; Max Jacobson, unpublished memoir, MHS.

70 Teddy Kennedy realized: *The Billings Collection.*

71 'He couldn't get': Betty Spalding, author interview.

72 two of the secretaries: Larry Newman, author interview.

72 free to turn Kennedy down: Larry Newman, author interview.

72 'If you didn't': Susan Stankrauff, author interview.

72 'Friend, I'm too': confidential source, author interview.

73 'some of them had': Larry Newman, author interview.

74 'It's not': Larry Newman, author interview.

74 made a presentation: David Finley to Members Commission of Fine Arts, February 24, 1961, LC; Mrs Charles W. Engelhard Jr to Henry du Pont, n.d., LC; Press Release, February 23, 1961, LC.

74 enlisted du Pont: JBK to David Finley, March 11, 1961.

74 dinner dance: White House file for March 15, 1961, dinner.

76 asking Jack: Letitia Baldrige to Evelyn Lincoln, February 20, 1961.

77 'animated and happy': J. B. West, *Upstairs at the White House.*

77 'What have you been doing': Maud Shaw, *White House Nannie*, New American Library, New York, 1966.

78 'greatest success': Betty Spalding, author interview.

78 'to stay out of sight': Susan Stankrauff, author interview.

78 'pouting a little': Susan Stankrauff, author interview.

79 'Oh, he was': Betty Spalding, author interview.

79 his father's puppet: Charles Spalding, interview, JFKL.

79 ordered Jack to take his place: Betty Spalding, author interview.

79 invasion plans: Colonel Jack Hawkins to J. D. Esterline, January 4, 1961; C.I.A., 'Evaluation of Possible Courses of Action in Cuba,' January 16, 1961; C. Tracy Barnes to J. D. Esterline, January 18, 1961; 'Meeting on Cuba,' memo, January 22, 1961; 'Conclusions of Dean Rusk's Meeting on Cuba,' January 22, 1961; General Andrew Goodpaster, Memo of Conference of President Kennedy and Joint Chiefs of Staff, January 25, 1961; Richard Bissell, memo, 'Concept of the Operation,' January 26, 1961; General L. L. Lemnitzer to Robert McNamara, January 27, 1961; 'Memorandum of Discussion of Cuba,' January 28, 1961; JFK to Dean Rusk, January 31, 1961; McGeorge Bundy to JFK, 'Memorandum of February 8, 1961, Meeting with President Kennedy,' February 8, 1961; McGeorge Bundy to JFK, February 18, 1961; National Security Action Memoranda, March 11, 1961; Arthur Schlesinger to JFK, March 15, 1961; McGeorge Bundy to JFK, March 15, 1961; General David Gray, notes on meeting of March 15, 1961; General David Gray, notes on meeting of March 16, 1961; General David Gray, notes on meeting of March 29, 1961; General David Gray, notes on meeting of April 6, 1961; General David Gray, notes on meeting of April 11, 1961; General David Gray, notes on meeting of April 12, 1961; C.I.A., 'Cuban Operation,' April 12, 1961; McGeorge Bundy to Dean Rusk, April 13, 1961.

79 background on invasion: Peter Wyden, *Bay of Pigs: The Untold Story*, Simon & Schuster, New York, 1979; Peter Kornbluh, ed., *Bay of Pigs Declassified: The Secret C.I.A. Report on the Invasion of Cuba*, New Press, New York, 1998; Richard Bissell, *Confessions of a Cold Warrior*, Yale University Press, New Haven, 1996; Chester Bowles, *Promises to Keep*, Harper & Row, New York, 1971; Richard Goodwin, *Remembering America*, Little, Brown & Co., Boston, 1988; Arthur Schlesinger, *A Thousand Days*, Houghton Mifflin Co., Boston, 1965; Michael Beschloss, *The Crisis Years: Kennedy and Khrushchev 1960–1963*, HarperCollins, New York, 1991.

80 violated prior U.S. commitments: Chester Bowles to Dean Rusk, March 31, 1961.

80 'binding in law and conscience': Chester Bowles to Dean Rusk,

March 31, 1961.

80 whether an invasion could succeed: General Lyman Lemnitzer, notes of January 28, 1961 meeting with JFK, Dean Rusk, Joint Chiefs of Staff, et al., quoted in Naval Intelligence report, 'Review of Record of Proceedings Related to the Cuban Situation,' May 5, 1961.

80 'first dramatic foreign policy initiative': Arthur Schlesinger Jr to JFK, February 11, 1961.

80 additional cover: General David Gray's account of March 11, 1961 meeting with JFK, Lyndon Johnson, et al., in his May 9, 1961 Summary Notes.

80 revised Zapata plan: 'Revised Cuban Operation,' March 15, 1961; General L. L. Lemnitzer to Robert McNamara, March 15, 1961; McGeorge Bundy to JFK, March 15, 1961; General David Gray, Summary Notes, May 9, 1961.

81 'The Cuban adventure': Chester Bowles to Dean Rusk, March 31, 1961.

81 'not greater than': Chester Bowles to Dean Rusk, March 31, 1961.

82 'hadn't gone through': Edwin Guthman and Jeffrey Shulman, eds., *Robert Kennedy: In His Own Words*, Bantam Books, New York, 1988.

82 shadow of the past: Isaiah Berlin, interview, JFKL; Henry Brandon, interview, JFKL; Charles Spalding, interview, JFKL.

Chapter 4: A Family Drama

84 giant feather: Larry Newman, author interview.

86 'really wanted to do this': Michael Beschloss, *The Crisis Years: Kennedy and Khrushchev, 1960–1963*.

86 detected Joe's influence: Michael Beschloss, *The Crisis Years: Kennedy and Khrushchev, 1960–1963*.

86 polled his senior advisers: General David Gray, Summary Notes on meeting of May 9, 1961.

86 'a fruitless theoretical argument': Peter Wyden, *Bay of Pigs: The Untold Story*.

86 'become our Hungary': Arthur Schlesinger Jr to JFK, April 5, 1961.

87 background on Lady Dorothy Macmillan: Alistair Horne, *Harold Macmillan*, 2 vols., Viking, New York, 1989; Robert Rhodes James, *Robert Boothby: A Portrait of Churchill's Ally*, Viking, New York, 1991.

87ff Macmillan visit: Prime Minister's Diaries, April 4–9, 1961, BLO; Dean Rusk to American Embassy London, January 30, 1961; American Embassy London to Dean Rusk, February 2, 1961;

JFK to Harold Macmillan, February 23, 1961; Dean Rusk to JFK, March 4, 1961; Briefing Book for Macmillan visit, March 21, 1961; Scenario Macmillan Visit, March 28, 1961; Harold Macmillan to JFK, April 7, 1961; McGeorge Bundy to Charles Bohlen, May 4, 1961; David Bruce to Dean Rusk, May 10, 1961; Harold Caccia to George Ball, May 11, 1961; Background and Objectives of Visit, March 21, 1961; Dean Rusk to American Embassy France, April 8, 1961; memoranda of conversations, JFK–Macmillan: April 5, 1961, 11 a.m.; April 6, 1961, 3:45 p.m.; April 6, 1961, at the British Embassy dinner; and April 8, 1961, 10 a.m.

87 'being shot through ... ballet dancer': David Bruce to the Department of State, December 12, 1961.

88 'cocky young Irishman': Henry Brandon, interview, JFKL.

88 'rather an old horse': Harold Macmillan to JBK, February 14, 1964, BLO.

89 fundamental principles: Harold Macmillan to JFK, December 19, 1960.

89 use his own connection: Harold Macmillan to JFK, January 23, 1961; JFK to Harold Macmillan, February 2, 1961.

89 Laos: 'Laos and U.S.–U.S.S.R. Relations,' memorandum of conversation between JFK, Andrei Gromyko, et al., March 27, 1961; Llewellyn Thompson to Dean Rusk, April 1, 1961; L. D. Battle to Ralph Dungan, April 4, 1961; Harold Macmillan to JFK, April 28, 1961; JFK to Harold Macmillan, April 29, 1961; Charles Bohlen, interview, JFKL.

89 Key West meeting: Prime Minister's Diaries, March 24–26, 1961, BLO; Hervé Alphand, interview, JFKL; Charles Bohlen, interview, JFKL; Chester Bowles to Dean Rusk, March 24, 1961; Charles Bohlen to Chester Bowles, March 25, 1961; Harold Macmillan to JFK, March 26, 1961; JFK and Harold Macmillan, Joint Communiqué, March 26, 1961; Harold Caccia to JFK, March 27, 1961; McGeorge Bundy to JFK, April 4, 1961.

89 talk freely: Harold Macmillan to JBK, February 14, 1964, BLO.

90 background on Ormsby-Gore: David Ormsby-Gore, interview, JFKL.

90 appointment of Ormsby-Gore: Dean Rusk to JFK, May 25, 1961; David Ormsby-Gore to JFK, May 18, 1961.

90 'second home': Kathleen Kennedy to JFK, July 29, 1943, in Amanda Smith, ed., *Hostage to Fortune: The Letters of Joseph P. Kennedy.*

90 strong cocktails: Harold Macmillan, *Pointing the Way 1959–1961*, Harper & Row, New York, 1972.

90 'fallen': Harold Macmillan to JBK, February 18, 1964.

90 accept Macmillan's advice: Hervé Alphand, interview, JFKL.

91 budding friendship: Harold Macmillan to JFK, May 25, 1961.

91 Eisenhower on Laos: JFK, Notes on Meeting with Eisenhower, January 19, 1961; Robert McNamara to JFK, January 24, 1961; Clark Clifford to JFK, January 24, 1961.

91 urge Eisenhower to refrain: Harold Macmillan to Dwight Eisenhower, April 9, 1961; Harold Caccia to JFK, April 9, 1961.

92 Inga Arvad: Inga Arvad, unpublished memoir, MHS; Inga Arvad F.B.I. files; Frank Waldrop, 'JFK and the Nazi Spy'; Inga Arvad correspondence with JFK, JFKL.

93 tea for Lady Dorothy Macmillan: White House file for April 5, 1961, tea.

93 negotiations for summit with Khrushchev: David Bruce, diary entry, January 5, 1961; 'Current Intelligence Weekly Review,' January 19, 1961; Llewellyn Thompson to Dean Rusk, January 28, 1961; JFK to Nikita Khrushchev, February 22, 1961; Llewellyn Thompson to Dean Rusk, March 10, 1961; Llewellyn Thompson to Dean Rusk, April 1, 1961; Llewellyn Thompson to Dean Rusk, April 10, 1961; Llewellyn Thompson to Dean Rusk, April 11, 1961.

93 'get acquainted': Dean Rusk to Llewellyn Thompson, April 5, 1961.

94 while she rode: Eve Fout, author interview.

94 Spalding's role: Charles Spalding, interview, JFKL.

94 JFK asks Spalding's opinion: Charles Spalding interview, JFKL.

95 press conference: Public Papers of the Presidents of the United States, John F. Kennedy, 1961.

95 meeting later that afternoon: General David Gray, Summary Notes on April 12, 1961 meeting of JFK, Rusk, Bissell et al., May 9, 1961.

96 numerous books and documents: Briefing Papers for Karamanlis visit, April 17–20, 1961, annotated by JFK.

97 Initial reports: Admiral Clark to the Joint Chiefs, April 15, 1961; Admiral Dennison to the Joint Chiefs, April 15, 1961; Colonel Beerli, Memo for the Record, April 15, 1961.

98 Adlai Stevenson: Adlai Stevenson to Dean Rusk, April 16, 1961, 5 p.m.; Adlai Stevenson to Dean Rusk, April 16, 1961, 6 p.m.

98 retaliatory move in Berlin: Edwin Guthman and Jeffrey Shulman, eds., *Robert Kennedy: In His Own Words*; Charles Bohlen, interview, JFKL; Nikita Khrushchev to JFK, April 18, 1961; JFK to Nikita Khrushchev, April 18, 1961; Nikita Khrushchev to JFK, April 22, 1961.

99 he called Bobby: Edwin Guthman and Jeffrey Shulman, eds., *Robert Kennedy: In His Own Words*.

100 venereal infection: Dr William Herbst Jr, medical file on John
       F. Kennedy 1953–63.

100 Rusk's 9 p.m. call: Admiral Arleigh Burke, notes of conversation
       with JFK, May 16, 1961.

100 Stevenson's angry words: Adlai Stevenson to Dean Rusk, April
       16, 1961, 6 p.m.; Adlai Stevenson to Dean Rusk, April 16, 1961,
       7 p.m.

101 'I'm not signed on': Arthur Schlesinger, *A Thousand Days*.

101 paced the bedroom: Arthur Schlesinger, *A Thousand Days*.

101 Rusk's 4:30 a.m. call: General C. P. Cabell to General Maxwell
       D. Taylor, May 9, 1961.

102ff Karamanlis visit: Constantine Karamanlis, interview, JFKL; Ellis
       Briggs to Department of State, March 12, 1961; Department of
       State Memorandum of Conversation, Subject: Meeting of the
       Prime Minister with the President, April 19, 1961.

102 administered penicillin: Dr William Herbst Jr, medical file on
       John F. Kennedy 1953–63.

103 'rather be called': Edwin Guthman and Jeffrey Shulman, eds.,
       Robert Kennedy: In His Own Words.

103 Karamanlis luncheon: White House file for April 17, 1961,
       luncheon.

Chapter 5: The Magic Is Lost

105 bad news: McGeorge Bundy to JFK, April 18, 1961.

105–6 Congressional Reception: White House file for April 18, 1961,
       Congressional Reception.

106 situation at Red Beach: Rear Admiral John Clark to Admiral
       Robert Dennison, April 18, 1961, 5:12 p.m.

106 burned tanks and trucks: Rear Admiral John Clark to Admiral
       Robert Dennison, April 18, 1961, 5:12 p.m.

107 message from the beachhead: Rear Admiral John Clark to
       Admiral Robert Dennison, April 18, 1961, 11:52 p.m.

107 ordered six unmarked jets: Joint Chiefs of Staff to Admiral
       Robert Dennison, April 19, 1961.

108 Kennedy on Eisenhower: Constantine Karamanlis, interview,
       JFKL.

109 Stevenson's report: Adlai Stevenson to JFK and Dean Rusk,
       April 19, 1961.

109 She was reminded: Rose Fitzgerald Kennedy, *Times to Remember*,
       Doubleday, New York, 1974.

110 rested his head . . . put his arms around Jackie: Michael Beschloss,
       The Crisis Years: Kennedy and Khrushchev, 1960–1963.

111 as though he were dying: Rose Fitzgerald Kennedy, *Times to
       Remember*.

111 porcelain snuffbox: Lem Billings, interview, JFKL.

111–12 evening with Karamanlis: Constantine Karamanlis, interview, JFKL.

112 invitation to JBK: Department of State, telegram, May 27, 1961; Constantine Karamanlis to President Kennedy, July 24, 1961.

112 'acted as if': Arthur Krock, interview, JFKL.

113 poured out all that had happened: Rose Fitzgerald Kennedy, *Times to Remember*.

113 'complete victory': Wymberley Coerr to Dean Rusk, April 10, 1961.

113 'no further word': Wymberley Coerr to Dean Rusk, April 10, 1961.

113 Kennedy's reaction: Robert McNamara to General Lyman Lemnitzer, April 20, 1961.

113 'shattered': Chester Bowles, Notes on Cuban Crisis, April 20, 1960.

113 'an acute shock': Chester Bowles, Notes on Cuban Crisis, April 20, 1960.

113 'amateur': Edwin Guthman and Jeffrey Shulman, eds., *Robert Kennedy: In His Own Words*.

113 'Almost without exception': Chester Bowles, Notes on Cuban Crisis, April 20, 1960.

113 'he was really': Fred Dutton, interview, JFKL.

113 'beaten off': Robert Kennedy to JFK, April 19, 1961.

113 'a genuine sense': Chester Bowles diary entry, quoted in David Halberstam, *The Best and the Brightest*, Random House, New York, 1972.

114 'not inexhaustible': The Public Papers of the Presidents of the United States: John F. Kennedy, 1961.

114 'I didn't want': Richard Goodwin, *Remembering America*, Little Brown & Co., Boston, 1988.

115 'the atmosphere': Chester Bowles, Notes on Cuban Crisis, April 22, 1961.

115 'fire eaters': Chester Bowles, Notes on Cuban Crisis, April 22, 1961.

115 'I felt again': Chester Bowles, Notes on Cuban Crisis, April 22, 1961.

115–16 conferred with Eisenhower: Richard Reeves, *President Kennedy*, Simon & Schuster, New York, 1994.

117 Chuck, too: Charles Spalding, interview, JFKL.

117 'How can I': Betty Spalding, author interview.

117 'She was undone': Betty Spalding, author interview.

117 grave trouble: Chester Bowles to Kenneth O'Donnell, May 12, 1961.

118 impact of Bay of Pigs on JFK and JBK: Joseph Alsop, interview, JFKL.

118 Bourguiba visit: White House file, May 3, 1961.

118 'the first reactions': Arthur Schlesinger Jr to JFK, May 3, 1961.

119 'Kennedy has lost': Arthur Schlesinger Jr to JFK, May 3, 1961.

119 Khrushchev's response: Chester Bowles, interview, JFKL.

119 told Charles de Gaulle: JFK to Charles de Gaulle, May 5, 1961.

119 Cuba complicates Khrushchev meeting: Harold Caccia to McGeorge Bundy, April 24, 1961.

119 complained privately: McGeorge Bundy to JFK, May 16, 1961.

120 Judith Campbell: 'Alleged Assassination Plots Involving Foreign Leaders, An Interim Report of the Select Committee to Study Governmental Operations with Respect to Intelligence Activities, United States Senate,' United States Government Printing Office, Washington, 1975; Judith Campbell Exner, *My Story*, Grove Press, New York, 1977; Courtney Evans to Alan Belmont, 'Subject: Judith E. Campbell, Associate of Hoodlums, Criminal Intelligence Matter,' March 20, 1962, F.B.I. file.

120 'he would have gone to bed': Larry Newman, author interview.

121ff background on Max Jacobson: Patrick O'Neal, author interview.

121 the grotesque illusion: Patrick O'Neal, author interview.

121 JFK and Jacobson: Max Jacobson, unpublished memoir, MHS.

122 JFK's visit to Jacobson's office: Max Jacobson, unpublished memoir.

124 'took a lot of strain': Betty Spalding, author interview.

124 Canada visit: Angier Biddle Duke, interview, JFKL; Letitia Baldrige, interview, JFKL.

124 enthusiastically received: Letitia Baldrige, author interview.

125 'this Goddamned': Richard Reeves, *President Kennedy*.

126 ducked the phone calls: Burke Marshall, interview, JFKL.

126 'Get 'em!': John Siegenthaler, interview, JFKL.

127 Jacobson visits White House: Max Jacobson, unpublished memoir, MHS.

127 lack of control: Betty Spalding, author interview.

127 impeded sexual performance: Betty Spalding, author interview.

127 treats JFK: Max Jacobson, unpublished memoir, MHS.

Chapter 6: Hall of Mirrors

130ff French trip: JFK to Charles de Gaulle, February 2, 1961; JFK to Charles de Gaulle, February 23, 1961; Walter Stoessel Jr to Ralph Dungan, February 27, 1961; McGeorge Bundy to JFK, April 5, 1961; Harold Macmillan to JFK, April 28, 1961; Adlai Stevenson to JFK, May 24, 1961; McGeorge Bundy, Memorandum of Conversation with Ambassador Caccia, May

12, 1962; JFK to Harold Macmillan, May 22, 1961; Harold Macmillan to JFK, May 25, 1961; Talking Points for President, May 27, 1961; JFK to McGeorge Bundy, May 29, 1961; McGeorge Bundy to JFK, May 30, 1961; Martin (Geneva) to JFK, May 31, 1961; Charles Bohlen, interview, JFKL.

130 'Inept': Hervé Alphand, *L'étonnement d'être, Journal 1939–1973*, Fayard, Paris, 1977.

130–1 background on de Gaulle: Confidential Background Paper, President's Visit to de Gaulle, May 31–June 2, 1961, De Gaulle's Personality, Motivations and Essential Philosophy.

131ff the Kennedys' reception: Hervé Alphand, interview, JFKL; Charles Bohlen, interview, JFKL; Angier Biddle Duke, interview, JFKL; Letitia Baldrige, interview, JFKL.

131ff events of visit: Daily Programs and Scenarios; Security Schedules.

131 'given up all ambition': Memorandum of Conversation, President's Visit, Paris, June 1, 1961.

133 'upset and lost ... reason to despair': Hervé Alphand, *L'étonnement d'être, Journal 1939–1973*.

133 De Gaulle's view of Kennedy: Charles de Gaulle, *Memoirs of Hope: Renewal and Endeavor*, Simon & Schuster, New York, 1971.

133ff JFK's meetings with de Gaulle: Ambassador Gavin to Chester Bowles, May 31, 1961; memoranda of conversations, JFK–de Gaulle: May 31, 1961, 10:30 a.m.; May 31, 1961, 2:50 p.m.; June 1, 1961, 10 a.m.; June 1, 1961, 3:30 p.m.; June 2, 1961, 10:30 a.m.; June 2, 1961, 11:30 a.m.; June 2, 1961, 3:45 p.m; Talking Points Reviewing Conversations Between President Kennedy and President de Gaulle (May 31–June 2, 1961); Memorandum of Conversation, June 1, 1961, 3:45 p.m., Bohlen, Bundy, et al.

135 military involvement in Southeast Asia: Hervé Alphand, interview, JFKL.

135 'probably because': Kenneth O'Donnell and David Powers, *Johnny, We Hardly Knew Ye*, Little Brown & Co., Boston, 1972.

136 'Well, I'm dazzled': Hugh Sidey, *John F. Kennedy, President*, Atheneum, New York, 1964.

136 Jacobson's visits: Max Jacobson, unpublished memoir, MHS.

137 Power ... the single theme: Don Cook, *Charles de Gaulle: A Biography*, G. P. Putnam's Sons, New York, 1983.

142 talks ... gone well: Charles de Gaulle to JFK, June 3, 1961; JFK to Charles de Gaulle, June 3, 1961; JFK to Charles de Gaulle, June 10, 1961; Charles de Gaulle to JFK, June 26, 1961.

142 'a great future': memorandum of conversation, JFK–de Gaulle, June 2, 1961, 11:30 a.m.

142ff Vienna visit: Program and Scenario for Vienna Visit; Harold

Caccia to McGeorge Bundy, April 24, 1961; Harold Macmillan to JFK, April 27, 1961; Llewellyn Thompson to Dean Rusk, May 6, 1961; Nikita Khrushchev to JFK, May 16, 1961; Department of State Scope Paper, 'President's Meeting with Khrushchev,' May 23, 1961; Department of State Talking Points for President's Meeting with Khrushchev, May 23, 1961; Adlai Stevenson to JFK, May 24, 1961; Llewellyn Thompson to Dean Rusk, May 24, 1961; Department of State Background Paper, 'Soviet Aims and Expectations President's Meeting with Khrushchev,' May 25, 1961; Llewellyn Thompson to Dean Rusk, May 25, 1961; Allan Lightner to Dean Rusk, May 25, 1961; Mike Mansfield to JFK, May 26, 1961; Llewellyn Thompson to Dean Rusk, May 27, 1961; Memorandum for the President, June 2, 1961; Special Background Paper, 'Line of Approach to Khrushchev,' June 1, 1961; Biographic Briefing Book, President Kennedy's Meeting with Khrushchev, Vienna; George Kennan to Dean Rusk, June 2, 1961; Foy Kohler, interview, JFKL; Charles Bohlen, interview, JFKL; Peter Lisagor, interview, JFKL; Paul Nitze, *From Hiroshima to Glasnost*, Grove Weidenfeld, New York, 1989; Charles Bohlen, *Witness to History*, W. W. Norton, New York, 1973; Dean Rusk, *As I Saw It*, W. W. Norton, New York, 1990.

142   highly volatile: Allan Lightner to Dean Rusk, May 25, 1961.

142   'like a tomcat': Meeting between Eric Johnston and N. Khrushchev, Foreign Service Dispatch, October 10, 1958.

142   swelling of the vein: Memorandum for the President, June 2, 1961.

143   'If the meeting': Mike Mansfield to JFK, May 26, 1961.

143   'skilled at getting': Memorandum for the President, June 2, 1961.

143   Cuba complicates meeting with Khrushchev: Khrushchev to JFK, April 18, 1961; JFK to Khrushchev, April 18, 1961; Khrushchev to JFK, April 22, 1961; Harold Caccia to McGeorge Bundy, April 24, 1961; Llewellyn Thompson to Dean Rusk, May 4, 1961; Dean Rusk to Llewellyn Thompson, May 6, 1961; Memorandum of Conversation JFK–Ambassador Menshikov, May 16, 1961; Department of State to All Diplomatic Posts, May 18, 1961; Llewellyn Thompson to Dean Rusk, May 24, 1961.

143   'as a sign ... young man': Chester Bowles, interview, JFKL.

143   'would send in': Chester Bowles, interview, JFKL.

145   psychological profile: A. Gromyko to N. S. Khrushchev, Soviet Embassy Profile of John F. Kennedy, August 3, 1960.

146ff   talks with Khrushchev: memoranda of conversations, JFK–Khrushchev: June 3, 1961, 12:45 p.m.; June 3, 1961, 3 p.m.; June

4, 1961, 10:15 a.m.; June 4, 1961, luncheon; June 4, 1961, 3:15 p.m.; Talking Points Reviewing Conversations between President Kennedy and Chairman Khrushchev, June 3–4, 1961; Dean Rusk, Summary of Talks, June 4, 1961; Dean Rusk, Summary of Talks, June 5, 1961; Memorandum of Conversation with the President and the Congressional Leadership, June 6, 1961; Meeting of the Policy Planning Council, June 7, 1961; Report Department of State to All Diplomatic and Consular Posts, June 8, 1961; Department of State, Talking Points Reviewing Conversations Between President Kennedy and Chairman Khrushchev, June 12, 1961.

146 'drawn into a sort': Charles Bohlen, interview, JFKL.

146 'out of his depth': Charles Bohlen, interview, JFKL.

147 Jackie in Vienna: Revised Program for the Visit of Mrs John F. Kennedy to Vienna, Austria, June 2, 1961.

147 pale and exhausted: Paul Nitze, *From Hiroshima to Glasnost*.

147 'Not too well': Evelyn Lincoln, *My Twelve Years with John F. Kennedy*, David McKay Co., New York, 1965.

147 Khrushchev's opinion of JBK: Nikita Khrushchev, *Khrushchev Remembers*, Little Brown & Co., Boston, 1974.

150 'slug-fest of words': Mike Mansfield to JFK, May 26, 1961.

150 'Then there will be war': Dean Rusk, *As I Saw It*.

Chapter 7: In Her Own Right

152 Long afterward: Harold Macmillan to JBK, February 18, 1964, BLO.

152ff London visit: Prime Minister's Diaries, April 4–5, 1961, BLO; Harold Caccia to McGeorge Bundy, April 11, 1961; McGeorge Bundy to Harold Caccia, April 14, 1961; Harold Caccia to McGeorge Bundy, April 15, 1961; Harold Caccia to McGeorge Bundy, April 19, 1961; McGeorge Bundy to Harold Caccia, April 21, 1961; Harold Caccia to McGeorge Bundy, April 24, 1961; Harold Caccia to McGeorge Bundy, May 19, 1961; McGeorge Bundy to Harold Caccia, May 20, 1961; Harold Caccia to McGeorge Bundy, May 22, 1961; JFK to Harold Macmillan, May 22, 1961; JFK and Harold Macmillan, Joint Communiqué, June 5, 1961; McGeorge Bundy to Lucius Battle, June 8, 1961; McGeorge Bundy to JFK, June 9, 1961; Dinah Bridge, interview, JFKL; Joseph Alsop, interview, JFKL; William Douglas-Home, interview, JFKL; David Ormsby-Gore, interview, JFKL; British Program and Scenario for Visit of President Kennedy, June 4–5, 1961; McGeorge Bundy to Dean Rusk, n.d.

153 'Mr President': Alistair Horne, *Harold Macmillan*, vol. 2.

153 'tactical': Harold Macmillan, *Pointing the Way, 1959–1961*.

153 'an act': Macmillan's personal diary, June 11, 1961, quoted in Harold Macmillan, *Pointing the Way, 1959–1961*.

153 'because of his human reactions ... theoretical': Memorandum of Conversation, JFK and Harold Macmillan, April 6, 1961.

153 'get going some kind': David Ormsby-Gore, interview, JFKL.

153 'completely overwhelmed ... Hitler': Harold Macmillan to Queen Elizabeth, September 15, 1961, quoted in Alistair Horne, *Harold Macmillan*, vol. 2.

154 private luncheon: Harold Caccia to McGeorge Bundy, May 22, 1961.

155 Jack valued Ormsby-Gore's: Edwin Guthman and Jeffrey Shulman, eds., *Robert Kennedy: In His Own Words*.

155 JBK's Greek trip: Angier Biddle Duke, Memorandum of Conversation with Prime Minister Karamanlis, April 25, 1961; Angier Biddle Duke to JBK, April 27, 1961; Letitia Baldrige to Angier Biddle Duke, May 5, 1961; Letitia Baldrige to Pierre Salinger, May 27, 1961; Embassy (Athens) to McGeorge Bundy, May 31, 1961; Bennett (Athens) to Embassy (London), June 5, 1961; Constantine Karamanlis to JFK, July 24, 1961; JFK to Constantine Karamanlis, August 8, 1961; Schedule for 1961 Greek Trip.

156 lent him their house: Charles Wrightsman to JFK, June 9, 1961.

156 entourage: *Air Force One* Passenger Lists: Flight Andrews Air Force Base, Maryland, to West Palm Beach, Florida, June 8, 1961; West Palm Beach, Florida, to Andrews Air Force Base, Maryland, June 12, 1961; Charles Spalding, interview, JFKL.

157 nearly unbearable: Janet Travell, interview, JFKL.

158 Alsop's visit to Glen Ora: Joseph Alsop, interview, JFKL.

158 'not a simple viral infection': Janet Travell, interview, JFKL.

159ff Ayub visit: Program and Scenario for State Visit Ayub Khan, July 11–18, 1961; National Intelligence Estimate Prospects for Pakistan, July 5, 1961; Briefing Papers for Visit of Ayub Khan; State Department, Biography of Ayub Khan, July 6, 1961; memorandum of conversation, JFK–Ayub, July 11, 1961; Richard Goodkin to Evelyn Lincoln, July 11, 1961; Elizabeth Carpenter, interview, LBJL; Angier Biddle Duke, interview, JFKL.

160 Johnson argued: Memorandum of Conversation, Vice-President Johnson and President Ayub, May 20, 1961.

160–2 Mount Vernon dinner: Program for the State Dinner at Mount Vernon, July 11, 1961; White House file for Mount Vernon Dinner; Letitia Baldrige to JFK, Random Notes on the Pakistan Dinner, n.d.; Letitia Baldrige, interview, JFKL.

161 liked to see attention: Angier Biddle Duke, interview, JFKL.

166 'She knew': Larry Newman, author interview.

166–8 Berlin crisis: George McGhee to Foy Kohler, June 21, 1961; Memorandum of Conversation JFK–Aleksey Adzhubey, June 26, 1961; Dean Acheson to JFK, June 28, 1961; JFK to Charles de Gaulle, June 30, 1961; JFK to McGeorge Bundy, July 5, 1961; David Bruce to Dean Rusk, July 17, 1961; Joseph Alsop, interview, JFKL; Foy Kohler, interview, JFKL; David Ormsby-Gore, interview, JFKL.

166 'What could we do ... attack': Bundy memos, file 7/61.

166 'The prospect': JFK to Eleanor Roosevelt, July 28, 1961, FDRL.

166 'There is one area': Walter Rostow to Robert McNamara, April 24, 1961.

166 'I believe it': Robert Komer to JFK, July 20, 1961.

166 'a horror': Charles Bartlett, interview, JFKL.

167 'Our central problem': JFK to Harold Macmillan, July 20, 1961.

167 press for negotiations: Harold Macmillan to JFK, July 23, 1961.

168 Berlin Wall: Meetings, Berlin Steering Group, August 15, 1961, and August 17, 1961; JFK to Willy Brandt, August 18, 1961; Joseph Alsop, interview, JFKL; Foy Kohler, interview, JFKL.

168 resumption of underground nuclear testing: National Security Action Memorandum no. 87, September 5, 1961; JFK to Harold Macmillan, September 6, 1961; Harold Macmillan to JFK, September 7, 1961; JFK to Harold Macmillan, September 7, 1961.

168 to propose talks: Dean Rusk to Llewellyn Thompson, September 3, 1961.

168 Abel's visit: Elie Abel, interview, JFKL.

169 'Why would anyone': Elie Abel, interview, JFKL.

169 paper by two historians: L. H. Butterfield and Julian P. Boyd, 'The White House as Symbol,' April 14, 1961, LC.

173 note from Letitia Baldrige: Letitia Baldrige, memo, September 18, 1961.

174 background on Gene Tierney: Gene Tierney, *Self-Portrait*, Wyden Books, New York, 1978.

174 Sinatra had been present: Letitia Baldrige memo, September 18, 1961.

175 JBK's view of Sinatra and Rat Pack: Joan Braden, *Just Enough Rope: An Intimate Memoir*, Villard Books, New York, 1989.

177ff *Advise and Consent* luncheon: White House file for September 21, 1961, luncheon; Lew Ayres, author interview.

177ff background on Mary Meyer: Nina Burleigh, *A Very Private Woman: The Life and Unsolved Murder of Presidential Mistress Mary Meyer*, Bantam Books, New York, 1998; Timothy Leary, *Flashbacks: An Autobiography*, Jeremy Tarcher, Los Angeles, 1990; Betty Spalding, author interview; confidential source, author interview.

181 'courageous and excellent': Eleanor Roosevelt to JFK, September 25, 1961, FDRL.

186 Ormsby-Gores in Washington: David Ormsby-Gore, interview, JFKL; Remarks Addressed to the President of the United States by the Right Honourable Sir David Ormsby-Gore on the Occasion of the Presentation of His Letters of Credence as Her Majesty's Ambassador to the United States.

187 Nehru was coming: Memo from Harry Rositzke, Psychological Aspects of Prime Minister Nehru's Visit to the United States.

187 skepticism intensified: Jawaharlal Nehru to Harold Macmillan, September 13, 1961, quoted in Harold Macmillan, *Pointing the Way*.

188-9 Nehru visit: Briefing Book, Prime Minister Nehru's Visit November 6–9, 1961; Jawaharlal Nehru to JFK, November 17, 1961; JFK to Jawaharlal Nehru, November 28, 1961; Mrs Indira Gandhi, Briefing Papers for Nehru Visit; Angier Biddle Duke, interview, JFKL; White House file November 6, 1961, luncheon; John Kenneth Galbraith to JFK, November 28, 1961; Letitia Baldrige to Evelyn Lincoln, October 19, 1961; White House file November 7, 1961, dinner.

189 Washington talks: Memorandum of Conversation JFK–Nehru, November 7, 1961.

189 Report on General Taylor's Mission to South Vietnam, November 3, 1961.

190 dinner dance: White House file dinner dance, November 11, 1961.

191 Vidal incident: Arthur Schlesinger Jr, *Robert Kennedy and His Times*, Ballantine Books, New York, 1978.

192 'That was when': Betty Spalding, author interview.

193 'a lot of': Betty Spalding, author interview.

194 'let their pleasures': David Cecil, *The Young Melbourne*.

194 'what the hell': Betty Spalding, author interview.

194 Muñoz-Marín dinner: White House file, November 13, 1961, dinner; White House file, Pablo Casals.

195 Olympic Hotel: Larry Newman, author interview.

197ff Latin American trip: Program and Scenario for December 15–18, 1961; White House File for trip.

198 'there was more': Sue Vogelsinger, author interview.

198 'to carry out': Richard Helms to Robert Kennedy, December 13, 1961.

198 'serious disturbances': Embassy (Caracas) to State Department, December 14, 1961.

198 champions of progressive reform: Position Paper, President's Visit to Venezuela and Colombia, December 14, 1961.

199 Puerto Rican visit: Briefing Book, Puerto Rico, December 1961; Program and Scenario for Puerto Rico.

199 'had a gun': Sue Vogelsinger, author interview.

200 running a gauntlet: Larry Newman, author interview.

Chapter 8: Goddess of Power

202 'a little unsure': Evelyn Lincoln, *My Twelve Years with John F. Kennedy.*

203ff JFK's reaction to Joseph Kennedy's stroke: Charles Spalding, interview, JFKL; Letitia Baldrige, interview, JFKL.

204 Macmillan sent word: Harold Macmillan to JFK, December 20, 1961; Philip de Zulueta to McGeorge Bundy, December 20, 1961.

205 'a very effective': Harold Macmillan to Queen Elizabeth, December 24, 1961, quoted in Harold Macmillan, *At the End of the Day, 1961–1963*, Harper & Row, New York, 1973.

205 'There is a marked': Macmillan's personal diary, December 23, 1961, quoted in Harold Macmillan, *At the End of the Day, 1961–1963.*

205 In Bermuda: Prime Minister's Diaries, December 19–22, 1961, BLO; David Ormsby-Gore, interview, JFKL; Department of State Objectives Paper, December 16, 1961.

205 'concept ... longer': David Ormsby-Gore, interview, JFKL.

205 'country house conditions': David Ormsby-Gore, interview, JFKL.

205 'I think that not many': David Ormsby-Gore, interview, JFKL.

206 'everything possible': Harold Macmillan to JFK, December 22, 1961.

206 'it is not': Harold Macmillan to JFK, January 5, 1962.

206 'to try and bend': David Ormsby-Gore, interview, JFKL.

206 'trickery and bad faith': Harold Macmillan to JFK, December 23, 1961.

211ff dinner dance: White House file dinner dance, February 9, 1962.

211 took Ben Bradlee aside: Benjamin Bradlee, *Conversations with Kennedy*, W. W. Norton, New York, 1975.

211 swap of prisoners: William Tyler to Dean Rusk, January 2, 1962.

212 'Up comes Jack': Betty Spalding, author interview.

214 invasion of Goa: Jawaharlal Nehru to JFK, December 19, 1961; Dean Rusk to John Kenneth Galbraith, December 23, 1961; Memorandum of Conversation Dean Rusk–Aziz Ahmed, January 3, 1962; Robert Komer to McGeorge Bundy, January 6, 1962; Jawaharlal Nehru to JFK, January 30, 1962.

214 'The effect of': JFK to Jawaharlal Nehru, January 18, 1962.

215 visit to Nehru: Nehru to JFK, November 17, 1961; JFK to Nehru, November 28, 1961.

215 visit to Ayub Khan: William Rountree to State Department, August 24, 1961; McGeorge Bundy to JFK, September 25, 1961; JFK to Ayub Khan, September 29, 1961.

215 balancing act: Ayub Khan to JFK, January 18, 1962; McGeorge Bundy to John Kenneth Galbraith, March 18, 1962.

215–16 JBK in India: Jack McNally to Kenneth O'Donnell, February 5, 1962; Lucius Battle to McGeorge Bundy, February 26, 1962; memorandum of conversation, JFK–B. K. Nehru, February 28, 1962; Dean Rusk to John Kenneth Galbraith, March 2, 1962; Pierre Salinger to Jacob Javits, March 5, 1962; JFK to John Kenneth Galbraith, March 7, 1962; Schedule for Mrs Kennedy's trip, March 7, 1962; John Kenneth Galbraith to JFK, March 22, 1962; JFK to John Kenneth Galbraith, March 22, 1962; White House Social Files for India trip; Jawaharlal Nehru to JFK, March 25, 1962; G. T. McHugh file, First Lady's Trip India–Pakistan; John Kenneth Galbraith, *Ambassador's Journal*, Houghton Mifflin, Boston, 1969; Letitia Baldrige, interview, JFKL.

216–17 JBK in Pakistan: Schedule for Mrs Kennedy's Trip, March 7, 1962; Walter McConaughy to JFK, March 22, 1962; Walter McConaughy to JFK, March 24, 1962; JFK to Ayub Khan, March 26, 1962; Walter McConaughy to McGeorge Bundy, March 28, 1962; Walter McConaughy to JFK, April 10, 1962; Letitia Baldrige, interview, JFKL.

217 Hoover lunch: 'Alleged Assassination Plots Involving Foreign Leaders, An Interim Report of the Select Committee to Study Governmental Operations with Respect to Intelligence Activities, United States Senate.'

218 'extracurricular activities': Cartha DeLoach to Mr Mohr, April 19, 1960, F.B.I. file.

218 wired to advise him: JBK to JFK, March 19, 1962; John Kenneth Galbraith to JFK, March 21, 1962; John Kenneth Galbraith to Dean Rusk, March 22, 1962.

219 'borderline paranoid addict': Ralph Greenson to Anna Freud, December 4, 1961, LC.

219 Sardar: JBK to JFK (Palm Springs); JFK to JBK, March 26, 1962; G. T. McHugh file, First's Lady's Trip India–Pakistan.

220–2 steel crisis: Charles Spalding, interview, JFKL; Charles Bartlett, interview, JFKL.

221 'an affront': Theodore Sorensen, *Kennedy*, Harper & Row, New York, 1965.

221 'to lose a public': Clark Clifford, *Counsel to the President.*

222 'a common measure': JFK and Harold Macmillan to Nikita Khrushchev, February 7, 1962.

222 When Khrushchev did reply: Nikita Khrushchev to JFK, February 10, 1962.

222 Britain and U.S. decline: JFK to Nikita Khrushchev, February 14, 1962.

222 Khrushchev's angry reply: Nikita Khrushchev to JFK, February 21, 1962.

222 letter written without consultation: JFK to Nikita Khrushchev, February 24, 1962.

223 'Eisenhower did not bother': Harold Evans, *Downing Street Diary: The Macmillan Years 1957–63*, Hodder and Stoughton, London, 1981.

223 'Our purpose': 'Prime Minister Macmillan's Visit to Washington, April 27–29,' April 20, 1962.

224–5 Macmillan's visit: Department of State Objectives Paper, April 20, 1962; Prime Minister's Diaries, April 25–29, 1962, BLO; Program for the Informal Visit to the United States of Harold Macmillan, April 25–29, 1962; David Ormsby-Gore, interview, JFKL; memoranda of conversations, JFK–Macmillan: April 28, 1962, 11 a.m.; April 28, 1962, 3:30 p.m.

224 'we should not': memorandum of conversation, JFK–Macmillan, April 28, 1962, 11 a.m.

224 'The whole thing': memorandum of conversation, JFK–Macmillan, April 28, 1962, 11 a.m.

225 'in their own houses': David Ormsby-Gore, interview, JFKL.

225 'really set the seal': David Ormsby-Gore, interview, JFKL.

225–6 JBK visit to Joseph Kennedy: Rita Dallas, *The Kennedy Case*, G. P. Putnam's Sons, New York, 1973.

Chapter 9: Eyes in the Portraits

227 tennis story: Larry Newman, author interview.

227 'rigidly in control': Larry Newman, author interview.

228 'Jackie had her': Larry Newman, author interview.

228–30 Malraux visit: Hervé Alphand, *L'étonnement d'être, Journal 1939–1973*; Memorandum of Meeting, JFK, Alphand, Malraux, May 11, 1962; Embassy (France) to Department of State, May 28, 1962.

230 Bundy laughed off: McGeorge Bundy to JFK, n.d.

230ff Background on Marilyn Monroe: Barbara Leaming, *Marilyn Monroe*, Weidenfeld & Nicolson, New York, 1998.

234 'See the editors': Richard Reeves, *President Kennedy.*

234 'He wanted': Senator George Smathers, author interview.

234 'She stopped bothering': Senator George Smathers, author interview.

235 'bugged': Larry Newman, author interview.

235 'eyes ... wall': Larry Newman, author interview.

235 'Is that one': Larry Newman, author interview.

235 drive past his office: Patrick O'Neal, author interview.

235–6 dinner dance: White House file, June 1, 1962, dinner dance.

236 'He would ... like him': Larry Newman, author interview.

237 trip to Mexico: White House File, State Visit to Mexico, June 29–July 1, 1962; Briefing Book, Mexico Trip; Roger Abraham, Embassy (Mexico), September 13, 1962 Report of Kennedy Visit; Senator Mike Mansfield, interview, JFKL.

237 'solidly with': Brigadier General Edward Lansdale to Special Group (Augmented), July 5, 1962.

237 'astounding': Roger Abraham, Embassy (Mexico), September 13, 1962 Report of Kennedy Visit.

238 'the mother of': Larry Newman, author interview.

238 'Sir ... insecure': Larry Newman, author interview.

239 laid down the law: Secret Service Memorandum, To: James J. Rowley, From: Children's Detail, July 25, 1962.

239 'You would think': Larry Newman, author interview.

240 'Where's the President?': confidential source, author interview.

240 'He loves pleasure': Hervé Alphand, *L'étonnement d'être, Journal 1939–1973*.

240 'He toots away': Dean Acheson to Harry Truman, May 3, 1962.

241 'In reading the ... race itself': JFK to Nikita Khrushchev, July 17, 1962.

242 'liked a new': Lem Billings, interview, JFKL.

242–3 Mary Meyer's visit to Leary: Timothy Leary, *Flashbacks: An Autobiography*.

243 Cord and Mary Meyer: confidential source, author interview.

244–5 Alsop dinner: Alsop entertainment records, July 17, 1962 dinner.

245 'wasn't the only': Betty Spalding, author interview.

245 Rattlesnake Mountain: memo, 'Paul R. Fout property,' August 1, 1962.

247 'Please put': Rose Fitzgerald Kennedy, *Times to Remember*.

247ff JBK's trip to Italy: White House social files; E. C. Kenney to Captain George Burkley, July 11, 1962; Letitia Baldrige to Michael Chinigo, July 17, 1962; Letitia Baldrige to Stanislas Radziwill, July 30, 1962; Carmine De Martino to Letitia Baldrige, July 30, 1962; Letitia Baldrige to JFK, August 7, 1962; Anne Lincoln to Costantino Cutolo, September 7, 1962; Anne Lincoln to Paolo Caruso, September 7, 1962.

248 'low key': Mary Taylor, author interview.

248 'She was very': Mary Taylor, author interview.

248 'a good impression': Mary Taylor, author interview.

249 'to cement relations': Mary Taylor, author interview.

249 'the best rapport': Larry Newman, author interview.

249 'Let them have': Larry Newman, author interview.

252 threatened to picket: Concerned Citizens of America Committee press release, August 29, 1962.

252 to invite himself: Janet Auchincloss, interview, JFKL.

253 'I can hardly': Mary Taylor, author interview.

Chapter 10: A Critical Moment

254 trouble had started: Memorandum of Discussion in Secretary Rusk's Office at 12 o'clock, 21 August 1962, Subject: Cuba; Arthur Schlesinger Jr to McGeorge Bundy, August 22, 1962; Central Intelligence Memorandum, Subject: Recent Soviet Military Aid to Cuba, August 22, 1962; Memorandum of Meeting with President Kennedy, Subject: Cuba, August 23, 1962; National Security Action Memo No. 181; Roger Hilsman to George Ball, August 25, 1962.

254ff background on Cuban Missile Crisis: John McCone, memo, The Cuban Situation, October 17, 1962; Memorandum of Conversation JFK–Andrei Gromyko, October 18, 1962; John McCone, notes on meeting with Robert Kennedy, October 20, 1962; JFK to Harold Macmillan, October 22, 1962; John McCone, notes on October 22, 1962 meeting with Congressional Leadership, October 24, 1962; JFK to Nikita Khrushchev, October 22, 1962; Nikita Khrushchev to JFK, October 23, 1962; JFK to Nikita Khrushchev, October 23, 1962; Robert Kennedy to JFK, October 24, 1962; Dean Rusk to Ambassador Hare, October 24, 1962; Walter Rostow to JFK, October 24, 1962; Nikita Khrushchev to JFK, October 24, 1962; JFK to Nikita Khrushchev, October 25, 1962; Dean Rusk to Adlai Stevenson, October 25, 1962, 2 a.m.; Adlai Stevenson to Dean Rusk, October 25, 1962, 2:30 p.m.; Roger Hilsman to Dean Rusk, October 25, 1962; John Scali to Roger Hilsman, n.d.; Dean Rusk to Adlai Stevenson, October 26, 1962; Nikita Khrushchev to JFK, October 26, 1962; Adlai Stevenson to Dean Rusk, October 26, 1962; Nikita Khrushchev to JFK, October 27, 1962; Adlai Stevenson to Dean Rusk, October 27, 1962; JFK to Nikita Khrushchev, October 27, 1962; Robert Kennedy to Dean Rusk, October 30, 1962; Nikita Khrushchev to JFK, October 28, 1962; JFK to Nikita Khrushchev, October 28, 1962; Dean Rusk to Adlai Stevenson, October 28, 1962; memo of meeting, Dean Rusk and David Ormsby-Gore, October 28, 1962; Notes on

Meeting between Ambassador Menemencioglu and William Tyler, October 29, 1962; Nikita Khrushchev to JFK, October 30, 1962; Foy Kohler to Dean Rusk, October 31, 1962; Charles Bartlett, interview, JFKL; David Ormsby-Gore, interview, JFKL; Joseph Alsop, interview, JFKL; Dean Acheson, interview, JFKL; John McCone, interview, LBJL; Elie Abel, interview, JFKL; Janet Travell, interview, JFKL; Robert Kennedy, *Thirteen Days*, W. W. Norton, New York, 1969; Theodore Sorensen, *Kennedy*; Arthur Schlesinger Jr, *A Thousand Days*; Arthur Schlesinger, *Robert Kennedy and His Times*; Kenneth O'Donnell and David Powers, *Johnny, We Hardly Knew Ye*; Pierre Salinger, *With Kennedy*, Doubleday, New York, 1966; Robert McNamara, *In Retrospect*, Times Books, New York, 1995; Dean Rusk, *As I Saw It*; Harold Macmillan, *At the End of the Day, 1961–1963*; Roger Hilsman, *To Move a Nation: The Politics of Foreign Policy in the Administration of John F. Kennedy*, Doubleday, New York, 1967.

254 'some form of': Current Intelligence Memorandum, Subject: Recent Soviet Military Aid to Cuba, August 22, 1962.

255 minority position: John McCone, interview, LBJL.

255 August 29 flight: Ray Cline to Marshall Carter, September 3, 1962.

255 remained unclear: McGeorge Bundy to JFK, August 31, 1962; Roger Hilsman to Dean Rusk, September 1, 1962; Walter Rostow to JFK, September 3, 1962.

256 'Were it to': State Department Bulletin, September 24, 1962.

256 Dobrynin summoned: Theodore Sorensen, Memorandum, September 6, 1962.

257 'defensive in nature': Theodore Sorensen, Memorandum, September 6, 1962.

257 continued to believe: John McCone, interview, LBJL.

257 Soviets warned: Central Intelligence Agency Memorandum, Subject: Soviet Statement on Cuba, September 12, 1962.

258–9 Breakers dinner: Harold Beale, interview, JFKL.

259 consensus of C.I.A. analysts: The Military Buildup in Cuba, September 19, 1962, Submitted by the Director of Central Intelligence.

259 'would indicate': The Military Buildup in Cuba, September 19, 1962, Submitted by the Director of Central Intelligence.

260 Ayub Khan: Program for Informal Visit of Ayub Khan, September 24–27, 1962.

260ff new crisis: Edwin Guthman and Jeffrey Shulman, eds., *Robert Kennedy: In His Own Words*; Burke Marshall, interview, JFKL; Nicholas Katzenbach, interview, JFKL; Talking Points for JFK Conversation with Governor Barnett; Draft Presidential Statement Mississippi; Transcripts of JFK–Barnett Telephone Conversations; JFK to Ross Barnett, September 29, 1962; JFK Executive Order Providing Assistance for the Removal of Unlawful Obstructions of Justice in the State of Mississippi; C. V. Clifton to JFK, October 3, 1962; Taylor Branch, *Parting the Waters*, Simon & Schuster, New York, 1988; Edwin Guthman, *We Band of Brothers*, Harper & Row, New York, 1971.

262 disclose the secret deal: Burke Marshall, interview, JFKL.

262 two speeches: Burke Marshall, interview, JFKL.

263 'I haven't had': Taylor Branch, *Parting the Waters*.

263 'The Attorney General': Taylor Branch, *Parting the Waters*.

264 highly sensitive: Joseph Alsop, interview, JFKL.

264 'a dismal account': Theodore Sorensen, *Kennedy*.

265 'a probability': John McCone, Memorandum of Discussion with McGeorge Bundy, October 5, 1962.

265 the latter that the Soviets: John McCone, Memorandum of Discussion with McGeorge Bundy, October 5, 1962.

266 approved a U-2 flight: Roswell Gilpatric, Notes on a Meeting with the President, October 9, 1962.

267 dinner party: White House file, dinner October 10, 1962.

268 to see Timothy Leary: Timothy Leary, *Flashbacks: An Autobiography*.

268 shown Kennedy photographs: John McCone, Memorandum on Donovan Project, October 11, 1962.

268 withheld until after the elections: John McCone, Memorandum on Donovan Project, October 11, 1962.

268 'a probability': John McCone, Memorandum on Donovan Project, October 11, 1962.

268 'We'll have to': John McCone, Memorandum on Donovan Project, October 11, 1962.

269 928 photographs: Chronology of Air Force Actions During the Cuban Crisis, 14 October–30 October 1962.

269–70 Joseph Kennedy's visit: Luella Hennessey, interview, JFKL.

270 'He can't do': Kai Bird, *Color of Truth: McGeorge Bundy and William Bundy*, Simon & Schuster, New York, 1998.

270 decided to wait: McGeorge Bundy to JFK, March 4, 1963.

270 a struggle between great men: Isaiah Berlin, interview, JFKL.

271 Bohlen's visit: Charles Bohlen, interview, JFKL; Charles Bohlen, *Witness to History*.

272 'I think we'll … missiles': Ernest R. May and Philip Zelikow, eds., *The Kennedy Tapes*, Harvard University Press, Cambridge, 1997.

272 'psychological factor': Ernest R. May and Philip Zelikow, eds., *The Kennedy Tapes*.

273 Alsop dinner: Isaiah Berlin, interview, JFKL; Joseph Alsop, interview, JFKL; Charles Bohlen, interview, JFKL; Katharine Graham, *Personal History*, Vintage, New York, 1998; Joseph Alsop, *I've Seen the Best of It*; Susan Mary Alsop, *To Marietta From Paris*, Doubleday, New York, 1975; Charles Bohlen, *Witness to History*.

274 meeting with Gromyko: Memorandum of Conversation JFK–Gromyko Meeting, October 18, 1962.

274 'more barefaced lies': Robert Lovett, interview, JFKL.

274 'only defensive': Memorandum of Conversation, JFK and Andrei Gromyko, October 18, 1962.

275 'It will lead ... Munich': Ernest R. May and Philip Zelikow, eds., *The Kennedy Tapes*.

275 'choleric': Roswell Gilpatric, interview, JFKL.

276 'they stood motionless': Janet Travell, interview, JFKL.

Chapter 11: Valediction

277 'He wanted Jackie': David Ormsby-Gore, interview, JFKL.

277 'our world position': Minutes of the 505th Meeting of the National Security Council, October 20, 1962.

278 'The best we can offer': Robert McNamara, Notes on Meeting with President Kennedy, Robert Kennedy, et al., October 21, 1962.

278 'come unseen': David Ormsby-Gore to Harold Macmillan, October 22, 1962, quoted in Harold Macmillan, *At the End of the Day*.

279 'enough to merit': David Ormsby-Gore to Harold Macmillan, October 22, 1962, quoted in Harold Macmillan, *At the End of the Day*.

279 would send word: JFK to Harold Macmillan, October 21, 1962.

279 de Gaulle: JFK to Charles de Gaulle, October 22, 1962.

279 dinner dance: White House file, October 23, 1962, dinner dance.

279 the Grazianis: Letitia Baldrige to Benno Graziani, October 9, 1962.

280 'share whatever happened': Theodore Sorensen, *Kennedy*.

280 'one more woman': White House file, October 22, 1962, dinner.

280 highly-charged encounter: Senator Mike Mansfield, interview, JFKL.

281 'We're either': Ernest R. May and Philip Zelikow, eds., *The Kennedy Tapes*.

282ff Macmillan consultations: Prime Minister's Diaries, October 22–28, 1962, BLO; Harold Macmillan to JFK, October 22, 1962; JFK to Harold Macmillan, October 22, 1962; Harold Macmillan to JFK, October 25, 1962; Harold Macmillan to JFK, October 26, 1962; JFK to Harold Macmillan, October 27, 1962; Harold

Macmillan to JFK, October 27, 1962; McGeorge Bundy to Harold Macmillan, October 27, 1962; Philip de Zulueta to McGeorge Bundy, October 27, 1962; David Bruce to Dean Rusk, October 28, 1962; Harold Macmillan to JFK, October 28, 1962; JFK to Harold Macmillan, October 28, 1962; Philip de Zulueta to McGeorge Bundy, October 28, 1962.

283 'You must have': transcript of telephone conversation, JFK–Macmillan, October 22, 1962.

283 Jackie and six guests: White House file, October 22, 1962, dinner.

284 informal dinner: White House file, October 23, 1962, dinner; David Ormsby-Gore, interview, JFKL.

284 'the same instructions': Robert Kennedy to JFK, October 24, 1962.

285 'stopped or turned back': Record of Action of the Third Meeting of the Executive Committee of the National Security Council, October 24, 1962.

285 'The Soviet Government': Nikita Khrushchev to JFK, October 24, 1962.

286 challenge postponed: memorandum of telephone conversation, Dean Rusk and George Ball, October 24, 1962.

286 'hold up': memorandum of telephone conversation, JFK and George Ball, October 24, 1962.

286 'take the necessary': JFK to Nikita Khrushchev, October 25, 1962.

286 told Macmillan: transcript of telephone conversation, JFK–Macmillan, October 25, 1962.

287 'rather unofficial': transcript of telephone conversation, JFK–Macmillan, October 26, 1962.

287 a letter arrived: Nikita Khrushchev to JFK, October 26, 1962.

287 'obsolete and': Summary Record of the Seventh Meeting of the Executive Committee of the National Security Council, October 27, 1962.

287 'set great store': Thomas Finletter to Department of State, October 25, 1962.

287 selling out an ally: Summary Record of the Seventh Meeting of the Executive Committee of the National Security Council, October 27, 1962.

288 pilot killed: Summary Record of the Eighth Meeting of the Executive Committee of the National Security Council, October 27, 1962.

288 'almost inevitable': Summary Record of the Eighth Meeting of the Executive Committee of the National Security Council, October 27, 1962.

288 Jupiter missiles: Ernest R. May and Philip Zelikow, eds., *The Kennedy Tapes*; Dean Rusk, *As I Saw It*; Robert Kennedy to Dean Rusk, October 30, 1962.

289 'It was indeed': Harold Macmillan to JFK, October 28, 1962.

289 outcome of the crisis: Charles Bohlen to Dean Rusk, October 28, 1962; Robert Komer to McGeorge Bundy, October 19, 1962; Pierre Salinger to JFK, October 31, 1962; Carl Kaysen to McGeorge Bundy, October 31, 1962; Charles de Gaulle to JFK, November 2, 1962; Sherman Kent to John McCone, November 8, 1962; Memorandum of Conversation, David Ormsby-Gore–Dean Rusk, November 9, 1962; Brubeck to McGeorge Bundy, November 9, 1962; Memorandum of Conversation Chester Bowles–Anatoly Dobrynin, November 15, 1962; Memorandum Prepared by the Central Intelligence Agency, Soviet Policy in the Aftermath of the Cuban Crisis, November 29, 1962; Memorandum of Conversation Averell Harriman–Anatoly Dobrynin, December 18, 1962.

290ff dinner party: White House file, November 8, 1962, dinner.

291 'a glow': Isaiah Berlin, interview, JFKL.

291 'a little ill': C. L. Sulzberger, *The Last of the Giants*, Macmillan, New York, 1970.

291 'pretty': C. L. Sulzberger, *The Last of the Giants*.

292 'I didn't approve': Betty Spalding, author interview.

292 'disgusted': Betty Spalding, author interview.

292 'like God ... virgins': Richard Reeves, *President Kennedy*.

292 'Jack had appeal': Jewel Reed, author interview.

293 dinner dance: White House file, November 9, 1962, dinner dance.

293 'Do you mind': Betty Spalding, author interview.

293 'I didn't want': Betty Spalding, author interview.

295 scene at Crosby estate: Larry Newman, author interview.

295 'show': Larry Newman, author interview.

296 Skybolt: Department of State, 'Implications for the United Kingdom of Decision to Abandon Skybolt,' October 31, 1962; Robert McNamara, Conversation Notes, November 9, 1962; Dean Rusk to Robert McNamara, November 24, 1962; Memorandum of Conversation JFK–McNamara et al., December 16, 1962; Harold Macmillan to JFK, December 24, 1962; Henry Brandon, interview, JFKL; Richard E. Neustadt, *Report to JFK: The Skybolt Crisis in Perspective*, Cornell University Press, Ithaca, 1999; David Bruce to Dean Rusk, January 31, 1963.

296 Nassau meeting: Prime Minister's Diaries, December 17–21, 1962, BLO; Background Paper, 'Current Political Scene in the United Kingdom,' December 13, 1962; memoranda of

conversations, JFK–Macmillan, December 19, 1962, 9:45 a.m.;
December 19, 1962, 4:30 p.m.; December 20, 1962, 10 a.m.;
JFK to Harold Macmillan, December 21, 1962; Henry Brandon,
interview, JFKL; McGeorge Bundy, interview, JFKL; Roswell
Gilpatric, interview, JFKL.

Chapter 12: Indiscretion

299 'The Blue Room': James Abbott and Elaine Rice, *Designing Camelot: The Kennedy White House Restoration.*

300 the best in her: JBK to Joseph Alsop, August 31, 1964, LC.

300 eager to take the veil: Mary Barelli Gallagher, *My Life with Jacqueline Kennedy.*

301 background on Graham incident: Katharine Graham, *Personal History.*

301 'He would and will': Katharine Graham, *Personal History.*

302 conversation with Timothy Leary: Timothy Leary, *Flashbacks: An Autobiography.*

302 'didn't mean anything': Betty Spalding, author interview.

304 lunch at Voisin: Charles Spalding, interview, JFKL.

304 dinner dance: White House file, March 8, 1963, dinner dance.

304 fifty-mile hike: Max Jacobson, unpublished memoir, MHS; Charles Spalding, interview, JFKL.

306 JBK speaks of Bobby Kennedy: Benjamin Bradlee, *Conversations with Kennedy.*

306 promised to end it: confidential source, author interview.

307 claimed to be unconcerned: Adlai Stevenson to Marietta Tree, March 10, 1963, in Sarah Bradford, *America's Queen: The Life of Jacqueline Kennedy Onassis*, Viking, New York, 2000.

309 pretend to fly: Maud Shaw, interview, JFKL.

309 battlefields: James Reed, interview, JFKL; Ralph Horton Jr, interview, JFKL.

310 confided to Mr West: J. B. West, *Upstairs at the White House.*

311 'run into the sand': David Ormsby-Gore, interview, JFKL.

311 'What, then': Harold Macmillan to JFK, March 16, 1963.

312 Profumo: F.B.I. memo, Christine Keeler/John Profumo, Internal Security–Great Britain, June 19, 1963.

313 'It is hard': Arthur Schlesinger Jr to JFK, March 25, 1963.

314 In conversation with Chuck Spalding: Charles Spalding, interview, JFKL.

314 answered Macmillan's letter: JFK to Harold Macmillan, March 28, 1963.

315 revisions were flying: transcripts of telephone conversations, Kennedy–Macmillan, April 1963.

315 expressed the wish: Macmillan personal diary, April 13, 1963,

quoted in Harold Macmillan, *At the End of the Day, 1961–1963*.

315 'It was a difficult': Rita Dallas, *The Kennedy Case*.

316 'Good evening': Paul B. Fay, Jr, *The Pleasure of His Company*, Harper & Row, New York, 1966.

316 'We all have a duty': JFK and Harold Macmillan to Nikita Khrushchev, April 15, 1963.

317 Spalding–Meyer affair: Betty Spalding, author interview.

318 JFK's birthday party: White House file, May 29, 1963, birthday dinner.

318 'a loosening of': David Bruce to Dean Rusk, June 11, 1963.

318 'an electoral liability': David Bruce to Dean Rusk, June 11, 1963.

319 what scandal had done: Edward Lampson to Department of State, June 11, 1963; Jones, Embassy (London) to Dean Rusk, June 12, 1963.

319 present the girls personally: Larry Newman, author interview.

319 two girls: Seymour Hersh, *The Dark Side of Camelot*, Little Brown & Co., New York, 1997.

319 message arrived from Khrushchev: Nikita Khrushchev to JFK, June 8, 1963.

320 significance of speech: Henry Brandon, interview, JFKL.

321 'real greatness': Chester Bowles, interview, JFKL.

321 phoned Joe Alsop: Joseph Alsop to Evangeline Bruce, June 12, 1963, LC.

322 'a bit of a bother': Joseph Alsop to Evangeline Bruce, June 12, 1963, LC.

322 'taxing weekend trip': Joseph Alsop to Evangeline Bruce, June 12, 1963, LC.

322 'stayed so long': Joseph Alsop to Evangeline Bruce, June 12, 1963, LC.

322 'a small boy': Joseph Alsop to Evangeline Bruce, June 12, 1963, LC.

323 race as a moral issue: Martin Luther King, interview, JFKL.

323–4 Kennedy's address: JFK Remarks of the President, June 11, 1963.

326 'Whatever estimate ... democracy': David Bruce to Dean Rusk, June 15, 1963.

327 'one of the most ... sooner or later': David Bruce to Dean Rusk, June 18, 1962.

328 'the best oral sex': Evan Thomas, *Robert Kennedy: His Life*, Simon & Schuster, New York, 2000.

328 background on Bobby Baker: Bobby Baker files, LBJL; Bobby Baker, *Wheeling and Dealing*, W. W. Norton, New York, 1978.

330 Birch Grove visit: Prime Minister's Diaries, June 29–30, 1963, BLO; Harold Macmillan to JFK, July 4, 1963.

330 gifts were received: Dorothy Macmillan to JFK, July 1, 1963; Harold Macmillan to JFK, July 4, 1963.

330 'One of the biggest': James D. Horan and Dom Frasca, 'High U.S. Aide Implicated in V-Girl Scandal,' *New York Journal-American*, June 29, 1963.

331 liaison at the F.B.I.: Courtney Evans, interview, LBJL.

331 'expressed concern': F. J. Baumgardner to W. C. Sullivan, June 30, 1963, F.B.I. file.

331 JFK's reaction to *Journal-American* article: Embassy (London) to J. Edgar Hoover, June 30, 1963, F.B.I. file; Embassy (London) to J. Edgar Hoover, July 1, 1963, F.B.I. file; Branigan to W. C. Sullivan, July 1, 1963, F.B.I. file; Courtney Evans to Alan Belmont, July 3, 1963, F.B.I. file.

331 'Hatless': Harold Macmillan, *At the End of the Day, 1961–1963*.

332 'prior to his election … periods of time': Courtney Evans to J. Edgar Hoover, July 3, 1963, F.B.I. file.

Chapter 13: Private Grief

334–5 background on Rose Kennedy: Rose Kennedy, letters to her children, JFKL; Betty Spalding, author interview; Jewel Reed, author interview; Rose Fitzgerald Kennedy, *Times to Remember*; Joan and Clay Blair Jr, *The Search for J.F.K.*, Berkley Publishing Corporation, New York, 1976; Nigel Hamilton, *J.F.K.: Reckless Youth*, Random House, New York, 1992; Amanda Smith, ed., *Hostage to Fortune: The Letters of Joseph P. Kennedy*; Doris Kearns Goodwin, *The Fitzgeralds and the Kennedys: An American Saga*, Simon & Schuster, New York, 1987.

335 whip and snap: Capt. Tazewell Shepard Jr to Phillip H. Warren Jr, October 31, 1963.

335 JBK's activities: Mary Barelli Gallagher, *My Life with Jacqueline Kennedy*.

338 'whether an accommodation': Harold Macmillan to JFK, July 4, 1963.

338 'second prize': Harold Macmillan to JFK, July 4, 1963.

339 test ban negotiations begin: JFK to Nikita Khrushchev, July 12, 1963.

339 'to cross into East Germany': David Ormsby-Gore, interview, JFKL.

339 Walsh incident: James Reed, interview, JFKL.

340 'came down mad': Larry Newman, author interview.

340 'Say, you're': confidential source, author interview.

340 'Don't worry': Arthur Schlesinger Jr, *A Thousand Days*.

341 treaty was being initialed: Prime Minister's Diaries, July 25, 1963, BLO; JFK to Harold Macmillan, July 26, 1963.

341 'I found myself': Harold Macmillan to JFK, July 25, 1963.

341 Ormsby-Gores at Hyannis Port: David Ormsby-Gore, interview, JFKL.

341 tin of caviar: Nikita Khrushchev to JFK, July 27, 1963.

342 puppies: Traphes Bryant, interview, JFKL.

342 Graham suicide: Katharine Graham, *Personal History.*

344 'Dr Walsh': Mary Barelli Gallagher, *My Life with Jacqueline Kennedy.*

344 'This baby mustn't': Mary Barelli Gallagher, *My Life with Jacqueline Kennedy.*

344 'Mr President … as I can': Carl Sferrazza Anthony, *As We Remember Her.*

345 'he just kept': Pamela Turnure and Nancy Tuckerman, interview, JFKL.

346ff birth of Patrick: Janet Auchincloss, interview, JFKL; Richard Cardinal Cushing, interview, JFKL; Janet Travell, interview, JFKL.

346 best medical treatment: Roy Heffernan, interview, JFKL.

347 Luella Hennessey: Luella Hennessey, interview, JFKL.

348 'Nothing must happen': Janet Auchincloss, interview, JFKL.

348 in the hospital elevator: Larry Newman, author interview.

348 JFK's reaction to Patrick's death: Roy Heffernan, interview, JFKL; David Ormsby-Gore, interview, JFKL; Francis Morrissey, interview, JFKL.

349 As she later described the scene: Betty Spalding, author interview.

349–50 JFK tells children about Patrick: Maud Shaw, interview, JFKL.

350 funeral: Francis Morrissey, interview, JFKL.

350 'He put his arm': Richard Cardinal Cushing, interview, JFKL.

351 'vultures': Pamela Turnure and Nancy Tuckerman, interview, JFKL.

351 'Yes, I can': Pamela Turnure and Nancy Tuckerman, interview, JFKL.

351 'the right way': Pamela Turnure and Nancy Tuckerman, interview, JFKL.

352 One old friend: Betty Spalding, author interview.

352 flag be lowered: Capt. Tazewell Shepard Jr to Philip H. Warren Jr, October 31, 1963.

352 'seemed even more broken': Theodore Sorensen, *Kennedy.*

353 'The burdens': Harold Macmillan to JFK, August 14, 1963.

Chapter 14: A Study in Betrayal

354 'He was so': Betty Spalding, author interview.

354 'never seen anything … jerk': Betty Spalding, author interview.

355ff background on Vietnam: David Kaiser, *American Tragedy: Kennedy, Johnson and the Origins of the Vietnam War*, Harvard University Press, Cambridge, 2000; William Rust, *Kennedy in Vietnam*, Scribners, New York, 1985; Neil Sheehan, *A Bright Shining Lie*, Vintage, New York, 1989; David Halberstam, *The Best and the Brightest*; Robert McNamara, *In Retrospect*; Maxwell Taylor, *Swords and Plowshares*, W. W. Norton, New York, 1972; Ellen Hammer, *A Death in November: America in Vietnam 1963*, E. P. Dutton, New York, 1987; Dean Rusk, *As I Saw It*; George Ball, *The Past Has Another Pattern*, W. W. Norton, New York, 1982; Roger Hilsman, *To Move a Nation: The Politics of Foreign Policy in the Administration of John F. Kennedy*; Edwin Guthman and Jeffrey Shulman, eds., *Robert Kennedy: In His Own Words*; Lawrence Freedman, *Kennedy's Wars*, Oxford University Press, New York, 2000; Kai Bird, *The Color of Truth: McGeorge Bundy and William Bundy*; W. W. Rostow, *The Diffusion of Power*, Macmillan, New York, 1972.

356 'had not paid': Michael Forrestal, interview, LBJL.

356 'In the discussion': Roswell Gilpatric, Memorandum, Subject: President's Meeting with Joint Chiefs of Staff, January 3, 1962.

356 'to seize upon': Michael Forrestal, Memorandum of a Conversation between the President and Averell Harriman, April 6, 1962.

356 'showing signs': Michael Forrestal, interview, LBJL.

357 'an unpopular Vietnamese ... abroad': Chester Bowles to JFK, March 7, 1963.

357 'forced': Michael Forrestal, interview, LBJL.

358 'the changing ... involvement': Mike Mansfield to JFK, August 19, 1963.

358 intelligence report: Joseph F. Carroll to Robert McNamara, August 21, 1963.

359 'full of sadness': Ralph Martin, *A Hero for Our Times*, Fawcett, New York, 1983.

359 'the loss of': Ralph Martin, *A Hero for Our Times*.

360 generals wanted to know: Henry Cabot Lodge to Department of State, August 24, 1963.

360ff coup telegram: Michael Forrestal to JFK, August 24, 1963; Henry Cabot Lodge to Department of State, August 24, 1963, 6 p.m.; Henry Cabot Lodge to Roger Hilsman, August 24, 1963, 11 p.m.; Michael Forrestal to JFK, August 24, 1963, 4:50 p.m.; General Clifton's note on Forrestal memo to JFK, August 24, 1963, 4:50 p.m.; V. H. Krulak, Memorandum for the Record by the Joint Chiefs of Staff's Special Assistant for Counterinsurgency and Special Activities, August 24, 1963; George Ball to Henry Cabot Lodge, August 24, 1963, 9:36 p.m.; Michael

Forrestal to JFK, August 25, 1963, 5:34 p.m.; Michael Forrestal, interview, JFKL.

360 'the mastermind': Michael Forrestal to JFK, August 24, 1963.

360 'Averell and Roger': Michael Forrestal to JFK, August 24, 1963.

360 'But if he': Telegram from the Department of State to Embassy in Vietnam, August 24, 1963.

360 'may not remain ... action now': Michael Forrestal to JFK, August 24, 1963.

360 'Harriman, Hilsman': Michael Forrestal to JFK, August 24, 1963.

361 telegram arrived from Lodge: quoted in Michael Forrestal to JFK, August 25, 1963.

361 approve Lodge's request: Michael Forrestal to JFK, August 25, 1963.

362 'egregious end run': Maxwell Taylor, *Swords and Plowshares*.

362 'second thoughts': General Maxwell Taylor to General Paul Harkins, August 28, 1963.

362 'We are launched': Henry Cabot Lodge to Department of State, August 29, 1963.

362 'there is one': JFK to Henry Cabot Lodge, August 29, 1963.

362 'To be successful': Henry Cabot Lodge to JFK, August 30, 1963.

362 Onassis problems: A. Jones to Cartha DeLoach, October 16, 1963, F.B.I. file.

363 'You have ... forward to it': Pamela Turnure and Nancy Tuckerman, interview, JFKL.

363 Labouisse's recommendation: Henry Labouisse to Dean Rusk, September 3, 1963.

364 ring with emerald chips: Theodore White, notes of November 1963 interview with JBK, JFKL.

366 angry letters: White House Social Files, JBK Greek trip, 1963.

367 'very deeply touched': Pamela Turnure and Nancy Tuckerman, interview, JFKL.

367 John Jr on *Air Force One*: Maud Shaw, interview, JFKL.

367ff JBK's Greek trip: White House Social Files; King Paul and Queen Frederica to JBK, September 20, 1963; Nancy Tuckerman to Henry Labouisse, September 20, 1963; Nancy Tuckerman to Henry Labouisse, September 28, 1963; Franklin D. Roosevelt's appointment book for 1963, FDRL; A. Jones to Cartha DeLoach, October 16, 1963, F.B.I. file.

368 resumed their coup plans: Central Intelligence Agency in Saigon to the Agency, October 3, 1963.

369 eighteen months: Stanley Tretick, interview, JFKL.

369 Macmillan's resignation: Prime Minister's Diaries, October 7–18, 1963, BLO; JFK to Harold Macmillan, October 18, 1963.

371 ugly experience: Porter McKeever, *Adlai Stevenson: His Life and Legacy*, William Morrow, New York, 1989.

371 Galitzine dinner party: Hervé Alphand, *L'étonnement d'être, Journal 1939–1973.*

371 Mink Coat mob: Elizabeth Carpenter, interview, LBJL.

372 'binding in law': Chester Bowles to Dean Rusk, March 31, 1961.

373 Mollenhoff's private diary: Evan Thomas, *Robert Kennedy: His Life.*

374 marshaled F.B.I. files: Edwin Guthman and Jeffrey Shulman, eds., *Robert Kennedy: In His Own Words.*

374 'lies': Edwin Guthman and Jeffrey Shulman, eds., *Robert Kennedy: In His Own Words.*

374 meeting with Evans: Courtney Evans to Alan Belmont, October 28, 1963, F.B.I. file.

374 meeting with Hoover: J. Edgar Hoover to Clyde Tolson, November 7, 1963, F.B.I. file.

375 'rules out my ... entail': Henry Cabot Lodge to the Department of State, October 29, 1963.

376 call from Diem: Henry Cabot Lodge to Department of State, November 1, 1963.

376 'in a large ... headquarters': Dean Rusk to Henry Cabot Lodge, November 1, 1963.

376 which side had the advantage: General Paul Harkins to General Maxwell Taylor, November 1, 1963.

376 humane fashion: Dean Rusk to Henry Cabot Lodge, November 1, 1963.

377 'literally blanched': Robert McNamara, *In Retrospect.*

377 murdered: Henry Cabot Lodge to Department of State, November 2, 1963.

377 'leapt to his feet': Maxwell Taylor, *Swords and Plowshares.*

378 'the right instincts': David Ormsby-Gore, interview, JFKL.

379 'shook him personally': Michael Forrestal, interview, LBJL.

379 'Diem and Nhu': Central Intelligence Agency Station in Saigon to Lieutenant General Gordon Blake, November 3, 1963.

379 Kennedy's hopes for relations with Soviets: Memorandum of Conversation Anatoli Dobrynin–Llewellyn Thompson, September 10, 1963; JFK to Khrushchev (conveyed orally by Thompson via Dobrynin), September 13, 1963; Memorandum of Conversation JFK–Gromyko, October 10, 1963; Ormsby-Gore, interview, JFKL.

380 'Say I'm going': Pamela Turnure and Nancy Tuckerman, interview, JFKL.

381 Black Watch: White House file, Black Watch, November 13, 1963.

382 *Air Force One* to Florida: Passenger List, *Air Force One*, Idlewild Airport, New York, to West Palm Beach, Florida, November 15, 1963.

382 'If you want': Richard E. Neustadt, *Report to JFK: The Skybolt Crisis in Perspective*.

Chapter 15: Alone

383 Judicial Reception: White House file, Judicial Reception, November 20, 1963.

384 'I think she': Pamela Turnure and Nancy Tuckerman, interview, JFKL.

385 called Donald Barnes: Donald Barnes, interview, JFKL.

385 wanted Macmillan to read it: Richard E. Neustadt, *Report to JFK: The Skybolt Crisis in Perspective*.

385 'in snatches': Richard E. Neustadt, *Report to JFK: The Skybolt Crisis in Perspective*.

387 'big, hesitant smile': Notes of Mrs Johnson, June 15, 1964, LBJL.

387 'Mr President': Kenneth O'Donnell and David Powers, *Johnny, We Hardly Knew Ye*.

388 Johnsons came down: Lyndon Johnson, Vice-Presidential diary, November 21, 1963, LBJL.

388 riding trousers: memo, White House Mission Schedule, November 22, 1963.

388 audience was delighted: Notes of Mrs Johnson, June 15, 1964, LBJL.

389 'very impressed': Donald Barnes, interview, JFKL.

389 Texas Hotel: John C. Trimble, November 22, 1963, statement, LBJL.

389 mattress: John J. O'Leary, November 30, 1963, statement, LBJL.

389 'You were great': William Manchester, *The Death of a President*, Harper & Row, New York, 1967.

390 'Where's Jackie?': Elizabeth Carpenter, interview, LBJL.

390 sent word upstairs: Clint Hill, WCT.

390 'was packed': Elizabeth Carpenter, interview, LBJL.

390 'much expectation': Elizabeth Carpenter, interview, LBJL.

390 show up at all: Elizabeth Carpenter, interview, LBJL.

391 'almost the focus': Charles Roberts, interview, JFKL.

391 'departure from protocol': Hugh Sidey, *John F. Kennedy, President*.

392 efforts to stick close: JBK, WCT.

392 Accompanied by Hill: Clint Hill, SSIRT.

392 returned to the fence: Paul Landis, SSIRT.

392 'It's wonderful': Charles Roberts, interview, JFKL.

392 seating: Roy Kellerman, SSIRT.

392 red roses on the seat: Nellie Connally, notes on the assassination, LBJL.

392 follow-up car: William McIntyre, SSIRT.

392 motorcade details: Secret Service White House Detail, November 30, 1963, Final Survey Report.

393 very familiar: JBK, WCT; Theodore White, notes of November 29, 1963, interview with JBK, JFKL.

393 'the crowd lined': Paul Landis, SSIRT.

393 four occasions: Clint Hill, SSIRT.

393 ran alongside: Emory Roberts to James J. Rowley, November 29, 1963.

393 'Mr President.': Nellie Connally, notes on the assassination, LBJL.

393 crowd had thinned: Paul Landis, SSIRT.

393 'it would be': JBK, WCT.

393 took to be the backfire: Theodore White, notes of November 29, 1963, interview with JBK, JFKL.

393 to his right, then at her: Zapruder film and film stills; Gerald Posner, *Case Closed*, Random House, New York, 1993.

393 turned to the right: Zapruder film and film stills; Gerald Posner, *Case Closed*.

393-4 'What was it? ... smoke': Paul Landis, SSIRT.

394 'Oh, no': JBK, WCT.

394 'My God': Nellie Connally, notes on the assassination, LBJL.

394 first with her right, then both: Zapruder film and film stills; Gerald Posner, *Case Closed*.

394 spinal trauma: Gerald Posner, *Case Closed*.

394 wrapped her right arm: Paul Landis, SSIRT.

394 'I love you': JBK, WCT.

394 'They've shot': Clint Hill, SSIRT.

394 'as if she': Clint Hill, SSIRT.

394 feared she would fall: Dave Powers, WCT.

395 'grabbed her': Clint Hill, WCT.

395 'to keep the': Theodore White, notes of November 29, 1963, interview with JBK, JFKL.

395 'Jack, Jack': Clint Hill, WCT.

395 'He's dead': Theodore White, notes of November 29, 1963, interview with JBK, JFKL.

395 sensed he was dead: Theodore White, notes of November 29, 1963, interview with JBK, JFKL.

395 screeched to a stop: Nellie Connally, notes on the assassination, LBJL.

395 curled over the President: Emory Roberts, SSIRT.

395 begged her: Nellie Connally, notes on the assassination, LBJL.

395 would not budge: Emory Roberts, SSIRT.

395 'You stay': Emory Roberts, SSIRT.

395 fears of a conspiracy: Bill Moyers, memories of 11/22/63, LBJL.

395 'I cast one': Lady Bird Johnson, *A White House Diary*, Holt, Rinehart and Winston, New York, 1970.

395 reached over: Paul Landis, SSIRT.

396 'No, I want': Paul Landis, SSIRT.

396 'Cover up his': Paul Landis, SSIRT.

396 'Oh, no ... President': Paul Landis, SSIRT.

396 'How badly ... dead': United Press International compilation, *Four Days: The Historical Record of the Death of President Kennedy*, American Heritage Publishing Co., New York, 1964.

396 tried to lift his head: Diana Bowron, WCT.

396 'From a medical': Dr Charles Carrico, WCT.

396 'I'm not going': Theodore White, notes of November 29, 1963, interview with JBK, JFKL.

396 burst into tears: Theodore White, notes of November 29, 1963, interview with JBK, JFKL.

396 'Do you mean': Paul Landis, SSIRT.

397 'I'll take care': Theodore White, notes of November 29, 1963, interview with JBK, JFKL.

397 'bossy ... hours': Theodore White, notes of November 29, 1963, interview with JBK, JFKL.

397 'It's her prerogative': Theodore White, notes of November 29, 1963, interview with JBK, JFKL.

397 dropped to her knees: Dr Malcom Petty, WCT.

397 caught a glimpse: Dr Malcom Perry, WCT.

397 handed him a piece: Gerald Posner, *Case Closed*.

397 'Apparently': Dr Charles Baxter, WCT.

397 'With each compression': Dr Marion Jenkins, WCT.

398 'a great deal': Dr Jackie Hunt, WCT.

398 'Literally, the right': Dr Charles Baxter, WCT.

398 felt like intruders: Dr Marion Jenkins, WCT.

398 'so beautiful': Theodore White, notes of November 29, 1963, interview with JBK, JFKL.

398 reached under the sheet: Theodore White, notes of November 29, 1963, interview with JBK, JFKL.

398 four sheets and mattress cover: Doris Nelson, WCT.

398 'The Vice-President': Rufus Youngblood, WCT.

399 'You always think': Lady Bird Johnson, WCT.

399 'God help us': Lady Bird Johnson, WCT.

399 'He's gone': Lyndon Johnson, WCT.

399 'How about Mrs': Rufus Youngblood, WCT.

399 'I am not': Bill Moyers, memories of 11/22/63, LBJL.

399 to say goodbye: Theodore White, notes of November 29, 1963, interview with JBK, JFKL.

399 'little': Theodore White, notes of November 29, 1963, interview with JBK, JFKL.

399 'Do you think': Theodore White, notes of November 29, 1963, interview with JBK, JFKL.

399 memory of her husband: Theodore White, notes of November 29, 1963, interview with JBK, JFKL.

400 'She was walking': Charles Roberts, interview, JFKL.

400 ripped out four seats: Notes of Colonel James B. Swindal, Aircraft Commander of *Air Force One*, LBJL.

400 'I will be': Pamela Turnure and Nancy Tuckerman, interview, JFKL.

401 'Why did I': Theodore White, notes of November 29, 1963, interview with JBK, JFKL.

401 saturated with blood: Charles Roberts, interview, JFKL.

401 'ashen and quivering': Liz Carpenter, 12/63 notes on assassination, LBJL.

401 'She was in': Charles Roberts, interview, JFKL.

401 'I want them': Lady Bird Johnson, *A White House Diary*.

401 'It's going to be': Bill Moyers, memories of 11/22/63, LBJL.

402 'Well, it doesn't ... designate': George Burkley, interview, JFKL.

402 full military alert: Dean Rusk, *As I Saw It*.

402 'just didn't know': Nancy Dickerson, interview, LBJL.

402 'an international conspiracy': Merle Miller, *Lyndon: An Oral Biography*, G. P. Putnam's Sons, New York, 1980.

402 anxiety on *Air Force One*: Charles Roberts, interview, JFKL.

402 plot by the Cubans or the Soviets: Dean Rusk, *As I Saw It*.

402 'the beginning of': George Ball, *The Past Has Another Pattern*.

403 with rifles out: Nancy Dickerson, interview, LBJL.

403 'Where's Jackie?': Liz Carpenter, 12/63 notes on assassination, LBJL.

403 'streaked with tears': Liz Carpenter, 12/63 notes on assassination, LBJL.

403 drive to Bethesda: Paul Landis, SSIRT.

403 'She was very': Pamela Turnure and Nancy Tuckerman, interview, JFKL.

403 'They were not': Pamela Turnure and Nancy Tuckerman, interview, JFKL.

404 'I am going': Pamela Turnure and Nancy Tuckerman, interview, JFKL.

404 'Under no circumstances': Merle Miller, *Lyndon: An Oral Biography*.

404 the possibility that an assassin: George Ball, *The Past Has Another Pattern*.

404 gathered on the balcony: Pierrette Spiegler, author interview.

405 Alphand contacted: Hervé Alphand, *L'étonnement d'être, Journal 1939–1973*.

405 Soviet Union on state of national alert: United States Department of Justice memorandum, Reaction of Soviet and Communist Party Officials to the Assassination of President John F. Kennedy, December 1, 1966.

405 'deep personal regret ... activities': Foy Kohler to Dean Rusk, November 23, 1963.

406 'if facts permit ... unbalance': Foy Kohler to Dean Rusk, November 23, 1963.

406 'the public had': Llewellyn Thompson to Dean Rusk, November 24, 1963.

408 'It is a tragedy': Hervé Alphand, *L'étonnement d'être, Journal 1939–1973*.

408 'No ... with Mrs Kennedy': Dean Rusk, *As I Saw It*.

408 anonymous telephone call: Hervé Alphand, *L'étonnement d'être, Journal 1939–1973*.

408 Johnson made it clear: Merle Miller, *Lyndon: An Oral Biography*.

Chapter 16: My Dear Friend

410 'You have shown': Harold Macmillan to JBK, February 18, 1964, BLO.

412 sat down to write: JBK to Harold Macmillan, January 31, 1964, BLO.

412 replying two weeks later: Harold Macmillan to JBK, February 18, 1964, BLO.

413 unsent letters: JBK to Harold Macmillan, June 1, 1964, BLO.

414 put all thought of her husband out of her mind: JBK to Harold Macmillan, May 17, 1965, BLO.

414 not to send *Air Force One*: JBK to Lyndon Johnson, March 28, 1965, LBJL.

414 ceremony at Runnymede: Secret Service Memorandum From: Hanly To: Chief Subject: Security Survey Report for Trip of Mrs Kennedy and children to London, June 2, 1965.

414–15 JBK's thoughts at Runnymede and Birch Grove: JBK to Harold Macmillan, May 17, 1965, BLO.

415 in the aftermath of her trip: JBK to Harold Macmillan, May 17, 1965, BLO; JBK to Harold Macmillan, September 14, 1965, BLO.

Epilogue

416 advice of her brother-in-law: Joseph Alsop to JBK, February 26, 1965, LC.

417 the issue of the ambassadorship: Joseph Alsop to JBK, February 26, 1965, LC.

417 transferred his romantic investment: Joseph Alsop to Robert Kennedy, November 1964, LC; Joseph Alsop, interview #2, JFKL.

417 wrote to express his horror: Joseph Alsop to JBK, February 26, 1965, LC.

417 contrite letter: JBK to Joseph Alsop, March 4, 1965, LC.

417 She would later say: JBK to Harold Macmillan, January 19, 1968, BLO.

418 JBK's trip to Cambodia: JBK to Averell Harriman, October 19, 1967; Averell Harriman to JBK, October 19, 1967; Dan Newberry to Averell Harriman, October 24, 1967; Averell Harriman to JBK, October 25, 1967.

418 'renew contacts': Averell Harriman, Notes on Telephone Call from Marvin Kalb, February 7, 1968.

418 Macmillan's visit to New York: JBK to Harold Macmillan, January 19, 1968, BLO.

419 thrilled to the sight: Harold Macmillan to JBK, March 21, 1968, BLO.

419 death of Bobby Kennedy: Harold Macmillan to JBK, June 11, 1968, BLO; JBK to Harold Macmillan, n.d., BLO.

419 Macmillan's voice on television: JBK to Harold Macmillan, June 24, 1968, BLO.

419 letter to Joe Alsop: JBK to Joseph Alsop, September 8, 1968, LC.

420 wishes for her happiness: Harold Macmillan to JBK, November 11, 1968, BLO.

420 lifebuoy: JBK to Harold Macmillan, November 12, 1972, BLO.

420 reminiscing about Jack: JBK to Harold Macmillan, November 12, 1972, BLO.

421 value of Jackie's friendship: Harold Macmillan to JBK, December 13, 1972, BLO.

Index

Abel, Elie 168
Abel, Colonel Rudolf 211
Acheson, Dean 240
Adams, Abigail 106
Adenauer, Konrad 76, 95, 96
Advise and Consent (film) 174, 177, 182
Agnelli, Gianni 57, 249–51
Agnelli, Marella 249, 251
Algeria 269
Alphand, Hervé 132, 134, 154, 211, 228–9, 240, 251, 273, 312, 372, 405
Alphand, Nicole 132, 211, 273
Alsop, Joseph 43–7, 47, 59, 66–7, 75; seeks to calm Jackie 5; and JFK's fears of nuclear war 158; Jackie confides in 300; JFK dines with 197; Mary Meyer at dinner party given by 244–5; on JFK's sensitivity to criticism 264; gives dinner party 270–1, 273, 290; and Profumo scandal 313; JFK invites himself over to 321–2; Jackie raises possibility of ambassadorship with 417; and Bobby's assassination 419
Arvad, Inga 9, 35, 92–3, 217–18
Astaire, Adele (*formerly* Cavendish) 91
Astaire, Fred 91
Astor, Lord 313
Auchinloss, Hugh D. (stepfather) marries Janet Bouvier 6; Jackie's childhood relationship with 7; nature of 34; Jackie rides round estate of 21
Auchinloss, Janet (*formerly* Bouvier; mother): marital difficulties 5–6; finding fault with Jackie 7–8; cripples Jackie's self-confidence 9, 13, 16; Jackie considers life stultifying 12; and baby's death 16; and Jackie's appearance 24; and sense of discipline 23; and Jackie's post-operative illness 29–30; and JFK's proposal of marriage 31; and birth of Patrick 347; tells children of JFK's death 403
Ayres, Lew 174

Baker, Bobby 328, 368, 373–4, 381–2
Balanchine, George 52, 229
Ball, George 223, 361, 404, 408
Baldrige, Letitia 47–9, 59, 172–4, 351
Barnes, Donald 389
Barnett, Ross 260–62
Bartlett, Charles 9, 166, 285, 294
Bartlett, Martha 9, 285
Batista y Zaldivar, Fulgencio 171
Baxter, Dr Charles 397
Bay of Pigs 79–81, 94–118, 136–7, 143, 153, 155, 157, 160, 166, 168, 170, 175, 187, 220–21, 254, 263, 272, 278, 281, 289, 296, 311, 317, 320, 354, 357, 368, 372, 375
Beale, Harold 258
Behrman, S. N. 290
Bellow, Saul 229
Ben Bella, Ahmed 269
Berlin 97, 98, 115, 150, 157, 159, 166–8, 187, 206, 241, 245, 272, 279, 283, 329, 356
Berlin, Isaiah 290, 295

Berlin, Mrs Isaiah 290

Bermuda 204–8

Bermuda Conference 207, 223, 295

Bernstein, Leonard 229

Beyond the Fringe (theatrical show) 303

Billings, Kirk LeMoyne ('Lem') 36, 52–4, 70–1, 86, 97, 100, 159, 165; Indira Ghandi and 188; at dinner-dance 211; and JFK's birthday party 318; on holiday with JFK 336, 339; to accompany JFK to Virginia 372

Bissell, Richard 95, 99–100

Blanch, Lesley, *The Sabres of Paradise* 148

Black, Eugene 305

Blough, Roger 220

Bohlen, Charles 146, 204, 241, 245, 271, 290

Bolton, Oliver 368

Boothby, Robert 66, 87, 91–2

Boudin, Stéphane 57, 59, 141, 169–70

Bourguiba, Habib 118

Bouvier, Jack (father): marital difficulties 5–6; nature of 7; and Jackie's childhood development 8

Bouvier, Janet *see* Auchinloss, Janet

Bouvier, Lee (*later* Radziwill; sister): childhood difficulties 6; early relationship with mother 7; visits Jackie at White House 74–5; daughter christened 150, 152; Jackie gives dinner for 190; at Glen Ora 208; accompanies Jackie on Indian trip 215; rents Italian villa 239; and holiday in Italy 249–50; at White House dinner 279; at White House dinner party 290; dinner with 303; at Patrick's funeral 350; and Patrick's death 352; and Jackie's trip to Greece 362, 367

Bowles, Chester 80–1, 113–14, 269, 320, 321; and Bobby Kennedy 136; and US–Soviet summit 143; advises against further involvement in Vietnam 357; and Bay of Pigs 372

Boyd, Julian P. 169

Bradlee, Ben 94, 176, 211–13, 306, 380

Bradlee, Mrs Ben 213, 306

Browne, Malcolm 357

Bruce, David 66, 87–8, 152, 204, 322; and dinner for Macmillans 91; and Profumo affair 326–7

Bruce, Evangeline 48, 322

Buchan, John 81; *Pilgrim's Way* (UK title *Memory Hold-the-Door*) 11

Bundy, McGeorge 163, 193, 204; and Bay of Pigs 86, 119; and Jackie riding 230; at dinner given by Alsop 245; and Cuban Missile Crisis 265, 270, 272; and Vietnam 360, 372, 376; and Skybolt Report 385

Burke, Admiral Arleigh 106

Burkley, Admiral George 397, 400, 402, 404

Butterfield, L. H. 169

Cabell, General Charles 101

Caccia, Sir Harold 91

Callas, Maria 366

Campbell, Judith 22, 120–1, 165, 190, 196, 213, 217–18, 240, 256, 314

Canada: state visit to 76, 112, 118, 124, 127; Macmillan visit 91

Capeheart, Homer 268

Capote, Truman 236

Cardona, Dr Miro 220

Carpenter, Liz 317, 390, 401, 403

Carrico, Dr Charles 396

Casals, Pablo 194

Cassini, Oleg 174, 283

Castro, Fidel 79, 97, 101, 101–3, 106–7, 108, 113–14, 121, 198, 220, 237, 372

Cavendish, William, Marquess of Hartington 33, 89, 155, 329

Cavendish, Lord Charles 91

Cecil, Lord David 66, 86; *The Young Melbourne* 11, 66, 194

Chagla, Mahomedali Currim 67–8

Churchill, Sir Winston 11–12, 139, 405

CIA: and Bay of Pigs 79–80, 95, 97–9, 101, 105–7, 109, 115; and attempt to assassinate Castro 121; Cord Meyer and 179, 209, 243; and JFK's visit to South America 198; during Cuban Missile Crisis 254, 268, 271–2, 274; and Vietnam 360, 368

Clark, Blair 236, 307

Clark, Dr William 397

Clifford, Clark 56–7, 63, 169, 221

Coerr, Wymberley 113

Colombia 184, 198

Connally, John 318, 370, 387, 392, 394

Connally, Nellie 387, 392–3

Cooper, Gary 12

Cooper, John Sherman 68

Cooper, Lorraine 68

Costa Rica 310

Council of the Organization of American States 95

Coward, Noël 12, 85

Crosby, Bing 218, 295, 385–6

Cuba 79–84, 86, 90, 93, 95–119, 126, 128, 143, 153–4, 157, 162, 170, 175, 194, 220, 254–98, 320, 330, 356

Cuban Missile Crisis 244, 254–98, 300, 363, 376–7, 313

Cukor, George 230

Cushing, Richard, Cardinal 348, 350

Daily Sketch (newspaper) 263

Dallas Morning News (newspaper) 391

Davies, Marion 78

de Gaulle, Charles 11, 93, 125, 127, 131–43, 147, 149–50, 154, 156, 162; warns JFK about South East Asia 166; and Jackie's diplomatic skills 184, 384, 387; Bohlen seeks discussion about 271; and Bohlen 273; and Cuban Missile Crisis 279; vetoes British entry to EEC 312; projected visit to US 372; and JFK's funeral 405, 407–8; survives assassination attempts 412

de Gaulle, Yvonne 130–2, 135

de Valera, Eamon 404

Deering, Harold 65

DeMille, Cecil B. 10

Des Moines Register (newspaper) 373, 375

Devonshire (Andrew), Duke of 89, 155, 329

Devonshire, Duke of 33

Devonshire (Deborah), Duchess of 155, 197, 329

Devonshire, Dowager Duchess of 155

Dickerson, Nancy 402

Dickinson, Angie 54, 196

Diem, Ngo Dinh 358–61, 375–80

Dirksen, Everett 369, 375

Dobrynin, Anatoly 241, 256, 269, 281, 284, 288, 406

Dominican Republic 136

Douglas-Home, Sir Alec 404

Downey, Morton 239

du Pont, Henry 58, 74

Duffy, LaVern 374

Duke, Angier Biddle 161

Dulles, Allen 80, 263; and Bay of Pigs 105; leaves CIA 254

Dulles, John Foster 119

Dutton, Fred 113, 292

East Germany 150

Eisenhower, Dwight David 46, 59, 79, 88, 91, 99, 108; and Bay of Pigs 115–6, 194; JFK denounces 119; and racial unrest 125; and arms sales to Britain 296; and JFK's funeral 406

Eisenhower, Mamie 24, 46, 49, 59

Elizabeth II, Queen 31, 87, 153, 205, 414

Erhard, Ludwig 404

Ethiopia 366

European Economic Community 312

Evans, Courtney 331, 374

Fay, Paul ('Red') 54, 221, 315

Fay, Anita 315

Fell, Fifi 211, 213

Fine Arts Committee 55–6, 58, 74

Finland 184
Finletter, Thomas 287
Fitzwilliam, Lord 89
Fonda, Henry 174, 177
Forrestal, Michael 356, 360, 377, 379
Fox, Charles James 12, 194
Franco, Francisco 194
Frasca, Maria 331
Fraser, Lady Antonia 322
Fraser, Hugh 321
Freedman, Max 213
Freedom Riders 125
Fulbright, J. William 86, 281

Galbraith, John Kenneth 187-9, 217, 235
Galitzine, Irene 250, 367, 371
Gallagher, Mary 337-8, 346, 349
Gandhi, Indira 188-90, 218
Gargan, Ann 202
Gavin, General James 290
German Democratic Republic 333
Germany 329
Giancana, Sam 22, 97, 218
Gilpatric, Roswell 275, 356, 361
Ginsberg, Allen 243
Goa 214
Goldberg, Arthur 221
Goodwin, Richard 114
Graham, Katharine 301, 342-3
Graham, Phil 244, 273, 301-5, 314, 342-3
Graziani, Mr and Mrs Benno 249, 279, 283
Greece 108, 112, 155-6, 352, 363, 365, 383
Greenson, Ralph 232
Greer, William 399-400
Gromyko, Andrei 89, 145, 168
Guatemala 80
Guinea 266

Haddad, William 234
Halaby, Najeeb 267
Halberstam, David 358

Hamilton, Edith, *The Greek Way* 96
Hammerskjold, Dag 173, 181
Harkins, General Paul 375-6
Harriman, Averell 211, 339, 341, 356, 359-61
Harris, Jed 209, 308
Hartington, Bill *see* Cavendish, William
Hassan II, King of Morocco 370
Healy, G. P. A. 171
Hearst, William Randolph 92
Helms, Richard 361
Hennessey, Luella 347, 349-50, 355
Hepburn, Audrey 258
Hepburn, Katharine 62
Hill, Clint 227, 236, 248-50, 337, 392, 394-7
Hilsman, Roger 360
Hines, Jerome 171
Hitler, Adolf 32, 82, 92, 339
Hoover, J. Edgar 217-18, 221, 332-3, 355, 369, 374-5
Horan, James D. 331
Houphouët-Boigny, President and Mrs 234
How Green Was My Valley (film) 178
Huber, Father Oscar 398
Hughes, Sarah T. 400
Hungary 86, 143

Ikeda (Prime Minister of Japan) 158
India 159, 184, 214-15, 219, 269
Istomin, Eugène 229
Italy 249
Ivanov, Yevgeny 312
Ivory Coast 234

Jackson, Lady (Barbara Ward) 69
Jacobson, Max 121-4, 127-9, 136, 141, 143, 145, 147, 150, 176, 235-6, 304, 381
Jacobson, Nina 122, 129, 293, 304
Jaipur, Maharaja and Maharani of 279
Jefferson, Thomas 58
Jenkins, Dr Marion 397

Johnson, Lyndon Baines: and JFK's Inauguration 30; dinner in honour of 59; and Bay of Pigs 80; and White House reception 106; and Kennedys projected visit to ranch 388; in Dallas 392; Roberts fetches 395; and JFK's assassination 399; sworn in 400–1; and JFK's funeral 404, 408–9; relationship with Jackie 416; Bobby Kennedy challenges for presidency 419; and Cuban Missile Crisis 271; relationship with Jackie 158; visit to Pakistan 160; and visit to Texas 318

Johnson, Claudia 'Lady Bird' 76; and JFK's Inauguration 30; and White House reception 106; relationship with Jackie 158; experiences in Dallas 371; on Jackie 387; and Kennedy's projected visit to ranch 388; in Dallas 392; and JFK's assassination 395, 399, 401; persuades Jackie to leave JFK's casket 400; and JFK's funeral 409

Johnson, U. Alexis 408

Karamanlis, Constantine 96, 102–3, 108, 111–12, 115, 155

Karamanlis, Mrs Constantine 102–3, 111–12, 155

Kater, Florence 20

Katzenbach, Nicholas 262–3

Kazan, Elia 229

Keating, Kenneth 255

Keeler, Christine 312, 318, 326, 330

Kefauver, Estes 15

Kellerman, Roy 195, 396

Kennedy, Caroline (daughter): born 19; White House nurseries prepared for 49–50; Jackie takes on holiday 54–55; and JFK's arrival at Glen Ora 64; JFK plays with 85; Jackie rides with 94; and walk with Jackie 95; and Steve Smith Jr 97; Jackie spends time with 163–5; with JFK 164; joins parents 181; presents rose to Nehru 188; Jackie concerned for privacy of 197; with Jackie 201, 277; goes swimming 202; sees grandfather in hospital 207; at Glen Ora 208; JFK takes Mary Meyer to schoolroom of 212; riding 220; Jackie protective of 238; and projected holiday in Italy 239, 246; on trip to Italy 247–8, 250–5, 253; in Oval Office 266; in White House 291; at aunt's 303–4; at Camp David 309, 326; on holiday with JFK 336; riding pony 343; JFK checks on welfare of 347, 351; and death of Patrick 350; Jackie plays with 352; Jackie settles in White House 365; JFK spends time with 367; welcomes Jackie home 370; Jackie takes to Virginia 372; goes to school 380; at White House 381; told of father's death 403; and father's funeral 407, 409; as father's representative 414–15; gives Jackie sense of purpose 416; and Jackie's marriage to Onassis 419

Kennedy, Christopher (nephew) 336, 339

Kennedy, Edward (brother-in-law): and Lem Billings 70; JFK plays backgammon with 165; and father's stroke 203; Jackie on boat ride with 355; and JFK's funeral 409

Kennedy, Ethel (sister-in-law): and birth of Christopher 336; and christening of Christopher 339; Luella Hennessey with 347

Kennedy, Eunice (sister-in-law): and father's stroke 203; Jackie rents house to 239

Kennedy, Jacqueline (née Bouvier): and JFK's Inauguration 1–4; childhood 5–9; first meets JFK 9–10; early relationship with JFK 10–12; and JFK's early infidelities 13; and JFK's post-operative recovery 14; loses baby 15; early responses to JFK's infidelity 16–17; and JFK's bid for the Presidency 18; and birth of Caroline 19; and decision not to participate in public life 21; and birth of John Jr 22; tours White House with Mamie Eisenhower 23; and Inauguration balls 30; and JFK's proposal of marriage 31; and JFK's dead sister 33–6; early days as First Lady 39–59; at Glen Ora 60–66; and JFK's infidelity in the White House 66–7; and depression 69–70, 74–6, 118, 124; and Lee at White House 74–5; and father-in-law 77–9; and Bay of Pigs 82; returns to White House 84–6; and Macmillan 86–94; during Bay of Pigs 95–117; and state visit to Canada 124; and Jacobson 127–9, 235–7; and state visit to France 130–142; and summit with Khrushchev 144–51; popularity in Europe 156–7; return from Europe 157; and JFK's illness 158–9; relationship with Johnson 158; and visit of Ayub Khan 159–62; studies foreign policy 163–4; and JFK's continued infidelity 165; in Hyannis Port with JFK 167; concept of her role 169–70; as 'image-maker' 171–73; and Sinatra 175–7; and Mary Meyer 180–3; and state visitors 184–90; and Dr Jacobson 192; India trip postponed 195; and South American trip 197–200; and Joe Sr's stroke 202–3, 207; and JFK's affair with Mary Meyer 209–13, 245, 302–7, 321–7; visit to India and Pakistan 215–7; and spring schedule 220; and Joe Sr's recuperation 222, 225–6; and lunch with Macmillan 224; isolation of 228; entertains Malraux 229; and horse show 230–1; and Party Convention 230; expected to return to Washington 234; and Secret Service 236–9; Italian trip 248–52; during Cuban Missile Crisis 254–98; pregnant 299, 316–17, 335–47; happiness at Camp David 309; and

Boudin 310; and Joe Sr on government plane 315; and JFK's trip to Europe 329; and JFK's return from Europe 332; and mother-in-law 334–5; gives birth to Patrick 344–6; and death of Patrick 348–53; and effect of Patrick's death on JFK 354–5; JFK spends time with 359; JFK seeks comfort from 361; and trip to Greece 363–7, 370; agrees to accompany JFK to Dallas 371, 380; takes children to Virginia 372; and Vietnam 375–6; plans trip to Dallas 383; arrival in Texas 387–9; early success in Texas 388–90; arrives in Dallas 391; and JFK's death 393–401; at Johnson's swearing-in 400–1; accompanies casket to morgue 403–4; and JFK's funeral 404–9; and Macmillan's support 410–15; and sense of purpose 416; death 421

Kennedy, Janet (sister-in-law) 350

Kennedy, Jean (later Smith; sister-in-law): and husband's infidelities 37; Jackie invites to Glen Ora 97–8; and Jackie's popularity 157; and father's stroke 203; at dinner-dance 211; JFK visits 303–4; and birth of Patrick 346

Kennedy, Joan (sister-in-law) 355

Kennedy, Joe Jr (brother-in-law) 32–3, 200, 349

Kennedy, John Fitzgerald (husband) 221–4; as President-elect 1; compulsive infidelity of 3, 60, 66–7, 71–4, 165, 228, 237, 240; Jackie first meets 9–10; prizes Jackie's intellect 10–12; infidelity in early married life 13; and operation 14; and baby's death 16; decides to run for President 18; elected President 22; Inauguration 27–8; and Inauguration balls 30; early days of Presidency 40–59; devotion to family 61; and Glen Ora 62–3; at Glen Ora 64–6; and Jackie's depression 69–

Kennedy, John Fitzgerald – *contd*
70; and father 78–9; and Bay of
Pigs 79–82, 95–117; and Jackie's
return to White House 84–5; and
Macmillan 86–94, 152–5; depressed
117; and Freedom Riders 125; and
Jacobson 127–8, 235; and state visit
to France 130–42; and summit with
Khrushchev 142–51; and Ormsby-
Gore 155; and recurrence of back
trouble 157–8; illness of 159; spends
weekends in Hyannis Port 165; and
US involvement in Vietnam 166,
356–62, 368–70; and Jackie's
support as 'image-maker' 170–2;
and Sinatra 174–7; and Mary
Meyer 177–83, 191, 208–13, 242–
6, 302–8, 317–18, 322–8, 333; and
Jackie's support with state visitors
184–6; and Nehru 187–90; and
Taylor Report 193; at Camp David
194; and prostitutes 195–6; and
South American trip 197–200; and
father's stroke 202–4; meeting with
Macmillan 204–7; and Jackie's
'Tour of the White House' 213; and
Jackie's trip to India and Pakistan
215–17; and Marilyn Monroe 218–
19, 230–4, 247; and steel crisis 221–
2; at Malraux dinner 229; avoids
physical intimacy with Jackie 239;
and Jackie's Italian trip 247–53; and
Cuban Missile Crisis 254–98; and
Jackie's pregnancy 299, 334–47;
Jackie seeks approval of 300; happiness at Camp David 309; visits
Costa Rica 310; consults Macmillan about Khrushchev 311–12;
and Profumo scandal 313–15; sends
letter to Khrushchev 316; visits
Texas 318; and negotiations for test
ban treaty 319–21; and Profumo
affair 318; and civil rights 324; relationship with Macmillan 326–31;
effects of continued infidelity on
Jackie 334–5; and birth of Patrick
243–7; and death of Patrick 348–

53; effect of Patrick's death on 354–
5; and Jackie's trip to Greece 365–
7; and Macmillan's resignation
369–70; and trip to Dallas 371; and
'right conduct' 372; and Ellen
Rometsch 373; and Vietnam 375–
82; arrival in Texas 387–9; and
Jackie's success in Texas 388–91;
arrives in Dallas 391; shot 394–400;
funeral 404–9; Jackie exhausted
after funeral 410–11; Macmillan
and Jackie write about 411–15;
Jackie rebuilds life after death of
416–21; *Profiles in Courage* 14

Kennedy John Jr (son): birth 22, 69,
345–6; Jackie anxious about 23;
White House nurseries prepared
for 49–50, 54–5; Jackie takes on
holiday 59; improved health of 77;
Jackie spends time with 163, 197;
joins parents 181; Jackie concerned
for privacy of 197; with grandfather
201; grandfather concerned about
202; at Glen Ora 208; Jackie protective of 238; and sailing trip 246;
greets JFK 253; character 266; with
Jackie 277; unwell 285; at Camp
David 309, 326–7; and toy planes
316; with JFK 336; JFK checks on
welfare of 347, 351; and death of
Patrick 349; and photographers
351, 380; Jackie settles in White
House 365; JFK spends time with
367; photographs of 369; welcomes
Jackie home 370; Jackie takes to
Virginia 372; and Black Watch
Tattoo 381; told of father's death
403; and father's funeral 407–9; as
father's representative 414–15; gives
Jackie sense of purpose 416; and
Jackie's marriage to Onassis 419;
and father's funeral 407

Kennedy, Joseph Patrick (Joe Sr,
father-in-law): Palm Beach residence 1; orders JFK home 16; and
JFK's decision to run for President
18; and JFK's womanising 19; as

Ambassador in London 32, 43, 161; and Jackie 33–7; and Bobby's appointment as Attorney General 44; on Lem Billings 52; Jackie stays with 75; and JFK's presidency 77–9; and Bay of Pigs 81–2, 111; Macmillan and 88; and JFK after Bay of Pigs 109; and appeasement 154; on holiday in France 163; treatment of Rose 186; meets JFK and Jackie after South American trip 200; suffers stroke 202–8, 213; discharged from hospital 210; rehabilitation 222, 225–6; and JFK's adultery 233; at Jackie's birthday party 245; JFK visits 247, 260, 297, 350, 382; and Kennedy Foundation 260; political downfall of 269; stays at White House 270, 274–7; on government plane 315; taking pleasure in wife's humiliation 325–6; effects of infidelity of 334–5; fails to provide moral guidance to JFK 345, 355

Kennedy, Kathleen (Kick; *later* Marchioness of Hartington; sister-in-law): working on *Washington Times-Herald* 9; letters to JFK from 32; marries 33; relationship with JFK 34–7; entertaining friends 46; and Lem Billings 53; and Barbara Ward 69; and favourite music 85; relationship to Macmillans 88; and David Ormsby-Gore 90, 186; and Inga Arvad 92; recklessness of 139; in England 140; JFK lunches with friends of 154; providing interesting people for JFK 186; and sister-in-law 197; death 200; wanting her own way 219; and father's philandering 292; and Betty Spalding 305; and Hugh Fraser 321; JFK visits grave of 329; and Sissie Ormsby-Gore 341; JFK grieves for 349

Kennedy, Pat (sister-in-law): and father's stroke 203; Jackie rents house to 239

Kennedy, Patrick Bouvier (son) 347–55, 359, 361, 364–6, 370, 377, 386, 399

Kennedy, Robert (brother-in-law): and baby's death 16; appointed Attorney General 44; Susan Stankrauff and 72; and father 78; on Bay of Pigs 82; JFK confers with over Bay of Pigs 102–3; and Bay of Pigs 106, 113; and Freedom Riders 125; and Chester Bowles 136; and JFK's relationship with Ormsby-Gore 155; JFK visits 165; and heavy drinking 191; and JFK's visit to South America 198; and father's stroke 203; and Sinatra 218; and steel crisis 221–2; at dinner given by Alsop 245; and Cuban Missile Crisis 256, 270, 275, 284, 288, 296; and civil rights 260–3, 323; and physical fitness 304; Ben Bradlee on 306; and sex scandal 330–1, 355, 373–4; and birth of Christopher 336; and christening of Christopher 339; and death of Patrick 348; seeks to keep Hoover onside 369; escorts Jackie 383; and JFK's assassination 403; and JFK's funeral 409; leaves Johnson's government 416; Jackie seeks solace in 417; challenges Johnson for presidency 419; death 419

Kennedy, Rose (mother-in-law): Joe Sr impersonates 35; and Jack as head of the household 79; arrives in White House during Bay of Pigs crisis 102; and party at Greek Embassy 110–11; and JFK after Bay of Pigs 112; on holiday in France 163; Joe Sr's treatment of 186, 325–6; and visits to White House 200; and Joe Sr's stroke 202; and Joe Sr's mistresses 236, 334–5; at Jackie's birthday party 245; and Kennedy Foundation 260; and use of tranquilizers 337

Kennedy, Steve Jr (nephew) 303

Khan, Ayub 160–2, 171, 187, 199, 215, 217, 260, 266, 313, 384, 387

Khan, Aly 174

Khrushchev, Nikita 52, 76, 82, 93; and summit meeting 112, 119, 125, 142–51, 153, 160, 353; JFK asks de Gaulle about 133, 135; and Jackie 142, 184, 384; and Berlin 167; and nuclear testing 168; and separate treaty with East Germany 187, 241; Macmillan urges summit with 206–7; and arms race 222, 224; Ginsberg on 243; JFK urges clarity on 244; and Cuban Missile Crisis 254–6, 261; letter 277–96; and East-West relations 311, 312; and test ban treaty 319, 338–41; and JFK's assassination 405, 408

Khrushchev, Nina 147–8

Kilgallen, Dorothy 233

King, Martin Luther Jr 126, 323, 369, 375

Kline, Franz 229

Kohler, Foy 241, 405

Komer, Robert 166

Korea 193

Krock, Arthur 9, 22, 35

Labouisse, Henry 363

Landis, Paul 392, 395

Laos 89, 96, 148, 149, 154

Laughton, Charles 174, 177

Laura (film) 174

Lawford, Peter (brother-in-law): and Inauguration gala 1; and JFK's female companions 71; accompanies Jackie to White House 84; dines with JFK and Jackie 86; and Macmillan 91; Kennedys lunch with 173–4; JFK flies to New York with 181; JFK parties with 196; introduces Marilyn Monroe to JFK 218; and Marilyn Monroe 231, 247; JFK stays with 253; assembles women for JFK 295; at Crosby estate 366

Leary, Timothy 242–3, 268, 302

LeMay, General Curtis 275

Lemnitzer, General Lyman 80, 106

Life (magazine) 122

Lincoln, Abraham 171

Lincoln, Evelyn 163, 344; and JFK's female companions 120; and summit with Khrushchev 147

Lodge, Henry Cabot 352, 360–1, 372, 375–6, 383

Look (magazine) 369

Louis XVI, King of France 134

Luce, Clare Booth 48

McCloy, John 167

McConaughty, William 217

McCone, John 254, 259, 265, 268, 270

Macdonald, Torby 71, 251, 293, 381

MacLeish, Archibald 229

Macmillan, Harold 66–7, 76, 86–94, 96, 133, 146, 150, 152–5, 159; JFK takes advice of 167–8; Nehru tells he finds JFK boring 189; JFK's relationship with 204–6; and Dorothy's infidelity 213; in talks with JFK 222–4; and Cuban Missile Crisis 279, 282, 286–9; JFK makes plans to meet 294; in discussion with JFK after Missile Crisis 296; satirised 303; and Khrushchev 311–12; and Profumo affair 314–15, 318, 322, 326–31; and test ban treaty 319–21, 339–41; and moral basis for political decisions 323; provides moral guidance to JFK 346, 378; sends condolences on Patrick's death 352; resigns 369–70; and East–West relations 372; JFK damages politically 382; and Skybolt Report 385; delivers eulogy for JFK 406–7; supports Jackie 410–15, 419–21

Macmillan, Lady Dorothy (*née* Cavendish) 66, 76, 87–93, 152–5, 327, 411, 418

Macmillan, Sarah 87

McNamara, Robert 360; opposes Roosevelt appointment 42; and Bay of Pigs 80; dancing with Jackie 211; and Cuban Missile Crisis 288; and Vietnam 368, 377

Malraux, André 138–41, 156, 228–9, 299

Manchester Guardian (newspaper) 213

Mansfield, Mike 143, 358, 368, 375

Marshall, Burke 260, 262

Martin, Edwin M. 272

Mellon, Bunny 157, 167

Mellon, Paul 167

Mendl, Sir Charles and Lady 92

Meredith, James 260–4

Mexico 220, 237, 393

Meyer, Mary (*née* Pinchot) 20, 176, 177–83, 191, 208–13, 217, 236, 242–7, 256, 259, 266–8, 280, 283, 290–1, 301–8, 321–4, 333, 335, 340–4; Cord 177–80, 209, 213, 243; affair with Chuck Spalding 318; Walton and 359; on board Air Force One 365; JFK reaches out to 377–8; JFK revives affair with 386

Mikoyan, Anastas 405–8

Miller, Arthur 219, 229, 232

Miller, Isadore 232

Mollenhoff, Clark 246, 373

Monroe, James 58

Monroe, Marilyn 218–19, 229–35, 246–7

Morocco 370

Moscow 119, 330, 338

Mountbatten, Edwina 215–16

Mrs Miniver (film) 178

Muñoz-Marín, Governor and Mrs 194

Murray, Don 174

NATO *see* North Atlantic Treaty Organization

Nehru, Jawaharlal 187–90, 214–17, 384, 387

Nehru, Motilal 216

Neustadt, Richard 382

New York City Ballet 52

New York Journal-American (newspaper) 330–32

New York Post (newspaper) 234

New York Times (newspaper) 9, 60, 95, 114, 149, 154, 168, 249, 323, 375, 392

Newman, Larry 72–4, 166, 195, 200, 227–8, 236–9, 248–51, 295, 340

Newport: Jackie and JFK married in 12

News of the World (newspaper) 330

Newsweek (magazine) 211, 306, 392, 400

Ngo Dinh Nhu 258–61, 375–9

Nhu, Madame 357–60

Nicaragua 94, 101, 108

Nixon, Richard Milhous 27, 198; in TV debate 121, 128

Nolting, Frederick 352

North Atlantic Treaty Organization (NATO) 287

Novotny, Maria 331–2

O'Brien, Larry 400–2

O'Donnell, Kenneth (Kenny) 107, 134, 363, 391, 399, 402

Onassis, Aristotle 363, 366–8, 419

Onassis, Artemis 368

O'Neal, Patrick 121

Organization of American States 220, 283

Ormsby-Gore, David 80, 150, 155, 186; and JFK's relationship with Macmillan 296–7, 378; at dinner-dance 211; lunching with Macmillan 224; during America's Cup 259; gives party 266; and Cuban Missile Crisis 277–80, 282, 284; and Jackie's pregnancy 299; at Camp David 309; JFK confers with 310; delivers letter from Macmillan 312–13; at dinner with Alsop 322; on holiday with Kennedys 338–9; and test ban treaty 340, 379; at White House 381; and Skybolt Report 385; and Kennedy Memorial Trust 414; Jackie seeks solace in 418;

Ormsby-Gore, David – *contd*
　Sissie 155, 211, 224, 259, 266, 280,
　292; and Jackie's pregnancy 299; at
　Camp David 309; at dinner with
　Alsop 322; on holiday with
　Kennedys 338–9; Jackie asks to be
　godmother to unborn child 341;
　death 418
Oswald, Lee Harvey 402, 406–8

Pakistan 159, 184, 186, 215–6, 219,
　269
Palm Beach: Kennedy residence at 1
Paris: state visit to France 112
Paris-Match (magazine) 249
Parish, Mrs Henry II ('Sister') 49–51,
　55, 58, 63
Parsons, Louella 92
Patten, Susan Mary 66
Patterson, John 126
Paul, Colonel Michael C. 201
Paul VI, Pope 332
Pearson, Drew 381
Perier, Father Albert 65
Perry, Dr Malcolm 397–8
Peru 171
Peters, Roberta 171
Philip, Prince 414
Pidgeon, Walter 174, 178–82, 208
Pinchot, Mary *see* Meyer, Mary
Pinchot, Rosamund 209, 244, 308
Pinchot, Gifford Jr 265
Pitt, William 12
Powers, Dave 71, 73, 120, 134, 168,
　195–7, 218, 228, 239, 242, 252, 292,
　295, 314, 319, 340; and death of
　Patrick 348; and weekend at
　Crosby estate 366; on Houston
　crowd 387; and JFK's assassination
　394–6, 402
Powers, Gary 211
Prado, Dr Don Manuel 171, 176, 184
Prado, Senora de 172, 176
Preminger, Otto 173, 180
Profumo, John 313–14, 318, 322, 326,
　328, 369
Puerto Rico 184, 194, 199

Radhakrishnan, Dr Sarvepalli 318
Radziwill, Lee *see* Bouvier, Lee
Radziwill, Prince Stanislas 74, 150,
　152, 248–9, 303–4, 363, 367, 416
Ravello 239, 366
Ray, Satyajit 67
Rayburn, Sam 59, 106
Ready, John 393
Reed, Jewel 35, 259, 292–3
Reed, James 259, 293, 318, 339
Roberts, Charles 392, 400–1
Roberts, Emory 395
Rometsch, Ellen 328, 332–3, 355,
　368–70, 373, 385
Roosevelt, Eleanor 19, 135, 166, 181,
　290
Roosevelt, Franklin Delano 45, 47,
　139, 145, 271, 405; Sue 43, 46
Roosevelt, Franklin D. Jr 42–3, 363,
　367, 371
Rostow, Walter 166, 189, 356
Rothko, Mark 229
Rusk, Dean: and Bay of Pigs 79, 86,
　101, 107, 115; meets Macmillan 87;
　and dinner for Macmillans 91; and
　Berlin crisis 168, 241–2; and
　meeting with Macmillan 204; and
　Indian invasion of Goa 214; and
　talks with Macmillan 223–4; and
　Cuban Missile Crisis 271, 281, 283,
　287; and Vietnam 360–1, 376;
　absent from Washington 402; and
　JFK's assassination 404–6; greets
　de Gaulle 408; and JFK's funeral
　408
Russell, Mary 45–6
Russell, Richard 280
Rwanda 259

Salinger, Pierre: and Bay of Pigs 107
San Román, José Perez 107
Saturday Evening Post (magazine) 12
Schlesinger, Arthur Jr: and Bay of
　Pigs 80, 86, 96, 118–20; at White
　House dinner party 290; on
　Profumo scandal 313
Seaborg, Glenn 206

Selassie, Haile, Emperor of Ethiopia 366–7

Shaw, Maud 77, 165, 172, 181, 201, 246, 367

Shaw, Mark 122

Siegenthaler, John 101

Sinatra, Frank: and JFK's Inauguration 1; introduces JFK to Judith Campbell 22, 121; gives private dinner for JFK 30; records by 85; and friendship with JFK 175–7; JFK parties with 196; and Giancana 218

Smathers, George 106, 234, 308, 318

Smith, Jean see Kennedy, Jean

Smith, Steve 37, 97–8, 100

Smith, Steve Jr 97

Smith, Flo 211, 235, 303

Smith, Earl 303

Something's Got to Give (film) 230

Sorensen, Theodore (Ted) 81, 221, 256, 319

Soviet Union see Union of Socialist Soviet Republics

Spain 194

Spalding, Betty 34–5, 37, 42, 48, 71, 79, 116–17; at Wrightsman estate 118; in Hyannis Port 165; and Max Jacobson 192–3; JFK confides in 194; and Mary Meyer 209, 212–13, 317; at dinner-dance 211; at Jackie's birthday party 245; relationship with JFK 291–3; on White House guest list 305; and JFK after Patrick's death 354; Charles ('Chuck') 34, 48, 94, 117–18; at Wrightsman estate 118; and Jacobson 121–4, 127, 193; as JFK's companion 156; in Hyannis Port 165; at dinner-dance 211; at Jackie's birthday party 245; holidaying with JFK 251; at White House dinner-dance 293; dinner with 303; at lunch with JFK 304; as friend of Kennedys 305; JFK confides in 314; affair with Mary Meyer 317;

visits JFK after Patrick's death 354; and Bobby assassination 419

Spellman, Francis, Cardinal 350

Stalin, Joseph 405

Stankrauff, Susan 72, 78

Stern, Isaac 229

Stevenson, Adlai: Jackie confides in about loss of privacy 4; JFK nominates 15; and Bay of Pigs 98, 100, 109; and Indian invasion of Goa 214; and Jackie's 'candour' 306; Jackie confides in 307; in Dallas 301

Sudan 182, 184

Sulzberger, Mr and Mrs Arthur 61

Sulzberger, C. L. 249, 290–1

Sweeney, Joseph 223

Sweeney, General Walter Jr 278

Tagore, Rabindranath 216

Tartiere, Gladys 63, 245, 302

Taylor, General Maxwell 157, 189, 278, 288, 362, 368; and Vietnam 376

Taylor, Mary 248, 253

Thant, General U. 286

Thomas, George 44, 388

Thomas, Sissie 90

Thompson, Bill 71, 234, 239, 246, 293, 314; and Ellen Rometsch 328, 373

Thompson, Llewellyn 93, 143, 168, 274, 406

Tierney, Gene 174, 177

Touré, Sékou 266

Towers, Harry Alan 331

Travell, Dr Janet 28–30, 69–70, 100, 102, 123, 127–8, 157–8, 276, 343–4; and birth of Patrick 346

Tree, Marietta 306

Tretick, Stanley 369

Truitt, James (Jim) 244, 267, 301

Trujillo, Rafael 136–7

Truman, Bess 24

Truman, Harry S. 30, 56, 184, 240

Tuchman, Barbara, The Guns of August 224, 241

Tuckerman, Nancy 345, 351

Tunisia 118

Turkey 272, 287–8

Turnure, Pamela 19–20, 48–9, 182, 344–5, 384, 403

Tyler, William 223–4

Union of Socialist Soviet Republics (Soviet Union): and Bay of Pigs 86; and Berlin Wall 168; and exchange of spies 211; and Cuban Missile Crisis 254–98; and test ban treaty 338–39; and Vietnam 356

United Nations 98, 109, 173, 177, 181, 214, 282, 286

Unruh, Jesse 319

Vance, Cyrus 264

Vanderbilt, Cornelius 258

Venezuela 184, 198–200, 215, 393

Vidal, Gore 191

Vienna 142–3, 152, 156–62, 330, 353; summit with Khrushchev in 112

Vietnam 135, 166, 189, 193–4, 352, 356–62, 372, 375–81, 418

Vittorio Emanuele III, King of Italy 248

Vogelsinger, Sue 198

Vogue (magazine) 9

Walsh, Dr John 337, 339–40, 343, 346, 348, 404

Walton, William (Bill) 44–6, 157, 235, 245, 266, 280, 283, 293, 318; as 'beard' for JFK 324, 342; and

sadness of Kennedy household after Patrick's death 360, 361; and JFK's funeral 403

Ward, Barbara *see* Jackson, Lady

Ward, Stephen 330–31

Warnecke, John 267

Warren, Robert Penn 229

Washington, George 171

Washington DC and JFK's Inauguration 1–2; Jackie expects happy marriage in 12; JFK's Inauguration in 24–8

Washington Post (newspaper) 244, 301

Washington Times-Herald (newspaper) 9, 31, 34, 92

West, J. B. 37–9, 41, 74, 77, 280, 310, 338, 365, 403

Wheeler, George 28

Wheeler, Jane (later Suydam) 28–30

Whitney, Jock 88

Wicker, Tom 392

Williams, Tennessee 229

Williams, John 369, 373

Wilson, Edmund 229

Windsor, Wallis, Duchess of (formerly Simpson) 57

Winterthur Museum 58

World of Apu, The (film) 67–8

Wrightsman, Mrs Charles 58, 118, 228

Wrightsman, Charles 118, 228

Wyeth, Andrew 229

Yarborough, Ralph 318, 392